McMAHON'S
AMERICAN GARDENER

ADAPTED TO THE

CLIMATE AND SEASONS OF THE UNITED STATES:

CONTAINING

A COMPLETE ACCOUNT OF ALL THE WORK NECESSARY TO BE DONE

IN THE

KITCHEN-GARDEN, FRUIT-GARDEN, FLOWER-GARDEN, ORCHARD, PLEASURE-GROUND, VINEYARD, NURSERY, GREEN-HOUSE, OUT-HOUSE, AND FORCING-FRAMES,

FOR EVERY MONTH IN THE YEAR;

WITH

PRACTICAL DIRECTIONS AND A COPIOUS INDEX.

BY

BERNARD McMAHON

Eleventh Edition,
WITH A MEMOIR OF THE AUTHOR:

REVISED AND ILLUSTRATED UNDER THE SUPERVISION OF

J. JAY SMITH,
EDITOR OF THE "HORTICULTURIST."

FUNK & WAGNALLS
NEW YORK

Introduction Copyright © 1976 by
Funk & Wagnalls Publishing Company, Inc.

Published simultaneously in Canada by
Fitzhenry & Whiteside Limited, Toronto.

Manufactured in the United States of America

L.C. Card 75-29506
ISBN 0-308-10223-1
ISBN 0-308-10224-X (paper)

10   9   8   7   6   5   4   3   2   1

INTRODUCTION

EXACTLY EIGHTY YEARS before I was born the 11th edition of *McMahon's American Gardener* was published. By then it was already a classic reference work for anyone who wanted to be a gardener. It was practical and timely—and amazingly complete. This book is a facsimile edition of that rare compilation of knowledge.

Since childhood I have been fascinated by old books and magazines. Each time I dragged home musty magazines and books from the attics, cellars, and barns of our neighbors, my mother, a down-to-earth farm woman, would say, "Why do you want to bother with those nasty old things?" You must understand, by "nasty" she meant that mice and rats had nested around and amongst them, and by "old" that the content was outdated and therefore useless. Mama was only partly right, of course, and if she were alive today we would have a lot of fun discussing the content of this book, for it contains the very essence of what I learned from her about gardening.

McMahon's background was rich in knowledge and experience about what plants need in order to grow well, and when he came to America from England he set about adapting old rules to the new climate. Since the plant materials were mostly the same, it was largely a matter of observing the climate around his home in Philadelphia and practicing the science of gardening accordingly. Plants themselves have an amazing adaptability, and when you combine this with the day-to-day, month-by-month, year-in-and-year-out variability of the weather conditions existing in any garden or field, it becomes apparent that gardening is in fact an inexact science.

Yet, what McMahon communicates so masterfully is the essentials that each plant requires, and then he tells exactly how to provide these. True, his recommendations are based on real experience nearly a hundred years ago in Philadelphia, but one cannot read him without beginning to understand how his approach can be applied to any climate or time. In other words, McMahon knew how to cope. He was assiduous, to use one of his favorite words, in determining how best to provide for the needs of each plant. And then, with equal dedication, he wrote down his experiences, couching them in the form of how-to instruction for his readers.

McMahon was also a generalist with a broad range of interests in the world of plants. As you read him, you will discover his expertise encompasses everything from delicious grapes to beautiful gloxinias. He served strawberries to his guests in March, and describes in detail how you can do it too—without getting them from a sunnier clime. And there were tender spears of asparagus on his table in February, harvested that very day from sun- and manure-heated forcing frames. McMahon may have been a gardener, but in terms of today's values, he lived like a king.

McMahon's American Gardener is an account of all the work required in all kinds of gardening pursuits for every month of the year, literally a compendium of when and where to plant what, and how to care for it. But there is much more to this book. It is in fact a guide to living well off the land, conserving and improving natural resources, all the while harvesting food for the body and beauty for the soul. Were McMahon alive today he would likely be emphasizing such words as "self-sufficiency" and "survival." He was totally dependent on natural things. He had no fearsome pesticides, no plastic gadgetry. Yet McMahon was a phenomenally successful gardener.

If you read McMahon with an open mind, you will find enough information and ideas for a lifetime of gardening pleasure. One approach you might take is to study this book as a text in lessons of convenient length. Buy yourself a sturdy loose-leaf notebook with divider sheets for the twelve months. As you read, make notes of information that is uniquely suited to where you live, how you want to live, and what you want to grow—or build.

Construction projects for the garden are important to McMahon, and it is in this area that he most reminds me of my mother. She, too, was a great hand at putting together simple constructions that became climate modifiers in her vegetable garden. In western Oklahoma she was constantly battling extreme heat or cold, drought, and the wind—always the wind. A couple of cedar shingles to shield the sun and wind, with a bottomless tin can sunk in the ground to hold water, were all she needed for a remarkable survival record with transplants. And with a rig of four old boards and a discarded window screen she always managed to pick an early crop of leaf lettuce. All this despite violent spring windstorms that dried out the good Oklahoma earth, lifted it into the atmosphere, and blew its dust to Missouri—or maybe Illinois. McMahon is equally ingenious at the simple carpentry that makes life better, both for the gardener and for his plantings.

The author shows us how to build more complex structures as well. At a time when everyone who gardens is interested in having a greenhouse but wonders if fuel for winter heating will be affordable or even available, I am especially glad to have McMahon's detailed instructions for building cold frames, hotbeds and sun-heated greenhouses, which he refers to as "cold pits" in the diagram on page 380. His guidelines for cold frames and hotbeds are actually better and more complete than in any current books. But his constructions always have a purpose. Would you like homegrown cucumbers in January instead of the waxed and costly commercial product? McMahon tells you how. Or how about a winter supply of nutritious salading? You'll find explicit directions for growing lettuce, radishes, cresses, mustard, and rape, (which is, in case you didn't know, a leafy cabbage relative). And if you'd like something for dessert, follow the directions for growing pineapples in northern climates, beginning on page 479.

This book is almost awesomely all-inclusive. Yet, even the most esoteric information is sure to be of value to some readers. For example, how do you protect young trees planted in a pasture grazed by cattle? See the diagram and discussion on page 303. Or what if you grow more okra than you need to pick and a quantity of the pods ripen, dry and split open, revealing the round, gray seeds? On page 341 McMahon suggests that these seeds, "if burned and ground like coffee, can scarcely be distinguished therefrom." Now there's an idea. If the taste of good coffee is in a dried okra seed, does it necessarily also contain caffeine?

If you are concerned that a twentieth century, city-bred person might not understand the jargon of a nineteenth century, to-the-trowel-born gardener, simply turn to page 17. You'll discover not only that if you "rod your peas" you can triple the crop, but that within the context of McMahon's writing you will understand exactly what he means when he talks about "rodding." His advice about growing such food crops as cauliflower, artichokes, and melons makes current authors seem like rank amateurs. Sure, if you hate cauliflower, McMahon can be a terminal bore, but if you want to grow cauliflower to perfection, you will love his attention to detail.

"Detail" is an important word as applied to this book. McMahon gardened and wrote in a time when attention to detail was still thought to be an honorable, worthwhile pursuit. He studied—and lived—his chosen field in depth. Fortunately for us, this man had the discipline and ability to record what he experienced. When he grew pines and firs from seed, practical experience told him that "the writings of persons of considerable celebrity" disagreed with what he found to be true in his nursery.

The word "nursery" is also noteworthy here. Month by month McMahon gives nursery guidance that is directly applicable and timely for any person interested in the commercial propagation and growing of plants. The coverage on strawberries, beginning on page 506, is invaluable if you want to get into the berry business. Or to propagate wax plant, gesneria, clianthus, and gloxinia from "mere leaves," see page 477.

Whether your interests are private or commercial, McMahon's insights into the pruning and training of fruit trees are enlightening.

INTRODUCTION.

Within the helpful framework of a seasonal calendar of activities, he explains exactly when and how to prune all kinds of fruit-bearing plants—trees, brambles, vines. And then there are directions and diagrams for training fruit trees into fancy shapes, including all the traditional espalier patterns, as well as others that are virtually unknown today except to serious students of pomology.

When I think of McMahon I picture a devoted gardener who must have sweated as he trimmed hedges and pulled mean weeds from the flower beds he loved. And in the heat of the day, he most likely stopped to rest under the fruit-laden branches of the apple trees he husbanded. McMahon was a gentle man with the strength of an aristocratic peasant. He cared about what he wrote; so much so that today we recognize the wisdom of his words and the practicality of his ideas.

Yes, Mama, and those of you who read this, a writer like McMahon makes searching through forgotten literature a worthwhile pursuit for all of us.

ELVIN McDONALD
Southampton, New York
August 2, 1975

PREFACE TO THE ELEVENTH EDITION.

M'MAHON'S GARDENING is by far the most comprehensive, complete, and best work that has been written for America. The advantages of minute detail will be found to consist in teaching how to perform many important operations, which those having gardens should understand the rationale of, whether they practise them all or not. Improved machinery and apparatus have not superseded knowledge, and there are thousands of small gardens where many of these detailed operations may still be practised with economy and advantage.

The work has undergone great improvements in this edition, having been carefully read by one of our best practical gardeners, and in important particulars brought up to the knowledge of the day. The newer vegetables are carefully noted, and a very few passages that are not now relevant have been expunged, such as the long description of the mode of cultivation of madder, and substances that time has exploded in American gardens.

Wcod-cuts have been inserted to add interest to the work, and altogether the publishers present the volume with confidence to the amateur and the practical gardener, as one which will bear careful study. They have also procured a brief memoir of the author, that so valuable a mans name "may not perish from among the people."

ORIGINAL PREFACE.

THE general utility of HORTICULTURE, or the art of improving every kind of soil; of producing a plentiful supply of wholesome vegetables and fruits, so necessary to health in all countries, especially in warm climates; of cultivating the various plants designed by INFINITE GOODNESS to minister to the comforts of animal life, by correcting the divers maladies to which it is subject by nature, and still more so, in the human race, by intemperance; of raising many articles of luxury and commerce, as well as materials for ornamenting the whole face of the country—is too obvious to render any arguments necessary in favor of an attempt to facilitate the general acquisition of that useful branch of knowledge; but more especially in a country which has not yet made that rapid progress in Gardening, ornamental planting, and fanciful rural designs, which might naturally be expected from an intelligent, happy, and independent people, possessed so universally of landed property, unoppressed by taxation or tithes, and blessed with consequent comfort and affluence.

The neglect in these respects is, no doubt, to be attributed to various causes, among the most prominent of which is the necessity of having reference for information on those subjects to works published in foreign countries, and adapted to climates by no means according with ours, either in the temperature or course of the seasons, and in numerous instances differing materially in modes of culture from those rendered necessary here by the peculiarities of our climates, soils, and situations. And however excellent and useful these works are in the regions to which they are adapted, they tend to mislead and disappoint the young *American* Horticulturist, instead of affording him that correct, judicious, and suitable instruction, the happy result of which would give impulse to his perseverance.

To obviate this necessity, as much as is in my power, and to contribute my mite to the welfare of my fellow citizens, and to the general improvement of the country, I have undertaken this work, and arranged the matter according to the seasons of the year, that the reader may have an easy reference to the particular business to be performed in every month. By this means the subject becomes a daily amusement and study, applicable at the moment, and consequently leaving a lasting impression on the memory; which, if attended to for a few years, may make any person who has a taste for admiring and enjoying the magnificence, beauties, and bounties of Nature in its vegetable productions, a complete Master of the Art, and, if he pleases, his own Gardener.

In writing this treatise, I have had recourse to the best publications, American, English, French, and Latin, lest any useful suggestions or modern improvements in the art should escape my notice or recollection; still keeping in view, not only the difference of climate, season, and the necessary modes of culture in foreign countries, but also in the extensive region of which the United States are composed. It is, however, probable, notwithstanding all my assiduity and care in collecting as much information as possible with respect to *the most proper seasons* for sowing particular kinds of seeds, &c., in *the remote parts of the Union*, that I have fallen into some mistakes; for these, as well as typographical errors, to which a work of this kind is unavoidably subject, I solicit the reader's excuse; and shall consider myself under serious obligations to those whose personal friendship or patriotism shall induce them to inform me of any horticultural errors which I may have committed, or improvements that may be made, in order that the former be corrected, and the latter, if justified by experience, published in some future work, or edition of this.

The culture and management of Grape-Vines, and all other kinds of fruit-trees which can be cultivated with us to advantage, or even to indulge curiosity; the raising and planting of Thorn Quicks and other plants suitable for Live Hedges; the cultivation of Liquorice, Rhubarb, Sea Kale (*Crambe maritima*), Cork-tree, Manna, Ash, Tanner's Sumack (*Rhus Coriaria*), Paper Mulberry,

Mulberry-trees for feeding Silk-worms (and care of the insects), with every other plant, not already common, which appeared to me of sufficient importance, either in a commercial, manufacturing, or ornamental point of view, or as affording any of the luxuries or necessaries of life, have been treated of with due attention: and in order to accommodate the Agriculturist, I have given a classical catalogue of the most important and valuable grasses and other plants used in rural economy; and likewise pointed out the particular kind of soil, in which each plant cultivated as a grass, or exclusively on account of its foliage, has been found, upon repeated trials, to succeed best.

From an experience which I have had of near thirty years in PRACTICAL GARDENING, on a general and extensive scale; the particular pains which I have taken, not only to designate the necessary work of every month, but also the best methods of performing it; the avoiding of all unnecessary repetitions, so frequent in works of the kind, in order to render it as full of important matter as possible; the assiduous endeavors to make it useful in every State of the Union, and to induce an association of the science of Botany with practical horticulture, without which the latter can never be so advantageously conducted: it is hoped that this will be found to be the most useful and valuable GARDENER'S CALENDAR hitherto published in any country, but more particularly so to the citizens of the United States, for whose use it has been written, and to whom it is respectfully inscribed by the Author.

BERNARD M'MAHON.

Philadelphia.

BRIEF MEMOIR OF BERNARD M'MAHON.

BERNARD M'MAHON was no common man. He sought the American shores from political motives, as is understood, but what these were has not been determined; most probably it was necessary to fly from the persecution of government. He found American gardening in its infancy, and immediately set himself vigorously to work to introduce a love of flowers and fruit. The writer well remembers his store, his garden, and green-houses. The latter were situated near the Germantown turnpike, between Philadelphia and Nicetown, whence emanated the rarer flowers and novelties such as could be collected in the early part of the present century, and where were performed, to the astonishment of the amateurs of that day, successful feats of horticulture that were but too rarely imitated.

His store was in Second Street, below Market, on the east side. Many must still be alive who recollect its bulk window, ornamented with tulip-glasses, a large pumpkin, and a basket or two of bulbous roots; behind the counter officiated Mrs. M'Mahon, with some considerable Irish accent, but a most amiable and excellent disposition, and withal an able saleswoman. Mr. M'Mahon was also much in the store, putting up seeds for transmission to all parts of this country and Europe, writing his book, or attending to his correspondence, and in one corner was a shelf containing a few botanical or gardening books, for which there was then a very small demand; another contained the few garden implements such as knives and trimming scissors; a barrel of peas, and a bag of seedling potatoes, an onion receptacle, a few chairs, and the room partly lined with drawers containing seeds, constituted the apparent stock in trade of what was one of the greatest seed stores then known in the Union, and where was transacted a considerable business for that day.

Such a store would naturally attract the botanist as well as the gardener, and it was the frequent lounge of both classes, who ever found in the proprietors ready listeners as well as conversers; in the latter particular they were rather remarkable, and here you would see Nuttall, Baldwin, Darlington, and other scientific men, who sought information or were ready to impart it. Mr. M'Mahon was esteemed by these, and in several botanical works his knowledge is spoken of with great respect and consideration; Nuttall has named a much esteemed species after him, though by omitting the M' the circumstance has been little noticed.

After a long life of laborious and painstaking industry Mr. M'Mahon paid his last debt, and left the concern to the management of his wife, who conducted it under difficulties that would have appalled most women. She, however, continued to be successful, but was at length stricken with blindness; in this condition, she still occupied a seat behind the counter, and gave directions to assistants, having a kind word and a piece of intelligence for all who frequented the shop. Her foreman supplied the flowers, seeds, plants, and bulbs for a considerable length of time, but at last she too disappeared, the store was closed, and the business passed into other and more enterprising hands.

The writer of this very imperfect memoir, which he regrets there are not materials extant to make more complete, has been favored with the following letter from the able and well-known botanist, Dr. William Darlington, which will fitly close this record of a useful man.

WEST CHESTER, June 15, 1857.

MY DEAR SIR,

I am much gratified to learn that a new edition of M'MA-HON'S "*American Gardener's Calendar*" is in press. That work was among the earliest of its kind in our country, and I have always regarded it as among the best. It is at once comprehensive and complete; and, moreover, remarkable for its judicious, practical, common sense views of the subject.

I had the pleasure of knowing BERNARD M'MAHON, in my youthful days. He was, I believe, one of those *Exiles of Erin* who sought and found a refuge in our country, near the close of the last century. In the autumn, I think, of 1799, he passed some weeks at my native village of Dilworthtown, in Chester County, in order to avoid the ravages of yellow fever, in Philadelphia, where he resided; and in that rural retreat I first knew him. I renewed the acquaintance in 1802, 3, and 4, while attending the medical lectures in the University of Pennsylvania, by which time he had established his nurseries of useful and ornamental plants: and I ever found him an obliging, intelligent, and instructive friend. He was a regularly educated gardener, of much experience, and great enterprise. He gave the first decisive impulse to *scientific horticulture* in our State; and to him we are mainly indebted, among other favors, for the successful culture and dissemination of the interesting novelties collected by LEWIS and CLARKE, in their journey to the Pacific. When, in 1818, Mr. NUTTALL published his *Genera of North American Plants*, he named a beautiful shrub "in memory of the late Mr. BERNARD M'MAHON, whose ardent attachment to Botany, and successful introduction of useful and ornamental Horticulture into the United States, lay claim to public esteem:" and although the genus has been reduced by later botanists to a section of *Berberis*, it is generally known by—and I trust will long retain—the popular name of MAHONIA.

It was a well-deserved tribute of respect, from one who intimately knew, and could justly appreciate the merits it commemorated: and I am happy in the opportunity, even at this late day, to add my own humble and inadequate testimonial to that of so accomplished a judge of botanical worth, as THOMAS NUTTALL.

Very truly yours,

WM. DARLINGTON.

THE GREAT CONSERVATORY AT KEW GARDENS.

ILLUSTRATIONS.

ILLUSTRATIONS.

JANUARY.

THE KITCHEN GARDEN.

PREPARATIONS FOR EARLY CROPS.

IN such parts of the Union where the ground is not at this time bound up with frost, continue to dig the waste quarters of your kitchen garden, first giving them such manure as they require; laying them in high sloping ridges, to sweeten and be improved by the frost, &c., more especially if the soil be of a stiff nature; by which method its adhesion is destroyed, the pores are opened for the admission of air, frost, rain and dews, all of which, abounding with nitrous salts, contribute, in a high degree, towards its melioration and fertility; and besides, a great quantity of ground thus prepared, can be soon levelled in the spring for sowing or planting; which, if neglected would require much time to dig in a proper manner, and that at a period when the throng of business requires every advantage of previous preparation.

When the ground at this time is frozen so hard as not to be dug, which is generally the case in the Middle and Eastern States, you may carry manure into the different quarters and spread it, repair fences, rub out and clean your seeds, prepare shreds, nails and twigs, for the wall and espalier trees, which are to be pruned in this and the next month; get all the garden tools in repair; and procure such as are wanting; provide from the woods a sufficient quantity of pea-rods, and poles for your Lima and other running beans; dress and point them, so as to be ready for use when wanted.

Here it may be well to remark, that many people who neglect to provide themselves with pea-rods at this season, when it can be so conveniently done, are necessitated, when the hurry of business overtakes them in spring, to sow their peas and let them trail on the ground; in which situation they will never produce, especially the tall-growing kinds, one-third as many as if they were properly rodded.

2

The various kinds of Early Peas will require rods from four to five feet high; the taller Marrowfat, Champion of England, and other tall-growing kinds, will require them to be from six to seven feet high, exclusive of the part to be inserted in the earth; they ought to be formed or dressed fan fashion, the lower ends pointed, for the ease of pushing them into the earth, and laid by, either under some shed, or in any convenient place, till wanted; one set of rods will, with care, last for three years. The same kind of rods that the tall-growing peas require, will answer for the generality of running Kidney Beans; the Lima beans requiring strong poles from eight to nine feet high.

If in this and the next month, you neglect forwarding everything that can possibly be done, in and for the garden, you will materially find the loss of such inattention, when the hurry and pressure of spring business overtake you. Every active and well inclined gardener will find abundant employment in the various departments of the garden at this season, and need not be idle, if disposed to be industrious, or to serve either himself or his employer.

FRAMING.

Many will think that the instructions hereafter given for the raising of early Cucumbers and Melons, in frames, are too diffuse; especially in a country which abounds in these kinds of fruit, produced in such quantities, in summer and autumn, without artificial heat, or very much trouble.

The remark may be just, but the principal motive for giving these lengthy instructions is, to exercise the young gardener in the art of managing Garden Frames in general; an art absolutely essential to every good Gardener, and which cannot be better exemplified than in the raising of early Cucumbers and Melons. And besides, these fruits coming into use at an early season, will be much valued and esteemed.

As several other kinds of kitchen garden vegetables are desirable at an early season, such as cresses, rape, lettuce, mustard, radishes, &c., to cut while young; asparagus, radishes, peas, kidney beans, &c., to be forwarded in early perfection; cauliflower and cabbage plants, to succeed those sown in September, and to produce a principal crop for early summer use; you should now provide the necessary supplies of hot stable dung, rich earth, and other requisites proper for their cultivation in hot-beds, as explained for each, under its respective head.*

HOT-BED FRAMES AND LIGHTS.

If not already provided with hot-bed frames and lights, you may get them made agreeably to the following instructions. Large frames

---

* The whole of these requirements may be more effectually secured by close and compact low houses, heated by hot-water pipes. Though more expensive at first, there is a final saving.

ought to be made of inch and half, or rather two inch plank, of the best yellow pine, nine feet two inches long, four feet ten inches wide, as high again in the back as in the front, to give the top a due slope to the sun and a proper declivity to carry off the wet when covered with glass lights, to move off and on occasionally; every joint ought to be tongued, the better to prevent the admission of cold air into, or emission of warm air out of the bed, but in such manner as the Gardener may think proper. The back and front are to be nailed to corner posts, so as to admit the ends to fit in neatly, which ends are to be made fast to the posts by iron bolts keyed in the inside, for the greater facility of taking the frame asunder when necessary; each end must be made one inch and a half higher than the back and front, so as that one-half its thickness may be grooved out on the inside, for the sash to rest and slide on, and the other half left for its support on the outside; when finished give it two or three good coats of paint before you use it, and with a little care and annual painting, it may last you twenty years.

These frames will take three lights of three feet wide each, each light containing five rows of glass panes, six inches by four, over-lapping one another about half an inch, which of all other sizes is the most preferable, on account of their cheapness in the first place, the closeness of their lap, their general strength and trifling expense of repairs; however, each person will suit his own convenience as to the dimensions of glass. Where the sashes when laid on the frame meet, a piece of pine about three and a half inches broad and near two thick, should run from back to front, mortised into each, for their support, and for them to slide on; in the centre of which, as well as in the ends of the frame, it will be well to make a groove five-eighths of an inch wide and near a quarter of an inch deep, rounded at bottom to receive and carry off any wet which may work down between the sashes.

But with respect to particular dimensions of frames, they are dif-ferent, according to the plants they are intended to protect, but gene-rally from nine to twelve feet long, from four feet eight inches to five feet wide, from eighteen inches to three feet six inches in the back, and from nine to eighteen inches in front, being for the most part twice as high in the back as in front, if not more.

The common kitchen garden frames may be of three different sizes, that is, for one, two, and three lights; the latter of which, how-ever, are the most material, and which are employed for general use: but it is necessary also to have one or two-light frames, the former as seedling frames, and the latter as succession or nursery frames, to forward the young plants to a due size for the three-light frames, in which they are to fruit.

EARLY CUCUMBERS AND MELONS.

As it is generally the ambition of most gardeners to excel each other in the production of early cucumbers, &c., all necessary prepa-ration should be made this month for that purpose, by preparing dung for hot-beds, in which to raise the plants; for they, being of a tender quality, require the aid of artificial heat under shelter of frames and glasses, until the middle or latter end of May, especially in the Middle and Eastern States.

But by the aid of hot-beds, defended with frames and glasses, we obtain early cucumbers, in young green fruit, fit to cut or gather in February, March, and April, &c., and ripe melons in May and June. The proper sorts of cucumbers for the early crops are the early Kenyon's free bearer, and Syon House, and Walker's Improved; of which the first sort comes earliest; but the latter is considerably the finest fruit, and greatly preferable for general culture.

The following cut represents a house built for forcing the cucumber, which may be done in the coldest weather with perfect success.

Fig. 1.

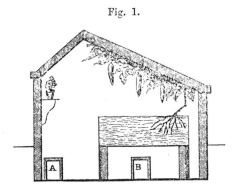

The house is heated by a flue A B, or still better by hot-water pipes and a boiler; such a house might be ten feet long and ten wide, as desired, and in it bushbeans, strawberries, &c., could be forced, and young flowering plants will here find a congenial atmosphere. There is no necessity of going to the expense of such a house where there are other buildings in which tender exotics are grown and a night temperature of 60° is kept, as a small space may be used for this purpose, and four or five plants trained up near the glass, will give a supply for a small family the whole winter.

If early melons are also required, there are several varieties of the fruit: the Cantaleupe is one of the best for its handsome growth, good size, and superior flavor; and is in much estimation.

The true *Cantaleupe*, or *Armenian warted Melon*, is very scarce in the United States; its fruit is large, roundish, and deeply ribbed, a little compressed at both ends, the surface full of *warted protuberances*, like some species of squash, the flesh reddish, firm, and of a most delicious rich flavor; of which there are several varieties, differing principally in color, and commonly called black rock, golden rock, &c.

This variety of melon derives the term Cantaleupe from a place of that name near Rome, where it was first cultivated in Europe— brought thence from Armenia, a country in Asia, in which is situated the famous Mount Ararat.

But it may also be proper to raise some of the others for variety; the Romana is a great bearer, comes early, but the fruit much smaller, though well flavored; the Polignac, Nutmeg, the best for general crop, and Minorca, are also fine melons; but it may also be eligible to raise two, three, or more of the best approved different sorts.

Observe, that in procuring these seeds for immediate sowing, both of cucumbers and melons, it is advisable to have those of two, three, or four year old, if possible, as the plants will generally show fruit sooner, as well as prove more fruitful than those of new seeds, which are apt to run vigorously to vine, often advancing in considerable length before they show a single fruit; but when seeds of this age cannot be procured, new seeds may be improved by carrying them a few weeks previous to sowing in your waistcoat or breeches pocket.

In order to raise early cucumbers and melons, you must provide a quantity of fresh hot stable dung, wherewith to make a small hot-bed for a seed bed, in which to raise the plants to a proper growth for transplanting into larger hot-beds next month to remain to fruit; for this purpose a small bed for a one or two-light frame may be sufficient, in which case two cart loads of hot dung will be enough for making a bed of proper dimensions for a one-light box, and so in proportion for larger.

Agreeably to these intimations, provide the requisite supply of good horse-stable dung from the dung hills in stable yards, &c., consisting of that formed of the moist stable litter and dunging of the horses together, choosing that which is moderately fresh, moist, and full of heat—always preferring that which is of some lively, warm, steamy quality; and of which take the long and short altogether as it occurs, in proper quantity as above. And being thus procured, proceed to make the hot-bed, or previously to forming it into a bed, if the dung is rank, it would be proper to prepare it a little to an improved state, more successful for that purpose, by forking the whole up into a heap, mixing it well together, and let it thus remain eight or ten days to ferment equally, and for the rank steam and fierce heat to transpire or evaporate in some effectual degree; and by which time it will have acquired a proper temperament for making into a hot-bed, by which treatment the heat will be steady and lasting, and not so liable to become violent or burning, as when the dung is not previously prepared.

Choose a place on which to make your hot-bed, in a sheltered dry part of the framing ground,* &c., open to the morning and south sun; and it may be made either wholly on the surface of the ground, or in a shallow trench, of from six to twelve inches deep, and four or five feet wide, according to the frame; but if made entirely on the surface, which is generally the most eligible method at this early season, it affords the opportunity of lining the sides of the bed with fresh hot dung, quite down to the bottom, to augment the heat when it declines, and also prevents wet from settling about the bottom of the bed, as often happens when made in a trench, which chills the dung, and causes the heat soon to decay.

Then, according to the size of the frame, mark out the dimensions of the bed, either on the ground, or with four stakes, making an

* Framing Ground is a part of the Kitchen Garden well defended from cutting winds, and well exposed to the sun; particularly intended for framing of all kinds, and generally inclosed with live or reed hedges, or board fences, the former being the most preferable.

allowance for it to be about four or five inches wider than the frame each way; this done, begin to make the bed accordingly, observing to shake and mix the dung well, as you lay it on the bed, and beat it down with the back of the fork as you go on; but I would not advise treading it, for a bed which is trodden hard will not work so kindly, and be more liable to burn that which is suffered to settle gradually of itself: in this manner proceed till the bed has arrived at the height of four feet, which will not be too much, making an allowance for its settling six or eight inches or more, in a week or fortnight's time; and as soon as finished, let the frame and glass be put on; keep them close till the heat comes up, then raise the glass behind that the steam may pass away.

The next thing to be observed is about earthing the bed, in which to sow the seed; and for which occasion should have a proper supply of rich, light, dry earth, or compost, ready at this season under some airy dry shed or hovel, covered at top to keep out rain, that the earth may be properly dry; for if too moist or wet at this time, it would prove greatly detrimental both to the growth of the seed and young plants, as well as be very apt to cake and burn at bottom next the dung by the strong heat of the bed; therefore, observing that for early hot-beds of cucumbers and melons should generally deposit a necessary quantity of proper earth, under some cover as above, either the beginning of winter, or at least a fortnight or three or four weeks previous to making the hot-bed, in order to have it in the dry, mellow state above mentioned, ready for immediate use when wanted.

Three or four days after the bed is made, prepare to earth it; previously observing, if it has settled unequally, to take off the frame and glasses, and level any inequalities; make the surface smooth, put on the frame again, and then lay therein as much of the above-mentioned earth as will cover the whole top surface of the bed about three or four inches thick; then fill two, three, or more middling smallish garden-pots with more of the aforesaid rich earth, place them within the frame on the hot-bed, put on the glass or glasses, and continue them till the earth in the pots is warm, and when that is effected sow the seeds in the pots, both of cucumbers and melons, each separately, more or less in each pot, according to the quantity of plants required, but generally considerably more of cucumbers than of melons at this season, covering in the earth near half an inch deep with the same earth.

This done, place the pots towards the middle of the bed, plunging the bottom part a little into the earth, drawing some of the same up round each pot at the same time; or in two or three days after, may sow a few seeds in the earth of the bed, to have a chance both ways; but by sowing in pots, if the beds should heat too violently, as is sometimes unavoidably the case, the pots can be readily drawn up more or less out of danger of burning the earth, &c., therein; and thus the sowing in pots in a new made hot-bed in full heat may prove of greater advantage than sowing in the earth of the bed with regard to more probable safety from burning.

After sowing the seeds, put on the lights or glasses close; but when the steam from the heat of the bed rises copiously, give it vent by raising one corner of the upper ends of the lights half an inch or an inch, which is also necessary in order to prevent any burning tendency from the great heat of the bed in its early state; 60° by night, and 80° with sunshine, will be a proper temperature.

Continue now to cover the glasses of the hot-bed every evening, about an hour before sun-setting, if mild weather, but earlier in proportion to its severity, with garden mats; and uncover them every morning, not sooner than between eight and nine o'clock at this season; and observe, in covering up in the evening, that as the bed will at first have a strong heat and steam within the frame, it may be advisable to cover only a single mat thick for the first three or four nights, as a thicker covering in the early state of the bed might be apt to occasion a too violent internal heat and steam of a burning nature; but as the great heat decreases, augment the covering, being careful not to suffer the ends of the mats to hang down considerably below the frame, over the sides of the bed, except in severe weather, which would draw up a hurtful strong steam from the dung, as well as confine the steam and heat too much, and keep the bed too stiflingly close from the external air, which would weaken the germination or sprouting of the seed, and the plants would come up weak and of a sickly yellowish hue; observe, therefore, these and the following precautions, in order both to prevent too great a heat in the bed, and that the plants may rise with a proper degree of strength and healthful growth.

Likewise observe, on the above considerations, that in covering up, or applying the night covering of mats over the glasses, during the time the strong heat and steam continue in the bed, it would be proper when the mats are put on in the afternoon to raise the upper ends of the glass or glasses, a quarter of an inch, or a little more or less, occasionally, both to give vent to the internal rank steam, and to admit a moderate degree of fresh air; and in which may fasten one of the covering mats to hang down a little over the part where the lights are occasionally opened to prevent the cutting external air from rushing immediately into the frame, especially after the plants are advancing; but this, necessary as it is, cannot be done with safety in very severe weather.

Great care is requisite that the earth in the pots have not too much heat, for the bed is yet very hot, and therefore let the degree of internal heat in the bed be daily examined; and, if anything of burning should appear, you can conveniently raise the pots farther from the dung, from which the danger proceeds, without disturbing the seeds or plants, and thereby prevent all injury from too much heat, provided you examine the bed every day, and give proper vent to the rank steam within the frame, while of a burning quality.

In two, three, or four days after the seed is sown, you may expect the plants to appear; when it will be proper to admit fresh air to them, by raising the upper end of the glass a little every day: and if the earth in the pots appears dry, refresh it moderately with a little water that has stood in the bed all night, just to take off the cold chill; applying it about eleven or twelve o'clock of the day, and principally only to the earth, about the roots, not over the tops of the plants; which done, shut down the glasses close for about half an hour or an hour, then opened again a little, and shut close towards the evening; when continue to cover the glass every night with garden mats. And at this time also, if the heat of the bed is strong and the weather not very severe, raise the glass a little behind with a prop, when you cover up in the evening, to give vent to the steam; and nail a mat to hang down over the ends of the glass that is raised, to break off the sharp edge of the external cold night air from the plants; but when the heat is more moderate, the glasses may be shut close every night, observing to uncover in proper time every morning, to admit the essential benefit of day-light, sun, and air, to the plants; being careful to continue the admission of fresh air at all proper opportunities in the day-time, to promote strength in the plants, otherwise they would run weak, and very long and feeble-shanked; raising the glass as before observed, and if windy or very sharp air, to hang a mat before the place as above.

On the day that the plants appear, sow a little more seed in the same bed, in the manner before mentioned; for these plants being liable to suffer by different causes at this season, it is proper, therefore, to sow a little seed at three or four different times in the same bed, at short intervals; for, if one sowing should miscarry, another may succeed.

When the plants, however, both of the first and succeeding sowings, are two, three, or four days old, they should be planted in small pots, which pots must be placed also in the hot-bed, in the manner following :—

Observe to fill the pots, the day before you intend to remove the plants, with some rich, dry earth, and set them within the frame till the next day, when the earth in the pots will be warm; then proceed to planting, take the plants carefully up in the seed-pots, raising them with your finger, &c., with all the roots as entire as possible, and with as much of the earth as will readily adhere about the fibres; and thus, the pots of earth being ready, and forming the earth thereof a little concavely hollow a small depth, place the plants in the hollowed part of the earth slopingly, with their roots towards the centre, and earth over their roots and stems near an inch thick; observing to plant three plants in each pot; and if the earth is quite dry, give a very little water just to the roots of the plants only; and directly plunge the pots into the earth on the bed, close to another, filling up all the spaces between with earth; and let every part of the bed within the frame be covered with as much earth as will prevent the rising of the rank steam immediately from the dung, which would destroy the plants by its pungency.

Be careful to examine the bed every day, to see that the roots of the plants do not receive too much heat; if anything like that appears, draw up the pots a little, or as far as you see necessary for the preservation of the plants, re-plunging them again to their rims when the danger is over.

Two or three days after planting, if the bed is in good condition, the plants will have taken root; though that is effected sometimes in twenty-four hours.

When the plants are fairly rooted, if the earth appears dry, give them a little water in the warmest time of the day; and if the sun shines it will prove more beneficial: let the watering be occasionally repeated very moderately, according as the earth in the pots becomes dry, and appears in want of a little moisture: and for this purpose always have some soft water set within the frame a few hours, to be ready to water the plants as you shall see occasion; but always with very great cautious moderation at this season.

If there is now a brisk growing heat in the bed, you should, in order to preserve it as long as possible, apply some outward protection of long stable-litter, straw, waste hay, dried fern, or leaves of trees, round the sides of the bed, raising it by degrees round the outsides of the frame.

This will defend the beds from cold piercing wind, heavy or driving rains and snow, if either should happen; for these, if suffered to come at the bed, would chill it, and cause a sudden decay of the heat, whereby the plants would certainly receive a great check.

If a lively heat be kept up, you may admit air to the plants every day, to strengthen their growth, by tilting the glasses in proportion to the heat of the bed, and temperature of the external air; generally observing, in this case, that when there happens a sharp cold air, or cutting wind, it would still be advisable to nail a garden-mat to the upper end of the glasses, to hang down over the place where the air is admitted, supported a little hollow or detached underneath, two or three inches from the frame; and it will thus break off and prevent the cutting external air from entering immediately into the frame upon the plants, and at the same time admit a proper degree of mild fresh air to a greater advantage: however, in calm, moderate weather, this precaution is not materially necessary.

About a fortnight, or a little more or less time after the bed is made, you will carefully examine the heat thereof, to see if it wants augmentation; and when the heat begins to decline considerably, remove the temporary protection of straw, hay, fern, or leaves from the front and back of the bed, if any was laid round it as before added; then apply a lining of fresh hot horse-dung, close to one or both sides as it shall seem necessary, by the heat being less or more decreased; for a constant regular degree of internal heat must be supported to resist the external cold, and continue the plants in a proper state of advancing growth; but if the heat is not greatly declined, it would be advisable to line only one side first, applying it to the back of the bed; and in a week or fortnight after, line the front, &c., forming the lining about fifteen or eighteen inches wide; but raise it very little higher than the dung of the bed, lest it throw in too much heat immediately to the earth and roots of the plants; covering the top with earth two inches thick to preserve the heat, and prevent the rank steam of the new dung from coming up and entering into the frame, where it would prove destructive to the plants; the lining will soon greatly revive the declining heat of the bed, and continue it in good condition a fortnight longer.

Ten or twelve days after lining one side, proceed as before, removing the protection of straw-litter, &c., if any, from the other side, and applying a lining of hot dung as above afterwards to both ends;—and these will again revive and augment the heat for another fortnight or more.

After performing the lining, if very cold, wet, or snowy weather prevail, it may be proper to lay a quantity of dry long litter all around the general lining, which will protect the whole from driving cold rains and snow, and preserve the heat of the bed in a fine growing temperature.

By applying these linings of hot dung in due time, and renewing them as there shall be occasion, you may preserve the bed in a proper temperature of heat of sufficient duration to continue the plants in a free growing state in the same bed until of due size for ridging out into the larger hot-beds, finally to remain to produce their heat.

Observe, however, that where there is plenty of hot dung, and every proper convenience, you may, in order to forward the plants as much as possible, prepare a second hot-bed, by way of nursery, about a fortnight after making the seed-bed, in order to receive the plants therefrom in their pots, when the heat begins to decline, plunging the pots in the earth as above directed; continuing to support the heat of this bed, as already explained, and in which the plants may be nursed and forwarded till they acquire a proper size for transplanting finally into the fruiting hot-beds. (See *next month.*)

When the plants have advanced in growth with their two first rough leaves, about two or three inches broad, and have pushed their two first running buds in the centre, or are a little advanced in the formation of one or two short runners, they are then of a proper size for ridging out into the large hot-beds, where they are finally to remain, which perform in proper time, according to the directions given in February under the article *Cucumbers.*

But in order to strengthen the plants in a more firm stocky growth, and to promote a production of fruitful runners, each plant must be stopped (as the gardeners term it), or topped at the first or second joint, *i. e.* the top of the first advancing runner, when formed in the centre.like a small bud, should be pinched or cut off close to the joint, as directed in February (which see), where the method of performing it is more fully explained.

CARE OF THE VARIOUS SORTS OF LETTUCES.

If you have lettuce plants in frames, or under hoop-arches defended with mats, let them enjoy the open air at all opportunities, by taking the glasses, or other shelters, entirely off, when the weather is mild and dry; but if the plants are frozen, let them, while in that state, be carefully protected from the hot sun, which would materially injure them.

In very wet weather, and when sharp cutting winds prevail, keep the glasses over them, observing, however, to raise the lights or glasses behind two or three inches, in mild days, to admit air to the plants; for, if they are kept too close, they will be drawn up weak, and attain to but little perfection ; but let the glasses be close shut every night.   In severe frosty weather keep them close night and day, and cover the glasses with mats, or straw, &c., both of nights and occasionally in the day-time, if the frost is rigorous ; also let the same care be observed to those under hoop-arches ; but let them have the full air in mild open weather.

Or where any lettuces are planted in a south border, close to a wall or board fence, &c., it would be advisable, in hard frost, to cover them as above.

In the above lettuces, in general, pick off all decayed leaves when any appear, keep them always cleared from weeds, and destroy slugs, which often greatly annoy them ; and in mild weather stir the surface of the earth between, which will much enliven the plants.

SOWING LETTUCES.

When lettuces have not been sown in autumn for early spring use, you may now sow any of the cos* or cabbage kinds, on a slight hot-bed under glasses, to be planted out in spring ; the young plants may be greatly forwarded, if pricked into another fresh hot-bed next month ; and in the latter end of March, or beginning of April, they will be strong, and fit for transplanting into warm borders ; a sufficiency may be retained in the frame to arrive at early perfection.

FORCING EARLY ASPARAGUS.

Hot-beds for forcing asparagus may be made with success any time this month, which will furnish young asparagus for the table in February and March.   It may also be forced under the stage of a warm green-house.

Observing, for this occasion, you must be furnished with plants that have been raised in the natural ground till of three or four years' growth, of proper size and strength to produce eligible crops of good sized asparagus shoots, when planted in a hot-bed ; and must be provided with plenty of good hot dung, wherewith to make substantial hot-beds, from three to four feet high, and with proper large frames and glasses to place on the beds, and garden mats for covering of nights, &c.

But for general particulars of the plants, and the necessary quantity, as well as of the hot-bed and other requisites—see the article *Forcing Asparagus* in February, which is equally applicable on the present occasion.

MINT, TANSEY, &C.

Make a small hot-bed for some mint, or plant the roots close together in boxes and place in the hot-house, when it is required at an

---

* The cos lettuces, however, are of little use in the North ; they are too tender to bear our severe winters, and soon run to seed in the summer ; consequently the cabbage kinds are best for all purposes.

early season, in young green shoots, for salads and mint-sauce, &c.
A bed for a small or middling garden frame, of one or two lights,
may be sufficient for supply of a moderate family; and in general
about two feet thick of dung; set on the frame, and lay about four
or five inches deep of earth on the bed, ready for planting.

Then having some roots of common spear-mint, place them upon
the surface, pretty thick, and cover them with earth about an inch
and a half deep; or you may place the roots in drills, and draw the
earth over them.

The mint will appear in about a week or fortnight, and will be in
fine order for mint-sauce, &c., and either to use alone as a salad, or
to mix among other small herbs.

By the same means you may obtain green tansy and tarragon.

SMALL SALADING.

Make a slight hot-bed, in which to sow the different sorts of small
salading, such as cresses, mustard, radish and rape, and likewise lettuce, to cut while young.

The hot-bed for these seeds need not be more than about two feet
thick of dung, and must be covered with a frame and glasses. The
earth must be light and dry, and laid about four or five or six inches
thick on the bed; then let small shallow flat drills be drawn from
the back to the front of the bed; sow the seed therein, each sort
separately, and very thick, covering them not more than a quarter of
an inch deep with earth; or, if but just covered, is sufficient, and the
plants will rise more expeditious and regular; or the seed may be
sown thick all over the surface of the bed, each sort separate; smooth
it down with the spade, then sift as much light earth over as will
just cover it, as above observed, and directly put on the glasses; or
in want of frames and lights, may use hand-glasses, observing in
general to cover the glasses every night, and in severe frosty weather,
with mats or straw litter, &c.

As soon as the plants appear, give them as much air as the state
of the weather will admit of, by raising the glasses on props; otherwise they will be apt to mould or fog, and spoil as fast as they come
up.

It must be remembered that where a regular succession of these
small herbs is required for salad, should repeat the sowings, at least
once a fortnight.

If you have not hot dung to spare to make hot-beds for this purpose, may sow in a sloping bed of natural earth, under a shallow garden frame, covered with glasses: allotting for this occasion some
warm compartments of rich earth in the *full sun :* preparing it in a
sloping manner fronting the south, a foot higher on the north side
than in front. Set a frame thereon, sinking the back part, &c., so
as to have the whole surface of the earth within six or eight inches
of the glasses; sow the salading, put on the glasses, cover them carefully with mats, &c., at night and in very severe weather, and you
need not doubt of success; though, generally, a hot-bed will always
prove the most effectually successful on this occasion.

CAULIFLOWER PLANTS.

Look over, in open weather, the cauliflower plants which were
raised and planted in frames last autumn for protection in winter, to
plant out in spring for an early summer crop; and where withered or
damaged leaves appear, let them be picked off; suffer no weeds to
grow among them, and stir the surface gently between, which will
enliven and cherish the plants.

In open weather let the plants have plenty of air every day, by
raising the glasses, or by taking them entirely off when the weather
is mild and dry; but generally continue the glasses over in rainy
weather: keep them close down every night, and do not open them
at all in severe frosty weather.

In severe weather cover the glasses every night with mats, straw,
or fern, &c., also, if there be occasion, in the day-time, in very rigorous frost; likewise, in such weather, lay some litter round the outsides of the frame, for this will be very serviceable in preventing the
frost from entering at the sides.

Cauliflowers under hand or bell-glasses must also have air every
mild day, by raising the glasses two or three inches on the warmest
side; in sharp weather keep them close; in severe frost lay some litter
round, and straw or mats over each glass; this will protect the plants
greatly; in *mild* dry weather the glasses may be taken off every day
for a few hours; but they must be kept close every night.

SOWING CAULIFLOWER SEED.

Sow cauliflower seed the beginning, middle, or any time this month,
to raise plants to succeed those sown in autumn; or also, in case none
were sown at that time for an early summer crop, or that they have
been killed by the severity of the winter; but in order to bring the
plants up soon, and forward them in growth, it will be necessary to
sow them in a slight hot-bed. Plants sown at this season, if well
managed, are to be more depended on for a general crop, than those
which were sown in autumn, as they are not so apt to button or run
to seed in April or May as the others, and will produce their flowers
within ten days as early; though such of the autumn raised plants
as do not button, generally produce larger flowers and earlier.

Make the bed as directed for cucumbers, in page 21, to about three
feet high, which, when settled, will fall to about two feet six inches,
and put a frame on; then lay four or five inches of rich earth over
the bed, sow the seed on the surface, but not until the violent heat
of the bed is over; cover it by sifting or otherwise, with light dry
earth, about a quarter of an inch deep, and then put on the glasses.

When the plants appear, let them have air every day that the
weather will permit, by raising the upper ends of the lights an inch
or two; and in *very mild weather*, the lights may be taken off entirely for a few hours in the warm part of the day: the plants must
not be kept too close, for that would draw them up so weak as to
render them of little value; therefore give them as much air as possible, consistent with their preservation and promotion of growth;

but let them be covered carefully at night, and in very severe weather.

Water them frequently, but sparingly, with water which has stood over night in the hot-bed; keep them free from weeds, and in one month they will be fit for transplanting into another hot-bed. (See *February.*)

SOWING CABBAGE SEED.

This is a proper time to sow a full crop of early cabbage seed, to raise plants to succeed those sown in September; the kinds most suitable are the early Wakefield, early York, early dwarf Battersea, and early Vanack; they are to be treated in every respect, as directed for the cauliflower plants, with this difference, that as they are somewhat more hardy, a less degree of heat will be sufficient.

Sow also some of the large late kinds of cabbage, such as the flat Dutch, drum-head, &c., likewise some of the red pickling cabbage; and plants from this sowing will be fit for use in July, August, &c., and will produce better and larger heads than if sown in April or May; and besides, they will immediately succeed the early summer kinds above mentioned.

SOWING CARROTS.

In some families young carrots are required as early as possible, and they may be forwarded by sowing the seed in a moderate hot-bed, about the end of this month.

Make the hot-bed about two feet thick of dung, and procure some light, rich, dry earth, which lay six inches thick on the bed. Sow the seed thinly on the surface, and cover it with the same kind of earth a quarter of an inch deep.

When the plants come up, let them enjoy the free air in mild weather, and cover them in cold nights, and also in very severe frost, whilst young; and when an inch or two high, thin them to about three inches asunder; and you will thus have young spring carrots for drawing in April and May. The early horn carrot is the best for this purpose.

SOWING RADISHES.

In order to have radishes as early as possible, recourse must be had to the assistance of hot-beds; therefore, any time in this month, make a moderate hot-bed for one or more garden frames, only about two feet and a half depth of dung, sufficient just to promote the early germination of the seed, and forward the plants moderately without running them up long shanked, &c. When the bed is made, set on the frame, lay in about six inches depth of good light garden earth, then having some seed of the best early-frame, olive or short-topped radish, sow it evenly on the surface, press it into the earth with the back of a spade, cover it nearly half an inch deep with light mould, and put on the glasses.

When the plants appear, give them a large share of air, either by taking the glasses, &c., entirely off, whenever it can be done with safety, even for half an hour at a time, or tilting them up high at one end, as the weather will permit, otherwise they will draw, or run up long shanked, and be spoiled; and after the plants have been up a few days, thin them regularly with your hand, where they stand too thick, and leave the strongest plants standing not less than an inch asunder. Support a gentle heat in the bed, when it declines, by applying a moderate lining of hot dung.

MUSHROOMS.

Mushroom-beds should be carefully attended to at this season. They should have sufficient covering to defend them *effectually* from the frost, rain, or snow; which should not be less than two feet thick; and if heavy rain or snow should have penetrated quite through the covering, this must be removed immediately, or your spawn will be in danger of perishing. Replace it with good covering of clean and dry wheat or other straw; and in order to defend the bed more effectually from wet and cold, it is advisable to spread some large garden mats, or canvas cloths, over the straw, which will greatly preserve the beds.*

ARTICHOKES.

Artichokes, if not landed up before, should not be neglected any longer, except the severity of the frost prevents it : in which case, as these plants are liable to suffer greatly by rigorous frosts, it is advisable to give some temporary protection, first clearing away the decayed and large old leaves, then apply a good thick covering of long, dry, strawy dung, or mulchy litter, close about each plant: but, if open dry weather, it would be most expedient to land them up; observing, preparatory to this, to cut away all the large and decayed old leaves close to the ground; then dig between, and earth up the plants, as in November and December.

But the work of landing up artichokes should always be performed in November or December; for which see the work of these months. It should never be omitted; for it is the most general effective method of preserving the plants in severe winters.

And after they are landed, if the frost should prove very severe, it will also be proper to lay light, dry, long litter over the rows : if the plants are of the true globe sort, too great care cannot be taken to preserve them; for sometimes a severe winter makes a great havoc among them; and, in spring, young sets to recruit the plantations may be very difficult to procure.

SOUTHERN STATES.

In Georgia, South Carolina, and such parts of the other southern States as are not subject to winter frosts, you may sow carrots, parsneps,

---

* The most economical and sure way to grow mushrooms is in a cellar or shed, where a temperature of 50° to 55° is maintained.

beets, spinach, lettuce, radish, celery, parsley, cabbage, cauliflower, borecole, broccoli, leeks, onions, &c., especially towards the latter end of the month.

Sow peas and plant beans of various kinds, earth up such peas and beans as are advanced in growth, rod and stake such of them as require it; plant out cabbage and cauliflower plants, earth up late celery, and tie up endive for blanching: and, in short, do all the work directed to be done in the kitchen garden for the month of *March*, where you will find ample instructions for performing the same.

In such of the southern or western States as frosts are prevalent in, at this season, the above work must be deferred till such period in next month, or even in March, as it can be done in, without danger from frost; with the exception of planting the Windsor-bean (*Vicia Faba*), and all the different varieties of that species, which ought to be planted as soon after the middle of January as it is possible to get the ground in a proper state of preparation to receive them: they are very hardy, are not subject to rot in the ground like kidney beans, provided it be dry; they thrive best in a heavy strong soil, and are seldom very productive in the United States, if not planted early.

THE FRUIT GARDEN.

PRUNING.

WHERE pruning was neglected in November or December, it can now be done; though the latter end of February is a preferable time in the middle States, and the beginning of March in the eastern; however, apple and pear-trees being perfectly hardy, may be pruned at any time during the winter months with safety; plums and cherries may also be pruned any time that the weather is tolerably mild: and as this month will answer extremely well in the southern States for pruning almost all kinds of fruit-trees, it may be useful to give at this time general instructions for performing the same, which may be referred to at any other period.

PRUNING ESPALIER AND WALL TREES.

As some people have not a sufficient idea of what is meant by *espaliers*, the following explanation, and instructions for forming them, &c., may not be unacceptable.

Espaliers are edges of fruit-trees, which are trained up regularly to a lattice or trellis of wood work, and are commonly arranged in a single row in the borders, round the boundaries of the principal divisions of the kitchen-garden; there serving a double or treble purpose, both profitable, useful, and ornamental. They produce large fine fruit plentifully, without taking up much room, and being in a close range, hedge-like, they in some degree shelter the esculent crops in the quarters; and having borders immediately under them each side, afford different aspects for different plants, and also they afford shelter in winter, forwardness to their south-border crops in spring, and shade in summer; and as to ornament and variety, what can be more delightful in spring, in the excursion of the walks, than the charming appearance which the trees make when covered with their showy bloom, differing in themselves, in those of different genera, species, and varieties; or in summer, to see the fruit of the different sorts advancing to perfection, and in autumn arrive successively to maturity? And as the trees are arranged all of an equal height, not exceeding six feet, closely furnished with branches, ranged horizontally at regular distances one above another, from the very ground upwards, the fruit hereby are exhibited to great advantage, and being low, and the branches fixed, are convenient to pull, and not liable to be blown down by wind.

An espalier has this advantage over a wall tree, that as being wholly detached, the branches have liberty to form fruit spurs on both sides, which in the wall tree cannot be effected but on one; in fact, common fruit-walls are unnecessary in the United States, except in the eastern and some of the middle States, where they are useful in forwarding to due perfection and favor some late kinds of superior peaches, grapes, and other late fruits; but when walls are built for other purposes, and are conveniently situated, advantage ought to be taken of them for raising fruit, observing to suit the various kinds to the various aspects.

Trellises are also used occasionally for wall trees, where the wall does not admit of nailing the branches immediately against it; also for training wall trees in forcing-houses and forcing-frames, and are formed according to different degrees of taste, for use and ornament, as well as of different dimensions, from four or five to six, or in forcing-houses, to seven, eight, or ten feet high.

For common espalier fruit-trees in the open ground, a *trellis* is absolutely necessary, and may either be formed of common stakes or poles, or of regular joinery work, according to taste or fancy.

The cheapest, the easiest, and soonest made trellis for common espalier trees, is that formed with straight poles being cut into proper lengths, and driving them into the ground in a range, a foot distant, all of an equal height, and then railed along the top with the same kind of poles or slips of pine or other boards, nailed down to each stake to preserve the whole straight and firm in a regular position; to which the branches of the espalier trees are to be fastened with small ozier-twigs, rope-yarn, &c., and trained along horizontally from stake to stake, as directed for the different sorts under their proper heads.

To render the above trellis still stronger, run two or three horizontal ranges of rods or small poles along the back parts of the uprights, a foot or eighteen inches asunder, fastening them to the upright stakes either with pieces of strong wire twisted two or three times round, or by nailing them.

But when more elegant and ornamental trellises of joinery work are required in any of the departments, they are formed with regularly squared posts and rails, of good durable timber, neatly planed

3

and framed together, fixing the main posts in the ground, ten or twelve feet asunder, with smaller ones between, ranging the horizontal railing from post to post in three or more ranges; the first being placed about a foot from the bottom, a second at top, and one or two along the middle space, and if thought convenient, may range one between each of the intermediate spaces; then fix thin slips of lath, or the like, upright to the horizontal railing, ten inches or a foot asunder; and paint the whole with oil color to render it more ornamental and durable; and in training the trees, tie their branches both to the railing of the trellis and to the upright laths, according as they extend in length on each side.

In either of the above trellises for a common espalier, five or six feet at most is a sufficient height, as, if much higher, the winds, having great power, would be very apt to loosen and displace them.

The permanent trellises ought not to be made till the second or third year after planting, except the trees have had as long a time of regular and judicious training; for while they are young, it will be sufficient to drive a few short stakes into the ground on each side of the trees in a straight line, to which the branches should be fastened in a horizontal position as they are produced, in order to train them properly for the espalier; these will be sufficient for the two or three first years, for should you make the regular espalier or trellis the first year the trees are planted, many of the stakes would rot before the espalier is covered. For directions respecting the planting espalier and wall-trees, see *March* and *October*.

TRAINING.

The following representations of the modes of training convey to the eye examples which it will be well to study:—

Fig. 2.

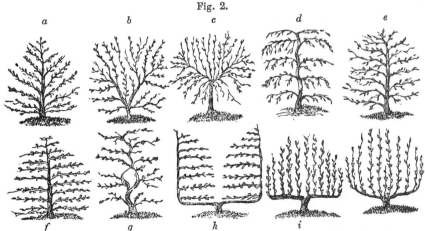

a. The herring-bone fan. *b.* The irregular fan. *c.* The stellate fan. *d.* The drooping fan. *e.* The wavy fan. *f.* The horizontal. *g.* The horizontal, with screw-stem. *h.* The horizontal, with double stem. *i.* The vertical, with screw shoots. *k.* The vertical, with upright shoots.

PRUNING APPLE AND PEAR-TREES IN ESPALIERS, OR TRAINED TO WALLS OR BOARD FENCES.

Apple and pear-trees being of the spur-bearing kind, and their mode of bearing similar, one method of pruning answers for both; they producing their fruit upon short natural spurs from the sides and ends of the branches, and the same branches continue bearing for many years, increasing their quantity of fruit spurs as they gradually advance in length; let it therefore be remarked, that in the general course of pruning those trees, their branches and shoots are not to be shortened, but generally trained along horizontally to the espalier and wall at their natural length, at least as far as there is scope of room to extend them; never shortened, except on particular occasions below explained, and the whole trained four to five or six inches asunder.

Keeping therefore this in mind, look over the general branches, in which observe, that in such advancing young trees as are still in training, requiring a further supply of young wood to form the head, be careful to select and retain a proper quantity of the best-placed last summer's shoots at full length, and generally a terminal shoot to each mother branch, and cut out all the superfluous and irregular ones; but in full-trained or old trees, still retaining the former trained or same individual bearing branches for many years, as long as they continue fruitful; and only examine any particular branches that appear worn out or decayed, or any that are too much crowded or very irregular, and let such now be pruned out; at the same time observe where any of the last summer's shoots are wanted to supply vacant spaces, and retain them accordingly; cutting out all the superfluous or over abundant *close* to the main branches; likewise, let all foreright and other irregular-placed shoots be cut away, carefully retaining the leading shoot to all the main branches where there is a scope to run them, so retaining the general branches and the necessary supply of young wood about four to five or six inches asunder, to be trained to the trellis or wall, &c., all at their full length as aforesaid; and, according as they advance in length, still continue extending them, or without shortening, at least as far as their limited space admits.

In the course of this pruning, have particular care to preserve all the natural fruit-spurs; but cut away all those formed of the remaining stumps of shorted shoots, for these rarely produce anything but a confusion of unnecessary wood-shoots every summer; and for which reason be careful, in pruning out the superfluous and irregular shoots, always to cut them off *quite close* from whence they originate.*

Then train in all the remaining proper branches and shoots at their full length, about from four to five or six inches asunder, as

---

* The better way to prevent superfluous lateral shoots is to pinch them into a few buds from time to time through the summer, and prune into one or two eyes in the winter. This practice will, after some two or three years, destroy the exuberance, and form fruit-buds, instead of wood-shoots.

aforesaid, without reducing them in length either in the summer or winter pruning.

By the above practice, the shoots of branches of these trees will, about the second or third year after they are laid in, begin to produce short shoots or spurs (as they are generally termed) about an inch or two in length, some not above half an inch; and from these the fruit is produced.

But if the branches of these trees were to be shortened, it would be cutting off the very part where blossom buds or spurs first begin to appear; and instead of those fruitful parts, they would send forth a number of strong wood-shoots. This plainly shows that the shoots which were intended for fruit-bearing must not be generally shortened, for if that is practised, the trees would constantly run to wood, and never produce any tolerable crop of fruit.

If, indeed, there is a want of wood in any part of these trees, then the occasional shortening of some of the adjacent young shoots may be necessary, whereby to promote a production of laterals the ensuing summer, to furnish the vacancy.

For instance, if there is any vacant part in the tree, and two, three, or more shoots are requisite to furnish that vacancy, and only one shoot was produced in that part the preceding summer, that shoot, in such a case, being now shortened to four or five buds, if it be strong, will produce three or four lateral shoots.

PRUNING PLUMS AND CHERRIES.

This is also a proper season to prune plums and cherries, either against walls or espaliers, especially where the weather is mild.

Let it be observed in the pruning of these trees against walls or espaliers, that, like the apples and pears, they being of the spur-bearing kind, producing the fruit upon short natural spurs or studs, emitted along the sides of the branches, or from two or three to many years old, so must accordingly retain the same branches many years for bearers, which must not be shortened in the course of pruning, but trained horizontally at their full length, about three or four to five or six inches asunder; also all young shoots of the last year's growth, as are now proper to be reserved in vacancies, to furnish the wall or espalier with bearing wood, must not be shortened; but every such shoot or branch must be left entire; and this should at all times be observed, which is the only certain method whereby to render the branches fruitful.

In the operation of pruning these trees, observe, as advised for the apple and pear trees, to give proper attention both in any young trees still under training, and in the fully trained older trees furnished with the requisite expansion of branches.

Observing, in the former, i. e., the young trees under training, that where further supplies of branches are required in order to form a proper expansion of bearers trained in regularity, should be careful to leave some best well-placed young shoots for that purpose, and cut out the improper and unnecessary, such as fore-right and other irregular placed growths; or also any superfluous or over-abundant shoots that may occur in particular parts of the trees, retaining the reserved proper shoots mostly at their full length, for training as above; and they will thus in from one to two or three year's growth, furnish natural fruit spurs for bearing; but generally sooner in the cherries than the plums, as some sort of cherries will probably bear fruit the same year on the young shoots now trained in : the morella in particular bears mostly on the one year old shoots. For observations thereon see *November.*

And in the full trained trees of the above sorts, look carefully over the general expansion; and where any occasional supply of young wood appears necessary, select and retain some best-placed proper shoots of last summer accordingly, either to furnish any present vacancy, or to train in between the main branches where it may seem expedient, in order to be advancing to a bearing state, ready to supply any apparent future occasion; but in the morella particularly, above mentioned, retain always a general supply for principal bearers : (see *November* :) and prune out all irregular and superabundant shoots close to the mother branches; and if casual worn-out or decayed old unfruitful branches occur, let them now be cut out, retaining young wood of proper growth, &c., to supply their place; preserving also, in all vacant spaces, a supply of the best young shoots at their natural length, as above advised, and a leading one to each branch; being careful to preserve all the short natural fruit spurs, and cut away close any remaining naked stumps of former shortened shoots : then, as soon as the tree is thus pruned, proceed to train in all the proper shoots and branches to the wall or espalier, at their full length as aforesaid, at the above mentioned distances : and all those thus treated will in two or three years' time send out many short shoots or fruit spurs, about half an inch or an inch in length; and from these spurs the fruit is always produced.

These spurs generally appear first toward the upper part, or that which was once the superior part of the one, two or three years old branches; and if shortening was to be practised, those parts would consequently be cut away where the blossom-buds would otherwise first made their appearance. Therefore, in the course of pruning apple, pear, plum, and cherry-trees, never shorten or top the young shoots that are left for a supply of bearing wood, nor any of the bearing branches, if there is room to extend them; and they will thus all gradually form themselves into a plentiful bearing state.

But if shortening was generally practised to these kinds of fruit-trees, as is the case with many pruners, it would prove their manifest destruction in regard to preventing their fruitfulness : for in the places where fruit-buds would otherwise naturally appear, there would advance nothing but strong wood shoots; so that the trees would be continually crowded with useless and unfruitful wood.

When, however, there is at any time a supply of wood wanted, then shortening particular shoots may be proper, as observed above for the apples and pears.*

* The reader will also consult with advantage the pages of the *Horticulturist,* and *Barry's and Thomas' Fruit Books* for remarks on pruning garden and orchard trees.

GENERAL OBSERVATIONS IN PRUNING ALL THE ABOVE TREES.

I observed above, that shortening the branches of apple, pear, plum and cherry-trees, was not proper in the general course of pruning; it, however, in some particular cases, is most necessary; for which take the following hints :—

For example, when the trees, for walls and espaliers particularly, are about one year old from the budding or grafting, either in the nursery, or newly planted against walls or espaliers, with their first shoot immediately from· the budding or grafting, at full length, it is proper to shorten or head down these shoots near the insertion of the bud or graft, to force out lateral branches, which is called heading down the trees; but this should not be done till February or March, cutting them down to four or five eyes; which will procure a production of lateral shoots near the head of the stock from these remaining lower eyes or buds, the following summer, in order for training in accordingly, that the wall or espalier may be regularly furnished with branches from the bottom. After this, the branches are to be trained along at their full length, except it appears necessary to shorten some or all of these lateral shoots, in order that each may throw out also two or three lateral branches to furnish that part of the tree more effectually; training the said lateral shoots also at their full length; but if there appear to be still more branches wanting, some of the most convenient of these last shoots may also be shortened, to promote their producing a farther supply of lateral branches, sufficient to give the tree its proper form ; for the great article in this training-pruning is to encourage and assist young wall and espalier fruit-trees in their first two or three years' growth, to produce shoots in proper places, so as to cover the wall or espalier regularly with branches from the bottom to the top.

But when the trees have acquired branches enough to effect the first proper formation of the head, they will afterwards naturally furnish further supplies to cover the wall or espalier regularly every way to the allotted extent, without any further shortening, except on particular occasions, when a vacancy happens in any part, according to the rule mentioned in the article of apples and pears.

There is one thing further to be observed in pruning apple, pear, plum, and cherry-trees ; and that is, when the trees have acquired branches enough to cover the wall or espalier at the distance above mentioned, then all those young shoots of the last summer's growth, that are not wanted in vacancies to form new bearers, must be cut off *quite close* to the place from whence they arise, leaving no spurs but the fruit-spurs that are naturally produced, which every branch will be plentifully furnished with if the above rules are observed.

PINCHING THE PEAR-TREE.

Nipping with the finger and thumb the soft young shoots, forms an excellent remedy for defects of growth. Following up this stopping at regular intervals of the tree's growth, the operator secures a profusion and regularity of lateral branches.   He does not wait till his plant has grown tall and misshapen, but as soon as he sees well formed buds in the axils of the leaves, he knows that by stopping the terminal growth these buds will be forced onward and produce lateral shoots.

An undue share of vigor in one or more shoots, weakens all the other parts of the tree by appropriating all the nutriment to themselves.   Fig. 3 represents a tree which became slightly bent, and this arrested the continuous flow of sap to the summit; the consequence was the development of a very strong shoot, which controlled the whole tree.   That strong grower pushing out with undue vigor, should have been checked, and thus an equal distribution of growth would be secured, that would leave, at the end of the season, a tree somewhat resembling Fig. 4.

Fig. 3.   Fig. 4.   Fig. 5.   Fig. 6.

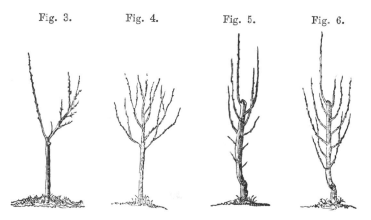

Pinching is an indispensable operation in the management of trees trained as dwarfs, pyramids, or espaliers.   Most trees have a natural tendency to grow most vigorously towards the top and at the extremity of the branches; this should be kept in continual check, for if one portion be permitted but for a short time to grow more vigorously than the others, the balance is destroyed, and much time and severe measures are required to restore it.

In the case of young trees that have been cut back for the purpose of producing the pyramid form, it often happens that three or four buds at the summit push so vigorously as to draw all the sap past those below them, and a tree something like Fig. 5 is the result.   If the upper shoots next the leader had been checked by pinching, the lower branches would have been benefited, and we should see a tree like Fig. 6.

PEACHES, NECTARINES, AND APRICOTS.

In the training and pruning of peaches, nectarines, and apricots, little or no difference is to be observed; they all produce their fruit principally upon the young shoots of the former summer, the fruit-blossoms rising directly from the eyes of the shoots; a plentiful supply of which must be reserved annually in every part, to train in for bearing; they also sometimes bear on the small natural spurs arising on the two or three years' wood, which generally occur more frequently in the apricots; and all such spurs should be carefully preserved, for they generally bear good fruit; keeping in mind, however, that the young yearling shoots are to be considered as the general bearers: observing that as the general branches and bearing shoots are to be trained to the wall or espalier horizontally, about three to four or five inches distant, we must prune out annually all super-abundant shoots, or that are more than can be trained in with proper regularity, likewise a considerable part of the old, or two last year's bearers; and, observing, that as a general supply of the best of the last year's shoots must annually be left in a regular manner in every part of the tree, to bear the fruit the succeeding summer, each of the said shoots must be shortened more or less, according to their strength, now in the winter pruning, as directed below, in order to encourage them to produce a more regular succession of bearing wood in the ensuing summer. The wood which is then produced, will bear fruit in the summer after that; and the same shoots both bear the fruit and a supply of successional shoots at the same time for future bearers, &c.

Before you begin to prune, in these trees particularly, it is proper generally to unnail and unbind all the young shoots which were nailed or bound in last summer, and great part of their respective mother branches; by which means you will have room to examine the shoots, and to use your knife properly.

In the course of pruning these trees, be careful to select the most promising and best situated shoots at the above distances, in a regular manner, advancing, as it were, one after another in every part of the tree, making room for them by cutting out all the other useless or unnecessary shoots, together with a proportionable share of the former bearers, before intimated, and old naked branches not furnished with bearing wood.

For example, you are to observe, that these young shoots are, as above hinted, produced principally upon those shoots, which were laid in last winter, and which produced the fruit last summer, and some casually on the older wood; but shall suppose many of the said shoots or branches, which were laid in last winter, to have produced each three shoots in summer, and that they now all remain, but that there may not be room to lay in more than one of the said shoots on each of the branches, it remains to be considered which of these three shoots on each branch is proper to be left; whether the uppermost, middle, or lower of the three: there is no general rule for this, but we will suppose the middlemost, in which case cut off the lower one quite close to the branch, and then that part of the branch which hath the upper shoot upon it must be pruned down to the middle one; so that there is only the middle shoot now remaining, which terminates or makes the end of the branch; but, if it is thought most convenient to leave the uppermost of the three, the middle and lower are to be cut away close to the branch; or, on the contrary, if the lower shoot only is to be left, cut off the branch with the middle and upper shoot thereon, close to the lower one; and if thought most proper to leave in any place two out of the three shoots on a branch, then the upper and lower are apparently most proper, provided they are the best shoots, and so cut out the middle one; or if two lower shoots appear best for your purpose, cut off the upper part of the branch with the top shoot close to the middle one; and, if to retain the two upper shoots, prune out the lowermost: there may not always happen to be just three young shoots on every year's branches, but I choose to mention that number, that I may be the better able in this small compass to explain and convey some idea of the method practised in pruning these sorts of trees.

At the same time observe, in the above general pruning, to retain the most promising well-placed shoots of the best middling, or moderately strong growth, and which appear the most fruitful, or likely to furnish a proper supply of blossom-buds, rejecting very weakly slender shoots, and such as are very long-jointed, likewise uncommonly thick spongy growths, as also remarkably rank luxuriants, cutting them all *clean out;* likewise the foreright and others ill placed, that could not be trained with proper regularity   And, as you proceed, cut out some considerable part of the past bearers of the last, or two or three preceding years, to make room for the above young supply, pruning them down to some eligible lateral shoots, or some occasionally to their origin, as it may seem expedient: also take out casual old naked branches, advanced of some considerable length, without being now furnished with lateral young bearers, or fruitful shoots, eligibly placed for training where wanted; pruning them either entirely out to make room for the more fruitful wood, or pruned down, more or less, to any more prolific well-placed young branch proceeding therefrom, and that is furnished with young shoots for bearing.

Next let it be remembered, that as you proceed in pruning these trees, most of those young shoots that are left to bear must be shortened, especially the smaller and middling, and those of moderate growth, both to strengthen them in their future production, and to promote their producing more certainly *a supply of successional lateral shoots* next summer, properly situated, so as to continue every part of the tree always well furnished with bearers; for without this precaution of shortening the shoots, many of them are apt to run up, producing laterals only, mostly towards the upper part, leaving the bottom naked, whereby the tree in time becomes devoid of bearing shoots below, so that the shortening should be performed, more or less, according to their strength, and that of the tree in general.   Though with standard trees of these kinds, shortening the shoots is not necessary, yet when trained to walls or espaliers, it certainly is, for the reasons above assigned.

For instance, if a tree is weak, or but a moderate shooter, generally leaving the shoots about five or six inches apart, for training in nearly at that distance, let them be shortened according to their strength; some of the weaker shoots to five, six, or eight inches; others of stronger growth to about ten or twelve, to fifteen or eighteen inches long; for the shortening should always be performed, more or less, according to the different shoots, and, in some degree, according as the blossom-buds appear situated higher or lower on the respective shoots; never shorten below all the said buds, in those shoots designed principally for bearing.

When a tree is in a moderate good condition, neither very vigorous nor weakly, but a middling strong shooter, the shoots may be left nearly about three to four or five inches asunder, and should be shortened rather less in proportion than the foregoing, but agreeable to the same rules in shoots of different growths; pruning some to about eight, ten, or twelve inches, others to fifteen or eighteen inches long, or more, according to their strength and situation in different parts of the tree, as well as in some cases the apparent situation of the blossom-buds, in being placed higher or lower on the respective shoots selected for bearers, as before observed.

But when any trees are of very vigorous growth in their general shoots, they must be shortened but moderately; or some shoots very little, in which some of the less vigorous may be cut to about twelve or fifteen inches; but in stronger shoots prune off only about one-third or fourth of their length, or some of the most luxuriant left mostly at their full length; for if the strong shoots of a generally vigorous tree were to be much shortened, it would occasion their shooting still more luxuriantly to rampant unfruitful wood; therefore the vigorous shoots should be very moderately shortened; and where they are general in a tree, it is advisable both to leave them closer and of much greater length than the shoots in moderate growing trees, that the exuberance of sap may be expended in the larger extent and expansion of wood, and the tree thereby in time become a more moderate shooter and a good bearer.*

Observe, however, in shortening the shoots in general, both in trees of moderate, middling, and strong growth, that in those shoots adapted for principal bearers the ensuing season, you should be careful not to cut away too low, or below all or most of the blossom-buds, or parts where they are expected to advance, being generally distinguishable from the leaf or shoot-buds by their round, plump, swelling appearance, the others being oblong, narrow, and flattish; and therefore should give proper attention to shorten accordingly in the shoots were the fruit-buds are apparent.

Likewise observe, that in shortening the bearing shoots or others of those trees, they should generally, where practicable, be cut to an eye or wood-but that is likely to produce a shoot for a leader the ensuing season; the shoot-bud eyes being distinguishable from the fruit or blossom-buds by their longer, flattish form; the others being roundish, swelling, and turgid, or may also, occasionally, prune to an eye having one or two blossom-buds, as frequently, from the same eye, shoot-buds are also formed on one side of the single or between the two twin blossom-buds aforesaid, and from which a good leading

---

* If all superfluous shoots be rubbed out during the summer, this exuberance of sap will be prevented, and the flow equalized over the whole tree.

shoot will be most likely produced, which is necessary to the welfare of the fruit; for where a leading shoot is produced at or near the extremity of a bearing branch, it draws nourishment to the fruit more effectually.

After having pruned one tree, let it be directly nailed or bound as you go on, observing to lay in the branches and shoots horizontally, perfectly straight, and parallel to each other at the above mentioned distances, nailing them all close to the wall, or tying them to the trellis in a neat manner.

PRUNE GOOSEBERRY AND CURRANT-TREES.

Gooseberries and currants bear both on the young one or two years' wood, and upon the several years' branches, generally upon small spurs rising naturally all along the sides; and in each winter-pruning it will be required to cut out any casual worn-out, decayed, and very irregular branches, and a proportionate supply of last summer's young shoots retained, and the rest pruned out.

In pruning gooseberries let them be always kept thin of branches, and these not permitted to grow ramblingly across one another, but all pruned to some regular order, so as the main bearers, or general branches and shoots, stand six or eight inches distant at the extremities; and generally either keep the middle somewhat hollow, or if permitted to run up full in the heart, keep it thin of branches, as above advised; so that you will now prune out any irregularities, &c., such as casual crowding cross-placed wood, and any worn-out or naked old branches retaining young shoots, where necessary to supply their place; and cut out all the superabundant lateral shoots of last summer, close to the old wood, only retaining here and there a good one in vacancies, or occasionally towards the lower parts, to be advancing to a proper state to supply the place of casual worn-out bearers; and generally leave, where practicable, a terminating or leading shoot to each main branch, either such as is placed naturally at or near the end of the branch; or, occasionally, where any branch is too long or rambling, prune it down to some convenient lateral shoot, &c., to remain for a terminal leader; and, in both cases, generally leave but one terminal to each branch; and all those shoots now retained, both lateral and terminal, should either be mostly left entire, and only shorten long stragglers, and very bending and reclining growths occasionally; or at least by no means shorten the shoots of these trees too much, for by cutting them very short, they are made to produce a deal of wood and but small fruit; and being so full of wood as to exclude the sun and free air in summer, the fruit cannot ripen well; and it likewise renders it troublesome to get at the fruit when fit to gather. Never clip the trees with garden shears, as is the practice of some ignorant persons.

Currant bushes should likewise be kept thin and regular, not suffering the branches to run promiscuously across each other; for when suffered to grow so irregular and crowding they produce but small fruit; and the great thicket of branches excluding the essential benefit of the sun, the berries will not ripen freely and regular, with a good flavor; observing therefore to keep the general branches thin, about six or eight inches asunder, in which, if any are too crowded or over abundant, prune out the most irregular; also any cross-placed branches, and casual worn-out old bearers, together with all the irregular-placed and superabundant young shoots of last summer, preserving only occasional supplies of the most regular ones in vacancies, and a leading one at the termination of each branch, agreeable to the rules exhibited above in pruning the gooseberry bushes; and the general upper shoots may be mostly shortened more or less where required to keep the head to a moderate extent, and a compact handsome growth.

Observe in pruning young gooseberry and currant bushes, let those designed for standards be pruned to a clean single stem, eight, ten, or twelve inches; and being careful to retain a requisite supply of the best young shoots properly situated above, to form the head accordingly, cut out the irregular and ill-placed; and the retained proper shoots may in some be moderately shortened, especially such as run away straggling from the rest; and any proper shoots advancing below may be permitted to remain entire till advanced equal with the others above, &c., that the whole may come on as equally as possible to form a regular head.

Currants and gooseberries trained against walls, palings, trellises, &c., should also have a necessary pruning and regulation in the general branches, or as may be required, cutting out the superabundant and irregular-placed shoots of last summer, or any casual too crowding and disorderly growing older branches, or such as appear unfruitful, or any of a worn-out or decayed state, and all dead wood; retaining young shoots advancing from below, and in the most vacant parts, shortened more or less, or left entire, according to room for extending them; and train the general branches, &c., three or four to five or six inches distant. For more particulars, see *October*.

FIG-TREES.

Fig-tree pruning is advised to be deferred till March or April, where see the method explained.

PROTECTING THE ROOTS OF NEW-PLANTED TREES.

If the weather should now prove severe, it will be proper to protect the roots of new-planted fruit-trees from being hurt by the frost, by laying mulch, or long dung litter, on the surface of the ground; particularly the choicest of the stone-fruit kinds—as peaches, nectarines, apricots, and any principal sorts of cherries and plums.

RASPBERRIES.

If you have neglected to afford the protection directed in November to your *Antwerp Raspberries*, you should no longer omit it; especially in those parts of the Union where severe winter frosts prevail. As to pruning and planting the various kinds, when not done in October or November, it will be better to defer this business till the latter end of February, or beginning of March; except in such of the States as the severity of the frost does not interrupt the tillage of the ground during winter; in which you can perform this business now with safety, agreeably to the directions given in October.

PRUNING THE RASPBERRY.

The accompanying figures represent the wood of the preceding summer's growth.

The portion with buds, marked *a a*, is from the upper part of the shoot; that with buds, marked *b b*, is taken from the lower part of the shoot or cane. The buds *a a*, can scarcely be termed blossom-buds, inasmuch as they do not contain the rudiments of flowers like the blossom-buds of larger fruit; but each of them possesses the power of producing a branchlet, and on this blossom-buds are formed. The buds *b b*, on the lower part of the cane, do not generally push unless the upper have been cut away, and then the lower are stimulated, producing, however, shoots and fruit later in the season than those obtained from the buds *a a*. Advantage has been sometimes taken of this, to procure a succession of fruit in autumn.

Fig. 7.

Raspberry shoots, or canes, growing up in one summer, and producing fruit in the next, and then dying to the ground, a succession having, meantime, sprung up, the pruning usually consists in the obvious operation of cutting away all the dead wood—that which has borne fruit; and, in the shortening that which is alive, thinning the canes so as to leave three, four, five, or six, from a plant, according to its strength.

An improvement may, however, be effected on this general mode. As the finest and best of these fruits are, in all cases, the produce of strong and well-ripened canes, it becomes necessary that the shoots should have every advantage afforded them. This may readily be effected by causing all the former year's canes to be cut down to the ground as soon as they have produced their crop, instead of allowing them to stand till the winter or spring; this removes an unnecessary incumbrance, and, at a season when sun and air are of infinite importance to the young canes, and, consequently, to the succeeding crop.

In autumn, or the early part of winter, the young canes should be shortened to about four-fifths of their original height, or to the place where the growth of the upper part of the shoot forms a sort of bending or twisting. They may then be either tied to stakes or arched, by tying their tips to those of the adjoining plant. When a late succession of fruit is desired, some plants may have all their shoots cut back to within a few inches of the ground.

FORCING EARLY STRAWBERRIES.

Now is a proper time, about the latter end of this month, to begin to make a hot-bed to raise a few early strawberries; those which are planted now in a hot-bed will produce fruit fit to gather in March or April.

About the middle or end of this month, provide for that purpose as much new horse-dung as will make a hot-bed about four feet high, for one or more three-light frames.

Let the dung be thrown in a heap, and let it lie about eight or ten days: in that time it will be in good condition to make the hot-bed.

But in this business, a tan-bark hot-bed, made in a bark-pit, defended with a proper frame and glasses would generally be more successful in fruiting these plants early.

But, previous to this, there should be a proper quantity of strawberry-plants potted, ready to place on the said hot-bed, as directed in *September*.

Having, however, prepared the dung for the hot-bed, make it for one or more frames, about three feet high, and directly set on the frame and lights, to protect it from wet, and draw up the heat sooner; and when the violent heat is over, lay therein either some dry light earth, or some waste tanner's bark of a decayed bark-bed, four or five inches thick; then bring in the plants and plunge the pots into the earth or tan, up to the rims, and close together as can be, filling up also all the interstices between with earth, &c.

When all the pots are plunged, put on the glasses, and keep them close till the steam arises in the bed, when it will be necessary to raise them a little behind, to let the steam pass off.

When the plants begin to push, let them have air at all opportunities, when the weather is favorable; for if kept too close, they will draw up weak, and not blossom well, and the blossoms would drop off, without being succeeded by fruit: you should frequently refresh them with a little water, and cover the glasses every night with mats, and support the heat of the bed by linings of hot dung.

N. B. In forcing strawberries, the plants may be taken up out of the natural ground with balls of earth, if not prevented by too hard a frost, and placed immediately in the earth of the hot-bed without potting them.   However, when it is intended to force strawberries, either in a common hot-bed, or in a hot-house, it would be the best method to plant some bearing plants in pots, in September or October, and so place the pots close together in a garden frame, till the time they are to be placed in the hot-bed.

But where there is the convenience of a pine-apple stove, or any kind of fruit forcing-house or hot-wall, &c., may raise plenty of early strawberries in great perfection, with but very little trouble : having some bearing plants ready in pots, place them in the hot-house, any-where near the glasses, giving frequent light waterings; they will fruit early in great abundance.

FORCING-FRAMES.

The great convenience of forcing-frames, either to force fruits or flowers into early perfection, or to preserve during winter, various kinds of exotic plants, may induce persons of taste to go to the expense of erecting such; to whom the following descriptions may not be uninteresting.

A forcing-frame is a sort of glass case, or light building, fronted with glass-frames, in which to force flowers and fruits to early perfection, by aid of artificial heat, either of dung, tanner's bark, or actual fire.

The general acceptation or meaning of forcing-frame is, a fixed erection full to the south sun; the length may be from ten to fifty or one hundred feet; the width from five to fifteen, and from five to ten feet high; having an upright back wall, of wood or brick; and a front of glass work, made sometimes in one continual range of slope, from near the ground in front to the top of the back wall; and sometimes with upright glass work, head high, ranging immediately along the front, and from the top of which a glass roof is carried to the top of the back or main wall; either of which may be for general use, for the reception of various sorts of flower-plants, small flowering shrubs, esculents, and dwarf fruit-trees, &c., occasionally, to force into bloom or fruit in winter, or early in spring and summer; whereby many sorts of the more curious flowers and fruits may be obtained some months before their natural season, which will be a great curiosity, and which is effected as aforesaid, by aid of dung, bark or fire heat; the first (dung heat), both by applying the dung principally against the outside of the back wall, and by forming it into a bed internally; the second (bark heat), by forming it into a bed, in a pit within side : and the third (fire heat), by having several returns of flues against the inside of the back wall, and that of the front and both ends, for the heat to pass along; each of which are hereafter described; for these kind of frames are of different construction, according to the sorts of plants chiefly intended to be forced; and the materials of heat, as dung, bark, or fuel, most convenient to be obtained for forcing them; so that the construction of each kind of frame is separately explained.

These frames may be employed to advantage in the vicinity of large towns for forcing various plants early for market, by the assistance of which you will have for sale, in February, March and April, various sorts of flowers, fruits and esculents that would not in their natural state of growth have appeared till May, June, or July.

But, for private use, where there is a roomy pine-apple stove, it may also be used, occasionally, for forcing many sorts of plants, flowers, and some sorts of fruits, with equal success, sufficient for the supply of a family.

However, where a considerable supply is required, a forcing-frame, distinct from the pine-stove, would be more convenient.

In either of these departments may be introduced for forcing, pots of strawberries, kidney-beans, roses, honeysuckles, jasmines, and any other flowering shrubs; likewise carnations, pinks, sweetwilliams, wall-flowers, stock-gilliflowers, narcissuses, jonquils and early dwarf tulips, and any other desirable flower-plants or roots that may be required early for curiosity; also several kinds of curious annuals, and other rare plants. You may likewise have several sorts of dwarf fruit trees, as early May and May-duke cherries, peaches, nectarines, apricots, figs, grapes, gooseberries, currants, raspberries, &c.

The general construction of each sort of these frames is explained under separate heads, according to the materials of heat used in forcing them, viz: by dung-heat, bark-bed heat, and by fire-heat.

By Dung-heat.—This is not only the most simple and cheapest kind of forcing-frame in its construction, but also considerably the cheapest in working, with respect to the article heat, as it may be forced effectually by substantial linings of hot dung against the back and ends.

This frame is formed with an upright back and ends of pine planking, and a sloping front of movable glass-lights; the length may be ten, twenty, or thirty feet, or more; the width from three to five, and five or six high: the frame-work should be of two inch pine planking, tongued, and closely joined, that no steam from the dung may penetrate into the frame, raised five, six, or seven feet high behind, and but ten or twelve inches high in front, raising both ends answerable to the front and back; the glass-work to range from the upright in front, sloping upward towards the back wall to about a foot width at top, there resting the ends upon proper framework of wood; and bars or bearers, three inches in width, must range sloping from the back to front, for the support of the lights, as in common hot-bed frames, and the top of all to be boarded wind and water tight; within side may be two or three ranges of narrow shelves along the back and ends for pots of small plants, and the bottom levelled on which to place pots of larger kinds; or you may have shelves rising one behind another, quite from the front half way up the back; so may place the lowest plants in front, the others in order behind them, rising gradually to the tallest in the back row.

From the above general sketch you will easily form an idea of the proper construction of a dung-heat forcing-frame, which you may improve as you shall see convenient.

This kind of frame may be used with good success where dung is plenty, and easily obtained; particularly for forcing roses or any other small flowering plants, whose flowers have merit in beauty or fragrance; you may also try pots of dwarf cherries, peaches, &c.; also pots of gooseberries, currants, and strawberries, carnations, pinks, and the like; having all the sorts in pots separately, and in which they are to be placed in the frame.

The season to begin to work this frame is January and February, and may be continued occasionally till May; but for any kind of fruit-trees, the beginning of February is time enough, though those plants of any kind that are designed to be forced may be placed in the frame a month or two before forcing time, to be occasionally protected with the glasses in hard frosts; but at other times let them enjoy the full air till you begin forcing.

The method of working this frame is thus: after having placed the pots of plants in regular order, the tallest behind, and the lowest in front, &c., then put on the lights, and having sufficient quantity of fresh stable-dung, full of heat, prepared as for common dung hot-beds, let it be piled up close against the outside of the back and ends a yard wide at bottom, drawing it gradually into a foot width at the top of the frame, finishing it somewhat sloping, to throw off wet; observing, that according as the dung settles or sinks down, a fresh supply must be added at the top to maintain the lining to the full height of the frame.

The lining will effectually throw in a fine growing heat, and soon set all the plants in motion; observing to give air in the middle of fine days by sliding one or more of the lights a little down, especially when the plants begin to push; give also moderate watering occasionally in mild sunny weather, and cover the glasses in cold nights with mats.

In three or four weeks, when the heat begins to decrease considerably, it must be renewed, either by entire fresh dung, or if new dung is scarce, by shaking up the old, taking the worst away, and mix the remainder with a due quantity of new, working the whole again in a pile close against the back and ends as before, which work must be repeated every three weeks or month, or as often as you shall see occasion, for the heat must be constantly preserved to a regular brisk temperature.

A frame of the above construction may be appropriated entirely for fruit-trees, planting them in a border prepared within the frame against the back part, and trained in the manner of wall-trees to a trellis, ranged five or six inches from the back erection, in which may be planted early dwarf cherries, peaches, nectarines, apricots, grapes, figs, currants, &c., so may be worked by dung-heat against the back of the frame as above directed; beginning in February, and continuing the glasses on, as well as support the dung-heat until May, and there is no doubt, with good management, but that the different sorts of fruit may be brought to perfection early.

But a dung-heat forcing-frame may be constructed of more capa-

4

cious dimensions, to admit of making a substantial hot-bed of dung internally, both to produce an increased degree of heat, and wherein to plunge pots of several sorts of flowering and esculent plants to bring them forward in growth, being assisted also with a lining of hot dung applied to the exterior of the back part of the frame, as explained in the foregoing; and for the internal hot-bed should form a bottom pit of proper width, length, and depth, making the bed therein a yard depth of good hot dung, covering the top with light dry earth, or old or new tan bark, six or eight inches thick, in which to plunge the pots of flowers, or those of early esculents, such as kidney-beans, peas, strawberries, salading, &c.

Bark-bed heat.—This kind of forcing-frame, or rather forcing-house, is worked by aid of a tanner's bark hot-bed, formed in a pit withinside the whole length.

This frame may be formed either of wood or brick-work, and fronted, &c., with sashes of glass like the former; the length may be ten, twenty, or thirty feet, or more, eight or ten wide, and six or eight high; and may be constructed either nearly like the dung-heat frame, six or eight feet behind, and one in front, the ends conformable, and sloping frames of glass-work raised from the front, sloping either quite to the top of the back wall, or to incline only about one-half towards that part, meeting a covered roof at top, half way, which should be raised high enough in front to throw the water off behind, as well as to admit as much sun as possible to every part of the frame, or it may be constructed with an upright front of glass, head high, and a sloping roof of glass-work, ranging from the upright front to the top of the back wall, which is rather the most eligible form, both for convenience and benefit of the plants; either of which constructions may be erected detached, or against a south wall already built, which will serve for the back and save some expense; the ends may either be of wood or brick, and the glass-work in every part should be made to move on and off, as well as to slide backward and forward to give air, and to do other necessary work; and at one end, near the back wall, may be a door to enter occasionally, and withinside must be a pit for the bark-bed three feet deep, part sunk, and the greater part raised, continued the whole length and width, except about a foot and a half alley to go in to perform the necessary culture, as well as to view and gather the produce of the different plants.

The pit within is to be filled with new tan any time in winter or spring you intend to begin forcing, though January is soon enough, and the beginning of February is not too late; the bark will support a growing heat three months, and if then stirred up to the bottom, will renew its heat, and continue it two months longer.

In this frame may plunge in the bark-bed pots of roses, or any other choice flowering shrubs you would force into an early bloom; likewise may place pots of strawberries towards the front and top glasses; and pots of kidney beans and early dwarf peas may be placed in any part of the frame; also pots of dwarf fruit-trees, before mentioned, pots of double pinks, carnations, and any other moderate growing fibrous-rooted perennials, as well as any sorts of bulbous or tuberous-rooted flowers, as narcissuses, jonquils, tulips, anemones, ranunculuses, hyacinths, and various other sorts.

The heat of the bark-bed will effectually warm the earth and internal air sufficiently to forward any sorts of hardy flowers and fruits to perfection at an early season; observing, that although they do not always flower and fruit so abundantly as in the full ground, yet, if there are but a few of any sort, a month or two before their natural season, they, if for sale, will sufficiently pay; and if for private use, they will always be acceptable as a rarity and curiosity in the family.

Fresh air must be admitted in fine sunny days at all opportunities, by sliding some of the glasses more or less open, keeping them close at night; and in very severe weather, the glasses must be covered with mats, or closed with sliding shutters made for that purpose, particularly at night, which trouble might be avoided if there was a fire-flue, by which heat could be introduced to counteract the extreme rigor of the frost, when necessity required.

When the heat of the bark declines considerably, do not omit forking it over to the bottom, which will revive the decaying heat six or eight weeks longer.

A bark-heat forcing-frame, nearly of the above dimensions, might be contrived entirely for forcing fruit-trees, having a border within-side along the back wall, three or four feet wide; there plant young bearing dwarf fruit-trees of any sorts before mentioned, at six or eight feet distance, in the manner of wall or espalier trees, training them also in the same manner as directed for the respective sorts in their natural state of growth. The bark pit should here be almost half sunk; and in the beginning of February fill the pit with new tan-bark, which will soon set the trees into bloom, and will ripen their fruit early.

But the *most eligible* general forcing-frame for various sorts of plants, is one of the above mentioned construction, having also flues for fire-heat; the walls must be of brick-work, having two or three returns of flues formed of the same materials, running the whole length of the back wall within, and one or two along the front and ends, by which to convey fire-heat occasionally in severe frosts, cold nights, and in all very cold and intemperate weather, which will be a great improvement in very early forcing, so that this kind of frame will be nearly of the plan of a stove or hot-house.

In default, however, of any of the above kinds of bark-heat forcing-frames, one might be effected by a common bark-pit, made in any dry sheltered situation, with a brick wall, to any convenient size, and covered with glass lights. This pit is to be principally above ground and filled with good fresh tan to the depth of four feet, in which you may plunge pots of roses, or any other shrubs, any sort of low herbaceous flowering plants, fibrous or bulbous rooted; kidney-beans, strawberries, &c.; observing, however, that in severe frost, the wall of this pit must be protected by hot dung, leaves or straw, in order to prevent the frost penetrating into the bed, and it must be carefully covered with mats at night, and even in the daytime in very severe weather.

By Fire-heat.—This kind of forcing-frame is worked by actual fire, burned in a furnace *behind*, at one end or middle, from thence communicating the heat by internal flues or funnels, running the whole length of the back wall in three returns, one above another, and continued in a flue round the front, and the frame thus constructed is often employed for ripening several of the more valuable fruit-trees at an early season, or for forwarding such to perfection which do not ripen freely without artificial aid.

This frame or forcing-house, must be formed of brick-work, at least the back or main wall, for the convenience of having fire and flues, and the whole front, &c., must be glass, like the other sorts; the length may be from twenty to forty feet or more, though one fire will not warm more than that length; the width may be from five or six to twelve or fifteen feet, and height eight or ten. It may be contrived either of moderate width for one row of trees only, to range against the back wall, or may be capacious enough to have a range of trained wall-trees behind, as just mentioned, and some small half standard, ranging also from the back to the front.

If it is therefore intended to have a narrow frame for only a row of trained trees behind, the width from four to five or six feet is sufficient, having the back or main wall formed of brick or stone, as aforesaid, eight or ten feet high, with several flues withinside, returned over each other, running the whole length of the wall; in the front must be a low wall a foot high, on which to lay a plate of timber, and from which are ranged glass frames or lights in one continued slope to the top of the back wall, there received into proper framework; but for the greater convenience, the lights may be in two tiers or ranges, an under and upper tier, the upper range made to slide up and down over the others, but so as all the glass-work can be moved away occasionally, to admit the full air to the trees after the work of forcing; the whole bottom space within this frame must be of good loamy earth, or any good garden mould, two spades deep, which must be dug or trenched in the common way; then plant a range of trees behind, towards the wall, and two or three yards asunder, erecting a trellis behind them, upon which to train the branches as against a wall or espalier; besides these trees, there may be other inferior plants set in the border or in pots, in front of the trees, as strawberries, dwarf kidney beans, dwarf peas, &c., dwarf roses or the like, that will not rise high enough to shade the fruit-trees in the back range.

A frame of this construction, forty feet long, may be worked by one fire; but if longer, two furnaces for fires will be requisite.*

But to have a more capacious frame both for trained trees and low standards, it may be of any length from twenty to fifty feet or more, but must be ten or fifteen feet wide, having an upright back wall of brick ten feet high, with flues as above directed, and a low wall in

---

* Hot water circulated through cast iron pipes is much better than common flues, and though more expensive on first erection, is afterwards most economical. One fire, if large enough, may be made to heat several large houses.

front one or two feet high, on which is erected upright glass-work, four or five feet perpendicular; and from the top of these, a sloping roof of glass frame, continued to the top of the back wall, supported upon proper bearers three feet or three feet six inches distance, having the top glasses in two ranges, an upper and under range, as before advised, both of which, and those of the upright in front, made to slide and move away occasionally : in this frame there will be room to walk under the glass-work in any part, and there will be also due room for the trees, both dwarfs and low standards; and then having the whole ground space withinside of loamy or other good earth, as in the other frame, you may plant your trees, some in one range against the back wall, as peaches, nectarines, apricots, grapes, figs, &c., six or eight feet asunder, erecting a trellis for training them upon, and in front of these may be planted rows of young cherries, both in small standards, half standards, and dwarfs; the full standards to have about five feet stems; each sort, both trained trees and standards, to be planted when about from three to four or five years old, as soon as they acquire a bearing state, with regular heads of two or three feet extent at first planting. Having procured the trees and the ground ready for their reception, may then plant one range of the choicest sorts as before noticed, next the back wall two or three yards asunder, the others in rows from back to front, at six or eight feet distance, the tallest behind and the lowest in front, at three or four feet distance in each row, making each row range against the intervals of the trained tree behind; or if they are all standards, and half standards, there will be more room for several sorts of smaller plants under them; and as their branches will be nearer the top glasses, it may be of particular advantage ; and in the intervals may be planted some low currants, gooseberries, raspberries, strawberries, dwarf beans. kidney beans, &c. But a frame of these dimensions is sometimes planted entirely with standards, more particularly cherries, as being more moderate shooters and soonest arrive to a bearing state, so as to bear any tolerable quantity of fruit; planting them five or six feet distance : sometimes standard plums, apricots, peaches, and nectarines are also planted, and vines to train up under the glasses.

A frame of these dimensions, twenty-five feet long, may be worked by one fire ; but if more than thirty feet in length, two furnaces for fires, with each its set of flues, will be necessary.

With respect to the age of trees for both the above kinds of fire-heat forcing-frames, they should be from three to four or five years old, with regular heads of branches, two or three feet extent, and just arrived at a tolerable bearing state ; no very vigorous shooters must be admitted, but such only as assume a moderate, regular growth, and are *trained* in the nursery until they have acquired a proper size, each as directed under its respective head, whether as wall trees or standards; they are to be transplanted into the frame in October or November to remain for forcing ; but should be permitted to have a year or two's growth here before you begin forcing them, that they may be firmly rooted; during which time all the glasses should be entirely away, that the trees may have the full air till forcing time is nearly arrived ; or may occasionally have trained bearing trees of small sizes in pots, which is the best for this speciality, if they have been in good growth for one season at least, and so removed in their said pots into the frame at the proper season as above.

In both the above kinds of forcing-frames, you may also plant some grape-vines on the inside of the front glasses in the full ground, and conduct the shoots along up towards the glass-work to a sort of slight trellis, keeping the branches quite thin; and they will ripen early fruit in great perfection.

The season for beginning to make the fires for forcing the trees in either of the above described fire-heat frames, is any time in January, though about the middle or towards the latter end of that month, or beginning of February, is, for the general part, rather the most successful time to begin the general forcing to have a good crop ; for if the trees are forced very early, there will be some danger of their miscarrying ; as, if they should come into blossom when severe weather prevails, that air cannot be freely admitted at intervals, they seldom set any tolerable crop of fruit; more particularly, cherries, peaches, nectarines and apricots ; therefore, by beginning to make the fires about the time above directed, the trees will be in blossom about the middle of February, when we may expect some fine sunny days for the admission of a moderate portion of fresh air, which is essentially necessary to promote the natural impregnation of the fruit, and improve its free growth; for if kept too close they are apt to drop off in their infant state.

The fires are to be lighted in the furnace every afternoon about four or five o'clock, and if kept burning till ten or twelve, it will sufficiently heat the flues to warm the internal air of the house till next morning, when, if very cold, frosty, or cloudy damp weather, a moderate fire may also be made occasionally ; and by no means force the trees too much, for a moderate warmth will prove the most successful;* and thus continue the fires occasionally till towards the latter end of April, but less in proportion as the weather grows warmer.

Fresh air must be occasionally admitted in fine days, by sliding some of the glasses a little open, and, as the trees advance to blossom and fruit, the days grow longer, and the power of the sun greater, allow a greater proportion of air accordingly.   Likewise give frequent waterings to the borders.

Thus your trees will be in full blossom in February, and some will ripen fruit in April, particularly cherries and strawberries ; you may also expect early apricots, peaches and nectarines, in May, and plums and early grapes in June.

After the fruits of the different sorts are all gathered, the glasses should be taken entirely away, that the trees may have the full air during summer; and in December they should be placed upon the frame again ready for forcing in January.

---

* In forwarding all stone fruit the thermometer ought to range from 45°
to 50° at night, and 60° to 70° in the day while in, and for a short time
after the blossoms are expanded.   Grapes will be the better with an
average of 10° higher.

With respect to pruning the trained trees, that is those that are
trained as wall trees against the trellis, &c., they are to be pruned
and trained every summer and autumn, each sort according to its
kind, as other wall trees, and as directed under all their respective
articles; and as to the standards, their requisite pruning is principally in autumn, to cut out any irregular growth, and thinning out
any crowding shoots, for the branches must be kept thin and regular,
clear of each other, six or eight inches distant; and any stragglers
which extend in length considerably, should be reduced to order; and
as the branches in general become so long as to press against the
glasses, or spread too much, they should also be reduced a little, to
preserve them within due compass, observing always, when shortening the standards, it is necessary to cut to a bud situated on the outside of the shoot or branch, making the cut on the inside.

Every autumn, after pruning the trees, the borders must be digged
carefully one spade deep.

It must be remarked that the trees in these frames or houses, if
annually forced, are not so durable nor plentiful bearers as those in
the full air; therefore, when you shall see any become weak, sickly,
or bad bearers, others should be ready in training, or procured from
the nurseries to plant in their stead; and in this no time should be
lost.   Here is the main advantage of growing in pots.

But to continue the same trees more effectually in health, and in a
bearing state, some have a double portion of walling and framing
planted, but more particularly that of the first described fire-heat
frame, which is sometimes contrived to move or slide along from one
place to another, for one framework and glasses to serve two portions
of walling, so that being alternately worked, one part one year, the
other the year after, each portion of trees will have a year of rest in
their natural growth, and will succeed each other in due order for
forcing, whereby the health and vigor of the trees will be better supported, and each year a greater crop of fruit may be expected than if
the same trees were successively forced every year.

HOT WALLS.

Hot walls are ranges of brick or stone walling faced with glass,
generally running due east or west, fronting the south and inclosing
a space of several feet width, furnished with internal fire flues, &c.,
wholly for forcing fruit-trees to early production.   But as hot walls
and forcing-houses are nearly similar in their construction, use, and
general management, to forcing-frames, reference should be had to
that article for their general explanation.

VINERIES.

Various buildings have been contrived to effect the ripening of the
more choice kinds of late grapes, which cannot be effected in the open
ground, as likewise to force the earlier sorts, so as to have them fit
for the table in May, June and July.   The constructions of these
kinds of buildings are different, though all answering the same pur-

pose : some are constructed with flues ranging within the wall where the vines are trained up ; but as the vines would receive more heat at times by being closer to the wall than is proper, a lattice-work is generally detached therefrom, to which the branches are trained, and the whole is covered with a range of sloping glass ; but the more common method is to train them under the sloping glasses of the hot-house, or other similarly constructed stoves or forcing-frames ; in such places the vines are generally planted close to the outside, and introduced through holes contrived for the purpose in the upright timbers of the front-lights, as low down as can conveniently be done.

In some vineries the vines are planted near the front, in the inside, and trained up to neat trellises made for that purpose close under the roof or sloping glasses. This is the best in all cases.

SOUTHERN STATES.

In the southern States, especially such of them as have not severe winter frosts, you may plant apple, pear, peach, nectarine, apricot, cherry and plum-trees, both for espaliers and standards : plant also almonds, quinces, gooseberies, currants, raspberries, and every other kind of hardy fruit bearing trees and shrubs, which are usually planted either in the fruit-garden or orchard.

You may also prune each and every of the above kinds, according to the directions given in *this month, March* and *October ;* and in the two last months you will find ample instructions, both for preparing the ground and planting the various kinds of fruit-trees above mentioned.

THE ORCHARD.

The Orchard is a department consigned entirely to the growth of standard fruit-trees for furnishing a large supply of the most useful kinds of fruit ; in which you may have as standards, apple, pear, plum, cherry, peach, apricot, quince, almond, and nectarine-trees ; also mulberries, filberts, medlars, and berberries ; Spanish chestnuts and English walnuts ; which two latter are more particularly applicable for the boundaries of *large* orchards, in which they will screen the other trees from impetuous winds and cold blasts, all of which are to be arranged in rows at the distances directed in *March* and *October ;* in which months you will find ample directions for raising, propagating, and planting the various kinds of fruit-trees necessary for all the departments.

But sometimes orchards consist entirely of apple-trees, particularly when apples are wanted in large quantities for cider or whiskey making ; and sometimes whole orchards of very considerable extent of peach-trees, when the fruit is designed for distillation ; likewise entire orchards of cherry-trees, but particularly within a moderate distance of large cities and towns, where sale can be obtained for the fruit; pear orchards are also extensive where people are in the habit of making perry.

A general orchard, however, composed of all the before mentioned fruit-trees, should consist of a treble or more proportion of apple and peach-trees, because they are considerably the most useful fruits, particularly the former, as they, exclusive of their use in distilling and cider-making, may be continued for table use, in the different sorts, the whole year round.

But the misfortune is, that too frequently after orchards are planted and fenced, they have seldom any more care bestowed upon them. Boughs are suffered to hang dangling to the ground, their heads are so loaded with wood as to be almost impervious to sun and air, and they are left to be exhausted by moss and injured by cattle, &c.

By a redundancy of wood the roots are exhausted unprofitably, the bearing wood is robbed of part of its sustenance, and the natural life of the tree unnecessarily shortened, whilst the superfluous wood endangers the tree by giving the winds an additional power over it, and is injurious to the bearing wood, by retaining the damps and preventing a due circulation of air.

The outer branches only are able to produce fruit properly; every inner and underling branch ought therefore to be removed. It is common to see fruit-trees with two or three tiers of boughs pressing so hard upon one another, with their twigs so intimately interwoven, that a small bird can scarcely creep in among them. Trees thus neglected acquire, from want of due ventilation, a stinted habit, and the fruit becomes of a crude inferior quality.

The trees are very often almost entirely subdued by moss, which kills many, and injures others so much that they are only an incumbrance to the ground and a disgrace to the country. This evil may easily be checked by scraping and rubbing off the moss at this season of the year, with a rounded iron scraper, &c., when men have little else to employ them, and only seek work in idle, expensive, and unprofitable amusements. Draining the land, if too retentive of moisture, will sometimes prevent or cure moss, or digging round the trees on the approach of winter, or in spring, and bringing fresh mould, or the scouring of ponds and roads, or the rubbish of old walls, well prepared and pulverized, and laid round them. Whatever contributes to the health of the tree, will cure, or in some degree mitigate, this and other diseases.

These considerations ought to induce to an examination of your standard apple, pear, plum and cherry-trees, &c., and where found necessary, to thin their branches, scrape and rub off moss, cut off all dead or irregularly placed limbs and branches, and also any luxuriant unfruitful shoots, and such branches as appear to be in a decaying or cankery state, all of which must be cut off *close* to where they were produced, or to some healthy leading branch or shoot; *for the bark cannot grow over a stump*, because there is no power to draw the sap that way, for which reason always cut rather a little within the wood.

Smooth the cut parts, and if the amputations are large, apply thereto a light covering of the *medicated tar* below mentioned, which is to be laid on with a painting brush; if under an inch in diameter, it is scarcely worth while to go to that trouble, for such, when well pruned, will heal and cover freely.

Be particular to use a saw in taking off all the limbs and branches that are too large for the knife, and smooth the cut parts with either your pruning-knife or a neat draw-knife, which answers better for large amputations.

The *medicated tar* is composed of half an ounce of corrosive sublimate, reduced to a fine powder, and then put into a three pint earthen pipkin, with about half a gill of gin, or other spirit, stirred well together, and the sublimate thus dissolved. The pipkin must then be filled by degrees with common tar, and constantly stirred till the mixture is intimately blended. This quantity will be sufficient for two hundred trees. Being of a very poisonous nature, it should not be suffered to lie carelessly about the house. The sublimate dissolves better when united with the same quantity of the spirit of hartshorn or of sal ammoniac. This mixture being apt to run, consistency may be given it by mixing it with either pounded chalk or whiting.

The above composition will be found eminently useful, as no worm of any kind can live near its influence, and no evil whatever will arise to the trees from its poisonous quality; it yields to the growth of the bark, and affords a complete protection to the parts against the influence of the weather.

A solution of corrosive sublimate, made as directed under the head *Orchard* next month, will be found the most effectual wash that can be applied to peach and other trees for the destruction of the worm which so generally annoys them.

Those who wish to apply Forsythe's or Barnes's compositions, will find instructions, both for making and applying them, under the head *Orchard* in *March*.

When pruning is judiciously done, fruit-trees will come into bearing sooner, produce more abundantly, and continue in vigor for nearly double their common age. No branch of your orchard trees should ever be shortened unless for the figure of the tree or the reasons before mentioned, and then it should be taken off *close*, as before observed, to where it was produced, or to a leading shoot. The more the range of branches shoot circularly, a little inclining upwards, the more equally will the sap be distributed, and the better will the tree bear. The ranges of branches should not be too near each other, that the fruit and leaves should all have their full share of sun, and where it suits, the middle of the tree should be so free from wood that no branch crosses another, but all the extremities point upwards.

If any of your particularly valuable fruit-trees are partly decayed, or in a bad state of health, and you wish to attempt their restoration by judicious pruning and the application of good composition, you must defer it till March, or when the sap begins to ascend in spring, which will be manifest by the swelling of their buds; then prune them and apply the composition as directed in *March*.

I am not an advocate for much doctoring with old decayed or sickly
tree, but the reverse; therefore recommend as the most preferable
way to replace such with young healthy trees, so soon as they show
strong symptoms of decay. Whenever you meet with a tree, the
fruit of which you esteem, propagate it immediately *whilst* in *health*,
by budding or grafting, &c.; and if it should afterwards get into a
declined state, replace it with one of the same, or some other good
kind. Never propagate from a sickly tree if you can well avoid it,
for its disorder will be carried with the buds or grafts, and in all probability will ultimately work their destruction.

For the method of propagating fruit-trees, &c., by budding or inoculation, see the *Nursery* in *July*.

GOOD AND BAD PRUNING OF FOREST-TREES.

The annexed wood-cuts will explain the effects of judicious and
injudicious pruning better than a lengthened disquisition. Fig. 8
represents a tree of thirty years' growth, which has been regularly
and properly pruned. Fig. 9, a tree of the same age, which has been
neglected as to pruning during its early growth, and has now been
pruned in a way too frequently practised—namely, by sawing and
lopping off the branches, after they have attained a large size. Fig.
10 shows the bad consequences of neglecting early pruning, in the

| Fig. 8. | Fig. 9. | Fig. 10. |

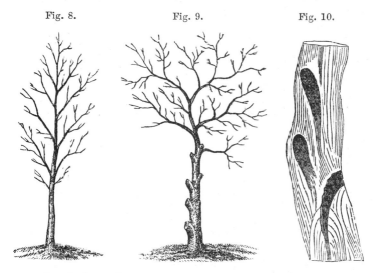

case of a plank cut from an ash-tree which had been pruned by lopping off the large branches many years before it was felled. The cuts
in this case had been made several inches from the bole, and the
branches being very large, the stumps left had become rotten. The
enlargement of the trunk had not, however, been stopped, for the
new wood had covered over all the haggled parts, in some places to

several inches thick. Yet the effects of the previous exposure to the action of the weather, by injudicious pruning, is strikingly marked by the decayed state of the parts connected with the branches which had been amputated ; progressive pruning of deciduous trees, commenced while they are young, if it is to be practised at all, will produce no such blemishes when the timber is cut up. In a school for gardeners or indeed in every school, these effects should be demonstrated by examples of bad pruning ; the best collection of such is to be found in the economic museum of Sir William Hooker's foundation at Kew Gardens, but it would be very easy to collect specimens for exhibition at horticultural societies and State and county fairs.

THE VINEYARD.

The cultivation of the vine merits the attention and support of every lover of his country. The practicability of producing *Wine* in the United States, cannot be doubted ; the experiment has been made successfully in Pennsylvania, Ohio, Kentucky, Missouri, and South Carolina. Nothing is now wanted but the liberal and spirited exertions of the citizens to carry it to such perfection, especially in the middle and southern States, as in the course of a few years to produce a sufficient supply for home consumption, and, in time, a large quantity for exportation.*

WORK TO BE DONE IN THE VINEYARD.

In severe weather, when other work cannot be performed, prepare poles for the support of the vines ; these, for sake of durability, ought to be made of red cedar, white oak, or chestnut, split and seasoned, and to be made one inch and a half or two inches square, and six and a half or seven feet long, pointed at the lower end ; and if that part which is to be inserted in the ground, and about three inches above it, say fifteen inches, be dipped in boiling pitch, it will be of considerable advantage ; if this is not convenient, let that part be slightly scorched in the fire, which will prevent their rotting so soon as they otherwise would. Round poles, such as are used for hoops, of about two inches diameter will do, but these soon rot, and will require to be replaced every two or three years, when the former would last, if made of the heart of well-grown timber, fifteen or twenty years. Sticks of four or five feet long may also be made for the purpose of supporting young vines during the first and second years of their growth, after which they are to be taken away to answer a similar purpose, and replaced with the tall poles ; those may be made one inch and a quarter square, pointed, and dipped in pitch as above.

* This is now being carried out to a prodigious extent ; the neighborhood of Cincinnati alone furnishes about one million gallons of first quality.

You may also at this season cart manure into the vineyard, and spread it as directed in *February*, repair old fences, and prepare posts and rails, or boards for new ones; examine your ploughs, harrows, spades, shovels, hoes, mattocks, and all your other tools, and have such as need it repaired; purchase any new tools that may be wanted, and have all your necessaries in readiness for the opening of the spring.

In such of the southern States as have mild winters and early vegetation, vines may now be pruned, as directed under the head *Vineyard* in February, but with them, November would be a much more eligible time for this work. In the middle States you must defer the pruning of vines to the last week or ten days in February, not later, except in extremely severe weather, but on no account later than the first week of March, for soon after that period the sap begins to ascend, after which, were you to prune them, they would bleed so copiously from where the wounds were inflicted, as to greatly exhaust and injure them, and even totally to destroy some. In the eastern States this work may be done between the first and tenth of March, according as the spring may be early or late, observing that it is safer to prune *too early* than *too late*.

Under the head *Vineyard* in March, you will find general instructions for the different methods of propagating and cultivating the *vine*, both as espaliers, and in the field way; likewise concise descriptions of the various kinds which have been generally cultivated, either for table use or making wine; and also, observations on the kinds most likely to succeed in the various parts of the Union.

THE NURSERY.

THOUGH this is not a period in which much business can be done in the Nursery, especially in the middle and eastern States, it may be well to call attention to that eminently useful department; in order that those who have not yet attempted it, may have time to consider of its utility, and to determined, when the season arrives in which it can be commenced.

The many advantages which every lover of improvement and planting may derive from having a nursery of his own, especially in such a country as this, where public nurseries are so scarce and frequently so remote, as to render it extremely inconvenient to procure such trees as may be wanted; the expenses of transportation to a considerable distance; the length of time the trees have to be out of ground, and the consequent uncertainty of their growth; the hazard of procuring the intended or even good kinds—except the proprietors are men of experience, knowledge, and integrity—are strong inducements to the establishing small and convenient nurseries, in which the owners may raise such kinds of fruit and forest-trees, ornamental shrubs and other plants, as may be pleasing and profitable to themselves, useful to posterity, and ornamental to the country.

The raising of Osage orange, buckthorn, thorn-quicks and other plants, suitable for making live hedges, ought also to command attention; especially in such parts of the Union as timber is getting scarce and dear in. The planting and establishing of such hedges must ultimately be resorted to, and the sooner it is commenced the better.

Conscious of the great utility of such establishments, I shall in the course of this work give such ample and minute instructions, for the raising and propagation of fruit and forest-trees, ornamental trees and shrubs, thorn-quicks, &c. &c., as may lead the most inexperienced persons to a complete knowledge of the business; which may be pursued upon a small or a more extensive scale, as it suits.

In the nursery may also be raised all sorts of hardy herbaceous plants, both fibrous, bulbous, and tuberous-rooted, for adorning the flower garden, pleasure-ground, and to plant for medical use, &c.

EXTENT, SOIL, SITUATION, &C.

With respect to the proper extent or dimensions of a nursery, whether for private use or public supply, it must be according to the quantity of plants required, or the demand for sale : if for private use, from a quarter to half an acre or more may be sufficient, which must be regulated according to the extent of garden ground and plantations it is required to supply; and if for a public nursery, for any general cultivation, not less than three or four acres of land will be worth occupying as such, and from that to fifteen or twenty acres or more may be requisite, according to the demand.

The soil for a nursery, requires particular attention. It ought to be naturally good for at least one full spade deep, or if more, the better; always prefer a loamy soil of a moderately light temperament, which cannot *naturally* be too good, notwithstanding what some advance to the contrary, even though the trees should afterwards be removed into a poorer soil. Reason teaches, that young trees growing vigorously and freely in a good soil, will form numerous and healthy roots, and when they come to be afterwards planted in worse land, they will be able, from the strength of their constitution and multiplicity of roots, to feed themselves freely with coarser food. On the contrary, young trees raised upon poor land, by having their vessels contracted and their outward bark mossy and diseased, will be a long time, even after being removed into a rich soil, before they attain to a vigorous state. If the roots of the young plants have not a good soil, or sufficient room to strike in, there will be little hope of their furnishing themselves with that ample stock of roots and fibres which is necessary to a good plant, and with which every young tree ought to be well furnished, when removed for final transplantation.

Most authors who have written on the kind of soil most suitable for a nursery have differed in their opinions, even so far as to be almost quite contradictory to one another; and the common opinion is in favor of the soil being the same, nearly similar, or rather worse, than that into which the trees are to be finally planted. But this is setting out upon a very wrong principle; for, were a nursery to be established on a poor gravel or stiff clay, the plants raised on such would be poor, small, hide-bound, starved things, very unfit for planting in any land.

If an animal was to be only half fed, from its first having life, for one year, I believe that such would never grow to be of a large size of its kind, if afterwards it was put into better keeping; but suppose it was put to harder fare, it would certainly make a poor figure. If this same animal had been moderately fed for one year, and then put into worse feeding, it would have made a better beast.

Some will say that these observations are unnecessary, as the ground in which *fruit-trees* are generally planted is for the most part good, being particularly selected for that purpose, and that a soil similar thereto will do very well; granted, provided the ground be naturally good; but if these people had a large extent of poor gravelly soil, or stiff clay, to plant with forest or ornamental trees, live hedges, &c., would they seek out a similar spot for a nursery, to raise plants for planting the same? If so, they would discover their mistake when too late. This is the error I wish to correct, being very desirous that every attempt towards this kind of improvement should prove successful; and in order to effect this, it is necessary to set out on right principles.

It is very wrong to enrich nurseries with *dung*, particularly until it is very old, and almost turned into earth; although many eminent nurserymen dung their ground very plentifully, yet they do it with great judgment, and never plant trees until it is well rooted and mixed with the mould, so as to be quite incorporated, and generally take a crop or two of vegetables before they plant trees therein.

It is not absolutely necessary that the soil should be exceedingly rich, nor over carefully manured; a medium between the two extremes is best; such as any good substantial garden ground; or good mellow pasture land, having the sward trenched to the bottom, will do very well for the growth of trees.

As to situation, it ought to be somewhat low, but dry, fully exposed to the sun and free air, and, if possible, where there is the convenience of water for the occasional watering of young seedlings and newly planted trees, &c.

As to a small nursery for private use, it may be formed out of part of the kitchen garden, if large enough, or some other convenient place; or it may be made somewhere convenient to the pleasure ground, if any, and so contrived as to lead insensibly into it by winding walks, so as to appear to be part of the same.

FENCES, PREPARING AND LAYING OUT THE GROUND.

A fence round the whole ground is necessary : this may either be a hedge and ditch, or a paling; the former is the cheapest, and in the end most durable; though in some places where rabbits abound, paling fences at first are eligible for preserving the nursery from the depredations of those animals which often do great mischief to the young plants by barking and cropping them : a good hedge and ditch fence, however, may be made very effectual against the inroads of both men and brutes; and the most eligible plant for this purpose is the hawthorn; but a paling, or other similar close fence, either in general or part, would be extremely useful, against which to train young wall-trees to a proper growth for garden or espalier plantations.

The ground must then be all regularly trenched one or two spades deep, according as the natural depth of the soil will admit, for by no means dig deeper than the natural good soil, being either one spade, one and a half, or two spades deep.

Then, having trenched the ground, proceed to divide it by walks into quarters and other compartments; a principal walk should lead directly through the middle or some principal part of the ground, which may be from five to eight or ten feet wide, according as it shall seem proper for use or ornament, having a broad border on each side; another walk should be carried all round next the outward boundary, four or five feet wide, leaving an eight or ten feet border next the fence all the way; then may divide the internal part by smaller cross walks, so as to form the whole into four, six, or eight principal divisions, which are commonly called quarters.

One or more of the divisions must be allotted for a seminary, i. e., for the reception of all sorts of seeds for raising seedling plants to furnish the other parts; therefore divide this seminary ground into four feet wide beds, with foot-wide alleys at least between bed and bed: in these beds should be sown seeds, &c., of all such trees, shrubs and herbaceous plants as are raised from seed; and which seeds consist both of the various sorts of kernels and stones of fruit, to raise stocks for grafting and budding; seeds of forest and ornamental trees, shrubs, &c., and seeds of numerous herbaceous perennials, both of the fibrous-rooted and bulbous-rooted tribes: the sowing season is both spring and autumn, according to the nature of the different sorts, which is fully illustrated in their proper places; and when the young tree and shrub seedling-plants so raised are one or two years old, they are to be planted out in nursery-rows into the other principal divisions; but many kinds of herbaceous plants require to be picked out from the seed-beds, when but from two to three or four months old, as directed for each under their own respective heads. On the other hand, most kinds of bulbous seedlings will not be fit for planting out in less than one or two years.

Part of the nursery ground should be allotted for stools of various trees and shrubs for the propagation by layers, by which vast numbers of plants of different kinds are propagated. These stools are strong plants of trees and shrubs, planted in rows three or four feet distant every way, and such of them as naturally rise with tall stems, are, after being planted one year, to be headed down near the ground, to force out many lower shoots conveniently situated for laying.

And as to cuttings, suckers, slips, offsets, &c., those of hardy trees, shrubs, and plants, may be planted in any convenient compartment, and in shady borders, &c., and for the more tender kinds should allot some warm sheltered situation.

The other principal divisions, therefore, of the nursery-ground, are for the reception of the various sorts of seedling plants from the above seminary quarters, also for all others that are raised from suckers, layers, cuttings, &c., there to be planted in rows from one to two or three feet asunder, according to their natures of growth; observing to allow the tree and shrub kinds treble the distance of herbaceous perennials. Of the tree and shrub kinds, some are to be planted for stocks to graft and bud the select sorts of fruit-trees upon, and other choice plants, which are usually propagated by those methods; others are trained up entirely on their own roots without budding or grafting, as in most forest and other hardy tree kinds, as also almost all the sorts of shrubs. Here they are to remain to have two, three, or several years' growth, according as they shall require, for the several purposes for which they are designed in their future situations in the garden and plantations, &c., which are directed in their respective cultures.

In a complete nursery it is also proper to allot some dry, warm, sheltered situation in the full sun, on which to have occasional hotbeds of dung or tan for raising and forwarding many sorts of tender or curious exotics, by seed, cuttings, suckers, slips, &c., and for which purposes you should be furnished with eligible frames and lights, hand-glasses, garden-mats, and other relative requisites.

GENERAL MODE OF ARRANGING THE PLANTS OF THIS DEPARTMENT.

In the distribution of the various sorts of plants in the nursery, let each sort be separate; the fruit-trees should generally occupy spaces by themselves; the forest-trees, &c., should also be stationed together; all the shrub kind should be ranged in separate compartments; allot also a place for herbaceous perennials: a warm place should likewise be allotted for the tender plants, and defended with yew, juniper, or private hedges, or a reed hedge, &c., in which compartments you may station all such plants as are a little tender whilst young and require occasional shelter from frost, yet are not so tender as to require to be housed like green-house plants, &c., so that in such compartments there may also be frames of various sizes, either to be covered occasionally with glass-lights, or some with mats, to contain such of the more choice of the above tender kinds in pots, to be nursed up a year or two, or longer, with occasional shelter, till hardened gradually to bear the open air fully.

The arrangement of all the sorts in the open ground must always be in lines or nursery-rows, as formerly observed, to stand till arrived at a proper growth for drawing off for the garden and plantation; placing the fruit-tree stocks, &c., for grafting and budding upon, in rows three feet asunder, if for dwarfs, but standards four feet, and a foot and a half or two feet in the lines; though after being grafted and budded, they then commencing fruit-trees, &c.; if they are to stand to grow to any large size, they should be allowed the width of five feet between the rows. Forest-trees should also be placed in rows four feet asunder, and eighteen inches distance in the rows, varying the distance both ways according to the time they are to stand; the shrub kind should likewise be arranged in rows about two feet asunder, and fifteen or eighteen inches distant in each line; and as to herbaceous plants, they should generally be disposed in four

5

feet wide beds, or large borders, in rows, or distances from six to
twelve or eighteen inches asunder, according to their nature of growth
and the time they are to stand.

By the above arrangement of the various sorts of hardy trees,
shrubs and herbaceous plants, in rows at those small distances in the
nursery, a great number of plants are contained within a narrow
compass, which is sufficient room, as they are only to remain a short
time; and that by being thus stationed in a little compass they are
more readily kept under a proper regulation for the time they are to
remain in this department.

In the public nurseries they often plant many kinds of seedling
trees and shrubs in much closer rows at first planting out than the
distances above prescribed, not only in order to husband the ground
to the best advantage, but by standing closer it encourages the stem
to shoot more directly upward, and prevents them expanding themselves much anywhere but at top; as for instance, many sorts of
evergreens that are but of slow growth the first year or two, such as
the pine-trees, firs, and several others, which the nursery gardeners
often prick out from the seminary, first into four feet wide beds, in
rows lengthways, six inches asunder; and after having two years'
growth there, transplant them in rows a foot asunder; and in two
years after give them another and final transplantation in the nursery,
in rows three feet asunder, as observed above; and by these different
transplantings it will encourage the roots to branch out into many
horizontal fibres, and prepare them better for final transplantation,
which is the more particularly necessary in several of the pine and
fir kinds and several other evergreens.

With respect to the different methods of planting nursery plants,
after being raised either by seed, layers, cuttings, &c., it is performed
in several ways to different sorts; some are pricked out by dibble,
especially small seedlings, others are put in by the spade, either by
trenches, slitting-in, trenching, or holing, and some are drilled in by
a spade or hoe.

As to most of the tree and shrub kind, sometimes the young seedling-trees and shrubs are pricked out from the seminary by dibble;
sometimes they are put in by the spade in the following method:
first, having set a line to plant by, strike the spade into the ground
with its back close to the line, and give another stroke at right angles
with it, then set a plant into the crevice made at the second stroke,
bring it close up into the first made crevice even with the line, and
press the mould close to it with the foot, then proceed to plant
another in the same way, and so proceed till all are planted. A
second method is for plants with rather larger roots; strike the spade
down with its back close to the line, as aforesaid, and then with a
spade cut out a narrow trench close along the line, making the side
next the line perfectly upright; then placing the plants upright
against the back of the trench close to the line, at the proper distances before mentioned; and, as you go on, trim in the earth upon
their roots; when one row is thus planted, tread the earth gently all
along close to the plants, and then proceed to plant another row. A
third method of planting out small tree and shrub plants is, having

set the line as above, then turning the spade edgeways to the line, cast out the earth of that spit, then a person being ready with plants, set one in the cavity close to the line, and directly taking another such spit, turn the earth in upon the roots of the plant, and then placing another plant into the second cut, cover its roots with the earth of a third spit, and so on to the end; but sometimes when the roots are considerably larger, holes are made along by the line wide enough to receive the roots freely every way, so covering them in, as above, as you go on, observing always to press the earth gently with the foot close to the roots, and close about the stems, to settle the plants firmly in their proper position.

Herbaceous fibrous-rooted plants are, for the most part, planted with a dibble, except when the roots are large and spreading, or such as are removed with balls of earth, then they are more commonly planted by holing them in with a garden trowel, or small spade.

Bulbous and tuberous-rooted plants sometimes are planted with a dibble, but many sorts may also be planted in drills drawn with a hoe. These sorts are also sometimes planted as follows: rake or trim the earth from off the top of the beds from about three to four inches deep into the alleys, then place the roots in rows upon the surface, thrusting the bottom a little into the ground, and immediately cover them with the earth which was drawn off into the alleys for that purpose, spreading it evenly over every part, so as to bury all the roots an equal depth.

As to the tender kinds of exotic plants that require occasional shelter whilst young, many of them should be potted, in order for moving to a warm situation in winter, or some into frames, &c., to have occasional shelter from frost, by glasses or mats, as they shall require; hardening them, however, by degrees, to bear the open air fully in the nursery the year round.

And the most tender kinds that require the aid of a green-house or stove, must all be potted and placed among the respective plants of those conservatories.

GENERAL CULTURE OF THE PLANTS OF THIS DEPARTMENT.

With respect to the management of the various hardy nursery plants :—

Those designed as stocks for fruit-trees should have their stems generally cleared from lateral shoots, so as to form a clean, straight stem, but never to shorten the leading shoot until it is decayed, or becomes very crooked, in which case it may be proper to cut it down low in spring, and it will shoot out again, training the main shoot for a stem, with its top entire for the present, till grafted or budded.

But in the above nursery culture of the fruit-tree kind, some sorts designed for principal wall or espalier trees should, when of one year's growth from grafting and budding, be transplanted against some close fence in the nursery, either a wall, paling, or trellis, &c., and their first graft or bud-shoot headed down in the spring, to promote an emission of lower lateral shoots and branches, in order to be regularly trained to the fence in a spreading manner for two years or more, or till wanted, whereby to form the head in a regular spreading growth for the intended purpose of garden trees, which in the public nurseries in particular should always be ready in proper training to supply those who may wish to have their espaliers, &c., covered as soon as possible by means of such ready trained trees.

A similar training, both for wall and espalier fruit-trees, may be practised to some principal sorts in the nursery rows in the open quarters of ground by arranging their branches in a spreading manner, to stakes placed for that purpose.

But for standard fruit-trees, they should be trained with a clean single stem, five or six feet for full standards, by cutting off all lateral shoots arising below; half standards trained with a three or four feet stem, and dwarf standards in proportion, by the same means; and as to the heads of the standards, it may be proper in some to have the first immediate shoots from the graft or bud when a year old pruned short in spring to procure several laterals, in order to form a fuller spread of branches, proceeding regularly together from near the summit of the stem that the head may advance in a more regular branchy growth.

Forest-trees, in general, should be encouraged to form straight clean single stems, by occasional trimming off the largest lateral branches, which also promote the leading top-shoot in aspiring straight and faster in height; always suffering that part of each tree to shoot at full length, that is, not to top it, unless, however, where the stem divides into forks, to trim off the weakest, and leave the straightest and strongest shoot or branch to shoot out at its proper length to form the aspiring top, as above.

The different sorts of shrubs may either be suffered to branch out in their own natural way, except just regulating very disorderly growths, or some may be trained with single clean stems from about a foot to two or three high, according as you shall think proper with respect to the sorts or the purposes for which you design them in the shrubbery; but many shrubs appear the most agreeable when permitted to shoot out laterally all the way, so as to be branchy or feathered to the bottom.

Each species of fruit-trees, as soon as grafted or budded, should have all its different varieties numbered, by placing large flat-sided sticks at the ends of the rows, for which purpose some nurserymen use the spokes of old coach wheels, or anything about that size of any durable wood, painting or marking the numbers thereon, 1, 2, 3, &c., on different sticks, entering the numbers in the nursery book, with the name of the varieties to which the number-sticks are placed; whereby you can at all times readily have recourse to the sorts wanted.

The same method may be practised to any other trees, shrubs, or herbaceous plants, especially the varieties of particular species, when they are numerous, as in many of the flowery tribe, such as auriculas, carnations, tulips, anemones, ranunculuses, and the like.

With respect to watering the nursery plants, this may be very requisite in dry hot weather in spring and summer to seed beds, and tender seedling plants while young, and when first planted out, till

they have taken good root; also occasionally to new-layed layers,
and newly planted cuttings in dry warm weather; but as to hardy
trees and shrubs of all sorts, if planted out at the proper time, that
is, not too late in spring, no great regard need be paid to watering,
for they will generally succeed very well without any; indeed, where
there are but a few, you may, if you please, water them occasionally,
if it proves a very dry spring in April and May; but where there
are great plantations, it would be an almost insupportable fatigue,
and a great expense.

Every winter or spring the ground between the rows of all sorts
of transplanted plants in the open nursery quarters must be digged;
this is particularly necessary to all the tree and shrub kinds that
stand wide enough in rows to admit the spade between; which work
is by the nurserymen called *turning-in;* the most general season for
this work is any time from October to the latter end of March; but
the sooner it is done the more advantageous it will prove to the
plants. The ground is to be digged one spade deep, proceeding row
by row, turning the top of each pit clean to the bottom, that all
weeds on the top may be buried a proper depth to rot: this work of
turning-in is a most necessary annual operation, both to destroy
weeds and to increase the growth of the young nursery plants.

In summer be remarkably attentive to keep all sorts clean from
weeds; the seedlings growing close in the seminary beds must be
hand-weeded; but among plants of all sorts that grow in rows wide
enough to introduce a hoe, this will prove not only the most expeditious method of destroying weeds, but by loosening the top of the
soil it will prove good culture in promoting the growth of all kinds
of plants; always perform this work of hoeing in dry weather in due
time, before the weeds grow large, and you may soon go over a great
space of ground, either with a common drawing hoe, or occasionally
with a scuffling hoe, as you shall find the most convenient.

According as any quarters or compartments of the nursery ground
are cleared from plants, others must be substituted in their room
from the seminary, &c., but the ground should previously be trenched
and lie some time fallow to recruit or recover its former vigor; giving
it also the addition of manure, if it shall seem proper; and after
being trenched in ridges, and having the repose only of one winter
or summer, or a year at most, it will sufficiently recover its vegetative force, and may be planted fresh.

It will be of advantage to plant the grounds with plants of a different kind from those which it occupied before.

The tender or exotic plants of all kinds that require shelter only
from frost, whilst young, as formerly mentioned, and by degrees become hardy enough to live in the open air; should such of them as
are seedlings in the open ground have the beds arched over with
hoops or rods at the approach of winter, in order to be sheltered with
mats in severe weather; and those which are in pots, either seedlings
or transplanted plants, should be removed in October in their pots
to a warm sunny situation sheltered with hedges, &c., placing some
close under the fences facing the sun, where they may have occasional covering with mats in frosty weather; others that are more

tender may be placed in frames to have occasional covering either of glass lights or mats, &c., from frost; observing of all those sorts here alluded to, that they are gradually to be hardened to the open ground, and need only be covered in frosty weather; at all other times let them remain fully exposed, and by degrees, as they acquire age and strength, inure them to bear the open air fully; so as when they arrive at from two or three, to four or five years old, they may be turned out into the open ground. The sorts requiring this treatment are pointed out under their proper heads in the different months.

The green-house kinds of all sorts, or such as require constant shelter in winter, are to be managed as directed under the article GREEN-HOUSE.

And the hot-house or stove-plants, or such as require constant shelter all or the greater part of the year, together with the aid of artificial heat, are to be managed as exhibited under the article HOT-HOUSE.

WORK TO BE DONE IN THE NURSERY.

Young apple and pear-trees may now be pruned agreeably to the rules laid down in March; though if your stock of these is not very numerous, and that you are desirous to have so much work done out of the way when the hurry of business comes on in spring, it will be quite as well to defer doing it till the end of February or beginning of March.

Trim up the stems of forest and other hardy trees where they require it; this may be done when little else can in the nursery; for if it is performed in frosty weather the trees will receive no harm by the operation, especially the hardy deciduous kinds.

Carry well-rotted dung or compost, and lay it on such parts of the nursery as require it. This may be necessary to such particular quarters as have been lately cleared, and that are intended to be planted again with a fresh stock in autumn, taking off a summer crop of vegetables previous thereto; and when the frost permits, let it be trenched in regularly one full spade deep at least. If the necessity requires it this ground may be planted with young trees, &c., in spring.

In severe weather, when out-work cannot be done, make label-sticks; and have them in readiness when wanted, to mark the various kinds and varieties of fruit and forest-trees, shrubs, plants, &c., which you intend to plant or propagate in spring; the largest to mark rows of fruit-trees, &c., should be about the size of a coach-wheel spoke, and for sake of durability, made of white oak, or some other good durable wood, with the numbers marked or painted thereon; such will last you for several years : small kinds for labelling flowers, or the various sorts of small seeds which you intend to sow, may be made of old or new shingles, or pieces of good pine, cut and split to such lengths as you desire; form these neatly, and when you are going to use them, rub one side of the upper end for about two inches with white oil-color paint; on which, while yet wet, write your num-

ber, or the name of the plant at full length with a black-lead pencil;
this will endure any kind of weather for one year at least, and be
legible for several years, when placed in pots, with GREEN HOUSE or
HOT-HOUSE plants.

CARE OF TENDER AND YOUNG SEEDLING TREES.

Take great care now of all the tender kinds of seedling trees,
shrubs, and other young plants of similar quality raised from seed,
or by other means, last year or before many kinds will, in hard frost,
need shelter, particularly the young seedling plants of the cedar of
Lebanon, &c., China arborvitæ, the tender kinds of pines and firs,
and the seedling plants of cypress, and such like kinds of young
seedling evergreens, which will all need occasional protection in severe
weather: and therefore, at the approach of the first hard frost, the
pots or boxes, &c., containing them should be removed into a garden
frame, or some other convenience of occasional shelter, and in the
time of hard frosts the glasses and other covering put on; but they
must be kept constantly open in mild weather, when it can be done
with safety to the plants.

The tender seedling plants which are growing in beds, and require
shelter in time of frost, should be covered at such time with mats;
first erecting some hoops across the bed, and the mats to be drawn
over them occasionally for defence of the plants.

Likewise some of the more hardy kinds of young plants may be
sheltered in bad weather by laying some straw, fern, or long dry litter
lightly over them; this will protect the tender tops and roots from
the frost.

But this covering must not be suffered to remain longer than
necessary to defend the plants.

Likewise any curious or tender young evergreens, &c., that are
planted in pots, should be placed under shelter in severe frosts; such
as arbutus or strawberry tree, magnolia grandiflora, cistuses, China
arborvitæ, English and Portugal laurels, &c., placing them in a
frame, or where they may be defended either with glasses, mats or
other covering in rigorous weather.

SOUTHERN STATES.

Dig the ground, if open weather, between the continuing rows of
young trees and shrubs of all sorts.

But previous to performing this work, give any necessary pruning
to the shrubs and trees, especially the deciduous kinds; then let the
ground be digged one spade deep: as you go on trim off any straggling roots of the trees and shrubs; and in digging, give every spit a
fair turn off the spade that the weeds on the surface may be buried
properly.

Transplanting of young forest and ornamental trees in the nursery,
and where required, may be performed any time this month if the
weather is open and the ground not too wet.

Particularly deciduous forest-trees, &c., of the hardy kinds, may be removed any time this month if mild weather; but this should not be generally practised to evergreens this season, especially where smart frosts may be expected to follow.

Prune honeysuckles and roses, and all other kinds of hardy deciduous flowering shrubs that want it, training each with a single stem, and trimming their heads as you shall see occasion; that is, either to cut out or shorten all straggling shoots in such manner as you shall see necessary to keep their heads somewhat to a regular form.

In open and settled weather you may now transplant, where necessary, most sorts of hardy deciduous flowering shrubs, both in the nursery order, and for shrubbery plantations, &c., in a dry soil; but where the soil is apt to lodge wet there should not be any planted therein before February.

Plantations of fruit tree stocks, for grafting and budding upon, may be made at any time of this month, if mild open weather. Many of those raised from seed, &c., last spring, or the year before, will be fit for this, digging them up out of the seed-bed, &c., with their full roots, and let them be planted in nursery rows, three or four feet asunder, and fifteen or eighteen inches distant from each other in the rows; and when they have attained one or two years' growth in these rows, will be proper for budding and grafting. See the *Nursery* in *October* for the method of planting; that of *March* for grafting, and *July* and *August* for budding.

You may still make layers in open weather of many sorts of deciduous trees and shrubs that you desire to increase.

This work of laying down the branches of shrubs and trees to propagate them, is very easily performed; and there are a great many kinds of trees and shrubs to be increased by this operation, in the manner following:—

In the first place it must be remarked, that the young branches that were produced last summer, are the most proper parts to be layed; for these will put out roots more freely than the branches that are a year or two older. Observing further, that many of the shrub kinds branching out near the earth, afford an opportunity of laying them with great facility, but such as run up with tall stems, and those of the tree kinds, require that some strong young plants, principally deciduous, with stems one, two, or three inches thick, be cut down near the ground a year or two before to form stools to furnish a supply of shoots near the earth, convenient for laying therein. The ground must be dug about the shrub or tree that is to be layed; and as you go on bring down the branches, and fasten them in the ground with hooked pegs, observing to lay down all the young wood on each branch into the earth, covering therewith the body of each layer three or four inches deep, and fastening each also with a peg, if necessary, and raise the tops upright out of the earth.

But in laying some hard-wooded trees and shrubs it is necessary to slit the layer by making a gash with a knife on the under side, slitting it an inch or more upward, so laying that part in the earth, keeping the gash a little open, which will greatly assist the rooting by promoting the emission of fibres at the cut part. And this may also be performed to the same advantage in the laying of trees and shrubs in general. Or you may give the young shoot a twist in that part which you intend laying in the earth, by which method it will root more freely than if laid down without it.

Those which are layed in this or next month will be tolerably well rooted by next autumn, and may then be separated from the tree, and planted in the nursery to get strength.

Cuttings of many kinds of flowering shrubs and trees may also still be planted; and there are vast numbers of plants that may be propagated by this method. There is hardly any tree or shrub but what may be increased either by this method, or by layers or suckers from the root.

The manner of propagating trees or shrubs by cuttings is this: the cuttings must be young shoots of the last year's growth, which must be cut with a sharp knife from the tree or shrub you desire to propagate; they must be from about six or eight to twelve or fifteen inches long, according to their strength and manner of growth; let them be planted in rows eighteen inches asunder, and from five to eight inches distance in the row, and every cutting inserted two-thirds of its length into the ground.

Propagate gooseberries and currants by *cuttings*, as directed in *October;* and prune such of the old plants as require it, agreeably to the directions given in this and that month.

In open weather, you should, as much as possible, forward the digging and trenching vacant compartments of ground, where young trees and shrubs are to be planted in this and next month.

Now prepare some ground where it is not wet, for the reception of stones and kernels of hardy fruits, to raise a supply of stocks for the purpose of budding and grafting upon.

These may be sown any time this month, observing to sow them in beds four feet wide; cover the stones an inch and a half deep with earth, and the kernels half an inch: the plants will appear in March, April, and May, when they must be kept clean from weeds, and moderate watering in dry weather will be serviceable when they are newly come up. Some of them will be fit for transplanting in nursery rows next November.

Sow the various kinds of hawthorn, holly, red cedar, yew, mezereon, juniper, sweet bay, English and Portugal laurel berries; likewise the seeds of hornbeam, ash, spindle-tree, bladder-nut, and all the other kinds of tree and shrub seeds which require a year's preparation previous to sowing, as noticed in *February.* The sooner now these kinds of seeds are sown the better, *provided the ground be dry, and that it works loose and light.*

For particular instructions respecting the sowing of these seeds, &c., see *February* and *March.*

THE PLEASURE, OR FLOWER GARDEN.

ORNAMENTAL DESIGNS AND PLANTING.

The district commonly called the Pleasure, or Flower Garden, or pleasure-ground, may be said to comprehend *all* ornamental compartments or divisions of ground surrounding the mansion; consisting of lawns, plantations of trees and shrubs, flower compartments, walks, pieces of water, &c., whether situated wholly within the space generally considered as the pleasure-garden, or extended to the adjacent fields, parks, or other out-grounds.

In designs for a pleasure-ground, according to modern gardening, consulting rural disposition in imitation of nature, all too formal works being almost abolished, such as long straight walks, regular intersections, square grass-plats, corresponding parterres, quadrangular and angular spaces, and other uniformities, as in ancient designs; instead of which are now adopted rural open spaces of grass-ground, of various forms and dimensions, and winding walks, all bounded with plantations of trees, shrubs, and flowers, in various clumps; other compartments are exhibited in a variety of imitative rural forms, such as curves, projections, openings and closings in imitation of natural assemblage; having all the various plantations and borders open to the walks and lawns.

For instance, a grand and spacious open lawn of grass-ground is generally first presented immediately to the front of the mansion, or main habitation; sometimes widely extended on both sides to admit of a greater prospect, &c., and sometimes more contracted towards the habitation; widening gradually outwards, and having each side embellished with plantations of shrubbery, clumps, thickets, &c., in sweeps, curves, and projections towards the lawn, with breaks or opens of grass-spaces at intervals between the different plantations; together with serpentine gravel walks, winding under the shade of the trees : extended plantations ought also to be carried round next the outer boundary of the pleasure-ground, when extensive; in various openings and closings, having gravel walks winding through them, for shady and private walking; and in the interior divisions of the ground, serpentine winding walks and elegant grass openings, ranged various ways, all bordered with shrubberies and other tree and shrub plantations, flower compartments, &c., disposed in a variety of different rural forms; in easy bendings, concaves and straight ranges, occasionally; with intervening breaks or opens of grass-ground, both to promote rural diversity and for communication and prospect to the different divisions; all the parts of the pleasure-ground being so arranged, as gradually to discover new scenes, each furnishing fresh variety, both in the form of the design in different parts, as well as in the disposition of the various trees, shrubs and flowers, and other ornaments and diversities.

In designs for a pleasure-ground, according to modern taste, a tract of ground of any considerable extent may have the prospect varied and diversified exceedingly, in a beautiful representation of art and nature, as that in passing from one compartment to another, still new varieties present themselves in the most agreeable manner; and even if the figure of the ground is irregular, and the surface has many inequalities, the whole may be improved without any great trouble of squaring or levelling; for by humoring the natural form, you may cause even the very irregularities and natural deformities to carry along with them an air of diversity and novelty which fail not to please and entertain most observers.

In these rural works, however, we should not abolish entirely the appearance of art and uniformity; for these, when properly applied, give an additional beauty and peculiar grace to all our natural productions, and set nature in the fairest and most beautiful point of view.

But some modern pleasure-grounds, in which rural design is copied to an extreme, are often very barren of variety and entertainment, as they frequently consist only of a grass lawn, like a great field, having a running plantation of trees and shrubs all round it, just broad enough to admit a gravel walk winding through it, in the serpentine way, in many short twists and turns, and bordering at every turn alternately upon the outward fence and the lawn; which are continually obtruded upon the sight, exhibiting the same prospect over and over, without the least variation; so as that after having traversed the walks all around this sort of pleasure-ground, we find no more variety or entertainment than at our first entrance, the whole having presented itself at the first view.

Therefore, in laying out pleasure-ground, the designer ought to take particular care that the whole extent be not taken in at one view; only exhibiting at first a large open lawn or other spacious open compartment, or grand walk, &c., terminated on each side with plantations of curious trees, shrubs, and flowers, exhibiting only some openings at intervals, and behind these have compartments of the like plantations, with grass openings gravel walks, water, and other ornaments: so that a spectator will be agreeably surprised to find that what terminated his prospect only served as an introduction to new beauties and varieties.

It is impossible to exhibit any regular direction for planning an extensive pleasure-ground, as the different figures and situations, &c., of the ground may require different designs, therefore general hints only can be given.

SKETCH OF THE DESIGN.

The following general sketch may be varied according to the situation and extent of the ground, and may be useful to persons who are inexperienced in designs of the kind.

With respect to situation, this must be immediately contiguous to the mansion house, whether high or low situated; remarking, however, that a somewhat elevated situation, or the side or summit of some moderate rising ground is always the most eligible on which to erect the chief habitation, arranging the pleasure-ground accordingly; such an exposure being the most desirable, both for the beauty of the prospect and healthfulness of the air : there are, however, some level situations, forming plains or flats, that possess great advantages both of soil and prospect, and also the beauties of water, without too copious damps or moisture ; there are also some large tracts of ground, consisting both of low and high situations, as level plains, hollows, eminences, declivities, and other inequalities, which may be so improved as to make a most desirable pleasure-garden, as the scene may be varied in the most beautiful manner.

The extent of pleasure-ground may be varied according to that of the estate or premises, and the fortune of the owner; so may be from even a quarter or half an acre to thirty, forty, or more.

The ground should be previously fenced, which may be occasionally a hedge, paling, or wall, &c., as most convenient.

With respect to the arrangement of the several divisions, the following general sketches are on a supposition of a considerable tract of ground; and if the piece of ground is small, greater simplicity of design must be observed.

First, an open lawn of grass-ground is extended on one of the principal fronts of the mansion or main house, widening gradually from the house outward, having each side bounded by various plantations of trees, shrubs, and flowers, in clumps, thickets, &c., exhibited in a variety of rural forms in moderate concave and convex curves and projections, to prevent all appearance of a stiff uniformity; introducing between the plantations, at intervals, breaks or openings of grass-ground communicating with the lawn and internal divisions, in some places widely spread, in others more contracted; leaving also tracts for serpentine gravel-walks, some winding under the shade of the plantations, so conducted as to command views of the lawn and interior divisions occasionally, and at intervals of the most beautiful parts of the surrounding country.

This ground must be more contracted as it approaches near the mansion, that company may the sooner arrive in the walks of the shrubbery, wilderness, &c., under the shade and shelter of trees; but the outward extension on each boundary should widen gradually towards the extreme termination, to give an air of grandeur, and admit of a full prospect from and to the mansion.

Each boundary must be planted with a choice variety of ornamental trees and shrubs, deciduous, and evergreens, arranged principally in several clumps; some consisting of lofty trees, others being entirely of the shrub kinds, and consisting of trees, shrubs, and herbaceous plants together; in all of which arrange the taller growing kinds backward, and the lower forward, according to their gradation of height, embellishing the front with the more curious low flowering shrubs and evergreens, interspersed with various herbaceous flowering perennials, all open to the lawn and walks.

In the general arrangement, the great art is to vary the prospect of the different divisions so as they may variously present an air of novelty and source of convenience and entertainment.

Around towards the outward boundary fence is generally arranged a plantation of trees and shrubs, in varied easy sweeps, and broad enough to admit of a serpentine walk through the whole extent, under cover of these trees and shrubs, for private and shady walking; with breaks and openings here and there to admit of prospects, both to the lawn and surrounding country.

In various parts of the pleasure-ground leave recesses and other places surrounded with clumps of trees and shrubs for the erection of garden edifices, such as temples, grottos, rural seats, statues, &c.; and if water from some upper spring or head can be led in a winding course through the lower parts in gentle meanders, it will have a charming effect.

Other internal divisions appear with an air of grandeur and magnificence when exhibiting a spacious opening of grass-ground, bounded by the noblest trees and shrubs in various elegant clumps, groves, groups, and straight ranges, and the opening terminated by some fine open prospect, grand piece of water, or ornamental building.

Another part shall appear more gay and sprightly, displaying an elegant flower-ground or flower-garden, designed somewhat in the parterre way, in various beds, borders, and other divisions, furnished with the most curious flowers, and the boundary decorated with an arrangement of various clumps of the most beautiful flowering shrubs and lively evergreens; each clump also bordered with a variety of the herbaceous flowery tribe.

Another division, sometimes to diversify the scenery, presents a *wilderness* in irregular partitions of plantations, having intervening spaces of grass-ground and gravel walks extended in various directions; some by winding mazes or labyrinths into openings formed in different parts; the boundary plantation of this division being generally planted in close assemblage with serpentine walks between; some leading in private meanders towards the interior parts, or breaking out sometimes into other walks that are open and spacious, both of grass and gravel occasionally, conducted in serpentine turns to cause the greater variety; some places being closely bordered with tall trees to effect a gloominess and perfect shade; the different walks leading now and then into circular openings, each being surrounded with plantations as aforesaid, making the principal walks terminate in a grand opening in the centre of the wilderness, in which may be some ornamental edifice or fine piece of water, &c.

Straight ranges of the most stately trees are sometimes arranged on grass-ground in different parts, in contrast with irregular plantations, and produce a most agreeable effect, which, though prohibited in many modern designs, always exhibit an air of grandeur; being arranged sometimes in single rows, others double, or two ranges at certain distances, forming a grand walk: in other parts, several regular ranges of trees together, in the manner of groves; the whole combined, forming a diversity pleasing to the senses, and conducive to health by exciting to the salutary exercise of walking.

In other parts are sometimes discovered eminences or rising grounds, as a high terrace, mount, steep declivity, or other eminence, ornamented with curious trees and shrubs, with walks leading under the shade of trees, by easy ascents, to the summit, where is presented to the view an extensive prospect of the adjacent fields, buildings, hamlets, and country around, and likewise affording a fresh and cooling air in summer.

Regular compartments and figures, in various forms, are also sometimes introduced in some extensive grounds for variety, in contrast with the irregular works, and still to preserve some appearance of the remains of ancient gardening; such as straight walks verged with borders, square spaces, circles and octagons, &c., inclosed with low clipped hedges, hedge-work formed into various devices, detached evergreens formed into pyramids and other regular figures, regular grass-slopes formed on the side of some declivity or rising ground, elevated terraces, clumps of trees surrounded with low evergreen hedges, straight avenues of trees in ranges, &c.; a little of each being judiciously disposed in different situations, may prove an agreeable variety by diversifying the scene in contrast with the rural works before mentioned.

Sometimes a bleak declivity, rocky ground, or rough vale is made to exhibit a wild and uncultivated scene, and tends to set off the improved parts to great advantage.

Pieces of water are always, where possible, exhibited in the most conspicuous points contiguous to the termination of the main lawn or other spacious openings, representing sometimes a lake, basin, &c., and sometimes a natural river winding its course through different divisions, and its termination concealed by a curious turn, making it appear to lose itself in the adjacent plantations.

With respect to the walks, some ought to be made of gravel and some of grass; the former for common walking and the latter for occasionally walking in the heat of summer, which, in dry, hot weather, may be more agreeable than the gravel walks; therefore, some of each sort is proper both for convenience and variety.

Gravel walks, however, should lead all round the pleasure-ground and into the principal internal divisions, so as to have dry and firm walking at all times of the year; for frequently, but particularly in winter and in wet weather, grass walks are very uncomfortable and even unhealthy to walk on. These walks should be of proportional width in different parts, and larger and smaller in proportion to the extent of the ground.

As to the distribution of gravel walks—first a magnificent one, from fifteen to twenty or thirty feet wide, should range immediately close and parallel to the front of the house, and be conducted directly across the lawn into the nearest side shrubberies; from this main walk other smaller ones, from five to ten or fifteen feet wide, according to the extent of the ground, should branch off at proper intervals, directed in the serpentine way—some leading through the *outer* boundary plantations as already hinted—others into the internal divisions, and others carried along the boundary plantation of the main lawn; all of which walks being conducted through the different parts in order to afford the convenience of shade and retirement occasionally, as well as to enjoy the variety of the trees, shrubs, and flowers, variously presenting themselves at different turnings: for the walks having various sweeps and windings discovering only a moderate length at once, every turning produces new varieties, and should likewise be so contrived as at proper intervals to discover openings for prospects into different principal divisions of the ground, having in some places the plantation of trees, shrubs and flowers bordering close upon the walks; in other parts have on one side of the walks considerable grass spaces running into the plantation in one or more concave curves to form the greater diversity.

In some places the winding of walks should be gradual and moderate; in others, exhibit sudden turns and sweeps—some displaying magnificent projections in the plantation; others, spacious openings bordered with curious plants; in other parts a close thicket, which sometimes may seem to terminate the walk, when by a sudden turn it breaks out all at once into some grand open division, spacious open walk, an avenue or elegant piece of water, open groves, &c.; and in other parts a walk suddenly divides into two or three divisions leading different ways in gradual sweeps, each separation being formed by a projecting clump of shrubbery work or group of trees, &c., and each division of the walk is conducted by such varied serpentine turns as soon to be concealed from the other by the intervening compartments.

Sometimes, a spacious gravel walk is extended in a perpendicular line immediately from the front of the house dividing the lawn, or extended on both boundaries and in other directions, with a wide border on each side, either straight or sometimes a little serpentined, and planted with the most curious low flowering shrubs, evergreens and herbaceous flowering plants.

All these gravel walks should be laid with the best gravel, six or eight inches deep at least, but if more the better.

All the open grass spaces may be considered as grass walks, whether formed in the manner of walks, or as breaks or divisions between the various plantations, all of which serving both for communication to different parts and to render the ground more rurally ornamental, and for occasional walking in dry weather in summer; but some tracts of considerable width and length formed into grass walks leading to different divisions, having each side bounded with clumps of trees, shrubs and flowers, gives an air of grandeur to the place, allotting smaller breaks or opens of grass branching off between the plantation compartments, as formerly mentioned.

The grass-ground may be formed either by sowing grass seed or by laying it with turf, cut from some common; but in extensive works turfing the whole would be an endless expense; therefore seed is the most eligible for the principal space in very large gardens.

Water being so ornamental in all garden designs, no pains should be spared to introduce it where possible; but where it admits of a constant running stream from some adjacent upper spring, its beauties may be rendered admirably fine, as it may be conducted in meanders through the plantation, so as to effect a beautiful assemblage of verdure and water together; and if it should be continued to any considerable length, one or more ornamental Chinese bridges may be carried over it at convenient places, which will have a beautiful effect and serve for communication with the opposite divisions on each side of the rivulet.

Cascades and other waterfalls have also a fine effect, where there is a constant plentiful stream and the situation proper to give the water a due fall from a higher to a lower part, upon a parcel of rugged stones, to increase the noise and break and disperse the water.

In some grounds, by their natural situations, water may be obtained at a moderate expense; as sometimes a contiguous vale or meadow, bounded by rising ground, and with a brook or rivulet constantly running through it, may be easily thrown into the most agreeable form; and sometimes large springs issuing from an upper ground, and running down a moderate descent between two rising grounds to some vale below, may either form one entire lake, &c., or be contrived by making proper heads at distances to form several lakes strung together, as it were, one above another, up to the beginning of the spring; each head may form a beautiful waterfall or cascade, having the rising grounds on each side embellished with plantation clumps.

Lakes and artificial rivers may also be contrived in a flat or level ground, where there are any contiguous brooks that can be conducted to supply them with water.

All pieces of water should generally be contrived in a natural imitation, as much as the situation will admit; and its boundary on all sides should be grass-ground to some considerable width, sloped off as easy as possible, corresponding with the other adjacent grass-ground, to admit of a prospect of the water at some distance.

On the verges of large compartments of water, some Babylonian or Weeping Willows, disposed in particular situations, singly at distances, sometimes in concave and projecting parts, terminations, &c., will have a very agreeable effect in their long, bending, arched branches, and numerous pendulous shoots, suspended over the water in a loose waving manner, sometimes sweeping the surface thereof; and when arrived to some considerable growth in their numerous low pendent branches suspended all round, display an air of peculiar solemn grandeur.

The various compartments of ground intended for the different plantations should be digged or trenched for the reception of the plants, particularly for all plantations of shrubbery, and wilderness quarters, flower compartments, &c.; and the ground for clumps should, if not thought too expensive, be raised above the common level in a gentle swell; especially all detached compartments, such as shrubbery clumps, and flower partitions; and most other detached compartments of ground for any kind of ornamental planting in gardens. These should generally be raised in a moderate rounding swell gradually from each side to the middle; or for any continued side plantation, it may be raised in a gentle slope; for the swelling and sloping figure always strikes the eye the most agreeably, as well as shows the plants to the best advantage.

But where intended to have groves of stately trees, or any straight ranges of trees, either single or double lines, forming a walk or avenue, it is most in character to dispose them all on grass-ground, in which they will appear most rural and beautiful.

Likewise elegant ornamental trees, both as single standards and in detached groups or clumps, appear the most beautiful when disposed on spacious openings of grass-ground.

All the plantation compartments of shrubbery, wilderness, &c., should be planted with some considerable variety of different sorts of trees, shrubs, and flowers, artfully disposed in various arrangements; the tallest behind, the lowest forward and the different sorts so intermixed as to display a beautiful diversity of foliage and flowers, disposing the more curious kinds contiguous to the principal walks and lawns.

As trees and shrubs are of two different tribes, deciduous and evergreen kinds, those of each tribe should be mostly planted in separate clumps, in which they will effect the most agreeable variety; and in some places exhibit clumps composed of both sorts to cause the greater diversity; and many of the most conspicuous deciduous compartments may be embellished towards the fronts with some showy evergreens, thinly dispersed, which will appear ornamental and lively in winter, when the deciduous plants are destitute of leaves.

In planting the several shrubbery clumps, &c., some may be entirely of trees, but the greater part an assemblage of trees and shrubs together; some entirely of the low shrub kind, in different situations, between and in front of the larger growths; likewise should intersperse most of the shrubbery and wilderness compartments with a variety of hardy herbaceous flowery plants of different growths, having also here and there clumps entirely of herbaceous perennials : the distribution or arrangement of the clumps and other divisions of the different kinds, both trees, shrubs, and flowers, should be so diversified as to exhibit a proper contrast, and a curious variation of the general scene.

And in the disposing the various trees, shrubs, and other plants in their respective compartments, observe, for the most part, to place the tallest towards the middle or back part, and the lower forward towards the front, according to their natural stature of growth; observing also to intermix the different sorts in each clump, &c., in such order as to display a diversity of different foliage and flowers as aforesaid, as well as to exhibit a conspicuous variety. Likewise placing the various sorts at such proportionable distances and dispositions according to their various growths as each may have full scope to spread its head, and so as the prospect of one may be no interruption or impediment to the growth and appearance of another, but all so judiciously arranged as to set off each other and appear distinct, and to proper advantage from the contiguous lawns, walks, and other divisions.

In planting any continued or running plantation where *shady walks* are designed, particular care is requisite in arranging a due share of the taller trees and shrubs nearer the walks; and in such order as to produce the desired effect; particularly in the continued

6

plantation of shrubbery-work around the outward boundary and other running plantations.

These plantations for shady walks are highly necessary to retire to occasionally for shelter from the various changes and injuries of the weather; they afford shade from the scorching rays of the summer's sun, shelter from tempestuous winds and cold blasts, and opportunity for private and contemplative walking, almost at all seasons of the year.

But where very close and gloomy shade is required in any particular parts for diversity, some trees and tall shrubs should be arranged nearer to the verge of the walks, backed and fronted with a variety of hardy shrubs, in such order as to produce the desired effect.

The planting in groves and avenues should consist principally of the tree kind, and such as are of straight and handsome growth, with the most branchy, full, regular heads, and may be both of the deciduous and evergreen tribes, but generally arranged separately; groves and avenues should always be in some spacious open space, formed into grass-ground, either before or after planting the trees; and in planting the groves it is most eligible to arrange the trees in lines, in some places straight rows, others in gentle bendings, or easy sweeps, having the rows at some considerable distance, that the trees may have full scope to display their branchy heads regularly around; and in some places may have close groves to form a perfect shade.

Avenues and walks of trees may be formed either entirely of deciduous trees, or of evergreens; but the deciduous kinds are in most estimation for this purpose; however, avenues and grass walks, planted with fine evergreen trees, make a beautiful appearance, and will always command admiration. In both sorts the trees are most commonly disposed in rows, one on each side of the avenue, though sometimes grand walks of trees may be both in single straight lines and in double rows, to exhibit the greater variety; planting the trees generally, both in avenues and walks, at proper distances, to have full scope to branch out regularly around and display their beautiful heads and foliage.

Thickets may be composed of all sorts of hardy deciduous trees planted close and promiscuously, and with various common shrubs interspersed between them, as underwood, to make them more or less close in different parts, as the designer may think proper. They may also be of evergreen trees, particularly of the pine and fir kinds, interspersed with various low-growing evergreen shrubs.

In some open spaces of grass-ground, such as spacious open lawns, or other considerable open fields, &c., you should dispose some of the most beautiful trees and elegant shrubs detached, both separately as standards or single objects, and in groups, from two or three, to five, ten, or more, in different groups or clumps, some irregularly, others in curves, straight lines, &c., for variety; arranging both single standards and groups a considerable distance asunder, not to obstruct the prospect, and at such varied distances as if they had grown there by chance.

It very frequently happens that on the spot or tract which is designed for a pleasure-ground, are found large stately trees of considerable standing, properly situated to be introduced into the design; and sometimes numbers in suitable assemblages for constituting groves or thickets, and some for single standing groups or clumps, &c.; these should be preserved with the utmost care, as it would require many years to form the like with young plantations; and although the trees should stand ever so close, irregular, or straggling, with proper address in thinning and regulating them, where necessary, they may be made to become beautifully ornamental to the place, and to prevent a considerable expense.

In some spacious pleasure-grounds, various light ornamental buildings are introduced as ornaments to particular departments; such as temples, towers, banqueting-houses, alcoves, grottos, rural seats, cottages, fountains, obelisks, statues, and other edifices; these, and the like, are usually erected in the different parts, in openings between the divisions of the ground, and contiguous to the termination of grand walks, &c.

These kinds being very expensive, are rather sparingly introduced; sometimes a temple is presented at the termination of a grand walk or opening, or sometimes a temple, banqueting-house, or bower is erected in the centre of some spacious opening or grass-ground in the internal divisions; other parts present alcoves, bowers, grottos, rural seats, &c., at the termination of different walks; and rural seats are placed in different parts by the sides of long walks, under the shade of trees, &c., for places of rest.

Fountains and statues are generally introduced in the middle of spacious openings; statues are also often placed at the terminations of particular walks, sometimes in woods, thickets, and recesses, upon mounts, terraces, and other stations, according to what they are intended to represent.

Sometimes, also, there are exhibited root-houses, rock and shell-work, ruins, and other rustic devices, representing hermitages, caves, &c.; such being generally stationed in some retired or private situation; these kinds of buildings being commonly arched or vaulted, are, for the most part, covered with a coat of earth and turfed with grass, so as to appear like a sort of mount or hillock, and planted with some little clumps of shrubs, &c., having private walks leading to the entrance.

In some parts are exhibited artificial rock-work, contiguous to some grotto, fountain, rural piece of water, &c., and planted with a variety of sexatile plants, or such as grow naturally on rocks and mountains.

Ornamental bridges over artificial rivers, or any rural piece of water in some magnificent opening, so as to admit of a prospect thereof, at some distance from the habitation, have charming effects.

Let it be particularly remarked, that although water, when exhibited with due taste and handsome design, adds considerable to the beauty of pleasure-grounds; yet, in districts subject to diseases occasioned by the effluvia arising from marshes and stagnant water, it ought to be cautiously introduced; a due regard to health will of course prevent its introduction, especially in large sheets, where likely to become stagnant. When such are admitted, they should always be situated in a clay or gravelly soil, and possess a sufficient head or stream to render the change of their contents frequent.

A foss, or ha-ha, is often formed at the termination of a spacious lawn, grand walk, avenue, or other principal part of parts of the pleasure-ground, both to extend the prospect into the adjacent fields and country, and give these particular parts of the ground an air of larger extent than they really have; as at a distance nothing of this kind of fence is seen, so that the adjacent fields, plantations, &c., appear to be a continuation of the pleasure-ground.

A foss, or ha-ha, is a sunk fence, ditch-like, five or six feet deep, and ten, twenty, or more wide, and is made in different ways according to the nature of the ground. One sort is formed with a nearly upright side next the pleasure-ground, five, six or seven feet deep, faced with a wall of brick, or stone, or strong post and planking, &c.; the other side is made sloping outward gradually from the bottom of said wall, till it terminates as near a level as possible.

It being absolutely necessary to have the whole of the pleasure-ground surrounded with a good fence of some kind, as a defence against cattle, &c., a foss being a kind of concealed fence, will answer that purpose where it can conveniently be made, without interrupting the view of such neighboring parts as are beautified by art or nature, and at the same time effect an appearance that these are only a continuation of the pleasure ground. Over the foss in various parts may be made Chinese and other curious and fanciful bridges, which will have a romantic and pleasing effect.

DESIGN FOR A VILLA GARDEN.

To lay out a rural residence satisfactorily, it is necessary to study the form and location of the ground, as well as to consult with, and ascertain the particular requirements of the family. It would be an easy matter to offer a series of designs, many of which might be useful to those in need. I conceive, however, that it will serve a more useful purpose to select a sketch as it occurs in practice, as many opportunities are presented of taking advantage of existing features and turning them to account in the general improvement. Individual taste must be recognized in the disposition of the various adjuncts to a dwelling. While some desire the purely ornamental character to predominate, others have more utilitarian objects in view. The most numerous class are those who wish to have a little of everything—vegetables, fruit, flowers, and ornamental trees —as shown in the following design. It was required to arrange the grounds, although limited in extent, so as to appropriate a small spot for flowers, as well as have a few of the most desirable ornamental trees disposed on the lawn, with convenient walks for their inspection. Flowering shrubs had also to be kept in view; a small space was also desired for cultivating some of the smaller kinds of fruits, and lastly, a portion had to be reserved for vegetable culture.

In arranging these various parts, the principle of *distinctiveness* has been kept prominently in view. On the west side, the short walk leading from the street to the principal entrance of the house, leads through a small flower-garden, consisting of a few simple figures geometrically arranged. The grape-arbor forms a very appropriate division between the ornamental and vegetable ground, and its proximity to the house renders it useful and convenient as a shady resort in summer. The open spaces of grass form a relieving contrast to the groups of trees and shrubs, and suggest a feeling of extent; a principle that is seldom adopted in small places, although it is most important; the same space of ground dotted over with plants, would appear confused, monotonous, and confined. The fruit garden, which is separated from the ornamental planting by an arbor-vitæ hedge, is adapted for dwarf pear-trees, strawberries and raspberries. The pears are arranged parallel to the walks, inclosing a space for strawberries. The raspberries are planted on a narrow border close to the fence. Currant and gooseberry bushes are planted along the walks in the vegetable garden, the whole being excluded from the stable-yard and road by an evergreen hedge.

References to Plan.—A. House. B. Barn. C. Rose clumps. D. Central figures of flower garden E. Lawn. F. Grape-arbor. G. Vegetable grounds. H. Fruit department. K. Yard. L. Piazza. S. Rustic seat. V. Vase. The ground measured 120 feet by 200 feet.

The entire ground is level and elevated; in order, therefore, to improve the architectural appearance of the house, the first floor is elevated three feet six inches above the surface, and connected with it by a small turf terrace.

A few of the principal trees are named below, with reference to their location. Owing to the method I have adopted in indicating the position of the plants on the lawn, I could not conveniently refer them to numbers on so small a scale. They are selected chiefly in regard to color and diversity of foliage. Those nearest the walks are mostly deciduous shrubs, planted sufficiently apart to allow full development. An annual pruning in of the strongest branches will improve their appearance when thus arranged, but not *clipped* into a formal shape. The masses of shrubbery shown by distinct outlines are thickly planted in the first instance, attention being given in the arrangement with a view to a gradual thinning out of the least desirable, as may be found necessary to allow space for the more select kinds. The line of shrubbery included between the walk and boundary north and east of the house, is planted in like manner, with the addition of a few hemlock and Norway spruce firs and other smaller sized evergreens, on purpose to shelter from cold winds.

The following named trees are placed as indicated by the figures on the plan: 1. Magnolia purpurea, Purple Magnolia. 2. Magnolia conspicua, Chandelier Magnolia. 3, 4. Cedrus Deodar, Deodar Cedar. 5, 6. Abies canadensis, Hemlock Spruce. 7. Liquidambar styraciflua, Sweet Gum. 8. Fagus sylvatica purpurea, Purple Beech. 9. Acer campestre, English Maple. 10. Chionanthus Virginica, Virginia Fringe Tree. 11. Magnolia tripetala, Umbrella Magnolia. 12. Rhus cotinus, Mist Bush. 13. Cytisus laburnum, Golden Chain. 14. Virgilea lutea, Yellow Wood. 15. Halesia tretraptera, Silver

Bell. 16. Larix Europa, European Larch. 17. Celtis occidentalis, Nettle Tree. 18. Acacia julibrissin, the Julibrissin Tree. 19. Juglans regia, Madeira Nut. 20. Berberis purpurea, Purple Berberry.

Fig. 11.

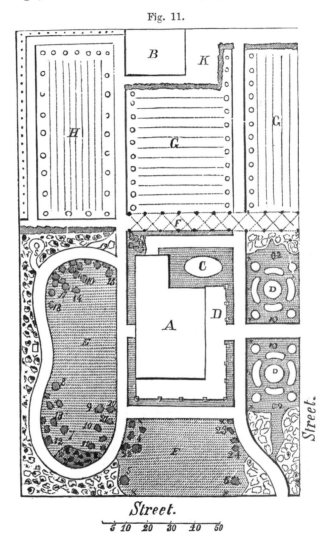

21. Pyrus Japonica, Japan Quince. 22. Buxus sempervirens arborea, Tree Box. 23. Euonymus Japonica, Evergreen Euonymus.

At D in the flower-garden, a plant of the weeping cherry, and the * shows the position of sugar maples for shade.

OF ANCIENT DESIGNS.

Designs in ancient gardening for a pleasure-ground, consulted uniformity in every part, exact levels, straight lines, parallels, squares, angles, circles, and other geometrical figures, &c., all corresponding in the greatest regularity to effect an exact symmetry and proportion.

Straight walks were everywhere observed, and all arranged parallel and crossing one another in regular intersections; generally a grand one of gravel was extended in a straight line immediately from the front of the main house, having each side verged either with a regular straight border of earth, furnished with a variety of flowers, &c., and sometimes having a verge of grass three or four feet wide, then a border, embellished as above with various plants; this main walk being often intersected by others at regular distances, so as sometimes to divide the spaces immediately in the front of the house into four, six, or more equal squares, some of which were sometimes formed into parterres, sometimes only naked grass-plats, or other uniform divisions; and often the whole garden was thus divided by straight, parallel, and intersecting walks, into many regular squares and angles without any variation.

Grand parterres were very commonly presented immediately on the front of the main house, having a grand walk of grass or gravel directly from the house through the middle, or dividing the parterre ground into two divisions.

A parterre is a spacious level spot of ground divided into many partitions, of different figures and dimensions, by means of edgings or lines of dwarf-box, &c. or by verges of grass-turf and tracks of sand, fine gravel, shell, and scroll-work, &c.

These works were in great estimation in ancient gardening, and were commonly situated directly in front of the house, generally the whole width of the front, or sometimes more.

The general figure of a parterre is an oblong or long square; because the rules of *Perspective*, or the natural declension of the visual rays in *optics*, a long square sinks almost to a square, and an exact square appears much less so than it really is, when viewed at a distance; therefore, parterres were generally made twice as long as broad.

These were bounded by a long bed, or border of earth, and the internal space within divided into various little partitions or inclosures, artfully disposed into different figures corresponding with one another, such as long squares, triangles, circles, various scroll-works, flourishes of embroidery, and many other fanciful devices; all of which figures were edged with dwarf-box, &c., with intervening alleys of turf, fine sand, shells, &c.

The partitions or beds were planted with the choicest kinds of flowers, but no large plants to hide the different figures, for such were intended as a decoration for the whole place long after the season of the flowers was past.

Though parterres in general are now become rather unfashionable, a little of that kind of work might still be permitted for variety's sake, though not immediately in front of the house as heretofore. A spacious lawn, bounded with rural shrubberies, is the most eligible situation for such; but a plain parterre of a moderate extent, either formed with lines of box, or with turf, might be introduced in some of the more internal parts, and distributed either into plain or complex departments, or beds of earth for flowers, so as to answer the purpose of a flower-garden for the most curious sorts; it will have an agreeable effect in forming a contrast with the more rural scenes.

In the more interior parts, large tracts of ground were frequently divided by straight grass-walks into many square and angular divisions of wilderness, each division surrounded by regular hedges of various kinds of trees and shrubs, kept in uniform order by annual clippings; having the interior part of each quarter planted with trees and shrubs, which were in a manner concealed by the hedges from persons in the adjacent walks, so that hardly anything but close hedges, the same thing over again, appeared to view on each side of the walks; and all the walks generally led into uniform openings of grass, particularly to a grand circle or octagon, forming some central part.

Frequently there were partitions of regular hedge-work, particularly of evergreens, surrounding large squares of grass-ground, designed as pieces of garden ornaments; the hedge-work being often formed into various uniform devices, such as pilasters, arcades or arches, porticos, galleries, amphitheatres, pavilions, cabinets, bowers, pediments, niches, and cornices; likewise regular arbors, having the sides formed into arcades, and sometimes the top vaulted; and with various other formal imitations, all performed in hedge-work, which were often so arranged and trained, as to effect an air of grandeur and art. High hedges were also in great repute, as boundaries to grand walks and avenues, sometimes carried up from fifteen or twenty to thirty or forty feet high; sometimes trained perfectly close from the very bottom to top; others open below a considerable way, and formed into regular arches, &c., all of which sometimes appeared magnificent and ornamental, but were troublesome and expensive to keep in order, on account of their great height : however, all sorts of hedge-work were generally esteemed so ornamental in ancient gardening, that almost every division was surrounded with regular hedges of one sort or other, presenting themselves to view in every part, shutting out all other objects from sight; but in modern designs, such hedges are rarely admitted; every compartment of the plantation being left open to view from the walks and lawns, in order to afford a full prospect of the various trees, shrubs and flowers, which consequently are more beautiful than continued ranges of close hedges; but for the sake of variety, a little ornamental hedge-work might still be introduced in some particular parts of the ground.

Labyrinths or mazes of hedge-work, in the manner of a wilderness, also prevailed in many large gardens.

A *labyrinth* is a maze or sort of intricate wilderness plantation, abounding with hedges and walks, formed into many windings and turnings, leading to one common centre, extremely difficult to find out, designed in large pleasure-grounds by way of amusement.

Detached trained figures of evergreens, as yew, cypress, juniper, holly, box, and various other close-growing evergreen plants, were also very predominant in ancient designs, and generally disposed in regular ranges along the borders and other verges of grand walks; being trained by clipping into various formal shapes, as pyramids, obelisks, columns, &c., in a variety of forms, with other formal figures, all placed in the most exact arrangement.

Straight rows of the most beautiful trees, forming long avenues and grand walks, were in great estimation, considered as great ornaments.

Regular grass slopes also greatly prevailed in most old gardens as ornaments to particular divisions; sometimes such were formed at the beginning of some rising ground, and sometimes at the termination or lower part; frequently canals and other pieces of water were bounded by a range of them, and likewise the sides of terraces and other elevated places. Moderate grass slopes, also, often formed a boundary to some open spaces, such as bowling-greens, flower garden, &c., forming a sort of terrace all around, and frequently having a gravel walk at top; these slopes were always formed with the greatest regularity and exactness, which in some situations were very ornamental.

Regular terraces, either on natural eminences or forced ground, were often introduced by way of ornament for the sake of prospect, and of enjoying the fresh air in summer; they were of various dimensions with respect to height, from two to ten, or twenty feet according to the nature of the situation and purpose they were designed for; some being ranged singly, others double, treble, or several, one above another on the side of some considerable rising ground in theatrical arrangement.

For the sake of diversity, some of the more elegant regular works ought still to be admitted, which would form a beautiful contrast with the general rural improvements, and diversify the whole scene, so as to have a most enchanting effect.

GENERAL CARE AND CULTURE.

With respect to the general culture of the ground, neatness must ever be observed in every part; the walks, lawns, shrubbery, clumps, &c., and the several compartments of trees, shrubs, and flowers, kept duly furnished with a proper stock of the various plants.

In the provision of plants, both of the tree and shrub kinds, let it be remarked, that when such are taken out of the woods or swamps, and planted in open exposures, they seldom succeed; therefore the better way will be to propagate them in your nursery, either by cuttings (of such as grow that way) or by seed; and when arrived there at a proper size, they may be transplanted into the pleasure-ground or elsewhere with success.

The gravel walks must always be kept free from weeds and all sorts of litter, and should be rolled at least once every week or ten days in summer, particularly the principal walks; previously trimming the edges, especially if verged with grass-ground, and sweeping off all loose litter.

The rolling in summer should be occasionally performed immediately after showers of rain, particularly the first after any continuance of very dry weather, to settle all the loose parts compact and smooth; in winter the rolling should also be occasionally performed, observing that it is improper to break up the walks at that season in rough ridges, as often practised, to remain in that unsightly manner till spring, whereby they are rendered useless at a time when there is hardly any dry or safe walking upon grass or other parts; besides, they have a disagreeable and slovenly appearance.

I would therefore advise to let the walks remain undisturbed, at least until spring, when, if the surface be foul or mossy, they may be broken up, the top turned to the bottom, and immediately raked and rolled, and rendered in a fit condition for walking on.

All the principal grass walks and lawns within the limits of the pleasure-ground, especially such parts as are intended for walking on, should also be kept perfectly neat by frequent mowing in summer to keep the grass short, close and fine; give also occasional rolling, both to clean up the scattering worm-casts and to render the surface smooth and firm. Always make choice of a dewy morning or moist weather for the work of mowing, as the short grass will cut much better then than when dry: be careful to have each mowing performed with an even hand, not to score, or leave the mark of the scythe at each stroke, which has a most disagreeable appearance, and directly after rake up all the swarths of grass into heaps and carry them away.

Rolling the grass should be occasionally performed, between the times of mowing, in order to continue the surface always firm, even, and of a close, smooth appearance.

In extensive pleasure-grounds, and large extended lawns, walks, &c., the rolling is sometimes done by horses, having a very large roller furnished with horse-shafts, and the horses' feet occasionally muffled, especially when the ground is rather soft, to prevent their cutting the surface of the grass in holes.

Keep all grass-ground clear from litter, such as fallen leaves of trees, &c., which may be expeditiously effected by a light broom or besom on a long handle.

The edges of all principal grass walks and those of grass-ground next to gravel walks in particular, should always be kept close and even, and dressed once or twice a year at least, with an *Edging-Iron*, which ought to be made of the best steel, and kept very sharp; this instrument is made somewhat in the crescent form, and about nine inches in diameter, pretty much like a saddler's cutting-knife, rounded below at the edge part, and with a socket above, upright in the middle, in which to fix a straight handle of wood, about four feet long; with this instrument a man can dress as much grass-edging in a day as three men with spades, do it much neater, and without wasting the edges of the borders.

The above dressings ought particularly to be given previous to turning the gravel-walks; at other times during the summer the edges may be trimmed occasionally as the grass grows rank, either with a pair of garden shears, or with shears made for that purpose, exactly in the form of sheep-shears, but a little larger and longer in the blades.

The shrubbery plantations should generally be all suffered to take their own natural growth, and branch out into full heads, only just giving a little occasional trimming to any very irregular growths, such as retrenching or reducing any very luxuriant rude shoots, or considerable ramblers running wildly from all the other branches. Cut out all dead wood and keep all the shrubs from entangling with one another, so as the head of each shrub may appear distinct, and show itself to proper advantage.

The ground of the principal shrubbery plantations, in which the shrubs stand distant, not covering the surface, should be digged every year, late in autumn, or in spring, previously giving the shrubs any necessary pruning as above observed; this operation gives health and vigor to the plants, kills weeds, and gives the place an air of culture, and a lively neat appearance.

After this general digging, the ground must be kept clean from weeds all summer, by occasional hoeing in dry weather, which with a scuffling-hoe may be expeditiously performed.

Particular care must be taken of the flower borders, &c.; they must be neatly and carefully dug in autumn, and pointed and dressed afresh in spring, according as the various plants grew up, let such as need support have sticks placed to preserve them upright; and as the herbaceous perennials and annuals have done flowering and their stalks decay, cut them down close, clearing off all decayed leaves and other rubbish.

All kinds of hedge-work and detached trained figures of evergreens should be clipped twice a year—that is to say, in June and in September, for without this, they will not have that neat, handsome appearance that inspires admiration and does credit to the person under whose care they are.

For further particulars, see the work under this head in the different months.

THE FLOWER GARDEN.

A commodious piece of good ground for a flower garden, situated in a convenient and well-sheltered place, and well exposed to the sun and air, ought to be allotted for the culture of the more curious and valuable flowers.

The form of this ground may be either square, oblong, or somewhat circular, having the boundary embellished with a collection of the most curious flowering shrubs; the interior part should be divided into many narrow beds, either oblong, or in the manner of a parterre; but plain four feet wide beds arranged parallel, having two feet wide alleys between bed and bed, will be found most convenient, yet to some not the most fanciful.

In either method a walk should be carried round the outward boundary, leaving a border to surround the whole ground, and within this, to have the various divisions or beds raising them generally in a gently rounding manner, edging such as you like with dwarf-

box, some with trift, pinks, sisyrinchium, &c., by way of variety, laying the walks and alleys with the finest gravel. Some beds may be
neatly edged with boards, especially such as are intended for the finer
sort of bulbs, &c.

In this division you may plant the finest hyacinths, tulips, polyanthus-narcissus, double jonquils, anemones, ranunculuses, bulbous-
irises, tuberoses, scarlet and yellow amaryllises, colchicums, fritillaries, crown imperials, snow-drops, crocuses, lilies of various sorts,
and all the different kinds of bulbous and tuberous-rooted flowers,
which succeed in the open ground ; each sort principally in separate
beds, especially the more choice kinds, being necessary both for distinction's sake and for the convenience of giving such as need it protection from inclement weather ; but for particulars of their culture,
see the respective articles in the various months.

Likewise in this division should be planted a curious collection of
carnations, pinks, polyanthuses, and many other beautiful sorts,
arranging some of the most valuable in beds separately ; others may
be intermixed in different beds, forming an assemblage of various
sorts.

In other beds you may exhibit a variety of all sorts, both bulbous,
tuberous, and fibrous-rooted kinds, to keep up a succession of bloom
in the same beds during the whole season.

Here I cannot avoid remarking that many flower gardens, &c., are
almost destitute of bloom during a great part of the season ; which
could be easily avoided, and a blaze of flowers kept up, both in this
department and in the borders of the pleasure-ground, from March
to November, by introducing from our woods and fields the various
beautiful ornaments with which nature has so profusely decorated
them.   Is it because they are indigenous that we should reject them?
Ought we not rather to cultivate and improve them ?   What can be
more beautiful than our Lobelias, Orchises, Asclepiases, and Asters;
Dracocephalums, Gerardias, Monardas and Ipomœas ; Liliums, Podalyrias, Rhexias, Solidagos and Hibiscuses; Phloxes, Gentianas, Spigelias, Chironias, and Sisyrinchiums, Cassias, Ophryses, Coreopsises
and Cypripediums; Fumarias, Violas, Rudbeckias and Liatrises; with
our charming Limodorum, fragrant Arethusa, and a thousand other
lovely plants which, if introduced, would grace our plantations and
delight our senses ?

In Europe, plants are not rejected because they are indigenous ;
on the contrary, they are cultivated with due care ; and yet here we
cultivate many foreign trifles, and neglect the profusion of beauties
so bountifully bestowed upon us by the hand of nature.

WORK TO BE DONE THIS MONTH.

Prune such of your ornamental shrubs, &c., as need it, particularly
the hardy deciduous kinds ; all decayed, ill-placed and straggling
branches ought to be cut off close to where they were produced, and
such others shortened as are growing in a disorderly way, always
taking great care to form the heads in a full and handsome manner,

that they may appear well furnished and display the beauty of their foliage and bloom in due season.

Great care should be taken at this time of the choicest kinds of flowering plants and other tender kinds in pots—they should be carefully protected from severe frosts, by giving each sort suitable covering.

AURICULAS.

The best auriculas in pots should be well protected from excessive rains, snow or sharp frosts; which will preserve them in strength to flower in great perfection.

The choicest varieties of these plants should always be removed in their pots, about the beginning of November, and placed in frames, or in a bed arched over with hoops, in a warm, dry situation in the full sun, where they can be occasionally covered when the weather is unfavorable; but let the covers be kept constantly off in the daytime when the weather is mild and dry.

CARE OF CARNATIONS.

Take great care to protect your fine carnations that are in pots from hard frosts, excessive rains and snow; for notwithstanding the plants being hardy enough to stand the winter in the open air, it is advisable to defend the choicest sorts in bad weather, to preserve them in good strength for flowering in the greatest perfection.

These pots should be plunged in a raised bed of dry compost, in the beginning of winter, and the bed arched over low with pliant rods or hoops at that time; this will be of great advantage to the plants, if you are careful to draw mats over the arches when the weather is severe.

But if the pots were to be placed in garden frames it would be still better, if you take care to put the glasses over them in rigorous weather and at night; but be careful to give them as much free air as possible by day, when the weather permits; either by taking the glasses totally off for a few hours, or tilting them up behind.

CARE OF CHOICE HYACINTHS AND TULIPS.

In severe frosty weather it would be of beneficial advantage if the beds, wherein you have deposited the choicest kinds of hyacinths and tulips, or any other curious bulbous roots, be covered either with an awning of mats, or, in default thereof, with straw, fern, leaves of trees, or dry long litter; but it must be removed as soon as the severe weather is over

Old decayed fine tan is a good article to cover hyacinths, tulips, and other bulbs with; it may be laid on one inch, or one inch and a half deep, immediately previous to the commencement of the severe winter frost, and need not be removed, as it will keep down the weeds in spring, and protect the roots from intense heat and drought during their period of ripening.

RANUNCULUSES AND ANEMONES.

The beds or frames in which are planted your choice kinds of ranunculuses and anemones, should be carefully protected from frost by laying tan, earth, or litter round the outsides of the frames, and carefully covering them at nights and in severe weather with glasses, or with boards laid lengthwise or across the frames, with mats or other covering on top, but carefully observing to give them plenty of air every day that the weather is tolerably mild, for if too much confined they will draw up and be good for nothing.

Plant ranunculuses and anemones in mild, dry, open weather, if you have any now out of the ground, and the frost will admit of your working it; these now planted will succeed those which were put into the ground in October or November.

For their reception choose a dry situation where the ground is of a light, rich nature. Let it be well digged, breaking the earth fine, and form it into beds of three and a half or four feet wide; rake the surface smooth, and then plant the roots. These roots, after planting, should be protected, as above, from severe frost and too much wet; either of which would, at this season, materially injure them.

For the particular method of preparing the beds and planting roots, see the work of October.

In warm, dry, and well sheltered situations, in the middle States and generally in the southern States, these beautiful flowers may be planted in the open borders in small patches with other kinds, and will there make a very agreeable appearance. You may plant four or five roots in a small circle of about six inches diameter, one in the middle and the rest round the extreme part of the circle; and let these patches or clumps be from two or three to five, ten, or twelve feet asunder, and the roots be covered from one to two inches deep, according to the lightness of the ground.

The above practice, however, of planting those roots in patches about the borders is meant principally for the common sorts; for it is necessary to plant the fine varieties together in narrow beds or frames, as above, in order both to have the opportunity of protecting them occasionally in severe weather, and that when in flower they may display a spacious show together in their various colors, stripes, and tints, in the different varieties; and also in the spring, when the plants are in bloom, they can be more readily sheltered from great rains or too much sun, both of which would hasten the decay of the flowers; and as the pleasure of admiring the bloom is the only intention of cultivating these flowers, no pains should be spared to protect the more beautiful sorts.

PLANTING TULIPS.

Tulips, if you have any out of the ground, should now be planted the first settled open weather, to blow late, and to succeed those planted late in autumn.

Let this be done as soon as the weather will permit; for if these roots are kept much longer out of the ground, they will blow very poorly. If they are to be planted in beds, let them be made three or four feet wide, raised two or three inches, somewhat rounding, that they may throw off the redundant wet of heavy rains, and remain dry during winter.

If intended to plant any of the inferior sorts in the borders, in assemblage with other flowers, they may either be planted in a single row towards the front, or some dotted singly, or by three together, to effect a greater variety; but these flowers, when planted in the borders, make the best appearance in little clumps; that is, in a circle of about six or eight inches, plant four or five roots, and about from three or four to five or ten feet farther, plant another such clump, and so proceed, in a varied order, towards the front and middle.

Observe that hyacinths, tulips, and other hardy bulbs, which, to do them justice, ought to be planted in October, or early in November, should have lighter or more shallow covering, in proportion to the length of time they are kept out of ground after that period; for instance, tulips, which ought to get four inches of light covering in October, will not be able to bear more than three in December, two and a half in January, two in February, and one and a half if kept up till March; for many of the bulbous kinds become so exhausted by keeping them too long out of the ground, that if planted at the usual depth they have not strength to bear up through it, and ultimately perish. However, this partial remedy ought by no means to induce to the keeping of bulbous roots out of ground after their proper season; but by attending to it, roots may be preserved that would otherwise perish, and which, by planting in due time the succeeding season, may produce tolerably good flowers, and an increase of their kinds.

Be particular never at any season, nor under any circumstance, to give less covering to any kind of a bulbous or tuberous root when planted in the open ground than one inch over the crown or upper part.

PLANTING CROCUSES AND SNOW-DROPS.

Any sort of crocuses may still be planted if dry mild weather; generally planting them along the edges of the flower borders, next the walks, and in flower beds, &c., commonly within five or six inches of the edge, either in a continued row, or dotted in little patches planted about one inch and a half deep: though those designed for the borders appear to greater advantage when disposed in small patches than in any other way. Draw a small circle with your finger, about four or five inches diameter; in the middle plant one root, and plant three or four round the edge of the circle; about eighteen inches or two or three feet farther make another circle, and plant the roots as above; and so proceed to the end of the border, &c., or you may vary the patches in having some near the edge, and others more towards the middle; observing, if you have different kinds, to plant each sort separate; and if you plant the first patch with yellow crocuses, plant the next with blue, and so proceed with others of different sorts.

Snow-drops may also now be planted in the same manner as the crocuses; but neither of them, when planted so late, flower well the spring following—the former, in particular, will totally perish if kept much longer out of the ground. These kinds ought to have been planted in September, or early in October, for being flowers of early bloom, they do not agree with being kept up after their proper time of planting.

When you desire a considerable increase of crocuses or snow-drops, take up the roots but once in two years; if you let them remain longer, though the increase will be numerous, the roots become very small and produce but poor flowers.

PLANTING VARIOUS SORTS OF BULBS.

Jonquils, ornithogalums, narcissuses, hyacinths, bulbous irises, Persian irises, gladioluses, fritillaries, crown imperials, or any other kinds of hardy bulbous flower roots that yet remain above ground should now be planted as soon as the weather will permit. Mild dry weather ought to be chosen for planting these and all other kinds of bulbous roots, and see that the ground is not too wet.

When it is intended to plant any of the common sorts of the above, or other kinds of bulbous roots in the borders, they may be planted in the manner mentioned above for the common tulips, &c., observing particularly that the longer you keep them out of the ground after October or November the shallower they must be planted.

FLOWERS TO BLOW IN THE HOUSE.

Several sorts of bulbous roots may be placed upon bulb-glasses of water for blowing in the apartments of the house, such as hyacinths, narcissuses, jonquils, early -dwarf tulips, bulbous irises, &c. The glasses for this purpose are to be had at the seed and glass shops. Being made concave at the mouth, they contain each one root, and are to be filled with soft water, and one root placed in each glass with its bottom touching the water, placing the bottles upon a shelf or chimney-piece of some warm room, or in the inside of a warm window, and if where the sun comes it will be an additional advantage; but in severe frost remove them to the interior part of the room where a fire is kept. They will soon shoot their roots down into the water, which, when become very foul or fetid, should be renewed with fresh occasionally; they will thus blow very agreeably early in the spring, and may be greatly forwarded if placed in a hot-bed or hot-house.

You may plant various sorts of bulbous and tuberous flower roots in pots for blowing in a house, such as hyacinths, narcissuses of all kinds, early tulips, crocuses, anemones, ranunculuses, or any other spring flowering kind. Having small pots or boxes filled with light sandy earth, plant the roots therein *just over their crowns*, and place the pots near a window; when the roots begin to shoot, give occasional light waterings, and they will flower in good perfection at an early season.

BLOWING FLOWERS EARLY IN HOT-BEDS, ETC.

Many sorts of bulbous, tuberous, and fibrous-rooted perennial flowers, if planted in pots, and now placed in a hot-bed, hot-house, or any forcing department at work, will shoot and flower early without much trouble, only to give occasional watering. Pots of roses, dwarf almonds, double-blossom cherry, peach, &c., may also be placed in the forcing houses for early bloom.

CARE OF PERENNIAL FIBROUS-ROOTED PLANTS IN POTS.

Double wall-flowers, double stocks, double sweet-williams, and any other of the choicer kinds of perennial plants in pots, should be well secured from severe frosts. If these plants in pots are placed in frames, let the glasses or other covering be kept over them at all times when the frost is keen, or occasionally in very wet weather; but in mild dry weather the plants must not be covered in the daytime.

Take care now of all other choicer kinds of fibrous-rooted perennial plants in general, which are in pots, to secure them from frost.

Those plants which are in pots should, where there is not the convenience of frames, be plunged to their rims in a dry and warm border, and at night and in severe weather be covered with garden-mats, supported on arched hoops placed low over such bed or border.

SEEDLING FLOWERS.

Boxes or pots of any tender or choice kinds of seedling flowers should be covered in frosty weather either with mats, long litter, fern, or the like, which should be laid a good thickness over them, and close round the sides, or remove them under a garden-frame and glasses, &c., which will be the better way.

Likewise beds of the more tender and curious sorts of seedling flowers, in the common ground, should also be covered in hard frosts with mats or long dry litter, but remove the covering when the weather is mild.

PROTECTING FLOWERING-SHRUBS.

If you have hardy flowering-shrubs or evergreens in pots, you should, to protect their roots from the frost, plunge the pots to their rims in the ground (if omitted doing in November or December), and cover the pots with some tan, leaves of trees or dry litter, allotting them for this purpose a dry, warm situation, where water is not apt to stand.

But any tenderer or more curious young evergreens, &c., in pots, should have the protection of frames or occasional covering of mats, &c., in severe weather.

Protect also the roots of the choicer kinds of new planted flowering shrubs and evergreens from frost. This is done by laying dry

7

mulchy litter on the surface of the ground, close round the lower part of the stem of each, as far as their roots extend or rather farther.

Likewise support such new-planted shrubs as require it with stakes, that they may not be displaced by the wind.

GRASS AND GRAVEL WALKS.

The grass and gravel walks should all be kept in decent order, especially in the principal parts of the garden and pleasure-ground : suffer no leaves of trees or other litter to remain thereon, for such would give them an unbecoming appearance.

SOUTHERN STATES.

Where mild weather is now prevalent and the ground not bound up by frost, you may plant all kinds of hardy deciduous trees and shrubs; and towards the latter end of the month, especially where smart frosts are not expected to follow, you may plant the different kinds of hardy evergreen trees and shrubs.

Plant cuttings and make layers of such kinds as you wish to propagate by these methods : plant dwarf-box for edgings, which is superior to every kind of plant for that purpose. Transplant suckers from the roots of roses and such other shrubs as produce them, and are worthy of cultivation.

Hedges of the various kinds of hawthorn, hornbeam, beach, elm, privet, white mulberry, &c., may now be planted. Make and repair grass and gravel walks; keep such as are made in clean and neat order, and give them occasional rollings.

Sow hardy annual and perennial flower seeds, and do the various other works directed to be done in the flower garden and pleasure-ground in March.

THE GREEN-HOUSE.

A green-house is a garden building fronted with glass, serving as a winter residence for tender plants from the warmer parts of the world, which require no more artificial heat than what is barely sufficient to keep off frost, and dispel such damps as may arise in the house, occasioned by the perspiration of the plants or a long continuance of moist weather.

A very considerable share of the vegetable creation, which in their respective native countries grow naturally in open fields, &c., in all seasons, require, when cultivated in less favorable climates, protection in winter; but observe, however, that those of the green-house department, being from the warmer parts of the world, require protection from frost only, not needing aid of artificial heat like stove plants, which are generally natives of the hottest regions, except in very severe weather; but the aid of a moderate fire, burned in a furnace contrived outside, either in the end or back wall, communicating the heat to the flues or funnels ranging along the inside, will be necessary not only in severe frosts, but also in moist foggy weather; a moderate fire now and then will dry up the damps, which would otherwise prove pernicious to several of the more tender kinds, especially to those of succulent habits.

A green-house should generally stand in the pleasure ground, and if possible, upon a somewhat elevated and dry spot fronting the south, and where the sun has full access from its rising to setting; the building ought to be of brick or stone, having the front almost wholly of glass-work, ranging lengthwise east and west, and constructed upon an ornamental plan.

As to its general dimensions, with respect to length, width and height, it may be from ten to fifty feet or more long, according to the number of plants which you intend it should contain, and its width in the clear, from ten or fifteen to twenty feet; though for a middle sized house fifteen or eighteen feet is sufficient; its height to the top of the upright front glasses equal to its width; as to erecting rooms over it, as is commonly directed, I disapprove of, such being not only an additional and unnecessary expense, but they give the building a heavy appearance; on the contrary all pieces of garden architecture ought to display a light, gay, and sprightly taste.

The walls of the back and ends should be carried up three bricks, or about two feet three inches thick, the more effectually to keep out frost; a furnace ought to be erected outside, either in the back wall or one of the ends, as before observed, communicating with flues within, ranging in two or three returns along the back wall, with only a brick on edge, with the plastering between them and the inside; also one flue running along the front and end walls, raised wholly above the floor; and as to the front of the building it should have as much glass as possible, and a wide glass door should be in the middle, both for ornament and entrance, and for moving in and out the plants; a small door at the end for entrance in severe weather will be found of considerable utility.

The width of the windows for the glass sashes may be five or six feet, and the piers between them may be either of timber, six, eight or ten inches wide, according to their height, or if of brick or stone, they must be about two feet wide, sloping both sides of each pier inward, that by taking off the angles a more free admission may be given to the rays of the sun; the bottom sashes must reach within a foot or eighteen inches of the floor of the house, and their top reach within eight or ten inches of the ceiling; and if brick or stone piers two feet wide, folding shutters may be hung inside to fall back against each pier.

In the modern construction of green-houses, in order to have as much glass as possible in front, the piers between the sashes are commonly made of good timber from six to eight or ten inches thick, according to their height, so as to admit as great a portion of light and heat of the sun as may be; and, on the same account, one-half or one-third of the roof is formed of glass-work, made in the manner of hot-bed lights, the remainder being either covered with slate or shingles and tarpaulins, or very strong canvas fixed on rollers, to be let down over the roof-glasses in very severe weather; you may also have large canvas cloths upon rollers to let down occasionally before the windows, or in default of such, you may nail up garden mats.

Let one-third of the front side of the roof, for the whole length of the house, be formed of glass-work, and the back wall raised, so as that a horizontal ceiling may be carried from the upper part of these lights to it, which will cause the back half of the roof to be somewhat more flat than the front. Ornamental wood-work may be erected outside along the top of those lights to give a light appearance to the roof. Or, if the house be small, you may carry the entire roof with a gentle slope from the front to the back wall, which must be made of a proper height for that purpose; one-third or one-half of such roof may be made of glass-work, from the termination of which carry the ceiling on a level to the back part of the house.

The better to confine the air warmed by the sun in the day-time, and to prevent the cold air from rushing in on the approach of night, when that within begins to cool, and consequently to contract in bulk, I would advise to have all the panes in the roof-lights neatly and closely puttied where they overlap one-another; and to have either one, two or three of those lights, in proportion to the length of the house, so constructed, as to slide down and up a few feet by means of pulleys, in order to give vent to the foul air generated in the house, which naturally ascends to the upper part. The sized glass, recommended in page 11, for hot-bed lights, is what I would particularly recommend for these roof-lights, being not only the strongest but by much the cheapest.

The windows, or upright front-lights, must be made with large panes of glass, &c., to admit the more light, as well as to give a handsome appearance to the house; the upper half of each window must be so contrived as to slide down, and the lower half up occasionally, to admit air to the plants when necessary.

If a spacious and ornamental window be placed in each end (if the house be detached), to receive the benefit of the rising and setting sun, it will be of considerable advantage; these particularly should have good close shutters either inside or outside, and be kept shut every night during the winter, and also in the day-time in very severe weather, except while the sun immediately shines on them. If the front is so contrived that inside shutters to the windows cannot be conveniently hung, outside sliding shutters should be made to be used only when necessity requires.

But let it be particularly observed, that all the lights, cases, doors, and wood-work of the house be made of good seasoned wood, and well painted, to prevent either their swelling by wet or shrinking by drought; that all parts be well jointed and fitted together, so as to be as nearly air-tight as possible.

A house constructed on this plan will very seldom require the assistance of fire-heat, which ought always to be used with great caution in a green-house; it will admit light, collect heat, and give health, beauty, and vigor to all the plants.

Some green-houses, for large collections of plants, have two wings of smaller dimensions added to the main building, one at each end, in a right line, separated sometimes from it by glass partitions and sliding sashes for communication, the front almost wholly of glass, and part glass roofs, as above observed; thus, by these additional wings, the green-house will consist of three divisions, whereby the different qualities and temperatures of the various plants can be more eligibly suited. The middle or main division may be for all the principal and more hardy, woody or shrubby kinds, which require protection from frost only; one of the wings may be appropriated for the succulent tribe, and the other for the more tender kinds that require occasional heat in winter, yet can live without the constant heat of a stove or hot-house.

Many green-houses, as they are commonly built, serve more for ornament than use; their situation to receive the south sun being the only essential that seems to be regarded towards preserving the health of the plants which they are intended to protect. It is rare to find one that will keep plants in good health during the winter, either by reason of their situation in moist places, their want of a sufficiency of glasses to attract heat and admit a due quantity of light, or of the glasses not being constructed so as to slide up and down occasionally, as they ought—as well to suffer the foul air to be discharged as to admit fresh. Sometimes where a green-house has been well considered in these points, all is confounded by the introduction of a mettle stove and pipes, which never can be managed so as to give, when necessary, that gradual and well regulated heat, which will protect the plants without injuring them; and, besides, both the stove and pipes unavoidably emit in the house a quantity of smoke, which seldom fails to annoy the plants. It does not unfrequently happen when such a house is intrusted to the care of an ignorant or negligent person, that the whole collection is destroyed in one night by excessive heat, or at least rendered of very little value; this is an evil which ought to be carefully guarded against.

For the particular method of erecting the furnace and flues, see the article HOT-HOUSE, for this month, with which it agrees in every respect, only that one range round the house and two along the back wall will be sufficient; and that the flues may or may not be erected close to the walls, at pleasure.

On whatever plan the green-house is constructed, let the whole inside, both ceiling, walls and flues, be neatly finished off with good plaster and white-wash, and all the wood-work made with the most critical exactness, of good seasoned timber, particularly the doors, sashes and sash-frames—the whole to be painted white—and let the bottom or floor be paved with large square paving tiles, or some similar materials.

The floor of the green-house should be raised at least twelve inches above the level of the ground, and higher in proportion as the situation is moist or springy—for damps sometimes arise during the winter months which prove very pernicious to plants.

In the green-house should be tressels, which may be moved in and out, upon which rows of plants should be fixed so as to place the pots or tubs of plants in regular rows one above another, whereby the heads of the plants may be so situated as not to interfere with each other.   The lowest row of plants or those nearest to the window should be placed about four feet from them that there may be a convenient breadth left next the glasses to walk in front; and the rows of plants shou d rise gradually from the first, in such a manner that the heads of the second row should be considerably advanced above the first, the stems only being hid, and so on for the whole.   At the back of the house there should be allowed a space of at least four feet for the conveniency of watering the plants, and particularly to admit a current of air around them.   There may also be narrow temporary open stairs of boards erected at one end, leading to a platform erected at the back on a level with the highest part of the stage, which will be found very convenient for watering as well as for common access to the highest and most remote plants; and also to place thereon near the back wall pots and tubs of deciduous plants, which would appear very unsightly in the front of the stage, observing that the boards of such platform be laid one inch at least asunder for the free admission of the circulating air.

If two or three air-holes be made in the back wall a little above this platform, or even below it, about six inches square in the outside and twelve inside, with close shutting doors towards the outside and within, both opening inward, they will be found very useful in mild weather for ventilating the house and driving off any foul air from the back part.   In these holes, between both doors, you may stuff in any kind of wadding to prevent air coming in that way but when wanted.

Never crowd the plants, for when pent in too closely a stagnant rancid vapor is generated, which often occasions a mouldiness upon the tender shoots and leaves, very destructive to the plants; neither should too great a proportion of succulent plants ever be placed in this department.

THE CONSERVATORY.

The green-house and conservatory have been generally considered as synonymous; their essential difference is this—in the green house the trees and plants are either in tubs or pots, and are placed on stands or stages during the winter till they are removed into some suitable situation abroad in summer.   In the conservatory the ground plan is laid out in beds and borders, made up of the best compositions of soil that can be procured, three or four feet deep.   In these the trees or plants taken out of their tubs or pots are regularly planted in the same manner as hardy plants are in the open air.   This house is roofed as well as fronted with glass work, and instead of taking out the plants in summer as in the green-house, the whole of the glass roof is taken off, and the plants are thus exposed to the open air, and at the approach of autumn frosts the lights are again put on, and remain so till the May following.

This building being furnished with flues, &c., may be used as a green-house at discretion by introducing stages instead of beds, and in that case the glass roof may be permanently fixed.

WORK TO BE DONE IN THE GREEN-HOUSE.

In mild days, when the weather externally is moderate and calm, let the windows be opened a little for the admission of fresh air about ten or eleven o'clock, and about two or three in the afternoon let them be shut close again; but the time of opening and the time they should be kept so must always be determined by the weather, for there are many changes sometimes in a few hours at this season. The upper lights may be let down a few inches for the admission of fresh air as well as to let out the foul air of the house, even when the under lights cannot be raised with safety.*

In frosty weather the windows must be kept constantly closed, and if very severe let the window shutters be shut every night, and even occasionally in the daytime when the frost is extremely rigorous, and no sun; or, in default of shutters, on this occasion let garden-mats be nailed up against all the windows, or strong canvas hung on rollers be let down before them, and remove the small or more tender plants in front as far from danger as possible.

Keep the plants perfectly clear from decayed leaves, and as clean as possible from any considerable foulness, and every part of the house clean and free from litter of fallen leaves, &c., all of which is essential at this time for the prosperity of the plants in general.

When the weather is foggy or very wet, it will be proper to keep the windows and doors close.

Water must be given to such plants as you see require it, but let that be given in very moderate quantities, and always, if possible, take the opportunity of a mild day, and if sunny the better. In the forenoon from eleven to twelve or one o'clock is the proper time of the day for watering at this season, and generally prefer soft water for this occasion.

But very little water must be given at this season of the year to any of the aloes, sedums, or any other of the succulent plants.

Let it likewise be observed that such of the woody exotics—as oranges, myrtles, geraniums, &c.—as you shall see necessary to water, should have but a very moderate quantity given them at any one time.

In such green-houses where there is the convenience of flues for occasional fire-heat in very rigorous weather, you should in time of continued severe frost make moderate fires in an evening and morning, just sufficient to warm the inclosed air enough to resist the frost; also in very foggy or moist weather may make a very moderate fire to expel the damp, which often proves pernicious to some of the more delicate exotics of this department.

---

* The opening of these under or front windows during cold weather is the cause of most of the mildew so often complained of. In the middle of winter always lower the temperature by opening the top ventilators.

THE HOT-HOUSE.

Hot-houses or Stoves, are buildings erected for preserving such tender exotic plants, natives of the warmer and hottest regions, as will not live in the respective countries where they are introduced, without artificial warmth in winter.

Though there are great varieties of these stoves, yet they are reducible to two, the dry stove and the bark stove. They are both comparatively of modern invention; the first, as far as I can learn, not having been in use more than one hundred and twenty-one years, being introduced by Mr. Watts, gardener at the apothecaries' garden at Chelsea, near London, who in the year 1684, contrived flues under his green-house; the latter being much posterior, not having been brought into repute till about the year 1720, when Mr. Le Cour, of Leyden, in Holland, discovered its utility for the propagation of the pine-apple, which had never before been brought to good perfection in Europe. Before the use of bark-beds was introduced, all stoves or hot-houses were worked by fire-heat only, hence they obtained the name of stoves.

These stove departments are generally constructed in an oblong manner, ranging in a straight line east and west with the glass front and roof fully exposed to the south sun, and in dimensions may be from fifteen or twenty to fifty or a hundred feet long, by twelve or fourteen to sixteen feet wide in the clear, and commonly from ten to fourteen feet high in the back wall, by five or six in front, including the wall and upright glasses together, and furnished with flues round the inside of the front and end walls and in several returns in the back wall for fires, and with the whole roof overhead sloping to the south entirely of glass-work, supported on proper cross-bearers.

Stoves of much more capacious dimensions are frequently erected by persons of fortune and curiosity, for the cultivation of the taller growing kinds of exotics, which shall be taken due notice of after the less expensive and more generally used kinds are described.

THE BARK STOVE.

The Bark Stove is so called, as being furnished with an internal pit for a bark bed, as well as with flues for fire-heat, and was formerly the most universally used, as being the most eligible for the general culture of all kinds of the tenderest exotics, as well as for forcing several sorts of hardy plants, flowers and fruit to early perfection; but its complex arrangements may now be dispensed with by the more simple and efficient hot-water apparatus; the bark being designed to effect a constant moderate moist heat all the year round, and the flues used occasionally for fire-heat in winter or during cold weather, to produce such an additional warmth in the internal air as may be requisite at that season; the bark bed is productive of a uniform moderate growing heat of long duration, and was considered to be adapted for the reception and growth of the most tender exotics, which require to be kept constantly plunged in their pots in it, such as pine-apple, &c., in order to enjoy the benefit of that durable, moist bottom heat about their roots, peculiar to bark beds, whose heat also evaporates and warms the air of the stove at all times, that even the plants on the surrounding shelves are comforted by its influence; so that with the aid of fire-heat in winter regulated by a well graduated thermometer placed constantly in the stove distant from the fire place, and as much in the shade as possible, there are hardly any exotics from the hottest regions of the world, either woody, herbaceous, or succulent, but may be cultivated in it, by replacing them in such different situations as their nature may require.

In the arrangement of the plants in this stove, some require the bark-bed, others succeed in any part of the house, and others, such as the succulents, require the dryest situation near the flues; many of the more tender, herbaceous and shrubby plants, natives of the hottest countries, generally succeed best when plunged in the bark-bed, though many sorts, both herbaceous and woody, thrive tolerably well in any part of the bark stove.

Such stoves as are intended principally for pine-apples, and for forcing flowers, strawberries, and some sorts of culinary esculents, &c., may be only ten or twelve feet high behind, which generally answers better for such than those of more lofty dimensions; or by raising the bark-pit within wholly above the surface, and sinking the front walk about a foot, the roof may be lower, and such plants by that means be brought nearer to the glass, which proves extremely advantageous to their growth.

When stoves are erected for cultivating and bringing to the greatest possible perfection the taller kinds of exotics, they are made from sixteen to twenty, or even to twenty-five feet high in the back wall, with width in proportion, by only six feet height in the front glasses, in order to suit low as well as high plants; and with the roof sloping quite from the top of the back wall to the front, and wholly of glass-work, having a capacious bark-pit within, formed towards the front; behind which is sometimes a pit of earth, either on a level with the bark-pit or with the back wall, to receive particular plants; in rear of this is a walk, between which and the back wall is formed a border of good earth, to receive the tallest growing plants which are intended to be cultivated. In this kind of stove you may cultivate exotics, &c., from the lowest to almost the highest stature, by placing those of the shortest growth forward, the tallest behind, and so on according to their several gradations of height.

However, these very lofty and capacious stoves are not recommended for general use, they being both very expensive in erecting and in the consumption of a great quantity of fuel, and not so well calculated for the growth of the general run of exotics as stoves of a moderate height, and the hot-water apparatus.

Flues ought not to be erected along the back wall in such stoves as have plants trained thereto or growing immediately close to them; and one range round the front and ends will not be sufficient to keep up a due warmth in such large houses in severe weather, without consuming an immense quantity of fuel, and at times raising a scorching heat in the parts of the house next to this single range, by over-heating it in order to force through it a heat sufficient to keep the entire of the house warm; this can never protect and promote the growth and health of plants so well as that gradual glow of moderate warmth issuing from flues of several returns, carried under the walks or other convenient places, as well as round the front and end walls, either in double or single ranges, and especially under the back walk, over which broad planks may be laid, resting on loose bricks, for the convenience of walking during the winter season; from these the heat will be equally diffused through the whole house, and to produce which, half the fuel will not be necessary that must be consumed in keeping the house warm by a single range round the front and ends only.

In the erection of stoves it will not be necessary to have the ends glazed more than half the width of the house, or at most, to within eighteen inches of the doors, leaving that much for piers between the doors and the upright end sashes; the remainder may be carried up with brick as high as the roof lights.

In stoves that are so long as to require two fires, each with its respective ranges of flues, it will be proper to make a glass partition in the middle, and to have two tan-pits, that there may be two different degrees of heat for plants from different countries; and were a range of stoves built all in one, and divided by glass partitions at least half the width of the house towards the front, it would be of great advantage to the collection, because they may have different degrees of heat according to their different natures, and likewise the air in each division may be shifted, by sliding the glasses of the partitions, or by opening the glass door which should be made between each division, for the more easy passage from one to the other.

In the warmest of these stoves or divisions, should be placed the most tender exotic trees and plants. These being natives of very warm countries, should be plunged in the bark-bed, and over the flues may be shelves on which to place the various species of Cactuses, Euphorbiums, Mesembryanthemums, and other very tender succulent plants which require to be kept dry in winter.

As in this stove are placed the plants of the hottest parts of the East and West Indies, the heat should be kept up equal to that marked *Ananas* upon the botanical thermometers, and should never be suffered to be more than eight or ten degrees cooler at most, nor should the spirit be raised above ten degrees higher in the thermometer during the winter season, both which extremes will be equally injurious to the plants.

The roofs of some stoves are so made, that the glasses do not slide either up or down, which is an evil of great magnitude; for where the sun is so powerful in the months of April and May, as it is in every part of the United States, the superabundance of heat collected in the house on very hot days, cannot be discharged by the doors and sliding upright sashes in front, which forces the plants into an extreme state of vegetation, and renders them unfit to bear the open air towards the latter end of May, when otherwise the greater number of them might be brought out with safety, without receiving

such a check by the transition, as many cannot recover during the
summer, and causing many more to appear much less beautiful than
they otherwise would, were they gradually inured to the open air in
the hot-house before their being brought out, by occasionally sliding
open the roof as well as the front glasses, and never letting the heat
arise in the house to too high a degree.

NURSERY AND SUCCESSION STOVES.

Besides the main bark-stove already described, it is very convenient
to have one or two smaller, such as a nursery-pit and a succession
stove, particularly where there are large collections, and more especially in the culture of pine-apples one serving as a nursery-pit, in
which to strike and nurse the young offspring crowns, and suckers of
the old pines for propagation; the other as a succession-house for receiving the year old plants from the nursery-pit, and forwarding them
a year to a proper size for fruiting as succession plants, to furnish the
main stove or fruiting-house every autumn, to succeed the old plants
then done fruiting.

These smaller stove departments prove materially useful in the
culture of pines particularly to raise and nurse the young plants,
until arrived at a proper age and size to produce fruit, then moved
into the main stove or fruiting-house, which being thus supplied
from these smaller stoves, with a succession of fruiting-plants annually, without being crowded or incommoded with the rearing of
the said succession plants, proves a particular advantage, not only in
the culture of the fruiting-plants, as they often require a higher degree of heat than the succession plants at particular times, in order
to forward and improve the growth of their fruit, but it is also making the best advantage of this main department, to have the bark-bed
instantly filled with fruiting-plants only, producing a full crop of
proper sized pine-apples every year, which could not always be effected
with such certainty and perfection without the aid of these succession-stoves, because the pine-plants in their infant state require sometimes different management from the fruiting-plants, particularly in
respect to the degree of fire-heat, which, in general, should be more
moderate than for the fruiting-plants, lest too much should force them
into fruit in their minor growth, when incapable of producing such
in any tolerable perfection.

Therefore, these smaller succession-stoves may be erected as ap-
pendages to the main house, or may be detached at some little distances, as may be convenient; though if the situation admits, it may
be both more convenient and ornamental to join them in a line with
the main stove, one at each end, and nearly of the same construction,
but smaller both in length, width and height, if thought proper:
these are sometimes formed in the manner of a common detached
bark-pit, without any upright glasses in front, having a wall all
around, five or six feet high behind, gradually sloping at each end
to about four feet in front, and with only sliding glasses at top, more
particularly the nursery-stove, commonly and simply called the pit,
because the whole internal space in length and width is often allotted

entirely as a pit for a bark-bed without any walk within, or door for entrance, the necessary culture being performed by sliding open the glasses at top, and the flues for the fires being formed in the upper part of the back wall above the surface height of the bark-bed : however, it may be more eligible to form the succession-stove particularly, nearly like the main one, with erect glasses in front and sloping sashes at top, with a door for entrance, and an alley or walk next the back wall at least, or more eligible if continued all round the bark-pit.

Observing, however, if these smaller stoves are joined to the end of the main one, they may be divided from it only by a sliding glass partition for communication with each other, particularly the succession and main stove, but with separate furnaces and flues to each department, because the young pine plants do not at all times require the same degree of fire-heat as the older pines, especially those of proper size for fruiting, so that by having separate fires, the heat can be regulated accordingly.

The nursery stove or pit may be of smaller dimensions in respect to width and height than the succession house, if thought convenient; and if designed wholly as a pit without any path or walk within, six or seven feet width may be sufficient, by five or six high in the back wall, and four in front, the whole internal space being filled with tan three feet deep to form the bark bed, serving chiefly as a nursery in which to strike and nurse the annual increase of crowns and suckers of the *ananas* or pine plants the first year; also to raise many tender plants from seeds, cuttings, &c., without incumbering the main stove; and when they are forwarded to such a state of growth as to require more room, they are removed to the succession house.

But the succession house may be nearly on the plan of the main stove, though of smaller dimensions both in the width and height, and is intended to receive the year old pine plants from the pit or nursery stove. In order to plunge them at greater distances, sufficient to give the whole proper scope to take their full growth another year, when they will generally be arrived to a proper size for fruiting the year following, being previously removed in autumn to the main fruiting stove to succeed the old fruiting plants, which generally by September have all yielded their produce, are then removed away and their place supplied by a sufficient quantity of large plants from the succession house, being arrived to a proper state of growth to produce fruit next summer; the largest succession house is at the same time replenished with the plants from the nursery pit, which next autumn will probably be also arrived to a proper size for removing to the fruiting house to succeed the others, and the nursery-pit supplied with young crowns and suckers of the year, from the fruit and old plants, to strike and forward them in ready successions for the above occasions.

Thus by having the different stove departments always furnished with pine plants of three different stages of growth, succeeding one another regularly, *i. e.* the nursery pit containing the yearly crowns and suckers, the succession pit the one and two year plants, and the main stove the fruiting plants, a constant succession is thereby annually obtained, for the same individual plants never produce fruit but once; they, however, produce a plentiful supply of crowns and suckers which commence proper plants, attaining a fruiting state in regular succession.

However, in many places, the situation or convenience not admitting but of one common stove to raise and forward the pines and other exotics in their different stages of growth, at least with probably the assistance only of a small detached bark-pit, or a bark and dung hot-bed under a large garden frame, to strike and nurse the yearling crowns and suckers of the pines, &c., of each year, until they are about a year old, then moved into the stove; where, with the proper requisite culture, are produced not only very good pine-apples, but also many curious exotics, flowers, other fruits, &c., at an early season.

But having a main stove with two smaller ones adjoining nearly on the same plan as above hinted you can always, with greater certainty, obtain a regular annual succession of fruiting pines in perfection.

A private passage or small door, made from the back shed into the hot-house, close to one of the ends, or at any convenient place, will be found extremely useful in severe weather for entering into the house to examine the temperature of the heat, or to do the other necessary work, when it would be ineligible to open the outer doors.

It would be an eligible way, for persons who have large collections of exotics, to have the green-house in the middle, with a stove and glass case at each end; the stoves to be next the green-house, and the glass cases at the extremities, made exactly in the same manner as the bark stoves, and to range with them.

These glass cases being furnished with flues, but no bark-pits, are in fact dry stoves; they may be kept of different temperatures of heat, and ought to be furnished with roof and front coverings of some kind to be used occasionally. The bark stoves may also be kept of different temperatures, so as to suit the various habits of the plants.

Thus by contriving the green-house in the middle, and a stove and glass case at each end, there will be a conveniency for keeping plants from all parts of the world; which cannot be otherwise maintained in good health, but by placing them in the different degrees of heat, corresponding with that of their native countries.

THE DRY-STOVE.

This stove differs in no wise from the bark-stove, but in not having a bark-pit; it is furnished with flues as the other, and consequently produces a more dry heat; being intended principally for the culture of some very succulent tender exotics of parched soils that require it to be kept always dry. Persons who have full collections of exotics prefer this kind of stove, in order to deposit the most succulent kinds therein, separate from plants which perspire more freely, lest the damp occasioned by such perspiration, and the more frequent watering of these kinds, should be imbibed by the succulents and injure them.

However, most of the tender succulent kinds are cultivated and preserved in the bark-stove, placed on shelves, and in dry situations, with very good success.

In this kind of stove are erected movable shelves or stands above one another, theatre ways, on which to place the pots of the various kinds of plants intended to be kept therein.

Stoves have been constructed on various other plans, according to the fancy of the owners or their desire to try experiments; some circular, some crescent form, and others ranging north and south, with double roofs and upright sashes, all of glass-work; but these not being found to answer as well as those described, it is unnecessary to take further notice of them.

For the various kinds of *forcing-frames*, and their respective uses, see pages 47 and 48.

PINES.

At this season the pinery hot-house requires good attendance, for some of the pines will now, towards the end of the month, begin to show fruit; and your assistance is at no time more necessary than when the fruit first appears, especially in one particular, the supporting a proper bottom heat; for if the heat of the bark-bed is not kept up at that time, the young fruit will receive a check more than may be imagined; as, notwithstanding the air of the house can be sufficiently warmed by the flues, yet these plants also require always a moderately brisk growing heat to their roots, but especially when the fruit is young; and without that assistance, they will not advance freely in the first growth, and being checked therein, will be much inferior in size to what they otherwise would have been.

Examine therefore carefully at this time, the heat of the bed in which the pots of pines are plunged; and if you find it very faint, take up all the pots, and let the bed be forked up to the bottom. But before you proceed to this, if the heat is found much decayed, or the bark considerably wasted, or become very small or earthy, it will be advisable to add at the same time some new tan, first removing away some of the wasted bark at top and sides, and then fill up with new bark, working the old and new well together. When that is done, let the pots be replunged again to their rims, in a regular manner. This will enliven the heat greatly; and, if done in proper time, the young fruit will grow freely.

Let the fires be made very regularly every evening and morning, and take care that they are not made too strong, for that would be of very bad consequence; and to avoid this, have a thermometer placed in the hot house, as a direction to regulate the degree of heat. Let the thermometer range from 70° at night to 85° or 90° with sun light.

Water should be given to the pine-apple plants once a week, or so often as it may seem necessary, and always very moderately; and let as little as possible fall into the heart or between the leaves at this season.

For the conveniency of watering the pines and other plants that are plunged in the bark-bed, a long pipe, made of tin, would be eligible to use occasionally; this should be in three different joints, in order that it may be shortened or lengthened as you see it convenient: one of these joints should have a funnel made at the largest end, that by pouring the water out of a handy watering-pot, into the funnel, the water is conveyed to the pots in any part of the bed with greater exactness, without pouring it into the heart of the plants.

All other tender exotic plants in the hot-house or stove should be supplied with water as they require it.

The woody kinds will require it often, those of the succulent tribe but seldom; or at least but very little must be given them at a time.

Be sure to have soft water for watering the different sorts of plants, for which purpose you may have a tub or cistern in some convenient part of the house to contain it, in which it is to remain till the cold chill is completely off.

In the management of the plants in the bark-bed there must be a particular regard had to the temperature of the bark, which should be about 90°, and the air of the house, that neither be too violent, as also to water them frequently but sparingly, especially the shrubby kinds, because, when they are in a continual warmth, which will cause them to perspire freely, if they have not a proper supply to answer their discharge, their leaves will decay and soon fall off.

In very severe weather, when necessity requires strong fires to be kept up for any length of time, and that the internal air becomes thereby of a dry and parching nature, it will be well to sprinkle the flues occasionally with water, to raise a comforting steam in the house, and to restore the air to its true atmospheric quality, which is always most congenial to the health of plants.

Every plant in the hot-house or stove should be kept perfectly clean from dust or any sort of foulness; if anything of that nature appears on their leaves, let the large-leaved sorts be washed with a sponge, &c., the others by occasionally watering them all over the top.

KIDNEY BEANS RAISED IN THE HOT-HOUSE.

Those who have the conveniency of a hot-house may raise early kidney beans with little trouble. The early cream-colored dwarf, early China and Mohawk, are proper sorts for this purpose.

The method is this: Fill some large pots or oblong narrow boxes with rich dry earth, and place them on the top of the surrounding wall of the bark-bed, or upon any of the shelves near the glasses, observing to plant four or five beans in each about an inch deep, or, if oblong boxes, of about two feet length, plant the beans triangularways along the middle, two or three inches asunder; and thus the pots, &c., being placed as above, the beans will soon sprout and come up.

When the beans have sprouted, sprinkle the earth with a little water, which will help the plants to rise; when they are up, water them frequently.

Let the plants be supplied with proper waterings two or three times a week, and they will grow freely, and produce plentiful crops of beans in March and April.

Plant a successional crop in a fortnight or three weeks after, in small pots, ready for turning out with balls of earth into the larger pots, &c.

OF CUCUMBERS IN THE HOT-HOUSE.

Cucumbers are sometimes raised early, in tolerably good perfection, in the hot-house.

This is effected by sowing the seed or planting young plants in large pots, or oblong narrow boxes, which are to be placed in a convenient situation in the hot-house near the glasses. The boxes for this purpose may be the same length and depth as for kidney-beans. Fill the pots or boxes with rich earth, and place them up near the top glasses, behind or upon the top of the back or end flues, with the bottoms raised or detached two or three inches that the heat of the flues may transpire freely, without injury to the plants.

But the best situation in the hot-house for cucumber plants is to place them by means of supports within about fifteen or eighteen inches of the top glasses, nearly under or towards the upper ends of the superior tiers of lights, not to shade, &c., the other plants below.

The seed may either be sown in small pots and placed in a dung hot-bed or in the bark-bed in the hot-house to raise the plants, or may be sown at once in the pots or boxes, six or eight seeds in a small patch, or in a box of two or three feet long you may sow two such patches; and when the plants are up they should be thinned out, leaving two or three of the strongest plants in each place.

Or, if you raise the plants first in small pots plunged in the bark-bed or in a dung hot-bed, let them be afterwards transplanted, with a ball of earth about their roots, into the boxes or larger pots.

When the runners of the plants have advanced to the outside of the pots or boxes, you may fix up some laths to support the vines or runners, which should be fastened thereto. Let them have water frequently, for they will require a little every other day at least.

EARLY STRAWBERRIES IN THE HOT-HOUSE.

Strawberries may be brought to early perfection in the hot-house; and, if desired, this is the time to begin to introduce therein some pots of good bearing plants.

The Longworth's prolific, large early scarlet and alpine strawberries are the kinds that succeed for forcing; for this purpose they should be taken up and planted in proper sized pots, either in the months of September or October, as then directed, and protected in garden-frames, till wanted for forcing; but, if the weather permits, you may take them up at any time, with balls of earth about their roots, planting one good plant in each pot—always observing to choose those of two or three years old and which are full of bearers.

Place these pots towards the front of the hot-house, near the glasses, and let them have water frequently, especially when they are in blossom and setting young fruit but observing at these times not to water too freely over the flowers for fear of washing off the impregnating farina, giving it chiefly to the earth in the pots.

OF FLOWERING PLANTS IN THE HOT-HOUSE.

You may now introduce into this department many kinds of flowering plants, to be forced into bloom at an early season, such as honeysuckles, African heaths, double-flowering dwarf almonds, and cherries, &c ; also pots of pinks, carnations, daisies, double sweet-williams, rockets, wall and stock-gilly flowers, &c., and pots or glasses of any kind of bulbous roots, planted either in earth or water, may also be introduced, with a variety of curious annual flowers, which may be sown in pots and forwarded there to early perfection.

RAISING PLANTS AND CUTTINGS.

Fig. 12.

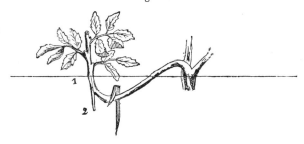

Many shrubs and plants that are difficult to raise by cuttings may be increased by layers. A layer may be defined as a cutting only partially separated from the plant. The branch is bent down to the ground, and, at the bend, a cut is made half through the shoot, cutting upwards for about half an inch. Some plants do as well as if the shoot is twisted at the bend ; anything to check the flow of sap will cause a root formation. The figure shows the appearance of a layer. The line at 1 represents the surface. At 2, the cut part is shown, and strong branches will require to be kept in place by a stout peg, as here represented. Nearly all plants, even fir-trees, may be increased by this practice.

FEBRUARY.

DESIGNS FOR A KITCHEN GARDEN.

THE Kitchen Garden is a principal district of garden-ground allotted for the culture of all kinds of esculent herbs and roots for culinary purposes, &c.

This may be said to be the most useful and consequential department of gardening, since its products plentifully supply our tables with the necessary support of life; for it is allowed that health depends much on the use of a proper quantity of wholesome vegetables, so that it is of the utmost importance for every person possessed of a due extent of ground to have a good kitchen garden for the supply of his family. This garden is not only useful for raising all sorts of esculent plants and herbage, but also all the choicer sorts of tree and shrub fruits, &c., both on espaliers and standards; and the annual cultivation of the ground by manuring, digging, hoeing, &c., necessary in the culture of the esculent herbage, greatly encourages all sorts of fruit-trees, preserves them in health and vigor, so as always to produce large and fair fruit; for which reason, in the kitchen garden should always be planted the choicest sort of fruit-trees, particularly for espaliers and walls; likewise some standards, if set a considerable way asunder, so as not to shade the under crops too much; and when the trees are judiciously disposed, there will be nearly the same room for the crops of herbaceous esculents as without them; so that this garden may be reckoned both as a kitchen and fruit garden.

As to the situation of this garden, with respect to the other districts, if designed principally as a kitchen and fruit garden, distinct from the other parts, and there is room for choice of situation, it should generally be placed detached entirely from the pleasure-ground; also as much out of view of the front of the habitation as possible, at some reasonable distance, either behind it or towards either side thereof, so as its walls or other fences may not obstruct any desirable prospect either of the pleasure garden, fields, or the adjacent country; having regard, however, to place it, if possible, where the situation and soil is eligible, as hereafter illustrated; and if its situation is unavoidably such as to interfere with the pleasure gardens, so as its fences may be thought disagreeable to view, they may be shut out from sight by intervening plantations of shrubs and trees.

But as in many places they are limited to a moderate compass of ground, and in others, though having scope enough, require but a small extent of garden, you may, in either case, have the kitchen, fruit, and pleasure garden all in one; having the principal walks spacious, and the borders next them of considerable breadth; the back part of them planted with a range of espalier fruit-trees, surrounding the quarters; the front with flowers and small shrubs; and the inner quarters for the growth of the kitchen vegetables, &c.

SITUATION, SOIL, WATER, EXTENT, ETC.

As to situation, it can only be observed in general, that both high and low, if the soil be suitable, will produce good crops of esculent herbage and fruits, though a moderately low situation is the most preferable, as being less exposed to the influence of cold cutting winds in spring, and more retentive of moisture during the summer months, which are advantages worthy of attention both on account of the early and of the other principal crops. A situation having a moderate slope is very eligible for this purpose, as in such a spot there will not be any danger of water standing, nor of being too wet at any season; and if it slopes towards the south, is is the more desirable, as it will not only be better defended from the cold north-westerly winds, but by its exposure or aspect inclining to the sun, you may always expect to have the earliest crops; or when the situation is in some parts a little elevated or gently sloping, and in others low and moist, it may be some advantage, as the higher or sloping ground will suit some early crops, and serve for wintering several sorts of plants that are impatient of copious moisture in that season, such as artichokes, spinage, corn, salad, lettuce, &c.; and the low ground will be eligible for late summer crops, as beets, kidney-beans, cauliflowers, cabbages, lettuce, and several others. However, as to choice of situation and soil, this only is practicable in large estates; but where persons are limited to a moderate space, they must be content with such as nature affords; observing in this case, that if the natural soil is of a proper temperament and depth, you need not be under any great anxiety about the situation if it is moderately dry, and not apt to be overflowed in winter; even in that case, it may be remedied or greatly helped, by digging two or three long, narrow canals, and from these some under-ground hollow drains, the earth from which will help to raise the contiguous ground higher, and the water in the canals will be convenient for watering the plants. Remarking that a situation too wet in winter should be guarded against as much as the nature of the place will admit; for in such land you can never have early nor good general crops, nor will the fruit-trees be prosperous.

With respect to soil, that for a kitchen garden of all others, requires to be naturally good, of depth enough for the growth of the large perpendicular esculent roots, as carrots, parsneps, red beet, horse-radish, &c., also for the growth of fruit-trees, a very material article; so that the proper soil for these general purposes should, if possible, be from about a foot and a half to two feet deep, or more; but much less than a foot and a half depth will be a disadvantage; so much depends upon the quality of the soil for a kitchen and fruit garden, that where there is scope of ground to choose from, we cannot be too cautious at first in fixing on a proper spot where the soil is good and deep enough, as above, before gravel, clay, or other bad soils are come at, which should always be more particularly attended to when designed to furnish the ground with a choice collection of fruit-trees, either for walls, espaliers, or standards ; for, without a due depth of good earth, these will neither bear well nor be of long duration.

Different sorts of soils are met with in different parts, as loamy, clayey, sandy, &c. A loamy soil, either of a brown or black color, is the best that can be for this purpose, more particularly a light sandy hazel loam, which always works pliable at all seasons, not apt to be too wet and cloggy at every shower of rain, nor bind in dry, hot weather; this soil, however, although in many places it is the most general superficial earth, is not common to all parts. A clayey, strong, stubborn soil, is the worst of all earths, and must be mended by sandy materials, ashes, and other loosening light substances. A sandy soil is common in many places, which is of a very light, sharp nature; this must be fertilized by plenty of rotten dung and strong earths, when they can be easily procured.

It is observable that ground which constantly produces good crops of grain and grass, is also proper for the growth of all esculent herbs and fruit-trees.

Choose, however, the best soil you can, according to the situation and extent of your ground, and if it happens to prove unfavorable art must assist; for if it is of a light sandy nature, it may easily be mended by adding a quantity of any kind of rotten or other good dung; and if of a very light, sharp, hungry temperament, earths of stronger substance, such as loam and the like, if it can be easily obtained, must be added occasionally, along with plenty of dung, working the whole with the natural soil of the garden ; and should your garden be of a clayey, cold, damp nature, add light materials, both of rich composts and light sandy soils; nothing is more proper, where it can be had, than plenty of coal ashes, &c., for opening and warming all tough, stubborn, cold soils.

.Water is a very essential article in a kitchen garden in summer, to water all new transplanted plants and others that cannot subsist without a due supply of moisture during the drought of that season ; therefore, in large gardens, where practicable, one or more reservoirs of water should be contrived in the most convenient part of the ground, either in basins or narrow canals, and supplied with water from some contiguous spring, river, brook, pond, well, &c.

The necessary space of ground proper for a family kitchen garden, may be from about a quarter of an acre, or less, to six or eight acres, or more, according to the appropriated limits of ground, the number and demand of the family, the consumption by sales, or the expense the proprietor would choose to bestow on the making and general culture. A kitchen garden of an acre will nearly employ one man, especially if it be furnished with espalier and other fruit-trees, and so in proportion to a garden of smaller or larger extent : a garden of the above size will produce a very plentiful supply of esculent herbage and fruit sufficient at least for a family of ten or fifteen persons ; but on large estates, and where the family is considerable in proportion, and not limited to space of ground, three or four acres of kitchen garden may be necessary; and some very large families have them of six or eight acres extent.

If the produce is intended for sale, the garden must be large in proportion to the demand.

FENCES FOR INCLOSING THE GROUND.

With respect to fences for inclosing the ground, it is most necessary to have an effectual fence of some sort around the kitchen-garden, both for security of the produce and to defend tender and early crops from cutting winds.

Previous to fencing the ground, the proper shape or form for the garden is to be considered; the most eligible form of a kitchen-garden is that either of a square or oblong square; but the figure may be varied as the necessity of the case may require; keeping, however, as near as possible to the square or oblong form, especially if the ground is to be fenced with materials for training fruit-trees; no other shape answers so well for that purpose; for trial having been made of circles, ovals, semicircles, angles, &c., none succeed near so well as the square form.

Different sorts of fences are used for inclosing this ground, as walls, palings, and hedges, &c.

Sometimes board fences or palings are used, both for protection and for training fruit-trees to. When such are intended for trees, the boarding should be tongued and closely joined edge to edge, so as to form a plane or even surface for the commodious training the branches.

In gardens where no wall trees are intended, a hedge, or bank and hedge is a very proper fence; which may be so trained as to form both an effectual fence against men and beasts, also to shelter particular parts of the ground for raising early crops: a hawthorn hedge is the most proper, though other sorts may be used.

No fencing, however, for a kitchen-garden where intended to have wall trees, especially in the more northerly parts of the Union, is equal to brick walls, which are considerably stronger, warmer, and more durable than paling fences; and their natural warmth, together with their reflection of the sun's heat, is the most effectual for the growth and ripening of the latest and more delicate kinds of fruit.

Hot walls for forcing by fire heat, &c., are often erected in large kitchen-gardens; for an account of which see page 55.

PREPARING AND LAYING OUT THE GROUND.

The whole ground should be regularly trenched two spades deep; observing if the soil is poor or of bad quality, and wants amendment, either of dung or any of the materials before mentioned, such must previously be added, and then trenched in betwixt the bottom and top pits, so as next year when it comes to be digged again, and the compost being well meliorated, will be worked up and mixed with the natural soil.

Do not omit enriching and improving the borders of the wall* and espalier trees, by adding a considerable portion of rotten dung; and if the natural soil is not good, add also, if possible, some good loamy earth from the surface of a field or pasture common, either to the whole, or rather than fail, a few barrowfuls at first to each place where a tree is to stand, and improve the rest afterwards by degrees at leisure.

The ground must be divided into compartments for regularity and convenience. A border must be carried round close to the boundary walls or fences, not less than five, but if six or eight feet wide, the better, both for raising various early and other kitchen crops, and for the benefit of the wall trees, if any, that their roots may have full scope to run in search of nourishment; and moreover, the annual digging and stirring the ground for the culture of the herbaceous esculents, greatly encourages the trees; hence the utility of having a broad border. Next to this border a walk should be continued also all around the garden of proper width, as mentioned below; then proceed to divide the interior parts into two, four or more principal divisions and walks, if its extent be large; first, if the ground is of some considerable width, a straight walk should run directly through the middle of the garden; and another, if thought necessary, may be directed across the ground, intersecting the first; and if the garden extends any considerable length, two or more such cross walks may be necessary; the width of the walks may be from about five to ten or twelve feet, in proportion to the extent of the garden; and each of the quarters should be surrounded with a five or six feet wide border; and a range of espalier fruit-trees may be planted along towards the back part of each border, so that every quarter will be inclosed with an espalier, which will be ornamental in growth, and profitable in the annual production of superior fruit of different kinds.

I would not, however, by any means advise dividing small or moderate-sized gardens into too many walks and small quarters, especially if they are to be surrounded by espaliers, which would render them too confined for the proper growth of culinary herbage; besides, it would be wasting too much of the ground in walks.

In one of the quarters a place should be allotted for the framing ground; that is, a place for making the hot-beds for raising early cucumbers, melons, and other tender plants; fixing on a spot for this purpose, full to the sun from rising to setting, sheltered as much as possible from the northerly winds, and conveniently situated for bringing in the dung for the hot-beds.

This place, if not so situated as to be sheltered by the walls or other fences of the garden, it will be of much advantage to inclose it with a close fence of some kind, serving both to break off the winds, and by having a door to lock, will preserve your crops more

---

* Observe that all trees planted against and trained to either paling or board fences, &c., producing fruit on one side only, are denominated wall trees, as well as if planted to actual brick or stone walls; in contradistinction to espalier trees, which produce fruit on both sides.

secure; these fences may be six or seven feet high in the back or north side, with both the side fences sloping gradually to about five feet high in front, which should always be lowest to admit the sun freely.

With regard to the borders and walks of this garden, the outer borders adjoining the walks should be neatly formed, the edges made firm and straight, and the walk gravelled, or laid with other dry materials.

The edges of the borders in small gardens are frequently planted with box, &c., especially in gardens where the kitchen and pleasure-ground are all in one; sometimes part are edged with under shrubby aromatic herbs, as thyme, savory, hyssop, and the like, but unless these are kept low and neat they appear unsightly; some, however, use no planted edgings at all in kitchen gardens, only have the edge of the border made up even, treading it firm that it may stand, then cut it straight by line; sometimes along the top of this edging is planted a row of strawberries, a foot or fifteen inches asunder; they will bear plentifully and have a good effect, observing to string them several times in summer to preserve them near and within due compass.

Sometimes grass-walks are used, but these are rather improper for general use in kitchen gardens, especially in such parts of the garden where wheelbarrows are obliged to come often, which would cut and greatly deface them; besides, they are apt to be wet and disagreeable in all wet weather and in winter; but if any are intended for summer's walking, they should be only in some dry part of the garden, and never let them be general, for besides the aforementioned inconveniences, they are apt to harbor slugs and other crawling vermin, to the detriment of the adjacent crops.

The espaliers should be planted in one range round each main quarter, about four or five or six feet from the outer edge of the border, in proportion to its width, and from about fifteen to twenty feet asunder, according to the sorts of fruit-trees you plant.

Within the espaliers in the quarters, you may plant some standard and fruit-trees of the choicer sorts, at fifty feet or more distance each way, especially the large growing standards, that they may not shade the ground too much.

Likewise in the quarters may be planted the small kinds of fruit-shrubs, as gooseberries, currants and raspberries, in cross rows, so as to divide the quarters into breaks of twenty or thirty feet wide, or more; others in a single range along near the outward edges, or some in continued plantations, placing the bushes nine feet asunder in each row, and if kept somewhat fan-spreading the way of the rows, they will not encumber the ground, and will bear very plentiful crops of large fruit; besides, between these rows you can have various early and late crops of vegetables.

In many places, however, as formerly noticed, there is but a small compass of ground, or so limited as to be obliged to have the kitchen, fruit, and pleasure-gardens all in one, or at least often all within the same general inclosure, in which case, if any distinct part of the ground is required for ornament, a portion of it next the house may be laid out in a lawn or grass-plat, bounded with a shrubbery, beyond which have the kitchen-ground, separating it also from the other with shrubbery compartments: the kitchen garden may also be laid out with ornamental walks and borders, having a broad border all round, and next this, a walk from five or six to eight feet wide, carried all round the garden, in proportion to its size, and if the ground is of some considerable width, may have one of similar dimensions extended directly through the middle; and next the walks have a border of four or five to six or seven feet wide, carried round the quarters or principal divisions, which border, if raised a little sloping, from the front to the back part, will appear better than if quite flat; planting a range of espalier fruit-trees along towards the back edge of the border, so as immediately to surround the quarters, allotting the out-sides of the borders for small esculents or flowers, and small flower-ing shrubs, having the edges planted with box, &c., or some with strawberries and other edging-plants, and the walks neatly laid with gravel or other materials before mentioned; the inside, within the espaliers, to be the kitchen-ground, dividing it, if thought necessary, by rows of gooseberry, currant, and raspberry plants.

But when necessary to have the whole space of the kitchen gar-den employed for real use, no ground should be lost in ornamental borders and walks: have a border all around the boundary fence, five or six feet wide, except the south borders, which should be seven or eight feet broad, because of their great use for raising early crops; and have a walk around the garden, not more than a yard to five or six feet wide, allowing the same width for the middle walks, or so as to admit of wheelbarrows passing to bring in the manure, &c., and may either have a four feet wide border all around each quarter next the walks, or not, as you shall think proper; laying the walks neatly with any gravelly materials, or with coal ashes, &c., so as to have dry walking and wheeling with a barrow in all weathers.

GENERAL CULTURE OF THE GROUND.

With respect to the general culture of the kitchen garden, it con-sists principally in a general annual digging, proper manuring, sow-ing and planting the crops properly, pricking out, planting, and trans-planting various particular crops, keeping the ground clean from weeds, and watering the crops occasionally in summer.

As to digging, a general digging must be performed annually in winter or spring, for the reception of the principal crops; also as often as any new crops are to be sown or planted at any season of the year, remarking that the general digging for the reception of the main crops of principal esculents in spring, I should advise to be performed by trenching either one or two spades deep, besides the paring at top, though except for some deep rooting plants, as carrots, parsneps, &c., one good spade deep may be sufficient for common trenching, unless on particular occasions, to trench as deep as the good soil admits, to turn the exhausted earth to the bottom and the fresh to the top to renew the soil. However, you should be careful not to trench deeper than the proper soil; and the trenching only one spade deep, will much more effectually renew the soil than plain digging; and by paring the top of each trenching two or three inches deep into the bottom, all seeds of weeds on the surface are thereby buried so deep that they cannot grow;* and I should likewise advise that the general digging be performed principally, especially in stiff ground, before the setting in of the winter frosts, or early in spring; but it would be better if done some considerable time before the season for putting in the crops, that the ground might have the advantage of fallow, to meliorate and enrich it, and always let the ground be trenched in rough ridges, that it may receive all possible benefit from the sun, air, rains, frosts, &c., to fertilize and pulverize the soil before it is levelled down for the reception of seeds and plants; and this levelling down will be an additional improvement in breaking, dividing, and meliorating the earth. Plain digging, however, may be sufficient for most of the slight crops, especially in summer or autumn, after the ground has been trench-digged in the general winter or spring digging.

As to manure—any kind of dung, or compost of dung and earth, is proper; and if this could be suited to the nature of the soil, it would be of greater advantage, that is, for ground of a strong, heavy, cold nature, have for manure a compost of well-rotted dung, ashes, or any sandy earths; and if light sandy ground, have the moistest sort of dung and heavy earths; though any kind of well-rotted dung will suit as proper manure for almost every soil, but none better than the dung of old hot-beds, which is the most common manure in kitchen gardens, being horse-stable dung, first used in hot-beds, where it becomes rotted to a soft, moist temperament of an extremely enriching quality, and suits almost all kinds of soil and plants, or some of the same quality from dung-hills is equally eligible; but well-rotted neat's dung is also very good, particularly for light grounds; or a compost of different kinds, as horse dung, neat's dung, hog's dung, farm-yard dung or mulch, ashes, lime-rubbish broken small, sawdust, rotten tan, having all lain together till well rotted, will make excellent compost manure.

The manuring or dunging the ground may be necessary every year or two; for all crops being of an exhausting nature in every soil, the vegetative vigor of the soils must be supported accordingly by a proper application of manure; but once every two or three years, at farthest, the ground in general will want amendment; though, where there is plenty of dung, give it as far as it will go every year, especially for the principal crops, such as onions, cauliflowers, cabbages, &c., for as the different crops exhaust the soil, the addition of dung fertilizes and renews it, which when duly applied in proper quantities, the various crops will not only be much finer, but arrive to earlier perfection than in poor starved ground.

But for some particular crops, ground which has been well manured the year before, will be more eligible than if immediately fresh dunged the same year; such as for some of the long fusiform-rooted kinds, as carrots and parsneps, &c., unless the dung is perfectly rotted,

* When the good soil is less than two feet deep, the under base, or inferior portion, my be loosened and left in the bottom.

mellow and mouldy, that these long roots can readily make their way straight through in their perpendicular, downward growth; for when the dung manure is rank and lumpy, it is very apt to impede the young descending radicle, and occasion the main root to fork or grow crooked, more especially the carrots, which also in some fresh-dunged ground are sometimes apt to canker.

All manuring should generally be performed in winter or spring, to be dug in at the general annual digging, taking opportunity of frosty or very dry weather to wheel in the dung for the principal manuring, as it may then be performed more easy and clean without clogging or spoiling the walks, or tearing up the ground; laying it in heaps by barrowfuls at equal distances; afterwards spread it evenly, and dig it in one spade deep or more.

In regard to cropping the ground, the proper situation for, and method of raising the different plants, is fully explained in the different months under their respective heads; I will therefore only hint here, that it is eligible to allot the driest, warmest, and most sunny situation for the early crops, and the other parts for the main crops.

The south borders are proper for raising the earliest plants, as early peas, beans, radishes, spinage, lettuce, carrots, small salad-herbs, kidney-beans, &c.; the east and west borders for succession of early crops, and the north borders, which, being shady and cool, serve for raising and pricking out many small plants, slips and cuttings in summer; though all these borders, in every exposure, may be made useful at all seasons. The borders next the espaliers are proper for crops of small plants at all seasons of the year, as lettuce, endive, spinage, small salad-herbs, strawberries, and several others, both to stand and for transplantation, according to the mode of culture of the different sorts; and by keeping all the borders constantly well furnished with various esculents, disposed according to their different growths, they, besides their usefulness, effect a delightful variety.

In the internal parts, called the quarters, should always be raised the larger principal crops, such as cabbages, cauliflowers, broccoli, coleworts, peas, beans, kidney-beans, onions, leeks, carrots, parsneps, beets, potatoes, turnips, artichokes, celery, general crops of lettuce, spinage, horse-radish, &c.

As many of the esculent plants succeed best in rows, such as peas, beans, cauliflowers, and all the cabbage kinds, transplanted lettuces, endive, potatoes, artichokes, Jerusalem artichokes, celery, and some others, particular regard is requisite that the rows are at proper distances for the plants to have full scope to grow, and would advise that all the tall-growing sorts, sown in drills, such as peas, beans, kidney-beans, &c., for early crops, have their rows ranging north and south, if possible, that the sun may shine on each side of the rows more effectually, as well as on the ground between the rows; both of which are of more advantage to early crops than may be generally imagined; for when the rows range east and west, one row shades another, so that when the plants grow up, they cannot all receive an equal benefit of the sun.

The great art in cropping a kitchen garden, is to make the most of every part of the ground where necessary, by having each quarter well occupied with as many crops annually as possible, as practised by the experienced market gardeners and others, who have occasion to cultivate the whole kitchen ground to every possible advantage, often having two or three different crops advancing in successive order together on the same compartment, especially where the principal crops are in wide rows, as in cauliflowers, cabbages, beans, &c. Other kinds are frequently inter-cropped, at proper periods, with those of peculiar growth in the respective sorts; not to impede each other nor the principal crops above intimated. Sometimes slight crops of quick growth are sown to come off soon, or by the time the others begin to advance considerably; or sometimes, in the advanced state of the main crops, they are inter-cropped with others of a more continuing and larger growth to be coming forward, ready, as the others are going off; fully occupying the same spot in a succession of crops in some advanced growth, whereby both time and ground are occasionally gained, though, where there is a plentiful scope of kitchen ground, especially in private gardens, any considerable inter-cropping would be unnecessary, as generally each sort raised separately will, in some degree, be superior; however, on the other hand, as in many places the kitchen ground is much limited, it is incumbent on the occupier or cultivator to inter-crop occasionally where it can be done with a good prospect of success, agreeably to the above intimations. With regard to the different methods of sowing and planting the different crops, these shall be designated in the course of the work.

Destroying weeds is a most necessary culture in the kitchen garden, which must be very particularly attended to; for the success of the crops greatly depends thereon, and without a full determination to keep them clean, it is in vain to sow or plant any.

The utmost attention is necessary never to suffer weeds to perfect their seeds in any part, whether in cropped or vacant quarters, or on dung-hills or compost heaps, as they would lay the foundation of several years' trouble to extirpate them; for, as in digging and hoeing the ground, some of the seed would be buried near the surface, and others much deeper, at every time of stirring the earth, a fresh crop of weeds would arise from the same stock of seeds, which verifies the saying, "One year's seeding makes seven years' weeding."

WORK TO BE DONE IN THIS MONTH.

The various preparations for early crops, noticed last month, in page 17, &c., I would again recommend to your particular attention, as you ought to " take time by the forelock" at this season, and have as much as possible in a state of forwardness, in order to ease the great press of business which will naturally come on next month.

CUCUMBERS AND MELONS.

Where the raising of early cucumbers and melons was not begun last month, it may now be commenced the beginning or middle of this, with a greater prospect of success; observing exactly the same method of making the seed hot-bed, sowing the seed, and the general management of the bed and plants, as directed under the head *Cucumbers*, &c., in the kitchen garden for *January*.

RIDGING OUT EARLY CUCUMBERS AND MELONS.

If the cucumber and melon plants which were raised last month, or the beginning of this, have not suffered by any of the accidents that are attendant on them at this season, the former are now, and the latter will, in the course of this month, be arrived to a proper growth for ridging out into a larger hot-bed, finally to remain.

A new bed or beds, for one or more large frames, should therefore be prepared in due time for the reception of these plants, and made in the same manner as directed in January, pages 21 and 22; observing that such must be three feet and a half, or four feet high when finished; for a less depth of dung will not produce the necessary heat which these plants require at this inclement season; and, besides, if the beds were made of a more shallow depth their heat would be soon spent, and lining could not be applied to them with so much advantage: for the latter reason particularly, they must be made wholly above ground.

The bed being finished, put on the frame or frame and lights, which will defend it from wet, and bring up the heat the sooner, tilting the upper ends of the lights a little that the steam may pass off. In a week after the bed is made, if it has settled unequally, take off the frame and make the bed level, then immediately put it on again for good.

After this let the state of the bed be daily examined with good attention; and when you find the violent heat is over, lay in the earth, but be sure to let that first pass away.

The earth for this purpose should be rich and tolerably dry; for that is a material article to be regarded at this season. The earth proper for cucumbers may be either any prepared compost of rich loam and rotten dung, or of the temperature of light rich kitchen-garden soil; but to prepare for this you ought, about the latter end of September, or in October (if the most convenient), to take from some quarter of the kitchen-garden, which is naturally light and dry, and well enriched by manure, a sufficient quantity of earth, and throw it up in a heap ridge-ways, in some dry place, open to the sun and air; mixing therewith at the same time some good rotten dung, breaking and blending the whole well together; a due quantity of this compost-heap should be carried into some shed or other sheltered place, open in front to the sun or free air, a month or a fortnight at least before you want it, that it may be preserved perfectly dry for earthing the bed.

Then, when the bed is in order, lay about half a bushel or rather more of earth under the middle of each light, rising each parcel of earth in a round hillock about ten inches high; let the spaces between the hills and quite to the sides of the frame be covered with the same sort of earth, only two or three inches thick at this time, while the bed is in strong heat for fear of burning, as explained below; but which, when the heat is become moderate, is by degrees to be augmented till raised as high as the top of the hills, as hereafter directed.

The reason for laying the earth in little hills, and not earthing the bed fully at once, is by way of precaution in case of violent afterheat, in which case it will more readily pass off in steam between the hills; and likewise, because we may venture to use the bed some days sooner than if it was earthed all over at once to the full thickness; for if the bed should burn after the plants are in, you can more readily prevent the earth and also the roots of the plants from being burnt thereby, by drawing the earth away from around the bottom of the hills if it burns, and supplying the places with more fresh mould.

As soon as the bed is earthed as above, put on the glasses, and by the next day the hillocks of earth will be warm; if they are, level the top of each a little, so that they may be about eight or nine inches deep; then proceed to put in the plants, the cucumbers, and melons separately, in different hot-beds, or distinct frames, &c.

Previous to this observe, that as having last month directed the plants to be pricked into small pots, three in each separately, and as they are now to be turned out of these pots with the balls of earth entire, and planted, one pot of plants in each of the above hills, I would intimate, in this final transplanting, that two of the best cucumber plants and only one melon, would be sufficient to remain, cutting the others away as soon after planting as you are able to distinguish which are most likely to do well; however, it is advisable, previously to transplanting, that, in order to have the whole ball of earth adhere closely about the roots, to give the pots some water the day before; and the method of planting is this: having some pots of the strongest plants ready, place your hand on the surface of the pot, taking the stems of the plants carefully between your fingers, then turn the mouth of the pot downwards, and strike the edge gently on the frame, the plants with the ball of earth to their roots will come out entire; then making a hole in the middle of each hill of earth, place one pot of plants with the ball entire in each hole, closing the earth well around it, and about an inch over the top, bringing the earth close around the stems of the plants; this done, shut down all the lights close for the present, till the steam rises again strong, then they must be tilted a little behind, in proportion, to give it vent.

The plants being ridged out finally into the beds where they are to remain for fruiting, you must be careful to give them fresh air every day, by raising the glasses a little for its admission, and for the great steam to pass off; and it is necessary to cover the lights every night with mats, putting them on about half an hour before the time of sun-setting, or a little earlier or later as the weather happens to be either mild or severe, and uncover them in the morning as soon after the sun begins to shine on them, or after sun-rising, as the state of the weather will permit: in covering up, observe, that while the bed is very hot, and the steam copiously rising, never to let the ends of the mats hang down over the dung outside of the frame, which would draw up a hurtful steam, and stifle the plants.

Air must be admitted to them every day when the weather is any way favorable, by raising the upper ends of the glasses from about half an inch to an inch or two, or in proportion to the sharpness or mildness of the outward air and internal heat and steam of the bed.

In giving the plants air, it is a good method at this season, especially in severe cutting weather, to fasten a mat across the ends of the lights were tilted, to hang down detachedly over the place where the air enters the frame; the mat will break the wind and sharp air before it reaches the plants, and yet there will be a due proportion admitted without exposing them directly to it, and there will also be full liberty to let the steam pass off.

Likewise, in covering the glasses on nights with mats, if there be a strong heat and great steam in the bed, let the lights be raised *a little* behind when you cover up; let them remain so all night, and use the mats as above mentioned, to hang down low before the place where the glasses are raised; but this must be done with caution in very severe frost.

One great article to be attended to now is to support a constant temperate heat in the hot-bed, so as to keep the plants in a regular growing state—about 65° at night and 70° to 80° in the day. The first thing to be observed towards this is that in six or eight days after ridging out the plants, provided the heat of the bed is become moderate, it will be very proper to give some outward protection of dry, long litter, waste hay, fern, straw, leaves of trees, &c., laying it close around the sides a foot thick, and as high as five or six inches up the sides of the frame; but this will be particularly serviceable in very wet weather, but more especially in driving cold rains or snow, and also if there be cold piercing winds, all of which would chill the bed, and, without the above precaution, would sometimes occasion such a sudden and great decay of the heat as to prove the manifest destruction of the plants; whereas the above lining will defend the bed, and preserve a fine heat till the dung begins naturally to decline or decay of itself, which is generally in about three weeks or a month after the bed is made, when the warmth of it must be renewed by adding a lining of fresh hot dung close to its sides and ends.

But for the first week or ten days after the plants are ridged out into this hot-bed, mind that their roots have not too much heat; for it sometimes happens that a bed after the mould and plants are in (the earth confining the heat and steam below in the dung) will begin afresh to heat so violently as to be in danger of burning the earth at the bottom of the hills, and without some precaution is taken the burning will soon reach the roots of the plants; therefore, for the first week or ten days, let the bottom of these hills be at times examined by drawing away a little of the earth below; and, if any burning appears, remove the burnt earth, replace it with new, and, by drawing some away quite around, let the hills be kept as narrow as they will just stand, so as to support the plants, and let them remain till the danger of burning is over, when you may replace it again.

When the great heat abates, or the roots of the plants begin to appear through the sides of the hills, then add some fresh, light, rich earth all around them. About three days after you may lay some more; and in two or three days after that you may earth the bed all over to the full thickness. But before you lay the fresh earth to the sides of the hills, let it be first laid a few hours, or for one night in the frame, up towards the sides, that it may acquire an equal degree of warmth with that in the bed; then, being applied as above, it will not be in danger of chilling the roots of the plants.

The next particular care is that of lining the hot-bed when the heat declines; therefore, when the heat of the bed begins to decrease much, let a lining of the best hot dung be applied in due time to the back or front of the bed, or to both if the heat is very much declined. The dung for this purpose should be prepared in the same manner as that for making the bed. Remember, that if there was a lining of dry litter laid around the sides of the bed to defend it from wet, &c., as before directed, this must first be removed before you apply the lining; then line the sides of the bed about from twelve to fifteen or eighteen inches wide, according as the heat is less or more declined, which should be raised about four or five inches higher than the dung of the bed, to allow for settling. Lay some earth on the top of the lining to keep the rank steam of the fresh dung from coming up that way, which, if it did, would be apt to enter the frame at the place where the lights are raised to admit air, and prove of bad consequence to the plants.

OF STOPPING OR TOPPING THE ABOVE PLANTS.

The young plants, both cucumbers and melons, should be stopped or topped, if not done before, at the first joint, by pruning off the top of the first runner-bud, which is necessary to promote a stocky growth, and cause them to put forth lateral shoots at the first and second joints to form fruitful runners, and from these others of the same nature will be produced.

This operation should be performed when the plants have two rough leaves, and when the second is about an inch broad, having the first runner-bud rising at its base. The sooner this is detached the sooner the plants acquire strength and put out fruitful runners. It is to be done in the following manner :—

You will see arising, in the centre of the plant, at the bottom of the second rough leaf, the end of the first runner, like a small bud, which bud or runner, being the advancing top of the plant, is now to be taken off close, and may be done either with the point of a penknife or small scissors, or pinched off carefully with the finger and thumb; but, whichever way you take it off, be careful not to go so close as to wound the joint from whence it proceeds.

Having thus pruned or stopped the plants at the first joint, they will by that means very quickly get strength, as will plainly appear in a few days, and, in about a week or ten or twelve days after being thus treated, will each begin to send forth two or three runners, which runners will probably show fruit at their first, second, or third joints; for, if the main or first runner was not to be stopped as above, it would perhaps run half a yard or two feet in length, without putting out more runners to fill the frame, or probably without showing a single fruit—for it is upon these lateral shoots or runners, produced after stopping the plants, that you may expect fruit to appear in any tolerable time in the season. But let it be also observed that when the said lateral shoots have three joints, and that if any of them do not then show fruit at either of these, it will be proper to pinch off the top of such shoots at the third joint, which will promote their putting forth a supply of two or three new shoots, some or all of which will most likely be fruitful; and after this, according as they advance in growth, train the runners along in regular order, cut out casual very weakly vines, and thin others where very irregularly crowded. Thus, if the bed is well managed and the plants are forward, those of the cucumbers will probably produce proper sized fruit at the end of this month or beginning or middle of the next, but the melons not so soon by six or eight weeks. (See next month.)

OF SOWING CUCUMBER AND MELON SEED.

As there may be many persons who did not begin last month to sow cucumbers for an early crop, it will here be proper to take notice that the beginning, middle, or any time of this month is still a good time to begin that work, making a hot-bed for sowing the seed as directed in *January*, pages 21 and 22.

Those which are sown early in this month, will, with good management, produce fruit in the end of March, or beginning of April; and those sown in the middle or latter end of the month will have fruit in the end of April, and will bear plentifully in May.

The beginning of this month is a very good time to sow melons for a full crop in the frames.

The seed hot-bed which is to be made now, either for cucumbers or melons, must be of the same dimensions; and the seeds sown, and plants managed as directed last month.

But observe, that to be well supplied with cucumber or melon plants, either to plant in new beds, or to have a reserve in case of accidents happening to any already planted out, it will be very proper to sow some seeds at three different times this month.

These may be sown in such cucumber hot-beds as are already made and in cultivation, and when fit to prick out, plant them in small pots as directed last month, which may be plunged in the back part of the same bed, where they may be kept till wanted, either for new, or to supply any deficiency in the present beds.

FORCING ASPARAGUS.

Hot-beds for forcing early asparagus may be made any time this month, for which purpose you must be provided with proper plants; these are previously raised in the natural ground from seed, as hereafter directed, which being transplanted from the seed-bed into others duly prepared for their reception, and having two or three years' growth there, they then are of the proper size and strength for forcing. But observe that in those parts of the Union where the ground is subject at this season to be bound up by frost, previous precaution will be necessary, in order to secure a supply of plants when wanted for this purpose; therefore, before the setting in of the severe winter frost, cover a sufficient number in the beds wherein they are growing, with as much dry litter or leaves of trees, &c., as will effectually keep the ground from being frozen, so that you can remove it, and take up the plants conveniently when wanted.

Or you may, on the approach of severe frosts, take up a sufficient quantity with as little injury to the roots as possible, which may be planted in sand or dry earth in a warm cellar, in the same manner as directed for planting them in the frame, covering their crowns about an inch, observing not to crowd the plants for fear of their becoming mouldy; and in mild weather ventilate the cellar as often as possible, to prevent any bad effect to the roots from stagnant air; but when it can be done, it will be much better to take up the plants out of their beds according as you want them.

The necessary quantity for a three-light frame is from three to four hundred plants, and so in proportion for any number of frames; the plants in such beds ought to be set very close, in order that by having as many as possible in each frame, they may produce a proportionable supply to recompense sufficiently for the trouble and expense of forcing them.

A bed for this purpose is to be made in like manner as those directed for cucumbers in pages 21 and 22, but very substantial; then put on the frame, and earth it all over six or seven inches deep, for the immediate reception of the plants.

The bed being made and earthed as above, and a sufficient quantity of plants in readiness, proceed to planting by raising at one end a small ridge of earth about three or four inches high, against which place a row of plants close to one another, drawing some earth to the bottom of the roots, then place others against these in the same manner, and so continue until the frame is full, all having their tops or crowns upright and of an equal level. When the whole bed is thus planted, cover the crowns of the roots all over with light, rich earth, about two inches deep, which concludes the work for the present.

You may now put on the lights, which are to be kept open, raised high behind, or slided down every day, except in very severe weather, but at night let them be closed; give all the air possible so that you do not suffer the earth in the bed to be frozen or chilled, by rain or snow, till the buds begin to appear when you are to give them another covering of three or four inches of the same kind of mould as before, so that the crowns may be covered in the whole about six inches deep.

But it must be remarked that for the first week or fortnight after the bed is made and the asparagus planted, that the state of its warmth should be every day carefully examined; for that purpose thrust two or three sharp pointed sticks down betwixt the roots into the dung in different parts of the bed; when upon drawing up the sticks once or twice a day, and feeling the lower ends, you can readily judge of the degree of heat, which, if found very violent, threatening to burn the earth and scorch the roots of the plants, it must be moderated by boring with a long, thick stake several wide holes in the dung on each side of the bed, also in the earth just under the roots, to admit the air, and to let the rank steam and burning quality of the dung pass off more freely; but when the heat is become moderate, the holes must be closed again.

Likewise observe when the heat is on the decline, it will be very proper to lay a quantity of dry long litter round the sides of the bed, which will preserve a fine kindly growing heat, and will defend the bed from being chilled by heavy rains, snow, &c.

In the next place, when you find the heat of the bed beginning to decline considerably, you should prepare to renew it as soon as possible, which is to be done by applying a lining of hot dung to the sides, as for cucumber and melon beds.

Fresh air must be admitted in fine weather daily, especially if the heat of the bed is strong when the buds begin to appear through this last covering of earth; for fresh air is necessary both to give them color and prevent their drawing up too fast and weak; therefore in fine sunny days, either tilt the upper ends of the lights an inch or two, or shove them a little down, as may be convenient; but keep them close in cold or very bad weather, and always at night.

Continue to cover the glasses every night, especially after the plants appear, with mats or straw.

The bed, if made and managed as above directed, will begin to produce asparagus abundantly in four or five weeks, and provided the heat be kept up, will continue producing buds in great plenty for about three weeks.

The method of gathering the asparagus in hot-beds is to thrust your finger down gently into the earth, and break the buds off close to the roots; but the cutting them with a knife, as practised in the natural ground would, by reason of the buds coming up so very thick, destroy as many or more than you gather.

When it is intended to have a constant supply of asparagus in the winter and spring seasons, till that in the natural ground comes in, you should make a new hot-bed every three weeks or a month.

A quantity of fresh plants must also be procured for every new bed; for those which have been forced in a hot-bed, are not fit for any use afterwards, either in the natural ground or elsewhere.

When designed to raise asparagus plants for forcing, you should sow some seed every year in a bed of rich earth, as directed in March; observing when the plants are one year old, to transplant them into an open compartment, in rows, nine inches asunder, and about the same distance between the rows. When they have two or three summers' growth, they are then fit to take up for forcing; but if they stand three years before you take them up they will produce much larger buds.

It is necessary to have three different pieces of ground always employed at the same time with asparagus plants for the above purpose; that is, one for the seed-bed with seedling plants, which should never

stand longer than one year before transplanted the other two pieces
to be occupied with transplanted plants; one to be a year's growth
from the time of planting before the other, by which method of sowing a quantity of plants every spring, you will, after the first three
years, obtain a fresh supply of proper plants every year of eligible
age and growth, as above, for forcing.

In those States where there is not severe frost to be encountered at
this season, asparagus may be forced as directed above, without the
assistance of a *frame and lights;* but in lieu thereof you must arch
the bed over with hoops, and protect it from heavy rains and cold
with bass mats or other convenient covering, laid over these hoops;
and the earth on the beds must be confined, either with a shallow
frame or with straw bands or ropes, three or four inches in diameter,
fixed down neatly along the edge of the bed, with sharp pointed
wooden pegs.

MUSHROOMS.

Take care that the mushroom beds are still well defended from
heavy rains and frost, both of which would destroy the spawn.

The covering of straw should not be less than fourteen or sixteen
inches thick on every part of the bed; and at this season it would be
proper to continue some large garden mats spread over the straw covering, to secure the bed more effectually from wet and cold; and observing, that if the wet at any time has penetrated quite through any
part of the covering, the wet straw should be removed, and replaced
with some that is clean and dry.

If these beds are made under open sheds constructed for that purpose, it will be a great advantage, particularly in protecting them
from too much wet, which is very injurious to them, especially during
the winter season.

New mushroom beds may now be made where wanted; for the particular method, see *October.*

KIDNEY BEANS.

Where early kidney beans are wanted, you may, in the beginning,
or any time this month, make a hot-bed for raising them; let this be
made, as directed for cucumbers, to the height of three feet, and long
enough for one or more frames, which, with their glasses, put on immediately; when the heat is come up, level the bed and cover the
dung seven or eight inches deep with rich light earth, then draw
drills from the back to the front a foot asunder, and an inch deep;
drop the beans therein two or three inches apart, and smooth over the
surface of the bed.

Or you may sow the beans thick in a small hot-bed, or in pots
therein to raise the plants about an inch in growth, then transplant
them into a large hot-bed as above, to yield their produce.

The best sorts for this purpose are the early cream-colored dwarfs,
early speckled, white and yellow dwarfs; because these kinds are of
an early nature, and do not run so strong or rampant as the other
sorts.

When the plants begin to appear, raise the lights a little behind every mild day, to admit fresh air to strengthen their growth : give also occasional gentle waterings, continue the same care in their advancing state, and support a proper heat in the bed ; they will thus afford an early produce in April, &c.

But where there is a hot-house you may raise early kidney or French beans, generally with much less trouble and more certain success than in hot-beds, as above.

SMALL SALADING.

Continue to raise in hot-beds a regular supply of small salading, such as cresses, mustard, rape, radishes, lettuce, &c., as directed in January, pages 28 and 29, which must be sown every eight or ten days, in order to afford a proper succession ; for at this season such are more acceptable, and to many persons more palatable, than at any other period of the year.

Towards the latter end of the month, in the middle States, and in all parts to the southward, you may begin to sow lettuce, and the other different kinds of small salading on warm well sheltered south borders, especially if the great winter frosts have passed away.

For this purpose dig the ground neatly, giving it an advantageous slope towards the sun, rake the surface fine, and draw shallow drills from north to south about three or four inches distant ; sow the seeds therein, each sort separate, very thick, and earth them over not more than a quarter of an inch deep. If the season proves favorable, you may expect tolerable success ; but the more certain way would be to cover these beds with frames and glasses, which would not only forward them to perfection at an earlier period, but also protect them from the various accidents incident to such early crops in unfavorable seasons.

When these plants, both under cover and in the open ground, begin to come up, they sometimes, by rising very thick, raise the earth in a kind of cake upon their tops, which consequently retards their growth ; they may be assisted by whisking the surface lightly with your hands, &c., to separate the earth, after which, the plants will rise regularly.

When those coming up in the open ground happen to be attacked with morning hoar frosts, and like to be a sunny mild day, if before the sun rises full upon them you water them with fresh pump or well water poured out of a watering-pot, with the head on, to wash off the frosty rime, it will prevent their turning black and going off.

CAULIFLOWER PLANTS.

The beginning of this month plant your autumn sown cauliflowers in hot-beds, to flower in April and May ; garden pits or frames constructed of stone is what is generally used and preferred now for forcing instead of the wooden frames directed in page 18 : however, where stone cannot conveniently be had wood will answer by being regularly lined with fresh dung, as directed in page 25. Stone pits are generally made larger than wood, say twenty-four feet long (which will require six sashes, each four feet wide by five feet ten inches long), six feet deep at the back, and four feet six inches in front; to be about two feet ten inches below the surface; the wall to be from one foot to eighteen inches thick. In these frames you can raise any kind of vegetables that are wanted early; or small flowers, such as roses, carnations, stock-gilly, wall flowers, mignonette, heliotrope, nerembergias, pæonies, or any low growing plants that you wish to bloom at an early season. By placing the pots at the back side, they will not interfere with cauliflowers, melons, or any other plants raised in a hot-bed, while they are small. In making the hot-bed, observe the directions in January, page 21, except that by having the bed below the surface you can use a foot or eighteen inches of old leaves or tan in the bottom; and then finish off as directed for cucumbers and melons. Plant the cauliflowers about two feet distant every way; and between the cauliflowers you may plant lettuce and sow radish or turnip seed; white turnip is the best for this purpose: these will be used before the cauliflowers bloom. It will be necessary to look over the cauliflowers to see if any show flowers before they attain their proper size, in which case, pull them up and plant others in their place. Those early autumnal sown plants which you have in frames, and that you are endeavoring to protect with a covering of boards and mats, &c., without the assistance of glass, should never have powerful sunshine admitted to them while in a frozen state; for its sudden action upon these tender plants, whilst in that condition, would prove their total destruction; therefore admit it only at intervals, when weak, until the plants and ground around them are completely thawed.

The cauliflower plants which were raised from seed sown last month, should, as soon in this as they may arrive at a sufficient size, which is about four or five inches, be transplanted into a new moderate hot-bed, which will greatly strengthen and forward their growth.

Make the bed two feet and a half high and put a frame on, lay on six inches deep of rich earth, when this is warm prick the plants therein two or three inches apart, and give them a little water; as soon as they have taken root give them plenty of air; and in mild warm days take the glasses totally off, but let them be carefully covered every night and the glasses only raised a *little* behind in cold weather.

Plants thus treated will become strong and well rooted, bear transplanting much better than if left in the seed-bed, and produce larger and better heads; for, by transplanting, the tap-roots are checked, and the plants push a number of lateral roots, which afford them nourishment and strength; they become short-stemmed and stout, and consequently more fit for a final and successful transplantation than if suffered to remain in the seed-bed.

Were these to be transplanted again, early in March, into another bed, it would be an additional advantage; it is by the neglect of this necessary treatment that we have so few good flowers, for the plants, when continued in the seed-bed till finally transplanted, become long and spindling, tender and unfurnished with roots or fibres; when planted out, for want of a sufficiency of roots, they are not able immediately to extract the necessary supply of nourishment from the earth, consequently become stunted, and either button, or grow so miserably as never to produce a good head.

When transplanted and furnished as above, and the proper season arrives for planting them out in the open ground, they are to be taken up separately with a hollow trowel or transplanter, preserving as much earth as possible about the roots of each plant, and deposited where they are to flower; thus treated they will scarcely be sensible of the removal, will continue in a constant and regular state of vegetation, and if protected for a few days with garden pots or other suitable coverings from too powerful a sun, and regularly at night, for ten or twelve days after planting, you may reasonably expect the desired success.

As it is from these early sowings that the greatest success may be expected in the United States, every care should be taken to promote their early growth and strength, in order that they may arrive at due perfection before the commencement of the severe summer heat, which is found so injurious to all late cauliflowers.

Continue to give a due quantity of air to your cauliflower plants at all favorable opportunities; for, as observed in *January*, it is an extremely essential article.

SOWING CAULIFLOWER SEED.

Sow some cauliflower seed in a hot-bed the beginning, middle, or at any time this month, but the earlier the better, to succeed those sown in January, or in case none were sown at that time; for the method of doing which, see page 29.

If you have not the convenience of glass lights, these plants may be raised with good success in *paper frames*, or, with particular attention, you may succeed with coverings of mats, or boards and mats.

PAPER FRAMES.

These frames are made either like the cover of a wagon or the roof of a house, and covered with oiled paper instead of glass. They have a frame of wood at the base, to which in the former broad hoops are fastened, bent over circularly. The width of the frame should be near five feet, the length nine or ten; the distance between the hoops not more than a foot, and there should be several rows of strong pack thread or rope yarn running from hoop to hoop all over, distant from each other about eight inches, and other lines crossing and intersecting these between the hoops or ribs of the frame, which arrangements of lines are of essential service for the more effectual support of the paper when pasted on the frame, and to strengthen it against the power of winds and heavy rains.

The other sort of frame may be made with slips of pine or neat laths, fastened to a roof-tree at the top, and to the base-frame at bottom. The panels or lights ought to have hinges alternately at each side, to open outward for giving air occasionally on the side from the wind, or on both sides if the weather is mild, and also for performing other necessary culture.

The paper for this purpose should be of the larger, strong printing or demi kind; which, previously to pasting on the frame, should be moderately damped with water, that it may not sink in hollows after being fixed; as soon as thus prepared, proceed to paste it on, sheet by sheet, using for this purpose the very best kind of paste; and contrive to have whole ones along the ridge-rail above, extending lengthways and across, to join regularly with the sheets below; pasting the whole in the most regular and secure manner to the frames, ribs, and pack-thread; and if, at the intersections of the latter, a small square or round bit of the same paper is pasted on the inside and to the large sheets over those parts, it will give additional strength against rain and winds.

After the paper is thus pasted on, and *perfectly dry*, then it must be oiled over with linseed oil, either raw or boiled; the latter, I think, is rather apt to harden the paper and cause it to crack, therefore would prefer the former. Having, however, the oil and a painter's soft brush, lay it on lightly, and brush the outside of the paper all over, equally in every part, which done, place the frame in some dry, covered shed, there to remain till the whole is thoroughly dry, then it may be used when wanted, and will answer extremely well for various purposes.

If the base-frames are well painted with the following composition they will last a long time. To every six pounds of melted pitch, add half a pint of linseed oil, and a pound of brick dust well pulverized, mix them all together and use them warm. This is the best pigment for all timber exposed to the weather, for no moisture can penetrate through it.

You may also form lights of the above kind for your common hotbed frames when glass cannot be conveniently had, which will answer a very good purpose.

These covers of oiled paper are used not only for early cauliflower and cabbage plants, but also for early salading, cucumbers, &c., and are excellent for covering cuttings of exotic and other plants, and for various other purposes.

CABBAGE PLANTS.

Continue to protect your autumn-sown cabbage plants from the severity of the weather, agreeably to the general precautionary directions given in the month of *October*, which see. But be very particular that such as are in frames, and consequently under occasional protection, which renders them still more tender than those protected under the shade of bows, &c., and that have got frozen either in consequence of neglect in covering, or of the extreme severity of the weather, are not to be exposed to the influence of the sun whilst *shining strongly*, until they are gradually thawed, and also the earth in which they stand; but at intervals when the rays are not too powerful, you may admit them to the plants, in order to accomplish this end the sooner; but it must be done with great precaution. This observation is not only applicable to cabbage and cauliflower plants, but to all other plants under similar circumstances.

The cabbage plants which were sown last month, should as soon in this as they have arrived to the height of three or four inches, or their leaves to the size of a quarter dollar, be transplanted into a new hot-bed, at the distance of three or four inches, plant from plant, every way; in order to promote their growth, give them strength, and the better to prepare them for planting out in the open ground, as soon as the season arrives for that purpose.

Previous to transplanting either these or cauliflower plants, see that the earth of the new bed is arrived at a proper degree of warmth, so that the plants when planted therein, may receive no check, but strike out new roots and fibres immediately. Let them be constantly kept in a moderate state of growth, admitting plenty of air to them at every favorable opportunity; for if neglected in this very essential point, they will grow weakly and slender, and never turn out to good advantage; therefore, let the air be given as often as it can be done with safety, but cover them carefully every night, and even in the day-time, in extremely severe weather.

SOWING CABBAGE SEED.

This is a good time to sow a full crop of cabbage seeds, such as the early Wakefield, early York, early dwarf Battersea, early sugar-loaf, &c.; these may be sown in a hot-bed, as directed for cauliflowers, any time this month, but the earlier the better, especially if none were sown in January: these will come to perfection at an early and very acceptable time.

Towards the latter end of the month, you may sow these kinds on a warm south border, to be covered with frames and glasses, or on slight hot-beds made in warm situations, and covered with paper frames, or with boards and mats occasionally.

Oiled paper covers will do extremely well for this purpose, and may be used to much advantage where glass lights cannot be had.

Sow also some red pickling-cabbage, flat Dutch, large drumhead Savoy, and other late cabbage seeds to succeed your early summer crops; these will produce larger heads and earlier, than if sown much later. Many people never think of sowing these late kinds at this time, which is an egregious omission, and ought not to be copied by any person who wishes to have a regular succession, and in the greatest perfection, of this invaluable vegetable.

The method of sowing these seeds in hot-beds being so similar to that of cauliflowers, a repetition is unnecessary; therefore see page 29. Always observe to give the plants plenty of air, in order to harden and strengthen them, and to prevent their spindling up in a weakly manner, more especially if you do not intend to transplant them into another hot-bed before their being finally planted in the open ground.

But notwithstanding all this precaution, you must not omit to keep them constantly in a growing state, and duly protected from the in-

clemencies of the weather; and when the beds wherein they are growing become cold and destitute of that warmth so necessary for the
above purpose, you must give them a slight lining of fresh horse-dung,
to renew the slow temperate heat so congenial and necessary to these
plants at this season.

SOWING CELERY.

Towards the end of this month, if the weather permits, prepare a
small bed of light rich earth in a *warm border*, to sow some celery
seed therein for an early crop; the best kinds to sow are the solid
white, and red celery, both of which are excellent.

Break the earth very fine, and either sow the seed on the surface,
and rake it in lightly, or rake the surface smooth, sow the seed thereon, and cover it with light earth, sifted over near a quarter of an inch
deep; or the ground being formed into a three or four feet wide bed
and the surface raked, then with the back of the rake trim the earth
evenly off the surface about a quarter of an inch deep.into the alley,
sow the seed on the bed, and with a spade cast the earth over it
evenly and rake the surface smooth.

Though this seed may not come up for a length of time, there will
be no danger of its perishing in the ground, and it will be in a state
to receive the first advantage of the growing season: if a frame and
lights or hand-glasses can be spared to put over it, they will greatly
forward its growth; when raised in this way, though it will not be
so early, it will not be so subject either to start to seed or to pipe,
as if sown and forced in a hot-bed.

But those who wish to have celery as early as possible, should sow
the seed on a slight hot-bed, and cover it with a frame and lights, or
with hand-glasses, or in default of these, cover at night and in bad
weather with mats placed on hoops stuck archwise over the beds to
support them, being careful in either method, when the plants are
come up, to admit the free air every mild day.

There should not be many of these early sown plants planted out
for a continuing supply, only a few to come in before the general
crop, for they will soon pipe and run to seed.

SOWING RADISH SEED.

Towards the end of this month, if the weather is mild and the
ground open, you may dig a warm border to sow therein some early-
frame, short-top, white and red turnip-rooted radish seeds, to draw
for salads in April and early in May. Dig another piece at the same
time for salmon-radish, which will succeed the former.

Let them generally be sown broad-cast on the surface, either in a
continued space, or in four or five feet wide beds, and rake them in
with an even hand; or in sowing large crops in one continued space,
if quite dry light ground, it is eligible, before raking in, to tread
down the seed lightly, then rake it in regularly.

You may sow among these crops of radishes, a sprinkling of spinage and lettuce seed; the spinage will come in after the radish, and the lettuce after the spinage.

The radishes sown last month must be carefully protected by covering the glasses at night and in very severe weather with mats, &c., and they must have plenty of air occasionally, otherwise they will not root well.

In order to have radishes tolerably early or to succeed those sown in January, let some of the early kinds above mentioned be now sowed on a slight hot-bed, as directed in page 30, and treated as there advised, or you may sow them on such beds under cover of oiled paper frames or of mats; but radishes are not apt to root well under covering of mats, especially when necessity requires them to be kept on for any considerable length of time, unless you are extremely careful to give them as much air and light at every opportunity as possible consistent with their safety.

SPINAGE.

Sow some prickly-seeded spinage, it being the hardiest kind, about the latter end of the month. Let some dry warm ground be prepared for this purpose, and sow the seed thereon thin and regular, either broadcast and raked in or in drills a foot asunder, or on four feet wide beds—being careful that in either case the seed be not covered more than from an inch to half an inch deep, according to the lightness or stiffness of the ground.

The smooth-seeded round-leaved kind is the best to sow during the remainder of the spring and early summer months, but for this early sowing, the prickly-seeded being more hardy, is preferable.

☞ I am well aware that in far the greater part of the eastern States the ground is generally, during the whole of this month and a considerable part of March, so bound up with frost as not to be dug or cultivated; but this not being the case in the middle States, except in very severe seasons, and not in all the southern States, I am induced to give these directions for the sowing of early crops, and where the state of the weather permits they may be practised to advantage, and where not the business must be deferred a little longer.

SOWING LETTUCE SEED.

If the weather be mild and the ground in good condition, you may, about the latter end of this month, sow some lettuce seed on a south border, which ought to be well defended by a wall, hedge, or board fence, &c. The kinds most suitable to be sown at this time are the early curled and common cabbage lettuces, if intended to be cut up for small salading, in which case they are to be sown very thick on the surface, after the ground has been raked tolerably well, and then raked in; or they may be sown in beds or drills, according to fancy, observing that these seeds require but a very slight covering.

You may also sow any other kinds of lettuce, such as the white or green cos, Egyptian and spotted cos, which are excellent kinds;

or, if for cabbaging or heading, you may sow the white Silicia, grand admiral, large Mogul, brown Dutch, or Malta cabbage lettuces, all of which form good hard heads. For this purpose they must be sown very thin, and when arrived at a due size be transplanted in rows into the different borders, &c., as directed in March, leaving a sufficient quantity to occupy the seed-bed, which will head earlier than those that shall have been transplanted.

If these be covered at night and in very unfavorable weather, either with mats or boards, &c., it will greatly forward their growth.

But in order to have a few in a more advanced state for transplanting, and also for early small salading, you may sow any of the above kinds in a hot-bed, those for the latter purpose very thick, and for the former pretty thin. The cos lettuces, not growing flat or in a spreading manner, are peculiarly adapted for sowing in hot-beds at this season; but either of the kinds may be sown, and with due care and proper thinning be brought to good and early perfection.

Lettuces which have stood the winter closely planted in frames should, about the end of this month, be thinned to about nine inches, or, if expected to grow very large, a foot asunder. The plants which are drawn out may be planted into other frames, or into warm borders where they can be well protected with mats or some suitable covering, till they are inured by degrees to bear the open air; but if the weather is unfavorable and you have not a sufficiency of frames to receive the plants, it will be better to defer this work till next month, being particular to pick off all decayed leaves, and to stir the earth a little about the roots.

SOWING CARROT SEED.

When carrots are desired at an early season, some seed may be sown in a slight hot-bed in the beginning or middle of this month. Make this bed two and a half feet high, put on the frame, and cover the bed with light dry earth six or eight inches deep; sow the seed thinly on the surface, and cover it about a quarter of an inch with the same kind of earth. When the plants are up give them plenty of air, and thin them as they advance in growth. Keep the glasses well covered at night, and in extremely severe weather and in April you may expect handsome roots. The early horn is best for this purpose.

This seed, if sown as above, towards the latter end of the month, will succeed very well without the assistance of glass, if the bed is carefully covered at night, and occasionally, as the weather may happen to be severe, in the daytime, with garden mats, &c. You may also about the end of the month sow a small quantity of carrot seed, on a warm border of light, dry, rich earth, and, if the season proves favorable they will succeed tolerably well, and be fit for use at a very acceptable period, for the method of doing which see *March.*

PARSNEPS AND BEETS.

Parsneps being very hardy plants and the seeds remaining in the ground a long time before they vegetate, may be sown as early in this month as the ground can be got in a proper condition to receive the seed, which ought always to be a principal consideration, for nothing can be worse than to work ground whilst too wet. I would not, however, advise to sow more at this time than what may answer for a first early crop.

Sow a small quantity of beet-seed on a warm border in drills for a first crop; but this ought not to be done till about the end of the month.

Observe that seeds which are sown in the open ground at this time, cannot have much advantage, as to earliness, over those which may be sown two weeks later; therefore would advise never to sow seeds till the ground is in a good dry state, and proper condition to receive them.

SOWING PEAS.

Towards the latter end of this month, prepare a dry and well situated piece of ground for an early crop of peas, the Sangster's early, early frame, and early emperor, are the kinds most suitable for this crop, but more particularly the first, though the others are excellent, and will immediately succeed the early frame.

Sow each sort separate, and pretty thick, in rows or drills three feet asunder, covering them not more than about an inch and a half; or if the ground be very loose and light, two inches deep; but if it is of a stiff nature, one inch will be sufficient.

But in order to give the first early crops a greater advantage, prepare a south border of dry light earth for their reception, and raise the earth into narrow sloping ridges, about a foot broad at the base, and nine inches high, and at the distance of three feet from each other; ranging these in a southwest direction from the north side of the border; then on the easterly sides of these ridges, about half their height, sow your drills of peas, giving them the same depth of covering as above directed. In this situation they will have all the advantage of the morning and mid-day sun, lie dry, and will consequently advance in vegetation much more rapidly than if sown in the ordinary way.

RAISING PEAS IN HOT-BEDS, ETC.

Where a few peas are particularly required in the most early season, they may be obtained by sowing some of the early dwarf kinds in a hot-bed, to remain, or rather to be transplanted from that into another; either of which methods should be performed early in this month if neglected in last. These may be sown in a large hot-bed in rows from the back to the front of the bed, to remain: or it would be rather more eligible to sow them thick on a small hot-bed, to be transplanted into a larger when about an inch or two high: and if you have any in an advanced state you may now transplant them as above, to remain for bearing. But if you have the convenience of a hot-house or forcing-house of any kind, you may easily and expeditiously raise them therein, by either sowing the seeds or planting the plants, if in a state of forwardness, in large pots, and depositing these in convenient places in those houses.

N. B. A large quantity of the fallen leaves of trees laid around all your hot-beds, as high as the upper parts of the frames, especially those which contain tender plants, will afford them a very necessary protection, by preventing the frost from penetrating through the sides and ends of the frames, and at the same time they will produce a lasting and comforting heat in the beds.

PLANTING BEANS.

By beans I mean the *Vicia Faba* of Linnæus, and not the *Phaseolus vulgaris*, or kidney beans.

A full crop of these should be planted as early in this or the next month as it is possible to get them into the ground; for it is from the early sown crops of these, that any tolerable produce may be expected in the United States, especially in the middle and southern parts.

For this purpose, as soon as the weather will permit, dig an open quarter of good ground, observing that a strong heavy soil is the most suitable, but see that is not too wet when you work it; in which plant a full crop of the early Mazagan, early Lisbon, long-podded, white-blossom, large Windsor, toker, Sandwich, and other kinds : by planting these different varieties at one time, they will come into bearing in regular succession, according to their different degrees of earliness. You need not be under any apprehension of their being injured by the weather, as they are of a hardy nature, and will not suffer by any frost which may overtake them, except in very extraordinary cases.

Plant the small early kinds in drills three feet asunder, and the beans two or three inches distant in the rows, or they may be planted two rows in each drill, four inches distant each way, and covered two inches deep.

The large kinds, such as the Windsor, toker, Sandwich and broad Spanish, should be planted at the distance of four feet, row from row, and somewhat thinner than the small kinds. These may also be planted occasionally by dibble, but drilling is the more expeditious and better way.

You may continue planting these kinds once a week till the end of March, but those planted after that season will not be so productive.

These kinds may be forced in like manner as peas if desired; for their further treatment, see following months.

SOWING PARSLEY SEED.

Sow some of the common and curled parsley seeds in drills, on some warm border, to produce an early supply; the seed will remain a long time in the ground before it comes up, but there is no danger of its perishing.

MUSHROOMS.

The same care that was directed last month in page 31, must be continued with due attention to your mushroom beds; being particular to preserve them effectually from frost and wet, either of which would destroy the spawn, and render your beds unproductive.

ARTICHOKES.

If the weather is extremely severe, and you have not attended to it before, lay some dry long litter over the rows of your choice globe artichokes, which will tend greatly to their preservation.

SOUTHERN STATES.

In Georgia, South Carolina, and other parts of the more southern States, this will be a very principal month with the inhabitants for making their kitchen gardens; for the method of doing which I can only refer them to the kitchen garden for *March* and *April*, the work recommended to be done in these months being quite applicable with them at this season.

In the more northerly of the southern States, much work can be done in the kitchen garden this month; but the next will be their important period, to which I refer them.

THE FRUIT GARDEN.

PRUNING WALL AND ESPALIER TREES.

Peaches, nectarines, and *apricots,* should, in the middle States, be pruned about the latter end of this month; the beginning of next will be a good time in the eastern States. This must be duly attended to before the buds are much swelled, for then many of them would be unavoidably rubbed off in performing the work.

Examine these trees well, and cut away all such parts as are useless, both in old and young wood, and leave a proper supply of the last year's shoots for next summer's bearing; all old wood that has advanced a considerable length, and produced no young shoots proper for bearing this year, nor support branches that do, are useless, and should now be cut out to make room for better; observing that a general successional supply of young bearing wood, of the best well-placed shoots of last summer, must now be retained in all parts of the tree at moderate distances, to bear the fruit to be expected the ensuing season, at the same time cut away all the ill-placed and superfluous shoots and very luxuriant growths, together with part of the former year's bearers, &c., to make room for the successional bearing shoots, as observed in *January.*

As you proceed, let the supply of reserved shoots be shortened each according to its strength. Shoots of a vigorous growth should be shortened but a little ; that is you may cut off about one-fourth of the original length ; those of a moderate growth should be shortened more in proportion by cutting off about one-third ; for instance, a shoot of eighteen inches should be shortened to twelve or thereabouts, and observe the same proportion according to the different lengths of the shoots.

But for the more particular method of pruning these trees, see the work of the fruit garden in *January,* pages 40, 41.

PRUNING OF APPLES AND PEARS, ETC.

Prune apples, pears, plums and cherries, against walls or espaliers; and, if possible, let the whole of them be finished this month.

In pruning these trees, observe, as directed last month, that as the same branches or bearers remain many years in a proper fruitful state, continue them trained close and straight to the wall or espalier, not shortening their ends, but still continue training each at full length as far as the limited space admits, and laying them in about four, five, or six inches asunder.

In the next place observe, that if the branches be anywhere much crowded, that is, if the bearing or principal branches are closer than four, five, or six inches from one another, some should be pruned out: observing, in this case, to take off such as are badly situated, and particularly such as appear to be the most unlikely to bear, by being either worn out, or, at least, not well furnished with fruit-spurs, as mentioned last month. Likewise observe, that when necessary to make room in any particular part of the tree, to train more regularly any eligible branches which are evidently well adapted for bearing; room must be made for them by cutting out such barren branches as above described ; and in any trees where the general branches are trained considerably too close, and crowding in a confused irregularity, let some of the most unserviceable and irregular growths be cut out in a thinning order, in different parts of such trees, to make room for training the other more useful and eligible branches, in a proper expansion, at regular distances.

When any old or large branches are to be taken out, let them be cut off close to the places from whence they arise, or to any eligible lateral branches which they support, and that you shall think convenient to leave ; in cutting off either old or young branches never leave any stumps.

After cutting out any large branches, let such as remain near that part be unnailed or unbound, in order to be brought higher or lower,

as you shall see necessary, to train them all at equal distances; or
when there are several large branches to be taken out in different
parts, the whole tree should be unnailed or unbound, then you can
more readily train the general branches and bearers in exact order.

Next, let it be observed, that where a supply of wood is wanted,
leave some of the best situated of last summer's shoots, such as
directed to be retained in the summer pruning, to fill up the vacancies; and generally leave a leading one at the end of each branch
where you have room to train them. But all others of the last year's
shoots, not wanted for the above purpose, should every one be cut off
close to the places from whence they proceed, leaving no spurs but
what are naturally produced. The proper fruit-spurs are such as
were described last month, being produced on the sides and ends of
the branches, short, robust, and from about half an inch to an inch
or two in length.

Let these fruit-spurs be well attended to in pruning, carefully
preserving all those of a fresh, plump, robust growth; but those of
a worn-out or rugged unsightly appearance, or that project considerably long and irregular from the front of the branches in a foreright
direction, should generally be displaced, in order to preserve the
regularity of the trees, taking care to cut them off close, by which
new ones will be encouraged in places contiguous.

Having, in the course of pruning these trees, left most of the general shoots and branches at their natural length, as before advised, in
all places where there is full scope to extend them, let them be all
trained regularly in that order, and nailed straight and close to the
wall, or nailed or tied to the espalier about four, five, or six inches
distant. For the management of young trees of these sorts, see the
work of the *Fruit Garden* in *March*, and for the methods of pruning
and treating your standard fruit-trees in this department, see the
article *Orchard* in *January*, pages 56, 57, and 58, and also the same
head both in this month and *March*.

FANCY TRAINING OF FRUIT-TREES.

It is a favorite theory of some writers that fruitfulness and bar-
renness in plants and trees are influenced by the mode of training.
Constraining fruit-trees within limited bounds, we know, answers a
good purpose. Hayward, an English writer on the subject, has explained various modes, which we here repeat for the amusement of
amateurs. The following, in brief, is his method:—

If it be desired to train fruit-trees so as to fill a circular space, they
are best trained with their branches reversed; they thus bear a great
deal of fruit in a small space, and are protected from high winds
without stakes. Obtain plants with one upright stem, of from three
to four feet in height, and at this height let them throw out from
four to six branches three or four feet long, like Fig. 13. Bring
down the branches at the winter pruning and fix them to a hoop
with willow or twine, thus, Fig. 14. The sap will not now flow in
sufficient quantity down the branches to form wood branches at their
ends, but the buds will readily form for blossom buds and fruit.

The wood shoots will be thrown out on the upper sides of the reversed branches, and in winter may be cut out or brought down as
before for a second tier, as in Fig. 15; and, on the same principles,

Fig. 13.   Fig. 14.   Fig. 15.

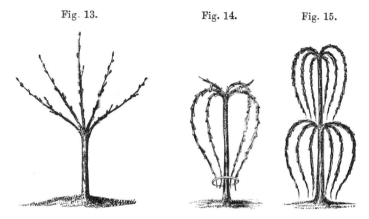

may be carried to a greater height.   Remove all collaterals as soon
as discovered, and as the reversed branches are worn out they must
be cut away, and fresh ones brought down.   Two tiers will be as
much as will be manageable or useful.
    The "spiral cylinder" is well adapted to small gardens.   Prune
and manage the tree so that it shall form four or six branches of
nearly equal size near the ground, Fig. 16.   When these are three
to five feet long, fix six rods or stakes into the earth for supports, in
a circle about the root, as in Fig. 17, the centre dot marking the
root and the others the rods.   Each branch is then to be brought
down, and, being fixed to the rod near its base, the branch is to be

Fig. 16.   Fig. 17.   Fig. 18.

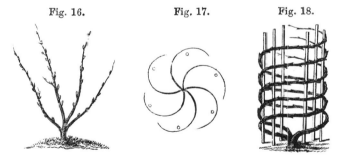

carried round in a spiral manner, on such an elevation as will form
an inclination of fifteen degrees, each being fixed in the same manner; thus all will move in the same direction, like so many cork-
screws, as we see in the Cereus tribe in windows, wound round upright sticks, Fig. 18.
    As trees trained in this manner need never exceed the bounds
    10

allotted them on a border or bed, a greater number may be planted, and a greater quantity of fruit produced in a given space, than can be the case when they are trained in any other manner. Pear and apple-trees thus treated should always be on dwarf-growing stocks.

FIG-TREES.

Except in the southern States, it will not be advisable to attempt pruning your fig-trees till towards the end of next month, or beginning of April, to which I shall refer you for particular remarks and directions.

PRUNE AND PLANT GOOSEBERRY AND CURRANT-TREES.

Gooseberries and currants should be pruned now, if omitted in the former months, both in the standard bushes and those against walls, fences, &c.

In pruning the common standards, observe to cut away all cross-growing branches, and regulate such as advance in a straggling manner from the rest; or where the branches in general stand so close as to interfere let them be thinned properly, so that every branch may stand clear of the other, at a regular moderate distance, and prune out the superabundant lateral and other unnecessary shoots of last summer. (See the *Fruit Garden* of last month, page 43, and also *October*.)

Let these shrubs be always trained with a single stem, clear of branches, six or eight inches to a foot from the ground, as directed in the former month.

Likewise to currants, &c., against walls, give a necessary pruning and regulation, as directed in *January*, &c.

Gooseberry and currant-trees may be planted towards the end of this month, if the weather permits, both in standards for the general plantation, at six to seven or eight feet distance, and some against walls, board-fences, &c., for earlier fruit, but principally currants, and let these for the most part be of the best red and white sorts.

You may occasionally plant a few of the best kinds of gooseberries to north walls, which is the most suitable situation for them in our climates; next to that east or west walls; but plant only very few to those fronting the south, as in such a situation the sun would in summer be much too powerful for these shrubs.

For the method of propagating and raising them, see the work of the *Nursery* in *March* and *October*.

RASPBERRIES.

Raspberries may be pruned towards the latter end of this month, especially if the weather be tolerably mild, in doing of which observe to clear away all the old decayed stems which bore fruit last season, and to leave four or five of the strongest of last year's shoots standing on each root to bear next summer. All above that number on every root must be cut off close to the surface of the ground, and all straggling shoots between the main plants must also be taken away.

Each of the shoots which are left should be shortened, observing to cut off about one-fourth of their original length.

The shoots of each root when pruned, if considerably long and straggling, may be tied two or three together; for by that method they support one another so as not to be borne down in summer by the weight of heavy rains or violent winds.

When you have finished pruning, or as soon after as possible, dig the ground between the plants, observing as you dig to clear away all straggling growths in the intervals, leaving none but such as belong to the shoots which are left to bear.

New plantations of raspberries may be made about the latter end of this month, where the severe winter frosts are over and the ground in proper condition; but where this is not the case, that work must be deferred till next month or until the soil is in a fit state for cultivation. For the method of making these plantations see the *Fruit Garden* in *March* and *October*.

The Antwerp raspberries, which had on the approach of winter been laid down and covered with litter, &c., on account of their being somewhat more tender than the common kinds, ought not to be disturbed till the opening of good weather in March, unless their buds begin to swell too freely.

STRAWBERRIES.

Continue to force early strawberries as directed last month in pages 46 and 112, which see.

Having two or three years old bearing plants in pots, as then directed, plunge them into the hot-beds, and manage them as there advised.

Be careful to admit plenty of air to the plants at every favorable opportunity, by setting up the glasses behind every mild day, and at intervals give gentle waterings to the earth in the pots around the plants, not pouring it over them, especially while they are in flower.

When you find the heat of the beds to be on the decline, renew it by adding a lining of fresh horse-dung to the sides or ends, or to both, as necessity may require; and be very particular in covering the glasses every night with mats or other covering.

This is also a very successful time to place pots of strawberry plants in the hot-house, or in any forcing-house; they will in these places bear well, and in early perfection.

FORCING EARLY FRUIT IN FORCING-HOUSES.

The beginning of this month, if not done before, you may proceed to forcing fruit-trees in hot-walls, peach-houses, cherry-houses, &c., by aid of fire or other artificial heat the proper sorts are peaches, nectarines, apricots, cherries, figs, vines, plums, &c.; having young trees for this purpose that are arrived to a bearing state, and planted

a year or two before the borders, &c., of the forcing departments; or
you may have some also in large pots or tubs, to remove therein at
forcing time occasionally. The trees may be both as wall-trees and
espaliers, training the branches to a trellis erected for that purpose,
and some may be in dwarf standards; you may also have some
cherries, both in small-headed standards, half standards and dwarfs;
and vines trained up under the sloping glasses. (See *Hot-house, December.*)

Let moderate fires be made every afternoon and evening; and if
there is a pit within the forcing-house, in which to have a bark or
dung hot-bed, you may make the bed a week or ten days before you
begin the fires; and if a bark-bed is intended, fill the pit with new
tanner's bark; or if a dung hot-bed, make it with fresh, hot horse-
dung; and when it has settled down six or eight inches, lay that
depth of tanner's bark at top. These beds will support a constant
moderate warmth in which you may plant pots of dwarf-cherries and
of scarlet and Alpine strawberries, which will have fruit very early,
and in great perfection. Continue making fires every evening, and
support them till ten or eleven o'clock to warm the air of the house
till morning, when the fire may be renewed moderately, but not constantly the whole day, except in very severe weather, especially if
there is the assistance of a bark hot-bed; unless it is required to forward the trees as much as possible. However, where there is no internal hot-bed you must continue a constant, regular, moderate fire heat.

With this management the trees will soon begin to advance in
blossom-buds, &c., when you must be careful to continue a regular
moderate heat in the house.

Admit fresh air to the trees every mild day when sunny, especially
after they begin to bud and shoot, either by sliding down some of
the upper sloping glasses two or three inches, or drawing some of the
uprights in front a little way open, shutting all close towards the afternoon, or as soon as the weather changes cold; giving air more fully as
the warm season increases, and as the trees advance in blossom and
shooting.

Give also occasional waterings both to the borders and over the
branches of the trees before they blossom; but when in flower and
until the fruit is all fairly well set, desist from watering over the
branches, lest it destroy the fecundating *pollen* of the anthers destined for the impregnation of the fruit.

The fires may be continued till towards May, being careful never
to make them stronger than to raise the internal heat to about 60°
of *Fahrenheit's* thermometer, in peach and cherry-houses, and 70°
in vine-houses; for in vineries, having only principally vines in
forcing, the heat is generally continued stronger, as they bear it in a
higher degree, whereby to forward the fruit to the earliest perfection.

According as the fruit advances to full growth, continue assisting
them by waterings, and give them free air every warm sunny day;
and when advancing towards ripening, encourage a strong heat in
the middle of the day, by admitting less or more air, in proportion
to the power of the sun, to forward their maturity, and promote a
rich flavor.

Thus the fruits will ripen earlier by two months or more in some, than their natural time of perfection in the open ground and full air.

In the above forcing departments you may also place pots of currants, raspberries, and strawberries, &c.

THE ORCHARD

The feelings of a lover of improvement can scarcely be expressed on observing the almost universal inattention paid to the greater number of our Orchards, and that people who go to a considerable expense in planting and establishing them, afterwards leave them to the rude hand of nature, as if the art and ingenuity of man availed nothing, or that they merited no further care; however, it is to be hoped that the good example and the consequent success of the careful and industrious, will stimulate others to pay the necessary attention to these departments, and thereby to serve themselves as well as the community at large.

At this season you can conveniently perform the very necessary and important works of pruning, of scraping and rubbing off moss and other parasitic plants, and of manuring the ground where wanted; and as much depends on these dressings, they should by no means be neglected, more especially as this is a very eligible time for performing them, and one with which other business does not frequently interfere.

For the method of pruning these trees and other necessary observations, I refer you to the article *Orchard*, last month, page 56, &c.

Where trees are much overrun with moss, it may be removed as directed in page 57, or a strong man with a good birch broom in a wet day would do great execution. The best method of destroying moss on young trees, is to rub all the branches affected, in spring or autumn, or in both if necessary, with a hard scrubbing-brush and soap-suds. This will not only remove the moss, but tend considerably to prevent its sudden return.

Canker in a great measure arises from animalcules, or small or very minute insects or worms, &c., of various kinds; where this is the case, cut out the whole of the cankered part, clean to the sound wood, wash the part well with the following solution, and also all other parts that seem to be in the least affected, then give it a light coat of the medicated tar prescribed in page 58.

Dissolve a drachm of corrosive sublimate in a gill of gin or other spirit, and when thus dissolved incorporate it with four quarts of soft water. This solution will be found to be the most effectual remedy ever applied to trees, both for the destruction of worms of every species, and of the eggs of insects deposited in the bark. No danger to the trees is to be apprehended from its poisonous quality, which in respect to them is perfectly innocent.

Peach-trees which are annoyed by worms, should, towards the end of this month, particularly near and a little under the surface of the ground, be carefully examined, and where any are found they must be picked out with the point of a knife, and with as little injury to the bark as possible, for by lacerating the rind or bark in a careless manner, which is too frequently the case on these occasions, this vehicle, which nature has provided for carrying up the nourishment extracted by the roots, being destroyed, the trees must of course perish, or be weakened in proportion as it is injured.

This being done, wash all the trunks or stems of the trees, as well as any other parts in which you suspect these vermin or their embryo eggs to be lodged, with the above solution, and also the wounded parts, after which apply with a brush a slight dressing of the medicated tar to each and every of the wounds inflicted by picking out the worms. This will preserve your trees in health and fruitfulness much longer than if left to the mercy of these destructive intruders.

As to manure, it is well known that where hogs and poultry are constantly running over the ground, the trees seldom fail of a crop, which is the best proof that manure is necessary. Any manure will suit an orchard, but the sweepings of cow-houses, hog-pens, slaughterhouses, poultry and pigeon-houses, emptying of drains, &c., are more disposed to facilitate the growth and promote the health of fruit-trees, than stable manure. However, any kind of manure is better than none at all.

ON ROOT-PRUNING.

When a tree has stood so long that the leading roots have entered into the under strata, they are apt to draw a crude fluid, which the organs of the most delicate fruit-trees cannot convert into such balsamic juices as to produce fine fruit. To prevent this evil, as soon as a valuable tree begins to show a sickly pinkiness upon the leaves, or the fruit inclining to ripeness before it has acquired its full growth, at the same time the bark becoming dry, hard, and disposed to crack, let the ground, as soon in the spring as the frost is out of it, be opened for three or four feet round the tree, and with a chisel cut close to the horizontal roots every one that you find in the least tending downward. Should there be any mouldy appearance or rottenness among the roots, cut such out effectually, and wash the others clean with a weak lye or soap suds. If the ground be wet, place a few flat stones under the places where you cut off the descending roots, to prevent the young roots which may be produced again from about the cuts taking a perpendicular direction, and to give them a lateral inclination.

As the roots invariably collect the sap from the extreme points, this cutting compels the horizontal ones to work and exert themselves, and if there be any energy left, they will soon throw out fresh fibres, and thus collect a more congenial sap for the support of the tree and fruit. At the same time, in the filling in of the earth, add a quantity of good rotten manure, and cover the ground thinly over with the same, as far as the roots may be supposed to extend; wash the stem and branches with soap-suds, or if any worms are perceivable, with the mercurial or corrosive solution, and water the ground round the tree at intervals in very dry weather, till you perceive it pushing vigorously.

There is not a more powerful agent for producing the canker and other disorders than these descending roots. Canker indeed may arise from an improper soil, a vitiated sap, animalculæ, and the want of free circulation of the fluids: the last is often caused by injudiciously shortening too many of the leading branches. The medication before recommended will stop the progress of the evil on the parts to which it is applied; but the canker may again break out on the other parts of the same tree, and that arises very frequently from the roots striking into a cold and unfriendly soil.

The fuids being once vitiated by any subterraneous cause, canker is not the only evil; insects are' invited thereby to deposit their eggs in the bark, which in due time become crawling maggots; these feed on the sap of the trees, devouring the inner bark and rind as they proceed, until the period of their chrysalis; which having undergone, they take wing and fly off, and in their progress seldom fail to lay the foundation of similar mischief.

From this may be inferred the necessity of making a judicious choice of proper ground for your fruit-trees, and paying due attention to their cultivation and health; for it is quite as presumable, if not more so, that the vitiated juices of the trees invite the worms, than that they are the original cause which produces it.

When any of your fruit-trees are growing extremely luxuriant, and continue to produce no fruit, though having arrived at a proper age for that purpose, they may be forced into a bearing state by opening the ground around them and cutting through a few of their largest roots, but especially the descending ones; the deprivation which will arise from this, of their extraordinary resources, which was the cause of their running into such a luxuriancy of wood, will soon bring them into a bearing state; but be careful that you smooth with a chisel or other sharp instrument, the roots at the amputations, and not have them in a mangled state, which might bring on diseases that probably would destroy the trees.

The following extracts, taken from a communication made by that ingenious citizen, DOCTOR JAMES TILTON, of Wilmington, Delaware, and published in the first American edition of the *Domestic Encyclopædia*, by Messrs. Birch and Small, Philadelphia, are worthy of attention; and the laudable efforts of that gentleman, both in agricultural and horticultural pursuits, are highly meritorious and deserving of emulation.

" Curculio, a genus of insects belonging to the *Coleoptera* or *Beetle* order. The species are said to be very numerous. The immense damage done by an insect of this tribe to the fruits of this country, of which there is no similar account in Europe, has given rise to a conjecture with some naturalists, that we have a peculiar and very destructive species in America.

"The manner in which this insect injures and destroys our fruits, is by its mode of propagation. Early in the spring, about the time when the fruit-trees are in blossom, the *Curculiones* ascend in swarms from the earth, crawl up the trees, and as the several fruits advance, they puncture the rind or skin with their pointed rostra, and deposit their embryos in the wounds thus inflicted. The maggot thus bedded in the fruit, preys upon its pulp and juices, until in most instances the fruit perishes, falls to the ground, and the insect escaping from so unsafe a residence, makes a sure retreat into the earth; where, like other beetles, it remains in the form of a grub or worm during the winter, ready to be metamorphosed into a bug or beetle as the spring advances. Thus every tree furnishes its own enemy; for although these bugs have manifestly the capacity of flying, they appear very reluctant in the use of their wings; and perhaps never employ them but when necessity compels them to migrate. It is a fact, that two trees of the same kind may stand in the nearest possible neighborhood, not to touch each other, that one shall have its fruit destroyed by the curculio, and the other be uninjured, merely from contingent circumstances which prevent the insects from crawling up the one, while they are uninterrupted from climbing the other.

" The curculio delights most in the smooth skinned stone fruits, such as nectarines, plums, apricots, &c., when they abound on a farm: they nevertheless attack the rough-skinned peach, the apple, pear, and quince. The instinctive sagacity of these creatures directs them especially to the fruits most adapted to their purpose. The stone fruits more certainly perish by the wounds made by these insects, so as to fall in due time to the ground and afford an opportunity to the young maggot to hide itself in the earth. Although multitudes of these fruits fall, yet many recover from the wounds, which heal up with deeply indented scars. This probably disconcerts the curculio in its intended course to the earth. Be this as it may, certain it is, that pears are less liable to fall, and are less injured by this insect than apples. Nectarines, plums, &c., in most districts of our country where the curculio has gained an establishment, are utterly destroyed, unless special means are employed for their preservation. Cherries escape better on account of their rapid progress to maturity and their abundant crops: the curculio can only puncture a small part of them during the short time they hang upon the tree. These destructive insects continue their depredations from the first of May until autumn. Our fruits collectively estimated must thereby be depreciated more than half their value.

" It is supposed the curculio is not only injurious above ground, but also in its retreat below the surface of the earth, by preying on the roots of our fruit-trees. We know that beetles have, in some instances, abounded in such a manner as to endanger whole forests. Our fruit-trees often die from manifest injuries done to the roots by insects, and by no insects more probably than the curculio. In districts where this insect abounds, cherry-trees and apple-trees, which disconcert it most above, appear to be the special objects of its vengeance below the surface of the earth.

" These are serious evils to combat, which every scientific inquirer is loudly called upon to exert his talents; every industrious farmer to double his diligence, and all benevolent characters to contribute their mite.

"Naturalists have been accustomed to destroy viscious insects by employing their natural enemies to devour them.

"We are unacquainted with any tribe of insects able to destroy the curculio. All the domestic animals, however, if well directed, contribute to this purpose. Hogs, in a special manner, are qualified for the work of extermination. This voracious animal, if suffered to go at large in orchards, and among fruit-trees, devours all the fruit that falls, and among others, the curculiones, in the maggot state, which may be contained in them. Being thus generally destroyed in the embryo state, there will be few or no bugs to ascend from the earth in the spring, to injure the fruit. Many experienced farmers have noted the advantage of hogs running in their orchards. Mr. Bordley, in his excellent *Essays on Husbandry*, takes particular notice of the great advantage of hogs to orchards; and although he attributes the benefits derived from the animals to the excellence of their manure, and their occasional rooting about the trees, his mistake in this trivial circumstance does by no means invalidate the general remarks of this acute observer. The fact is, hogs render fruits of all kinds fair and unblemished, by destroying the curculio.

"The ordinary fowls of a farm-yard are great devourers of beetles. Poultry in general are regarded as carnivorous in summer, and therefore cooped sometimes before they are eaten. Every body knows with what avidity ducks seize on the tumble-bug (*Scarabæus carnifex*), and it is probable the curculio is regarded by all the fowls as an equally delicious morsel. Therefore it is, that the smooth stone fruits, particularly, succeed much better in lanes and yards, where the poultry run without restraint, than in gardens and other inclosures, where the fowls are excluded.

"All the terebinthinate substances, with camphor and some others, are said to be very offensive to insects generally. Upon this principle, General T. ROBINSON, of Naaman's Creek, suspends annually little bits of board, about the size of a case-knife, dipped in tar, on each of his plum-trees—from three to five of these strips are deemed enough, according to the size of the tree. The General commences his operations about the time or soon after the trees are in full bloom, and renews the application of the tar frequently while the fruit hangs on the tree. To this expedient, he attributes his never failing success. Other gentlemen allege, that common turpentine would be still better; being equally pungent and more permanent in its effects. Some have sown offensive articles, such as buckwheat, celery, &c., at the root of the tree, and have thought that great advantages followed.

"*Ablaqueation*, or digging round the trees, and making bare their roots in winter, is an old expedient of gardeners for killing insects, and may answer well enough for a solitary tree a year or two; but the curculio will soon recover from a disturbance of this sort, and stock the tree again.

"In large orchards, care should be taken that the stock of hogs is sufficient to eat up all the early fruit which fall from May until August. This precaution will be more especially necessary in large peach orchards; for, otherwise, when the hogs become cloyed with the pulp of the peach, they will let it fall out of their mouths, and content themselves with the kernel, which they like better; and thus the curculio escaping from their jaws, may hide under ground until next spring.

"A young orchard should not be planted in the place of, or adjacent to an old one, that it may not be immediately infested with the curculio.

"It is also apparent from what has been said, that great advantages might result from an association or combination of whole neighborhoods against this common enemy. Although an intelligent farmer may accomplish much, by due attention, within his own territory, the total extermination of the curculio can hardly be expected but by the concurrent efforts of whole districts."

For further particulars respecting fruit-trees, see the article *Orchard* in *March*.

THE VINEYARD.

To the preparatory and other necessary work, recommended in *January*, to be done in the vineyard, page 60, I again call your particular attention; if it is put off till March, you will then find the consequent embarrassment of such neglect; therefore let every preparation be made in this, as well as the last month, that the season will admit of.

The beginning of this month will be a good time to cart manure into the vineyard; laying it down in the most elevated places possible for the ease of wheeling it on barrows down among the rows of vines; this ought to be perfectly rotted, and of a quality suited to the nature of the soil; well rotted cow-dung is the best manure for ground of a very hot nature, but, if very cold or stiff, which ought to be as much avoided as possible in the planting of a vineyard, it may be improved by well rotted horse-dung or street dirt; when these cannot be had, any kind of well incorporated rich compost or other manure may be used.

If the vineyard be on the declivity of a hill, and your vines are not more than one, two, or three years old, scatter a good shovelful or two of this manure principally on the upper side of each plant, observing that none of it reaches within six inches of the stem; for if placed close thereto, slugs, worms, and the embryos of various insects, so frequently found in dung and other manure, would take shelter about the stock, penetrate down along its roots, and might materially injure it at a future period. But when these are exposed, without the advantage of this protection, to the severe frosts of the season, the greater number of them will be destroyed thereby.

The manure so placed, its nutritive parts will be washed down by rains, and the whole, by the necessary culture, will ultimately be brought to the roots of the plants. When the vineyard happens to be on level ground scatter the manure as above, equally around the plants.

If your vines are four years old or more, let it be cast all over the ground, as by this time the roots will be extended to a considerable distance in every direction and prepared to receive nourishment at all points.

PRUNING OF VINES IN THE VINEYARD.

In the middle States, the last week of this month will be an excellent time to prune vines, unless it should happen to be extremely severe; in which case it will be better to defer the pruning for a few days longer, but on no account later than the first week in March, which latter period will be a good time to commence that business in the eastern States, allowing there the same latitude in similar cases; but the more to the southward the earlier ought this to be done; for if deferred till the sap begins to ascend, serious evils will ensue to the plants, in consequence of bleeding too copiously from the wounds. Let it be observed that the sap begins to rise six weeks or more before the buds expand into leaves.

Such plants as are but one year old from the cuttings must be cut down to one or two good buds each, according to their strength, always cutting about an inch above the bud in a sloping manner, and on the opposite side thereto, observing that the lowermost bud, next the old wood, is never reckoned among the good ones.

Such of these young plants as have made more than one shoot last season must be deprived of all, by cutting them off as close as possible to the old wood, except the strongest and best placed; which prune as above directed, and cut off such part of the old wood, close to this shoot, as appears above it, in order that the bark may grow over it and the stem become whole and sound.

Your two year old plants must be similarly treated, with this difference, that you may leave two good buds to each in order to form as many strong shoots for the next season.

The three year old plants must be headed down to two good buds, leaving not more than two shoots to each plant, which will produce four for the ensuing season; and these, if the plants be in good health, will yield fruit very handsomely that year.

The fourth year of a plant leave it three of the best shoots, heading them down to good buds each; and observe to cut off the extra branches close to where they were produced, and in like manner any decayed wood, as well as the spurs or stumps occasioned by last year's pruning; by which treatment all the parts will get covered with bark, and the stock to be continued in health and vigor.

According as your vines increase in age and strength, you may leave from four to eight shoots on a plant, in proportion to its strength, each headed down from two to four or five good buds, always leaving the greatest number of buds on the most vigorous shoots.

When a vine is extremely vigorous and well furnished, you may head one or two of its best shoots at the height of three or four feet which will bear an abundance of fruit ; but the others must be headed down to two or three buds each, in order that they may produce good wood for the ensuing year's bearing and not too much fruit ; for those which you headed so high must be effectually cut out close to where they were produced in the next pruning.

Having finished your pruning, see that each plant has a good firm stake to support the young shoots when produced and advancing in growth, and if it be vigorous and of many shoots, a second, or even a third, would be more eligible.

Some inconsiderate persons may think that eight are too few for a full grown vine ; but if they consider that the eight shoots so pruned may produce, on an average, twenty-four, and each of these bear three bunches of grapes, making in all seventy-two, they will probably view the matter in a different point, especially when they consider that the ground, occupied by this plant, is no more than about six feet square. However fond people may be to see their vines bear great quantities of fruit, the over-bearing of them, especially while young, and indeed at any period, is allowed on all hands to injure them materially.

You are particularly to observe that the young shoots of last summer's growth are the only bearing wood ; that is, they produce new shoots which bear fruit the same season ; therefore if you expect a regular supply of grapes, you must manage your plants so as to have an annual succession of new wood, which you cannot expect if the vines are suffered to overbear.

The above being the method of managing vines in vineyards, the heads being formed near the ground, which is the present practice in most of the vine countries, I shall now proceed to give some directions for the pruning of such as are trained against walls, trellises or espaliers.

PRUNING OF VINES AGAINST WALLS, TRELLISES, AND ESPALIERS.

In order to have well formed espaliers and wall-vines, &c., you must train the two first good shoots, produced by the plant, horizontally, one to each side, within a foot or a little better of the ground, and continue them in that direction, from year to year, to whatever extent you may think desirable.

The first year these must be deprived only of the decayed wood on the extremities, and of any secondary shoots proceeding from the axillas of the leaves, unless they have run to the desired extent : the second year they will produce shoots from the joints, which are to be trained either upright, serpentine form, or fan-fashion, according to fancy, at the distance of about twelve inches from each other ; the third year head each of these down to one good bud, and train them up as before directed ; the fourth, and every succeeding year, make choice of the strongest shoots, say every third one, and head them down to from ten to twenty buds each, more or less, according to the strength of the mother plant, goodness of the ground, and roundness of the wood, but never leave wood that is not round, for such seldom bears fruit. The other shoots are to be headed down to one or two good buds each, which are to produce young wood for the next year's bearing, as those left to bear this season must be cut down next, in order to produce a succession of young wood; and so continue in their management from year to year.

When you meet with old vines which have been neglected, and having a great quantity of naked wood, as is generally the case, cut them down near to the ground, and they will not fail to produce you plenty of young wood, which you can train to your liking, but you will have no fruit for that year. Or you may cut out every other branch, leaving the old ones to produce fruit that season; but these must be cut down the next year in order to produce young wood, and a well furnished tree.

When arbors are to be formed of grape-vines, the shade being as much an object as the fruit, you are to train them so as to cover the place handsomely, and at the same time to produce as much and as good fruit as possible, by not permitting the leading branches or shoots to crowd together, but to spread evenly and thin over the whole place: this must be done by judicious pruning and careful training, always bearing in mind the preceding general directions.

For the methods of propagating and planting grape-vines, and the various kinds thereof, see the *Vineyard* in *March.*

SOUTHERN STATES.

This will be a principal time for propagating vines by cuttings, layers, &c., and planting vineyards in most of the southern States: for the methods of doing which, see the *Vineyard* in *March.*

THE NURSERY.

☞ The various instructions given in the course of this month, for the nursery, as far as they relate to work which is to be done in the open ground, are on the presumption that the severe winter frosts, have, towards the end of the month, disappeared, and that the ground at that time is in a fit state for cultivation; at least, sufficiently so for the reception of plants of a very hardy nature, and such as, if planted, could receive no injury whatever from any subsequent frost or severity of weather, and that will succeed better by taking the earliest possible advantage of the season: moreover, it is the better way to have as much of your business done at as early a period as possible, the better to enable you to meet the great pressure, which, with respect to planting, sowing, grafting, &c. &c., must be attended to in March.

But when the weather in the latter end of this month is severe, or the ground bound up by frost, there is no alternative but to defer the business till the arrival of a more favorable period.

PROPAGATING BY CUTTINGS, ETC.

Plant cuttings of gooseberries and currants according to the rules laid down in next month and in *October;* these will form tolerable branchy heads by the end of summer, and will produce fruit in a year or two after.

Be careful to train these trees always with a single stem, six or eight to ten or twelve inches high before you form the head.

Plant also cuttings of honeysuckles, and other *hardy* flowering shrubs and trees; as many different sorts may be propagated by that method.

The cuttings must be shoots of the former year's growth : choose such as have strength, cutting them from the respective trees and shrubs in proper lengths; or long shoots may be divided into two or more cuttings, which should not be shorter than eight inches, nor much longer than twelve. Plant them in rows two feet asunder, at six or eight inches distance in the row, putting each cutting two-thirds of its length into the earth.

Most kinds which are thus planted now, will be well rooted by next October.

PROPAGATING BY SUCKERS.

Many kinds of trees and shrubby plants furnish abundance of suckers from the roots for propagation, particularly robinias, roses, lilacs, syringas, and many other hardy kinds : the suckers may now be separated from the parent plants, each with some roots, and planted either in nursery-rows for a year or two, or the largest, at once, where they are to remain.

PROPAGATING BY LAYERS.

The latter end of this month, you may make layers of all such shrubs and trees as are increased by that method, though the best time to do this is between the first of October and end of November, but where it was omitted at that period it may now be done, and most kinds will still succeed.

In making layers of any kinds of trees or shrubs, observe to dig round the plant that is to be layed, and as you go on, bring down the shoots or branches regularly, and lay them along in the earth, with their tops above ground, fastening them securely there with hooked pegs, and then let all the young shoots on each branch be neatly layed, and cover them five or six inches deep with earth, leaving the top of each three or four to five or six inches out of the ground.

It may be of advantage in laying some of the more hard-wooded kinds, to gash or slit the layers an inch or better by an upward cut on the under side, as intimated in the *Nursery*, page 70.

Most kinds of layers which are now layed, will be tolerably well rooted and fit to be transplanted by next autumn, some not till the second year ; but for general instructions, see the *Nursery* in *October.*

TRANSPLANTING LAYERS.

Take off the layers of such hardy shrubs and trees as were layed down last year, and which still remain on the stools.

Let these layers, as soon as they are taken off, be trimmed and planted in rows in an open situation two feet or more asunder, according to the size of the plants, and the plants about twelve or fifteen inches distant in rows.

PRUNING, ETC.

Should the weather permit, you ought towards the latter end of the month to dig the ground between the rows of your nursery trees and shrubs, first giving them such necessary pruning as may be wanted; but if the ground is then bound up with frost, you may perform the latter and defer the former work, till the frost is away, which then must be done without delay, especially where the ground is tolerably dry.

Trim up the stems of such young, hardy fruit and forest-trees as require it, especially the deciduous kinds, and also prune off all disorderly rambling shoots, so as to bring them into a neat and handsome form.

Prune also the hardy flowering shrubs in nursery rows, whereby to regulate any disorderly growths, and to give them a becoming appearance.

In doing this work, it would generally be proper to prune or train the young plants mostly to short, single stems below; and where the heads of any shrubs are very irregular or run out in rambling shoots, let them be reduced to some order and form, by cutting out or shortening such as may require any regulation, whereby to form a somewhat orderly shape in the general head. Likewise suckers arising from the roots should generally be cleared off, and, if carefully detached with some roots to each, the best of them, if wanted, may be planted in nursery rows at proper distances; they will make good plants in two or three years' time, and the mother plants being cleared therefrom, will be preserved in a more regular proper growth.

After the above occasional pruning, let the ground be dug between the rows of the continuing shrubs, if not done before; digging it one spade deep in a neat, regular manner, to remain in good cultivated order all the spring and ensuing summer.

SOWING STONES TO RAISE STOCK FOR GRAFTING, ETC.

As early as possible this month sow the stones of plums, peaches, nectarines, apricots and cherries, &c., which were preserved in sand or earth from the time of the fruit being ripe till this period; for unless they were preserved in this way, few of them will grow; these may either be sown in drills, or broadcast in a bed, and covered from an inch to two inches deep, according to the lightness of the soil and the proportionate size of the stones. I am by no means an advocate for covering seeds of any kind too deep, never having had good success from such. If the above sorts are covered but lightly, they will easily grow through it, and when up you can refresh them by sifting fresh earth over them, if in beds, and if in drills, by drawing it to their stems.

SOWING HAWS FOR THE RAISING OF THORN-QUICK.

Having collected a sufficiency of fruit of the various kinds of hawthorn which you desire to propagate, the autumn twelve months previous to the time of sowing, which is, as *early* in spring as it is possible to get the ground in a good state of culture to receive them, proceed to sowing as hereafter directed.

When you collect these seeds in autumn, mix them with equal quantities of light sandy earth, and lay them in that state on the surface of a dry spot of ground in your best inclosed garden, where they cannot be disturbed by hogs, &c.; form this mixture into a narrow, sloping ridge, tapering to the top, and covering it with light, loose earth two inches thick all over; the April following, turn this ridge, mixing the whole together, and form it again in the same way, covering in like manner as before with two inches deep of light, loose earth; repeat this again in the months of July and August, by which the seeds in every part will be equally prepared for vegetation. A trench must be cut round this ridge to prevent any water from lodging about the seeds, for this would rot many, and injure others, especially in the second winter, when the stones would be losing their cementing quality, and begin to open; for until this is effected, the kernels cannot vegetate. Hence the necessity and great advantage of not burying the stones in the earth, as injudiciously practised by many; for if so treated, they would not have the advantage destined by nature for their due preparation, and would labor under many other disadvantages, as hereafter noticed.

It is well known, that many kinds of seeds when buried in the earth below the power of vegetation, remain in an inactive state for several years, even those whose nature it is to vegetate the first season when properly exposed; how much more so must it be with seeds of such tardy vegetation as haws, and many other sorts; but by being thus exposed to the influence of the sun and air, and frequently turned as before directed, all become equally and sufficiently prepared, and will not fail when sowed in due season and suitable soil to reward the judicious cultivator with an abundant crop.

When those seeds are buried deep, and not mixed with a due quantity of earth as before observed, they are subject to ferment too powerfully, and also to be injured by too much wet, and will never be found, more especially when large quantities of them are together, to vegetate equally—those near the surface and sides of the pit doing tolerably well—some of the others not growing until a full year after being sowed, and the greater number not at all.

There is not the least danger to be apprehended from frost injuring the seeds whilst so much exposed to it in those ridges; however, it will not be amiss to strew a light covering of long litter over them on the approach of winter, which will keep them dry, and consequently in a better state for sowing when the season arrives.

The above mode of preparation is the result of the Author's experience for upwards of twenty years, being in the habit of raising several millions of thorn-quicks annually.

Your haws being prepared as above, make ready a piece of good, rich ground, neither upon an elevated situation, nor too low; in the former, the summer drought would be unfriendly, and in the latter, they would be subject to mildew; this must be done as early in spring as you can get the ground to work freely and pulverize well; for the haws begin to throw out roots at a very early period, and if not sown at this time or before, a great number of those roots will be broken off in the act of sowing, and thereby totally lost; the others which escape this accident, having their radicles extended on the surface, penetrate the earth at the extreme points of those roots, forming right angles with the parts already produced, by which means they can never drive up the seed-leaves with as much vigor as if the radicles descended immediately in a perpendicular direction from the stones of the fruit; hence the necessity of early sowing.

The ground, however, must not be wrought while wet, or at least the seeds should not be covered with wet or heavy earth, nor too deep, for if the surface should cake or become stiff in consequence of dry weather ensuing, few of these young plants having broad seed-leaves could bear up through it; therefore you must be very cautious in that point; and if the earth of your bed is not light and dry enough for this purpose, you must carry as much as will cover the seeds from some dry compost heap, or some quarter of the garden where it can be found in a suitable condition.

On examining your haws, if you find the earth in which they are mixed any way clogged with too much moisture, so that the parts and seeds would not separate freely in the act of sowing, mix therewith a sufficient quantity of slack-lime or wood-ashes, to accomplish that end.

Having everything in readiness, and your ground well dug, *and raked effectually as you proceed in the digging*, still presuming that it is in the best possible state of preparation, lay it out into four feet wide beds, leaving twelve or fourteen inches of an alley between each, and with the back of the rake push off into these alleys about three-quarters of an inch of the fine raked surface of the beds, one-half of each bed to the one side, and the other to the opposite; this done, sow your haws thereon, earth and all, as they had lain, so thick that you may expect a thousand plants at least after every reasonable allowance for faulty or imperfect seeds (there being many of these), on every three or four yards of your beds; (I have often had that number upon as many feet); then, with a spade or shovel cast the earth out of the alleys evenly over the beds, covering the seeds not more than three-quarters of an inch deep, and not more than half an inch if the earth be any way stiff; after which, rake the tops of the beds *very lightly*, taking care not to disturb the seeds, in order to take off the lumps and to give a neat appearance to the work.

11

The business being thus finished for the present, should you at a future period perceive, especially when the plants are beginning to appear above ground, any stiffness on the surface occasioned by dry weather, give the beds frequent but *gentle* waterings, till all those innocent prisoners are released from their bondage, after which you will have pleasure and profit in their progress.

But this is not all; the whole of your former trouble will be totally lost, unless you are particularly careful in keeping these beds effectually free from weeds from the moment the plants appear above ground, till they are fit to be planted in hedge-rows, and even then, until they have arrived at a sufficient size not to be injured by such.

It was an old practice to sow these seeds as soon as ripe, covering them about an inch deep; but the loss of the ground during the long period in which they lie dormant, the trouble and expense of weeding them all that time, the numbers pulled up and exposed to animals of various sorts, and I may say the exposure of the whole to mice, squirrels, &c., have very justly induced to the abandonment of that mode of culture.

Indeed, they may be sown with considerable safety the November twelve months after they are ripe, being previously prepared as before directed, there is no impediment in their way at that season, but their long exposure to the depredations of mice, &c., which are extremely fond of their kernels; as to frost they value it not. However, upon the whole, I prefer the *early* spring sowing, and have generally practised it with the best success.

Many of these plants, and indeed the greater number, if the ground be good, will be fit for planting into the face of *ditches* the autumn or spring following, and the entire of them that time twelve months; but if they are intended for forming upright hedges, the strongest of the year old plants must, in the month of March, or very early in April, be drawn out of the seed-beds, their long taproots cut off, so as to shorten them to the length of five or six inches, and then planted into nursery rows about two feet asunder, and the plants to be about six inches distant in these rows; having there two or three years' growth, they will be in prime condition for that purpose; the remaining plants may be taken up the spring following, and treated in the same way.

It often happens that an after-growth of young plants arises in the seed-bed the second year, particularly when the haws have not been well prepared; these seldom come to anything : but if you pursue the method already prescribed, you may depend on a good and general crop the first year.

The various kinds of hawthorns that, on account of their spininess might suit for live hedges, are the following; all being indigenous in the United States, except the first, which is the kind principally used in Europe for that purpose.

1. *Cratægus oxyacantha,* or common European hawthorn, or whitethorn. *Leaves obtuse subtrifate serrate.*

With a robust trunk, branching from the bottom upwards to ten or fifteen feet high, the branches armed with spines; leaves obtuse, trifid and sawed, with numerous clusters of flowers from the sides and ends of the branches, succeeded by bunches of dark red fruit, commonly called haws; flowers two-styled, sometimes three or four.

2. *Cratægus coccinea*, or great American hawthorn. *Leaves cordate-ovate, gash-angled, smooth; petioles and calyxes glandular; flowers five-styled.*

This rises, when detached, to the height of near twenty feet, with a large upright trunk, dividing into many, strong, irregular, smooth branches, so as to form a large head. Leaves large and bending backwards; they are about four inches long, and three and a half broad, having five or six pairs of strong nerves, and become of a brownish red in autumn. The flowers come out from the sides of the branches in umbels or large clusters; they are large, make a noble show early in May, and are succeeded by large fruit of a bright scarlet color, which ripens in August or September. The branches are marked with irregularly scattered dots; thorns axillary, stout, spreading very much from the rudiments of the branches. Peduncles pubescent, corymbed.

3. *Cratægus crus galli*, or cockspur hawthorn. *Leaves subsessile, glittering, coriaceous; calycine leaflets, lanceolate subserrate; flowers, two-styled.*

Stem strong, ten to fifteen feet high, bark of the stem rough, of the branches smooth and reddish. Leaves lanceolate, three inches long, and about one inch broad in the middle, serrate, of a lucid green, alternate; at many of the joints are smaller leaves in clusters; thorns axillary, very strong, two inches in length, and bending like a cock's spur. Flowers axillary, in roundish clusters, generally two together, petals white, with a blush of red; styles three; fruit globular, of a red color. It flowers the latter end of May.

4. *Cratægus tomentosa*, or woolly-leaved hawthorn. *Leaves wedge-form ovate, serrate, somewhat angular, villose underneath.*

This has a slender shrubby stem about six or seven feet high, sending out many irregular branches, armed with long slender thorns. The flowers are small, proceeding from the sides of the branches, sometimes single, and at other times two or three upon the same peduncle, having large leafy calyxes, and being succeeded by small roundish fruit. The flowers appear the latter end of May, and the fruit ripens in September.

5. *Cratægus cordata*, or maple-leaved hawthorn. *Leaves cordate-ovate, gash-angled, smooth, petioles and calyxes without glands; flowers five-styled.*

This rises with a strong woody stem about five or six feet high, sending out many spreading branches which incline to a horizontal position. Leaves different in form, some indented at the petiole, others not: they are generally about an inch and a half long, and nearly of the same breadth in the middle, ending in acute points, and their borders cut into several acute parts, which are sharply serrate; they are of a bright green, and stand on very slender petioles, about an inch in length. The branches are armed with a few pretty long slender spines. The flowers come out in small bunches from the sides of the branches; stamens eight; styles four; fruit round, containing two seeds.

Branches spotted with white; leaves cut into three, five, or seven segments, accuminate, the size of birch-leaves. Petiole very slender, shorter than the leaves: corymb compound: bractes at the base of the peduncles, solitary, subulate, very small, deciduous: flowers somewhat smaller than the European hawthorn: teeth of the calyx very short, obtuse, falling off when the fruit is ripe: styles five: fruit an oblate spheroid, scarlet, the size of a red currant: the navel loose, naked: stones five, tops filling up the navel, and naked. It flowers the last of the genus.

6. *Cratægus pyrifolia*, or pear-leaved hawthorn. *Leaves ovate-elliptic, gash-serrate, somewhat plaited and hirt, calyxes a little villose, leaflets linear-lanceolate serrate, flowers three-styled.* This species is sometimes unarmed.

7. *Cratægus elliptica*, or oval-leaved hawthorn. *Leaves elliptic, unequally serrate smooth, petioles and calyxes glandular, fruit globular, five-seeded.*

8. *Cratægus glandulosa*, or hollow-leaved hawthorn. *Leaves obovate-wedge-form, angular, smooth, glittering; petioles, stipules, and calyxes glandular; fruit oval, five-seeded.*

This has very stout thorns. It flowers in May, and is a very beautiful shrub.

9. *Cratægus flava*, or yellow pear-berried hawthorn. *Leaves ovate, wedge-form, angular, smooth, glittering; petioles, stipules, and calyxes glandular; fruit turbinate, four-seeded.*

There are often small leaves on the thorns, which in this and the following species, are slender, and a little bent at the ends; it flowers in May.

10. *Cratægus parviflora*, or gooseberry-leaved hawthorn. *Leaves wedge-form-ovate gashed serrate; calycine leaflets gashed the length of the fruit; flowers five-styled.*

This is of humble growth, seldom rising more than five or six feet, sending out a great number of branches, which are interwoven and armed with very long slender spines. The leaves are scarcely an inch long, and some are not more than half an inch broad, but others are almost as broad as they are long; they are serrate, and have very short footstalks. The flowers are produced at the ends of the branches, generally one coming out from between the leaves, but sometimes there are two or three, one below the other at the axils; they have large leafy calyxes, much longer than the petals; they are small, have twelve or more stamens, and four styles. The fruit is small, and of an herbaceous yellow color when ripe.

There are many other varieties of the hawthorn in the United States; but these being generally unfurnished with spines, are not so suitable for hedges as those described. Of the above, the first, second, and third sorts, where they can conveniently be had, are the best kinds to cultivate; but either of them will answer that purpose very well. The cultivation of all the species is similar.

For further particulars, and for the best methods of planting hedges, as well as the several kinds of trees and shrubs most suitable for them, see the *Nursery* in *March*.

SOWING VARIOUS KINDS OF HARDY TREE AND SHRUB SEEDS, WHICH REQUIRE A PREVIOUS PREPARATION.

Ash, hornbean, red cedar, mezereon, juniper, holly, yew, spindle-tree, bladder-nut, and lauruses of various kinds, with many others, will require the same preparation as directed for haws; they must be sown at the same time, and covered only in proportion to the size of their seeds; that is, the smaller seeds will require not more than a quarter of inch of covering, and the larger, from half to three-quarters of an inch, in proportion to the lightness of the soil. Always avoid, at this season particularly, sowing seeds of any kind too deep, especially if the ground is of a heavy binding nature, or too wet at the time of working it.

SOWING KERNELS OF APPLES, PEARS, AND QUINCES.

So soon as you find the ground in a good dry state, sow the kernels of apples, pears, and quinces, to raise stocks for budding and grafting on. The sooner that this can be done the better. It will be necessary to have these kernels preserved, either in sand or earth, from the time they were taken out of the fruit till the time of sowing, or to take them at that time immediately fresh out of the fruit; for when long exposed to the dry air they lose their vegetative quality.

CARE OF TENDER AND YOUNG SEEDLING TREES AND SHRUBS.

In order to avoid repetitions and make room for other important matter, I refer you for instructions on the above subjects to page 71, observing that the same care and management recommended there will be necessary during the whole of the winter months.

By one night's neglect at this season you might lose what cost you the labor of months; therefore diligent care and attention is particularly requisite during severe weather.

HOT-BEDS FOR SOWING TREE AND SHRUB SEEDS IN.

Make hot-beds for sowing therein some of the more curious kinds of tree and shrub seeds. These are to be made as directed for cucumbers in page 20, and fully as substantial; sow the seeds either in pots or long narrow boxes, covering each kind with light dry earth in proportion to its size; then plunge these pots and boxes to their rims in the earth of the beds, but not till after the violent heat has passed away; sprinkle the earth in these pots frequently but very lightly with water till the plants are up, after which you may give it in proportion to their apparent necessity.

Keep the beds carefully covered at nights and in desperately severe weather, and when the heat declines renew it by adding a lining of fresh horse-dung to the sides and ends occasionally.

SOUTHERN STATES.

The various works recommended to be done in page 71, this month and *March*, in the *Nursery*, may be now practised with good success in Georgia and South Carolina and various other parts of the more southern States. This being their proper period for grafting, I refer them for general observations and instructions on that head to the work of the *Nursery* in *March*.

THE PLEASURE OR FLOWER GARDEN.

HARDY ANNUAL FLOWER-SEEDS.

About the latter end of this month, if the weather is mild and dry, you may sow many sorts of hardy annual flower-seeds in borders and other parts of the pleasure-garden.

The sorts proper to sow at this time are larkspur and flos Adonis, scarlet pea, sweet-scented and Tangier peas, candy-tuft, dwarf lychnis, Venus's looking-glass, Lobel's catch-fly, Venus's navelwort, dwarf poppy, Nigella, annual sunflower, oriential mallow, lavatera, and hawk-weed, with many other sorts.

Some of these, if sown now, particularly the Larkspur, flos Adonis, sweet and Tangier peas, will flower much better than if sown at a later period.

All the above seeds must be sown in the places where you intend the plants to flower, in beds, borders, pots, &c. They must not be transplanted, for these sorts will not succeed so well by that practice. The following is the method :—

The flower-borders having been previously dug, dig with a trowel small patches therein, about six inches in width, at moderate distances, breaking the earth well and making the surface even; draw a little earth off the top to one side, then sow the seed therein, each sort in separate patches, and cover it with the earth that was drawn off, observing to cover the small seeds near a quarter of an inch deep, the larger in proportion to their size; but the pea kinds must be covered an inch deep at least.

When the plants have been up some time, the larger growing kinds should, where they stand too thick, be regularly thinned, observing to allow every kind, according to its growth, proper room to grow.

For instance, the sunflower to be left one in a place, the oriental mallow and lavatera, not more than three; the rest may be left thicker. (See *May*, &c.)

PLANT HARDY HERBACEOUS FIBROUS-ROOTED FLOWERING PERENNIALS.

Towards the end of the month, if the weather be mild and open and the ground dry, you may plant, where wanted, most sorts of hardy fibrous-rooted flowering pla♠, both of perennials and biennials, such as lobelias, Phloxes, Dracocephalums, polyanthuses, primroses, London-pride, violets, double camomile, thrift, gentianella, hepaticas, and saxifrage.

Plant also rose-campion, rockets, catch-fly, scarlet lychnis, double feverfew, carnations, pinks, sweet-williams, columbines. Canterbury-bells, monk's-hood, Greek valerian, tree primrose, foxglove, golden rods, perennial asters, perennial sunflowers, hollyhocks, French honeysuckles, and many others.

In planting the above, or any other sorts, particularly at this early period, observe to preserve balls of earth about their roots, to dispose them regularly, and intermix the different kinds in such order as there may be a variety of colors, as well as a regular succession of flowers in every part during the flowering season.

AURICULAS.

The choice kinds of auriculas in pots must now be treated with more than ordinary care, for their flower-buds will soon begin to advance; therefore the plants should be carefully defended from frost and cold heavy rains.

This must be done by a good covering of glass and mats, but every mild and dry day the plants must be entirely uncovered.

Any old decayed leaves should be picked off as they appear, the earth loosened at the top of the pots, some of it taken out and replaced with good fresh compost mould. This will encourage the pushing of young roots from immediately under their leaves, which will greatly strengthen the plants.

Be very cautious, however, not to force those plants at this season, for that would prevent their flowering in any tolerable perfection; all they require is to be protected from severe frost, snow, cutting winds, and cold rains; they are to have no bottom heat whatever, nor are the glasses to be kept close in any kind of sunshine that might produce a strong heat in the frame; on the contrary, they must get as much air as possible, by taking the glasses off every sunny or mild day, and replacing them at night and in cold weather; and when you cannot take them totally off, raise them a little behind, or slide them either up or down, at every favorable opportunity. A little frost will not do them much injury, especially until their flower-buds begin to appear; but after that, they must be carefully protected therefrom: cold heavy rains is their utter enemy at all times, against which you must carefully guard.

SOW AURICULA AND POLYANTHUS SEEDS.

Auricula and polyanthus seed may be sown any time in this month; they will grow freely, and the plants from this sowing will rise well. The seeds may be sown in boxes, or large pots filled with light rich earth, and covered about the eighth of an inch deep; then place the pots or boxes in a hot-bed frame at work, give them fequent but light sprinklings of water, both before and after the plants appear, and a reasonable proportion of air at favorable opportunities : by this means you will have a fine crop of seedlings, handsomely advanced towards the beginning of May ; when, after all danger from frost is over, (for these being tenderly raised, would be subject to injury therefrom), take the pots or boxes out of the frame, and place them where they can have only the morning sun till ten o'clock, and that of the afternoon after five, during the remainder of the summer.   The midday sun you must carefully guard against, for it would totally destroy your plants.

Snails and slugs being utter enemies to these plants, whilst in a seedling state, it will be necessary, so soon as you sow the seeds, and before placing the pots and boxes in a hot-bed, or under the protection of glasses without bottom heat, for either method will do, to make lines of short, coarse, strong hair, about half an inch or better in diameter, to tie round each pot or box, immediately under the rim ; the line being tied, trim the long loose hairs around it with a pair of scissors, to a quarter of an inch in length, which short prickly hairs will, as often as snails or the like approach it, in the act of ascending the sides of the pots or boxes, prick them, cause them to change their course, and thereby finally protect the young plants from enemies which would in a few hours, totally eat up the finest crops, particularly the auriculas.

TULIPS, HYACINTHS, ANEMONES AND RANUNCULUSES.

Defend the beds of the more curious or valuable tulips, hyacinths, anemones, and ranunculuses, from frost, snow, and cold or excessive rains ; the plants will now begin to appear above ground, and the beds wherein the finest of the flower-roots are planted, should now, where intended, and if not done before, be arched over with hoops ; and in frosty or extremely bad weather, let mats or canvas be drawn over them, in some measure to defend the advancing flower-buds.

This, where it can be conveniently done, should not now be omitted to the choicer kinds, when required to have them blow in their utmost perfection ; for although they are hardy enough, yet, being protected in their early flower-buds from inclement weather, both in this and the next month, the blow will be much finer than if fully exposed ; however, this care is not necessary for the common kinds, either in beds or borders.

The early anemones and ranunculuses which were planted in September or early in October, and are consequently in a considerable state of forwardness, will still require greater protection than such as were late planted ; for the rudiments of their flowers being in a somewhat advanced state, would be greatly injured if too much exposed, especially to the great extremes of our mid-day sun, and the severe night frosts prevalent at this season ; therefore, by protecting them carefully from the rigor of the one, you do not expose them so much to the power of the other ; but when both are suffered to act alternately with their full respective force upon these, as well as upon many other of the more tender kinds of flowers and esculents, a disorganization of their parts is the immediate consequence, and an untimely death their ultimate end. This is a "golden rule," which ought to be assiduously observed with respect to every plant that is not sufficiently hardy to bear the frosts of our rigorous winters.

For the convenience of affording all the above choice kinds a suitable protection, they ought to be planted in beds of rich compost mould, surrounded with a hot-bed or other temporary frame, with tanner's bark or other protection drawn up on the outsides thereof, all around as high as the upper parts, which will prevent the frost from penetrating and injuring the plants next the frame. Over this frame you can lay a covering of boards and mats when necessary, or if you have not mats, straw or other suitable covering may be used. Frost will enter the beds notwithstanding this kind of care, but not in sufficient force to do much injury, for these plants are tolerably hardy, and require only to be protected from its too powerful influence, as well as that of the sun.

The plants must be exposed to the full air constantly, except while freezing sufficiently strong to bind up the earth, and at night or during the prevalence of cold, heavy rains or snow. Such of the preceding and other hardy bulbs, &c., as yet remain out of ground, ought to be planted as soon as possible; observing the directions given in page 95, &c. Anemones and ranunculuses if carefully preserved, will yet succeed very well.

CARNATIONS AND PINKS.*

Your choice carnations and pinks which were planted in pots and plunged in beds under the protection of frames and coverings, ought, for the present, to be managed in every respect as above directed for the protection of anemones, ranunculuses, &c. By this treatment you may expect to be rewarded with a bloom of these charming flowers in the highest degree of perfection.

Towards the end of this month, if the weather is mild, but not otherwise, you may transplant such as were raised last year from layers into large pots, or into the open borders, &c., where you intend them to blow; but this would have been better if done in autumn. Also such seedling plants as were raised last season, may, under similar circumstances, be transplanted into any beds or borders which are ready for their reception, always observing to remove them with balls of earth around their roots. For further particulars, see next month.

TENDER ANNUALS

The latter end of this month will be a suitable period for preparing to sow some of the more valuable and curious sorts of tender annuals; such as the fine kinds of double balsams, tricolors, mesembryanthe-

---

* The Remontant class of these flowers is now becoming more generally, and deservedly so, cultivated. As they are perpetual bloomers they ought to be in every collection. All the kinds are readily propagated from slips in a gentle hot-bed, or warm green-house.

mums or ice plants, Browallia's sensitive plant Ipomœa Quamoclit, and many others.

Therefore, provide some new horse-dung, and let it be thrown up in a heap, and in eight or ten days it will be in good condition to make the bed. Let this be made about three feet high of dung, levelling the top, and then set on the frame and glasses. When the burning heat is over lay on the earth, observing that, for this use, it must be rich, light, and perfectly dry, and broken pretty small by rubbing it between the hands; the depth of earth on the bed must be about five or six inches, making the surface level and smooth.

The seed may either be sown on the surface, observing to sow each sort separate, covering them about a quarter of an inch, or rather less, with light earth; or you may draw some shallow drills with your finger from the back to the front of the bed, sow the seeds therein, and cover as above; or you may sow them in pots and plunge these into the earth of the hot-bed. But if you intend sowing in pots, and you have the convenience of tanner's bark, lay on eight or nine inches, or a foot deep of it all over the bed in place of the earth, to plunge your pots therein, in which case two and a half feet deep of dung will be sufficient.

As soon as the plants appear, admit fresh air to them every day when the weather is any way mild, and let them have now and then gentle sprinklings of water. Mind to cover the glasses every night, and in bad weather with mats; or if boards are first laid on, and then covered with mats, they will afford an additional protection.

But in raising the above annuals, if it is required to be saving of hot dung and trouble, and there are cucumber or melon hot-beds at work, you may sow them in pots and place them in these beds to raise the plants; which may afterwards be transplanted or pricked into other pots in the same, or into a nursery hot-bed, to forward them to a proper size. For the further management of these plants, see *March* and *April.*

SOWING TEN-WEEK STOCK AND MIGNONETTE.

The ten-week stock is a beautiful annual; none makes a more agreeable appearance in pots, and in the borders, &c., and it continues a long time in bloom. The mignonette imparts a sweet and agreeable odor, for which purpose it is extremely worthy of cultivation.

When these plants are wanted in early perfection, the seeds of either may be sown, towards the end of this month, in a slight hot-bed, or in a very warm border, to be covered with a frame and glasses; but by sowing the seed in the former it will bring the plants on much sooner, though, in the latter, they will be tolerable early, and being raised in a more hardy manner may be planted out into the borders with better success; yet, when they are wanted for an early blow in pots, the hot-bed is preferable.

Sow the seeds either in pots or on the surface of the bed, covering them with light, dry earth about the eighth of an inch deep, or a little more, and give them gentle occasional waterings, and the necessary protection from the inclemencies of the weather, and plenty of air at proper opportunities. Towards the latter end of April these may be planted into the open borders, or wherever they are destined to remain, with good success. The mignonette, being very impatient of transplanting, ought to be taken up with as much earth as possible around the roots, and so transplanted with particular care.

But if your plants stand thick in the seed-bed, some of them, when they have been up about three or four weeks, or when about an inch high, may be pricked out either into a slight hot-bed, which will forward them considerably, and some into small pots to be placed therein, three plants in each; others may be planted on a warm border, three inches asunder, and covered with hand-glasses; after they have stood a month all those not potted should be planted where they are to remain.

STOCKGILLY-FLOWERS AND WALL-FLOWERS.

The choice double and other stockgilly-flowers and wall-flowers which you have in pots, and under the protection of any kind of covering, should never be exposed to a *strong* sun whilst in a frozen state; they will stand the winter with very little protection from frost, but must be carefully guarded against the sun's influence at such times.

FORCING EARLY FLOWERS.

Where early flowers are required, either for ornament or for sale, you must prepare for this business in *October*, and then plant in suitable-sized pots the various kinds that you intend to force, such as carnations, pinks, sweet-williams, double daisies, and other fibrous-rooted plants. The earliest kinds of hyacinths, van-thol, and other early tulips, anemones, ranunculuses, jonquils, narcissusses of various sorts, dwarf Persian irises, crocuses in different varieties, and many other kinds of early flowering bulbs, having been protected in a suitable manner as heretofore directed; you may about the beginning of this month plant these pots, or such of them as you wish to force for the earliest bloom, in any forcing department now at work, such as hot-houses, forcing-houses of any kind, hot-beds, &c. By plunging the pots into the bark-pits or hot-beds you will have them to flower the sooner. As the hyacinths, carnations, and pinks advance, tie their flower-stems to neat sticks, or to pieces of painted wire stuck into the pots for that purpose.

You may likewise force pots of roses, honeysuckles, jasmines, double-flowering almonds, thorns, cherries, and peaches, and also any other early flowering and desirable plants by the same means.

Either of the preceding kinds may be forced in board forcing-frames, with the assistance of hot dung applied to the back and ends thereof, these being constructed of strong inch and a half or two inch plank, made eighteen inches high in front and five or six feet high in the back, the ends in proportion and length at pleasure, the width to be five or six feet, and the whole covered with sloping glasses.

Having such a frame in readiness, fill the inside thereof to a level with the front with fresh tanner's bark, into which plunge your pots; or, if you have not the convenience of bark, sink a pit into the earth about eighteen inches deep, which fill to the surface with fresh horse-dung; place the frame thereon, and add more dung till it reaches within six inches of the upper part of the frame in front, then fill the remainder to that level with good dry earth.

In either case plunge the pots to their rims in the bark or earth, and add a lining of good horse-dung to the back and ends of the frame to its entire height, which will produce a strong growing heat in the inside, sufficient for any purpose of forcing small plants. The glasses being placed on this kind of frame with a considerable degree of elevation, will receive the rays of the sun in a more direct manner than if not elevated so much, by which means more heat will be accumulated.

Shelves may be erected in this kind of frame towards the back part, if the plants intended to be forced are not large, and the lining can be renewed as often as necessary.

DRESS AND DIG THE BORDERS, BEDS, ETC.

When the weather permits, let the flower-beds and borders in general be thoroughly cleared from weeds and from every kind of litter, for neatness in those parts of the garden is agreeable at all times, but more particularly at this season.

Therefore, let the surface of the beds and borders be lightly and *carefully* loosened with a hoe in a dry day, and let them be neatly raked, which will give an air of liveliness to the surface, and the whole will appear neat and very pleasing to the eye, and well worth the labor.

Likewise, if any borders, beds, &c., were not dug last autumn or winter, it should now be done, ready for the reception of flower-plants, seeds, &c., that the whole may appear fresh and neat.

PRUNE FLOWERING SHRUBS.

Finish pruning the hardy deciduous flowering-shrubs where wanted. In doing this work, observe to cut out all dead wood, and where any of the branches are too long or grow straggling, let them be shortened or cut off close, as you shall see necessary; and likewise, where the branches of different shrubs interfere or run into each other, shorten them so that each may stand singly and clear of another, then all the different shrubs will show themselves distinctly and to the best advantage.

When the shrubs are pruned, let the cuttings be cleared away and the ground be neatly dug between and about all the plants, observing to take off all suckers arising from the roots. Nothing looks better in a shrubbery than to see the ground neat and fresh between the flowering-shrubs and evergreens, &c., especially in such clumps and other compartments where the shrubs stand distant.

But as sometimes particular parts of a shrubbery are on some occasions required to form a close thicket, in that case very little pruning or digging, &c., is wanted.

CARE OF GRASS WALKS AND LAWNS.

Grass walks and lawns should be kept extremely clean. In dry weather, as soon as the greater winter frost is over, roll them with a heavy roller to settle the earth which the frost had thrown up.

GRAVEL WALKS.

Keep the gravel walks perfectly clean and free from moss, weeds, or litter of any kind; let them be well rolled, to settle them after the winter frost, which will give them a fresh and neat appearance, and render them comfortable for walking on.

SOUTHERN STATES.

This is a very proper period in the southern States to sow annual, biennial, and perennial flower seeds, and to transplant the various kinds of fibrous-rooted herbaceous flowering plants; to plant out into the borders of the pleasure grounds all kinds of deciduous trees, flowering and ornamental shrubs; and, in short, to perform all the other works directed to be done either in this or next month, in the *pleasure* or *flower garden* compartments, which are suitable to that climate.

A COLD VINERY.

A simple lean-to cold vinery, as represented in the following sketch, may be prepared this month for planting in April.

Fig. 19.

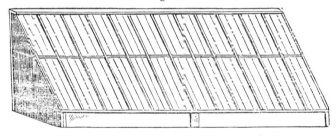

A lean-to cold vinery; scale ten feet to an inch.

It may be built against the south side of a barn or other building, and may be thirty feet long, twelve feet high on the back wall, and one foot in front, and fourteen feet wide. The ends should be double, and filled in with tan-bark for warmth. No fire is used, as the name indicates. The sashes are in two lengths, the upper ones to slide easily over the bottom ones, so that the house may be readily aired.

A hogshead sunk in one corner of the house will catch the water from the barn. The border may extend over the whole inside, running twelve feet outside in front. The dirt is to be first removed to the depth of two feet and eight inches, then filled up eight inches with broken bricks, stones, and lime rubbish, so as to form a thorough drain; the soil is then filled in two feet eight inches, to allow for settling.

In the border, place, say, fifty bushels of old bones, fifty bushels of pulverized charcoal, twenty-five bushels of oyster shells, a quantity of leather scrapings, twenty-five bushels of coal and leached ashes, twelve bushels of blacksmith cinders and iron filings, twelve loads of well decomposed manure, and the rest make up of street scrapings, garden soil, and sod from a pasture. The whole is to be first well mixed together and filled in on the last of March, and the vines should then be planted in the inside of the house, eight inches from the wall, one under each rafter; this makes the vines about three feet apart, and ten in front; the back wall may have eight vines.

The following are the best grapes for a cold vinery: Black Hamburg, white and red Frontignan; black St. Peters, Royal Muscadine or Fontainebleau, Palestine, Gray Tokay, Black Prince, Purple Chasselas, Decan's Superb, and Grizzly Frontignan. For its size and curiosity, De la Palestine.

If but one grape is to be cultivated in a cold grapery, it will undoubtedly be black Hamburg; if three, black Hamburg, white Frontignan, and Fontainebleau or Royal Muscadine.

A little study and attention will enable every one to have profitable crops in such a house. The best separate work on grape culture is that by William Chorlton.

THE GREEN-HOUSE.

Particular attention ought to be paid to the green-house plants at this season, in order to give them occasional waterings and fresh air, and if severe frost should prevail, to give the necessary protection.

In mild weather they will require refreshments of water now and then, and admission of external air whenever it can be given with safety, though all should enjoy an equal benefit of the latter; it is not so with respect to the former.

Oranges, lemons, and myrtles, and most other of the woody plants will require water frequently, but never give them much at a time, and none but when absolutely necessary.

The herbaceous kinds will also require occasional supplies of water, but less frequent, and in less quantities than the woody tribe.

Let the succulent kinds, such as aloes, sedems, mesembryanthemums, cactuses, &c., have water but very sparingly, and only when the earth in the pots is very dry.

Examine the tubs and pots separately to see which want water; let none be given but when necessary, and always very moderately; a little will be serviceable, but too much would be of bad consequence at this season.

Air should be admitted to the plants at all times when the weather is favorable, for that is a necessary article: they cannot thrive without it, nor continue a healthful lively appearance. Every day, when the weather is *mild*, let some of the windows be opened a little way for the admission of air, and take care that they are shut again in due time.

But be very particular not to admit sharp or cutting winds, or frosty air, into the green-house at this season ; to avoid which, you must never be absent while the windows are more or less open : for the changes of weather are so sudden, that a few hours' inattention might do irreparable injury to your plants, especially to the more tender kinds. The safest method now of admitting air, is by sliding down the upper tier of your front windows, less or more, according to the weather, which will not only admit the fresh, but discharge any foul air which has been generated in the house.

In frosty weather, keep your lights all close, and if very severe, defend the windows at night. If you have roof-lights, protect them as directed in *January*, page 100.

Fires may also occasionally be used, and indeed are indispensable at times ; but these ought never to be resorted to except when absolutely necessary, either to keep out the frost or to dispel damps ; and even then you are to be very cautious not to create *thereby* too strong a heat in the house, never above 40 or 45° of Fahrenheit's thermometer ; for this would cause your plants to push and get into a fresh state of vegetation, which would be extremely injurious to them during any of the winter months.

Another thing to be regarded, is to keep the plants of all kinds free from casual decayed shoots and leaves, for these are not only hurtful to the plants while in the house, but appear very unsightly ; therefore, whenever such appear, let them be constantly taken off ; keep also the pots, &c., and green-house, always neatly clean.

The latter end of this, or any time next month, you ought to loosen the earth in the top of the pots or tubs of your oranges, lemons, and other plants in general, and take out about an inch deep or more, adding some fresh in its stead ; this will prove very beneficial to the plants, and whoever will bestow this little dressing upon them, will see the advantage of it in a short time.

Your pots of Cape bulbs, such as Ixias, Gladioluses, Lachenalias, Moreas, Watsonias, Lapeyrousias, Walchendorfias, Tritonias, Antholizas, Cyanelias, and Oxalis versicolor—Babianas, Massonias, Geissorhizas, Melanthiums and Melaspherulas, &c., which are now in a state of vegetation, should be kept all towards the front of the house, and as near the glasses as possible, lest they should draw up weakly, and thereby produce but indifferent flowers.

HOT-BEDS FOR RAISING GREEN-HOUSE PLANTS.

Make hot-beds to sow tender exotic seeds in, observing to work the dung well, turning it over two or three times while it remains in the heap, at intervals of four or five days ; make the beds as directed for cucumbers, page 20, to the height of three feet six inches ; put on your frames, and lay eight or ten inches of good fresh tan even over the bed; if that cannot be conveniently had, lay on six inches of dry earth; when the bed comes to its heat, sow your seeds separately in pots, and plunge them into the tan or earth; some of these will not vegetate for a long time, and others frequently lie in the ground a whole year. When the heat of the bed is on the decline, add a fresh lining of hot dung, as directed for cucumber and melon beds. Or these seed may be sowed in pots, and plunged into the bark-bed in the stove.

Plant cuttings of Geraniums, Fuchsias, Myrtles, Hydrangeas, and other green-house plants in small pots, one or more in each, and plunge them into a hot-bed; they will now freely strike root and be fine early plants; these when they begin to grow must have plenty of air occasionally, and be carefully protected at night and in severe weather.

THE HOT-HOUSE.

As most hot-houses are frequently infested with various kinds of insects, which do very considerable injury to the plants, it may be of some importance to give a description of these, and also the most effectual methods of destroying them.

OF THE SPECIES OF INSECTS THAT INFEST THE PINE-APPLE PLANTS.

1. THE BROWN TURTLE INSECT. *Coccus hesperidum* of Linn. This species is not only found upon the pines and most other plants which grow in hot-houses, but also upon many plants which are in green-houses. These insects, after they are arrived at a certain age, fix themselves immovably to the leaves of the plant; but, before that time, though they generally appear motionless, yet on a close inspection, in a very warm day, many of them, and especially the smaller ones, may be perceived to move to different parts of the plant, being in appearance much like a turtle in miniature.

A sweet glutinous matter issues from these insects, this soon turns mouldy, and in time become quite black, which causes the plants to appear very unsightly. But as these insects do not, in any other respect, injure the pine-plants, I shall pass over them, and proceed to those of a more pernicious nature.

2. THE WHITE SCALY INSECT. This insect, as far as I can learn, has hitherto remained undescribed; neither *Linnæus, Geoffrey*, or *Schæffer*, seem to have known it.

This species is very nearly allied to the former, both of them being *Cocci*, and of the oviparous kind; it seems to be exactly similar to it in its manner of breeding, the process of which, curious naturalists have observed to be nearly as follows: The eggs which are discharged from the female, are pushed forward between the skin of the belly and the leaf of the plant, to which the insect adheres; in consequence of this, the skin of the belly becomes less distended, which enables the insect to afford a large covering to the eggs already excluded. When the eggs are all discharged, the skin of the belly retreats *close* to the back of the parent insect, which then appears like a mere scale. If the insect in this state be raised with the point of a needle from the leaf, a number of eggs may be perceived under it, of a pale red color, and very transparent, not unlike the roe (or eggs) of fishes; but with this difference, that they are not connected by a membrane, but loosely packed together. The mother, with a parent care, not only thus broods over her eggs till they are hatched, but continues to protect her young for a considerable time after, and either dies during the time she is performing this last office for them, or very soon after.

The males of both the above species are much less than the females, and appear very different from them; the latter, except just in their infant state, never assuming any other form than that of a scale, as already described; whereas the males of both kinds, in their last state, become flies; but neither of them can probably do any injury to the pine plants whilst they are in that form; for the *flies* of none of the *coccus* kind have been found, on the strictest examination by the most able naturalists, to have any organ by which they can take in nourishment. In that state, therefore, they can probably continue but a short time, the whole business of their lives being then destined to the impregnation of the females.

I have hitherto only taken particular notice of the *round* scale, or female insect, which is the most conspicuous, being far larger than the male. But a careful observer will readily perceive, where these *scales* are numerous, another set of smaller ones intermixed with them, which, if he be unacquainted with the natural history of these insects, he will hardly suspect to belong to the same animal, as they put on so different an appearance. They are semitubular, and their length scarcely exceeds the diameter of one of the small round scales, and their breadth is not more than a third or fourth part of their length. These, however, contain the males in one of their last stages, under which they assume the form of *nymphs*, and become flies. In order to be satisfied of this, a person need only break open, with the point of a needle, a few of these scales, when they are arrived at maturity, and he will perceive contained within each of them a very beautiful, but small fly, with all the characters of the flies of the *coccus* kind.

The length of this fly, from the head to the tail, exclusive of the wings, and those long hairs which are so characteristic of the flies of this kind, is about the thirtieth part of an inch: and the length, including the wings when folded one over the other, exclusive of the hairs before mentioned, is not more than the eighteenth part of an inch.

The insects of this last mentioned species are of a very pernicious nature. When the pines are infested with them, there will be much trouble and great expense in cleansing them, even to keep the insects under; and notwithstanding the greatest care, the plants will suffer much, and in time grow very unsightly; their leaves will appear

12

yellow and sickly, and generally a great number of yellow transparent spots may be seen all over them,

On the least neglect in destroying them, they will increase innumerably, and so beset the lower parts of the leaves next the stem of the plant (where they are most numerous) with scales, as nearly to touch each other. And as they pierce that part of the leaf immediately under the scale with their proboscis, they thereby not only draw out the nutricious juices themselves, but also destroy the tubes through which they flow. The upper parts of the leaves being thus deprived of their nourishment, consequently die. But these insects do not attack the roots, as has been frequently asserted.

3. THE WHITE MEALY CRIMSON-TINGED INSECT. This insect, as well as the former, I have not found to be noticed by naturalists.

This species also has all the characters of a *coccus*, but in all probability belongs to another genus. For whereas the two former species are undoubtedly oviparous, this seems to be viviparous. It is most probable that the young ones remain some time in the mealy down of the mother till they have acquired strength, and are arrived at such a degree of perfection, as to enable them to support themselves when they forsake the parent insect and disperse to different parts of the plant.

When this species is first perceived on the leaves of the pine, it appears to be nothing more than small particles of meal or powder collected together; but in a few days it assumes the form of a louse or bug, thickly covered with a fine meal or down of an oval form on its upper, and very flat on its under side, from whence proceed its legs, which are six in number. These, as well as many other particulars in the above, and preceding descriptions, are not to be distinguished without the help of glasses.

The last described species is of a more pernicious nature than the former; it attacks every part of the plant, from the top of its fruit even to the most extreme parts of its roots. These animals wedge themselves in between the protuberances of the fruit in a most surprising manner, so as not to be got out without difficulty, which not only makes the fruit appear very unsightly when it becomes ripe, but by robbing it of its nutricious juices is the cause also of its wanting flavor and being ill-tasted.

But the bad effects of this species on the *roots* of the plants are yet of a far worse consequence; for there, even at the bottom of the pots, they increase with an uncommon degree of rapidity, so as to become very numerous, and in the end to destroy the principal roots of the plants.

There have been various methods used for the extirpation of these insects, such as shifting the plants and washing their roots: decoctions from tobacco, wormwood, walnut leaves, henbane, and other herbs of a bitter or poisonous quality. Some have added to the above snuff, sulphur and pepper. These and many other remedies have been tried to very little purpose; at length, Mr. *William Speechly*, then gardener to the Duke of Portland, England, discovered and recommended in his excellent Treatise on the Culture of the Pine-apple, the following receipt, which, he asserts, "for the destruction of these insects, had never failed him; its efficacy being confirmed by nine years' experience. '

THE RECEIPT.

Take one pound of quicksilver; put it into a glazed vessel, and pour upon it one gallon of boiling water, which let stand till it becomes cold; then pour off the water for use. Repeat this on the same quicksilver (for it will retain its powers) till a sufficient number of gallons are provided to fill a vessel intended for the purpose. One in the form of a trough that will hold eight or ten gallons, is the most convenient, especially for the large-sized plants.

Then to every gallon of this mercurial water add six ounces of soft green soap, dissolved in a portion of the prepared water. Let the mixture stand till it becomes milk-warm, which is the degree of warmth it must be kept to during the time of dipping.

Before I proceed to the method of applying the above mixture to the plants, I cannot avoid calling in question, any virtue that may be attributed to a mercurial efficacy therein; first, as it is the opinion of the most experienced chemists, that crude mercury is not soluble, in any degree in pure water, whether poured on in a cold or boiling state; secondly, that if it contained any acid when put on, which might decompose a part of the mercury, the adding thereto of soap, would by virtue of its alkali, neutralize the acid, and thereby disengage and precipitate the mercury: therefore, it is at least very questionable, whether its efficacy is not exclusively attributable to the alkali of the soap.

If in place of the quicksilver or crude mercury above recommended, you were to substitute corrosive sublimate in the following or even in a greater proportion, there is no doubt of its effectually answering the end, without doing the shadow of injury to the plants.

Dissolve half an ounce of corrosive sublimate in a pint of gin or other spirits; when dissolved incorporate therewith four gallons of soft water, and it will be ready for use.

The soft soap may be added thereto, in the proportion above mentioned, but its alkali acting on the acid of the sublimate, will convert it into a mild muriate of mercury, and consequently render it much less active than before.

Previously let it be observed, that this dressing cannot be effectually applied with propriety to fruiting pines, either after they have started their fruit, or for two months before it, as disturbing their roots at that time would prevent their fruit growing to the full size; however, succession plants may be dressed at any period, but in the month of October that work can be done with the greatest success; and fruiting plants, if infested, may at any time be washed with the solution, which will destroy such insects as affect them above ground.

Before the plants are taken out of their pots, I would advise the brushing off a few of the scaly insects (as in a common dressing) especially towards the bottom of the leaves, where they will sometimes be so numerous as in appearance to lie one upon another, in which case the mixture might be prevented from penetrating to the bottom insects. I do not know that this business of brushing is absolutely necessary; but as the whole operation in a large hot-house may be performed in one day, the labor of a person or two extraordinary, for this purpose, can amount to but a very inconsiderable expense.

The leaves of the large-sized plants should then be tied together; they will be more manageable in this form than with their leaves loose, and less liable to be damaged. The plants should then be taken out of the pots, and divested of their long loose roots, as also a few of the decayed leaves at the bottom, and the rest washed clean.

The last species of insects (by gardeners most generally called pine bug) will sometimes conceal themselves in holes at the bottom of the stems of the plants, especially in large ones; and as the mixture might be prevented from penetrating into those holes, by the air contained in them, care should be taken to examine that part with great circumspection.

It may not be amiss in this place to observe, that the earth which comes out of the pine pots, together with the leaves and roots taken from off the plants, should be removed to a considerable distance from the hot-house. Also, that the pots out of which the pine plants were taken, should not be used again for that purpose, without first being put into boiling water.

The pine plants being now ready, let them be put either into the mixture, or the corrosive solution, in which they should remain, with every part covered, for the space of six minutes; then take them out, first letting the tops decline for the mixture to drain out of their centres. The vessel should be immediately filled with fresh plants, and those taken out set to dry with their root *downwards;* for by placing them in that position the solution, &c., will descend and penetrate to the very bottom of the leaves in the centre of the plant, whereby the insects which are concealed there will be totally destroyed. The mixture will change the plants to a sad green color, which will give them the appearance of being spoiled; but, as they become dry, they will in a great measure resume their proper hue.

During the operation it will be necessary to add a supply of hot mixture, in order to keep the whole to a proper degree of warmth, as also to make up the deficiency which must naturally happen.

It will be proper to do this work in a fine day, and as soon in the forenoon as convenient, that the plants may have time to dry, which they will do in a few hours, and then they must undergo the same operation a second time.

The process of the second operation being exactly the same as the first, a repetition thereof is unnecessary.

After the second dipping, a sponge should be used to remove any unsightly matter on the leaves of the plants. They should then be set to dry with their tops *downwards,* that the mixture may drain from every part, for it is necessary that every part of the plant should be quite dry before it is planted.

During the performance of the above operations, a sufficient number of laborers should be employed in getting the hot-house ready for the reception of the plants (as changing the tan, and cleaning every part of the hot-house); and if the inside of the roof were painted at the same time it would be better. Also, it might be serviceable, if a small fire was made in the pine pit with charcoal and sulphur, and the house shut up an hour or two to keep in the steam. But in case there are vines, or other plants, growing in the hot-house, this last operation must be omitted.

If the above work cannot be done in one and the same day, the pine plants may with great safety be set in a dry airy place for a day or two, provided they are not put into heaps, which would greatly damage them in a short time.

The mould intended for the pine plants at the first potting, should be light and fine; and I would recommend that the pots be small in proportion to the size of the plant, that each plant may be what gardeners term UNDERPOTTED; they will strike root both sooner and better than if put into larger pots, and at their next shifting they will go into proper sized pots with their balls and roots entire.

After the pine plants are replaced in the hot-house, it will be proper to shade the glasses in the middle of the day whenever the weather is warm and clear. The house should be constantly kept to a great degree of heat, which will be the means of making the plants strike sooner and stronger, it being evident that they cannot draw themselves weak while in an inactive state: however, as soon as the plants are perceived to grow, it will be necessary to give them by degrees a greater quantity of air.

Great care should be taken to prevent the roots of the plants from being injured by an over-heat of the tan, which may be done by raising the pots in case the tan should heat violently.

OTHER INSECTS FOUND IN HOT-HOUSES, WITH THE METHODS OF DE-
STROYING THEM.

Besides the different species of insects which are found so pernicious to the pine-apple plants, there are other kinds that infest most stoves, which frequently prove very troublesome; and although they are not injurious to the pine-apple, are yet very prejudicial to most other plants kept there, either for use or ornament.

1. THE APHIS. This insect is of the order HEMIPTERA. *Characters:* Rostrum bent inwards. Antennæ, setaceous and longer than the thorax. Wings, four on the males; females none. Feet six. They have generally two little horns or hairs placed on the hinder part of their abdomen.

Roses and various other plants are very subject to be overrun with these insects, and if no means are used to extirpate them, they will in a short time take such entire possession of the plants, that every part of the young wood will appear to be covered with them. They are commonly called lice. Many kinds of flowers and exotic plants which are kept in stoves are very subject to be annoyed with them.

These are easily destroyed three ways. 1. By fumigating the house with tobacco. 2. By dusting the infected plants with fine snuff or tobacco dust. 3. By a decoction or infusion of tobacco.

2. The ACARUS, commonly called the *Red Spider*. This is of

the *order* APTERA. *Characters:* Eyes placed on the sides of the head, remote from one another. Mouth or proboscis formed by a small pointed rostrum inclosed in a sheath. Antennæ shorter than the proboscis. Feet eight; they are oviparous.

This is a pest to almost every kind of plants, for this insect is not only pernicious to most plants kept under glass but also to many growing in the open air.

In hot dry weather the increase of these insects is exceedingly rapid, and when they become numerous they, by various means, commit great havoc on plants; for this insect with its proboscis perpetually wounds the fine or capillary vessels of plants and extracts their nutritious juices. It also works a web about the leaves and over the tender buds and tops of the plants in such a manner as nearly to suffocate them and prevent their vegetation.

This insect does not seem to be affected by fumigation made with any ingredients hitherto discovered, and it is probable that the apterous insects, or those without wings, are not so much affected by fumigation as the winged tribe.

However, the mixtures recommended for destroying the insects on the pine-apple will have the same effect on this. Plants greatly infested, and growing in pots, when their tops are not very large, may with great facility be dipped in a convenient vessel filled with those mixtures. The top of the plant need only remain a short time therein, and it should then be placed in a shady place to prevent its drying too rapidly.

These insects very frequently reside on the under side of the leaves, and, when very numerous, they work so thick a web thereon that it sometimes prevents the mixture from entering into certain hollow parts of the leaves, by which means a few escape unhurt, in which case it will be proper for the plants to undergo the same operation the succeeding afternoon, which will most assuredly destroy all that escaped before.

Large or climbing plants, when their leaves are large, as, for instance, the *vine*, must be dressed with the mixture by means of a *sponge*. This has the appearance of a tedious operation; but in a dark day, when the house is not very warm, a person will make considerable progress therein in the course of a few hours.

The keeping of the house in a moist state by watering the walks and flues late in the evening, and the frequent sprinkling of the plants with water, contributes to retard the progress of these insects, which are very impatient of much moisture. This reduces them to a temporary state of inaction, but will not destroy them.*

3. The THRIPS. *Order* HEMIPTERA. *Characters:* Rostrum small and obscure; antennæ as long as the thorax; body slender, of an equal thickness in its whole length; abdomen reflexible, being generally bent upwards; wings four, incumbent on the back of the insect,

---

* If a small portion of sulphur be applied on the cooler ends of the flues, or any part of the hot water pipes, it will effectually destroy Red Spider. Care should be used that it does not ignite, or the plants will also be severely injured.

narrow in proportion to their length and cross one another at some distance from their base; feet six, the tarsus of each foot having only two articulations.

This is also a very pernicious species of insect, and is very common in hot-houses, as well as upon plants in the open air; it is very minute, so much so as to be scarcely perceptible, generally concealing itself along the veins of the leaves, from whence it skips with great agility on being touched. It is a great enemy to the vine while the leaves are young and tender, whether they grow in the open air or under glass. The Cape jasmine, as well as many other plants, often falls a prey to these minute insects.

These may be destroyed by the same methods as the *Aphis*.

4. The ONISCUS, or *Wood-louse*. This belongs to the *order* AP-TERA. *Characters:* Antennæ setaceous, and bent-mouth, furnished with two palpi; head intimately joined with the thorax; body oval form, composed of several crustaceous plates; feet fourteen. They change their skin like many other apterous insects.

These are very common in the bark-pits, as well as in woods, houses, gardens, &c., but are seldom destructive except to young seedling plants on their first appearance above ground. This, how-ever, may be prevented by dusting the plants, whilst in that state, with fine snuff or tobacco dust.

5. The FORMICA, or *Ant*. This insect is so universally known as to render a description unnecessary.

These are often exceedingly numerous in hot-houses, and especially where the *Aphides* and *Coccus hesperidum* abound, for there is a sweet glutinous matter which issues from these insects (being either their excrements or produced by them from some other cause) that seems to be the principal incitement that draws the ant thither.

The ant may be destroyed with great facility by setting pots con-taining honey and water in the same manner as is practised for catching wasps, &c.

6. The COCCUS HESPERIDUM, or *Brown Turtle Insect*, already de-scribed, is not only an enemy to the pine-apple plant but also to many others both in the hot-house and green-house, therefore I am induced to take notice of it again.

This insect may be destroyed whilst young by fumigation, there-fore, where that operation is frequent they are rarely to be met with.

OF FUMIGATING THE HOUSE.

The house may be fumigated either by means of bellows invented for that purpose or by that of a smoking-pot. The most eligible seasons for this business are the spring and autumn, when, if neces-sity requires, it should be repeated every eight or ten days, till the proper effect is produced; but it may be done at any period, except when there are ripe fruit in the house, as then it would give them a smoky flavor.

Fumigation is best performed late in an afternoon or evening, and proves most efficacious when the weather is moist and calm; for the smoke is retained much longer in the house when the air is still and the cavities of the roof, particularly those between the squares of glass, filled with moisture.

The *Aphides* may be destroyed with a gentle fumigation; but the *Thrips* and *Coccus hesperidum* require a smoke so strong, that a person cannot distinguish an object farther than at the distance of five feet.

When a hot-house is greatly infested either with the *Aphides* or *Thrips*, the fumigations should be repeated every third or fourth night, for three or four times successively. The reason and necessity of these repetitions proceed from a probability that the smoke cannot affect the insect in the egg, and perhaps it may not have sufficient power over them in other of their states; therefore a fresh brood may naturally be expected in a few days.

CARE OF THE PINES.

Many of the pine plants will now appear set for fruiting, which may be distinguished by the short leaves in their centres; from that time they should be moderately watered and the house kept pretty warm; for when plants are kept cold at the time of forming their fruit, it generally causes many of them to be crooked, imperfect and misshapen. Therefore, under such circumstances, never let the heat fall lower than 55° of Fahrenheit, nor rise higher, by *fire-heat*, than 62°; a little air should, however, be admitted whenever the weather permits, and especially on sunny, warm days, when the heat rises to above seventy degrees. But in no case, nor under any circumstances, let the heat of the house fall below 52°, if possible.

As some persons may be furnished with *Reaumur's* and not with *Fahrenheit's* thermometer, it may be of use to give a comparative table of their scales, as well as the rules by which one can be converted into the other; observing that 32° of the latter, being the freezing point, is equal to 0 (or zero) of the former.

Reaumur's.	Fahrenheit's.	Reaumur's.	Fahrenheit's.
Degrees 16	68	Degrees 33	106.2
15	65.8	32	104
14	63.5	31	101.7
13	61.2	30	99.5
12	59	29	97.2
11	56.8	28	95
10	54.8	27	92.7
9	52.5	26	90.5
8	50	25	88.2
7	47.7	24	86
6	45.5	23	83.8
5	43.3	22	81.5
4	41	21	79.2
3	38.6	20	77
2	36.5	19	74.7
1	34.2	18	72.5
0	32	17	70.3

To convert the degrees of Reaumur into those of Fahrenheit: multiply the degrees of Reaumur by 9, and divide the product by 4; to the quotient add 32, and the amount will be those of Fahrenheit.

To convert the degrees of Fahrenheit into those of Reaumur: subtract 32 from the degrees of Fahrenheit; multiply the remainder by 4; divide the product by 9, and the quotient will be those of Reaumur.

Your fires must be continued every evening and night, being careful in very severe weather to keep them burning, and sufficiently supplied with fuel till so late a period that there can be no danger of the house becoming cold before morning. Indeed, unless your house is well constructed, there may be some severe weather in which it would be necessary to keep up the fires all night. There have been instances of careless persons intrusted with this work, who, in order to get to bed at an early hour, or to some idle frolic, have put down large and violent fires, which never fail to do injury to the plants, and sometimes to burst the flues; this practice is to be carefully avoided, as a moderate and steady heat is what always will insure the best success.

The fires are to be renewed very early in the morning, and continued until the heat of the sun is sufficient to promote a comforting warmth in the house; and in very cold and *dark* weather, it will be necessary to keep them burning all day.

It is very advisable, and indeed indispensable, for the health of the plants, to sprinkle the flues and floor occasionally with water, in order to restore the parched air of the house to its atmospheric quality; this will not only render great service to the plants, but tend to weaken the power of destructive insects; for these do not like a moist air, manifested by their greater increase in dry stoves, than in others.

A proper degree of heat must now be preserved in the bark-bed, for nothing can contribute so much to the free growth of the young fruit as a brisk bottom-heat; if the roots have not this advantage, it is impossible to make the fruits swell to any tolerable size.

Therefore, where the bark-bed was not stirred up the former month, to renew the fermentation, and revive the declined heat, it should now be done, for the heat will consequently now begin to be very faint, and by stirring up the bark almost to the bottom, it will bring on a fresh fermentation therein; by which means the bed will again recover a lively growing heat, the good effect of which will soon appear both in the plants and fruit, provided it be done in due time; but if the heat is greatly decreased, and the bark decayed, you may augment it at the same time with about one-third or fourth part of new tan, otherwise defer it till next month, which see.

However, where the work of forking up the bark-bed appears necessary at this time, agreeable to the observations above mentioned, it should, if possible, be done in the first week in the month; for if it is delayed much longer, the plants and fruit will certainly, for want of a due proportion of heat, be much checked in their growth. Observe, in the first place, to take all the pots out of the bed; then

begin at one end, and open a kind of trench, by taking out some of
the bark and carrying it to the other; this done, begin at said trench,
and with a fork, dig and work up the bark quite to the bottom, taking
care to break the cakes or lumps; mix all the parts well together,
and fill up at last with that taken out of the first opening. Having
finished, let the top be made level, and immediately plunge the pots
again to their rims as before. This work is so very necessary that
it should not on any consideration be omitted at the time above mentioned; that is to say, if the bark has much declined in its heat.

The bed being thus treated, it will soon renew its heat, and retain
the same well for six weeks or thereabouts.

At the expiration of that period, or some time in March or beginning of April, the bark will require to be stirred up again, and refreshed with about one-third, or at least one-fourth part of new tan;
after this it will retain a proper degree of heat till the fruit is ripe.
(See *March* and *April.*)

The bark-bed wherein the succession pine-plants are plunged, should
also be examined now with good attention; and if the heat is found
to be much decreased, the bed should be treated in the manner above
directed.

WATERING THE PINES.

The fruiting pine-apple plants should now have moderate refreshments of water, provided there be a good heat in the bark-bed : and
when there is a proper degree of that and moderate moisture together, it will make the young fruit swell very fast.

But in watering these plants, be careful to give it moderately at
each time. The rule is this : let the earth in the pots which contain
the plants, be kept just a little moist in a middling degree; and if
this is observed, the plants and fruit will thrive.

The succession pine-plants, that is, those which are to fruit next
year, must also be refreshed now and then with water; in watering
these, let the same rule be observed as just mentioned above.

Remember also to give water at times to the younger succession
pines, consisting of the last year's crowns and suckers.

In watering the pine-plants in general, you should still be cautious
to let none of it, or but as little as possible, fall into the centre of
the plants, where, being apt to lodge, it would prove detrimental, in
some degree, to these exotics at this season.

OF THE VARIOUS KINDS OF PLANTS IN THE HOT-HOUSE.

In some hot-houses there are kept many other sorts of curious exotics, besides the pines, both of the succulent and woody kinds, &c.,
and as they are all tender, being from the hottest parts of the world,
the same degrees of heat as recommended for the pine, will, generally speaking, be suitable for them; however, there are some of those
which, to do them the greatest possible justice, require a somewhat
greater degree of heat than the pine-apple, and others not quite so
much; therefore, when there is the convenience of different apart-

ments in a long range of hot-houses, all may be suited according to their respective necessities.

Let it be observed, that all tender plants which are kept in pots, the succulent tribe excepted, thrive much better when plunged in the bark-bed; but the tallest growing kinds must be planted in a border of suitable earth, near the back wall, to give them the greater scope for extending their heads.

All these kinds of plants should be kept remarkably clean from dust, or any sort of filth that may gather upon their stems, shoots, or leaves; and such ought always to be washed off as soon as it appears. There is nothing more necessary than cleanliness to preserve the health of plants; and where foulness is permitted upon any of them, it will not only close up those small pores which are so necessary to the growth of all vegetables, but will also render the whole plant unhealthy, which seldom fails to invite insects, and to increase them prodigiously in the house.

These plants must also be kept very free from decayed leaves; that is, when any such appear, let them be immediately taken off.

Water should also be given to all these plants at times; some will require but very little and seldom, and others will need it pretty often. Therefore, let good care be taken that every plant, according to its nature, be properly supplied with that article; but be sure never to give any sort too much at a time; and in giving it always make a distinction between the succulent, the herbaceous, and the woody kinds.

The latter will need water oftener, and more at a time, than either of the former; for some of those require very little moisture about their roots, and too much would rot the plants.

Let the woody kinds in general be moderately watered not less than once or twice a week; and it will be serviceable to sprinkle water sometimes all over the head or branches of these plants, especially the coffee tree, the pimento, or allspice, and all the tender Mimosas.

But the succulent kinds, such as the cactuses, mesembryanthemums, aloes, Euphorbias and the like, must not be watered oftener than once a week.

In watering these kinds let care be taken to give but little at each time, just sufficient to reach the bottom roots.

It will be an advantage to all these tender plants, both of the woody, succulent, and other kinds, when the surface earth in the pots casually crusts or binds, to stir and loosen it lightly a small depth.

ADMIT AIR.

Fresh air should now be admitted to the pines and other plants in the hot-house, at all times when the weather will permit.

But this, however, must only be done at this season, when the sun shines warm, and the air is quite calm and clear; then it will be proper to slide some of the glasses open a little way, in the warmest time of the day, particularly the roof-lights, shutting all close if the weather changes cold and cloudy, and always in proper time in the afternoon.

The best time of the day for the admission of fresh air, is from about twelve to one, two, or three o'clock ; but for the time of opening or shutting the glasses, let the weather be the guide.

OF KIDNEY-BEANS IN THE HOT-HOUSE.

Now plant some more kidney-beans of the early white, cream-colored, yellow, or speckled dwarfs, &c., in pots or boxes, and place them in the hot-house to succeed those planted last month; or if none was then planted, this is a very successful time, superior to the former month, for planting a good hot-house crop, and managed as directed in *January*, page 111.

Do not forget to refresh with water those kidney-beans which were planted last month ; they will require it two or three times a week : give also necessary waterings to the young beans advancing for successive crops.

OF BLOWING ROSES AND OTHER PLANTS EARLY.

You may now, in the beginning of this month, set pots of roses and honeysuckles, &c., in the hot-house ; or pots of bulbous roots, carnations, pinks, and double sweet-williams, or of any other desirable flowering plants, either of the shrub or herbaceous kinds, which you desire, by way of curiosity, to bring to an early bloom, supplying them, when in growth, with plenty of water.

Likewise, about the middle and end of the month, you may introduce more of the same sort of flowering-plants to produce flowers in regular succession.

You may also introduce pots sown with seeds of any desirable annuals, of moderate growth, to flower early, such as mignonette, balsams, ten weeks stock, &c. &c.

OF CUCUMBERS IN THE HOT-HOUSE.

Where it is desired to raise early cucumbers in the hot-house, some seed may be now sown as directed last month, or young plants planted therein from any common hot-bed. (See *Hot-house* for *January*.)

EARLY STRAWBERRIES.

You may now introduce into the hot-house, pots of the scarlet and alpine strawberries, either to succeed those of last month, or as a first introduction. Let them be two years' old bearing plants ; place them near the glasses, or plunge them in the bark-bed to forward them earlier, giving proper supplies of water.

If some fresh plants are taken into the hot-house every three weeks, you may obtain a constant supply of early fruit till those in the open ground ripen.

Or pots of strawberry plants kept in moderate dung hot-beds to forward them, may be removed in successive order into the hot-house; they will produce a supply of early fruit in regular succession.

MARCH.

THE KITCHEN GARDEN.

THE weather in this month, both in the middle and eastern States, is very unsettled; sometimes it proves dry and frosty, sometimes tolerably warm and comfortable, at other times cold and wet, with storms of strong winds, hail, snow and rain, which make a diligent attendance on the hot-beds absolutely necessary; otherwise, they often miscarry, and all the preceding trouble and expense are lost.

Let me here observe, that snow ought never to be suffered to remain but as short a time as possible, either on the hot-bed lights, covers, or about the beds; for the cold produced thereby, often penetrates through a slight covering, especially if there is not a strong bottom heat, and produces a kind of hoar-frost in the inside of the frame, which seldom fails to do considerable injury; and likewise, when suffered to lodge round the beds, it causes a sudden decline of the heat.

CARE OF EARLY CUCUMBERS AND MELONS.

Examine the state of the cucumber and melon hot-beds, and see if they are of a proper degree of heat, so as to preserve the plants in a state of free growth.

You must let the heat be lively, but moderate, by which means the ridged-out plants of good growth will show fruit plentifully, and these will swell freely and grow to a handsome size.

If you find the heat declined, apply a lining of fresh horse-dung, as directed in *January*, page 25, to which I refer you for general instructions on this subject.

Let the plants have fresh air every day, by raising the upper end of the glasses from about half an inch to one or two inches in height, in proportion to the heat of the bed and warmness of the weather; always more freely in sunny, calm, mild days, than when cloudy or a sharp external air; and when the weather changes colder, diminish the admission of air or shut down the glasses; and always shut close in proper time towards evening, about three or four o'clock, &c., according to the temperature of the weather.

Refresh them now and then with water; let this be given very moderately, and in a mild sunny day: the best time for doing this is from ten to two o'clock.

Cover the glasses with mats every afternoon as soon as the sun is off them ; or, if a dark day, and the weather is severe, at such period as you may think necessary, according to the degree of heat or cold that may be prevalent at the time; and uncover in the morning, if a sunny day, so soon as it shines on the beds, or, if otherwise, as early as may be consistent with the safety of the plants; for their being too much debarred from the light, causes them to become discolored and weakly.

As the early plants raised last month will have now advanced considerably into fruitful runners, and show fruit abundantly, especially cucumbers, let the runners or vines be trained out regularly along the surface of the bed at equal distances, and peg them down neatly with small hooked sticks. At this early season it will be of much utility to impregnate the young fruit of cucumbers with the farina of male blossoms. The flowers of cucumbers and melons are male and female, separate on the same plant, and the females produce the fruit; the males are often erroneously called false blossoms, and many persons in consequence of that notion pull them off; but they are so far from being false blossoms, that they are by nature designed to impregnate the female flowers to render them fruitful; for the antheræ in the centre of the male blossom being furnished with a fine powder, which being dispersed on the stigma in the centre of the female, the fecundation is effected, and the fruit in a day or two after will begin to swell, and which in cucumbers will generally, in about a fortnight, or within a few days under or over, according to the state or growth of the plants, be arrived to a proper size for cutting or gathering for the table, in young green fruit six to twelve inches long or more; so that without the assistance of the male blossom, the females having the embryo fruit at their base wither and decay, and the infant fruit turns yellow and drops off.

Therefore it is of importance to preserve a sufficiency of the male flowers, for the purpose of impregnating the females; and in the early culture of cucumbers, &c., it is eligible to carry some of the males to the female flowers; observing for this purpose to detach some new expanded male blossoms with the stalk to each, and holding the stalk between the finger and thumb, and pulling off the petal or flower leaf surrounding the male organ, then with the remaining antheræ or central part, touch the stigma in the centre of the female, twirling it about so as some of the farina or male powder of the antheræ may adhere thereto, a little of which being sufficient to effect the impregnation.

This operation is essentially necessary to be performed by hand, to early plants that are shut up in frames, before the lights or glasses' can be admitted sufficiently open to give free access to a large current of air, or flying insects, such as bees, &c., all of which assist in conveying the farina of the male blossoms to the females, as is evident in plants exposed to the open air.

The above operation of fecundating, or, as the gardeners term it, setting the fruit, should be performed the same day the flowers open and are fully expanded, which is the most essential period of their generative effect.

The female or fruit-bearing flowers are readily distinguished at sight from the males; the former having always the embryo fruit placed immediately under the base of the flower; or in other words, the embryo fruit issues forth with the flower-bud on its top, visible from its first eruption from the stem of the plant; but the male blossom is placed immediately on the top of its footstalk without any appearance of fruit under its base.

The same operation of impregnating or setting the fruit, as above, may also be practised on melons, which will have the same effect as in cucumbers; but as melons are only eatable when ripe, it will be five or six weeks longer before they attain full size and mature ripeness.

SOW CUCUMBER AND MELON SEED.

Sow in the above, or any new made hot-beds, the seeds of cucumbers and melons, at the beginning, and also about the middle, and towards the latter end of this month, to have a supply of young plants in readiness, either to plant into new beds, or to supply the place of such plants as may fail.

The sorts of cucumbers are the early Kenyon's free-bearer, Syon House, and Walker's improved.

But the Early Short Prickly and Long Green Prickly, are commonly cultivated for the early and general crop, the short prickly being the earliest, and are, therefore often sown for the first crop in the frames; but the Long Green Prickly is the best to sow for a main crop, either for the hand-glasses, or in the natural ground; it being both a plentiful bearer in long continuance, and the fruit attains the most handsome regular growth, six or eight to ten or twelve inches in length.

MAKING NEW HOT-BEDS TO TRANSPLANT CUCUMBERS, ETC.

Make hot-beds the beginning of this month to plant the cucumber or melon plants upon, which were sown the latter end of January, or any time in February; make the beds very substantial, fully three feet and a half or four feet high, having the dung previously prepared as directed in *January*, page 21, which will prevent a violent heat taking place after its being made; let the cucumber or melon plants be planted therein, and managed as directed in that month and in February.

There are many gardeners and others who cannot conveniently procure dung to begin to make hot-beds for cucumbers or melons at an early season. Where that is the case, it is not too late to begin now; and a hot-bed may be made the beginning or any time of the month, and the seeds of cucumbers and melons sown therein; the cucumbers from this sowing will be fit to cut towards the end of April, be in full bearing the beginning of May, and will continue fruiting a long time. The melons will come to perfection in June and July.

CUCUMBERS AND MELONS FOR BELL OR HAND-GLASSES.

About the eighteenth or twentieth, or any time towards the end of this month, is the time to begin to sow the cucumbers and melons which are to be planted under hand or bell-glasses.

They may be sown in any of the cucumber hot-beds now at work; or if not convenient, or there are no such beds made, make a hot-bed for that purpose, for a one, two, or three light frame, according to the quantity of plants required; sow the seed, and manage the beds as directed in the two former months. The plants will be ready for ridging out by the middle or towards the end of next month; the cucumbers will be in bearing the latter end of May, and the melons in July.

CAULIFLOWERS.

Where cauliflower plants were raised from seeds sown last month, they should as soon in this as they have arrived to the height of three or four inches, be pricked into a new slight hot-bed, made for that purpose, at the distance of three inches every way, and managed as directed in *February*, page 132.

By pricking out the plants on a little bottom heat, it will forward them considerably, and by thus transplanting, they will become strong and well furnished with roots, and consequently will succeed much better when planted out than if suffered to remain in the seed bed.

The autumn sown plants, and those which you had transplanted last month, from the January sowing, must now have plenty of air, and this in proportion as the season advances, and the weather grows warm, in order to harden them for bearing the open air, when planted out where intended for flowering, which cannot be done with safety in the middle States before the last week in this month, or rather the first in April; nor in the eastern States before the second week or middle of that month, unless you have hand-glasses to cover them, in which case they may be planted out any time that the ground is in good condition, after the middle of March.

The latter method I would recommend, provided the plants are large, the spring early, and that you have the convenience of hand-glasses, but not otherwise.

Though at this early period the ground best adapted for producing good cauliflowers is not always in a proper state for cultivation, which ought to be a principal consideration, either in the planting or sowing of any crops whatever, and never departed from, should the season prove ever so late.

Cauliflower seed may be sown the beginning of this month, as directed in *January*, page 29, which, if well attended to, and judiciously managed, and the great summer heats should not set in at an early period, will head tolerably well; but if these circumstances do not follow, a great number of them will not flower before late in autumn, and some not even then; such of these as do not flower before the setting in of the winter frosts, are to be treated as directed in the *Kitchen Garden* for *November*, by which treatment they will produce tolerable good heads, and at a very acceptable period.

You must be very particular during this month, especially when the weather gets warm, to give your cauliflower plants plenty of air, otherwise they will draw up weakly, and be good for nothing; but at the same time, do not let them be chilled, nor their vegetation checked, by exposing them too much in cold weather, or neglecting to cover them carefully at night; expose them fully to the air every mild and warm day, but not when the wind is sharp or cutting, and raise the glasses behind in more unfavorable weather.

On the judicious treatment given to these plants during this month depends, in a great measure, their future success; therefore, due and constant attention should be paid to them, agreeably to the rules already laid down.

As the beginning or early part of next month will be the principal period for planting out cauliflowers in the middle and eastern States, I am induced to defer the instructions for performing that part of the business till April; observing, however, that in every part of the Union it should be done as *early* in spring as the ground gets warm and into a good state of vegetation, not before; for, when that is not the case, the plants very frequently get chilled and stunted by the coldness of the earth and air, and seldom afterwards produce good heads.

You may sow some cauliflower seed on a warm border towards the latter end of the month, to produce their flowers or heads in October, &c.

CABBAGE PLANTS.

During the early part of this month the cabbage plants, which are in a considerable state of forwardness, must be well inured to the open air, the better to prepare them for planting out as soon after the middle of the month as the weather will permit. Those produced from later sowings in hot-beds will, to do them justice, require the same management as directed for cauliflower plants.

PLANTING AND SOWING CABBAGES.

As early in this month as you find the weather sufficiently favorable, which, in the middle States, is generally so about the fifteenth or twentieth, transplant cabbage plants of all kinds, particularly the early sorts, where they are to remain for heading; this, in warm situations and dry ground, may be done at an earlier period, according to circumstances.

Let them be planted in good ground enriched with dung, at two feet distance for the early York, sugar-loaf, and other early kinds; but the large late cabbage plants should be set a yard asunder.

The above distances are to be understood of such plants as are to remain to grow to their full size; but such of the forward kinds as are to be cut while young, may be planted closer; eighteen inches will be sufficient.

13

Plant out also a general crop of red cabbage plants, to head in August, &c., and allow them three feet every way, plant from plant.

Sow seeds of every kind of cabbage which you wish to cultivate. These may be sown in the open ground about the middle or as early in the month as the weather permits. The early as well as the late kinds should be sown now, in order to have a regular succession, or as substitutes in default of early plants, or for a general summer crop. The early Wakefield, early York, Battersea, and sugar-loaf, are best adapted for this purpose. The last kind, though not quite so early as the others, has a particular advantage over them, in not being liable to burst so soon after having arrived at perfection, and consequently may be kept a long time, either for use or market.

Sow also a full crop of the large flat Dutch, drum-head, large English, Savoy, and red pickling cabbages. The plants from this sowing will produce larger and better heads than if sown later.

Should the season prove favorable, by which you can get these seeds sown early in the month, it will be very proper to sow some more of each kind, about the end, for succession plants.

Some people never think of planting Savoys till late in spring. This is a great mistake, for the early sown plants will always produce larger and better cabbage-heads than the late.

In sowing the different sorts of cabbage-seeds, never let them be sown under the shade of trees, hedges, very *high* fences or buildings, for in such situations the plants are drawn up weak and long-shanked, and are more liable to be destroyed by vermin than in open exposures.

SOWING PEAS.

As early in this month as possible sow a full crop of peas. The kinds most proper for this sowing are the early-frame, emperor, and Charleton hot-spurs. Sow also at the same time some of the Champion of England, marrowfat, dwarf, or blue imperial kinds. These, or any of the late sorts, being now sown, will regularly succeed the early crops.

Sow peas from this forward once a fortnight or three weeks, to keep up a regular supply for the table young and in good condition; or it will be a good rule when the plants of a former sowing are up to sow another crop of the same sort for succession.

All the sorts of peas, except those which are intended for the first or early crops, which may be sown on south or warm borders, should be sowed in open situations, and by no means near low or spreading trees.

At this season, and from henceforward, let the early kinds be planted in drills three feet and a half asunder; the larger growing sorts five feet, and the largest, such as the champion, &c., six feet, giving them rods or sticks in proportion to their respective growths, by which means you will be certain of abundant crops.

It will not be advisable to sow any of the above kinds while the ground is tough and wet, always observing to have your ground in good working condition before you sow these or any other crops;

for, if otherwise, they cannot receive much benefit, but may considerable injury—observing at the same time that peas do not thrive in a heavy or clay soil.

The depth of covering which they require is from one to two inches, according as the ground may be either of a light or heavy nature, or in a dry or wet state at the time of sowing.

EARTHING AND STICKING PEAS.

Towards the latter end of the month the early sown peas will be advancing in growth, and must have earth drawn to their stems as they progress, which will greatly strengthen them and encourage their growth.

As to sticking peas, always be careful to have this done when they are about four inches high; for, if they fall to one side or the other, they with difficulty can recover their erect posture; and if they are double-sticked the better—that is, place a range of sticks on the one side, all in a regular declining manner, and another on the other side of the row declining in an opposite direction to the former, by which none can fall on either side. I cannot too much impress the necessity of rodding well, for on this in great measure depends the abundance of your crops.

PLANTING THE LARGE WINDSOR BEANS, AND OTHER VARIETIES OF THE SAME SPECIES.

As early in this month as possible plant a full crop of Windsor beans, and also of any of the other varieties which you esteem. The Mazagan and Lisbon are the earliest; the white-blossom bean is very delicious, and boils much greener than any other kind; but the green Genoa bears the heat of our climates better than either of the others, and therefore is the most suitable for late crops. The long-podded bean is very good, and bears well; but the Windsor, Sandwich, Toker, and broad Spanish kinds, on account of their great size and sweetness, are more esteemed for blanching than any other. The dwarf-cluster bean is a great bearer, never grows above a foot or fourteen inches high, and may be planted in rows either in beds or borders, the rows to be about two feet asunder; and as this kind branches out considerably from the root, the beans must be planted in single rows, and six inches distant from one another.

I have again to remark that it is from the early planted of these kinds that much produce may be expected, for when overtaken by the summer heat, whilst in blossom, these drop off prematurely; consequently the crops are poor and scanty

Continue planting these kinds once every ten days till the end of the month or beginning of next; and as the early crops advance, draw some earth up to their stems as directed for peas.

When beans are desired at as early a period as possible you may force some of the early Mazagan kind, in any of your forcing departments, observing, when the plants are in full blossom, to nip off their tops, which will cause their fruit to set and ripen sooner than if left to take their natural course.

Or you may, about the beginning of the month, plant a quantity of them close together in a hot-bed, to be defended with a frame and glasses, or with mats, &c., and when thus forwarded for two or three weeks, plant them into the open ground; observing to give them plenty of air whilst in the hot-bed, and when they have one or two inches growth therein, to plant them into some warm border, in rows two feet and a half or a yard asunder.

For further particulars, and the method of planting all the kinds, see *February.*

COVERING HALF-HARDY PLANTS.

For covering half-hardy plants, or screening from dry winds, various means are employed. In France a basket is constructed, of two semi-cylinders, constructed in the mode of straw

Fig. 20.

hives. To these are fixed solid feet of wood to drive into the ground. If it is necessary to shelter one plant from east or northeast winds, one cylinder is sufficient; but if it is a plant which you are forced to protect, is delicate, and requires a more complete protection, you inclose it between the two semi-cylinders, fixed one to the other by means of hooks represented in the drawing. A lid of the same construction, furnished at its edge with a circle of woodwork, is fitted, when necessary, on the cylinder, and thus, perhaps, offers a more effectual shelter against the severity of cold winds and excessive heat than any other. These sorts of shades are light to move, very solid, and very warm; for, letting but little of the exterior air penetrate, they preserve at night the heat which accumulates in the interior. They would also guard plants well from the sun, and thus offer a means of checking the natural perspiration of green

parts. Probably nothing could be invented more suitable for the protection of young plants, like the magnolia grandiflora, in this latitude, where the frozen sap is attacked by the sun, and the leaves in young specimens annually killed. For protecting the stems of grafted roses from the summer sun, they might be made of basket willows.

SOWING AND TRANSPLANTING LETTUCES.

As early in this month as possible, prepare a warm south border, and sow thereon, very thick, some of the early Silesia and white Dutch lettuces; in order to have it fit for cutting, with other small salading, at an early period, and to succeed such as you have forwarded in frames; let the ground be dry and light, and the seed either raked in or covered very slightly.

Towards the middle of the month, if the weather be mild and settled, you may sow in borders, beds or any open compartments of ground, different sorts of lettuce seed, such as the white, green, spotted, and Egyptian cos, grand admiral, white Silesia, Indian tennis-ball, New Zealand, Mogul, white and brown Dutch, &c., these are all most excellent sorts for this sowing, where variety of superior kinds are wanted.*

Every two weeks it will be necessary to sow other successional crops, so as to have a regular and constant supply either for market or family use.

The different sorts should generally be sown separate, and in digging the ground, let the earth be well pulverized. Sow the seed on the surface, and rake them in lightly, taking care not to draw the earth in heaps.

Or some of the cos kinds particularly, may be sown thinly among the crops of carrots, parsneps, leeks, &c.; some for transplanting, and others to remain for full growth.

In sowing lettuce it is of much importance to have good sorts, and such as will not run to seed before they attain full growth; these are not commonly to be met with, and are worth procuring.

As soon in this month as the weather gets mild and tolerably warm, transplant some of the lettuce plants from the beds or borders, where they have stood all winter, provided they stand too close. In doing this, observe to draw the plants out regularly, and let the strongest remain for heading at about ten inches distance; then loosen the surface of the earth between them, and clear away all decayed leaves and litter; after which, add a little fresh earth, which will give the plants new vigor, and considerably enlarge their growth.

Previously to planting out into the open borders any plants raised in hot-beds from the early spring sowings, you must be very particular to inure them to the open air, so that when transplanted, they may not receive a great check by too sudden a transition.

It will be of considerable service to these plants, when transplanted into the borders at this season, to cover them at night with mats or other light coverings, which are to be taken off early in the morning.

Should it happen that you have no lettuce plants in a state of forwardness for early salading, some may be now sown in a hot-bed, to forward for that purpose.

RADISHES.

Sow more seed to raise a supply of radishes to succeed those sown last month.

There should be some both of the salmon, olive shaped, and short top kinds, sown at three different times this month; that is, at the beginning, middle, and latter end, by which means there will be a due succession of young radishes for the table. Let this seed be

---

* White curled Silesia is one of the very best for all purposes, excepting the winter. It stands the sun without being scorched, and is tender, brittle, and sweet flavored.

sown now in an open compartment, observing the same method as in *February,* page 137.

Thin the early crops of radishes where the plants stand too close; pull up the worst and leave the others about two inches apart; clear them from weeds of all kinds, and as they advance in growth thin them by degrees by drawing them for the table.

In dry open weather, let the early crops in frames, &c., be moderately watered at intervals, to forward them in a free swelling state, as well as to render them mild and crisp for eating.

A thin sprinkling of radish seed may be sown among other general crops at this season, which will grow freely, and being detached, will form fine large crisp roots.

TURNIP-ROOTED RADISHES.

Now sow some turnip-rooted radish; there are two sorts, the white and the red, but the former is preferable to sow for the general supply; it grows like a young Dutch turnip, is very mild, agreeable to eat, and of early perfection.

Let the seed of both sorts be sown separately in an open space of light ground, and rake them in evenly.

When the plants have the first central rough leaves half an inch broad, thin them to about two inches apart.

SOWING SPINAGE.

Sow spinage every fortnight or three weeks to have a regular supply; for the plants of one sowing, in spring and summer, will not continue fit for use longer than that time before they run to seed. Let the seed be of the round-leaved or smooth-seeded kind; that being the most proper sort to sow at this season, its leaves being considerably thicker and larger than the prickly-seeded spinage.

This seed should be sown thinly either in beds or borders, and generally broadcast, in which method you may sow therewith a little radish-seed; when the seed is sown in light dry ground, tread it over lightly, and then rake it in regularly, or you may sow it in drills a foot asunder, and about half an inch deep.

Let it be observed, that spinage should not, at this season, be sown where the ground is much shaded with trees or bushes; for in such situations, the plants would be drawn up to seed before they arrive to half their growth.

Hoe or hand-weed the early crops of spinage, thinning the plants at the same time, but particularly those sown broadcast, to three, four, or five inches distance.

The crop of winter spinage, which was sown last autumn, will, towards the end of the month, be advancing in good perfection for use, and should be kept clear from weeds, and the earth between the plants stirred with a hoe; and in gathering the plants for use, if they stand close, should thin them out clean by the roots; but if they already stand at wide distances, only crop the large outer leaves as wanted, till they begin to run, then cut them clean up to the bottom.

CARROTS AND PARSNEPS.

Any time after the middle of this month that the ground is in good condition, you may sow carrots and parsneps for a full crop, particularly the latter; and also, a sufficient early crop of the former.

A spot of light deep loam, inclining a little to sand, and in an open situation, should be chosen for these crops; for their roots will thrive best and grow largest in such.

The ground should be trenched one good spade deep at least, observing in the digging to take but thin spits, and to break all the lumps fine, that the roots may have full liberty to run down long and straight; for if the earth is not well divided and separated, the roots are apt to grow both short and forked.

Then draw drills one inch deep and fifteen inches apart, sow the seed evenly, cover carefully with the feet, after which, rake the surface lightly, and the work is finished.

Previous to sowing carrot-seed, you should rub it well between your hands, mixed with some dry sand, to cause it to separate freely.

When the plants are about three inches high, thin the parsneps to six, and the carrots to four inches, plant from plant, in the rows.

Some people sow the seeds broadcast in beds tread them in, and then rake the ground; but this method should never be practised where the soil is stiff, inclinable to wet, or apt to bind. You may sow with these crops a few radish and lettuce seeds; of the latter any of the cos kinds are most suitable for this purpose, they not being subject to spread like the heading sorts.

SMALL SALADING.

Small salading, such as cresses, mustard, radish, rape, and turnip, &c., should, when a constant supply is wanted, be sown once a week or fortnight, in a warm border, observing to draw some flat shallow drills three inches asunder; sow the seeds therein, each sort separate, and cover them lightly with fine earth.

For the particular method of sowing and treating these seeds, see the work of last month, page 132.

If these young herbs, or any other of your early advancing crops, such as peas, beans, &c., are attacked with a hoar frost appearing on them in the morning, and a sunny day is likely to follow, let them be watered before the sun shines on them with spring or pump water, to wash and melt it off, which will prevent their turning black and spoiling.

CELERY.

If celery was not sown last month, let some seed be sown the beginning of this, to plant out in May, &c., for an early crop; sow some more of the same seed about the middle, or towards the latter end, for a succession crop. The seed should be sown in a bed or border of mellow rich earth, sowing it on the surface moderately thick, and cover it in lightly with fine mould not more than a quarter of an inch; or you may rake it in with a light and even hand. Water the bed frequently in dry weather.

Let it be observed that there are two sorts of celery; one known by the name of Italian or upright celery; the other called celeriac, or turnip-rooted celery. The first is that which is commonly culti-vated for the general crops, and of which there are several varieties, viz., common upright celery with hollow stalks, solid-stalked celery, red-stalked solid celery, &c.,* either of which being raised from seed sown as above, is afterwards planted in trenches for blanching their stalks, which are the principal useful parts; but the celeriac is gene-rally cultivated for its swelling bottom part; and being planted either on level ground, or in shallow drills, the roots of it swell like a turnip. (See *April, May, June*, &c.)

BROCCOLI.

Sow broccoli for early crops, &c., to come in for use in October, November, and December, &c.

Choose seed of the early purple, and some of the cauliflower broc-coli; sow a little of each kind about the middle or latter end of the month in an open bed of rich earth, and rake them in. When the plants come up, manage them as directed in *May, June,* and *July*.

SOWING BORECOLE, OR CURLED KALE.

Towards the end of this month you may sow a first crop of bore-cole for autumn service.

There are two principal sorts, the green and the brown, both very hardy plants, with tall stems, and full heads of thick fimbriate curled leaves, not cabbaging, and are desirable open greens for winter, &c.

Let this seed be sown in an open exposure, distant from trees and close fences, as in such situations they are apt to draw up too fast, with long weak stalks. Sow it broadcast, and rake it in evenly. For other particulars, see the succeeding months.

Borecole is extremely valuable for winter and spring greens, where the winter frost is not too powerful for it, particularly in all the southern States. It is the most hardy of the cabbage tribe, and in mild winters will stand tolerably well in the middle States. In the eastern States, it will require to be taken up before the winter frosts set in with much severity, planted in trenches up to the leaves, and covered occasionally with straw or other light covering. The heads may be cut off as wanted, and in spring the stems, if taken up and planted out, will produce an abundance of most delicious sprouts.

* Hollow stalked celery is not worth cultivating. *Seymour's White Solid* is one of the very best.

OF FORKING AND DRESSING THE ASPARAGUS BEDS.

This work should be begun about the latter end of the month. For the purpose of digging or forking these beds, you should be provided with a proper fork, having three short tines, six to eight or nine inches long, perfectly flat, about an inch broad, and the ends of them rounded and blunt. However, in want of such, it may be performed with a small short-pronged common dung-fork.

In forking the beds, be careful to loosen every part to a moderate depth, but taking great care not to go too deep to wound the crowns of the roots.

The above work of forking these beds is most necessary to be done every spring to improve and loosen the ground and to give free liberty for the buds to shoot up, also to give easy access to the sun, air, and showers of rain.

The beds being forked, they must afterwards be raked even, observing, if you do not rake them immediately after they are forked, to defer it no longer than the first week in April, for by that time the buds will begin to advance.

Before raking the above beds you may scatter thereon a few radish and lettuce seeds to pull up while young.

As to the method of gathering or cutting asparagus when advanced to a proper growth for the table, it is generally most eligible to be furnished with an asparagus knife, having a straight, narrow, tapering blade, about six or eight inches long, and about an inch broad at the haft, narrowing to about half an inch at the point, which should be rounded off from the back, observing, when the shoots are from about two to three or four inches high, they should be then cut, slipping the knife down perpendicularly, close to each shoot, and cut it off slantingly about three or four inches within the ground, taking care not to wound any young buds coming up from the same root, for there are always several shoots advancing therefrom in different stages of growth.*

PLANTING ASPARAGUS.

New plantations of asparagus may now be made, this being the proper season to remove these plants. It may be done any time in this month, when the weather is mild.

In making plantations of these plants, one great article to be considered is to make choice of a proper soil; choose the best the garden affords. It must not be wet nor too strong or stubborn, but such as is moderately light and pliable, so as it will readily fall to pieces in digging or raking, &c., and in a situation that enjoys the full sun.

The ground where you intend to make new asparagus beds should have a large supply of rotten or other good dung laid thereon several inches thick, and then regularly trenched two spades deep, and

---

* If the young shoots be allowed to grow six inches high and are cut off level with the ground, the whole is tender; all below the soil is tough and stringy.

the dung buried equally in each trench, twelve or fifteen inches below the surface.

When this trenching is done, lay on two or three inches of very short well-rotted manure all over the surface, and dig the ground over again eight or ten inches deep, mixing this top-dressing and incorporating it well with the earth.

The ground being thus prepared and laid level, divide it into beds four feet and a half wide, with alleys two feet wide between each bed.

At each corner of every bed let a firm stake be driven into the ground, to serve as a mark for the alleys.

Four rows of asparagus are to be planted in each bed, and ten or twelve inches distance to be allowed between plant and plant in the row, and let the outside rows of each bed be eight inches from the edge.

Next, let it be observed that the plants for this plantation must not be *more* than two years old; but most good gardeners prefer those that are only one, which are what I would recommend and choose to plant, as from experience I have found they generally take root much freer and succeed every way better than the former. The following is the method of planting them :—

Strain your line along the bed eight inches from the edge, then with a spade cut out a small trench or drill close to the line, about six inches deep, making that side next the line nearly upright; and when one trench is opened plant that before you open another, placing the plants upright ten or twelve inches distant in the row.

In planting these plants, observe that they must not be placed flat in the bottom of the trench, but nearly upright against the back of the trench or drill, and so that the crown of the plants may also stand upright, and two or three inches below the surface of the ground; let them be all placed an equal depth, spreading their roots somewhat regular, against the back of the trench, and at the same time drawing a little earth up against them with the hand as you place them, just to fix the plants in their due position, till the row is planted; when one row is thus finished, immediately with a rake draw the earth into a drill over the plants, and then proceed to open another drill or trench, as before directed ; plant it in the same manner, and cover in the plants as above, and so on till the whole is planted, then let the surface of the beds be raked smooth, and cleared from stones.

When the plants come up, keep them always free from weeds; but in the mean time, be cautious not to sow any early crops whatever among your young plantations, as is very injudiciously practised by many, for these would smother them in their growth, and greatly retard their progress.

Let it be next observed that it will be three years from the time of planting before the asparagus plants produce buds large enough to cut for use in any general gathering; though sometimes in rich, good ground, and a remarkably prosperous growth in the plants in the production of strong shoots, a few of the largest may be cut the second spring after planting, but I would advise not to cut many before the third year.

A plantation of asparagus, if the beds are properly dressed every year, as directed in the spring and autumn months, will continue to produce good buds for ten or twelve years or more.

In making new plantations, I have sometimes, instead of putting in young plants as above directed, sown the seed at once in beds where the plants are to remain; and, as by that practice the plants are not disturbed by a removal, they consequently cannot fail of producing a regular crop.

The beds being four feet and a half wide, and prepared as before directed for the plants, mark out four lines lengthways the beds; then along these line, at the distance of every nine or ten inches, dot in a few seeds, covering them about an inch deep. When the plants have been come up some time, they must be thinned, leaving only one of the strongest in each place, and carefully clear them from weeds.

A plantation of asparagus thus raised, will produce buds fit to cut the third spring after sowing, but will be very large and fine the fourth year.

For forcing asparagus, see *February*, page 128.

SOWING ASPARAGUS SEED.

This seed may be sown about the middle, or towards the latter end of the month, on four feet wide beds of rich earth. Sow it tolerably thin on the surface, clap it in with the back of a spade, cover it a little better than half an inch deep with earth out of the alleys, and then rake the beds smooth.

Or it may be sown thinly in drills, six inches asunder, and covered the same depth as above; give the beds, both before and after the plants are up, occasional waterings to strengthen them and forward their growth; and they must be kept very free from weeds, by a careful hand-weeding at different times during the summer.

When a quantity of asparagus for forcing is annually required, you must act as directed in *February*, page 128.

SOWING BEET SEED.

You may now sow some of the different sorts of beet; the red for its large root, and the green and white sorts for their leaves in soups, stewing, &c.

For this purpose make choice of a piece of rich deep ground; lay it out into four feet wide beds, push the loose earth into the alleys, then sow the seed tolerably thin and cover it with the earth out of these alleys to about three-quarters of an inch deep. Or let drills be drawn with a hoe, near an inch deep, and a foot or a little more asunder; drop the seeds thinly therein and cover them over the same depth as above. Or you may sow the seed on a piece of ground, rough after being dug, and rake it well in.

Likewise you may now sow the Mangel Wurtzel, root of scarcity, or great German beet, for its large leaves to boil as spinage, its thick fleshy leaf-stalks to dress as asparagus, and its roots for boiling before they become of a very large size. The leaves and roots are excellent food for cattle; producing, during summer, an uncommon abundance of foliage; the outside leaves, for this purpose, may be stripped off every eight days during the season, but if large and well developed roots are wanted for winter fodder, the leaves are better to be left on.

SOWING ONION SEED.

In order to have onions in good perfection the first year from seed, which can certainly be effected in the middle, but more particularly in the eastern States, you must be careful to fix upon a suitable soil, which is a strong, light, rich loam; always avoiding that which is subject to become parched or bound up by heat and drought; or that, in consequence of too large a proportion of sand, is likely to become violently hot in summer, for this is extremely injurious to those plants by causing them to come to an untimely maturity, manifested by the extraordinary perfection that onions arrive to in the moderate climates of Europe, where they have not to encounter a violent summer heat.

If this ground had been strongly manured in November, and then thrown up into high sloping ridges, it would be much improved and meliorated by the frost, &c., and could now be easily and expeditiously levelled for sowing.

When this is not the case you may now give such ground a good coat of well-rotted cow dung, or other good rotten manure, and dig it a full spade deep, incorporating the dung therewith and pulverizing the earth as you proceed in the digging; this should not be attempted till the ground it sufficiently dry to pulverize well and fall to pieces under the rake; but the earlier you can get it in this state, and the seed sown, the larger and better onions will you have.

There are various methods of sowing the seed; but first I will give you the one practised by the most judicious and careful gardeners.

As you proceed in digging the ground rake it well after you; that being done lay it out into three and a half, or four feet wide beds, with alleys between of about a foot wide; then with the back of a rake push off the light loose earth from the top of each bed into the alleys, one half to the one side, the other to the opposite; this done, and being provided with good seed, sow it thereon at the rate of one pound for every sixteen rods, and with a shovel cast the earth out of the alleys over the beds, covering the seeds evenly about half an inch deep; then rake the beds lightly, drawing off all the lumps into the alleys.

When the plants are up let them be kept very clean and free from weeds of any kind by a good careful hand-weeding, which is to be repeated, from time to time, as they require it; and where they grow too close thin them to about two inches, plant from plant, all over the beds; by these means you will have excellent onions for the table the first year.

Others dig the ground, levelling the surface evenly after them as they proceed in digging without raking it, and lay it out in beds as before; then sow the seed thereon and rake it in; and if the earth is light and dry they frequently tread it in with the feet before raking. Or the beds may be prepared, as in the first instance, and the seeds sown very thinly in drills a foot apart, either of which methods will do very well. The last is, however the best, as the push hoe can be used in extirpating the weeds, and loosening the surface.

But when they are raised upon an extensive scale the ground may be cultivated by the plough, and when harrowed very fine the seed may be sown in drills at the above distance, and the intervals between them kept clean by hoeing; the remainder must be carefully hand-weeded.

Sowing seed, to produce small seed onions, will answer better in *April,* which see. If sown in this month they would generally grow to too large a size for that purpose.

Of the several varieties of onion the Strasburg is the best for a general crop; it is a handsome bulb, generally assuming a roundish oval shape, is of firm growth, and keeps well for winter service.

The white Spanish and silver skinned onions are of a milder taste, but all the varieties generally turn out very profitable crops; the latter kinds rarely keep so well after January as the Strasburg.

The Portugal and Madeira onions are extremely fine; but they rarely attain with us as large a size as in these countries.

The red Spanish onion is highly esteemed for pickling on account of its deep blood-red color, and much cultivated for that purpose: it may also be used for any other purpose as well as the former kinds.

SOWING LEEKS.

Leek seed may be sown, and treated in every respect for the present as directed for onion seed.

PLANTING SEED ONIONS.

By seed onions is meant the *small* bulbs produced from seed sown last season, which should be planted out as early in spring as it is possible to get the ground in a good state for tillage; the southern States in particular have to depend on such for a general crop, as the summer heat is too powerful in these, and indeed in the middle States, except the ground is peculiarly suitable for the bulks arriving at a sufficient size the first year from seed.

Having prepared an open piece of strong ground, well dug and enriched with manure, you may proceed to plant these bulbs in rows, either by line and dibble, or by hoe; planting them not more than half an inch over the crowns: let the drills or rows be six inches asunder, and the onions three inches one from the other in the rows.

But for expedition sake, especially when there are large quantities to be planted, prepare an instrument, just in form of a common hay-rake, having four round teeth or pegs, either of wood or iron, placed in the head, at the distance of six inches from each other, four inches long, and near an inch in diameter, close to the head, tapering to a blunt point: this being in readiness, proceed to mark out your ground into two feet wide beds, leaving a twelve inch alley between each; then pull this rake along each bed from one end to the other, pressing it down as you proceed, by which it will make four regular drills in each, for the reception of the small onions, which you are to plant by hand in these drills, at the distance above mentioned, and just so deep as that you can cover the crowns, by drawing a little earth over them with the hand as you proceed.

By the same method you may plant these onions in beds of any dimensions you please, either lengthwise or across the beds.

The *Allium canadense*, or tree onion, merits culture both as a curiosity in producing the onions at the top of the stalk, as well as for their value in domestic use, particularly for pickling, in which they are excellent, and superior in flavor to the common kinds; they may also be used for any other purposes that onions are.

It is perennial, and propagated by planting the bulbs in spring or autumn, either the root-bulbs, or those produced on the top of the stalks; the latter if planted in spring as directed for the other kinds will produce very fine, handsome sized onions of excellent flavor.

The root-bulbs increase greatly by offsets, and should be taken up once in every two or three years, when the stems decay in autumn, and replanted again to produce a supply of top-bulbs.

GARLIC, ROCAMBOLE, AND SHALLOTS.

Prepare some beds of good ground, four feet wide, in which to plant garlic, rocambole, and shallots; of which procure some best bulbs or roots; divide the garlic and rocambole into cloves, and the shallots into offsets, as they admit; plant them in rows, lengthwise the beds, eight or nine inches asunder, by six inches distance in each row, and two or three inches deep.

They may be planted either with a dibble or in drills drawn with a hoe.

CIVES, OR CHIVES.

Cives, a small species of onion, growing in large tufts, are useful in a family in the spring, &c., as a substitute for young onions, both in salads and culinary purposes; they are propagated by slipping the roots, and this is a proper time to plant them; the method is to part or take off some slips from the old roots several small offsets together, and plant them in beds or borders about six to eight, or nine inches distance.

In slipping or parting the above roots, observe to preserve eight, ten, or more of the small bulbs together in a cluster, and in that manner to plant them.

They are to be planted with a dibble or trowel, making holes for them at the distance above mentioned, putting one cluster of roots, as above, in each hole, and closing the earth well about them. They will soon take root, and increase very fast into large bunches, of many years' duration.

TURNIPS.

Sow turnips for a first early crop, about the middle, or towards the latter end of this month, in an open situation, and where the ground is light.

The proper sort to sow now is principally the early Dutch and six weeks turnip, they being the best sort to sow at this season in gardens, but especially for the first and second crops; excepting in very cool and moist localities, turnips do not succeed during the summer months.

SCORZONERA AND SALSAFY.

The latter end of this month you may sow scorzonera and salsafy; these plants are in some families much esteemed for their roots, which are the only parts that are eaten, except the salsafy, as explained below.

The roots run pretty deep in the ground, in the manner of carrots and parsneps, and are boiled or stewed, and eaten either alone or with flesh-meat, like young carrots, &c.

But the salsafy is estimable both for its roots as above, and for the young shoots rising in the spring from the year old plants, being gathered while green and tender, are good to boil and eat in the manner of asparagus.

Dig one or more beds for each of the above, in an open situation. Sow the seed either in shallow drills, six inches distant, and earthed over half an inch, or sow on the surface, covered from the alleys, and the beds then raked; they are all to remain where sown, and the plants thinned in May to from four to six inches distant.

LARGE ROOTED PARSLEY.

Sow the seeds of Hamburg, or large rooted parsley; this is cultivated for its large parsnep-like root: let the seeds be sown in an open situation, either in shallow drills, or on the surface, and raked in evenly; when the plants are two or three inches in growth, they must be thinned to six inches distant, that the roots may have room to swell.

SKIRRETS.

Skirret seed may be sown tolerably thin, on beds of good earth and raked in, or they may be propagated by parting their roots, and planting them at six or eight inches distant. The fleshy tubers of these roots are considered very delicious.

SOWING PARSLEY.

Parsley seed may be sown in a single drill along the edge of the quarters or borders of the garden; it will make a useful and also a neat edging, if not suffered to grow rank, especially the curled parsley;

or if large supplies are wanted for market, it may be sown in continued rows nine inches asunder, or upon the general surface, trod
down and raked in.

SOWING CHERVIL AND CORIANDER.

Sow chervil and coriander for soups and salads, &c.; draw shallow
drills for these seeds eight or nine inches asunder: sow each sort
separate, and cover them about half an inch deep with earth.

These herbs are all to remain where sown, and the chief culture
they require is to be kept clear from weeds; but as the plants soon
run up for seed, you should sow a small portion every month.

CRAMBE MARITIMA, OR SEA KALE.*

The *Crambe maritima,* or Sea Kale, being yet very little known
in the United States, though a most excellent garden vegetable, and
highly deserving of cultivation, it may be of importance to the community to give some account of this plant, and the most approved
methods of cultivating it.

This plant is found growing spontaneously, though locally, on the
sea shore of the southern parts of England, as well as in similar
places in many other parts of Europe.

It is of the same natural class as the cabbage, but differs from it
and most of the Tetradynamus plants of LINNÆUS, in having a round
seed vessel, containing one seed only; its root is perennial, running to
a great depth, growing to great thickness, and branching out widely,
but not creeping: its full grown leaves are large, equalling in size,
when the plant grows luxuriantly, those of the largest cabbage, of a
glaucous or sea-green hue, and waved at the edges, thick and succulent in their wild state, dying away and disappearing entirely at the
approach of winter. Seedling plants when raised in spring, produce
the first year radical leaves only; the second spring most of them
throw up a flowering stem, a foot or more in height, which, expanding
into numerous branches, forms a magnificent head of white or cream-
colored flowers, having a honey-like fragrance; these, if the season
proves favorable, are followed by abundance of seed.

As an article of food, the Crambe maritima appears to be better
known in England than in any other part of Europe; it is in that
country only that its value is rightly appreciated and its culture
carefully attended to.

On many parts of the sea coast of England, especially of Devonshire, Dorsetshire, and Sussex, the inhabitants from time immemorial
have been in the practice of procuring it for their tables, preferring
it to all other greens. They seek for the plant in the spring where
it grows spontaneously; and as soon as it appears above ground, they
remove the pebbles or sand with which it is usually covered to the

* This vegetable ought to be cooked in a pan, the inside of which is
lined with block tin or porcelain; if exposed to an iron surface, it will get
black and be of bitter flavor.

depth of several inches, and cut off the young and tender leaves and stalks, as yet unexpanded and in a blanched state, close to the crown of the root. It is then in its greatest perfection. When the leaves are fully grown they become hard and bitter, and the plant is not eatable.

The more curious, desirous of having it at hand and in their immediate possession, have now, in many parts of the maritime counties of England, introduced it into their gardens; and in Devonshire particularly there is scarcely a good garden to be found without a plantation of it for the use of the table. It is also cultivated for sale in various parts of England, particularly Bath, Chichester, &c.

It is to be observed that the sea kale is delicate eating only when young, and that it is highly improved by being blanched. In the cultivation of this plant it becomes necessary to blanch it before it is fit for the table. To effect this it must be covered in some way or other before the flowering stem, which constitutes the chief eatable part, and its attendant leaves show the least sign of emerging from the crown of the root.

Cultivators have differed widely respecting the mode of treating this plant; many, conceiving that stones or gravel and sea sand are essential to its growth, have gone to the expense of providing it with such, not aware that it will grow much more luxuriantly on a rich sandy loam, where the roots can penetrate to a great depth without reaching the water, in which, if they are immersed, they are apt to rot. The plant will succeed almost in any soil, provided it be dry. Its luxuriance will depend chiefly on the manure with which the soil is enriched, but, of all others, a deep, rich, sandy loam is its favorite soil.

The most usual mode of raising the sea kale is from seed. It may also be raised from cuttings of the root and that with the greatest certainty; but seedlings make the finest plants. Some find a difficulty in making the seeds vegetate; this may be attributed to their being old, buried too deep in the earth, or sown too late in the spring. The most proper time for sowing the seed is in October, or as early in the spring as the ground can be got in a fit condition to receive them, and an inch is the proper depth to cover them. They rarely vegetate in less than six weeks after being sown, even in the most favorable season; and some will remain in the ground for twelve months before they vegetate. Should the season prove dry, it will be necessary to water the ground where the seeds are sown, and the plants after they appear, frequently.

It is the best practice to raise young plants immediately from seed on the bed where they are intended to remain; by this means the plants receive no check in their growth. When you have formed your bed, which should be raised somewhat above the level of the ground, being previously trenched very deep and enriched with the best rotten manure, make each bed wide enough to hold two rows of plants, the space between each plant in the row fourteen inches, and between each row a foot and a half. Sow about six or eight seeds, as before directed, on each spot where your plant is intended to remain. This number is directed in order to guard against accidents,

14

as every seed may not vegetate, or at least not the first season, which would be a losing year; besides, some of those that do may be destroyed by worms or insects. Should all of them succeed they are easily reduced to three plants. This reduction, however, need not be made too hastily. During summer your bed of course must be kept perfectly clean from weeds. If, for the sake of a more certain crop, you are disposed to make your plantation of the cuttings of the roots, you may take such as are about half an inch or a little more in diameter, and cut them into pieces of about two inches in length, burying each in an upright position about three inches under ground, in the same kind of bed and at the same distances as you would have sown the seeds. The middle or latter end of this month will be a proper season in the middle States for doing this; earlier in the southern States, and somewhat later in the eastern.

Or if, for the sake of forwarding your plantation and gaining time, you make use of plants instead of seeds or cuttings, presuming that it is possible for you to procure them, they should be those of a year old, and taken up with due care out of the seed-bed. Trim off the extreme part of the root, and let each plant be planted in a perpendicular manner so deep as that its crown will be one inch under the surface. The period before mentioned for planting cuttings will be the proper time for transplanting these. If their flowering-stalks be cut for food the same season, it will weaken the plants considerably, and hence, even in point of time, there is little gained by using such; for most of the seedling plants in your bed, if they have been properly managed, as well as your plants from cuttings, will flower, and of course be fit to cut the second year.

In November cover your beds with a thick coat of rotten dung or leaves; this, at the same time that it protects your plants from frost, will bring them more forward, and add to their luxuriance; about the middle of March, in the middle States, it will be necessary to cover your plants for blanching; the most ready mode of doing which, is to draw the earth up with a hoe over the crown of the root, so that each plant shall be covered to the depth of ten or twelve inches; some blanch it by heaping on it sea sand, some common sand and pebbles, and others with large garden pots inverted, and placed immediately over the plants, stopping up the holes at the bottoms; this last is the neatest and cleanest mode.

The finest or at least the largest sea kale, is that which is produced from seedling plants the first year of their flowering, as the great produce of the plant then centres in one flowering stem; afterwards the crown of the root ramifying into many heads, a greater number of stalks are produced, which are more slender but not less delicate.

When your plants have been covered in either method, three, four, or five weeks, according to the early or late period of covering, examine them, and if you find that the stalks have shot up three or four inches, you may begin cutting; should you wait till all the shoots are of a considerable length, your crop will come in too much at once, for in this plant there is not that succession of growth which there is in asparagus; you may continue cutting till you see the head of flowers begin to form, and if at this time you uncover it entirely, and let it proceed to that state in which the broccoli is usually cut, and use it as such, you will find it an excellent substitute ; and this greatly enhances the value of the plant, as broccoli does not stand our winter frost, and can only be had when carefully protected as directed in *November*, but this plant is sufficiently hardy to bear our severest frost without much injury.   You are not to weaken the roots too much by over-cutting, for in that case you would injure their next year's bearing ; they are to be indulged as you do asparagus with several uncut shoots to grow up during summer, to carry on a proper vegetation, to strengthen and enlarge the roots.

Such as are partial to this plant may force it in any of the winter or early spring months, nothing more being necessary than to place over each plant a large garden pot, as in one of the modes of blanching already recommended, and cover the pots with a sufficient quantity of hot horse-dung ; the heat of the dung brings forward the plant, while the pot keeps it from coming in contact therewith ; and as the growth of the plant is by this means greatly accelerated, it is of course rendered more tender as well as sweeter.

These plants may also be forced in frames as directed in *January* and *February* for asparagus, observing to take up such plants for this purpose as are sure to flower ; trimming their side roots and shortening their long tap-roots to the length of nine or ten inches, or twelve in very large plants, and placing them in a frame on a hot-bed, and in a suitable depth of earth, at the distance of four to six inches asunder ; as the plants used thus, will be rendered of little or no value : where this practice is used, it will be necessary to have a regular succession of plants for the purpose.

In cutting the plants for the table, care must be taken not to injure the crowns of the roots by cutting the shoots too close to them.

The sooner this delicious esculent is dressed, after it is cut, the better.   Twenty minutes boiling, in general, is sufficient to make it tender : this process is the more to be attended to, as the goodness of the article greatly depends on it ; that which is young, recently cut or forced, will be done in less time ; when properly boiled it is to be served up in the manner of asparagus ; it dresses well by stewing, and makes an excellent pickle.

As an esculent vegetable it is found to be very wholesome, and most people who have tried it prefer it to asparagus, to which it is related, in point of flavor.

When the crop is sufficiently cut, level the earth all over the beds, keep them free from large weeds during the remainder of the season, and cover them in *November*, as before directed.

This plant will grow extremely well in such soil as suits asparagus, having it prepared in the same manner as for that, and would be very profitable to cultivate for sale near cities and large towns.

SPRING DRESSING OF ARTICHOKES.

As soon in this month as the very severe frosts are over, any long light litter with which your artichokes are covered must be raked off

into the trenches ; and when you perceive the young shoots beginning
to appear above ground, or rather one or two inches up, not before,
proceed to levelling down the beds into the alleys or trenches, rounding them in a neat manner, then dig and loosen all the ground around
the plants ; at the same time examine the number of shoots arising
on each stool or root, selecting three of the strongest and *healthiest
looking* on every stool to remain ; all above that number are to be
slipped off close to the root with your hand, except you want such to
make new plantations with ; in which case, any extra number for that
purpose are to remain on the mother plants until they are about eight
or ten inches high from their roots or junction with the old plants,
when they are to be *slipped* off and planted as hereafter directed,
leaving only three of the best shoots on each crown as before, closing
the earth in again about the crowns of the roots, and drawing it a
little up to the remaining suckers.   Observe that in every part of the
Union this dressing is to be given when the plants are in the above
described state, whether that happens in February, March, or April,
occasioned by the difference of climate, or the earliness or lateness
of the spring.

PLANTING ARTICHOKES.

In making new plantations of artichokes, select for that purpose a
piece of deep, rich, sandy loam, that is not subject to retain too much
wet in winter, nor to be parched up with drought in summer, having
a gentle slope sufficient to carry off any moisture that might lodge
in the trenches between the rows; for that is much more destructive
to their roots in winter than the most severe frost ; when both these
enemies attack the plants with their combined powers, they seldom
fail to accomplish the work of destruction ; but from the frosts there
is not much to be apprehended if the plants lie dry.

Having fixed upon a proper soil and situation, lay on it a good
quantity of rotten dung, and trench the ground one good spade or
eighteen inches deep, incorporating the manure well therewith, and
pulverizing the ground effectually in the digging; then proceed to
take of the slips mentioned before in the dressing of artichokes,
slipping them off the mother stools with all the roots or fibres which
they may have thrown out, rejecting such as appear unhealthy, and
closing the earth up after you to the remaining shoots.   These being
provided, pull off any loose hanging leaves, and trim the fibres ; then
plant them with a dibble, about four or five inches deep, in rows five
feet asunder, and two feet plant from plant in the row, leaving part
of their green tops above ground, and the hearts of the plants free
from any earth over them, and give each plant a little water to settle
the earth about its roots.

Or, if you have seedling year old plants in a seed bed, you may
take them up, and after shortening their tap-roots a little and dressing their leaves, plant them as above.

Such young plantations, if kept clear from weeds, and now and
then watered in dry weather, will yield good artichokes the following
autumn, but will produce larger fruit, and more abundantly next

year. You may sow a small crop of lettuce, radish, or spinage, &c.,
the first year between these rows, especially if you wish to make the
most of your ground.

A plantation of artichokes will continue to produce good heads for
five or six years, but it must be observed, that if you wish to have a
succession of this fruit, you must make a small plantation every
spring, for the young plants will not produce their heads in perfection
till after the crops of the old standing ones are over.

SOWING ARTICHOKE SEED.

There are two principal varieties of the garden artichoke; indeed
Mr. Miller makes two species of them; the *cynara scolymus*, or
French artichoke, and the *cynara hortensis*, or globe artichoke.

The first being the sort which in former times was most commonly
cultivated in France, is generally known by the title of French
artichoke. The leaves are terminated by short spines, the head is
oval, and the scales do not turn inward at the top like those of the
globe artichoke; the heads are of a green color, the bottoms are not
near so thick of flesh, and have a perfumed taste, which to many
persons is very disagreeable, so that it is seldom cultivated where the
globe kinds can be procured.

Of the second, there are two varieties, the green and the red
fruited, both extremely fine. The head is globular, a little compressed at the top, the scales lie close over each other, and their ends
turn inwards so as closely to cover the middle.

The leaves of the globe artichoke are of a bluer cast, with more
and deeper jags on the cliffs than those of the French; they have
small inert prickles like the latter but not so perceptible; the leaves
of the French sort are larger, much wider, and of a paler color. The
great openness of the scales in the head of the French artichoke is a
leading character; it also rather draws up to a point in the middle,
whereas, the globe kind is quite flat at top. The color of the fruit,
in the red variety of the globe artichoke, is a reddish-brown, or rather
a dusky purple with a tinge of green.

After the above descriptions it will be unnecessary to recommend
which kind to sow; but being provided with good fresh seed of either
sort that you desire to cultivate, prepare a piece of ground as
directed for the young plantations, and at the distances there mentioned sow a few grains of seed in each spot where a plant might be
set, covering them about three-quarters of an inch deep with light
fine earth; when they appear keep them very clean and free from
weeds during the whole summer and autumn, and in *November* you
will find the method of their winter treatment, as well as that of the
old plants. Any extra plants that may arise are to be transplanted
into new beds the spring following.

In the course of the season you may have crops of cauliflowers,
cabbages, dwarf-kidney beans, spinage, lettuces, &c. &c., between the
rows; keeping them at a sufficient distance from the young artichokes, so as not to smother or cause them to draw up weakly.

Or sow these seeds in a bed so thin as you may expect the plants to rise at the distance of six inches, allowing for imperfect seeds and accidents, cover them as above, and in the spring following transplant them as before directed.

CARDOONS.

The *cynara cardunculus*, or cardoon artichoke, has been a long time used for culinary purposes, such as for salads, soups, stewing, &c.

The stalks of the leaves being thick, fleshy, and crisp, are the eatable parts, being first blanched by landing them up like celery, to two or three feet high, to render them white, tender, and of an agreeable flavor, which otherwise would be rank and bitter; they are in perfection in autumn and winter.

Sow the seeds towards the latter end of this month or beginning of next, broadcast, in a bed of rich earth, and cover them about three-quarters of an inch deep; when the plants are three inches high thin them to four or five inches distant, that they may not be drawn up weak; keep them free from weeds, and towards the latter end of May or beginning of June they will be fit to plant where they are intended to remain for perfection. For their further treatment see *May*, &c.

Or, as these plants are rather impatient of transplanting, you may sow the seeds at the distances directed in May for the plants, a few seeds in each spot, and as they advance thin them, leaving only the best plant in each of those squares.

ALEXANDERS, OR ALESANDERS.

The *Smyrnium olusatrum*, or common Alexanders, are used for culinary purposes as the cardoons, and blanched in like manner. The whole plant is of a strong, warm, and aromatic nature, and the leaves and seed are sometimes used for medicine.

The seed of this plant should be sown in autumn soon after it is ripe, for if kept out of the ground till spring, few of them will come up till that time twelve months; however, when you sow the seed in spring, let it be done as early as possible, and sown pretty thick in drills eighteen inches asunder, covering the seeds near an inch deep; when the plants are up thin them to six or eight inches distant in the rows, and as they advance in growth draw the earth up to their stems as you do to celery, in order to blanch and whiten them, that they should be crisp and tender for autumn and winter use; in the spring following, such as remain will shoot out again vigorously, let the earth then be hoed up close to each plant, and in three or four weeks they will be blanched and in a fine condition for use.

When these plants are desired I would recommend them to be sown where they are to remain, in any of the autumn months; in that case they will rise freely in spring, and become fine vigorous plants.

PROPAGATING VARIOUS POT AND MEDICINAL HERBS.

The latter end of this month will be a good time to plant cuttings or slips of hyssop, thyme, winter savory, rue, rosemary, lavender, wormwood, southern-wood, sage, and any other under-shrubby kinds; in taking off the slips of any of these sorts give a preference to the suckers if any, that is, such as have a few fibres attached to them ; from such as are not furnished with these, take off slips or cuttings of the young healthy outward shoots produced last year, from about six to ten inches long, according as they occur, observing to slip or cut them clean off close to the parts from whence they proceed. Let these be planted in a bed or border six inches apart, and inserted two-thirds of their lengths into the ground; they will take root freely by observing to water them in dry weather, and in September will be well rooted, and may either then, or in October, be transplanted wherever destined to remain ; or the slips may, in the first instance, be planted in such places.

Propagate tarragon, tansy, chamomile, common fennel, marsh-mallows, pot-marjoram, baum, burnet, horehound, spearmint, pepper-mint, feverfew, official scurvy-grass, catmint, celadine, pennyroyal, or *mentha pulegium*, angelica, lovage, gromwell, and any other peren-nial herbaceous plants, and also thyme, hyssop, and winter-savory, by parting their roots or by slips therefrom ; the best time for sepa-rating the roots of each and every of the above kinds, is just when they *begin* to advance *a little* in growth. All the above kinds may be planted in four feet wide beds, in any tolerably good ground, having twelve to eighteen inch alleys between, and placed in rows length-wise in the beds, allowing proportionate distances according to their respective growths; or the small growing kinds may be planted in borders, or any other convenient places that are open and well exposed.

The best time to gather any of the preceding kinds for distillation, or to preserve in a dry state for medicinal purposes, &c., is when they are in the first stage of their flowering.

You may, towards the latter end of this month or any time in the next, sow seeds of either, or all of the above mentioned kinds, and also of the following annual plants, for medicinal and culinary pur-poses, viz: borage, sweet fennel, sweet marjoram, sweet basil, sum-mer savory, fenugreek, pot marigold anise, and likewise clary, cara-way, smallage, and foxglove, &c.; the four last are biennials and do not flower till the second year, but their leaves may be used at any time when arrived at a sufficient size. . All these seeds should be sown separately in beds of rich earth, and covered from the eighth of an inch to half an inch deep in proportion to their size, either in the broadcast way or in drills, or the low growing kinds may be sown in single drills along the edges of borders, particularly thyme, hyssop, and winter savory, &c., and when the plants are arrived at a sufficient size, they may be thinned and transplanted into any beds or quarters that can be spared for that purpose.

DILL.

This plant is extremely valuable as an ingredient in pickles, to which it gives a most exquisite flavor : the seeds when ripe are frequently used for that purpose, but it is the more general practice when they are formed, and not yet perfect, to cut off the umbels or heads, and then use them as above.

This seed should be sown in any of the autumn months after being ripe, and will come up the spring following, for when kept out of ground till the latter period, one-third of it and perhaps less, will not vegetate till that time twelve months, but if sown very early in March, and thick, you may expect a tolerable crop that season ; sow it broadcast on four feet wide beds, covering it, if sown in autumn, half an inch, and if in spring, a quarter of an inch deep ; when the plants come up, thin them to six inches distant, and the same season they will perfect their seeds, which, if any are suffered to shed, will not fail to come up plentifully the next year.

FINOCHIO, OR AZORIAN FENNEL.

The Finochio has very short stalks, which swell just above the surface of the ground to three or four inches in breadth, and near two thick, being fleshy and tender ; this is the part which is eaten when blanched with oil, vinegar and pepper as a cold salad.

For the cultivation of this plant, make choice of a good spot of light rich earth, not dry nor very wet, for in either extreme it will not thrive. Sow the seeds pretty thin in shallow drills about eighteen inches asunder, covering them half an inch deep ; when they come up thin them, leaving the best plants six inches distant from one another : about the beginning of July your first crop, if sown in March, will be fit for blanching, at which time you are to earth it up as you do celery, and in three weeks after it will be in a good condition for use. To have a regular succession of this plant, some seed must be sown every three weeks during the season, and your late crops may be preserved in winter as you do celery.

CAPSICUMS OR RED-PEPPERS, TOMATOES, AND EGG-PLANTS.

The different varieties of the capsicums, tomatoes, and egg-plants being in much estimation for culinary purposes, you should sow some of each kind now in pots, and forward them in your hot-beds, so as to have strong plants ready for planting out into the open ground as early in May as the night frosts shall have totally disappeared. Each and every of these kinds bear transplanting extremely well, and from this sowing you may expect early and abundant crops. For further particulars, see *April, May,* &c.

PLANTING OUT CABBAGES, BEETS, TURNIPS, ETC., FOR SEEDS.

As early in this month as the weather gets open and tolerably mild, plant out such cabbages, beets, carrots, turnips, parsneps, &c.,

as you have preserved during the winter to raise seed from; the cabbages are to be planted in rows four feet asunder, one foot distant from each other in the rows, and up to their heads in the earth; the others may be planted in four feet wide beds, at the distance of ten or twelve inches root from root, or in rows at pleasure; observing to tie up the shoots to stakes placed for that purpose, as they advance for seeding, to prevent their being broken down by winds, heavy rains, &c.

PLANTING POTATOES.

Potatoes may now be planted for an early crop as soon as the weather opens, and the frost is entirely out of the ground; let the soil in which you plant them be moderately light, a little enriched with dung, and advantageously situated.

Be careful to procure the earliest kinds, from which select a quantity of the best formed and soundest roots, and of a tolerable size; these are to be cut into sets, a week before planting, in order that the wounds should have time to form a dry crust; for if planted at this season immediately after being cut, they would imbibe too much moisture, many of them rot, and all would be greatly weakened thereby; cut each root into two, three or more pieces, according to their size; minding particularly that each cut be furnished with one or two good eyes or buds, which is sufficient. They are then to be planted in rows two feet and a half asunder, the sets to be nine inches distant in the row, and three or four inches deep. Should severe frost ensue protect them by laying some long litter or wispy dung over the drills.

HORSERADISH.

This plant is cultivated by cuttings of the root, either cut from the top an inch or two long, or some old roots cut into pieces of that length, or by small offsets that arise from the sides of the main root, retaining the crowns or top shoots or as many as possible.

Being furnished with these sets, choose in an open situation a light and rich soil, which trench regularly two spades deep, at the same time giving it a good dressing of manure; then beginning at one end of the ground, range a line, and with a large dibble make holes about ten inches deep, all of an equal depth and about six inches asunder, dropping as you go on, one set or cutting into each hole, with the crown upright, taking care to fill or close the holes up properly with the earth, and let the rows be two feet asunder. Or you may plant them as you advance in the digging or trenching of the ground, at the same depth and distances, covering each row when set in with the earth of the next course, and so proceed till all are planted. After this, level the surface of the ground even, observing to keep it free from weeds until the plants are so far advanced as to be strong enough to overbear and keep them down.

With this management the roots will be long, straight, and free from many small lateral offsets, and the second year after planting will be fit for use. It is true they may be taken up the first year, but then the roots will be slender; therefore it is the better way to let them remain till the second, when they will be in a fine condition; and if in taking up the roots you take care to leave some offsets still remaining, you will have a successional supply for many years.

LIQUORICE.

The *glycyrrhiza glabra*, or cultivated liquorice, is a plant that brings enormous profit to the industrious cultivator: it is of considerable importance in medicine, and consequently in great demand by the druggists and apothecaries; and also by porter brewers, being a very material ingredient in that article. Of 4000 quintals, or nearly two hundred tons, annually exported from Spain, the far greater part is considered to be purchased by the porter brewers of London. About Pontefract, in Yorkshire, England, where it is cultivated in great perfection, an acre of well-grown liquorice is considered to be worth one hundred pounds sterling; therefore, due attention should be paid to its culture in the United States, where it will grow to the greatest possible perfection; thereby to prevent the necessity of importing large quantities of it annually from Europe, at a considerable expense, and in a much inferior condition to what it could be had if cultivated at home. In hopes that this may be attempted by some spirited persons, who may have the welfare of their country, as well as their own at heart, I shall proceed to give the method of bringing this valuable plant to the utmost perfection.

The liquorice delights in a light sandy rich soil, which should be three feet deep at least, for the goodness as well as the profits arising from the culture of this plant is proportionate to the size and length of its roots. The ground in which you intend to plant it should be highly manured and well dug the autumn before, that the dung may be perfectly rotted and mixed with the earth. Immediately previous to planting, trench the ground three spades deep, if the natural soil be good that depth, and lay it very light. When your ground is thus prepared you should furnish yourself with fresh plants, taken from the sides or heads of the old roots, observing that each has one or two good buds or eyes, otherwise they are subject to miscarry. These plants should be from six to ten inches long, and perfectly sound.

The best season for planting them in the middle States is the latter end of March, or just when their buds *begin* to show symptoms of fresh vegetation, which must be done in the following manner, viz: first strain a line across the ground, then with a long dibble put in the roots so that the whole plant may be set straight in the ground, with the top about an inch under the surface, in a straight line, and about a foot or a little more asunder, and two feet distance from row to row. You may then sow a thin crop of radishes, onions, lettuces, or any other small-growing crops, in drills, between the rows, keeping the whole clean, particularly the rising plants of liquorice, during the summer and autumn. In the November following, you should carefully hoe and clean the ground. The shoots and leaves being then decayed, cut them off and spread a little rotten dung on the surface, the virtue of which will be washed into the ground by the rains, and the plants greatly improved thereby.

In the March following you should slightly dig the ground between the rows, burying the remaining part of the dung; but in doing this you should be careful not to injure the roots. Let nothing now be either sowed or planted between the rows, but keep them always clean; and in autumn, when the stalks of the liquorice are decayed, cut them down close to the surface of the earth as before.

The same work is to be repeated annually till the plants are three years old, when they will be fit for taking up—that is, slightly stir the ground every spring and autumn, keeping down the weeds in summer by hoeing—but after the first or second year the stalks will shoot so vigorously as soon to cover the ground and greatly retard the growth of weeds.

The proper season for taking up the roots is November, for they should not be taken up until the stalks are fully decayed, nor deferred till the sap begins to circulate afresh in spring, for in either case the roots would be apt to shrivel and diminish in weight, which would be a loss to the cultivator, as it is by weight they are always sold.

The method of taking up the roots is by trenching the ground, beginning at one side and opening a trench close to the first row, three spades deep, or to the depth of the roots, at which work three or four spadesmen are generally employed at a trench. One goes on with the top spit, a second with the next, and another with the third, and the fourth commonly gets to the bottom of the roots, having a mattock to assist him occasionally to clear them. As he takes them up he throws them on the top of the ground, and in this manner they proceed from row to row till the whole plantation is taken up.

The small side roots are then trimmed off, the best divided into lengths for fresh sets, which are to be carefully preserved in earth till the time of planting, if not planted immediately, and the main roots are washed clean, dried, and tied in bundles for sale.

When liquorice is intended to be cultivated on a large scale, the rows may be planted three feet distant, and the labor of hoeing performed with a small plough.

If not sold immediately after having been taken up, the cultivator must be careful not to suffer them to be put together in large quantities, lest they should become mouldy, as this vegetable, unless preserved in a dry place, is very liable to such corruption.

RHUBARB.

There are several species of this plant, but the *rheum palmatum*, or true officinal rhubarb, is that which merits particular attention. It is a native of China and Russian Tartary, has braved the climate of St. Petersburg, grows to good perfection in Scotland, as far north as Perthshire (lat. 56°); also in England, Turkey, and various other parts of Europe; is an article of considerable consumption, consequently of national importance, and highly deserving of attention in the United States.   It grows to the greatest possible perfection among the Tartarian mountains, from Selin to Thibet, without any other culture than what is afforded by the scraping of the Marmots; and shall we despair of bringing it to perfection where soil and climate are perfectly congenial, and nothing wanted but the enterprise of a few spirited individuals to make a commencement?   There is no doubt that if the culture of this and liquorice were duly attended to that the crops would more than amply repay the cultivators; and although a partiality to articles of customary culture is in the way, it is to be hoped that new and necessary plants will, from time to time, be introduced and cultivated with advantage to the individuals and the nation at large.

The following is the mode of its culture : Having procured a sufficient quantity of seed of the true kind, select a piece of light rich sandy loam, such as answers for asparagus, and after giving it a good coat of manure, trench it two or three spades deep, if the good soil admits; after which, level the top neatly and lay it out by line into squares of four feet, at the angles or intersections of which you are to form little circles with your finger about six or eight inches in diameter, and on each scatter a few seeds, then cover them with light fine mould three-quarters of an inch deep.   The seeds should be sown as early in spring as possible, or, if this had been done in November, they would vegetate in spring with more certainty.   When the young plants appear, keep them free from weeds, and in dry weather give them frequently a little water, but not much at a time; and above all things protect them from the mid-day sun till they get considerably strong, for, if exposed fully to this, during their infant state, few of them would escape destruction thereby.   Were you to place a piece of board on end, about fifteen inches broad and two feet and a half high, at the south side of each hill, leaning a little over the plants, this would answer the end effectually without depriving them of the benefit of the circulating air.   The first season is their critical period, having survived that they have nothing to fear afterwards.   Onions, lettuces, or any other low-growing crops may be either sown or planted in the intervals for the first year, so that they are kept at a proper distance from the young plants.   The supernumerary plants, one being sufficient to be left in each of these places for ultimate perfection, may be transplanted the spring following into new plantations, similarly prepared and at the same distance.

The November following, all the leaves being then decayed, cover the crowns of the plants two inches deep with earth from the intervals; and if there is danger of any wet lodging, throw up trenches, rounding the beds as is commonly done to asparagus, and for the first winter, lay some dry litter over the plants.   In the March following, strip the covering till you just perceive the tops of the plants, give all the ground a slight digging and dress it neatly after you, observing to keep the beds well hoed, and always free from weeds.

Thus proceed every autumn and spring, till the roots have four years' growth, when some of them may be taken up for use; but it is generally admitted that their medicinal virtues increase until they are eight or ten years old.

You must be very circumspect in the choice of ground; particularly, that it is not subject to lodge wet, for this plant by no means agrees with too much moisture, preferring a rich dry sandy loam to any other kind of soil.

Rhubarb may also be propagated by offsets from the old roots, or by sowing the seed in seed-beds, and transplanting them when a year old into such beds and at the same distances as before directed for sowing the seed; but they always produce larger and better roots when sown where they are to remain.

The proper time to take up the roots for use in autumn, after the leaves and stalks are totally decayed; when taken up, wash them clean, trim off the small fibres, and lay them in an airy place to dry, for four days, then rasp off the outward skin, which greatly obstructs the quickness of drying, from the pores not being laid open for the herbaceous moisture to exhale; the mere stripping off the bark will not be sufficient, the rasping it off, and the lacerating of the outward part of the root adjoining it will be necessary; for the lateral pores must be opened to permit the confined watery fluid to exude freely. Then cut them in slices, which string on pack-thread so as not to touch, and hang them up in a stove-room, to be kept constantly warm till they are effectually dry. Should the season even prove hot enough for drying them in the sun, the former method would be preferable, for, by exposing them so much to the sun and light, they would be greatly impaired in the color, and perhaps some of their finer parts dissipated thereby; but culinary heat is free from that objection, and at the same time possesses all the advantages of quick drying. The drying of the roots, without suffering them to get mouldy must be carefully attended to, as a neglect in this point would render all your former industry fruitless, and it is considered among the cultivators as a difficult task.

The marks of the goodness of rhubarb are, the liveliness of its color when cut; its being firm and solid, but not flinty or hard; its being easily pulverable, and appearing, when powdered, of a bright yellow color; on being chewed, its imparting to the spittle a deep saffron tinge, and not proving slimy or mucilaginous in the mouth.

The true officinal or palmated rhubarb has numerous root-leaves, large, rough, of a roundish figure, deeply cut into lobes and irregularly pointed segments on long, smooth, round footstalks. Stem-leaves, one at each joint, issuing from a membranous sheath successively smaller upwards. Flowers surrounding the branches in numerous clusters, and forming a kind of spike. Corolla or flowers of a greenish-white.

The species cannot be mistaken if you attend to its superior height, the ferruginous or reddish-brown color of the stem branches and petioles or leafstalks, the particular palmate form of the leaves, and the elegant looseness of the little panicles of flowers which display themselves on erect, round, hollow, jointed, slightly scored stems branching towards the top, and from six to eight feet high.

THE RHEUM RHAPONTICUM, OR COMMON RHUBARB.

This has a large thick root, which divides into many strong fleshy fangs, running deep into the ground; the outside of a reddish-brown color, and the inside yellow, from which arise several leaves, in number according to the size of the root; those come up folded in the spring, and afterwards expand themselves; they are smooth, of a roundish heart shape, having very thick footstalks of a reddish color, which are a little channelled on their lower part, but flat at the top. When the plant grows on very rich land, the footstalks of the leaves are over two feet long, and as thick as a man's wrist; the leaves also are often three feet long, and as much in breadth, having several strong longitudinal veins running from the footstalk to the borders of a deep green, and waved on their edges, having an acid taste, but particularly the footstalks, which are very frequently used, and much esteemed for tarts and pies. The flower-stalks grow from four to five feet high, and are terminated by thick, close spikes of white flowers. Its roots afford a gentle purge, but is of much inferior quality to the former, and may be cultivated the same way as directed for that. The best varieties are Myatt's Victoria and Linnæus, and Cohoon's Seedling.

TART RHUBARB (RHEUM RHAPONTICUM).

The seeds should be sown this month in a rich sandy soil; and if the plants come up too thick, thin them; a good method for doing so is to let them stand in stools four feet distant every way, two or three plants in each, as it is more convenient for blanching, which is very easily done in the following manner: clear the ground around them from the old leaves or stems, place a large size flower-pot or small keg over each stool, and then cover it about two feet thick all around with good warm manure, and it will be finely blanched by the beginning of May. Or the old plants may be bedded in soil in a warm cellar, before winter, in which case it may be had much earlier for use. The plants for this purpose should be three years old. Many persons do not take this trouble, but it will more than repay, being much greater in quantity and better in quality than if suffered to grow naturally, and the stalks used without blanching. It is much more esteemed now for pies and tarts than formerly, and is considered very wholesome for children: in many parts of England it is stewed and used as apple butter is here.

THE JERUSALEM ARTICHOKE.

The *helianthus tuberosus*, or tuberous-rooted sunflower, commonly called the Jerusalem artichoke. "This root," says Parkinson, an ancient English writer, "our ancestors boiled tender, and then being peeled, ate them sliced and stewed with butter, wine and spices—thus they were a dainty for a queen, being as pleasant as the bottom of an artichoke;" hence probably that name originated, as they bear not the least resemblance in growth to an artichoke.

The roots being the eatable part, are large fleshy tubers, much resembling a potato, are in perfection in autumn and all the winter, and are wholesome palatable food when properly dressed.

They are raised by sets or cuttings of the root, preparing the sets and planting them as directed for potatoes, in rows three feet asunder, four or five inches deep, and eighteen inches distant from one another in the rows: they increase abundantly, will thrive in any tolerable soil, and cannot easily be got out of the ground again, for the least bit will grow. It is a native of Brazil, and a striking instance of how tropical productions may gradually and successfully be introduced and naturalized in colder climates.

SOUTHERN STATES.

This is a very principal month in the southern States for gardening; all manner of work hitherto directed, may now be performed there successfully. In South Carolina and Georgia they may now sow the seeds of melons, cucumbers, squashes, tomatoes, egg-plants, okras, red peppers, &c., as directed in the kitchen garden for *April* and *May*.

THE FRUIT GARDEN.

PRUNING PEARS, PLUMS, CHERRIES, APPLES, ETC.

As early in this month as possible finish pruning your cherries and plums, also your apple and pear-trees before the end thereof, whether as espaliers, standards, or wall trees. Peaches, nectarines, apricots, almonds, quinces, &c., should also be pruned early in the month, if not done before. For the particular method of pruning espalier and wall trees, see the Fruit Garden for *January* and *February*, pages 32 and 142; and for that of the standards, the *Orchard*, pages 57, 150, &c. This should be particularly attended to, and the pruning of all kinds of fruit trees finished before their buds begin to push.

PRUNING AND TRAINING YOUNG APRICOT, NECTARINE, AND PEACH-TREES, ETC., FOR ESPALIERS AND WALLS.

Now is the only proper time to head down young wall or espalier trees, &c., preparatory to their first training; such as apricot, peach, and nectarine-trees planted against espaliers or walls any time since last October with their first shoots, from budding at full length, which, when a year old, should always be headed down low, to force out lower branches to furnish the wall or espalier properly, quite from the bottom.

This should be done just as the trees begin to swell their buds; therefore watch the opportunity, and let them be headed accordingly at the proper time.

The heads should be cut down to about five, six, or seven eyes or buds from the bottom; and if there are two shoots from the same stock let them both be cut down as above.

By this practice the trees will produce some strong shoots near the ground, whereby they will be furnished equally with branches from the bottom to the top of the wall or espalier. But if the trees were not to be headed down as above, they would run up with a stem like a standard tree, and not furnish any branches below, within two or three feet of the bottom; whereby the use of such part of the espalier or wall would be lost.

Such young apricot, peach, and nectarine-trees as were headed down a year ago, and having each produced three, four, or more shoots the last summer, should now have these shortened to such length as may encourage each shoot to produce two or three new ones the same season.

The method is this: let each shoot be shortened generally in some degree of proportion to its strength; in some pruning off about one-half or third of their original length; and in others a little more or less, according to circumstances of growth and situation of the trees; as for instance, shoots of about two feet may be cut to ten, twelve, or fifteen inches, or a little longer in strong growths; for the strongest shoots should always be left the longest; and those about twelve to fifteen or eighteen inches pruned to six, eight, ten, or twelve inches in length; and so in proportion to the different lengths and degrees of strength, and particular situation of the respective shoots. (See *January*, &c.)

By this practice each of these shoots will probably produce two, three, or four new shoots the succeeding summer, so that by October each young tree, so treated, will be furnished with from twelve or fifteen to eighteen or twenty shoots, or more.

The trees may then be pruned according to the method directed for the older trees of that sort, observing still to shorten the young shoots, but in such a manner as they may both produce fruit and a supply of young wood, as in the full-bearing trees aforesaid; that is, generally to prune the weaker shoots about one-half, the stronger ones prune about a third or fourth of their length, according to strength and where situated, and the situation of the blossom and wood-buds on the respective shoots; then nail them straight and close to the walls, or tie them to the espalier with willow twigs, &c., three or four to five or six inches asunder. (See *Fruit Garden* in *January*, &c.)

PRUNING AND TRAINING YOUNG APPLE, PEAR, PLUM, AND CHERRY-TREES FOR ESPALIERS AND WALLS.

Any young dwarf apple, pear, plum, and cherry-trees, lately planted against walls or espaliers, &c., or still remaining in the nursery with their first shoots, of only a year or two old entire, should now be pruned down to a few eyes that they may put out some good shoots near the ground, to furnish the bottom of the wall or espalier therewith.

If the heads of these trees are but one year's growth from the bud or graft, let them be shortened to four or five eyes; observing to do it just as they begin to form buds for shooting.

Suppose they are two years from the bud or graft, and the first shoots were cut down, as above, last spring; let the shoots which were produced from them the last summer be also shortened now to six, eight, or ten inches.

The same rule holds good with these at first training as mentioned for the apricots and peaches; for it is on shortening properly the first and second year's shoots, from the budding and grafting, that the whole success depends for forming a useful and handsome tree; as when a young wall or espalier tree is well furnished with branches near the ground, these will readily supply you with more, in their turn, to furnish the wall or espalier upwards.

But in the common course of pruning apples, pears, plums, and cherries, their shoots and branches are not to be shortened; for after the young trees are furnished with a proper supply of branches below, their shoots must then be trained to the wall at full length, only shortening particular shoots when more wood may be required to furnish that part, or where they grow too crowded; as directed in page 34, &c.

PRUNING FIG-TREES.

Some prune fig-trees the latter end of autumn, which is a very wrong practice, where severe winter frosts are prevalent; as the young shoots, which are *the only bearing wood*, are liable to be killed in hard winters. If they were pruned in that season, and no more left than what might then appear necessary, and severe frosts afterwards destroy many of them, you would have no resource left.

Therefore the better way is to let the trees remain unpruned till this time, and if some have been killed by the severity of the winter, there will be a chance, from among the whole, to find a sufficiency for your purpose, that have escaped. Observing, however, that the sooner this work is done, after the *severe frosts* are over, the better; for if delayed too long the trees would bleed, and be injured thereby; but in the southern States the late autumn pruning is preferable.

Fig-trees agree with, and in fact require, great heat; consequently in the eastern and middle States they will thrive and bear better when planted against walls, board fences, or espaliers, in warm exposures; therefore I shall give the method of pruning and training them to such.

In those southern States where they grow in the open standard way, they need no other pruning than keeping each on a neat single stem free from suckers, cutting out any dead or ill placed wood, thinning the young shoots where too crowded, but never topping any.

In pruning fig-trees, you must leave a sufficient supply of the last summer's shoots from the bottom to the extremity every way, in all parts where possible; and prune out the ill-placed and superfluous shoots thereof, with parts of the old bearers and long extended naked

15

old wood, to have due room to train the proper shoots, so that the tree may be equally furnished with a succession of young bearers at moderate distances; for these young shoots bear the figs the ensuing season; fig-trees always producing their fruit on the one year old wood only.

Leave the branches and shoots in general about five to six or seven inches asunder, all at full length; being careful to prefer the best middling strong shoots to retain for general bearers, cutting out the improper, superabundant, and useless old wood, quite close; pruning out any very rampant young wood, excessive long-jointed shoots, or very slender infirm growths, leaving the most promising and firm to supply the general expansion.

Take care always to train in every year some young shoots, at or near the bottom, that there may by a succession coming up regularly one after another, to supply the places of casual, long, old, naked branches, which will occur every season in some part or other of the tree; for such long-extended naked old branches or others, not furnished properly with young wood, should now be cut out, that there may be sufficient room to train the bearing shoots regularly and at proper distances.

In cutting out useless large branches, either too long extended or unfurnished with bearing wood, &c., let them be cut off close to the places from whence they proceed, to some convenient lower young shoots or branches, leaving no stumps.

The young branches of fig-trees must not be shortened or topped, but leave each at full length; for if they were, it would not only cut away the part where fruit would have appeared, but also occasion them to run much to wood, and thereby never produce half a crop; so only cut off casual dead ends.

The tree being pruned, let the general branches and bearers be directly trained in and nailed to the wall or fence, or made fast to the espalier in regular order, extending them horizontally, at equal distances, six or seven inches from each other.

PLANTING AND PROPAGATING FIG-TREES.

Plant fig-trees where wanted, this being rather the best month in the year for removing them ; they will now take root in a very short time.

In planting figs, you may either procure trained young trees that are arrived to a bearing state, and plant them at fifteen or twenty feet distance, or as they are propagated in general, either by the suckers which arise from the roots of the old trees, or by layers, or cuttings, young plants of these may be planted at once where they are to remain, that they may establish their roots more effectually without being disturbed by removal : therefore in default of trained trees, some good plants or suckers of moderate growth, and such as are firm and well ripened, may be procured and planted at once where they are to remain ; and others may be planted in the nursery, for training a few years.

To raise them by layers, select young branches of one or two years' growth, laying them in the earth four or five inches deep, with the tops as erect as possible; they will be well rooted by next spring, when they should be separated from the old tree and planted either in the nursery or where they are to remain.

To propagate them by cuttings, make choice of the ripest and most perfect of the last year's shoots, from twelve to fifteen inches in length, cutting them off with an inch or two of the two years old wood at their base, leaving the tops entire and uncut. Plant these cuttings six or eight inches deep, in good soil, and in rows two feet and a half asunder, and a foot distant from one another in the rows; here they may remain for two years when they will be in a fine condition for planting where wanted.

They may also be propagated by sowing the seed in long narrow boxes the beginning of this month, placing them in a hot-bed to forward their growth; and about the middle of May, remove these boxes into the shade where they can have the morning sun till ten o'clock, and the afternoon sun from four; giving them water when necessary, and protecting them the winter following from frost, either by placing the boxes of plants in the green-house, or in garden frames. When a year old they may be planted out as directed for cuttings, and treated afterwards in the same way. This will be the best method to obtain new kinds; the seeds of the imported figs will grow freely if properly treated; they are to be covered when sown only about the eighth of an inch deep.

Layers or cuttings are preferable to suckers, as they are not so subject to produce suckers from their roots, after being finally planted, as the others.

Fig-trees may be trained in half or whole standards, and planted detached in sheltered sunny situations, keeping them free from suckers, permitting their heads to branch regularly around, and they will produce ripe fruit in good perfection: they produce more and better in a strong dry loamy soil than in a sandy parched one (though in soil they are easily pleased, provided it does not lodge water); for when planted in the latter, they are subject to cast their fruit in May and June, which, under such circumstances, in some measure, may be prevented by frequent waterings at that season: where they thrive well, they usually produce two crops in the season; the first on the former year's wood, and the second on the young shoots of the present, which is generally the most abundant.

The following are the varieties of this fruit that are generally considered as best worth cultivating, and are placed in the order of their ripening.

1. The brown or chestnut colored Ischia fig. The fruit is very large, globular, with a pretty large eye, pinched in near the footstalk, of a brown or chestnut color on the outside, and purple within; the grains are large, and the pulp sweet and high flavored.

2. The black Genoa fig. This is a long fruit, which swells pretty large at the top, the lower part slender; the skin of a dark purple color, almost black, has a purple farina over it like that on some plums; the inside is of a bright red, and the flesh is very highly flavored.

3. The small white early fig. This has a roundish fruit a little flatted at the crown, with a short footstalk; skin, when ripe, of a pale yellowish color, and thin; the inside white, flesh sweet, but not highly flavored.

4. The large white Genoa fig. This is a large globular fruit, a little lengthened towards the stalk; skin thin, of a yellowish color when ripe, and flesh red.

5. The black Ischia fig. Fruit short, middle sized, a little flatted at the crown, skin almost black when ripe; flesh of a deep red, and highly flavored.

6 The Malta fig. Fruit small, compressed at the top; greatly pinched towards the footstalk; skin a pale brown color; flesh the same, and very sweet.

7. The Murrey, or brown Naples fig. Fruit large and globular, of a light brown color, with some faint marks of a dirty white; flesh nearly of the same color, and well flavored; grains large.

8. The green Ischia fig. Fruit oblong, almost globular at the crown; skin thin, of a green color, but when fully ripe it is stained through by the pulp to a brownish cast; flesh purple, well flavored, and will stain linen or paper.

9. The Madonna fig. Fruit long, pyramidal, and of a large size; skin brown; flesh a lighter brown, coarse, and of little flavor.

10. The common blue, or purple fig. Fruit purple, oblong, and small; the tree a great bearer and very hardy.

11. The long brown Naples fig. Fruit long, somewhat compressed at the crown; footstalks pretty long; skin of a dark brown when fully ripe; grains large; flesh inclined to red, and well flavored. The leaves of this tree are deeply divided.

12. The yellow Ischia fig. Fruit large, of a pyramidal form; skin yellow when ripe; flesh purple, and well flavored; leaves very large, and not much divided.

13. The small brown Ischia fig. Fruit small, of a pyramidal form, with a very short footstalk; skin of a light brown; flesh inclining to purple, of a very high flavor; leaves less divided than any of the other sorts.

14. The Gentile fig. Fruit middle sized, globular; skin, when ripe, of a yellow color; grains large, and flesh well flavored.

The preceding are all the varieties of the *ficus carica,* or common fig-tree. There are upwards of fifty other *species* of fig described by botanists, but these are generally cultivated either on account of their timber or as curiosities.

I have been the more diffuse on this article, as the cultivation of the fig and its different varieties is not as well known in the United States as other kinds of fruit-trees, and as it may be cultivated in the greatest perfection, particularly in the southern States, while in the northern, an abundance of fruit may be obtained if the branches be laid down in the winter and covered over six inches with soil.

HEADING DOWN FRUIT-TREES.

For the method of pruning and heading down the various kinds of fruit-trees which have shown symptoms of decay, in order to attempt their restoration to health and bearing, see the *Orchard* this month.

PRESERVING THE BLOSSOMS AND YOUNG FRUIT OF WALL AND ESPALIER TREES.

It often happens, that at too early a period in spring, we have a forward and untimely vegetation, which throws our early blooming fruit-trees, especially those in warm situations, into a full blow of blossoms, which, if afterwards attacked by frost, proves their destruction. In such cases some of the choicer kinds of wall and espalier trees should be defended therefrom with mats, &c.

The mats for this purpose should be of the largest size; one end of them should be fastened with nails or hooks to the top of the wall, and let them hang down over the trees. The lower end of the mat should also be fastened down to prevent their being blown to and fro by the wind, which would beat the blossoms off.

When the weather is mild the mats should be taken off, for it is only at night, in sharp frosts and cutting frosty winds, that the blossoms require to be thus sheltered.

Or, to preserve the blossoms and young fruit, you may occasionally stick the trees with the cuttings of hardy evergreen trees and shrubs, sticking them between the branches in a somewhat spreading manner, so as the leaves may afford some protection to the blossom, and which I have found to be often very serviceable.

This should also be done just when the trees are coming into blossom, having cuttings of the shoots and small branches of laurel, yew, pine, and some other hardy evergreens, preserving the leaves to them, and being placed between the branches in the manner before observed, so as to shelter those which are in blossom; they must be permitted to remain constantly till the fruit is fairly set as big as large peas.

PLANTING FRUIT-TREES.

Fruit-trees of all kinds may be planted any time this month when the weather is open, with success, but the sooner in the month the better, before they begin to shoot; they will now take root in a short time, and with the assistance of a little water in dry weather, will grow freely.

Let every kind be planted at proper distances, both for espaliers and walls, and also in standards, that they may have room to grow without interfering with each other in the course of a few years; which is often the case in many gardens, more particularly with wall trees and espaliers.

Peaches, nectarines, and apricots should never be planted nearer than fifteen feet asunder, against walls or espaliers; nor need they be planted more than eighteen or twenty feet distant.

Apples and pears, for walls and espaliers, should be planted fifteen to eighteen or twenty feet asunder; but, in some cases, twenty-five

feet is a more eligible distance, especially for some sorts of free-shoot-
ing pears; though it appears considerable at first, yet if grafted, &c.,
upon free stocks, they will readily fill that space, and bear considerably better than if confined so as to require to be often shortened to
continue them within bounds; however, generally allow those on
dwarf stocks not less than fifteen feet, the others eighteen or twenty
feet distant.

Plums and cherries designed for walls and espaliers should be
planted from fifteen to eighteen or twenty feet distance.

The above distances advised in planting the different sorts of wall
and espalier trees, appear great when the trees are first planted; but
in a few years the advantage of allowing them proper room will be
manifest; and it should be observed to allow trees planted against
low walls a greater distance than for higher, in order that in default
of height, there may be proper scope to extend them horizontally.

For the particular soil and situation proper for the different kinds,
see the *Fruit Garden* in *October* and *November;* and also the *Orchard*
in this month.

Having the ground previously well prepared, open a *wide* hole for
every tree about a spade deep, or according to the size of the root,
and loosen the bottom well. Then prune the roots of the tree, that
is, cut off bruised or broken parts, and trim the ends a little of all
the very long straggling roots in general, prune out irregular shoots
of the head, then place the tree in the hole, break the earth well and
throw it in equally about the roots, and when all is in tread the surface gently round the tree.

New planted fruit-trees should be well secured from the violence
of the wind; if they are all standards in exposed situations, let them
be supported with stakes, and if wall trees, &c., with large heads,
planted against walls and espaliers, fasten their main branches
thereto.

☞ As the seasons for planting out fruit and other trees differ so
much in the climates of the United States, and even in the same
place in different seasons, the only sure guide is to plant all kinds of
trees as soon as their buds *begin* to swell, or rather a little before.

GOOSEBERRIES AND CURRANTS.

Prune gooseberry and currant bushes, where they are not yet done;
but let this work be finished the beginning of the month.

Keep the branches thin and the middle of the trees open and clear
of wood, so as to admit the sun and air freely, by which means the
fruit will be large and well tasted. Observe the rules exhibited in
January, page 43, *February*, page 146, and also in *October*.

From the beginning to the middle of this month, is a good time
to plant gooseberry or currant-trees; the former particularly require
rich ground, plenty of manure, frequent culture about the plants,
and to be kept on one stem. The best form for a well trained standard gooseberry, or currant, is that of a wineglass; if you expect good
fruit, you must be particular to keep them free from suckers.

Manure and dig the ground between the gooseberry and currant trees, which, as they are just advancing in bud, will now be of great service, in promoting a plentiful production of large good fruit.

For the best methods of propagating gooseberries and currants, see the work of the *Nursery* for this month.

PRUNING AND PLANTING RASPBERRIES.

Prune raspberries, when not done before, agreeably to the directions given last month, page 146 ; let this be done as early in the month as possible.

You may now make new plantations of raspberries, where wanted. Observe that the young shoots or suckers, which arise every summer from the old roots, are to be chosen for this purpose. These should be planted in good ground, and in an open situation ; if you dig in some rotten manure, it will be of considerable service to the plants, and promote a production of large fruit.

In choosing the plants for this plantation, observe to select the outward young suckers of strong and robust growth, all of last summer's production, not less than two feet, but the more eligible if from three to five feet long, with strength in proportion—digging them up with full roots, preferring those with roots the most fibrous, for this is material in those plants; and, as sometimes one, two, or more buds appear, formed on the root near the bottom of the stem, for next summer's shoots, such plants are particularly to be chosen, if to be had.

Fig. 21.

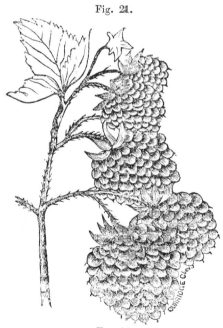

Fastolf.

Previous to planting shorten the shoots, cutting off about one-fourth of their length, trim the roots and cut away any old stumps or hard woody parts annexed thereto, then plant them in rows four feet and a half asunder, and from two to three feet distant in the rows; they will produce some fruit next summer, and more abundantly the second year, &c.

Fig. 22.

Dig the ground between your old plantations of raspberries after pruning, taking out the suckers, &c., as directed last month.

The Fastolf and Red Antwerp raspberries are among the most esteemed market varieties, and we therefore give their portraits.

Brinkle's Orange raspberry is considered one of the most desirable for private gardens, and has become much introduced.

Red Antwerp.

DIGGING THE FRUIT-TREE BORDERS.

Dig the fruit-tree borders as early in this month as you find the ground to work freely, previously giving them a good dressing of well rotted manure. This will be serviceable to the trees, the borders will appear neat, and be ready to receive any small crops, which may be proper to sow or plant therein.

STRAWBERRIES.

The strawberry plants will now begin to push, therefore the sooner they receive their spring dressing, after the weather becomes tolerably favorable, the better.

Clear the beds from weeds, and the plants from decayed leaves and old runners; it is most advisable to keep the plants in single bunches, clear of each other, so that there may be room to hoe between, and occasionally to dig round them with a narrow spade or trowel, by which means they will fruit in much better perfection than if crowded together.

The beds being cleared from litter, loosen the earth between the plants; and if you add a little fresh earth from the alleys, &c., to the beds, drawing it close to the plants, it will greatly strengthen them, and cause them to flower strong and bear plentifully.

Strawberries may be planted about the middle or latter end of the month, but if planted in September, or early in October, they would bear fruit the summer following; not but those planted now will take root freely and bear some fruit, but they will be few in comparison to those of the autumn planting; however, next year they will bear abundantly.

The proper sets for planting are the young offsets and runner plants of the last summer, which procure, of the strongest stocky growth, from beds of good plants that are in full perfection for bearing, and not from worn-out stools, taking them up with good roots.

Prepare for these plants a piece of good ground, either in the main quarters or in the borders; if loamy the better; and let some rotten dung be dug in. If in the main quarters, divide the ground into beds four feet wide, with alleys eighteen inches wide between them, or they may be planted in continued rows in the borders. Plant the strawberries of the scarlet kind fifteen inches asunder, and allow the same distance between plant and plant in the rows. But the large kinds, such as the hautboy and Chili, should be planted eighteen inches distant every way.

The Alpine or prolific strawberry, should likewise be planted fifteen or eighteen inches distant every way, that there may be room for their runners to spread and take root; this kind of strawberry being different in its manner of bearing from the others, for the runners often yield the largest and fairest fruit; this kind continues bearing ripe fruit from the latter end of May to October.

A farther supply of bearing strawberry plants in pots may still be placed in hot-beds and hot-houses, &c., to produce a succession of early fruit, and to afford a sufficient supply till those in the open ground ripen.

STRAWBERRY TILES.

A refinement in strawberry culture may be practised with advantage where expense is no object. *a*, a bed of young strawberry plants with the tiles placed around them. *b* shows the end of a bed, with

Fig. 23.

the tiles placed down without the plants. *c* shows the end of a bed with the fruit and foliage upon the tiles. It would be injurious to the plants to place these tiles around the plants early in the season, as they would deprive them of rain during the growing season; but, just as the blossom is appearing, it is an advantage, as the fruit would lie dry and clean on the upper surface. These tiles are so constructed, on flange-like edges, as to give a good circulation of air below.

FORCING FRUIT-TREES.

Continue the care of fruit-trees now forwarding in hot-walls and forcing-houses; such as peaches, nectarines, cherries, vines, &c.; let the fires be made every cold afternoon and morning, but regularly at night; and as the season advances in heat, and the sun's power increases, diminish the fires and admit more air; occasional waterings will be very necessary to encourage the fruit to swell and grow freely; but be particular towards the latter end of the month, when the sun gets powerful, to admit in proportion, and to manage the plants in every respect as directed in *February*, page 147.

THE ORCHARD.

PRUNING.

Finish pruning of all kinds of fruit-trees as early in this month as possible, according to the rules laid down under the head *Orchard* in *January* and *February*, to which I refer you for that, as well as other useful information.

In those parts of the Union where the winter is very severe and the weather changeable, autumnal pruning of fruit-trees is not advisable, particularly of stone fruit; for by pruning at that season, especially if many limbs are cut off, you are apt to bring on the canker. The exposure of the wounds, the almost dormant state of the sap, together with the additional check to its slow, but certain ascent to the extremities occasioned by the amputation of limbs, &c., predispose to mortification; whereas, in early spring, when the sap may be expected soon to follow the knife, the lips will quickly grow and heal over.

It is universally admitted, that the sap continues to flow, though slowly, in the milder parts of the winter days, and that it must rise continually during the winter months in evergreen trees, otherwise their foliage would wither; and also in deciduous trees (that is, such as shed their leaves in winter); because the branch of an evergreen tree will grow on a deciduous tree, and not lose its leaves in winter, as the Prunus Lauro-Cerasus, or European laurel, on a cherry; and the evergreen oak, on a common oak.

When pruning is judiciously done, and at a proper time, if the branches are small, a fresh bark and fresh wood will, in one season, completely cover the wounds; but if large, a time proportionate to the size will be necessary for their covering and healing; this process, however, is much accelerated by the application of a proper composition, which excludes the air and wet, protects the wounds from the effects of the various changes of the weather, the surrounding bark from any injury by insects of worms, and yields to its growth; all these ends will be effectually answered by an application of the *medicated tar* prescribed on page 58; and applied as there directed.

The following compositions have been much spoken of; I shall, therefore, publish them without any comments on their virtues, leaving the result to the experience of those who have, or shall have tried them; however, I must observe, that the methods of pruning old or decayed trees, recommended by MR. FORSYTH, and accompanying his instructions for making the composition, are very judicious, and should be duly attended to, whatever composition may be determined on for use afterwards.

ROYAL GARDENS, *Kensington*, May 11, 1791.

Directions for making a composition for curing diseases, defects, and injuries in all kinds of fruit and forest-trees, and the method of preparing the trees and laying on the composition, by WILLIAM FORSYTH.

"Take one bushel of fresh cow-dung, half a bushel of lime rubbish of old buildings (that from the ceilings of rooms is preferable), half a bushel of wood ashes, and a sixteenth part of a bushel of pit or river sand; the three last articles are to be sifted fine before they are mixed; then work them well together with a spade, and afterwards with a wooden beater, until the stuff is very smooth, like fine plaster used for the ceilings of rooms.

"The composition being thus made, care must be taken to prepare the tree properly for its application, by cutting away all the dead, decayed, and injured part till you come to the fresh, sound wood, leaving the surface of the wood very smooth, and rounding off the edges of the bark with a drawknife, or other instrument, perfectly smooth, which must be particularly attended to; then lay on the plaster about an eighth of an inch thick, all over the part where the wood or bark has been so cut away, finishing off the edges as thin as possible; then take a quantity of dry powder of wood-ashes mixed with a sixth part of the same quantity of the ashes of burnt bones, put it into a tin box, with holes in the top, and shake the powder on the surface of the plaster, till the whole is covered over with it, letting it remain for half an hour, to absorb the moisture; then apply more powder, rubbing it on gently with the hand, and repeating the application of the powder till the whole plaster becomes a dry smooth surface.

"All trees cut down near the ground should have the surface made quite smooth, rounding it off in a small degree, as before mentioned; and the dry powder directed to be used afterwards should have an equal quantity of powder of alabaster mixed with it, in order the better to resist the dripping of trees and heavy rains.

"If any of the composition be left for a future occasion, it should be kept in a tub or other vessel, and urine of any kind poured on it, so as to cover the surface; otherwise the atmosphere will greatly hurt the efficacy of the application.

"Where lime rubbish of old buildings cannot be easily got, take pounded chalk, or common lime, after having been slacked a month at least.

"As the growth of the tree will gradually affect the plaster, by raising up its edges next the bark, care should be taken, when that happens, to rub it over with the finger when occasion may require (which is best done when moistened by rain), that the plaster may be kept whole, to prevent the air and wet from penetrating into the wound."

ADDITIONAL DIRECTIONS FOR MAKING AND USING THE COMPOSITION.

To the foregoing directions for making and applying the composition, it is necessary to add the following :—

"As the best way of using the composition is found by experience to be in a liquid state, it must, therefore, be reduced to the consistence of pretty thick paint, by mixing it up with a sufficient quantity of urine and soap-suds, and laid on with a painter's brush. The powder of wood ashes and burnt bones is to be applied as before directed, patting it down with the hand.

"When trees are become hollow, you must scoop out all the rotten, loose, and dead parts of the trunk, till you come to the solid wood, leaving the surface smooth ; then cover the hollow, and every part where the canker has been cut out, or branches lopped off, with the composition , and, as the edges grow, take care not to let the new wood come in contact with the dead, part of which it may be sometimes necessary to leave ; but cut out the old dead wood as the new advances, keeping a hollow between them, to allow the new wood room to extend itself, and thereby fill up the cavity, which it will do in time, so as to make, as it were, a new tree. If the cavity be large, you may cut away as much at one operation as will be sufficient for three years. But in this you are to be guided by the size of the wound, and other circumstances. When the new wood, advancing from both sides of the wound, has almost met, cut off the bark from both the edges, that the solid wood may join, which, if properly managed, it will do, leaving only a slight seam in the bark. If the tree be very much decayed, do not cut away all the dead wood at once, which would weaken the tree too much, if a standard, and endanger its being blown down by the wind. It will therefore be necessary to leave part of the dead wood at first, to strengthen the tree, and to cut it out by degrees as the new wood is formed. If there be any canker, or gum-oozing, the infected parts must be pared off, or cut out with a proper instrument.

"Some months before the publication of the 'Observations on the Diseases, &c., in Fruit and Forest Trees,' I had tried the composition in a liquid state, but did not think myself warranted to make it public until I had experienced its effects through the winter. The success answered my most sanguine expectations ; and I have used it in that way ever since. By using the composition in a liquid state, more than three-fourths of the time and labor are saved ; and I find it is not so liable to be thrown off as the lips grow, as when laid on in the consistence of plaster ; it adheres firmly to the naked part of the wound, and yet easily gives way as the new wood and bark advance.

" The first time that I tried the composition in a liquid form, was upon an elm which had been planted about twenty years. It had been very much bruised by the roller, had several cavities in it, and was very much bark-bound besides. Having prepared the wounds, and applied the composition with a painter's brush, I took my knife and scarified the tree in four places; I also shaved off, with a draw-knife, all the cankery outer bark, and covered the whole tree with the composition, shaking the powder of wood-ashes and burnt bones all over it. A very heavy rain began in the evening and continued all night; yet, to my great surprise in the morning, I found that only some of the powder, which had not had time to dry and incorporate with the composition, was washed off. I now repeated the powder, and without anything more being done to the tree, the wounds healed up and the bark was restored so completely, that, three years ago, it could hardly be discerned where the wounds had been. The scarifications had also disappeared. Some of the wounds were thirteen inches long, eight broad, and three deep. Since the time when it was scarified, the tree has increased ten inches more in circumference than a healthy tree planted at the same time with it, about sixteen feet distant, which was not scarified."

BARNES'S COMPOSITION.

" Melt together in a large earthen pipkin, two pounds and a half of common pitch, and half a pound of common turpentine, then put in three-quarters of an ounce of powder of aloes, stir them all together, and set the matter on fire; when it has flamed a moment, cover it up close and it will go out, then melt it well and fire it again in the same way; this must be repeated three times (in the open air); after it has burned the last time melt it again, and put in three ounces of yellow wax, shred very thin; and six drachms of mastic, in powder; let it all melt together till perfectly well mixed, then strain it through a coarse cloth, and set it by to cool.

" When you use this composition, melt a small piece of it, and let it cool till it is just sufficiently soft to spread on the part where wanted, but it must not be laid on very hot."

When any of your old fruit-trees, which you particularly esteem, appear on the decline, and are grown thin of young wood, you may probably restore them by heading down such limbs as are in a bad state, to those parts where young shoot appear, and *close to the most vigorous;* but be careful not to do this generally the same season, for that would give too sudden a check to the sap, and in all probability destroy the tree totally. But if every other branch all over the tree were headed at proper lengths, each close to some young shoot, new healthy wood would be produced, which would soon come into bearing. The next spring after the first branches were headed, the remaining old branches may be cut out, as directed above; after which the head of the tree will be soon filled with bearing wood, which may afterwards be pruned as directed for other trees. This may be practised on either standard, wall, or espalier trees.

Peaches and nectarines will require to be treated with more caution than any other kinds; never head them lower down than you find young shoots or healthy branches, otherwise you will endanger their lives; and always cut close to the most vigorous of these, in order that the sap may be drawn that way, by which the wounds will heal and cover over. Indeed this caution will be generally useful, but more particularly with these.

When any of the trunks of your trees become hollow, cut out all the loose rotten wood, and also examine the roots, cutting off the injured, rotten, or decayed parts.

As you proceed in pruning, apply to the wounds either of the preceding compositions which you prefer, in the manner directed; but if your trees are annoyed with worms, the *medicated tar* is decidedly preferable.

Examine now your fruit-trees, particularly the peaches; and if annoyed by worms, either in their trunks, branches, about the surface of the ground, and a little under, pick out as many as you can with a sharp pointed knife, and with as little injury to the bark as possible; scrape off clean all the gum that appears on the stem or branches, and wash all these parts, and any other that you suspect to be infected with these insects or their embryos, with the corrosive solution described on page 149, which you may make twice or three times as strong as there directed, without the least fear of its injuring the tree; then dress the wounded parts with the medicated tar, as there directed.*

I have at the present time (January, 1805), and have had for several weeks, the roots of polyanthus-narcissuses, hyacinths, and other bulbs, growing in bulb-glasses, filled with a much stronger solution of the corrosive sublimate than that prescribed in page 149, and apparently in more health and vigor than those which are growing in pure water; I have also washed the leaves, stems, branches, and various kinds of tender plants with it, and poured it on the earth about their roots in large quantities, without any other effect than the destruction of the earth worms, and those which annoyed the plants.

Be very cautious not to leave any of the corrosive sublimate, or solution, in a careless manner in or about the house, for, with respect to animal life, it is a very active poison; so powerful that when administered medicinally, the quarter of a grain, being the two hundred and fortieth part of a drachm, is considered a sufficient dose for an adult person.

EXTENT, ASPECT, SITUATION, AND SOIL.

The extent of an orchard should be in proportion to the quantity of fruit required either for family use, distillation, cider, &c., or for public supply; and may be from half an acre to a hundred acres, or more.

As to aspect, that is not of as much importance as some people

---

* If a small mound be-formed around the base of peach-trees when first planted, composed of slaked lime and wood ashes, it will prevent these "borers" entering.

imagine, especially for apple, pear, and other hardy fruit-trees; for you will find these growing and bearing fruit in the greatest perfection in every aspect where the soil is suitable, and proper care taken of the trees; but the more tender and early flowering fruits, such as peaches and nectarines, &c., will require to be planted where they may have protection from the cold north and northwesterly winds; which, when accompanied by frost, often do considerable injury to their early bloom; and likewise, it will be necessary to give a warm exposure, especially in the eastern and middle States, to late ripening kinds, such as the heath-peach, &c., in order to bring their fruit to maturity in due season.

In the southern States a north aspect will be the most eligible for apple-trees, and perhaps for several other kinds.

With respect to situation, very thriving orchards are frequently found on high and low grounds, on declivities and plains, in various aspects and exposures; but this is in consequence of the natural soil being good; you should, however, avoid very low damp situations, particularly such as lodge water; for in very wet soils, no fruit-trees will prosper, nor will the fruit produced in such places be good; but a moderately low situation, free from wet, may be more eligible than an elevated ground, as being less exposed to tempestuous winds; but if having a gentle declivity the more desirable.

A proper soil being the grand and essential requisite, should be carefully selected, for on this depends much of your success; a good deep sandy loam, neither too dry nor wet, is the most suitable for all kinds of fruit-trees, and whether this be on high or low situations it should be preferred to every other. In the heaviest part of this ground you may plant apples and pears; in the lighter, plums and cherries; and in the lightest, peach, nectarine, and apricots. Gene-speaking ground that will produce good crops of natural grass, or kitchen garden vegetables, is suitable for an orchard; if of a loamy nature it will be a particular advantage; any soil, however, of a good quality, not too light and dry, nor too heavy, stubborn, or wet, and not less than one spade deep of good staple will be proper for this purpose.

Where the soil is naturally defective, such may be assisted by the application of proper manures and composts; applying them to the whole ground if but of moderate extent, or, if extensive, to the place where each tree is to stand, for the space of eight or ten feet in diameter, working it up with the natural soil.

This trouble, however, in extensive orchards would be very expensive; therefore those who have choice of ground should be very careful to fix upon a proper soil, such as would require but little assistance.

PREPARATION OF THE GROUND.

The preparation of the ground, for the reception of fruit-trees, is either by digging a spacious place for each tree, a general trenching of the ground, or by ploughing it. If the latter kind of preparation is intended, and that the ground has been under pasture for some years, you should plough the greensward the spring before you plant the trees, and also two or three times in the course of the summer following, to rot the sward, pulverize the earth, and to prevent the growth of weeds.

Early in October you should plough it again very deep, running the plough twice in each furrow, in order to make it deep and loose for the roots of the trees; which should be planted therein in the course of the same or next month; but if the soil be moist, March will be a much better season.

Or you may plough as above, eight or ten feet wide for each row of trees, leaving the remainder of the ground untouched.

In planting orchards on a grass ground, in very good soil, you may dig a hole for each tree capacious enough for the easy reception of all the roots, loosening the bottom well without disturbing any other part of the ground; but when it is trenched either wholly, or some considerable width along the place of each row of trees, it will consequently prove of disproportionate advantage.

Your orchard should get a good dressing of manure, once in two or three years, whether under crops of grain, or grass; this will prove very serviceable to the trees, and also more than repay your expenses in the abundance of the succeeding crops. If the ground is suffered to be exhausted by successive crops of fruit and grass, or grain without refreshing it occasionally by manure it will soon, if not extremely fertile, become unfit to produce either.*

Tillage is favorable to the growth of young trees; whereas in grass-ground their progress is comparatively slow for want of the earth being stirred about their roots, and being frequently injured by grazing stock. Where circumstances will allow it is best to plant fruit-trees on newly broken-up ground, and to cultivate the soil (refreshing it with manure as often as necessary), until the trees are well grown; then to lay it down to grass; for after that period the shade of the trees would do less injury to it than to any other crop; and besides, the pending boughs would render tillage inconvenient.

CHOICE OF TREES, ETC.

If not provided with trees in your own nursery, you must apply to some public nursery-man of integrity, who will not deceive you in the varieties of the kinds wanted: observe in the first place that the trees are healthy and fresh looking, without any blemishes or appearance of canker or worms in the bark; that they have been raised at proper distances, and not drawn up spindling; that their heads are well formed and well furnished; that their stems are stout, proportionate to their heads, straight, clean, free from suckers, and that they are not more than from two to four years old from the bud or graft, and that all have been worked, that is, budded or grafted, for otherwise, there would be no certainty of having good fruit, and besides, there would be much longer coming into bearing.

* There is little doubt but this want of nourishment is a primary cause of the supposed wearing out of many, otherwise, valuable orchards.

These are important objects, and such as you cannot be deceived in. Never make choice of larger trees nor higher in the stems than six feet, especially for general plantations, for they never thrive as well as young trees, and are subject to be dashed about by the wind after planting.

The next object is to see them taken up with care, so as to preserve all their roots as entire as possible; when taken up, prune off any broken or bruised parts of the roots, shorten long stragglers, and top the ends of the principal roots in general with the knife; always observing to prune these roots on the under side, and sloping outwards.

Let several varieties of each particular kind be chosen, such as ripen their fruit at different periods from the earliest to the latest, especially when they are wanted for the table; but by much a greater number of autumnal and late ripening kinds, than of the early sorts, particularly of the apples; for the early ripening fruits are of short duration, and only proper for temporary service. When you want apples or peaches for distillation, or cider-making, choose proper juicy kinds for that purpose, and quantities proportionate to your intentions.

METHOD OF PLANTING.

If the trees have been already trained so as to have full branching heads, they must be planted with those entire, only retrenching or shortening any irregular or ill-placed branches or shoots that take an awkward direction, or that grow across others or such as run considerably longer than the generality of the others, either cutting them clean off, close to the places from whence they proceed, or to some young shoot or small leading branch, as may appear most eligible for giving the tree an open spreading form, leaving no stumps or spurs.

Should you not be able to procure trees having furnished and well formed heads, and you are obliged to take such as are thin of wood, and running up tall, plant them, having their roots dressed as before, but without touching their heads for the present. So soon after planting as their buds begin to push, head them down to within six, eight, or ten inches of the place where you wish them to branch out for forming their heads; they will then throw out young vigorous shoots, which you may afterwards train and thicken, or make thin at pleasure, by judicious pruning in the following years; or should any of these young shoots in the course of the succeeding months take too great a lead of the others, you may top them in July, which will stop their rampant growth, and cause them to throw out side shoots that will still enlarge a foundation for numerous branches, and not carry off too much of the sap from the others.

Should it happen that any of your trees have large heads and but few or scanty roots, reduce their tops by a select and judicious pruning to a due proportion with their roots; for an ox fed only through a wren's quill, could not long exist. This will seldom happen, unless by accident or carelessness in the taking of them up, provided they are raised at proper distances in the nursery.

16

The arrangement of the trees in the orchard should be in rows, each different kind of fruit separate, and at distances proportionate to the nature of their growths. Apple and pear-trees may be planted at fifty feet distance every way; cherry and plum, at from thirty to forty; peach, nectarine, apricot, almonds, and quinces, at from twenty-five to thirty feet; and at still greater distances, if you are not limited in extent of suitable ground, and you intend to raise various crops between the trees. Pear-trees on quince stocks may be planted ten feet apart, and the other kinds on dwarf stocks, at half the distance, as mentioned above for each kind.

You should have great regard to the distance of planting the trees, which is what few people have rightly considered; for if you plant them too close, they will be liable to blights; the air being thereby pent in among them, will also cause the fruit to be ill-tasted; for a great quantity of damp vapors from the perspiration of the trees, and the exhalation from the earth mixed with it, will be imbibed by the fruit, and render their juices crude and unwholesome; besides, it is the opinion of some well informed naturalists and orchardists, that these vapors and perspiration of the trees, collect the heat of the sun, and reflect it in streams, so as to cause what is called a fire-blast, which is extremely hurtful to fruit, and most frequent where the orchards are open to the south sun.

Having your trees in readiness, proceed to stake or mark out the ground, according to the above or greater distances, placing a small stake or mark where each hole is to be made for the reception of the trees, which, if made *to range every way*, will have a very agreeable effect, admit the currency of air and sun's influence more effectually, and make the orchard still more convenient for tillage.

A wide circular hole must be dug for every tree, capacious enough to receive all the roots freely without touching the sides, but by no means of a greater depth than the natural good soil; if you make a deep hole, basin like, into the clay bottom, or unfriendly sub-soil, which is too frequently done, and plant the roots therein, even filling it round with good earth will not do, for as soon as it pushes its roots beyond this, they must enter into the bad and unfriendly soil, which will not fail to bring on the decay of the most healthy tree, and can never afford it suitable juices for perfecting delicious fruit; besides the lodgement of water about the roots in this confined basin in wet seasons, will cause the tree to become sickly, and to get overrun with moss, and full of canker.

When the holes are all ready, proceed to planting, placing a tree in each, having its roots trimmed as before, one person holding the stem erect, whilst another casts in the earth, previously breaking it small; let it be settled in equally between all the roots, by gently and frequently shaking the tree a little up and down, which will cause the mould to settle in close about all the small roots and fibres; and also to raise the tree gradually up, that the crown of the roots may not be more than about three or four inches below the general surface, even in the deepest soil. When the hole is filled up, tread it gently, first round the outside, then near the stem of the tree; forming the surface a little hollow, to admit of giving water, if found

necessary, with more convenience; and if on the top of all is laid
some inverted turf, and stones over this, to the width of the holes,
forming it into a sort of circular bank, it will support the tree, and
guard the roots from powerful heat, drought and parching winds;
observing that each tree stands perfectly upright, and that they
range exactly in their proper rows.

Should the earth be rather shallow, so that you cannot cover the
roots a sufficient depth with good soil, you must have some hauled
for that purpose to where each tree is to be planted, or collected to
such places, from the general surface, and bank the roots around
therewith; for there is no alternative between planting them in the
good soil, where their roots can take a wide extended horizontal
direction, and lie within the reach of the genial influence of heat,
rain, dew and air, and that of an untimely end if planted too deep.

When you desire to remove large trees of any kind, the best
method will be to open trenches about their roots, immediately previous to the setting in of the frosts leaving as much earth around
them as you think can be conveniently moved or carried with the
trees, cutting at a proper distance the large wide-spreading roots,
and leaving only as many uncut as are sufficient to prevent their
being blown down; when you find the earth sufficiently bound by
the frost, work in under, and take them up with the balls, place
them on a sled, and so carry them to their place of destination; previous to planting, smooth all the wounded parts, and prune or thin
their tops in proportion to their loss of roots.

When a defect in an old orchard is to be supplied, it will be necessary to take away the earth where the old tree stood to a proper
depth, and to the extent of a circle of ten feet in diameter, which fill
up with fresh earth previous to planting; for it seldom happens,
without this management, that young trees thrive, when planted
where old disordered ones stood.

If the orchard is much exposed to winds, it will be proper to stake
the new planted trees, to support them in their proper positions, and
secure them from being rocked to and fro thereby, which would
greatly retard their rooting—placing one or two strong tall stakes to
each tree; but in large trees, the most effectual method is to have
three stakes to each, placed in a triangle, meeting at top near the
head of the tree, wrapping a hay-band around that part of the stem,
to prevent its being barked by the stakes or ties; then tie the stakes
at top close to the tree, with some proper bandage, bringing it close
about the stem and stakes together, over the hay-wrapping, to secure
the tree firmly in an erect posture.

If your young orchard is laid down with grass, no cattle should
be turned into it to graze at large; unless each tree is previously well
secured with posts and railing, otherwise they will bark the trees, to
their very great injury, and eat off the tops of such of their young
shoots as they can reach; nor should large cattle be turned into any
orchards where the branches of the trees are yet low and within their
reach.

Where great quantities of fruit are wanted, large avenues of apple,
pear, peach, and cherry trees, &c., may be extended across neighbor-

ing fields, which will render them pleasant, and produce abundance
of fruit; or there may be single rows planted to surround fields, &c.,
which will be found extremely profitable, if in an honest neighborhood.

You may now plant the boundaries of large orchards with English
walnuts and Spanish chestnuts; these will not only afford you an
abundance of fruit, but protect the trees in general from the power
of tempestuous winds. A small quarter of the orchard may be
allotted to filberts, mulberries, medlars, berberries, &c., and this is a
proper time for planting them.

For the method of raising and propagating all kinds of fruit-trees,
&c., see the *Nursery* for this and the preceding month; and also
July.

THE VINEYARD.

The *Vitis vinifera*, or common wine-yielding *Vine*, is a native of
the warmer regions of Asia: it is found to be most successful in the
temperate climates, or between the 30th and 50th degrees of north
and south latitudes.

It is cultivated in the greatest perfection in the Island of Madeira,
lat. 32° north; and in every part of Europe as far north as the fif-
tieth degree of latitude; also at the Cape of Good Hope, about lat.
33° 50′ south, as well as in every corresponding parallel in Asia and
the civilized parts of Africa: yet there are people among us who
seem to despair of its being possible to cultivate it successfully in the
United States, and who by this kind of despondency publicly expressed, discountenance its cultivation. We have similar climates,
and as suitable soil and situations, as are to be found in any of the
countries where this plant is cultivated, and what to attribute this
infidelity to I am at a loss to know.* What do they perceive insalu-
brious in the air, or unfriendly to vegetable life in the soil of America, any more than in trans-atlantic countries; or are they led estray
by prejudiced European writers, whose envy, or want of knowledge,
or perhaps both, had prompted them to assert, that neither animals
nor vegetables arrive at as good or as great perfection in America as
in Europe? However, a little time and some industry will show
that this prejudice is erroneous, and that the *vine* can be cultivated
in the far greater part of the *Union*, to immense national, as well as
individual advantage.

The *vine* was originally introduced into Europe from *Asia Minor;*
and even in the days of *Lucullus*, the Romans were seldom able to

---

* The extreme variation of temperature in the northern States checks the
circulation of the sap, and produces mildew in the European kinds. They
can be and are, however, grown under glass to as great perfection as in
any part of Europe. Our native sorts are now being improved by fresh
seedlings, and there is now no doubt but our own country will soon equal
the finest quality.

regale themselves with its juice, very little wine being made at that time within the compass of *Italy;* and the foreign wines which they imported from *Asia* were so dear, that they were rarely introduced at an entertainment, and when they were, each guest was indulged only with a single draught. But in the seventh century of Rome, as their conquests augmented the degree of their wealth, this luxury was sought after with avidity, and wines became the object of particular attention. In the progress of their conquests, the westerly parts of the European continent was at once subjected to the *arms* and enriched with the *vines* of *Italy ;* its cultivation went on but slowly for some time in these countries, where it has since become a staple article of great national importance, perhaps occasioned by the same kind of doubts, fears, prejudices, and apprehensions that now operate against it in the United States; but these at length were surmounted by the industry of a few cultivators who had penetration enough to perceive its practicability, and who, no doubt, were amply remunerated, in consequence of being first in market with large quantities : others perceiving their fortunate success, copied their examples in expectation of obtaining like profits. Similar to this will be its progress in America, and those who first commenced the business by planting on an extensive scale, will assuredly reap the richest harvests.

The culture of the vine for some time will be an experimental business with us; however, the first object is to obtain the kinds that will immediately, or soonest, accommodate themselves to the different regions of the Union; perhaps those from Madeira, or the Cape of Good Hope, would best suit in the southern States; those from the south of Europe, in the middle; and those from Burgundy, Champagne, Switzerland, Bordeaux, or the banks of the Rhine, in the eastern States. Trials of this kind should be made, and the result carefully attended to; and, indeed, each and every of the States should give a fair trial to the vines of every country, from whence they can be procured; by which means, and by which only, they can discover those best adapted to their respective soils and climates.

There is not the least doubt but the vines of a temperate climate can be naturalized in any State in the Union in a very short time : for there is an astonishing facility in plants to accommodate themselves to soil and climate, and in very few more than in the vine. The *helianthus annuus,* or common annual sunflower, is a native of *Mexico* and *Peru;* and yet we all know that it now grows in every part of the Union where introduced, as well as if it were indigenous. The *helianthus tuberosus,* or what is commonly called the *Jerusalem artichoke,* is a tropical plant, being a native of *Brazil,* and is become naturalized to our climates, as well as to those of Europe, as far north as St. Petersburg, and perhaps farther. The cherry-tree, when first introduced into *Italy* by *Lucullus,* a Roman general, from the city of *Cerasus,* in *Pontus,* whence its name *Prunus Cerasus,* was there treated as a tender exotic; by degrees it had crept into *Britain,* where it was treated for some time in like manner; and experience now proves that it thrives in *America* as well as in *Italy, Britain,* or *Pontus* itself. Thousands of other instances could be adduced of the wisdom and goodness of the Creator in furnishing plants with those accommodating powers; but the vine has manifested itself in so many, and so universally, that it is unnecessary to recapitulate them; yet we frequently meet with people who say "it will *never* succeed here!!"*

It may, however, be proper to remark, that where the peach-tree perfects its fruit in open field culture, so will the vine; the latter is even capable of bearing greater degrees of heat, and of producing fruit in perfection in higher latitudes than the former, manifested by the quantity of wine made in many places in the south of England, from its productions in open vineyard culture; whilst there they could not have a single peach from a thousand trees cultivated in the same way, principally owing to the want of a sufficiency of summer heat to ripen the young wood; and mild as their winters are, in comparison to ours, they, under such circumstances, generally destroy the pithy and unripened shoots of the peach, without doing near so much injury to those of the vine. On the other hand, it is well known that the grape-vine will bear fruit abundantly, year after year, when forced in pine stoves, with pine-apples, where, if a peach was introduced, it would scarcely survive one season; at least it would not produce a single fruit worth eating the second.

Before entering on the general culture, I shall give a short description of the varieties of the grape hitherto cultivated in Europe, either for making wine, or for the table; many of which are now under trial at the *Spring-Mill Vineyard*, within fourteen miles of Philadelphia, the property of a company incorporated by the legislature of Pennsylvania, "for the promotion of the culture of the *vine*," and under the superintendence of Mr. Peter Legaux, an experienced vine-dresser, and a gentleman of worth and science.

These I shall divide into three classes, in the order of their ripening. 1. Those which ripen earliest. 2. Those which succeed them; and 3. The latest coming to maturity. Perhaps the first class might be best adapted for the more immediate culture in the eastern States; the second in the middle; and the third in the southern States. But, experiments on all the kinds that it is possible to procure, should be tried in each State of the Union; giving, at the same time, suitable soil and situation to each class, according to their periods of ripening; that is, to give the latest kinds the warmest exposure, &c.

FIRST CLASS.

1. The *White Frontinac*, or *Muscat Blanc*, is a high flavored grape, and has a peculiar rich juice when perfectly ripe; the bunches are large, and the berries, which are round, are very closely joined to each other, whereby some of them in wet seasons are apt to rot before they are ripe, which, in some measure, is owing to the thinness of

* Notwithstanding the sanguine expectations of our author, it has now been proved by experience that the exotic grape will not thrive and grow to perfection in our changeable climate, excepting in the most favored localities.

their skins: those who wish to have them in the best perfection, will thin them out when about the size of peas, whereby the air will have free admittance, and those which are left, will be larger and higher flavored.

2. The *Blue*, or *Violet Frontinac, Muscat Violet.* This has a small black berry, powdered with a fine blue or violet bloom, and is of an exalted vinous flavor. The berries grow close upon the bunches, which are very small.

3. The *White Sweet Water.* This is a very large round white grape. The berries grow close on the bunch, which is of a moderate size, and are replete with an agreeable juice. The skin and flesh of this grape are more delicate than of any other sort. The berries on the sides of the bunches next the sun, are clouded with spots of a russet color.

4. The *Black Sweet Water.* The berries of this variety are much smaller than the former; are black, roundish, grow in small, short, close bunches, and are replete with a very sweet juice.

5. The *Brick Grape.* The berries of this kind are small, inclining to an oval figure, and of a pale red or brick color. This is a very sweet grape, though not much admired.

6. The *White Muscadine*, or *Chasselas Blanc.* This is a round white berry, moderately large, with a thin skin and delicate juicy flesh. The bunch is well formed and of a pretty good size. This is an early grape and a great bearer.

7. The *Munier*, or *Miller's Burgundy Grape.* The berries are small, black, rather inclining to an oval figure, and grow close on the bunch, which is commonly short and small. The skin and flesh are delicate, possessing a sweet and pleasant juice. The leaves are distinguishable from most others by a hoary down, especially when young, being then almost white. This is an excellent bearer, and a principal grape to be cultivated for wine.

8. The *Small Black Cluster.* The berries and bunches of this grape are little different from the former, but the leaves have less down, and are smaller. This is a delicate sweet fruit, and is sometimes called the Burgundy grape.

9. The *Early Black July Grape, Morillon Noir*, or *Hatif Noir.* This has a small black round berry, replete with a sugary juice; the bunches also are small, and thin set but it is also a prolific bearer, and comes to the table at an early period.

10. The *Early White Grape*, from *Teneriffe.* The berries of this variety are round, white, and of a moderate size with thin skins and delicate juicy flesh, of an extraordinary sweetness. The berries and bunches much resemble the common Muscadine, to which it appears to have a near affinity.

11. The *Auvernat Noir* of *Orleans, Pineau* of *Burgundy*, or *True Burgundy Grape*, sometimes called the black morillon, is an indifferent fruit for the table, but is esteemed one of the best for making wine. It is of a middle size, somewhat of an oval, and of a fine black color; the bunches are longer than Miller's Burgundy.

SECOND CLASS.

12. The *Aleppo Grape.* This is a middle-sized, roundish grape, with a thin skin and delicate juicy flesh, of an exquisite vinous flavor. The color is commonly very various, some of the berries being white, others black, but the major part are curiously striped with black and white; but what appears most remarkable is, that the colors do not intermix, but are divided by straight lines as if painted. The leaves of this sort are in the autumn very curiously striped with red, green, and yellow, somewhat similar to the Aleppo lettuce.

13. The *Grizzly Frontinac.* The berries of this grape are round, tolerably large, and their color brown and red, intermixed with yellow. Both this and No. 1 possess a high, musky, perfumed flavor.

14. The *Black* or *Purple Frontinac,* or *Muscat Noir.* The berries of this variety are black when ripe, and covered with a kind of powder, which gives them a purple hue; are moderately large, round, and of a most exquisite flavor. They compose very long bunches. This has formerly been called the red Frontinac, and is one of the very best grapes. It is called at the Cape of Good Hope the black Constantia.

15. The *Red Frontinac,* or *Muscat Rouge.* This is a very fine grape and greatly esteemed. The berries are of a brick color, thin skin, moderate size, and juicy delicate flesh.

16. The *Black Hamburg.* The berries of this variety are large, inclining to an oval figure, and of a black color. They hang loosely on the bunch, and compose well-formed handsome bunches. The skin is thick, and the pulp hard; but, notwithstanding, it is a very valuable grape, being a good flavored fruit and a plentiful bearer.

17. The *Red Hamburg.* The berries of this sort are of a dark red, with thin skins and juicy delicate flesh. The size and figure of both the berry and bunch are nearly like the former. It is sometimes called the Gibraltar grape.

18. The *Malvoise.* The berries of this are small, rather inclining to an oval figure, and of a brown color. The skin is thin, and the flesh delicate, replete with a vinous juice. As the berries are powdered with a blue bloom, it is sometimes called the blue Tokay.

19. The *Genuine Tokay.* This is a white grape. The berries incline to an oval figure, and grow rather close on the bunch, which is of a moderate size. The skin is thin and flesh delicate, abounding with a very agreeable juice. This variety is very distinguishable by the foliage, the under side of the leaf being covered with a fine soft down, having the appearance of satin.

20. The *Lombardy Grape.* This has a large berry inclining to an oval figure, of a beautiful flame color. The bunches are regularly formed with shoulders, and frequently arrive to the weight of six or seven pounds. The leaves are much more divided than most other sorts, and the upper surface is of a deep green color. This is by some called the Rhenish grape, and by others the flame-colored Tokay.

21. The *Smyrna Grape.* This has a large red-colored berry of

an oval figure, with thin skin and delicate juicy flesh.   It forms long branches, with shoulders loosely connected.   The leaves in autumn die with purple edges.

22. The *Alicant*, or *Black Spanish Grape*.   The berries of this variety incline to an oval shape, are moderately large and black, and form exceedingly long unshouldered bunches.   The flesh is soft, juicy, and of an agreeable flavor.   The leaves in autumn are beautifully variegated with red, green, and yellow.   This is a pretty good fruit, and is sometimes, though incorrectly, called the Lombardy grape.

23. The *Black Muscadine*.   The berries and bunches of this variety are somewhat smaller than those of No. 7.   This is a very prolific grape, and makes a fine appearance on account of the black berries being powdered with a bluish bloom; but the flesh is not so delicate and juicy as the former.

24. The *Royal Muscadine*, *D'Arboyce*, or *Chasselas Blanc*.   This has a round white or amber-colored berry, of a moderate size, a thin skin, and a juicy soft flesh.   The bunches are generally exceeding large, sometimes arriving to six or seven pounds.   This variety is very distinguishable by the wood and foliage, generally growing remarkably gross and strong, and is considered an excellent table grape.

25. The *Malmsey Muscadine*.   This seems nearly allied to the preceding, but the bunches and berries are somewhat smaller, and the juice of a higher flavor, being remarkably sweet.   This is a good bearer, a very fine grape, and said to be one of those of which the Madeira wine is made.

26. The *Claret Grape*.   The berries of this are small, black, and inclining to an oval figure; they grow close and form small bunches. The juice is of a blood-red color, of a harsh taste, excepting the grapes are perfectly matured, and then it may be considered as an agreeable and delicate fruit.   The leaves change from green to a russet-red early in summer, and die a deep red in autumn.

27. The *Large Black Cluster*, or *Lisbon Grape*.   The berries are large and grow more oval than the two former varieties, which are black, and not so delicate, the juice being of a harsh and rough taste.   The leaves in autumn, when on the decline, change to a beautiful bright scarlet.   This is the grape of which the red port wine is made.

28. The *White Morillon*.   This has an oval white berry, of a moderate size, with thin skin and delicate juicy flesh   It grows close on the bunches, which are small.   The leaves are soft, being greatly covered with down on the under side, somewhat similar to the genuine Tokay grape, to which it appears nearly allied.

29. *Cat's Grape*.   This has a small oval berry, of a greenish-white color, with a thin skin and soft juicy flesh.   The berries grow close, forming small bunches.   The taste of this fruit before it is quite matured is disagreeable; but when perfectly ripe is very sweet and pleasing to some palates.

30. The *St. Peter's Grape*.   This has a pretty large berry, inclining to an oval form, and of a deep black color when ripe; the skin is thin, and the flesh very delicate and juicy.   This vine pro-

duces large shouldered bunches, and the leaves are much more divided than those of most other sorts.

31. The *Black Grape from Palestine.* This appears nearly similar to the preceding, but may probably be a distinct variety.

32. The *White Parsley-Leaved Grape,* or *Ciotat.* This is a variety of the parsley-leaved grape. The berries are round, white, of a moderate size, with thin skins and delicate juicy flesh, which is very sweet but not of a vinous flavor. The branches are of a pretty good size, almost similar to the white Muscadine. The leaves are finely divided, differing from any other sort. There is a variety of the parsley-leaved grape which produces *red* berries.

33. The *Black Lisbon Grape.* This has a large globular berry, black, thin skinned, and juicy. It has also large shouldered bunches, which not a little resemble the black Hamburg. This is a good grape.

34. The *Greek Grape.* The berries of this variety are of a moderate size, rather inclining to an oval figure, of a bluish-white color, and grow close, forming moderate sized handsome bunches. The leaves grow on very short footstalks, and bear a resemblance to those of the *Sweet Water.* It is a delicate and justly esteemed fruit.

35. The *White Corinth Grape.* This has a white, round berry, rather small, with a thin skin and very delicate juicy flesh, of an agreeable flavor. The bunches too are rather small. The berries, when perfectly ripe, are transparent, so that the seeds appear very distinctly.

36. The *White Muscat* of Lunel. The berries of this are large and oval, and when perfectly ripe are of a fine amber color, somewhat clouded with brown or russet, especially on the side next the sun. The skin is thin and the flesh delicate, replete with a vinous juice. As this grape is a very plentiful bearer, and forms pretty large bunches, it may justly be deemed a valuable sort.

37. The *Red Chasselas,* or *Chasselas Rouge* is very like the Chasselas Blanc, No. 6, in size and shape, but is of a dark red color. It is a very good grape, but ripens later than the white.

THIRD CLASS.

38. The *White Muscat of Alexandria,* or *Alexandrian Frontinac.* The berries of this are large and oval, the bunches long, and, when perfectly ripe, are of a fine amber color; the skin thick, pulp firm, the juice rich and vinous, and of a high musky flavor; the berries hang loosely, ripen well, and are in great estimation.

39. The *Red Muscat of Alexandria.* This resembles the former, only the berries are red; it is a most excellent grape, and highly worthy of cultivation.

40. The *Black Damascus.* The berries of this are large, round, and of a fine black color; the skin thin, the flesh juicy, and of an exquisite flavor. The same bunch commonly consists of different sizes; the small berries are without stones, and the large ones contain only one in each berry; this is an excellent sort.

41. The *Black Tripoli Grape.* This grape seems nearly allied to the black Damascus, but the bunches are always composed of large berries of an equal size, and with one stone in each. This circumstance of the berries being equal in size, renders the bunches of a more agreeable appearance ; the foliage in both are exceedingly beautiful in the fall, assuming a reddish hue, and very similar : this is a very good grape.

42. The *Red Grape from Syracuse.* This is a very large grape, of a red color and oval figure, somewhat irregularly formed ; the berries hang together loosely on the bunches, which are pretty large : this is a most excellent grape.

43. *Le Cœur Grape,* or *Morocco Grape.* This produces large berries in figure somewhat heart-shaped, and of a tawny grizzly color. The bunches are often composed of unequal sized berries, some of them exceedingly large ; these never contain more than one stone each, and the lesser-sized berries are always without stones. The footstalks of the berries are short, and singularly large, differing from most other sorts. This is a much esteemed grape.

44. The *Golden Gallician.* The berries of this variety are large, and of an oval figure ; the flesh hard, but of a tolerable flavor : these, together with the footstalks, are of a light yellow color.

45. The *Black Muscadel.* The berries of this are large, oval, and of a black color ; the skin thin, with a delicate juicy flesh. The same bunch contains berries of different sizes, some of them very large and long, but somewhat compressed at the ends : the leaves change in autumn to a beautiful scarlet.

46. The *Red Muscadel.* The berries of this sort are large, oval, and of a beautiful red color ; the skin thick, and the flesh hard, something like the raisin grape. The bunches frequently arrive to five or six pounds, and are most elegantly formed of berries of an equal size. This is one of the largest grapes. The leaves change in autumn to a beautiful red and green.

47. The *White Grape from Alcobaca.* This has a large oval, white berry with a thin skin and juicy flesh ; the bunches are large and long, without shoulders.

48. The *White Hamburg.* This has an oval berry, with a thick skin and hard flesh. As this variety is a plentiful bearer, and forms large bunches, it is much admired by some, but is not so valuable as either of the two preceding kinds. It is sometimes called the *Portugal Grape.*

49. The *Syrian Grape.* The berries are white, large, and of an oval figure ; the skin thick, and the flesh firm and hard ; the bunches well formed, and enormously large. Though this is generally considered as a coarse fruit, it has properties that ought to introduce it into every large collection. It is very prolific, and the bunches commonly grow very large, sometimes to upwards of twelve pounds, making a most beautiful appearance, and, when well perfected, may be called a very eatable fruit; they may without difficulty be kept many weeks longer than any other kind. This grape requires a very warm exposure.

50. The *Black Raisin Grape.* The berries of this variety are

oval and black, with a thick skin, and a hard, firm flesh. It forms long, handsome bunches.

51. The *White Raisin Grape*. The properties of this grape are nearly similar to the preceding, but the berries are white.

52. The *Damson Grape*. The berries of this variety are very large, oval, and of a beautiful purple color. They grow loose on the bunch, which is large. The leaves of this grape are large, and more thick and succulent than those of any other sort, and have something of the appearance of green leather.

53. The *Cornichon Grape*. The berries of a remarkable shape, about an inch and a half long; their breadth not half an inch. They taper from the stock, but not in a regular manner, and end in a blunt point, according to the French, something like a horn; but its figure is more like the long end of a small fish's bladder. The berries are white, with a thick skin, and a firm, sweet flesh.

54. The *New Muscat of Jerusalem*. This variety has large, round berries of a red color, nearly as large as middle-sized gooseberries.

55. The *Black Prince*. This has fine, large, black berries and the bunches grow to a large size, frequently to a pound and a half.

AMERICAN SPECIES OF VINE.

The following species of the vine are indigenous in America.

1st. The *Vitis sylvestris*, or common bunch grape.

2d. The *Vitis vulpina*, of Bartram; *V. Labrusca*, of Linn., or fox-grape.

3d. The *Vitis taurina*, of Bartram, or *Vitis Vulpina*, of Linn.; commonly called the bull or bullet grape.

4th. The *Vitis serotina*, or winter grape, by some called the Bermudian grape.

There are several varieties produced by the intermixtures of the above with one another, or with the varieties of the *Vitis vinifera*, which are called hybrids or mules; the most noted are, 1. Alexander's or Tasker's grape; 2. Bland's grape; 3. That called the Raccoon grape. And now may be added the Catawba, Isabella, Diana, Concord, Rebecca, Canadian Chief, &c., &c. From either of these hybrids, it is probable that good wine may be produced; but I shall leave that to the experience of those who have made, or wish to make the experiment.* At the same time, I would suggest the idea of grafting some of the best European kinds on our most vigorous native vines, which, no doubt, would answer a very good purpose.

SOIL AND SITUATION.

The first and most important thing to be considered in planting a vineyard, is the choice of *soil* and *situation;* for on these depends

---

* These experiments have since been carried out, and have proved eminently successful. There is now more than three million bottles of wine manufactured in the State of Ohio annually, principally from the Catawba. The improvement of our native grapes is progressing wonderfully.

much of the ultimate success. That best adapted for a vineyard, is a light, rich, deep loam; on a chalky, limestone, flinty, or gravelly bottom; it should be naturally from one to two feet deep, of good mellow earth, or made so by art; a deeper soil is unnecessary for any tree or shrub whatever, that is not cultivated on account of its roots; and although vines may shoot more vigorously in such, and produce a greater quantity of fruit, which, by the bye, is very questionable, yet they ripen later, and their juice is more crude than that of those which draw their nourishment from earth within the influence of the sun, air, rains, dews, &c.

The situation should be on an elevation inclining to the south, southeast, or southwest; and if having all these exposures, the better, as the various kinds could have different situations according to their natures and necessities. The ground should have a gradual descent, that the moisture may be drained off; but if too rapid, it will be more difficult to labor, as the plough cannot then be used; and besides, it will be less retentive of manure, and consequently will require a greater quantity, and more frequently administered. If at a *distance* there are large hills, or elevated woods, to defend it from the north and northwesterly winds, the better.

The immediate neighborhood should be open; and, if hilly, towards the north and northwest, the better   it should be free from swamps, or widely extended woods; for, under such circumstances, the air would frequently be replete with too great a quantity of moisture, occasioned by the perspiration of the trees, and the exhalations from the adjoining swamps, whereby both vines and fruit would be greatly subjected to what is called the mildew.   It has been observed in the middle States, particularly by Mr. Peter Legaux, of Spring-Mill, near Philadelphia, that the more easterly the exposure, the more are the vines and fruit liable to become mildewed; and that, in a southwest exposure, they are less subject to it than in any other.

Those who wish to cultivate grapes for the table only, and that have not the advantage of the kind of soil above described, need not despair of having good fruit for that purpose, as vines will grow and bear well in any dry and tolerably rich ground; that is, neither sandy nor light to excess, nor too clayey or binding; for a tolerable stiff loam will do well enough, with the assistance of good culture.

PREPARATION OF THE SOIL.

Having made choice of soil and situation, the next thing to be done is to prepare it for planting; in doing of which, the following method is to be observed: In the *spring*, if the soil is not naturally rich, give it a good coat of well-rotted manure, or compost; and immediately plough it in as deep as can be done, with *four or six stout horses or oxen*, and a strong plough; after it has lain a month, cross harrow it, and cleanse it from stones and the roots of noxious weeds. About the middle of June, cross plough it again as deep as possible; in three weeks after, harrow it, and clear off all the roots of weeds and large stones. Towards the latter end of August, plough it again, and harrow as before. In November, give it another very deep ploughing, and let it lay so all winter, without harrowing. As early in the month of March, following, as you find it sufficiently dry, and in good state for tillage, but not before, plough it *across the hill*, and as deep as you can, running the plough twice in each score : then harrow it well, and you have it in a fine state for planting.

In some ground, and very frequently in that extremely well adapted to the culture of the vine, the declivity is too great to cultivate it with the plough; in which case it must be done with the spade, and other manual implements; and it would be well if such land could be thrown or banked up into terraces, each capable of receiving one, two, or three rows of vines, the better to retain the necessary manure and moisture.

PREPARATIONS FOR PLANTING, ETC.

Being provided with a number of four feet stakes, in proportion to the quantity you intend planting, and made as directed in *January*, page 60, mark out your ground in rows ranging north and south, as well as east and west, by placing those stakes at intervals of six feet distance every way, so as it may be convenient to plough and harrow between the rows in these directions. This is meant for a south exposure; but in others, they are generally arranged up and down hill as well as across; though the former direction may be given to the rows in any situation, and perhaps with more advantage as to ease of culture, and benefit of the sun.

Six feet plant from plant, every way, will not be too great a distance, however it may appear at first view; especially in a country where Providence has been very bountiful in blessing its inhabitants with abundance of ground, as well as with everything else that tends to make an industrious man happy; for if planted too close, there will not be room for the sun and air to pass freely between the rows, to ripen the fruit, and dry up the moisture and autumnal damps, which would otherwise be imbibed by the fruit, and render it crude and insipid; and more particularly so when their stocks grow large, and their branches proportionably extend themselves on each side.

The next thing to be considered is the choice of proper sorts. It is worthy of particular notice, that the best grapes for eating are, for the most part, the worst for making wine. This is agreeable to the practice of cider-makers, who always prefer the rough, juicy, and austere kinds of apples to those that are considered best for the table, and also to that of the most skilful *Vignerons* of Europe, who are very particular in selecting such kinds of grapes whose juice, after being pressed and properly fermented, affords a vinous, rich liquor.

The *Auvernat Noir*, or true Burgundy grape, is the kind most preferred, and in the greatest repute in *Burgundy*, *Champagne*, *Orleans*, and most of the vine countries in France. The *Munier* is also in great repute; but as far as I have yet observed, I have seen no kind more likely to answer for making good wine in America than

the *Constantia*, or Cape of Good Hope grape,* and with either of
these the claret grape, to heighten and enliven the color, when red
wine is intended to be made.

But as this business is yet in its infancy here, and as the difference of soil and climate is well known to make a material change in
the produce of the same kind of grape, experiments must be made
on the various sorts, in order to ascertain which may best answer the
purpose.†

I shall now proceed to the different methods of propagating the
vine, and then to its planting.

PROPAGATION IN GENERAL.

The vine admits of being propagated in various ways: first, by seeds;
secondly, by layers; thirdly, by cuttings; and fourthly, by "eyes,"
or buds. This tree can also be propagated by grafting, inoculation,
and inarching.

Propagation by seed is undoubtedly the way to raise new kinds,
but is seldom practised, on account of the length of time and hazard
of obtaining better, or even as good kinds, as the original grapes
from whence the seeds were taken; but this should never deter, for
superior kinds may be obtained, and a seedling vine, *judiciously*
managed, will produce fruit in about seven years, or perhaps sooner.

PROPAGATION BY SEED.

When you raise vines from seed, always be sure to do it from the
very best kinds. The grapes for seed should be permitted to remain
on the plant until they are perfectly ripe. As soon as the seed is
taken from the pulp, it should be laid in some airy, but shady place,
to dry, and then carefully preserved in sand till spring. If, however,
the seeds were immediately sown in pots, and preserved in a hot-
house, green-house, or under the protection of glasses, till spring,
they would then more freely vegetate. Or, sow the seed in February
or March, and plunge the pots into a temperate hot-bed; when the
plants appear, they will require, from time to time, gentle sprinklings
of water, and protection from frost and cold. When so far advanced
as to have three or four joints each, they must be carefully staked
out, and planted each in a separate pot.

The greatest care will be required in the performance of the above
operation, as it will be beneficial to preserve as much of the earth to
the roots as possible; then plunge the pots into a gentle hot-bed;
give the plants a little water and occasional shade from a strong sun
till they have taken root; after which give them plenty of air occasionally, so as to inure them to the open weather, and have them fit

---

* This grape was imported from the Cape of Good Hope, some years ago,
by Mr. LEGAUX, of *Spring Mill*, Pennsylvania, before mentioned, who for
several years past has made wine from it, of a most excellent quality, and
also from the *Munier*.

† The Catawba is at present the best wine grape of America.

to turn out of the pots in July, with the balls of earth, wherever they are intended to remain; and from thenceforward they may be treated exactly in the same manner as recommended hereafter for plants raised from cuttings, only that they will require some slight protection from the frosts of the ensuing winter.

PROPAGATION BY LAYERS.

When the vine is intended to be propagated by layers, the best shoots of the preceding season that can be most conveniently brought to the earth, are to be chosen for that purpose. After making the ground light and fine with the spade, each shoot must be fastened with a hooked stick about five or six inches below the surface, with the tops somewhat erect, and cut so as to leave but two buds above ground; this work may be done at any time when the weather permits, from the middle or beginning of October till the end of March, or rather until and at the time of spring pruning; for, if done much later, the top of the layer where cut, and even the parts bent in the operation, would bleed, which would injure it considerably. Some give them a slit where inserted into the earth, but they will root freely with or without such.

During summer, if the weather proves dry, a little water occasionally would be of use to them, just as much as will keep the ground in a moist state. The autumn, or spring following, the layers may be taken off from the mother plants, their tops pruned, the extreme ends of the stems beyond the young roots cut off close to them, and so planted where they are to remain; but I would prefer doing this early in March.

This is a very useful and necessary operation when any of your plants in the vineyard are bad kinds, or in an indifferent state of health, for you can extend the end of a long shoot from a neighboring plant to where the bad plant was, or stands, entering it into the earth as before where you wish it to grow, and the next season you will have a fine vigorous plant; observing then to detach it from the mother vine by cutting off the connection close to its new established roots; or you may lay it all the way in the earth from the mother plant to where you desire its top to grow, and in a year disconnect them near to the old plant; this will be the better way, provided you lay it in deeper than the ordinary culture to secure it from being disturbed thereby. This the French call *Provigner la vigne*.

PROPAGATION BY CUTTINGS.

The method of propagating the vine by cuttings is in more general practice than by that of layers, and very justly; for plants raised in the latter way are found to be much inferior to those raised by cuttings, both in point of vigor and durability.

The particulars necessary to form a good cutting are principally these: 1st. The eye or bud should be large and prominent. 2d. The shoots moderately strong, round, and short jointed. 3d. The texture of the wood should be close, solid, and compact; but the best criterion of its maturity is its solidity, and having very little pith; it is absurd to expect good success or prosperous plants from wood imperfectly ripened.

Unskilful persons frequently choose remarkably strong shoots for cuttings; the extraordinary size is one of the least necessary requisites; indeed, exceeding strong shoots generally abound too much with pith, and are too long jointed to claim a preference.

In the proper pruning season, which, in the middle States, I conceive to be the latter end of February, or first week in March, much earlier in the southern States, and very little later in the eastern— take your cuttings from the old vines, near to where they were produced; cut off the lower end of each in a sloping manner, half an inch below a bud, and the upper end, in like manner, an inch above one, having the slope on the opposite side of the bud, and leaving the cutting from twelve to sixteen inches long; but twelve is sufficient, if short-jointed, and furnished with at least four or five good buds.

There can be but one *prime* cutting obtained from each shoot, though many persons cut these into several lengths, and plant them all, which should not be done except in cases of necessity, for the upper parts are never so well ripened as the lower, on account of these being produced at an earlier period, and having the advantage of the whole season to perfect their maturity. The upper parts being soft and spongy, admit the moisture too freely, which often preven s their growth, and even should they succeed they will not produce fruit so soon, nor will they bear so abundantly for many years as those whose wood is close, compact, and already organized for fructification.

Some people recommend taking off the cuttings with an inch or two of the two years' old wood annexed, but this is unnecessary, and even injurious, unless the species of plant which you are propagating is extremely pithy and spongy, like the fig; for the nearer we approach to nature's method by having as little old wood as possible about the root of a young plant, the better.

When the cuttings are thus prepared they should be laid in trenches close to each other, in some dry part of the vineyard, and covered with earth to within two inches of their tops, where they are to remain till you are ready to plant them; covering them in frosty or parching weather with some loose dry litter, which is to be taken off every mild day, that they may the more effectually be inured to the open air. This is the best method of preserving them, even during the entire winter. I do not approve of keeping cuttings for any length of time in close, dark, unventilated cellars; for in such places they become weak, blanched, tender and sickly, and seldom succeed well when planted out; besides, they have nothing to imbibe whilst there but foul air, which vitiates their juices, and brings on diseases and bad health.

17

GRAFTING GRAPE-VINES.

From the Horticulturist.

Fig. 24. Fig. 25. Fig 26.

Having had some experience in grafting the vine, I am desirous of informing your readers of my mode of procedure. I have visited several vineries in this State, and having had conversation with the proprietors, I have learned from them how very important it would be to grape-growers to be able to change one variety for another by an easy and sure way of grafting.

My practice is as follows: I try to have the eyes of my stock and scion swell at the same time. This I do by putting my scions in wet sand, and leaving them in the vinery. As soon as the eyes move, I take a sharp knife and cut my scions wedge-shaped, leaving only one eye. I next take my knife, holding the point down, making an incision in the stock as at 2, 2, Fig. 24; the scion is cut as at 3. I then fit my scion into the stock, as at Fig. 25, being careful to have the bark of both in close contact. I next tie with strong bass mats, and cover all over with grafting wax, as at Fig. 26, to prevent air and moisture getting to the incision.

This mode of grafting has the advantage of having the stock bearing fruit while the scion is making bearing wood. I have worked two vines this season, in the forcing-house of Mr. Joseph Breck & Son, and they are beginning to grow.—*Bonnard Denis*, Brighton, Mass.

METHOD OF PLANTING.

Having your ground prepared and marked out with stakes, as before directed, and your cuttings in readiness, so soon after the middle of this month as you find the soil dry and in good order, proceed to planting, in the following manner: Take up a number of your cuttings carefully, without injuring the buds, and place them in a bucket of dung water about six inches deep, the bucket having a handle for the convenience of carrying it from place to place; then, at each stake, make a hole with a spade, about a foot deep, and as wide as you please, but it will be better to have all these holes made the day before you commence planting; into each put one strong cutting, placing it a little sloping, and so deep that the second bud from the top may be just on a level with the general surface; immediately fill the hole with earth, pressing it gently with your feet to the cutting, and drawing the *loose* earth around so as to cover the second bud, before noticed, half an inch deep, which bud, so protected, will frequently make the most vigorous shoot, and often succeed when the top bud, exposed to the weather, will not; then drive down the stake, so as to make it firm, within three inches of the plant.

If your cuttings are not extremely good and fresh, and such as may be depended on, it will be the more certain way to plant two in each hole, the tops within a few inches of each other, and the lower ends sloping in opposite directions for the greater convenience, if both should succeed, of removing one without disturbing the other; these extra plants may be made use of next season to fill up vacancies, or to form a new plantation.

Cuttings are generally preferred for this purpose to rooted plants, as they are thought to establish themselves more effectually when not removed; however, when such are to be planted, keep their roots out of ground but as short a time as possible; and if immersed when taken up in a pap of earth and water, or dung and water, the better: plant them in the same manner as directed for the cuttings, pruning their heads, and observing to place their roots, after first shortening any long stragglers, in a spreading manner in the earth, and then cover them up as before.

It is necessary that each particular kind of grape should be planted in separate quarters, that they may all be gathered when ripe without injuring others; for, when planted in a mixed, confused way, the going through the different quarters to pull the fruit of a vine here and there is very inconvenient, and often the later ripening intervening kinds are injured thereby.

If your ground is intended to be cultivated, after planting, with the plough, you must leave sufficient head lands for the horses to turn in.

In the course of this month, as soon after pruning as the ground is dry and in good condition for tillage, plough and harrow between the rows of your former plantations of vines, previously giving such quarters as need it a dressing of well rotted manure; and dig, or give a deep hoeing to such places as cannot be come at with the plough.

THE NURSERY.

GRAFTING.

It is too difficult a task to state the precise time of grafting the various kinds of fruit and other trees, in the different climates and States of the Union; but as I cannot do this with precision, and must confine myself, in this article, to the periods most suitable for performing that operation in the Middle States, where I am best acquainted with the seasons, I will give such hints as will lead to a perfect knowledge of the true periods for grafting in every country and every place.

The best time for grafting, in the Middle States, is generally from the twentieth of March to the tenth of April, a few days earlier or later, as vegetation may happen to be in an advanced or retarded state, which sometimes makes a difference of ten or twelve days.

Grafting is always most successful when done at the period that the buds of your stocks are swelled, so as to be nearly ready to burst into leaf; this is the time in which the greatest success may be expected, and should be very particularly attended to; however, if done a few days before, or even when the stocks display several expanded leaves, there may be a tolerably good hit, provided the operation is judiciously performed.

Your scions or grafts must be taken off about a month or three weeks before this crisis, or so soon as you are able to perceive the least disposition in their buds to swell; for, if not cut off in proper time, the grafts will not take kindly, nor will they shoot so vigorously.

The proper sorts to begin with, in respect to fruit-trees, are cherries and plums, and, if you please, peaches, nectarines, and apricots; but the latter kinds are generally propagated by budding or inoculation. Pears, filberts, and apples may be grafted at the same time; but the latter may be deferred for ten days longer than either of the former, provided the scions were taken off in due time; pears will also agree with tolerably late grafting.

Before I proceed to the methods of grafting, it will first be necessary to mention what stocks are proper to graft the different kinds of fruit upon; for instance, apples should be grafted upon stocks raised from the kernels of the same kind of fruit; that is, any kind of apples; for the grafts or buds of these trees will not take well upon any other stocks.

It should be observed that for dwarf apple-trees for walls or espaliers, or for small standards, they should generally be grafted upon codlin apple stocks, raised either from suckers from the root, or by cuttings or layers; for the stocks raised from these are never so luxuriant in growth as those of the larger growing apple-trees; and consequently trees grafted upon such stocks will be slower in growth, and can more easily be kept within due compass, and will answer the purpose for dwarfs or espaliers, &c., much better than those grafted on larger growing kinds. Or, if required to have them of still more dwarfish growth for small gardens, you may use stocks of the Dutch paradise apple and Siberian crab, &c.

But for the general supply of apple stocks for common standards and large espalier-trees, they are raised principally from the seed of any sort of apples or wild crabs.

Pears are generally grafted or budded upon stocks raised also from kernels of any of their own kinds of fruits, or occasionally upon stocks raised from suckers; they likewise are very commonly grafted upon quince stocks, whereby to have trees of more moderate growths, to form dwarfs; and which are generally raised by seed, cuttings, layers, or suckers; and the pears grafted or budded upon these stocks are very proper for walls or espaliers, and occasionally for small standards. Sometimes also pears are grafted upon white thorn stocks; but this is improper for any general practice, not being so successful, and never producing so good fruit, as if grafted on stocks of their own family.

Cherries are propagated by grafting or budding them upon stocks raised from the stones of the common black or red cherry, or upon stocks raised from the stones of any other kind of the same fruit; but the first two are most esteemed for that purpose, because they generally shoot much freer than any other.

Plums are grafted or budded on stocks raised by sowing the seeds of any or either of the plum kinds; but those raised from the vigorous growing sorts are most preferable; they are also grafted on stocks raised from suckers, but such should not be used unless when seedling stocks cannot be had. Plums will likewise take on the apricot, but then the trees are not permanent.

The apricot proves the most durable on stocks of the plum kind. It will also grow on its own, and on peach and almond stocks; but on either of the last two it will not be durable.

For peaches and nectarines, several sorts of stocks are occasionally used; such as plum, peach, almond, and apricot stocks, all raised from the stones of the fruit, and the first kind from layers and suckers also. If a plum could be procured of such vigorous growth as to keep pace with the peach, it would be an acquisition of infinite importance; for on such, the peach would be as permanent as the plum itself. In Europe, all their peach-trees are worked on the plum; but with us, the growth of the peach is so rapid as in a few years to overgrow the stock, when wrought on any of the kinds of plum which we have yet procured. The kind particularly selected for this purpose in Europe is the muscle plum.

Almonds will take and grow on any stock which answers for the peach.

Medlars will grow on either medlar, white-thorn, pear, or quince stocks; but those of its own genera are preferable.

Filberts will succeed by budding or grafting on the common hazelnut tree, raised either from the nuts or by suckers from the roots.

The first thing to be done towards this work is to select the grafts, in the choice of which, the following directions should be observed. 1st. That they are shoots of the former year; for, when they are older, they never succeed well. 2d. Always to take them from *healthy fruitful trees;* for, if the trees from which they are taken be sickly, the grafts very often partake so much of the distemper, as rarely to get the better of it, at least for some years; and when they are taken from young luxuriant trees whose vessels are generally large, they will continue to produce strong shoots, but will be a long time coming into bearing, and are seldom so productive, as those which are taken from fruitful trees whose shoots are more compact, joints closer together, and whose system is already organized for bearing. 3d. You should prefer those grafts which are taken from the lateral or horizontal branches, to those from the strong perpendicular shoots, for the reasons before given.

When your grafts are cut off, open shallow trenches in a dry sheltered situation, and place them thinly therein, with their cut ends down, drawing up the earth so that they may be covered two-thirds of their length; then lay some light litter thinly over their tops to prevent their drying. If a small joint of the last year's wood be taken off with the scion, it will preserve it the better; for the old wood being more compact than the new, will prevent its imbibing too much moisture from the earth whilst kept there, and that can be cut away when you take them up for grafting. If grafts are to be carried to any considerable distance, it will be proper to pack them up in earth, and surround them with damp moss, if but a small quantity, to prevent its drying too soon.

Always prefer stocks which were raised in the nursery from seed; next to these, those raised from layers and cuttings; and, last of all, such as were produced from suckers; for the last will continue to throw up suckers from their roots, much more abundantly than any of the former, to the great annoyance of the borders, garden, or orchard, which are not only unsightly, but they also take off a great part of the nourishment from the trees.

When you intend to change the fruit of an old espalier or wall-tree, always graft on fresh healthy branches, and as near the trunk as such are to be found; ten or a dozen grafts may be necessary to furnish the tree, the more immediately, with the kind or kinds desired. For a standard, six or eight scions will be sufficient to answer a similar purpose, always observing to cut out the far greater part, if not the whole, of the old branches, previous to grafting, and the remainder, as the young grafts advance in growth.

For this purpose, you must be provided, 1. With a strong knife to cut off the heads of the stocks previous to the insertion of the grafts. 2. With a neat, small hand-saw, for occasional use, in cutting off the heads of some large stocks, for crown-grafting. 3. With a grafting-chisel and small mallet, for clefting large stocks, for the reception of the scions in cleft-grafting. 4. With a neat and very sharp pruning-knife for cutting and shaping the grafts, and for sloping and forming the stocks for their reception; and 5. With a quantity of new bass strings; or, if bass cannot be had, with soft woollen yarn, to tie the parts close, secure the grafts, and thereby to promote their speedy union with the stocks.

The next thing to be provided, is a quantity of grafting clay, which should be prepared at least ten days previous to its being wanted for use; to be applied closely around the grafts at the places of insertion into the stocks, and a little above, in order to prevent the air from exhausting the sap of the scions, before they could be supplied with a sufficiency from the stocks, and also to keep out wet, which would greatly obstruct the uniting of the parts; it is to be made in the following manner :—

Get a quantity of strong, fat loam, in proportion to the number of trees to be grafted; then take about a fourth part of fresh horse-dung, free from litter, or a third part of cow-dung, it matters not which you make use of; or, if you please, you may use a proportionate quantity of each, mixing them, or either of them, well with the loam; add to it a small quantity of hay, cut very fine, and also some salt, which will prevent it from cracking or drying too fast in hot or parching weather; work the whole well together, and add as much water as necessary; after which, beat and incorporate the mass effectually, after the manner of mortar, and continue so to work it every other day, adding a little water as it becomes dry, till the time you want it for use. Be very particular, during this period, not to expose it to frost or drying winds; and the more effectually you incorporate it, the better will it answer your purpose. Some people use a composition of bees-wax, rosin, and turpentine, melted together, to put round the grafts in the manner of clay, but laid on warm and much thinner. This I conceive to be too expensive, and am certain, from experience, that it does not answer the end a whit better, nor even so well as the former, if properly made.

Observe, that the stocks to be grafted, if intended for dwarf trees, for espaliers or walls, must be headed down to within five or six inches of the ground; but if for full standards, they may be headed and grafted at five or six feet high, or in fact at any height you please, even at the surface of the ground, but more particularly apples and pears; for you can afterwards train the graft on a single clean stem, as high as you like, and then top it, to cause it to throw out side branches for forming a head; this is the best method to treat stunted or ill formed stocks, but is not necessary for those that are well thriven and straight, for by it you would lose a year of their growth, as you can immediately form the head from the graft when inserted at a proper height; for dwarf and half standards, you may head and graft at the height of two, three, or four feet.

There are various methods of grafting in practice; such as whip-grafting, cleft-grafting, crown-grafting, side-grafting, root-grafting, and grafting by approach or inarching; but the two former are in more general use among experienced gardeners, particularly the first, as being every way preferable to any other, when the stocks are under an inch in diameter.

FIRST, BY WHIP-GRAFTING.

This kind of grafting is that most commonly practised in nurseries, as being both the most expeditious and successful, and may be performed upon smaller stocks than any other; for it is effected with the greatest success upon such as are from about half an inch or less, to near an inch in diameter; the method of performing the work is this:

Having the scions or grafts, knife, bandages, and clay ready, then begin the work by cutting off the head of the stock at some clear smooth part thereof, generally performing this by one clean slanting cut upwards, so as to form a slope on one side about an inch and a half or two inches in length; and make a notch or small slit from near the upper part downwards, a little better than half an inch long, to receive the tongue of the scion; then prepare the scion by cutting it to five or six inches in length, preferring the lower or thick part, and cutting the bottom end on one side also, in a sloping manner, the length of, and to fit the slope of the stock, as if cut from the same place, that the rinds of both may join as nearly as possible in every part, as if you were splicing a fishing-rod; but when the stock is much larger than the scion, this cannot be done so exactly, unless you insert it on the opposite side of the stock to the slope; however, that will not be necessary, provided you join the rinds or bark of both, so as to fit neatly on either edge or side of the slope; then make a slit upwards in the slope of the scion, so as to form a sort of tongue to fit that made in the slope of the stock, which insert therein, so that the rinds of both may join together exactly, at least on one side, and immediately tie the parts together with a ligature of bass, &c., bringing it in a neat manner several times around the stock and graft moderately tight, and fastened accordingly.

This done, clay the whole over near an inch thick on every side, from an inch below the bottom of the graft to the same above the top of the stock, finishing the coat of clay in a longish oval form, closing it effectually in every part, and tapering it up to the scion to prevent the wind, sun, or rain reaching the grafted parts till the union is effected; observing to examine it now and then; and if any part falls off, or cracks appear, such must be immediately repaired with fresh clay.

Expert nursery-gardeners generally perform whip-grafting with four cuts; two in heading and slitting the stock, and the same in sloping and turning the graft, inserting it immediately, being followed by one or two persons to tie and clay them.

This sort of grafting may also be performed, if necessary, upon strong young shoots of any bearing tree, if intended to alter the kind of fruit, or have more than one sort on the same tree.

By the middle or latter end of May, the grafts will be well united with the stocks, as will be evident by their shooting; the clay may then be taken off, but suffer the bandages to remain on till the united parts seem to swell, and be too much confined thereby.

SECOND, BY CLEFT-GRAFTING.

This is called cleft-grafting, because the stock being too large for whip-grafting, is cleft or slit down the middle for the reception of the scion, and is performed upon stocks from about one to two inches diameter, and may be practised with success where the rind of the stock is not too thick, whereby the inner bark of the scion will be prevented from closely joining that of the stock, which junction is absolutely necessary to form a complete union of the parts.

First, with a strong knife cut off the head of the stock; or if the stock is very large it may be headed with a small saw.

This done, fix upon a smooth part just below where headed, and on the opposite side to that cut away part of the stock, about an inch and a half, in a sloping manner upwards, so as the crown of the stock may not be more than about half an inch broad, which slope and crown are to be cut smooth and neat. Then prepare your grafts or scions in the following manner: observe to cut them into proper lengths of about six inches, with several eyes or buds to each: then take your sharpest knife, and pare away the bark and some of the wood at the lower end of the graft in a sloping manner, about an inch

and a half or near two inches in length on opposite sides, making it
have a wedge-like shape ; but let that edge which is to be placed outwards on the stock be left thicker than the other, and with the rind
continued thereon.   The graft being prepared, take your strong knife
or chisel, and place it on the middle of the stock, not across, but
contrarywise to the sloped part, and with a small mallet strike the
knife or chisel into the stock, observing to cleave it no farther than
what is necessary to admit the graft readily ; then place the knife, or
some small instrument, a little way into the cleft, at the sloped part
of the stock, to keep it open for the reception of the graft, which
directly introduce into the cleft on the top of the stock, at the back
of the slope; inserting it with great exactness, as far as it is cut,
with the thickest edge outwards, and so that the rind may meet exactly every way with that of the stock.   The graft being placed,
then remove the knife or wedge, taking care not to displace the scion;
this done, let it be tied and well clayed in the manner directed above,
in the work of whip or tongue-grafting.

Or, if you choose to put in two grafts, it may be performed on
large stocks, which must be twice cleft, parallel to each other, and so
fix the scions as above, in opposite sides.

This method of grafting may be performed occasionally on the upright branches of bearing trees when intended either to renew the
wood or change the sort of fruit.

When the grafts have shot five or six inches, take off the clay and
bandages, and cover the wounded parts of the stocks with fresh grafting clay, which will protect them from the influence of the weather,
and accelerate the growth of the bark over the wounds ; let this
claying remain on till it falls off of itself : this second claying is more
necessary to large than to small stocks, but will be very useful to
either.

THIRD, BY CROWN-GRAFTING.

The third kind of grafting is known by the name of crown-grafting, as sometimes three, four, or more grafts are inserted round the
crown of the stock, in a circular order, introduced betwixt the bark
and the wood.

This way of grafting is commonly practised upon such stocks as
are too large and stubborn to cleave, and is often performed upon the
branches of apple and pear-trees, &c., that already bear fruit, when
it is intended to change the sorts or to renew the tree with fresh bearing wood.

The manner of doing it is as follows :—

First, to cut off the head of the tree or stock level, or of any particular branch of a tree which you intend to graft, and pare the top
perfectly smooth ; then prepare your scions, which is done by cutting
one side flat and sloping, about two inches in length, making a kind
of shoulder at the top of the cut to rest on the head of the stock,
and pare off a *little* of the bark towards each edge of the graft ; then
prepare to insert it, which, in this order of grafting, must be effected
by introducing the sloped part down betwixt the bark and wood of

the stock ; first slitting the bark or rind from the top downwards clean through to the firm wood, two inches or two and a half in length ; and having a small thin wedge of iron or wood, open therewith the rind of the stock a little at the top of the slit, by introducing it gently down betwixt the wood and rind, far enough to make way for admitting the graft; then drawing it out, insert the scion with the cut sloped side towards and close to the wood of the stock, slipping it neatly down the length of its cut part, resting the shoulder thereof, prepared as above, upon the top of the stock, and in this manner you may put four, five, or more grafts, as may seem convenient, into each stock, and bind them round with strong bass.

When the grafts are all thus fixed, you must immediately apply a good quantity of well-wrought clay, bringing it close about the stock and grafts, observing to raise it at least an inch above the top of the stock in a rounding manner, so as to throw the wet quickly off, and prevent its lodging or getting into the work, which would ruin all.

This method of grafting is sometimes called shoulder-grafting, and grafting in the rind, and was much more in practice formerly than at present; for, although the grafts take freely, they are liable to be blown out by strong winds after they have made large shoots, which has frequently happened after three or four years' growth, so that when this method is practised, the evil must be remedied by tying some firm sticks to the body of the stock or branch that is grafted, to which the young shoots must be tied, or they must be made fast to some convenient support that will answer the same end ; or even tying them to one another, should the grafts take on *opposite* sides of the stock, will answer a good purpose.

This kind of grafting may be performed a week or ten days later than the other methods; for it will prove most successful if done when the sap begins to be in active motion, as then the bark of the stock will separate from the wood more freely to admit the graft.

When the scions are well taken, treat them as directed under the head Cleft-grafting.

FOURTH, BY SIDE-GRAFTING.

This is done by inserting grafts into the sides of the branches without heading them down, and may be practised upon trees to fill up any vacancy, or for variety, to have several sorts of fruit on the same tree.

It is performed thus : fix upon such parts of the branches where wood is wanting to furnish the head or any part of the tree ; there slope off the bark and a little of the wood, and cut the lower end of the graft to fit the part as near as possible ; then join it to the branch, first tongueing both as in whip-grafting, tie them with bass, and clay them over.

FIFTH, BY ROOT-GRAFTING.

This is done by whip-grafting scions upon pieces of root turned up about half an inch thick, either as the roots remain or separated, and immediately replanted.

Here it will be well to observe that grafting is frequently done, and very often with good success, without the assistance of grafting-clay or any other prepared composition. The method is this: head down your stocks near the surface of the ground, and graft them as low as you possibly can; bind them neatly, as in other cases, and draw the earth over the crowns of the stocks, so as to let one or two of the buds of each scion appear; look to them frequently, and if the earth sinks so as to expose the crowns of the stocks, cover them up again.

When the sciors are sufficiently taken, clear off the earth, unbind the bandages, and then replace it as before. Trees grafted in this way may afterwards be trained up, either for standards, half standards, espaliers or wall trees, at pleasure.

It sometimes happens that persons are under the necessity, in spring, of removing some stocks, when in the way of other business; in which case they are frequently taken into the house, and grafted in any method most convenient, then planted immediately: this is called by gardeners fire-side grafting, and often proves tolerably successful; but I would not recommend it, except in cases of necessity.

GRAFTING BY APPROACH, OR INARCHING.

This method of grafting is performed only when the stock and the tree from which you mean to propagate, either grow, or can be placed so near each other, that the intended graft may be brought to approach and join the stock, forming therewith, when grafted, a kind of arch, and not to be separated from the mother plant till a perfect union is formed: hence its name.

When intended to propagate any tree or shrub by this method, if of a hardy nature, and growing in the open ground, the requisite quantity of young plants for stocks should be planted around it, and when grown of a proper size or height, the work performed: or, if the branches of the tree designed to graft from, are too high for the stocks, these must be planted in pots (if a year previous to the operation, the better), and placed upon a temporary stage erected around the tree of sufficient height to answer the purpose.

In performing this work, make choice of a smooth part of the stock, and with which the intended graft can be conveniently brought to meet, marking on each the place of junction; then cut away the bark and a part of the wood, from two to three inches in length, both of the stock and scion; after which, make a slit upwards in the scion, so as to form a tongue, and another downwards in the stock, as directed for whip-grafting, and insert the one into the other, making all parts fit in an exact manner, particularly the rinds or barks, and tie them closely together with bass; after which, cover the whole with a due quantity of grafting clay, as directed in the other methods. In this mode of grafting, the scion is not separated from the tree until it is firmly united with the stock, nor is the head of the latter generally cut off till this time, though it is sometimes performed with the head of the stock cut off, under the idea that its whole efforts would then be directed to the nourishment of the graft, which is not of as much advantage as might be imagined.

If the plants which you inarch, are exposed to strong winds, it will be proper to make them fast, either to stakes stuck into the ground for that purpose, or to some other more convenient support to prevent their being displaced thereby.

The stocks and grafts are to remain for three months, or upwards, before you unbind them; at the expiration of that time, take off the clay and bandages, and if well taken, separate the graft from the mother plant, being careful to do this with a perfectly sharp knife, cutting it off with a slope downwards to the stock; and, if not done in grafting, the head of the stock must also be cut off close to the graft, and afterwards the stem kept free from any under shoots. If at this time the graft and stock, particularly if not extremely well united, were tied again *gently*, as before, fresh clayed, and those suffered to remain on for a month or five weeks, it would be of considerable advantage.

The walnut, fig, and mulberry, with many other trees, which do not succeed by the common methods of grafting, will take freely by this, and also various kinds of evergreens. It is in frequent use to ingraft a fruit-bearing branch upon a common stock of the same family, by which means you have a tree with much fruit in a few months, that would take perhaps as many years, when left to nature, before it would show a single one. This is frequently practised on orange-trees, and other green-house plants.

This method of grafting is not to be performed so early in the season as the others, it being most successful when the sap is flowing; in the Middle States, I would recommend doing it towards the latter end of April. But it is not to be practised where the other methods will succeed; for trees propagated in this way are always observed to grow more weakly, and never to the size of those which are propagated by budding, or the other modes of grafting.

GRAFTING PEACHES, NECTARINES, AND APRICOTS.

Peaches, nectarines, and apricots will succeed by grafting, but propagating them by inoculation is much preferable; however, if you graft them, let it be done early, always before they show flowers, having their scions taken off three weeks previous to the time of performing the operation, and deposited in the earth till that period, as before directed for those of other fruit-trees, in the choice of which you must be very particular, so as to get the best ripened young wood, round, plump, and short-jointed, and with very little pith; all these will take as freely on plump stocks as on their own kinds, and if intended for walls and espaliers will be more permanent, as they are not so subject to be destroyed by worms. Grafting may be also performed, to any desirable extent, on most kinds of forest and ornamental trees, such as elm, ash, oak, holly, althea-frutex, &c. &c., whose scions are not soft-wooded, nor too full of pith.

MANAGEMENT OF FRUIT-TREES GRAFTED AND BUDDED LAST YEAR.

Those fruit-trees which were grafted last year should now have their shoots shortened, that they may send forth lateral branches to form regular heads; if they are intended for espaliers or wall-trees, observe the method recommended in page 224; if for standards, the stems must be trained up to a proper height and then topped, or some of the shoots shortened, so as to produce handsome well furnished heads.

The stocks which were budded the last summer, and in which the buds still remain dormant, should now have their heads cut off a little above the budded parts; by which means the whole nourishment will go to the inoculations, which will soon begin to advance their first shoots.

In proceeding to do this, cut the head of the stock off, sloping behind the inoculated bud, either almost close thereto or about a hand's breadth above it; which part of the stock, remaining above, will serve for tying thereto the first shoot from the bud in summer, to secure it from the wind, but must be cut down close next spring.

The stumps left last season, for a similar purpose, should now be cut off close to where the bud was inserted, cutting them effectually in to the clean fresh wood, in order that the wounds may cover over and heal, which will be effected in one season, if no spotted or unsound wood be left.

TRANSPLANTING STOCKS TO BUD AND GRAFT UPON.

Make new plantations of stocks to bud and graft the different kinds of choice fruit upon.

Many of those raised from seeds, &c., last year, will now be ready for this purpose.

Let these be planted out, as soon in the month as the weather will permit, in rows three or four feet asunder, and at least twelve inches distant from one another in the row. They should be planted by line, either dibbling in the small plants, or the large ones trenched or holed in with the spade; or you may cut out small trenches by line, placing the plants therein at the above distance, and turn the earth in upon their roots, treading it gently along.

SOWING STONES TO RAISE STOCKS FOR GRAFTING.

Where plum, peach, apricot, and cherry-stones, &c. were neglected, or could not, in consequence of the weather, be sown last month, let it be done as early in this as possible, agreeably to the rules laid down in page 159, which see.

SOWING KERNELS OF APPLES, PEARS, AND QUINCES FOR STOCKS.

If the sowing of these were neglected, or impracticable last month, let it be done in this as early as possible, sowing them tolerably thick, in beds, and covering them with light dry earth, a little better than half an inch deep. These will be fit to plant out in nursery rows next season; but they would succeed much better if sown in October or November, if not carefully preserved in sand or earth, or unless they are, at the time of sowing, taken fresh out of the fruit. See page 165.

SOWING HAWS FOR RAISING THORN-QUICKS.

It will be necessary to sow your haws as early in this month as possible, if not done in the last, for the reasons assigned in the *Nursery* for *February*, page 160, &c., where you will find ample directions both for the preparation and sowing of the seed, &c.

You may, any time this month, particularly after the middle, or towards the latter end, take up your one or two year old seedling quicks, out of the beds where they were raised, and plant them into nursery rows, as directed at p. 160. Should it be your intention to let them remain in those rows to grow to a large size, the more immediately to make a fence, when planted out, set them at greater distances than there directed, but they always succeed best when planted young.

During the continuance of the plants in those rows, they must be kept free from weeds, and each spring and autumn it will be necessary to dig between them to loosen the earth, which will greatly strengthen and invigorate their growth.

LIVE HEDGES.

Live hedges are already become objects of serious importance, particularly in those parts of the Union in which timber has got scarce, and must inevitably become more so in a very rapid progression; therefore, the sooner the citizens turn their attention to the cultivation and planting of them, the greater portion of their benefits will they themselves enjoy, and the sooner will they lay the foundation of a rich inheritance for their children, and of an ornamental and useful establishment for their country.

Our farmers not being accustomed to the making of live hedges, may for some time be very tardy in attempting it; those of greater penetration will not hesitate a moment, but commence immediately; others will look on for years to see the result, which will be so much time, profit, and pleasure lost to themselves; and consequently a proportionate injury done to their posterity. Some will try the experiment; but in such a half way, negligent, slovenly manner, as to insure disappointment; I would advise such to hold fast by the *post and rail*, and not to lose time in doing more harm than good.

It has been asserted that any other than ground hedges, that is, such as are established on the plain surface without a ditch, are unnecessary in the United States; but why in the United States any more than in those countries that ages of experience and necessity have taught to give a decided preference to the hedge and ditch? Such may succeed in very good ground, and with uncommon care; but it is an incontrovertible and well known fact, that a hedge and ditch will make a more formidable fence, in three years, than a ground hedge will in ten.

Having now given my decided and unequivocal opinion as to which is preferable, for outward fences, I shall proceed to give the best instructions in my power for the formation of both; the more especially as the ground-hedge is the neatest and most eligible for *internal hedges* in gardens and pleasure-grounds.

The hawthorn, of all other kinds, is the most suitable for outward fences; and here I think it necessary to remark, that the common European white thorn, or *Cratægus oxyacantha* of Linnæus, appears to answer well in America, but is not of so rapid growth as our cockspur thorn, or *Cratægus crus galli;* the former makes a closer and thicker hedge, but not more formidable, nor so immediately as the latter. We have many varieties of native hawthorns, as described on page 164, &c., either of which will answer very well, and convenience must be considered in respect to choice; but when choice can be made, a preference should be given to the cockspur thorn, or rather to that kind which is observed to grow most luxuriantly in the neighborhood in which it is intended to be planted.

THE HEDGE AND DITCH.

The months of October, November, and December will be the most eligible periods in the southern States for making this kind of fence, particularly as their frosts can do no injury to the ditch, and the roots will have an early establishment, and consequently be the better prepared to encounter the summer heats. In the middle and eastern States, I would prefer doing this business in March, or early in April; as the ditch in that case would have one year's-advantage of the frost, which, in some kinds of soil, would have a considerable effect, particularly in the first year, by swelling the earth in the face of the ditch, causing it to moulder down, and thereby expose the roots of the quicks; but this can be obviated by leaving a scarcement in the front, as hereafter directed.

Strong year old quicks will answer very well for laying in the face of a ditch, but such as have had the advantage of two years' growth in nursery rows, after being transplanted when one year old from the seed-bed, will sooner form a good fence, or two year old plants from the seed-bed will answer a very good purpose. Be particular, in the taking of them up, not to injure their roots but as little as possible, and to sort them into three different lots, the smallest, larger, and largest, and also to plant each lot together; for the mixing of the small with the large is very injudicious, as the former in a little time would be smothered and overgrown by the latter, and vacancies consequently formed in the hedge.

Previous to planting, prune off the extremities of any long straggling and wounded roots, and also cut off the heads of the plants about seven inches above the earth-mark where they stood in the ground, and likewise any side branches that remain; let no consideration prevent your doing this, for on it depends much of your success.

Having your plants in readiness and dressed in this manner, lay them by the heels in the earth, to be taken up as wanted, lest their roots should become dry and be injured thereby. Then proceed to form your ditch, which should be four feet wide at least at top, narrowing with a gentle slope on each side towards the bottom, to the perpendicular depth of two feet and a half, where it should be one foot wide. The more your ground is subject to slip by heavy rains, the greater slope must be given to the bank side.

Begin by cutting the surface sod of the ditch into squares of convenient size, and about three inches deep, having previously lined out and cut both sides with a spade, sloping inwards as above intimated, and lay a row of them with the grassy surface under, six inches inward from the edge on the bank side; lay on top of this row of sods, two inches of the loose and mellow earth, that is, the best the ditch affords, and also a quantity of it behind them, for about eighteen inches or two feet, breaking it very fine with the spade; on this lay your quicks nearly in a horizontal manner, their tops being a little elevated, and at the distance of six inches one from the other, and so far in that three or four inches of their tops may remain uncovered when the ditch is finished. Spread the roots to advantage, and cover them well with the mouldy earth that dropped from the surface sod; this is necessary, in order to give their roots the advantage of the best soil, and should on no account be neglected. Then proceed to finish your ditch and bank, laying the remainder of the surface sods in front of the bank, as you had done with the first row, giving it exactly a similar slope to that of the ditch, and the whole bank such a form as if it was taken up at once out of the ditch and turned upside down. The scarcement left in front throws the bank so far back as not to bear heavily on the side of the ditch to crush it down, and it also will receive and retain a considerable portion of the rain that slides down along the face of the bank, by which means the earth in front will be kept in a more moist state than if no such thing was left.

Were you to lay in two rows of quicks in the front, the second eight or nine inches above the first, and the plants in each row nine or ten distant, placing those of the upper opposite the intervals of the lower, it would be the most effectual method of making a better and more immediate fence. A very slight paling, on top of the bank, that will defend the quicks for three years, will be sufficient; and if the land in front is not in cultivation, but under stock, a similar fence may be necessary to prevent their going into the ditch, and reaching the plants; but if you take particular care to keep them constantly wed, for the first two years, which is absolutely necessary or all is lost labor, they will have the less inducement to approach them.

There are many other methods of making hedge and ditch fences; but having found, from ample experience, the above to be most successful, I shall confine myself exclusively to it, lest too much speculation might lead people astray, and retard the progress of this important business.

GROUND-HEDGES.

The best method of planting a hedge on a level, or without a ditch, is to plough a slip of ground on each side of the intended line of fence the preceding spring, and having previously dunged it, to plant it with potatoes, taking the ordinary care to keep it free from weeds during the period of their growth. In autumn, the potatoes being removed, the entire slip should be ploughed deep, gathering it up towards the centre, and in October or March, having your quicks previously raised in the *nursery*, as directed in that department in February, to the height of two or three feet, take up the plants carefully without injuring their roots, prune off the extremities of the roots and any long straggling shoots of their tops, then plant them in a trench made along the centre of this slip of ground for their reception, at the distance of from six to eight inches from plant to plant, and settle the earth well into their roots; observing, previously to planting, to match the quicks; that is, to plant all the larger sized together, for it is improper, as before observed, to intermix the small and large, as the former would be smothered by the latter, which would occasion injurious and unsightly breaches in the fence.

If you have plenty of quicks, it will be of advantage to plant a double row at the distance of a foot from each other, in which case the plants may be set ten inches apart in the rows, placing those of one row directly opposite the intervals of the other. This method I would prefer to the former.

The quicks must afterwards be protected from cattle by palings or some kind of dead fences, till they arrive at a proper growth, not to be injured thereby; and for the two first years kept perfectly free from weeds; for without these precautions it will be in vain to plant them.

The quicks being tolerably close planted, will need no annual top clipping to thicken them; but it will be very proper to shorten occasionally any extraordinary vigorous top shoots, so as to keep them all pretty equal, and also such as branch out too much at the sides. However, it would be very advisable to give a slight dressing to the sides every October or March, for a few years, with a pair of hedge-shears, which may be done in a short time, narrowing the hedge a little towards the top to afford the benefit of the air, rain, and dews to the lower side shoots; this will encourage their growth, and cause the hedge to be well furnished from bottom to top.

When a hedge of this kind is to be made, it might be the most convenient way to plant it within a few feet of some established post and rail fence, and erect another as many feet from it on the opposite side, each at such a distance as would be sufficient to keep off cattle; here it would be effectually protected until arrived at a proper height and strength, when both these ranges of palings might be taken away to answer similar purposes; but again and again would I suggest the necessity of keeping the plants free from the annoyance of weeds during the first two or three years of their growth, after which they will be completely furnished and out of their power.

18

The autumn or spring following after planting, examine your hedge, and if any of the plants have died, or seem to be in a very bad state of health, replace them with others from the nursery, placing some fresh earth to the roots of each.

CRAB AND APPLE HEDGES.

The common wild thorny *crab* will make an excellent ground or ditch hedge, and will thrive in a poorer soil than the thorn; and hedges raised from the pippins of apples do tolerably well and form strong fences; the former is raised from the pippins, and the latter can be propagated in abundance by sowing the pumice *very thick*, immediately after being pressed for cider, on a bed of good ground properly prepared, and covering the whole with fine light earth near an inch deep; a few plants will appear soon after sowing, but a great crop will come up in spring, which may afterwards be used for stocks to graft on, and also for hedges, where more suitable kinds cannot be had.

HORNBEAM AND BEECH HEDGES.

Our indigenous kinds of *hornbeam* and beech will make admirable hedges; the seed of the former, which it produces here in great abundance, will require the same preparation and management in every respect as directed for haws on page 160, &c.

In Westphalia and other parts of Germany the hornbeam is in great repute for hedges. The German husbandman throws up a parapet of earth, with a ditch on each side, and plants his sets, raised from layers, in such a manner that every two plants intersect each other; then he cuts off the bark and a little of the wood from each, and binds them close together with a hay-band. The plants unite and form a living palisado, which, being pruned or dressed annually with discretion, will, in a few years, make an impenetrable fence. Most other kinds may be treated in the same manner.

The seeds or mast, as they are commonly called, of the *beech*, may be sown as soon as ripe, but as the ground-mice, squirrels, &c., are extremely fond of them, it will be the better way to preserve them in *dry* sand till March, to be then sown either in drills or broadcast in beds, covering them not more than half an inch deep; for, as they rise with very broad seed-leaves, they could never work up through a thick covering. The beech vegetates the first spring after the perfection of its seed; the hornbeam not till the second.

HONEY-LOCUST AND ELM HEDGES.

The *Gleditsia triacanthos*, or honey-locust, will make very good hedges; the seeds are to be sown in March, and covered half an inch deep; they will come up freely, and when a year old may be transplanted into nursery rows till of sufficient size to plant. If to be planted in the face of ditches, they will in the second year be in prime condition for that purpose.

The *elm* makes a good hedge, and is propagated by seed, suckers, or layers; when by seed it should be sown as soon as ripe, which, in the middle States, is between the 15th and 20th of May; it may be sought for and collected at that time, dried for four or five days, and then sown broadcast on a bed of good earth, covering the seed not more than a quarter of an inch deep; they will vegetate immediately, and when up, must be kept very clean and free from weeds. All kinds of elm may be propagated freely from *layers*, in the manner directed under that article.

HOLLY HEDGES.

Of all other plants there is none that makes a more durable, close and beautiful hedge than the *holly*, nor one that agrees better with the shears; it may be clipped and dressed to any form; the seeds do not vegetate till the second spring after their being ripe, and consequently must be treated as directed for haws, page 160, &c. They must remain two years in the seed-bed, and then should be planted either in the face of ditches, or into nursery rows, if intended for ground hedges; for which there is no equal as to beauty, shelter and closeness. The latter end of April is the best season to plant them: they never thrive well when taken out of the woods, but are very prosperous when cultivated by seed, though not of rapid growth for a few years.

WHITE MULBERRY AND LOMBARDY-POPLAR HEDGES.

The *white mulberry* makes a tolerably good hedge, and may be easily propagated by washing the seed out of the pulp when the fruit is ripe, drying and preserving it till the latter end of March, or beginning of April, when it may be sown on a bed of light rich earth, and covered about a quarter of an inch deep; the plants will appear towards the latter end of April, when they must be kept carefully weeded, and when a year old some of them will be fit to plant into nursery rows; the small plants may remain in the seed-bed a second year, and then transplanted either into the face of ditches or nursery rows as above. They are also cultivated by layers and cuttings, but not so successfully by the latter as by either of the former methods.

The *Lombardy poplar* is propagated by cuttings, which grow very freely; the most eligible size for these, though much larger are frequently used, are such as are from three-quarters of an inch to an inch in diameter, about twelve or fourteen inches long, and are to be planted two-thirds of their lengths into the earth. These and the mulberry bear clipping very well, but not being spiny, they never make formidable fences.

JUNIPER AND RED CEDAR HEDGES.

Juniper and *red cedar* make good garden hedges, particularly the former, and are very proper for affording shelter to such quarters of the garden or nursery as are set apart for the raising of tender plants in : both may be propagated abundantly from seeds, which do not vegetate till the second spring after ripening, consequently they must be prepared as directed for haws, and when sown, should not be covered more than a quarter of an inch deep ; they may remain in the seed-bed for two years, if not too thick, and then planted into nursery-rows ; or the largest may be taken up when a year old, and planted therein, provided that they have grown freely.   The juniper may be raised by cuttings, planted in a shady border towards the latter end of this month.

YEW AND PRIVET HEDGES.

Yew and *privet* make neat garden hedges ; they are both raised from seeds and cuttings, the latter planted in March, and the seeds of each are to be treated as directed for haws, not vegetating the first spring after ripening.

PYRACANTHA OR EVERGREEN-THORN HEDGES.

The *Mespilis Pyracantha,* or evergreen thorn, will make a tolerably good hedge ; it is propagated by seed, which will not vegetate till the second spring after ripening, and must be treated accordingly.

ROSE AND SWEETBRIER HEDGES.

Wild *roses* and *sweetbrier* are sometimes used for hedges, and may either be propagated by suckers, layers, or seeds.   The best way to cultivate them for hedges is by seed, which must be gathered in autumn when ripe, and preserved as directed for haws, till the spring following twelve months, and then sown.

ELDER, WILLOW, AND ALDER HEDGES.

The *elder-tree* is sometimes used for hedges, especially when a fence is wanted as soon as possible, being of a more speedy growth than any other kind commonly used for that purpose, though not the most effectual nor beautiful.   However, an immediate fence may be made of it, by planting large truncheons or cuttings of the straightest upright shoots and branches, from two or three to six feet long, planted either upright, a foot asunder, and wattled along the top to preserve them firm and even; or by planting them slanting across one another, checkerwise, forming a sort of lattice-work, which is the most effectual method.   In either way of planting, do not point and drive them in, as is commonly done, but make holes for their reception, twelve or fifteen inches deep, with a crowbar, then insert their ends, and make the earth fast about them : when driven down by force, the bark is frequently stripped, which in a great measure prevents their rooting freely, and pushing as vigorously as if carefully planted.

Various kinds of *willow* are found extremely useful to plant along the sides of watery ditches, brooks, rivulets or any marshy and moist situations ; and may be propagated by planting small cuttings, or large truncheons, as directed for the elder.   Either of these you may treat the following, or any succeeding spring, as the Westphalians do the hornbeam, noticed on page 274.

The *alder* is sometimes made use of as a fence in moist, swampy places; it is propagated abundantly by suckers, layers, or seed.   The seed, if sown in March, covered very lightly, and when up kept free from weeds, will grow prosperously.

BLACK-THORN HEDGES.

The *black-thorn*, or *sloe*, is a tolerably good shrub for a fence, but is subject to spread too much by suckers, by which it can be propagated ; but the best plants are always produced from the stones of the fruit, collected when ripe, and then sown or preserved in sand or earth till early in March, when you are to sow and cover them near an inch deep.   They will vegetate the first season.

PLUM-LEAVED VIBURNUM HEDGES.

The *Viburnum prunifolium*, or black haw, is an indigenous plant, and well adapted for hedges.   It may be propagated in abundance by collecting the berries in autumn, and managing them in every respect as directed for haws.

Note.—When you have but small quantities of such seeds as require a year's preparation previous to sowing, you may mix them with light sandy earth, which mixture put into garden pots, first placing a hollow shell, or something similar, with the concave side under, over the hole in the bottom of each, the better to suffer any extra moisture to pass off; then place the pots in some dry border up to their rims in the earth, but not deeper, observing to cast out the whole contents, rubbing and mixing it well together three or four times in the course of the following summer, and to sow the seed, as before directed, early in the second spring,; or you may use shallow boxes not deeper than six or eight inches, having their bottoms perforated with several holes, and covered with shells, &c., but by no means sink them in the earth deeper than their edges, as you have nothing to fear from the frost; but if covered in summer with moss, or anything that will keep the earth moderately moist, the better; or, during that season, you may plant the pots or boxes in some shady border.

OSAGE APPLE (MACLURA AURANTIACA).

The first of these plants introduced into this country, was brought by Messrs. Lewis and Clark, from the Rocky Mountains, and presented to the author.   It was esteemed by the Indians for making bows, and hence they called it bow-wood.   It ought to be in the collection of every person having trees or shrubbery, as its foliage is extremely rich and beautiful, in which it bears a close resemblance to the orange.   The fruit (which is said to be eaten by the Indians), is a large globular ball of a beautiful green color, composed of a pulpy substance something similar to the orange. It is easily propagated by seed, layers or cuttings, and is now becoming very valuable for hedging, as it is of much more rapid growth than the thorns, and is quite as impenetrable; it is not affected by the drought in summer, and is every way preferable for hedges : they should be planted eighteen inches asunder, or planted as a standard or ornamental tree ; it will attain a large size in a short time, and the branches may be trained to form a very pretty summer-house. Mr. Duke, of this city, has at his garden (formerly M'Mahon's), a tree under which thirty persons have dined. By recent discoveries in France it has been ascertained that the leaves are equally as good, if not preferable, for feeding the silk-worm; and the silk is considered equal in quantity and stronger than that raised on the mulberry.

ADDITIONAL OBSERVATIONS ON HEDGES.

It is not very eligible to mix two or more kinds of plants in any hedge, for they seldom grow equally, and the more vigorous sort will destroy the other; nor is it proper, for the same reason, to plant trees intended for timber among either.

Should you have a variety of the preceding kinds in forwardness for planting, it would be proper to observe, in the surrounding country, what soil and situation each kind thrives best when growing in a wild and uncultivated state, which will enable you to give to every one its favorite. This will be found of importance, and worthy of being attended to.

The European white thorn does not thrive well in a dry gravel or sand, nor in a cold spuey clay; a good strong loam is its favorite.

When young hedge plants of any kind become stunted and hidebound in consequence of the poverty of the ground, &c., it will be proper to head them down to within two inches of the ground, either in the months of October or March, cutting them off clean and smooth; observing, however, that this is not to be done to one here and there, but to the whole row out of the face, as far as they are in that condition. The summer following they will produce vigorous and prosperous shoots.

When you have crab hedges, which certainly forms very good and durable ones, you may encourage one vigorous straight shooting plant, at every fifty feet distance, by pruning and cleaning up their stems till out of the reach of cattle, retarding the ascending growth of the others by annual topping, then they may be grafted with any good kinds of cider apples, and in a few years will produce fruit in abundance.

Hedges raised from the pippins of apples may be treated in the same way; but you may suffer some to stand ungrafted, for many will yield very good cider fruit, and perhaps some may produce new and superior kinds. You will be able to judge by leaf, shoot, and bud, which are most likely to produce the best fruit, and which not, and manage them accordingly.

We have various other plants that might answer for live hedges, which due observation, and a little experience will point out; but, upon the whole, I am of opinion, that the *cockspur thorn* will answer a better purpose with us for outward, strong, and durable fences than any other.

PLASHING OF HEDGES.

This is a very necessary operation, especially when hedges are grown old, or have been so neglected as that gaps are formed in several places; and indeed it is the practice in countries where the greatest attention is paid to them, either to plash, or cut them all clean down to within six inches of the ground every fourteen or fifteen years. To perform this business, you must be provided with a good sharp hedge-bill, handsaw, and a pair of strong leather gloves that will reach up to your elbows, to protect your hands and arms from the spines or thorns; unless you are provided with these you will have a *bloody* job of it; but being so fortified it will be but a recreative amusement.

Then select some of the main upright stems at distances in proportion to the general growth of the hedge, to serve for stakes, which are to be cut off with the saw at the height of three or four feet from the roots; other stakes are to be drove down in those vacancies where growing ones do not occur, between which, as well as the former, to plash and lay the general branches observing that the shorter the shoots which are to be plashed, the closer the stakes should be to one another. The remainder of the hedge you are then to thin, leaving only a sufficiency of the best and longest middle-sized shoots, to lay down and work in between those stakes, cutting the others off in a sloping manner, within five or six inches of the ground, always preferring the saw to the bill, for this purpose, when it can be used conveniently. Proceed then to lay down the intended shoots, first lopping off the straggling side branches, and cutting or gashing occasionally such of the larger growths as are not pliant enough to yield and keep their intended stations, observing to cut them no deeper than what is absolutely necessary; lay and weave them in between the stakes almost to a horizontal position, all leaning one way, and their top extremities terminating as much as possible on the ditch side, if any; if not, equally on both. When the hedge is thus plashed, finish the top all the way with some of the longest and most pliant, but stout, of the shoots which were first cut out, previously divesting them of all their side branches, and working two together, lapping around and over one another between each stake, by which the whole plashing will be kept down to its proper birth; then with the hedge-bill or shears dress and lop off any projecting or straggling branches at the sides to within six inches of the hedge, and the work is finished.

Never lay your plashes too upright, but near to a level; by so doing, the sap will the better break out in several places, for the production and nourishment of a number of young side shoots, and not run so much to the ends, as it would if laid at a higher elevation. Also avoid crowding your plashes too much, and never lay in more than can *conveniently* be wove between the stakes, by which the young productions will have the benefit of the air, and grow much stronger than otherwise.

Old overgrown fences, which have been planted in the hedge and ditch way, may be *all* cut clean off with the saw, within six inches of their roots, and the fallen earth in the bottom of the ditch dug up and laid at the back of them; they will shoot vigorously, and soon form a fine fresh hedge.

Large ground hedges will be improved by cutting them down at intervals of ten or fifteen years, to the height of three, four, or five feet, and where vacancies occur, to fill them with plashing, always preferring, on these occasions, the saw to the bill, especially when the shoots are large.

CLIPPING WITH SHEARS.

The old method of clipping the yew, and other trees, is represented by the following cut; it is an ancient yew at Elvaston Castle, England, and is probably the best specimen now in existence. It forms a beautiful clipped arbor, fifteen feet square and twenty feet high, and very perfect, being surmounted by two peacocks, and over them two rings, all made with the shears.

Fig. 27.

THE PLANE, TULIP, AND NETTLE-TREES.

The *platanus occidentalis*, or plane-tree, commonly called the large buttonwood, and in some places, though very improperly, sycamore, is a valuable tree for shade, and many other useful purposes. It may be propagated, either by cuttings, layers, or seed; but the last method is much preferable to either of the former, not only with respect to this, but to every other tree bearing seed, which may be cultivated for its timber; and although it may appear more tedious at first, it will, in the end, be found the most expeditious and profitable. They may be sown either in November, when ripe, or in March, first breaking the balls of seed, and separating them effectually, mixing them with some dry earth or sand, and then sowing them even on the surface of prepared four feet wide beds in the nursery, and covering them about a quarter of an inch deep, or a little more, if the earth is fine and light: *too deep* covering is injurious to all kinds of *seed*, for nature never designed more than a sufficiency to promote and give action to vegetation. They will come up the first season, and the next or succeeding year may be planted into nursery rows.

The *Liriodendron tulipifera*, or tulip-tree, commonly, but very improperly called poplar, is best propagated by seed, which should be sown in November, when ripe, or preserved in sand or earth till March, and then sown, covering them half an inch deep. Those sown in November will all grow the spring following; but, if kept out of the ground in a dry state till spring, a great number of them will not vegetate till the next year.

The *Celtis occidentalis*, or nettle-tree, is propagated by seed which, if sown in November, when ripe, or preserved in earth or sand till March, and then sown, will generally vegetate the same season; but if the berries are kept dry till spring, the greater number of them will not grow till the next year. They should be covered about an inch deep.

MAPLES.

The *Acer argenteum*, or silvery leaved, and *Acer rubrum*, or scarlet maples, perfect their seeds in May, and should be sown immediately after having been collected; they will vegetate directly, and produce fine plants the first season, if kept free from weeds. The seeds of the former do not keep well till spring, but those of the latter will.

The sugar, Canada, ash-leaved, Pennsylvania, and mountain maples, and also the *Acer majus*, or sycamore, may be sown either in autumn or March, and will succeed well in either season; if sown in autumn, cover them about three-quarters of an inch deep; if in spring, half an inch will be sufficient. When about a foot high in the seed-beds, plant them early in spring into nursery rows, at proper distances.

CATALPA, SWEET-GUM, PAPAW, AND PERSIMMON.

The *Bignonia catalpa* will grow freely from seed, which is to be preserved in the siliques or pods till March, and then sown; or it may be propagated either by layers or suckers.

The *Liquidambar styraciflua*, or maple-leaved sweet-gum, grows freely from seed sown early in spring.

The *Annona triloba*, or common papaw, is a hardy plant, and may be propagated by sowing the seed about an inch deep, either in October, November, or March.

The *Diospyros virginiana*, persimmon, or American date plum, is best cultivated from seed sown in autumn, soon after ripe, or in March; if kept up till spring, some of them will not vegetate till the second year after sowing.

CHESTNUTS, WALNUTS, HICKORIES, AND OAKS.

About the middle of this month plant the nuts of the European and American eatable chestnuts, also of the horsechestnut, and likewise of the different varieties of walnuts and hickories, which you wish to propagate. All the above kinds should be sown in drills, first throwing the nuts into a tub of water, and rejecting such of them as swim, covering them with light rich mould about two inches deep. The drills may be three feet asunder, and the nuts planted about six or eight inches from one another in the rows.

The different varieties of oak succeed best when sown immediately after being ripe; but in that case, they have to encounter the depredations of mice, squirrels, &c., to avoid which, they may be kept in earth or sand till this time: but as most of them will be sprouted, you are to take them carefully up, without breaking the radicles, and plant them in drills two feet asunder, covering the acorns not more than three-quarters, or, at most, an inch deep, with light loose mould.

The whole of the above kinds may remain in these seed-drills for two years, keeping them at all times very free from weeds; and as they are generally, but more particularly the walnut kinds, subject to push down long tap-roots, and not to form many lateral ones, it will be proper, nay it will be necessary, in order to insure success in transplanting, when they have had one or two years' growth, to open, in the spring, a small trench close to each row, and then with a *very sharp* spade to cut the descending roots about six or eight inches under ground, casting back the earth when done. This will cause them to throw out a number of laterals, and the spring following you can transplant them with safety into nursery rows, at greater distances, to remain till wanted to plant out where finally intended.

ROBINIA, OR LOCUST-TREE.

The *Robinia pseudo-acacia*, or common locust-tree, is said to be superior to any other kind of wood for ship runnels, mill cogs, and fence posts, as well as for various other purposes. Its culture is very easy, as it may be propagated in great abundance by collecting the seeds in autumn when ripe, preserving them dry till March, then sowing them in a bed of good sandy loam, which is their favorite soil, and covering them half an inch deep. They will come up in the course of the following month numerously, for no seeds grow more freely, notwithstanding what some inexperienced persons assert to the contrary. They require no preparation whatever; sow them as above directed, and a good crop is certain. When a year old transplant them out of the seed-bed into nursery rows, four feet distant, and, plant from plant, one foot in the row. Having two or three years' growth in these rows they may be planted successfully in any warm and tolerably rich sandy ground. They may also be propagated by suckers, which they throw up abundantly; especially if some of their wide extending roots be cut through with an axe, &c.

The *Robinia glutinosa* is a charming plant; it produces in May numerous bunches of delightful flowers, grows to a good size, and is a great ornament in pleasure-grounds. It may be propagated by seed in like manner, or by grafting it on the former.

The *Robinia hispida*, or rose acacia, is a most beautiful flowering shrub, of humble growth, and may be propagated by suckers, which it produces in great numbers, or by grafting it on either of the above species.

THE ASH, LIME, AND SOUR-GUM.

The various kinds of *Fraxinus*, or ash, are propagated by seeds, which are to be prepared in the same manner as directed for haws, on page 160, &c., for they do not vegetate till the second spring after the seeds are ripe. All the kinds take freely by grafting on one another.

The *Tilia americana*, or American lime or Linden tree, together with every other species of the same genus, is easily propagated by layers, or by sowing the seeds in October or November, or in March, if preserved in dry sand till that time. Sow the seeds on an even surface, clap them in with the back of a spade, and cover them a little better than half an inch deep.

The *Nyssa integrifolia*, or upland tupelo-tree, or sour-gum, is propagated by seed, suckers, layers, or cuttings; if by seed sow them immediately when ripe, covering them an inch deep; some of them will come up the spring following, but many not till the second year. The better way would be to prepare them as directed for haws, and in the ensuing March examine them; if you then find many showing symptoms of vegetation, sow them; if not, let them remain till that time twelve months.

DECIDUOUS CYPRESS, WHITE CEDAR, AND ARBOR-VITÆ.

The *Cupressus disticha*, bald or deciduous cypress, grows to an enormous large size, the foliage of which is uncommonly beautiful during the summer months. It is propagated by sowing the seed in March, in beds of good mellow earth, covering them half an inch deep; they must be kept very free from weeds, and when two years old transplant them from the seed-beds into nursery rows.

The *Cupressus thyoides*, or white cedar, is propagated by sowing the seeds, which are very thin and flat when taken out of the cones, in boxes of light earth, taken from swampy ground, and covered about the eighth of an inch, or a little more, with loose rich mould sifted evenly over them; they must have frequent sprinklings of water, and when up, and the heat increases, the boxes must be removed into the shade. You must keep them very free from weeds, as many of the seeds will not grow till the second year. When they are two years old transplant them into nursery rows, in moist light swampy ground.

The *Thuya occidentalis*, or American arbor-vitæ, is propagated by layers and cuttings, or by sowing the seed as directed for the white cedar, with this difference, that it will not be necessary to procure swampy earth for it, as it thrives best in upland.

The *Thuya orientalis*, or Chinese arbor-vitæ, may be propagated in like manner as the occidentalis.

All the above kinds, if raised by seeds, will require some protection during the first two years, from very rigorous frosts.

PINES AND FIRS.

The pines and firs, though ranked under the same genus (*Pinus*), may be easily distinguished from one another, as the leaves of the former come out by two, three, or more, from the same sheath, and those of the latter singly. In the cedar of Lebanon and larch, they arise in bunches from the same bud, spreading out every way.

It is also to be remarked that all the pines have a tendency to drive down tap-roots, and therefore are more impatient of transplanting than the firs, whose roots generally take a lateral direction. The larch is the only deciduous plant of the whole family. As all these kinds are not only very useful, but extremely ornamental, and as none of them can be transplanted from the woods with good success, I shall be the more minute in giving the true methods of raising them, so as to insure thereby the growth and prosperity of the plants.

The *Pinus cedrus*, or cedar of Lebanon, is rather too tender for those parts of the Union where the winter frosts are very rigorous; but will succeed tolerably well in warm exposures in the middle States, if protected from its violence a few years, and be gradually inured thereto. The seeds when procured are always in the cones, and are extremely difficult to be got out; the method is, bore the cone through with a small gimlet direct in the *centre*, entering it at the but-end and working out at top; then drive in a round iron or hard wooden pin, and split the cones, after which, raise the scales one after another with a knife, and carefully pick out the seeds, which are very tender.

Having your seeds ready, sow them in a box of good fresh earth, covering them near half an inch deep; in the middle States, the first week in April will be the best time to do this, but early in March will be preferable, if you have a green-house or hot-beds to place the box therein; give them a little sprinkling of water frequently, just what will be sufficient to keep the earth moist, for much would rot or burst the seeds. When up, do not expose them too much to the sun at any time during the season, nor keep them in too confined a place; and on the approach of winter remove them into the green-house, or place them under the protection of glasses, and so treat them for two years, without removing them out of the seed-box. Then, early in April, transplant them carefully into separate pots, treating them all this time, and for two or three years more, as you do green-house plants; after which turn some of them with the earth out of the pots, and plant them in dry warm exposures.

The *Pinus pinea*, or Italian stone pine, grows to a considerable height, and is cultivated chiefly for its nuts and the beauty of its foliage.   In Italy and the southern parts of Europe, the kernels are frequently served up in desserts during the winter season, and are as sweet as almonds, but have a slight flavor of turpentine.   The cones are generally four or five inches long, and when for some time exposed to the sun, they open and drop out the nuts, which should be sown towards the latter end of March, in drills, and covered about half or three-quarters of an inch deep; when they have had one or two years' growth in these rows, cut their tap-roots as directed for walnuts, on page 282, and the next year you may transplant them about the first week in April, either into nursery-rows, at greater distances, or where they are to remain.

The *Pinus cimbra*, or Siberian stone pine.   There is a variety of this that grows in Switzerland, and higher up the Alps than any other pine, and is found on elevations where the larch will not grow. The stones are shorter than those of the Italian pine, and full as thick.   The wood is short, having scarcely any grain, and very fit for the carver.   The peasants of the Tyrol, where this tree abounds, make various sorts of carved works with the wood, which they dispose of in Switzerland among the common people, who are fond of the resinous smell which it exhales.   Both the varieties may be cultivated in the same manner as directed for the Italian stone pine.

All the other species and varieties of pines and firs may be successfully raised in the following manner :—

Being provided with good fresh seeds, for on this everything depends, prepare for their reception, *as early in the spring* as your ground will work free and light, and pulverize finely in the working, beds three or four feet wide, of rich loamy ground, by no means subject to burn or become parched with the summer heats; then sow the seeds on the surface, so thick as that you may expect, after all reasonable allowances for defective seeds, &c., *at least* a plant on every inch square of the ground, or at the rate of a pound of good seed to a bed three feet and a half wide and sixty long.   The sowing of them so thick is indispensable, for unless they completely cover the surface, they will, if not carefully shaded, be destroyed in their infant state by the summer heat; early sowing is also necessary, for they have nothing to apprehend from subsequent frosts, that their roots may be established before the heat overtakes them.   After the seeds are sown, sift over the smaller sized kinds about a quarter of an inch of fine, rich, light, mould, and over the larger, nearly half an inch, then place over the beds nets made for that purpose, or any old small-meshed fishing-nets, to keep off the birds, for all the kinds, when lightly covered, which is indispensable to their growth, generally carry up the seeds on their tops, and if attacked by birds, which are extremely fond of them, the far greater number will be destroyed.

The beds must be kept completely free from weeds of any kind, from the moment the seeds are sown during the continuance of the plants therein ; and if you perceive their leaves turn foxy in summer, by heat or drought, it will be necessary to give them occasional shade and water. In the month of June following, sift some fine, light, rich earth over the beds, so as to just come up to the foliage without covering it, which will protect their yet tender stems, prevent their being scalded by extraordinary heat, which often melts them away, so as to fall flat, whilst the foliage appears fresh ; and besides, it will help to retain the moisture about their roots and fibres.

The spring following, early in April, or as soon as you perceive an inclination in the buds to push, pull up the largest grown plants, of such kinds as have arrived at the height of three inches or upwards, but not otherwise, and plant them in drills made with a hoe or spade for their reception, eighteen inches or two feet asunder, and eight inches plant from plant in the rows, just so deep as that the earth may come up to their foliage ; close it well about the roots, and water them occasionally till sufficiently taken with the earth and growing freely, and if repeated occasionally during the summer and early autumn, the better ; always giving it about the setting or going down of the sun. The spring following, that is, when they have two years' growth in the seed-beds, take them all up out of the face with a spade without injuring the roots or fibres, and plant them as above, without attempting to trim them, but laying them in a spreading and horizontal manner in the drills. If the ground is good and the season proves favorable, a great number of the larch in particular will have grown to a sufficient size for transplanting into nursery rows by the ensuing spring.

When the plants have stood two or three years in these rows, they may be planted in others at greater distances, or finally where they are intended to remain ; observing, however, that the fourth or fifth year of their growth is the most successful period for a final transplanting, which ought always to be done, in the middle States, between the first and fifteenth of April, earlier in the southern, and not much later in the eastern States.

ALTHÆA FRUTEX, LABURNUM, AND SNOWY MEDLAR.

The *Hibiscus syriacus*, or althæa frutex, is propagated by sowing the seeds in March, which grow very freely ; all the varieties of it take well by grafting or budding on one another.

The *Cytissus laburnum*, or common laburnum, grows freely by sowing the seed in spring, and covering it as well as the former, about half an inch deep.

The *Mespilus canadensis*, or snowy medlar, is a beautiful and early flowering shrub, rises to a good height, and is a great ornament to pleasure grounds. It is propagated abundantly by seeds, which should be preserved in sand from the time of their being ripe till March, and then sown and covered about half an inch deep. If kept in a dry state till spring, some will vegetate the first season and some not till the second. It will take by grafting or budding it on any kind of medlar, or on the white thorn, pear, or quince.

THE JUDAS, SNOWDROP, AND FRINGE-TREES.

The *Cercis canadensis*, or American Judas-tree, is one of our most beautiful early flowering and ornamental plants; and may be propagated by sowing its seeds in March, as directed for the common locust-tree.

The *Halesia tetraptera*, or snowdrop-tree, is exceeded by very few shrubs for the beauty of its numerous white pendant flowers. It may be propagated by suckers or layers, or by sowing the seeds in November when ripe, or in March, and covering them near an inch deep with light rich mould.

The *Chionanthus virginica*, or fringe-tree, is a very ornamental shrub, and may be cultivated by layers, suckers, or seed. Sow the seeds when ripe in autumn, covering them an inch deep with very fine light mould, or preserve them in earth or sand till March, and then sow them as above; many will not rise till the second spring, so that it will be necessary to keep the ground very free from weeds all the time.

MAGNOLIAS.

The seeds of the different kinds of magnolia should be sown immediately after being ripe, or be preserved in damp sand or earth till March; for if kept dry till that time, very few, if any, will vegetate till the year following; and indeed may not until the second season, even if sown when ripe. They may also be propagated by layers and suckers, and by grafting and budding upon one another.

RHODODENDRONS, KALMIAS, AZALIAS AND ANDROMEDAS.

Each and every species and variety of the above beautiful families of plants may be propagated either by seeds, layers, or suckers. The finest plants are always raised from seed, and although the process may be thought tedious, it is worth attending to; the more especially as they do not always succeed well when taken from the woods, and that thousands may be raised in this way, which may be successfully removed to any place where wanted.

The capsules should be collected when the seeds are perfectly ripe, and if you intend to sow them immediately, which is certainly the better way, expose the capsules a few days to dry, but not to a powerful sun; they will then open, and the seeds will easily shake out; but if you do not intend sowing them till February or March, preserve them in the capsules till that time. To have a double chance sow some on shady borders of light, dry, loamy earth, and also in boxes, making the ground very fine and even on the surface, then sow the seeds thickly thereon, and cover them not more than the eighth of an inch deep, or rather so as barely to hide them. Immediately cover the beds or boxes with moss, in order to shade the surface and vegetating seed from the influence of the sun, or parching air; for when the small descending radicles are protruded, if the earth gets dry below them, all will be destroyed; and the seeds being so very minute, if covered deep, can never come up; therefore it will be necessary to give them shade and very frequently light sprinkles of water; the moss will prevent its washing the earth off the seeds, and will gently communicate the moisture to the surface thereof. When the plants begin to appear, thin the moss, and expose them, but by slow degrees, as they collect strength. If the boxes be placed in a green house, or under the protection of garden frames and glasses, from the time of sowing the seeds till the middle of May, it will be a great advantage; observing that the plants, when up, must be carefully protected from the mid-day sun whilst in an infant state. Towards the middle of May remove the boxes to some comforting shade, to remain there till the latter end of October, then place them in a warm exposure till the approach of severe frosts, when they may be put into a garden frame, and slightly protected during winter. Suffer the plants to remain in the seed boxes or beds till they have two years' growth, being careful to give them shade and water in summer, and some slight protection in winter, and in the beginning of April plant them out into nursery rows as directed for firs and pines, on page 284, in a shady situation and a loamy soil; covering the ground about their roots with moss to keep it moist till the plants are established; observing to give them occasional watering during the first summer and autumn after being thus planted out.

Note.—All other minute seeded shrubby plants, such as ericas, &c., when propagated by seed, should be treated in the above manner, with this difference, that they must have protection and heat in winter, in proportion to their necessities, and soil adapted to their respective natures. Such may also be raised under bell glasses, without the assistance of moss, as these confine the evaporations from the earth, thereby preserving the moist atmosphere around the plant, which prevents a greater exhalation of sap from the tender leaves, than the small radicles are yet able to extract and supply, which is frequently the cause of the sudden death and disappearance of various other crops in warm climates.

WEIGELA AMABILIS.

This beautiful new plant possesses such interest to the modern garden, from its blooming twice in the year, that we insert an illustration of the new favorite. Like W. rosea it is a native of China and Japan, and deserves to be grown by all who have space for a single shrub. It is preferable to the rosea.

Fig. 28.

Weigela Amabilis.

1. Calyx and pistil. 2. Corolla laid open. 3. Gland from the inner base of the tube of the corolla. 4. Transverse section of ovary—*magnified*.

CALYCANTHUS, FRANKLINIA, AND GORDONIAS.

The *Calycanthus floridus,* or Carolina allspice, commonly called the sweet-scented shrub, is deserving of a place in every pleasure-garden, on account of the delightful odor of its flowers. It is easily propagated by layers or suckers ; the most eligible time of laying it is in autumn, and by the spring following twelve months, they may be taken off and planted with good success.

The *Franklinia alatamaha,* of Bartram, is a most charming plant, and very deservedly worthy of cultivation ; it may be propagated in the same manner as the Calycanthus, as may also all the family of Gordonias, which are very ornamental shrubs.

RHUS, OR SUMACH.

The various kinds of *rhus* or *sumach*, may be propagated by suckers, layers, or seed. The seeds, if preserved in sand, and sown early in March, will rise freely the same season, and when one or two years old, may be transplanted into nursery-rows, and having had there two years' growth, may be planted where intended to remain.

THE CORK-TREE.

The *Quexcus suber*, or cork-tree, may be cultivated with good success in the southern States, and consequently deserves to be noticed among other articles of great national importance. It is a native of the south of Europe, and the northern parts of Africa. At present there are considerable woods of them between Rome and Naples, between Pisa and Leghorn, and also in Spain, Portugal, and the south of France.

The uses of the cork are well known amongst us, by sea and land, for its resisting both water and air; the fishermen who use nets, and all who deal in liquors, cannot do well without it. Some persons prefer it to leather for the soles of their shoes, being light, dry, and resisting moisture, whence the Germans name it *Pantoffel-holts,* or slipper-wood; it was first applied to that purpose by the Grecian ladies, whence they were called light-footed. The poor people in Spain, and other parts of the south of Europe, lay planks of it by their bed side to tread on, as great persons use Turkey and Persian carpets; they also employ it for bee-hives. For this last purpose, they roll the bark into a cylinder, or into a conical form, and it answers the end extremely well. It is also used for making cork jackets, which have been found eminently useful for mariners, passengers at sea, and for all those who resort to bathing-places for the benefit of their health; as such will enable the most timorous to swim with perfect safety.

Of the cork-tree there are two or three varieties, one with broad leaves, a second with narrow leaves, both evergreen, and one or two which cast their leaves in autumn; but the broad-leaved evergreen kind is the most common, and said to produce the best cork. The leaves of this are entire, about two inches long, and an inch and a quarter broad, with a little down on their under sides, having very short footstalks; they continue green through the winter, and generally fall off just before the new leaves come out, so that the trees are often bare for a short time. The acorns are very like those of our common white oak.

The exterior bark is the cork, which is taken from the tree every eight or ten years; but there is besides an interior bark which nourishes them, so that the stripping off the outer coat is so far from injuring the trees, that it is of real service; for when it is not taken off they seldom last longer than fifty or sixty years in health; whereas trees which are barked every eight or ten years will live one hundred and fifty, or more. The bark of a young tree is porous and good for little; however, it is useful to take it off when the trees are twelve or fifteen years old, for without this it will never be good. After eight or ten years the bark will be fit to take off again ; but the second peeling is of little use. At the third peeling it will be in perfection, and continue so for upwards of one hundred and fifty years—for the best cork is taken from old trees. The time for stripping is in July, or early in August, or when the second sap flows plentifully : the operation is performed by slitting it down on one side, raising the edges, and then it will peel off readily.

Having procured the acorns in good condition, they are to be treated in every respect as directed for other kinds of oak, on page 282 ; but if they are planted at once where intended to remain for full growth, it will be much the best way ; in which case, particular care must be taken to keep them free from weeds during their infant state, and to protect them from the annoyance of cattle till grown out of their reach. The sooner the acorns are planted after having been procured the better, for when long kept in a dry state they lose their vegetating power, like every other kind of oak.

Curse them! exclaims the peevish planter ; I shall never live to cork a bottle with them. Have patience, good sir ; you have no objection to throw by a few dollars in an iron chest for posterity, never to come in contact with the light of the sun during your existence, and which will always be depreciating in value as the circulation of paper currency increases, and from several other circumstances, a few of which, if laid out on planting cork-trees, would be rapidly accumulating wealth for your children, and rendering a real service to your country, besides, every day you walked out, you would have the pleasure of beholding your little family of trees prospering in health and beauty, humbling their boughs before you, and in their silent language returning you grateful thanks for your fostering care, and promising to reward your offspring for the friendly protection which you afforded them in their minor days.

TANNER'S SUMACH.

The *Rhus coriaria*, or elm-leaved sumach, is a plant which should be introduced and cultivated, particularly in the southern States, where it will prosper in great perfection. It grows naturally in Italy, Spain, the south of France, the Levant, about Aleppo, Rama, and near Algiers, in Africa. The branches are used, instead of oak-bark, for tanning leather ; but the great and particular necessity of its introduction into the United States is, that without it our tanners, who are both numerous and industrious, cannot manufacture what is called Turkey or Morocco leather in good perfection ; for it is with this plant exclusively that that valuable article is tanned in the eastern world ; and a substitute for it has not yet been discovered in America.

It has a strong woody stem, divided into many irregular branches, and rises to the height of eight or ten feet or more ; the bark is hairy, and of an herbaceous brown color when young. The leaves are composed of seven or eight pair of leaflets, terminated by an odd one ; these leaflets are about two inches long, and half an inch wide in the middle, and are of a yellowish green color. The flowers grow in loose panicles at the ends of the branches, each panicle being composed of several thick spikes of flowers, sitting close to the footstalks; they are of a whitish herbaceous color, and appear in June and July, and are followed by numerous roundish compressed seeds.

It may easily be propagated by seed, which, if sown soon after being ripe, or preserved in sand or earth till spring, will grow freely the first year; but if kept dry till spring, they do not generally vegetate till the next season. It can also be propagated by suckers, which it produces pretty freely, or by layers. It is tolerably hardy, and will thrive in warm exposures in the middle States.

MULBERRY-TREES AND SILK-WORMS.

The *Morus alba*, or white mulberry, is a native of China, Cochin-China and Japan, and according to Gmelin, of Persia. It grows well in the United States, and may be cultivated to great advantage for the feeding of silk-worms, as well here as in France, Spain, or Italy. In Spain, Mr. Townsend informs us that, in the Province of Valencia, they prefer the white mulberry; but in that of Grenada, they give a preference to the black. The Persians generally make use of the latter; and it has been asserted, upon very good authority, that worms fed with the black mulberry produce much better silk than those fed with the white. But the leaves of the black should never be given to the worms after they have eaten for some time of the white, lest they should burst.

Sir George Staunton, in his embassy to China, says that the trees he observed in that country did not appear to differ from the common mulberry-trees of Europe; that some of them were said to bear white, and some red or black fruit, but that often they bore none; and that the tender leaves growing on young shoots of the black mulberry are supposed to be the most succulent.

About the year of Christ 551, two Persian monks, employed as missionaries in some of the Christian churches established in India, penetrated into the country of Seres, or China. They there observed the labors of the silk-worm, and became acquainted with the art of working up its productions into a variety of elegant fabrics. They explained to the Greek Emperor, at Constantinople, these mysteries, hitherto unknown, or very imperfectly understood, in Europe; and undertook to bring to the capital a sufficient number of those wonderful insects. This they accomplished by conveying the eggs of the silk-worm in a hollow cane. They were hatched, and afterwards fed with the leaves of a wild mulberry-tree, and multiplied and worked in the same manner as in those climates where they first became the objects of human attention and care. Vast numbers of these insects were soon reared in different parts of Greece, particularly in the Peloponnesus. Sicily afterwards undertook to breed silk-worms with equal success, and was imitated, from time to time, in several towns of Italy. In all these places extensive manufactures were established, with silk of domestic production.

From the reign of Justinian, it was mostly in Greece and some of the adjacent islands that silk-worms were reared. Soon after the conquest of Constantinople by the Venetians, in the year 1204, they attempted the establishment of the silk manufacture in their dominions, and in a short time the silk fabrics of Venice vied with those of Greece and Sicily.

About the beginning of the fourteenth century, the Florentine manufactures of silk became very considerable. It was introduced much later into France; the manufacture of silk, though considerably encouraged by Henry IV., not having been fully established there till under Louis XIV., by Colbert.

"It is an established and well-known fact that both the white and black mulberry-trees grow as well in almost every part of the United States as in any country on earth; and also that silk has been raised and manufactured into a most excellent fabric, under the direction of that great and venerable patriot, and friend of mankind, Dr. BENJAMIN FRANKLIN. That so useful a pursuit should be suffered to die away in a country as well adapted for it as any in the universe, is as extraordinary as it is unfortunate and injurious to the real interest of the nation."

Trees which are designed to feed silk-worms should never be suffered to grow tall, but rather kept in a sort of hedge; and instead of pulling off the leaves singly, the young twigs should be cut off with them on, which is much sooner done, and not so injurious to the trees. This is the more interesting as the mulberry makes a tolerably good hedge and can be used with advantage for both purposes.

The raising and manufacture of silk, as well as every other new establishment, can only be brought to perfection, and consequently into repute, by the industry of some wealthy individuals, or by established companies whose united efforts will surmount the difficulties which always present themselves in new undertakings: for we every day see those that deal in small quantities in any way of life, or in any commodities whatever, generally unsuccessful, whilst at the same time, others possessed of wealth, or in established societies, dealing *largely* in the same articles, acquire vast property and riches; merely from being able to afford constant and regular employment for the people engaged in the business, and having due attention paid to every department thereof.

The vast wealth of Lyons, and of various other places, gained from the labors of this little insect, plainly show that where no accommodations or materials are wanted to employ a multitude of hands in a regular society or combination of undertakers, the silken manufacture must answer; and that people may grow rich thereby, as well in America, as in any other country, if similarly pursued, is too self-evident to bear contradiction.

With a view and expectation that this business may be attempted successfully, I shall contribute my mite by giving the best information that I have been able to acquire on the subject; not in the least doubting but that better may be easily obtained, for the introduction of this important work.

The first object is to raise a sufficient quantity of mulberry-trees, of both the white and black kinds, which are very easily propagated, as directed on page 275. The cultivating of both kinds I think the more necessary, from the different opinions entertained of their utility for this purpose, and the universal admission of either kind answering the end.

The next is to procure the eggs, about the beginning of May, or when the mulberry begins to expand its leaves, to lay them on paper or flannels placed on shelves, in warm exposures, where they may have the heat of the sun to hatch them. In Sicily, boarded or frame houses are commonly erected for this purpose in the fields, among the mulberry-trees, with a number of shelves rising one above another, and a large table in the middle of the room, on which, when they are hatched, to lay over them the young twigs bearing the leaves intended for their food, which must be removed and renewed as often as necessary; keeping them always clean from dead leaves, and their own dirt. A man and boy will attend all the worms that come from six ounces of eggs, and those, one year with another, will spin twenty pounds weight of silk.

The method of clearing off their dirt is this; spread a net over the worms, on which lay fresh food; they will all crawl through the meshes to feed on the leaves, when they may be taken up without the least injury, and their shelves cleaned effectually: after which lay fresh twigs with leaves on the shelves; over these lay the nets and they will return to their former places, when the nets may be laid by till wanted again for a similar purpose. In some countries the worms are suffered to feed and work upon the trees, but their being subject, under such circumstances, to the ravages of birds, unfavorable changes of weather, &c., they are generally kept in houses or sheds erected for that purpose.

In Turkey, the worms are fed in long barns, made, both walls and roofs, of reed or cane; when they are fed, and afterwards spin their clues upon these reeds. In Italy and Spain, they are kept to feed in the same rooms wherein the people live and do their other household affairs, feeding them on shelves and tables without more curiosity.

It is observed, that the worms are commonly sick three or four times during their feeding, generally about ten days after they are hatched, and at weekly periods afterwards. Their best treatment, during these times, is to give them but little food while sick. The whole time of their feeding is about seven weeks; and as they get strength and grow bigger, it need hardly be said that you must give them more and oftener. The leaves should not be given to the worms whilst wet with the dew or rain.

When they have fed their due time they begin to look clear, and a little of the yellowish cast, and to prepare for work; at every time, but at this more particularly, they should have plenty of air. Then small branches, divested of their leaves, are laid over them and in their way, upon which they mount and attach themselves, and in a few days each will cover itself all over with silk so as to be seen no more, till suffered to work its way out for the business of propagation.

In about two weeks they commonly finish their balls, and soon

after cut their way out, and couple for procreation; the balls so perforated are then good for nothing; but it is necessary to suffer a sufficient number to come out in this way, to produce a sufficiency of eggs
for the next season's brood. The others, when they have done working, and before they begin to cut through, should be all put into an
oven just sufficiently hot to kill the worms.

The method of winding the silk off the balls, is first to find their
ends, which is not difficult, and then put about a dozen or fifteen
of them into a basin of hot water, wherein is dissolved a little *gum
tragacanth*, commonly called *gum dragon;* and thus they will be
easily wound. Sometimes the balls are gummy, in which case they
should be thrown into a hot clean lye of wood ashes, and after that
into scalding pure water, which will cause them to wind freely.

When the animal is protruded from the egg, it is a small blackish
worm, very active, and naturally crawls about in search of food; at
this period it should be fed with the youngest and most tender leaves;
in eight or ten days it will increase in size to about a quarter of an
inch in length. It is then attacked with its first sickness, which is
a kind of lethargic sleep, for about two or three days' continuance ;
during which time it changes its skin, preserving the same bulk. It
undergoes similar sickness and changes three or four times, at intervals of about eight days, before it arrives at its full size; which
is from an inch and a quarter to an inch and a half in length ; and
the intervals between these changes, and consequently the periods of
its arrival at maturity for work, are said to vary in different climates,
which is very probable.

After it has formed its cocoon or ball of silk, and undergone its
change in the heart of it, it comes forth a heavy, dull-looking moth,
with wings, but these it seldom uses for flying ; it only flutters and
crawls slowly about in quest of its mate ; soon after copulation the
female lays its eggs, and both die without tasting food in this stage
of their existence.

When in the worm or caterpillar state, they are of a blackish, or
a milk or pearl color ; the former are esteemed the best. The body
is divided into seven rings, to each of which are joined two very short
feet. It has a small point like a thorn exactly over the anus. There
are a considerable variety of breeds, some of which possess qualities
much superior to others. This is a particular of much importance
to be adverted to at the time of beginning to breed; for it will make
a great difference in the profit to the undertaker. The eggs, when
obtained, should be kept in a cool, dry place, neither exposed to heat
nor to excessive frosts, till wanted for hatching the ensuing season.

The *Morus nigra*, or black mulberry, is more esteemed for its fruit
than the white, and when cultivated for such, layers or cuttings from
good fruit-bearing trees ought to be preferred to raising them by
seed ; for monoecious trees, until arrived at a good age, bear male
flowers chiefly and very little fruit. The cuttings, if taken off in
March, rightly chosen, and skilfully managed, will do very well;
though, in general, they do not take as freely in this way as many
other trees ; however, if placed under bell-glasses, they will strike
with great certainty ; but where there is no such conveniency, the

ground about them should be covered with moss to prevent its drying ; and where this is carefully done, they will want but little water, and will succeed much better than with having too much wet.

The *Morus rubra*, or red American mulberry, is admired by some on account of the pleasant acidity of its fruit, and is said to answer the end of feeding silk-worms very well. It is cultivated like every other kind, by layers, cuttings, and seed.

The white mulberry prospers best in a moist rich loam, the black, in a dry sandy soil, and the red in a mean between both these kinds.

The *Morus multicaulis.* Since the preceding was written this new variety of the mulberry has been introduced to the attention of the American public. Its introduction marks a new era in the silk history of the United States. It has already become so rapidly and extensively known that little more need be said upon it here than to remark that it differs from the other varieties, particularly from the white or Italian mulberry, in the luxuriance with which it sends up its " many stalks ;" the increased size of the leaf, and the small portion of refuse left by the worms in feeding. It also is distinguished by its foliage, furnishing food for the worms to considerable extent during the first season of its growth, and in great abundance after the second and third year. The product from the seed is so uncertain, and the propagation by layers and cuttings so easy, that the preference is invariably given to the latter mode of cultivation. A good rich soil, aided by compost or well fermented manure, should be chosen when the planting is intended simply for multiplying the trees, though for feeding the worms the preference is decidedly in favor of a foliage grown on a dry, sandy or gravelly loam, the latter furnishing silk of a better quality, with less risk of endangering the life of the worm. As to the particular mode of cultivation, it is generally conceded to be as simple as that of corn. The ground should be ploughed in the fall, and again in the spring.

The " *Silk Worm*," a valuable periodical, published by Mr. Thomas C. Clarke, of this city, and devoted to the advancement of this rapidly increasing business, furnishes the following directions for planting, which we find corroborated by other writers on this subject, as well as by practical cultivators.

" There are four methods of planting these trees. 1st, by budding under glass ; 2d, by cuttings laid out at the usual season ; 3d, by layers of whole trees; and 4th, by layers of sections or parts of trees.

" The cuttings should always be made at least with one bud, and that within a quarter to half an inch of the end intended to be next the surface. When they are *budded*, there should be a box made about two feet on the back and eighteen inches in front, covered with glass lids with hinges of iron or leather, so that they may be aired. This box should be filled two-thirds full with rich mould, or mould enriched with well-rotted manure. The cuttings should be inserted in this in a sloping direction at an angle of 45°, the upper end towards the north, the bud below the surface half an inch, and the whole box towards the south. The cuttings should be from a quarter to half an inch apart, so that the mould may be all around each cutting. They should be placed in this position about the 1st of March, and let remain to the 15th or 20th of May. The late frosts should be all over when removed, and they should be placed in well prepared soil with a trowel dibble, the soil pressed well around them, and well watered if the weather be not rainy. The planting of these should, if possible, be done in rainy or at least cloudy weather.

"The cuttings of the second method should be inserted in the soil without dibble, the upper end to be about one inch under the soil, if the mould be loose, or even with the soil if the mould be stubborn. When they come up an inch or two, let the hoe draw carefully mould around them.

"By the third method, the ground is prepared as for corn, well broken with the harrow, and if necessary, the roller ; and let a cultivator be run with one horse, from three to four feet, in parallel lines, forming a furrow as for corn.

"The trees are laid horizontally, the root of one to the top of another from one end of the row to another, the root laid deeper than the tree, and let the hoe cover them about one or one and a half inches.

"The fourth method is by cutting a tree up into pieces of from twelve to fifteen inches, and laying them in the furrow, prepared as in the last method, so as to leave a space between each piece equal to the length of the cutting."

THE PAPER MULBERRY, AND METHOD OF MAKING PAPER OF ITS BARK.

The *Morus papyrifera*, or paper mulberry. This tree makes very strong vigorous shoots, but seems not to be of tall growth; it drives up an abundance of suckers from the roots, by which it is easily propagated. The leaves are large, some of them entire, others cut into two, three, or four lobes, sporting themselves into various forms, and scarcely two to be found alike on the same tree, especially while young; they are of a dark green, and rough to the touch on the upper surface, but pale green and somewhat hairy on the under side, falling off on the first approach of frost in autumn. Their fruit is little larger than peas, surrounded with long purplish hairs, when ripe changing to a black purple color, and full of sweet juice.

It is a native of Japan and the South Sea Islands ; and according to Mr. Miller, of China and *South Carolina*, whence he received the seeds. The inhabitants of Japan have, for ages, been in the habit of making paper from its bark : they cultivate the trees for this purpose, on the mountains, much in the same manner as we do osiers, cutting them all down for use every autumn after the leaves are fallen.

The finest and whitest cloth worn by the principal people at Otaheite and in the Sandwich Islands, is made of the bark of this tree; which they frequently dye red. The bread fruit-tree makes a cloth inferior in whiteness and softness, worn there chiefly by the common people.

Paper making having a connection in this instance with objects of my attention, and the probable use it may be of to the community, induces me to give additional publicity to the following method of manufacturing it from the bark of the paper mulberry-tree; the more especially as such has been attempted last year, and with good success, by the laudable exertions of Mr. William Young, proprietor of the Brandywine paper-mills, in the State of Delaware. It is extracted from Martyn's edition of Miller's *Gardener's Dictionary*, and quoted by him from *Kæmfer*. I am not certain what kind of mulberry Mr. Young had used for that purpose, nor whether it was the bark of the roots or branches he manufactured, but some of the paper I had seen printed on, and it promised well. It is very probable that either *species* might be manufactured into paper, but I am induced to think that the paper mulberry, from the vigorous growth of its *young* shoots, is more likely to answer the end than any other.

"The young shoots being cut down in autumn after the leaves are fallen and divided into rods of three feet in length, or shorter, are gathered into bundles to be boiled. If the shoots are dry, they must be softened in water twenty-four hours. The bundles are bound very close together, and placed erect in a large copper, properly closed: the boiling is continued till the separation of the bark displays the naked wood. Then the stalks are loosed out of the bundles and allowed to cool; after which, by a longitudinal incision, the bark is stripped off and dried, the wood being rejected. When this bark is to be purified, it is put three or four hours in water, when being sufficiently softened, the cuticle, which is of a dark color, together with the greenish surface of the inner bark, is pared off. At the same time the stronger bark is separated from the more tender, the former making the whitest and best paper; the latter a dark, weak and inferior kind. If any bark appears that is old, it is set aside for a thicker paper of worse quality. Into this last class they throw the knotty parts of the bark, and those which have any fault or blemish.

"The bark is now boiled in a lye that is clear and strained; care being taken to stir the substance as soon as it begins to boil with a strong reed, and to pour in of the lye gradually as much as is necessary for stopping the evaporation and restoring the liquor that is lost.

"The boiling is to cease when the materials can be split by a slight touch of the finger into fibres and down.

"Next it is to be washed, which is a thing of some moment; for if washed too short a time, the paper will be strong indeed, but too rough, and of an inferior quality; if too long, it will be whiter, but of a fat consistence, and less fit for writing. Being sufficiently washed, the materials are put upon a thick, smooth, wooden table, and stoutly beat by two or three men, with battons of hard wood, into a pulp, which being put in water, separates like grains of meal. Thus prepared, it is put into a narrow vat; an infusion of rice, and a mucous water of the infusion of the root of Manihot being added to it. These three are to be stirred with a clean slender reed, till reduced into a homogeneous liquor of a due consistence. The prepared liquor is now put into a larger vat, from whence the sheets are poured out one by one, and placed in heaps upon a table, covered with a double mat; a small thread of reed being placed between the sheets at the edge, and projecting a little, so that they may be taken up singly when wanted; the heaps are covered with a plank of wood the size of the paper, upon which stones are put, at first of a light weight, but afterwards heavier, that all the wet may be pressed out by degrees. The following day, the weights being removed, each sheet is taken up by itself, and the operation is finished."

The preceding is the process employed by the Japanese, and whether we regard the expedition or labor, or the quantity and quality of the product, it seems to admit of much improvement.

Instead of reducing the subject to a *pulp* by battons, in the manner above described, that might be done more effectually by grinding it, in the way practised with rags.

The color might be rendered as elegantly white as that of any other substance, by means of an immersion, first in oxygenated muriatic acid, afterwards in a solution of alkali, and finally, washing it in pure water. By these means it is probable that the portions thrown aside for paper of inferior qualities, might be wrought into that of prime excellence.

The decoction of rice and of the root of Manihot, can have no possible advantage over the size commonly used for giving to the paper the necessary firmness and texture.

THE CALABRIAN OR MANNA ASH.

There are two particular *species* of ash, from which that useful drug called manna is collected, in the kingdom of Naples, &c , and which might be cultivated in the southern States to advantage; therefore I am induced to give some account of them.

1. The *Fraxinus ornus*, or flowering ash, which is the principal kind cultivated for manna. The leaflets are ovate-oblong. serrate, petioled; flowers with petals.

2. The *Fraxinus rotundifolia*, or round-leaved ash, which also produces it, but not in as great quantities as the former. Leaflets roundish, acutish, doubly serrate, subsessile; flowers with petals. Both these kinds may be raised from seeds as directed on page 283, or by grafting or budding them on any other species of ash. They are natives of Italy, Sicily, and the southern parts of Europe.

They also cultivate in Sicily the *Fraxinus excelsior*, or common European ash, for that purpose; which induces me to think, that if the above kinds were grafted *low*, on any of our American species, it would not prevent their yielding as good manna as if established on their own roots. Doctor Cullen supposes " manna to be a part of the sugar so universally present in vegetables, and which exudes on the surface of a great number of them." The qualities of these exudations he thinks are " very little, if any, different." The principal trees known to produce these mannas, in different climates and seasons, are the larch, orange, walnut, willow mulberry, and some different kinds of oak; which latter are found growing between Merdin and Diarbecker, and also in Persia near Khounsar.

In Sicily, the three species above mentioned, with the view of obtaining manna from them, but more particularly the first, are planted on the declivities of hills, having eastern aspects. After ten years' growth the trees first begin to yield manna, but they require to be much older before they afford it in any considerable quantity. Although the manna exudes spontaneously from the trunks and branches, yet in order to obtain it more copiously, incisions are made through the bark, by means of a sharp crooked instrument, a slice of which is taken off, about three inches in length and two in breadth; they leave the wounds open, and by degrees the manna runs out. The season thought to be most favorable for instituting this process, is a little before the dog-days commence, when the weather is dry and serene. The incisions are first made in the lower part of the trunk, and repeated at the distance of an inch or two from the former wound, still extending them upwards as far as the branches, and confining them to one side of the tree, the other side being reserved till the year following, when it undergoes the same treatment. On making these, a thick white juice immediately begins to flow, which gradually hardens on the bark, and in the course of eight days acquires the consistence and appearance in which the manna is imported, when it is collected in baskets and afterwards packed in large chests. Sometimes the manna flows in such abundance from the incisions, that it runs upon the ground, by which it becomes mixed with various impurities, unless prevented, which is commonly attempted by interposing large concave leaves, stones, chips of wood, &c. The business of collecting it, generally terminates in those countries in September, when the rainy season sets in.

That manna is got in quantities on the leaves of trees, is an opinion taken from the doctrine of the ancients, and received as incontestible without consulting nature; for all those who are employed in the gathering of it, know of none that comes from the leaves; therefore, that with which the Israelites were so peculiarly favored, could only have been produced through miraculous means, and is consequently out of the province of the naturalist. The best manna is what exudes from the tree very slowly, and is collected clean; this is always more dry, transparent, and pure, for when it flows copiously it concretes into a coarse, brown, unctuous mass.

METHODS OF PROPAGATING TREES AND SHRUBS BY LAYERS.

There are few trees or shrubs, if any, but may be increased in this way. The nursery gardeners who want to propagate large quantities of various hardy kinds, of which they cannot easily procure seeds, and which by experience they do not find to grow freely by cuttings, establish what they call stools, of the different kinds intended to be propagated, particularly of the deciduous tribe, and also some evergreens. For this purpose they plant in different quarters, stout, healthy plants, at the distance of four or five feet from one another every way, and head them down; these throw out near the earth a number of young shoots, some of which may be laid in the autumn or spring following; these stools, as they are commonly called, continue for many years, always laying down the shoots of the last season, and every year successively they produce abundance for the ensuing year's laying, still taking them off either in autumn or spring as they become well rooted. The elm, linden, mulberry, and maple, do extremely well in this way, but it is seldom practised on any of the pine family. The far greater number of kinds will be well rooted and fit to take off in one year after laying, some not till the second, and others not until the third year; but the latter are very few.

The ground in these quarters should always be kept free from weeds, be manured occasionally, and dug every autumn and spring, being careful not to disturb the layers.

After the layers are taken up, the stools must have all the wounded parts taken away, and any old branches cut off pretty close to the stems, the next season these will produce new shoots, which may be laid the autumn or spring following.

The best season for laying all the kinds that do not root freely, is autumn, and the young shoots of the preceding summer's growth, should be preferred; these should be tongued as hereafter directed. The free rooting kinds may be laid either in autumn or spring, as convenient.

Though branches may be laid at any time, yet the best season for laying hardy trees, that shed their leaves, is October or November; for such as are tender early in March; evergreens may either be laid at the latter period or in June or July.

When the branches or twigs cannot be bent down into the ground lay them in boxes or pots, filled with good earth and elevated to the necessary places by blocks, tressels, or benches. Too much of the head of the layers must not be left on, and the smaller, the less should be left out of the ground, except they are twigs of the former year's growth, and intended for timber trees, in which case they should not be topped.

Many trees and plants will not put out roots from old wood branches; yet if the young shoots of the same year be laid in July, they will often root very freely; but as those shoots will be soft and pithy, they must not have too much wet, which would cause them to rot; cover, therefore, the surface of the ground with moss, which will prevent its drying too fast, and a little water will suffice.

In many kinds of the young shoots of the same year, if laid in June or July, they will be well rooted by the November or spring following, and may then be taken off.

When layers are to be made from green-house shrubs, or other plants in pots, the laying should be generally performed either in their own pots, or in others placed convenient for that purpose.

Sometimes the branches of trees are so inflexible as not to be easily brought down for laying, in which case they must be half cut through, as practised in plashing hedges, and by that means brought down; or when they are got too old for plashing, or the nature of the wood will not bear that operation, they may be thrown down on one side, by opening the earth and loosening or cutting the roots on the opposite.

There are several methods of performing this operation.

1. Having well dug the ground and made it very light, take some of the most flexible and free-growing shoots, and lay them into it about six inches deep, pegging them down with hooked sticks if necessary, leaving the end of the layer a foot or a foot and a half, or more if the twig be young and healthy, out of the ground, with its head as erect as possible; keep them moist during the summer season, and if of a free rooting kind, they will take root and be fit to be taken off and removed in the autumn or spring following, if not, they must remain another season.

2. Tie a piece of wire tight around the bark of the layer, at the place you intend to lay in the ground, and half an inch below a bud; twist the ends of the wire so that they may not untie, as the shoot swells, prick the parts above and below the wire with an awl in several places, and then lay it in the ground as before directed. This method will succeed when the other fails.

3. Slit the shoot underneath a joint or bud up the middle, and about an inch long, or a little better, according to the size and nature of the layer, forming a sort of tongue, nearly the same as directed for carnation layers; laying that part in the earth and raising the top upright, so as thereby to separate the tongue of the slit from the other part and keep it open; then apply the earth as before. This is the most universally practised and successful mode, when any preparation of the shoot is necessary to promote its rooting.

4. Twist the part of the branch intended to be layed in the earth as you would a willow twig, this greatly facilitates the emission of fibres, and layers of numerous trees and shrubs may be forwarded exceedingly in rooting by this method.

5. Cut the bark nearly all around, a little below a joint or bud, taking out small chips thereof in several places below the cut, and lay that part in the earth. Some sorts will root more freely by this than any other mode.

6. Thrust an awl through a shoot at a joint in several places, laying that part in the earth, and it will emit fibres from the wounds.

After laying, in either of the above methods, there is no particular culture necessary, except in the heat of summer to give occasional waterings to keep the earth moist about the layers, which will greatly promote their rooting, and which, if effected the first season, they should be taken off in the autumn or spring following.

ADDITIONAL OBSERVATIONS ON PLANTING.

Plants are always most prosperous when propagated by seed, which is nature's favorite method.

Evergreen plants are best fit for transplanting from the seed-beds into nursery-rows when they have attained the height of from four to six inches, and deciduous kinds, when from six to twelve inches high.

Layers should not be suffered to remain on the mother plants longer than until sufficiently rooted, which will be effected by some in six or seven months, if laid in spring; by far the greater number in one year, and by others, not in less than two or three.

Tonguing or twisting the layers, &c., is necessary for such kinds as do not strike freely, but not for those that do.

All kinds of *seedlings* should be transplanted in spring, the deciduous earlier than the evergreens.

October or November is the best time for the *final* transplanting of all kinds of hardy deciduous trees, if the ground in which they are to be planted is dry, and not subject to become too wet in winter; but early spring planting does best in most soils.

Evergreens of every kind succeed best when planted in spring, provided it be done to each respective kind *immediately* before its vegetation commences.

Watering is very useful when given in small quantities and frequently; but the reverse when in large quantities, and but seldom.

Every kind of tree, whether deciduous or evergreen, grows to a larger size when finally planted out at the age of four years, having remained one or two in the seed-bed, and two or three in the nursery-rows, than at any other subsequent period.

Walnuts, oaks, and every other tree that has a tendency to drive down perpendicular or to tap roots, always grow to larger timber when the seeds are sown where intended to remain, and never transplanted.

PROTECTING TREES FROM CATTLE.

The beauty of individual specimens, as well as groups of trees, is often marred, to a great extent, by the means employed to protect them from cattle. None of these are more objectionable than the abomination termed a crate. Where such heavy-looking and unsightly objects are thickly placed, as they often are, the effect is disagreeable in the extreme; as they have to be endured for years, any substitute that will afford equal protection without their objectionable appearance, should be readily adopted.

Fig. 29.

The accompanying sketch illustrates a contrivance which combines both support and protection from cattle, and is also neat in appearance. This fence by being entirely below the eye, is very little seen, and the supports of the tree, being of wire, are scarcely to be distinguished, except upon close examination. If the whole were of iron, it would, of course, be still less objectionable, on the score of appearance. The uprights of the fence.

as given in the sketch, are supposed to be stout piles, six in number, driven into the ground at an angle of about 45°, at a sufficient distance from the tree to prevent cattle from reaching the stem or branches. The uprights should be about three feet six inches out of the ground. They are connected by rails placed horizontally, and sufficiently close to prevent sheep from getting between them. From the tops of three or four of these uprights, stout wires are fixed, the upper ends meeting at the tree, where they are attached to a collar, which should be somewhat larger than the stem it is to surround; the intervening space is then to be filled with leaves, hay, or moss, and properly secured, to prevent damage to the bark. These wire supports are, of course, only required when the tree is newly planted; by employing them, stakes—which are rarely effective and always objectionable in appearance—are entirely dispensed with.

PROPAGATION OF TREES AND SHRUBS BY CUTTINGS.

Various trees and shrubs may be propagated by cuttings, and this month, especially in the middle States, is a good time for planting all the hardy deciduous and evergreen kinds that grow in that way, observing to plant the former in the early part of the month, and the latter towards the end of it.

When you intend to propagate trees for timber, or for a tall state-ly growth, be particular never to take the cuttings from horizontal branches, for they will never have an inclination to grow in a spread-ing manner; always make choice of perpendicular shoots, and par-ticularly those that terminate the branches; these will most certainly produce the straightest and handsomest trees, and be little inferior to those raised from seed; of this I have had ample experience, and found it uniformly to be the case.

But when you intend the plants for hedges, wildernesses, or thick-ets, the same precaution is not necessary; though in propagating any kinds of erect-growing shrubs for detached plants in the pleasure garden, I would recommend it, as they will be less subject to spread and injure other herbaceous flowering plants growing near them.

Large shoots cut into lengths, are often used, and will do tolerably well, provided they are selected as above; but I would ever prefer what gardeners term cock-shoots, or those retaining the terminating buds. The soft and pithy sorts will succeed better with having an inch or two of the former year's wood annexed to the cuttings, but all the hard wooded kinds are much better without it.

For this purpose dig one or more beds or shady borders, &c., where the ground is somewhat mellow and not wet; let the earth be well broken with the spade, and rake the surface smooth.

Take off the cuttings with your knife from the trees or shrubs that you want to increase; let them be of the last summer's shoots, cut-ting them off from about six or eight to ten or fifteen inches long, according as they may occur in the different sorts of trees, &c.; plant them in rows, each cutting about half or two-thirds of its length into the ground; close the earth well about them, and in dry weather let them be occasionally watered.

The tacamahaca, white, black, trembling; Lombardy, Canada, Athenian, Carolina, heart-leaved, smooth-leaved, and various leaved poplars, and all the varieties of willow may be propagated in this way; also, the plane-tree, tupelo-tree mulberry, and alder; with the sea buckthorn, elder, tamarisk, some kinds of solanum, honeysuckles, diervilla, privet, trumpet-flower, virgin's-bower, Carolina kidney bean-tree, passion flower, jasmine, periploca, jew, juniper, savin, arbor-vitæ, Portugal and English laurels, and immense numbers of other trees and shrubs.

Cuttings of all sorts planted a year ago, and that are well rooted, may now be transplanted or quartered out into open nursery rows, to advance in proper growth, and to have occasional training for the purposes intended.

GRAFTING FOREST TREES AND ORNAMENTAL SHRUBS.

The latter end of this month will be a good time to graft the various kinds of forest trees and flowering and ornamental shrubs which you mean to propagate in that way; such as elms, ash, oaks, hollies of various kinds, robinias, double-flowering thorns, altheas and cherries, &c. There are very few hard-wooded plants but will take in this way when grafted on stocks of their own families, and indeed there are many instances of plants taking on stocks of a different genus, as the pear on the white thorn the peach on the plum, &c. &c.

TRANSPLANTING YOUNG TREES AND SHRUBS.

All hardy kinds of deciduous trees and shrubs may now be transplanted, either into nursery rows, or finally where intended to remain; always observing to do this in mild weather, and when the ground works freely and is in a good condition to receive them. In the middle, and particularly in the eastern States, the removal of evergreens should not be commenced before the beginning of April, and then finished towards the middle of that month, if the season proves favorable. Hollies are best removed towards the end of April.

WEEDING SEEDLING TREES AND SHRUBS.

Look over the seed-beds of young trees and shrubs: if weeds appear on them, let them be carefully picked out by hand in time before they mix their roots with those of the plants.

WATERING SEEDLING TREES, ETC.

In dry, warm weather, it will be proper to refresh the seed-beds of small young trees and shrubs with water now and then; a little at each time will do; let this be done early in the morning.

DIGGING VACANT GROUND, ETC.

All requisite digging and trenching of vacant quarters of ground
20

in the nursery, designed for plantations of young trees, shrubs, &c., this spring, should now be completed as soon as possible, in due time for the reception of the respective plants intended, which, in the deciduous kinds particularly, should be mostly or generally finished by the middle or latter end of this month, and the evergreens soon after that time. (See *April*.)

Finish all digging between the rows of young trees, &c., in this month if possible ; and also in all parts where planting is intended this spring, provided that the ground will work freely.

PROPAGATING GOOSEBERRIES AND CURRANTS.

The only proper method of propagating gooseberries and currants, is by cuttings; suckers should never be resorted to except in cases of necessity, for such will always produce others numerously from their roots, which carry off the nourishment that ought to go to the support of the fruit; and besides, they form such thickets as to smother and deprive them of the benefit of a free circulating air.

The proper cuttings for planting are the shoots of the last summer's production, of straight, clean growth ; they should be taken from healthy trees, and such as are remarkable, according to their kinds, for bearing the finest fruit; let each be shortened from about ten to twelve or fifteen to eighteen inches long, according to its strength.

Previous to planting, cut off every bud as close as possible to the shoot, except three, four, or five near the top, which are to be left to form the head of the plant. Some people imagine that the buds on those parts inserted in the earth grow into roots, which is by no means the case, nature never having designed them for such ; the roots or fibres always strike out through the clean and smooth bark, but generally a little below a bud, and sometimes at the lower extremity of the cutting from between the bark and the wood. In some kinds these' buds decay and die away, but in gooseberries and currants they always rise in suckers, and from these others innumerably, which always rob the fruit, and often render even the best kinds not worth their room in the garden.

Your cuttings being thus prepared, plant them in rows eighteen inches or two feet asunder, and about eight or nine inches apart in the rows, always inserting them at least six inches into the earth, and if the shoots are sufficiently long, eight or nine, leaving from four to ten inches, according to circumstances, of a clean stem between the surface earth and lowest left bud, upon which to establish the head. Having had one or two years' growth in these rows, they may be planted out either in autumn or early in spring, where intended for fruiting, but autumn is the most preferable season.

Gooseberries, of all other fruit-trees, require the richest soil. The situation should neither be too high nor too low, nor the soil much inclined to gravel or sand, a deep rich loam is their favorite. Where this fruit is expected in the best perfection, the ground between and about the trees must be kept free from weeds, and dug every spring and autumn, and strongly manured once a year with old well-rotted cow-dung; they must be judiciously pruned, and each tree kept to a single stem, without any suckers, which must be dug up or stripped off whenever such appear. But all the culture on earth will not produce good fruit unless you have good kinds, for there are *crab* gooseberries as well as crab apples, and as great a variety of the one kind of fruit as of the other.

THE PLEASURE, OR FLOWER GARDEN.

HYACINTHS.

The choice kinds of hyacinths should now be protected from severe frost, for if permitted to penetrate so far into the soil as to reach the bulbs, especially about the time that the plants begin to appear above ground, it will produce a singular effect, by causing some of them to shoot forth or discharge their stems or blossoms; but if at this time the roots become entirely frozen they are in danger of being destroyed, or at least so weakened as to produce but indifferent flowers.

TULIPS

When your choice tulips appear above ground, if on examination any distemper or canker is discernible on the foliage, about this time, either above or a little below the surface of the soil, it should be carefully cut out with a sharp knife, and the wounded part left exposed to the sun and air, which will presently heal it : a fine dry day should be made choice of for the foregoing operation.

If the surface of the beds appear to be of too close and solid a texture, it should be carefully stirred up, about two inches deep, which will admit the air more freely to the stems, give vent to their exudations, and encourage their growth.

Should the weather prove extremely severe, a slight covering of mats, placed on arched hoops over the beds, will be very serviceable to them. But this care or attention is not necessary for the common kinds, growing promiscuously in the borders, &c.

RANUNCULUSES AND ANEMONES.

Continue to protect your choice kinds of early planted ranunculuses and anemones, as directed on page 168 ; they will now require particular attention, as the rudiments of their flowers will be advancing, which would suffer greatly if too much exposed to nipping frosts.

Finish planting the ranunculuses and anemones that are yet kept out of ground for a successional bloom, which is to be done agreeably to the directions given in *October*.

Ranunculus roots will lay in the ground several days after planting, before they begin to vegetate; during this period they become very much swollen by imbibing the moisture of the soil, and are in this state extremely susceptible of injury from frost, much more so than when vegetation has actually taken place.

As soon as the bed is planted, if hard frosts are likely to ensue, a sufficient quantity of dry straw should be placed near it, ready for covering when necessity requires, which should be kept on only during severe frosts, or such as would be likely to penetrate to the roots, as the effects of covering too long or too much would be as destructive as the reverse, by causing the roots to become mouldy, than which nothing can be more prejudicial.

Anemones are somewhat hardier than ranunculuses, and therefore do not *require* so particular care, but if such is afforded them, it will cause them to blow in greater perfection.

PLANTING BULBS OF VARIOUS KINDS.

As early in this month as possible, finish planting all your hardy kinds of bulbous roots, such as hyacinths, tulips, polyanthus-narcissus, jonquils, star of Bethlehem, &c. &c., as they must be considerably weakened by being kept too long unplanted, observe the directions given on pages 93 and 94, under the article *tulips*.

AURICULAS.

The first favorable weather that occurs in this month, divest the auricula plants of their exterior decayed leaves, and by the middle of the month, the operation of earthing up, as it is termed, should commence; that is to say, the surface earth of the pot should be taken away about one inch deep, and fresh compost, with the addition of a little loam, should be substituted in its stead : this will contribute greatly to the strength of the plants and the vigor of their bloom; at the same time it will afford a favorable opportunity to separate such offsets as shall appear possessed of a sufficiency of fibres to be taken off at this early season : these offsets, when properly planted in small pots, should be placed in a frame, in some warm sheltered situation, till their roots are established.

The fine auriculas should now be protected from very severe frost, cold cutting winds, or excessive rains, for these would injure them and prevent their blowing in good perfection ; but they must have plenty of air in mild weather, and not be debarred from warm moderate showers of rain, which will now prove beneficial.

When the weather proves very dry, let them be refreshed moderately with water, just to keep the earth a little moist about their roots, but too much would materially injure them. For their further treatment see next month, &c.

SOWING AURICULA AND POLYANTHUS SEEDS.

If you have neglected last month to sow auricula and polyanthus seeds, to raise new varieties, sow them as early as possible in this, agreeably to the directions given on page 176.

CARNATIONS.

Being provided with some of the finest and most valuable carnations, for with the common sorts it will not be worth while to take much pains, you should proceed to the potting of them between the middle and latter end of this month.

The proper compost for these flowers is as follows, viz :—

One-half fresh, sound, loamy earth, taken from the surface of a rich pasture ground, turf and all, and not more than four or five inches deep.

One-third, or a little more, of old horse-dung, such as had been a year previously used for hot-beds.

One-sixth coarse sea or river sand.

These ingredients ought to have been mixed together in autumn, laid in a heap about two feet thick, in an open exposure, and turned three or four times during winter, so as that all the parts may be well incorporated and have the benefit of the frosts; early in March it should be gathered into a round conical heap to drain and become dry, and when sufficiently so, and wanted for use, pass it through a *coarse* screen or sieve to reduce its parts, and take out stones or any other extraneous substance which it contains.

The pots made use of for spring potting, should be ten inches wide at the top, five inches at the bottom, and eight inches deep in the side, with a hole in the centre of the bottom an inch in diameter.

The pots are first to be nearly half filled with compost, previously placing an oyster-shell or such like, with its hollow side downwards, over the hole in the bottom of each : the compost is to be higher at the sides than at the centre of the pots, and the plants intended for them, which are supposed to have been wintered in small pots containing three plants each, are to be carefully turned out with the earth adhering to them in a ball; and after rubbing off half an inch of the surface of the old mould around the plants, above their fibres, cleaning them and cutting off the points of their decayed leaves, the ball is to be carefully placed in the centre of the pot, and the space between it and the sides filled up with the prepared compost.

If your plants have been wintered one plant in each pot only, a size much smaller than the above will be sufficient to shift them into, but when three plants grow and flower together in a large pot, they appear to more advantage.

This being done, give the plants a little water, and observe that the earth comes no higher up their stems than it did in the former pots, nor should the compost come nearer than within an inch of the top of the rim, after it has been gently shaken or struck against the ground in finishing; as an inconvenience will attend its being too full when the operation of laying comes to be performed, which requires some additional mould on the surface, for the layers to strike into.

When the plants are thus potted off for bloom, they should be placed in an open airy part of the garden under an arch of hoops, that in case of cold drying winds, heavy rains, or cold frosty nights, mats may be thrown over, to preserve them from the effects of such unfavorable weather. In this situation they are to remain, always open to the air, except in the cases above mentioned, and be kept regularly watered with soft water, as often as appears necessary, from a fine rosed watering-pot. For their further treatment, see next month, *May*, &c.

The plants which were planted in large pots last autumn, where they are to remain to flower, should now have the old mould taken out as near to their roots as possible, without disturbing them, and replaced with fresh compost, after which, treat them as above.

The common carnations in beds, borders, &c., may be removed towards the latter end of this month and planted where desired.*

PINKS.

The culture of pinks is much less difficult than that of carnations; they are hardier, more easily propagated, increase more abundantly, and are less liable to incidental casualties than the latter.

A good fresh loamy soil, dug and well pulverized, about twelve or eighteen inches deep, and well manured and mixed with cow-dung, two years old, is all the preparation that is necessary for this charming flower.

The plants designed for the principal bloom should be planted where intended to blow in September or early in October, as they do not flower quite so well if removed later in the season; they should be planted at about the distance of nine inches from each other, and the bed should be laid rather convex or rounding, to throw off excess of rain; but will require only a slight covering or protection in case of frost; and this only for the superior kinds.

The beds should be kept free from weeds, and the surface stirred up a little if it inclines to bind.

They may also be propagated now freely, by slips from their roots, or removed if necessary. If desired to have them in pots, you may pot a few of the finest kinds as directed for carnations.

POLYANTHUSES.

Your finest kinds of polyanthuses and double primroses may be treated in every respect as directed for auriculas, if desired in pots; if not, they may be removed at pleasure, between the middle and latter end of this month, and large roots divided for increase; but this should not be done to those which you intend to flower strongly, till their bloom is over, immediately after which, you may slip them or divide their roots. They are impatient of heat and drought, and love the reverse, shade and moisture: they are very hardy, and seldom perish except by the summer heats, which frequently destroy them, unless the necessary precautions are taken.

* The Remontant, or Ever-blooming Carnations, are now become indispensable in the flower garden. They will strike readily from cuttings, and should be propagated afresh each season.

DOUBLE DAISIES.

These beautiful little flowering plants may, about the end this month be taken from the winter repositories and planted for edgings in *shady* borders; for if planted in open exposures, the summer heat will totally destroy them, unless they are removed into the shade as soon as their first bloom is over.   The roots may now be separated for increase, as every shoot of them, if *slipped* off, will root freely. They may also be removed into pots with balls of earth adhering to their roots, where they will blow handsomely, but it would have been better if they were planted in these in September or October.

GIVING FRESH EARTH TO VARIOUS PLANTS IN POTS.

Give some fresh earth to the pots of double wall-flowers, double stock July flowers, double sweet williams, rockets, rose campions, catchfly, campanulas, scarlet lychnis, and such like plants, which were potted last autumn or before.

In doing this, clear the plants first from decayed leaves, and take some of the earth out of the tops of the pots, but not too deep to disturb the roots of the plants; then fill up the pots again with fresh earth, and give some water; this will strengthen their roots, and the plants will shoot freely and produce large flowers.

PRICKING OUT EARLY ANNUALS.

If any tender annuals were sown last month, such as cockscombs, tricolors, Ipomœas, sensitive plants, ice plants, balsams, &c., in order to have them in perfection at an earlier period than common, make a new hot-bed towards the middle or latter end of this, in which to prick them to forward their growth.   Let the hot-bed be about thirty inches high, and make the top even; then set on the frame; and when the great heat is over, let the earth be put in; let it be light, rich, and perfectly dry, and lay it equally over the bed six inches thick; when warm, prick the plants therein at three or four inches distant each way, or some may also be pricked in small pots, one good plant in each, and plunged in the earth of the bed; giving the whole a little sprinkling of water; then let the glasses be put on, observing to raise them behind a little every day to admit air and let out the steam; shade the plants from the sun till they have taken fresh root.

When they are rooted and begin to push, they should have fresh air every day; therefore let the upper ends of the glasses be raised an inch or two or three in height to admit it; but shut them down towards the evening, and cover them every night with mats; remember to sprinkle them with water occasionally, giving but a little at each time.

Keep up the heat of the bed by occasionally lining with hot dung. Thus these tender annuals are to be continued forwarding in growth till May; then, when the frost is totally gone, finally transplanted into large pots, flower borders, &c.

SOWING TENDER ANNUALS.

A hot-bed may be made the beginning or any time this month, in which to sow the seeds of tender annual flowers, such as the ice plant, sensitive plant, browallias, &c.

Make the bed and sow the seed as directed in last month. Or a few plants may be raised in pots in any cucumber or melon hot-bed now in cultivation, to a proper size for transplanting. (See *April.*)

The plants raised from the above sowings will blow strong and beautiful in May, June, July, &c.

Remember they are not to remain in the hot-bed where raised, but are to be transplanted, some into pots, and some into the borders. (See *April* and *May.*)

SOWING HARDY ANNUAL FLOWERS.

Any time this month that the ground is in good condition, you may sow in the borders and other flower compartments, a variety of hardy annuals, such as large and dwarf annual sunflowers, sweet pea of every kind, larkspur, flos-adodis, persicaria, Tangier peas, Nigella, Venus's looking-glass, Venus's navelwort, double dwarf poppy, Lobel's catchfly, dwarf-lychnis, snails, horns, hedgehogs, caterpillars, mignonette, china-aster, horse-shoes, belvidere, candy-tuft, honey-wort, convolvulus-minor, cyanus, china-hollyhock lavatera, curled mallow, winged pea, china pink, ten weeks' stock, and many other sorts, which will flower better if sown early than if delayed to a late period; though all of the above will succeed very well if sown in the beginning of next month.

These should be sown, each kind separate, in patches in the different borders and flower beds, &c., finally to remain where sown; or a few, when grown to a sufficient size, may be carefully transplanted into such borders and places as you desire. For the method of sowing them, see page 166.

SOWING VARIOUS KINDS OF FIBROUS-ROOTED PERENNIAL AND BIENNIAL PLANTS.

Perennial and biennial flower-seeds, of most kinds, may be sown, in the middle and southern States, towards the latter end of the month; in the eastern States, the middle or latter end of April will be preferable.

It is to be observed that these kinds do not flower the same year they are sown; but all the sorts of them will flower strong, and in good perfection the year after.

As every one may not know the meaning of perennial and biennial plants, the perennials are those which continue on the same roots many years, producing new flower stems annually, such as everlasting sunflower, scarlet lychnis, perennial asters, &c. The biennials are only of two years' duration, being sown one year, flower and perfect their seed the next, and soon after die, or become of a dwindling growth, such as honesty, tree-primrose, tree-mallow, &c.

Many kinds are proper to be sown now, such as carnations, pinks, sweet-williams, wall-flowers, and stock July-flowers of all sorts; also rose-campion, scarlet lychnis, columbines, Greek valerian, polyanthus, auriculas, scabiouses, and Canterbury bells.

The seeds of hollyhocks, French honeysuckles, rockets, honesty, or satin flower, tree-primrose, broad-leaved campanula, and fox-gloves; snap-dragon, bee-larkspur, with seeds of most other sorts of perennial and biennial plants, may be sown.

All the above, and other hardy perennial and biennial flower-seeds, are to be sown in beds of light earth in the open ground.

For the method of sowing them, see the *Flower Garden* for next month.

DIG THE BORDERS, ETC.

Dig the borders and flower compartments, &c., and make them smooth; they will then be ready to receive the seeds of annual flowers and plants of other kinds; besides they will appear fresh and neat.

TRANSPLANTING PERENNIAL PLANTS.

Where there are vacancies in any of the beds, borders, or other parts of the garden, they may now be filled up with many different kinds of perennial and biennial flower plants, and will all blow the same year.

Many principal sorts may now be planted, such as lychnises, rose-campions, rockets, catch-fly, campanulas, carnations, pinks, and sweet-williams, double feverfew, golden rod, perennial sunflowers, perennial asters, and French honeysuckles; also columbines, Canterbury bells, monk's-hood, fox-gloves, tree-primroses, scabiouses, snap-dragon, lobelias, irises, bee-larkspur, double ragged robin, valerian, and most others of the like sorts.

Plant also dwarf fibrous-rooted flowers in the borders &c., they will take root freely in a short time; such as polyanthuses, double chamomile, London pride, violets, hepaticas, thrift, primroses, saxifrage, gentianella, lilly of the valley, &c.

In planting the intended different kinds, dispose them variedly, the larger growing sorts more or less back; and the smaller forward towards the front and middle.

Give water at first planting, and afterwards occasionally in dry weather, till the plants are fresh rooted; by which they will grow freely, and all flower the same year in their proper seasons

HOE AND RAKE THE BORDERS.

Loosen with a hoe or small spade, the surface of those beds or borders which were dug and planted with flowers of any kinds last autumn, or any time since.

Let this be done in a dry day, hoeing, or lightly digging and stir-ring the earth carefully between the plants, taking care of the shoots of bulbous roots, &c., which are now just peeping through the sur-face; clearing away all decayed leaves of the plants, weeds, and every sort of rubbish, and then let the beds or borders be neatly raked even and smooth.

By thus loosening the surface of the borders, the first growth of seed-weeds will be retarded, it will greatly promote the strength of the flowers, and the whole will appear clean and agreeable.

PRUNING SHRUBS, AND DIGGING THE CLUMPS IN THE SHRUBBERY.

Finish pruning all sorts of flowering shrubs and evergreens which require it, observing the directions of the two former months.

Dig the ground in the clumps or borders if not done in the former month, which will prove beneficial; the ground being turned up fresh will appear neat, and the plants will show themselves more agreeably.

PLANTING DECIDUOUS FLOWERING SHRUBS, ORNAMENTAL AND FOREST TREES.

Where deciduous flowering shrubs or trees are wanted in any of the pleasure grounds, they may now be planted with good success, such as common and Persian lilacs, snow-drop tree, fringe-tree, blad-der-nut, rose-acacia, bladder-senna, angelica-tree, Azalea, honey-suckles, Calycanthus, New Jersey tea, Judas-tree, clethra, papaw, leather-wood, fern-leaved Comptonia, Amorpha, dog-wood, double flowering thorns, cherries and peaches, snowy-medlar, Euonymus in sorts, Fothergilla, althea-frutex, Franklinia, Guilandinia, sassafras, swamp magnolia, Benjamin-tree, witch-hazel, St. Peter's-wort, dou-ble altheas, of various colors; corchoras japonica, evergreen or sweet-scented China honeysuckle, purple magnolia, pyrus japonica, purple beech, copper beech, fern-leaved beech, Norway maple, sorbus hy-brida, jasmine, rhus cotinus, or Venetian sumach, Dierville roses, and all kinds of hardy deciduous shrubs; and also the tulip-tree, lime-tree, poplars of every kind, catalpa, chestnuts of every sort, sour and sweet gum, elm, maple, walnut, hickory, plane-tree, horn-beam, beech, nettle-trees, ash, honey-locust, oak, poplar, &c. &c.

In planting trees for timber allow them the proper distances for the purposes intended; if for close plantations, or by way of coppices or underwood for gradual thinning and falling for poles and other small purposes, every seven, eight, or ten years; you may plant them in close rows only four, five, or six feet distant; and when they have attained growths proper for the first thinning, select the handsomest plants at regular distances to stand for timber, and thin the rest; but when designed to have the whole to stand for a full plantation of large standards before they are thinned, plant them at from ten to fifteen or twenty feet distant.

DIRECTIONS FOR PLANTING ALL SORTS OF TREES AND SHRUBS.

All flowering and evergreen shrubs, ornamental trees, &c., designed for the shrubbery and other plantations, should be planted at such distances that they may not crowd each other as they grow up; for they always show themselves best when they stand separate at moderate distances. Shrubs of all kinds designed for detached clumps particularly, should be planted not less than three to four or five feet asunder, that the different kinds, according to their growths, may generally remain distinct; but where a thickety growth is required in particular compartments, a closer plantation may be formed of different common shrubs.

Let all the tree kinds be allowed proper room, proportionate to their respective growths, and according as they are designed for open or close plantations, or clumps, groves, avenues or thickets, &c.

In planting shrubs and trees of every kind, let all convenient expedition be made in doing it, so that they may be planted as soon as possible after they are taken up, or brought from the nursery or elsewhere; that their roots may not be dried by the sun and wind; but when brought from any distance, and they cannot be immediately planted, untie the bundles, lay the roots in a trench, and cover them with earth to lie till the places allotted are ready to receive them.

In preparing for planting, dig a round aperture for each shrub or tree from half a yard to two or more feet wide, according to the size of the roots, and a spade deep, capacious enough to receive them freely, and loosen the bottom well. Then having the shrubs, &c., ready, prune off broken or bruised roots, and any irregular productions of the heads, and place them in the holes upright, break the earth well, and throw it in equally about the roots, which cover a proper depth, shaking each plant gently as the earth is filled in, to cause it to settle close between all the roots and fibres; tread it moderately to fix the plant firmly in an upright position, making the top of the earth a little hollow round each to hold water when given in dry weather; and if they are watered as soon as planted, it will settle the earth about all the roots more effectually, and promote their fresh rooting; it would be of advantage in general, but more particularly to any of the more tender or curious shrubs, &c., to lay some long litter on the surface to preserve the moisture about the roots in dry weather.

Immediately after planting, fix stakes to such tall plants as require support, and let them be fastened thereto.

PLANTING EVERGREENS.

Evergreen trees and shrubs may be planted with good success any time this month in most of the southern States, but in the middle States that should not be attempted before the last week therein; nor in the eastern States before the beginning or middle of April; these kinds are always most successfully planted when done *imme-*

diately before their respective vegetations commence; which is a rule that ought to be carefully observed. (See the *Nursery* and *Pleasure Garden* for next month.)

PLANTING ROSES.

You may plant roses any time this month that the weather will permit; and indeed there is a particular advantage in planting some every ten days, even to the middle of May, for the flowering of them may be retarded in this way, and the bloom of those delightful shrubs continued for a much longer period than if all were planted at the same time; but such as are planted after the twentieth of April, should the season prove dry, will require shade and water until they have taken fresh root. The early planting, however, will be the most successful in growth, and flower in greater perfection than the others.

PLANTING BOX EDGINGS.

Box, of all other plants, makes the neatest and most beautiful edgings, and this is a very successful time to plant it, particularly in the middle States; in the other States it should be planted on the spur of the earliest spring vegetation; for although it is an evergreen, its taking and growing freely by slips or cuttings, causes it to agree with early planting better than those kinds that do not easily propagate in that way; and, moreover, it is very hardy and seldom injured by winter frosts.

To make neat edgings you should get some short bushy box, and let it be slipped or parted into moderately small slips of not more than from eight to ten inches long; if any of them have roots or fibres, the better, but the cuttings or slips will all grow if planted early, and kept moderately and occasionally watered. The long woody roots of such as have them must be trimmed, and all the plants, slips or cuttings, made pretty much of a length.

The method of planting is this: stretch your line, if for a straight edging, along the edge of the bed or border, let that part be trodden lightly and evenly along to settle it moderately firm, and with the spade make it up full and even according to the line; then on the side of the line next the walk, let a small neat trench be cut out, about six inches deep, making the side next the line perfectly upright, turning the earth out towards the walk or alley.

The box is to be planted in this trench close against the upright side next the line, placing the plants so near together as to form immediately a close compact edging, without being too thick and clumsy, and with the top of the plants as even as possible, all an equal height, not more than an inch or two above the surface of the ground; and as you proceed in planting, draw the earth up to the outside of the plants, which fixes them in their due position; and when you have planted the row out, then with your spade cast in the earth almost to the top of the plants, and tread it neatly and closely thereto; when the edging is planted, let any inequalities of the top be cut as even and neat as possible with a pair of shears.

Where there are any gaps in the former planted edgings, let them now be made good; for, when ragged and uneven, they have a disagreeable appearance.

Or where any old edgings of several years' standing have been permitted to run up rude and spreading, nothing in a garden looks more unsightly; and should be taken up, slipped, trimmed, and replanted in a neat, regular order.

For an account of the various plants generally used for edgings and the methods of planting them, see the *Flower Garden* next month. They may all be planted towards the latter end of this, if the weather proves favorable.

PLANT HEDGES.

Finish planting all the kinds of deciduous hedges as early in the month as the weather permits, and if the season proves very favorable, you may, in the last week thereof, plant evergreen hedges. For the methods of doing which, see the *Nursery* for this month.

China arbor-vitæ forms a very ornamental hedge for a flower garden. The American makes the best hedge.

CLEAN THE PLEASURE GARDEN.

Every part of this garden should be now well cleaned and put into the best order. Give the flower borders, beds, &c., a general spring dressing, by digging, hoeing, and raking; let the edgings of box, &c., be regulated where disorderly, and the gravel-walks be well cleared from weeds and litter, and occasionally rolled.

Keep the grass lawns, walks, &c., now well cleared from litter and worm-cast earth, which appears unsightly, and spoils the compact evenness of the sward; give them, therefore, occasional rollings with a heavy roller, whereby to preserve a clean, even, firm surface, neat to appearance, and that can be mowed close and regular with greater facility.

The edges of all the grass walks and lawns should now be cut even with an edging-iron (see page 91), which will add greatly to the general neatness.

MAKING GRASS-WALKS AND LAWNS.

The sooner in this month that you can make any grass-walks, lawns, or grass-plats, that may be necessary, the better; as the roots will have time to establish themselves before the great droughts and heats commence. Turf, when it can conveniently be got, is always preferable to sowing grass-seed, but in extensive lawns, the latter, of necessity, must be resorted to. The best turf for those purposes, is that of a close-fed pasture or common, where the sward is tough, and the grass short and fine.

This natural turf is generally composed of Kentucky blue grass

(*Poa pratensis*), and our native variety of white clover (*Trifolium repens*). They are the best for lawns in all cases as they do not "burn out," and form a close sward.

If you have much to lay, you should be provided with a *turfing iron*. This instrument is formed with an iron plate for the cutter, six or seven inches wide, rounding at the edge, very sharp, and about a foot long, pretty much in the form of a spade; and at the tread, it is forged or connected to a long bent iron handle, the bending so formed as to admit of the plate or cutter resting flat on the ground, in the proper position for flaying the turf; the iron handle at top being either formed like the handle of a spade, or having a socket near the plate to place a crooked wooden and properly headed handle therein. With this instrument, turf can be taken off with much more convenience and expedition than with a spade; but when it cannot be conveniently had, a spade may do very well.

It will also be necessary in order to go completely about your work, to have a *racer* or sward-cutter. This should have a stout wooden handle, about four feet long and bent a little in the lower end, having about four or five inches of the point end of an old scythe, placed *transversely* in the lower extremity, with the point downwards, projecting an inch and a half, with the edge forward and made fast in a slit in the handle with a couple of rivets; so that when pushed before you, it may expeditiously cut the sward as you race it along.

Having this instrument, strain a line tight, first lengthwise, then strike the racer into the sward close to the line, run it along, it will expeditiously cut its way and divide the turf to a proper depth; directly place the line a foot farther, and race it out as before, and so proceed to as many widths as may be wanted, then with the line placed crosswise, race out the sward in yard lengths. Being thus divided, the turf-cutter with his turfing iron proceeds to cut them up, about an inch and a half thick, which he can do with great expedition; and according as they are cut, each should be rolled up with the grass side inward, as close and firm as possible, for the more ready carrying and removing them without breaking.

Let the ground where the turf is to be laid, be made as even as possible, that it may settle equally thereafter, and rake the surface smooth. In laying them, make the edges join close every way, and as soon as laid, the whole should be immediately well beaten, with a wooden beater, and afterwards rolled with a heavy stone, or iron roller.

GRAVEL WALKS.

Now is the time to begin to turn gravel walks where the surface is dirty, &c., especially in the middle States, observing, that this is to be done where necessary in all parts of the Union as early as possible in spring.

The gravel walks which display a dirty surface, or are annoyed with weeds, should be turned as early in this month as the weather gets dry and comfortable, in order to render them neat and convenient for walking on. For the method of doing which, as well as that of their general formation and treatment, see the *Flower Garden* for next month, to which I particularly refer you, and advise as much of that work to be done in this as the weather and hurry of business will permit.

Such gravel walks as were broken up and laid in ridges the beginning of winter, which is a very bad practice, as noticed on page 90, should now be levelled down, formed dressed, and rolled, as directed next month.

The necessity of due attention being paid to all your walks, on the opening of spring, is so evident, that it is scarcely necessary to urge it; the having them neat and newly dressed will give a gay and sprightly appearance to the whole garden.

RATIONALE OF DRAINING LAND.

So many gardens consist of a clay soil which it is necessary to success to drain, the following should be studied by those who wish to understand the necessity of the oft repeated advice as to drainage, whether they be gardeners or farmers.

The reason why drained land gains heat, and water-logged land is always cold, consists in the well-known fact that heat cannot be transmitted *downwards* through water. This may readily be seen by the following experiments :—

Experiment No. 1.—A square box was made of the form represented by the annexed diagram, eighteen inches deep, eleven inches wide at top, and six inches wide at bottom. It was filled with peat, saturated with water to *c*, forming to that depth (twelve and a half inches) a sort of artificial bog. The box was then filled with water to *d*. The thermometer *a*, was plunged, so that its bulb was within one and a half inch of the bottom. The temperature of the whole mass of peat and water was found to be $39\frac{1}{2}°$ Fahr. A gallon of boiling water was then added; it raised the surface of the water to *e*. In five minutes the thermometer *a* rose to 44°, owing to the conduction of heat by the thermometer, and its guard tube; at ten minutes from the introduction of the hot water, the thermometer *a* rose

Fig. 30.

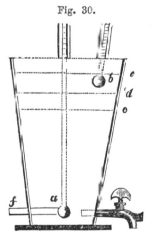

to 46°, and it subsequently rose no higher. Another thermometer, *b*, dipping under the surface of the water at *e*, was then introduced, and the following are the indications of the two thermometers at the respective intervals, reckoning from the time the hot water was supplied :—

				Thermometer b.	Thermometer a.
	20 minutes	.	.	. 150○	46○
1 hour	30 "	.	.	. 101	45
2 hours	30 "	.	.	. 80½	42
12 "	40 "	.	.	. 45	40

The mean temperature of the external air to which the box was exposed during the above period was 42°, the maximum being 47°, and the minimum 37°.

Experiment No. 2.—With the same arrangement as in the preceding case, a gallon of boiling water was introduced above the peat and water, when the thermometer a was at 36°; in ten minutes it rose to 40°. The cock was then turned, for the purpose of drainage, which was but slowly effected, and, at the end of twenty minutes, the thermometer a indicated 40°; at twenty-five minutes 42°, whilst the thermometer b was 142°. At thirty minutes, the cock was withdrawn from the box, and more free egress of water being thus afforded, at thirty-five minutes the flow was no longer continuous, and the thermometer b indicated 48°. The mass was drained and permeable to a fresh supply of water. Accordingly, another gallon of boiling water was poured over it, and, in

3 minutes,	the thermometer a	rose to	77○
5 "	" " "	fell to	76½
15 "	" " "	"	70½
20 "	" " "	remained at	71
1 hour 50 "	" " "	" "	70½

In these two experiments, the thermometer at the bottom of the box suddenly rose a few degrees immediately after the hot water was added; and it might be inferred that heat was carried downwards by the water. But, in reality, the rise was owing to the action of the hot water on the thermometer, and not to its action upon the cold water. To prove this the perpendicular thermometers were removed. The box was filled with peat and water to within three inches of the top; a horizontal thermometer, $a f$, having been previously secured through a hole made in the side of the box, by means of a tight-fitting cork, in which the naked stem of the thermometer was grooved. A gallon of boiling water was then added. The thermometer, a very delicate one, was *not in the least affected* by the boiling water in the top of the box.

In this experiment, the wooden box may be supposed to be a field; the peat and cold water represent the water-logged portion; rain falls on the surface, and becomes warmed by contact with the soil, and thus heated descends. But it is stopped by the cold water, and the heat will go no further. But, if the soil is drained, and not water-logged, the warm rain trickles through the crevices of the earth, carrying to the drain level the high temperature it had gained on the surface, parts with it to the soil as it passes down, and thus produces that bottom heat which is so essential to plants, although so few suspect its existence.

This necessity of warmth at the root undoubtedly explains why it is that hardy trees, over whose roots earth has been heaped, or having laid, are found to suffer so much, or even to die; in such case, the earth in which the roots are growing is constantly much colder than the atmosphere, instead of warmer.

It is to the coldness of the earth that must be ascribed the common circumstance of vines that are forced early, not setting their fruit well when their roots are in the external border, and unprotected by artificial means; and to the same cause is often ascribed the *shanking* or shrivelling of grapes, which most commonly happens to vines whose roots are in a cold or unsunned border.

THE GREEN-HOUSE.

The green-house plants should now have plenty of air admitted to them at all favorable opportunities, particularly as the weather gets warm towards the latter end of the month, but due attention must be paid, in any sudden changes, which are very frequent at this season, to preserve them from cold, cutting, or frosty winds; during the prevalence of which, the windows, &c. should be kept close, for such weather would ruin some of the tender kinds, and would be of bad consequence to all. It need hardly be said that the windows and doors must be kept close every night, and should imperious necessity require it, in the early part of the month, the flues heated at night to counteract the power of severe frosts.

Look over the tubs or pots every day, and see where water is wanting, and let such as require it be supplied therewith, taking care to use moderation in that case. Water will be serviceable to most of the plants, but especially to all the woody kinds, which will now require more frequent refreshments, if fine mild weather, but always in moderate quantities; and be still careful, on the whole, not to give too much water at a time, for that would prove the destruction of many kinds, and would be prejudicial to the plants in general, especially if a cold season, and while they are confined in the green-house.

Keep every plant in the house free from decayed leaves; that is, where such appear let them be immediately picked off; for these, if generally permitted to remain would injure the plants; besides, they appear disagreeable.

Any decayed or mouldy shoots should be cut clean off to the firm live wood, and where dust or any sort of filth appears on the leaves of the plants, let them be cleared therefrom: if those of the oranges, lemons, and other large-leaved kinds, are foul, have a sponge dipped in water and clean them therewith, one by one, and let the small-leaved sorts be cleaned by a brisk syringing all over their heads.

ORANGES, LEMONS, AND MYRTLES.

Where any of the oranges, lemons, and myrtles, &c., have naked or irregular heads, you may now towards the latter end of the month, if mild fine weather, begin to reduce them to some regularity. The branches or head may either be cut close, or shortened less or more to the place where you desire shoots to rise, to form the head regular, for they will break out in the old wood.

When any trees are thus headed down, it would also be an advantage to shift them, especially such as are of a weakly growth, in order to add a little fresh earth about their roots ; and the method is this : let the tree be taken out of its tub or pot, but preserve the ball of earth entire ; then trim off with your knife any very matted roots, or dry fibres round the outside, and also some of the loose old earth from the bottom and sides of the ball; and, having fresh compost ready, put some into the bottom of the pot or tub ; place the tree therein, fill up around the ball with fresh earth, and give it a little water.

But in heading down any of the green-house plants, if time will not permit, or that you think it not necessary to shift them as above, do not, however, fail to loosen the earth in the top of the tub or pots, and a little way down around the sides, and draw this loose earth out ; then fill up the tub again with new compost, and give some water.

But where any orange or lemon-trees are in a very weak or sickly unprosperous growth, it would be advisable about the latter end of this month, or beginning of next, to prune the heads and shift them into entire new earth, taking the plant clean out of the pot, all the old earth shaken entirely from its roots, and all mouldy and decayed roots cut off; then let the whole root be washed in water, and plant it again immediately in a tub or pot of new earth, taking care not to place it too deep, and give water moderately.

After this shifting, it would be a great advantage to the same plants if you had the convenience of a glass case, &c., in which previously to make a hot-bed of tan or dung, but tan is much preferable ; and if in this bed the trees are plunged, they will shoot sooner and more freely, both in root and top, to recover good strength, and a renewed head of branches of prosperous growth, early in the following summer.

HEADING DOWN MYRTLES, ETC.

Where myrtles or other similar exotics have decayed branches, or their heads thin, straggling, and irregular, they may now also be headed down, more or less, as it shall seem proper, and either shift them into some fresh earth, as directed above for the oranges, or some of the top mould within the pots taken out, and a little around the sides, then fill up with fresh earth and water them.

These trees with this management will shoot out again, and in four or five months' time will be furnished with entire new heads. Supply them duly with water.

SHIFTING PLANTS, THAT WANT IT, INTO LARGER POTS.

Any of the oranges, lemons, or myrtles, or other green-house plants that want larger pots, may be shifted therein, with some fresh earth, towards the end of this month, when the weather is mild.

In performing this, let each plant intended for shifting be turned out of its present pot with the ball of earth entire; but let any thickly matted or dry mouldy roots on the outside of the ball be pared off with a sharp knife; then set them in their new pots, and fill up the spaces with fresh earth.

Water them immediately after this, set them in their places in the green-house, and they will shoot freely both at the root and top.

CARE OF GERANIUMS OR PELARGONIUMS.

Examine the geraniums and other plants of a similar growth; the young shoots being somewhat succulent, are more liable to injury from the effects of a severe winter, or great damps, than the harder wooded exotics, so that sometimes many of them decay or mould, and which, where they occur, should now be pruned away: likewise pick off all decayed leaves.

Your geraniums will now show flowers, and it is necessary to give them plenty of water and as much air as the weather will admit of.

GIVING FRESH EARTH TO THE POTS OF GREEN-HOUSE PLANTS.

The orange and green-house plants in general, which do not require shifting, should at this time have some fresh earth added to the tops of their pots or tubs; it will encourage the plants greatly, and it is soon done.

First loosen the old earth in the tops of the tubs or pots, quite to the surface of the roots, but so as not to disturb them, and loosen it also down round the sides a little way, then take out the loose earth and fill up the pots with some that is new, and give them a moderate watering.

SOW SEEDS OF GREEN-HOUSE PLANTS, ETC.

A hot-bed may be made the beginning of this month to sow the seeds of tender plants, either of the green-house or stove kinds. The bed should be made either of hot dung, or fresh tanners' bark, and covered with frames and glasses; or if made of hot dung lay eight, ten, or twelve inches of tan-bark at top, either new or old, both in which to plunge the pots, &c., and to continue longer a regular heat.

The seeds should be sown in pots of light earth, and these plunged to their rims in the tan, and moderately watered at times, as you see occasion.

Where tan cannot be obtained readily, make the bed of hot dung, three feet high, set a frame on, and when the burning heat is over, lay on four or five inches depth of earth, then fill some middling small pots with fine light mould, sow the seeds therein, and cover them lightly with sifted earth, then plunge the pots in the earth on the bed, and put on the glasses.

Let the pots in general be frequently sprinkled with water, and when the plants appear, give them fresh air, by raising the glasses behind a little way. Observe to keep up the heat of the bed, by applying a lining of fresh hot dung, when it declines much, and protect them occasionally from the too powerful influence of the midday sun.

SOWING KERNELS OF ORANGES FOR STOCKS.

Now is the time to sow the kernels of oranges and lemons, in order to raise stocks to bud any of those kinds of trees upon.

The best method of sowing these kernels is this : fill some middle-sized pots with very good earth, sow the kernels in the pots, and cover them half an inch deep with earth, then plunge the pots into a hot-bed, and let them be frequently watered. (See the *Green-house,* next month.)

PROPAGATING BY CUTTINGS, LAYERS, ETC.

Propagate by cuttings and slips, various shrubby green-house plants, as myrtles, geraniums, fuchsias, oleanders, hydrangeas, jasmines, coronillas, justicias, &c. The young shoots planted in pots and placed in a hot-bed, will soon strike root and grow freely ; or where there is the convenience of bark-beds, either in a hot-house, or under any glass frames, &c., these, and many other sorts, if plunged therein, may be struck very expeditiously ; or, if at the same time, some are covered with a hand-glass, it will still more expedite their rooting, giving proper waterings.

Likewise propagate shrubby kinds by layers, and also different sorts by suckers, &c.

THE HOT-HOUSE.

FRUITING PINES.

It is on a due proportion of air admitted into the hot-house that the goodness of the pine plants in a great measure depends. The want of it will cause them to grow with long leaves and weak stems, which plants never produce good fruit.

On the other hand, air admitted in too great a quantity, or at improper times, will injure the plants, and cause them to grow yellow and sickly.

In the depth of winter, during the time that the plants are nearly in a state of inaction, the hot-house will require but very little air ; yet it will absolutely be necessary to take every favorable opportunity to let out the foul air and admit fresh, when it can be done with safety to the plants ; the letting down the glasses a little way, even for a *few minutes,* in the middle of the day, is of more importance than inexperienced persons can conceive, especially when there is a little sun and a mild wind. But at this season, particularly in the advanced part of the month, to have regard to the words *give air* on the botanical thermometers, is not necessary, for a little may with much safety be given, although the spirits should not rise higher than 62° of Fahrenheit, or six or eight degrees above temperate.

It will be necessary to continue a regular degree of heat in the house, as directed last month, by keeping up a fire-heat every evening, night, and morning, but more particularly in severe weather; and a constant heat in the bark-bed. As the heat of the weather increases, and the sun becomes powerful, the morning fires, in particular, must be regulated accordingly.

The fruiting-plants will now generally show fruit; they must, therefore, have very particular care, and not be suffered to want a sufficiency of bottom heat, air, or a reasonable portion of water.

Examine the bark-bed, and see if there is a proper heat, for upon that depends the success of having handsome and full-sized fruit. The great article is to preserve a *free growth* in the fruit from their first appearance to the time of their maturity; this must be done by keeping the bark-bed to a proper degree of heat, that is, it should be quite lively, for a faint heat will not answer the purpose; therefore, on examining the bed, if you find it much decreased, let preparation be made for its revival as soon as possible.

Provide for that purpose a quantity of new bark from the tanners the beginning of this month. The middle-sized bark is to be chosen, and such as has been at least a fortnight or three weeks out of the tan-vats.

The quantity of fresh bark necessary to provide at this time, should be equal to near one-third of what the bark-pit will contain. This, when brought home, if very full of moisture, and but little or no heat, should be thrown up in a heap to remain eight or ten days, to drain and prepare for fermentation. But if very wet, it should be first spread thin in an open, sunny place for two or three days to dry, and then be thrown in a heap.

When your bark is ready, and the bark-pit is declined in heat, the latter end of this month, or earlier if necessary, proceed to fork up and renew it as directed in page 185, and immediately replunge the pots. The whole of this work should be begun and finished the same day if possible.

The heat of the old bark, not being quite exhausted, will cause the new immediately to ferment, and if well proportioned and mixed, and it is done towards the end of the month, it will retain a kindly growing heat till the fruit is ripe. (For further particulars, see *January* and *February*.)

SUCCESSION PINES.*

As the length of the day and power of the sun increase, these plants will begin to grow freely, and from this time it will be neces-

---

* The best cultivators now dispense with succession stocks altogether. The under part of the bed is heated by hot-water pipes, the plants twined into the bed, and a good sucker allowed to take the place of the one fruited In this way a crop is annually secured from the same bed.

sary to keep them in a regular growing state; for if young plants receive a check afterwards, it generally causes many of them to start fruit. From this time forward they will require a little water occasionally, just what is only sufficient to keep the earth in a moderate state of moisture, for too much would injure them.

About the middle of the month or soon after, will be an eligible season for shifting them, in the doing of which, shake off the whole ball of earth, and cut off all the roots that are of a black color, carefully preserving such only as are white and strong. Then put the plants that are intended to fruit next season, in pots of eight or nine inches diameter at the top, and seven deep, with fresh mould entire.

The bed at this time should be renewed with a little fresh tan, and forked up in order to promote its heating, and the pots plunged therein immediately. The hot-house should be kept pretty warm till the heat of the tan begins to rise, as it will be the means of causing the plants to strike both sooner and stronger.

As soon as the bed gets warm, give the plants a sprinkling of water over their leaves, and when you perceive them to grow, give water according as they require it, and as the weather increases in heat give air in proportion.

VARIOUS SHRUBBY AND SUCCULENT HOT-HOUSE PLANTS.

The various kinds of shrubby and succulent exotics will require the same treatment this month as directed in the last, page 186, &c., but particularly observing to give them air in proportion as the heat of the weather increases, and water according to their respective necessities, as noticed in *February*.

PROPAGATION OF EXOTIC TREES, SHRUBS, AND PLANTS.

This is a very proper time to sow such seeds of rare plants as you are able to procure; those that are in good condition, and whose nature it is to vegetate the first season, will rise freely; but many kinds will not grow for three, four, five, or six months after sowing, and others not for a year; therefore, it will be necessary to have patience, and to take care all the time of the whole, as well the pots in which the plants do not rise, as those that do; if you have room to plunge them into the bark-pit, or into hot-beds at work, or made for the purpose, it will greatly facilitate their growth.

You may now propagate many kinds by suckers, cuttings, and layers, which should be duly attended to, particularly such as are scarce and difficult to be obtained.

RAISING EARLY FLOWERS, FRUITS, ETC. IN THE HOT-HOUSE.

Pots of any desirable flowering plants may still be introduced to forward an early bloom, such as pinks, fuchsias, hydrangeas, roses, carnations, and many others. (See *February*, &c.)

Also pots of strawberries and vines, as in the two former months, to continue the supply of early fruit.

Likewise, a few more kidney-beans, &c. (See last month and *January.*)

In hot-houses where grape-vines are trained in, from plants growing on the outside, and conducted up under the glasses, &c., they will, towards the end of this month, or earlier, according to the degree of heat kept up, be well advanced in young shoots, having fruit, which shoots should be carefully trained along in regular order, and all the improper and superfluous growths cut away.

APRIL.

THE KITCHEN GARDEN.

PREVIOUS to entering upon the work of the kitchen garden, &c. for this month, it will be proper to observe that a great portion of the open ground culture and sowing necessary to be done in some places in April, have been fully treated of in March, in order to accommodate those citizens of the middle States, whose gardens, from the nature of soil and situation, admit of early sowing, as well as a desire in many to have their crops at as early a period as possible, either for sale or family use; and also for the general accommodation of the more southerly States, that month being their principal season for gardening. But, in the eastern States generally, and in such parts of the middle States as the ground is naturally of a binding and heavy nature, this will be the most eligible period for sowing their general garden crops; always observing to sow the hardy kinds as early in the month as the soil, season, and situation will admit of, in order that the young plants may be established before they are overtaken by the summer heat and drought; but never, nor on any account should a stiff or moist ground be wrought till it gets so dry as to fall to pieces in the working, nor delayed till it binds and becomes hard. Let the spade not be applied till every particle of water, that is not in contact with the clay, is either drained away or drawn off by the air; nick that time and you will then find the earth to work freely, and not subject to bind afterwards; for if a clay is worked before this critical period it kneads like dough, becomes more tough, and never fails to bind when drought follows, which not only prevents the seed to rise, but injures the plants materially in their subsequent growth by its becoming impervious to the moderate rains, dews, air, and influence of the sun, which are all necessary to the promotion of vegetation.

On the other hand, a light sandy soil will be rather benefited by working it when moist, as such will have a tendency to make it more compact, and consequently more retentive of moisture.

The nearer the ground approaches to a sand the less retentive will it be of moisture; the more to a clay the longer will it retain it; and the finer the particles of which the clay is composed, the faster will it hold every small particle of water, and consequently be longer in drying, and become harder when dry; but earth of a consistence that will hold water the longest *without becoming hard when dry*, is that of all others best adapted for raising the generality of plants in the greatest perfection. This last described is called loam, and is a medium earth between the extremes of clay and sand.

The great art of improving sandy and clay soils, is to give to the former such dressings of clay, cow-dung, and other kinds of manure, as will have a tendency to bind and make it more compact, and consequently more retentive of moisture; and to the latter, coats of sandy earth, pond-mud, horse-dung, and such other composts as may tend to separate its particles and open its pores, thereby easily to discharge any superabundance of moisture, and cause it to approach as near as possible to a loam, which may be greatly assisted by summer and winter fallowing; for the winter frost and summer heat being the plough and spade of nature, have a power to separate the particles of earth, by the expansion of the particles of water lodged between and in contact with them, more effectually than the ploughs and spades made by the hand of man; but when art and nature act in co-operation, the business is more speedily accomplished. This is the foundation stone of horticulture and agriculture, and merits the serious consideration of every person concerned.

Let it not be understood that I am an advocate for late sowing or planting; I am the reverse, when it can be done under favorable circumstances.

The above remarks are applicable generally to all the other open ground departments, as well as to the *Kitchen Garden*; but particularly inasmuch as they have relation to the sowing of seeds.

CARE OF CUCUMBERS AND MELONS, ETC.

Examine your cucumber and melon beds, and if any have declined in heat, especially in the early part of the month, line them with fresh dung, as directed in page 25: this will be necessary, in order to obtain plentiful crops of fruit.

As the sun is now become very powerful, all kinds of plants which you have in hot-beds, will require abundance of air, and occasional shade, for if the beds were left close shut only for a few hours during the prevalence of a hot mid-day sun, the whole would be scorched to death: therefore you ought never to leave the garden at such times without first raising the glasses and giving shade to the plants if thought necessary.

MAKING NEW HOT-BEDS FOR CUCUMBERS AND MELONS.

In order to have successional crops of cucumbers and melons, you may in the early part of this month make new hot-beds, either for the reception of plants or for sowing the seeds; observing the directions given in the former months, as well for these, as the due attention which fruiting and other plants require.

MAKING HOT-BED RIDGES FOR CUCUMBERS AND MELONS.

Make hot-bed ridges about the middle of this month for the cucumber and melon plants raised last month, in order to be planted under hand or bell-glasses. For this purpose make trenches three feet wide and two deep, in a warm dry part of the garden, and fill them to the surface with good fresh horse-dung, as directed in *January* for other hot-beds, then you may either earth them directly, or in two or three days after when the dung will be settled, and the heat risen to the top of the bed, laying from seven to nine inches thick of light rich earth over every part.

When this is done and all the surface made smooth, lay on your hand or bell-glasses in the middle of the ridge four feet asunder, and keep them close down till the dung has thoroughly warmed the earth, then proceed to put in the plants.

You may plant under each glass two strong melon plants, or three cucumbers; observing, if possible, to remove and plant them with balls of earth about their roots.

As soon as they are planted, let them be moderately watered and directly set on the glasses; if sunny weather, and the sun powerful, shade them a little with a mat over each glass, and repeat the waterings occasionally, once or twice a week, according to the degree of warmth in the bed, and temperature of the weather; but let moderation be always observed in performing this work, especially when newly planted.

When the plants are well taken with the ground and growing freely, give them plenty of air, by raising the glasses on one side, and when they have grown so large as to run out under the glasses, let these be raised on brickbats, stones, or pieces of wood, to give full liberty to the plants, and do not take them off totally till towards the end of May.

Cucumber and melon seeds may be sown about the middle of this month, on ridges made as above, and protected with glasses; these will be much earlier than if sown in the beginning of May in the open ground, and much more profitable to market-gardeners.

PLANTING CAULIFLOWERS.

In order to have cauliflowers in good perfection, you must be provided with stout early plants, such as are strong, and in the middle States, perfectly fit for planting out early this month: being furnished with these, select a piece of very rich loam, rather inclining to moisture, but by no means wet, and such as will not be subject either to burn or become stiff and bound by severe drought, always avoiding sand or clay, as much as possible; give it at least four or five inches deep of well rotted cow-dung, or if this cannot be had, other old manure; dig or trench it one good spade or eighteen inches deep, incorporating the manure effectually therewith, as you proceed in digging or trenching.

Then in the first week of this month, take up your plants, which were managed as directed in the preceding month, with a transplanter or hollow trowel, one by one, preserving as much earth as possible about their roots, and plant them down to their leaves in rows three feet asunder, and the same distance plant from plant, in the rows, forming a little hollow (basin like) about eight inches over, and two deep, round every plant to receive water occasionally, till fit for earthing up; and which, *immediately* previous to landing the plants, should be filled with good compost earth, if convenient. Then give each a *little* water, which repeat at intervals of three or four days, till in a vigorous growing state, and afterwards occasionally. Or, after having first manured and dug the ground, you may make trenches as if for celery, in the direction of north and south; and in the bottom of each lay four inches deep of well rotted cow-dung, cast thereon five or six inches of earth, and point over the whole with a spade, mixing the earth and dung effectually: in these trenches plant your cauliflower plants at the above distances, and give occasional waterings as before.

To attempt planting cauliflowers in poor ground would be labor in vain; they love, nay, they require a deep, very rich, and moist loam, and agree exceedingly well with large quantities of manure.

You should be provided with hand-glasses, garden-pots, or covers made of two boards, each a foot long, and nailed together at right angles, to cover every plant at night and in very severe weather for two or three weeks after planting; observing to take them off early each morning, except the weather is desperate, and never to keep a dark covering over the plants longer than necessity requires.

This occasional protection is necessary to keep them in a constant and uninterrupted state of vegetation, for if stunted, at this period, by frost or too much cold, many will button, and very few produce large flowers.

The early cauliflower plants, under hand-glass, should have earth drawn up to their stems. This will be of a great service in promoting a strong forward growth.

The hand or bell-glasses may still be continued over these plants at night, and in cold wet weather; but in warm days, and when there are mild rains, let them be exposed to the free air; when the plants are considerably advanced in growth, the glasses should be raised proportionably high on props; first drawing a border of earth, two or three inches high or more, round each plant; then place the props upon that, and set the glasses thereon; but towards the end of this month, or beginning of next, they should be taken entirely away.

The above instructions will suit any part of the Union, except as to time of planting, which should, in every place, be on the eve of the first *brisk* spring vegetation, when no danger can be apprehended from subsequent frosts; and where this can be done in December, January, or February with safety, so much the better.

Young cauliflower plants, raised from seed sown last month, should now be pricked out into nursery beds, or some in a hot-bed, to forward them for final transplanting. (See page 192.)

SOWING CAULIFLOWER SEED.

Cauliflower seed may be sown, any time this month, in the open ground, to raise plants for heading in October, &c.

For the further treatment of cauliflowers, see *May*.

CABBAGES.

As early in this month as possible plant out your general crops of cabbage plants, observing to set all the early heading kinds at the distance of two feet every way, and all the late sorts at that of three feet.

As to soil and preparation, the nearer you approach in both to that directed for cauliflowers, the larger cabbages you will have; but where they are desired very early, you must adapt the soil and situation to that purpose.

Some of the cabbage and savoy plants which were sown in March, for a succession of young summer and autumn cabbages, and a forward autumn crop of savoys, should be thinned out and pricked into nursery-beds, to get strength before they are planted out for good.

Let this be done when the plants have leaves one or two inches broad; prepare beds of good earth about three feet and a half wide, in an open situation, and let the largest plants be drawn out regularly from the seed-bed, and planted in those prepared for them, at four or five inches distance every way. Water them immediately, and repeat it occasionally in dry weather.

The smaller plants which are left in the seed-beds, should be cleared from weeds; give them a good watering to settle the earth about their roots, loosened in drawing out the others; they will then grow strong, and in two or three weeks be in fine order for transplantation.

SOWING CABBAGE SEEDS.

Sow now a general assortment of cabbage seeds, such as early York, early sugar-loaf, and early Battersea, to succeed those sown in March, and large late Battersea, large late sugar-loaf, flat Dutch, drum-head, large English, large Scotch, flat-sided, and Savoys, for autumn and winter use. Sow also the seed of the red pickling cabbage, to succeed those sown in the former months. The earlier you sow all these kinds, the larger and better cabbages will you have.

Sow these seeds tolerably thin, in open beds or borders, and keep them free from weeds, till fit for planting out; or if they are transplanted into other beds, when about four inches high, it will greatly strengthen them, and render them in a much better condition for final transplanting.

SOWING BORECOLE, OR FRINGED CABBAGE.

The varieties of this are—1. Green curled.   2. Red curled. 3. Thick-leaved curled.   4. Finely fringed.   5. Siberian, or Scotch kale.

For the garden these may be treated in every respect as winter cabbages ; they are extremely hardy, and never so delicious as when rendered tender by smart frosts ; they are very valuable plants to cultivate, particularly in the more southerly States, as they will there be in the greatest perfection during the winter months ; they will also, if planted in a gravelly soil and in a sheltered warm situation, bear the winters of the middle States, and may be kept in great perfection in the eastern States if managed as directed on page 200, which see. The deliciousness of their sprouts in spring, surpasses everything of the kind, which they produce in great abundance. The seeds of either sort may be sown any time this month, and treated in every particular as directed for cabbages.

The green and red borecole, is also a very useful green food for sheep ; because, it is not only hardy, but if sown in time, will grow three or four feet high, and may in deep snows be got at by these animals, who frequently suffer much for want of food in such cases.

TURNIP-CABBAGE, AND TURNIP-ROOTED CABBAGE.

The turnip-cabbage produces its bulb or protuberance, which approaches to roundness, on the stem above ground, immediately under the leaves. It is eatable when young, and about the size of a tolerably large garden turnip. The bulb or protuberance must be stripped of its thick fibrous rind, and then it may be treated and used as a turnip. Some of their bulbs grow to twenty-three inches in circumference and weigh upwards of twelve pounds.

The seeds may now be sown and the plants afterwards treated as you do cabbage, only that in earthing up the plants when grown to a good size, you must be cautious not to cover the globular part, which is to be eaten. They are much more hardy than turnips, and in Europe are cultivated for the feeding of cows and sheep, as well as for table use ; in either case they treat them as they do cabbages, or sow them like turnips, and afterwards hoe them out to proper distances.

The turnip-rooted cabbage has an oblong, thick root, pretty much of the form of the winter radish, but very large, and is a valuable article to cultivate for cattle, as it produces, with proper care, from twenty-five to thirty tons per acre. It is extremely hardy, and very seldom injured by frost, and would be found an excellent sheep food in April, where the frosts are not overly desperate. It merits attention from the farmer, and is frequently used for culinary purposes in the same manner as the turnip-cabbage. The tops and sprouts make delicious greens in spring.

BRUSSELS SPROUTS AND JERUSALEM KALE.

The Brussels sprouts is an open-headed cabbage, grows very high, and is remarkable for producing a great quantity of excellent sprouts in spring.

The Jerusalem kale is one of the most hardy plants of the cabbage tribe ; it never heads, but the leaves, after being pinched by a smart frost, make most delicious greens, and boil greener than any other of the cabbage kind; it bears a very severe winter, and affords a grateful supply when most other plants perish.

Both these kinds are cultivated in the same manner as cabbages; their seeds may now be sown; but let it be observed, that they stand the winter frosts better when planted in a gravelly soil than in any other.

BROCCOLI.

There are several varieties of the broccoli, which are all but late heading varieties of the cauliflower, such as the Purple Cape, the Walcheren and white Cape, the green and black broccoli, with some others; but the purple and white Cape are in most estimation. The seeds should be sown in the early part of this month, if not before, and afterwards, when of due size, pricked out in beds at the distance of four inches apart and watered, there to remain till arrived of sufficient strength for planting in the quarters where intended to produce their flowers or heads.

The early purple broccoli, if sown early in this month and planted as you do cabbage, in good rich ground, will produce fine heads in October or November, very little inferior to cauliflowers, and by many preferred to them; the white will not flower so early, and in the middle and eastern States must be taken up in November and managed as directed in that month, by which a supply of this very delicious vegetable may be had in great perfection during all the winter and spring.

In such of the southern States as their winters are not more severe than in England, they will stand in the open ground, and continue to produce their fine flowers from October to April. In the middle, and especially in the eastern States, if the seeds are sown early in March on a hot-bed, and forwarded as is done with cauliflowers and early cabbage plants, and planted out finally in April, it would be the most certain method of obtaining large and early flowers. All these kinds produce heads exactly like the cauliflower, only that some are of a purple color, some green, some black, and the white kind so exactly resembles the true cauliflower, as to be scarcely distinguished therefrom, either in color or taste.

If any plants were raised in the preceding months, let some of them be pricked out now into nursery beds, to get strength for planting out finally.

PEAS

Continue to sow successional crops of peas every ten or twelve days, as directed in pages 140 and 194, to which I refer you for instructions.

You may now sow the dwarf-sugar and the dwarf Spanish-peas; they are both plentiful bearers, and do not require to be rodded, as they never rise more than from twelve to eighteen inches high. They are to be sown in drills two feet asunder, very thin, and covered about two inches deep.

Bishop's dwarf pea is, perhaps, the most prolific and profitable of the whole family; it bears most abundantly, and is very delicious; it rises to the height of from two and a half to three feet, according to the soil, and may, or may not be rodded, but if having some support, the produce will be the greater.

The tall crooked sugar pea is particularly worthy of cultivation, and should now be sown; its green pods, when young, are boiled like kidney-beans, and are uncommonly sweet and delicious; these grow to a considerable height, and require rods from seven to eight feet high, and to be sown in drills at least four feet asunder.

If you sowed no peas in the preceding months, the early frame, early Warwick, and Charleton kinds should now be sown for first crops; and for succession, the Champion of England, or the dwarf marrowfat, and blue imperial, and blue Prussian kinds. The Champion should be planted in drills at the distance of six feet at least, and be rodded or sticked to the height of six feet or more, by which you may expect very abundant crops. Rods from four to five feet high will answer for the early frame and other kinds, and also for the pearl peas and Essex-reading, all of which are very prolific bearers.

Draw earth to such rows of peas as are up and advanced a little in height, which will strengthen the plants and forward them greatly in their growth.

This earthing should always be performed, for the first time, when the plants are about three or four inches high.

Be very particular to rod or place sticks to such rows of peas as have attained the height of five or six inches; if this is not timely attended to, the crops will be greatly injured, for peas are never so productive as when rodded before they begin to fall to either one side or the other. For the method of doing which, see page 195.

PLANTING AND EARTHING UP BEANS.

In the early part of this month you may plant long-pod and Windsor beans, with every other variety of that species. These are always most productive when planted early; but if you are desirous of a succession of this kind of bean as long as possible, your late crops must be of the early Mazagan, early Lisbon, or green Genoa kinds, but more particularly the latter, as it bears our summer heat better than any of the whole family. For particulars, see page 195.

Such beans as are advanced in growth to the height of four or five inches must have some earth drawn up to their stems, which will greatly refresh and strengthen them.

LETTUCES.

Transplant lettuces of every kind that require it, where they stand too close; both those of the winter standing or such as were sown in any of the former months, and are now grown to a sufficient size.

Choose a spot of good ground for these plants, and if moderately dunged it will prove beneficial to their growth; dig the ground evenly one spade deep, and rake the surface smooth, then plant the lettuces about ten or twelve inches distant each way; water them immediately, and repeat it occasionally in dry weather till they have taken good root.

For the method of planting the kinds most deserving of cultivation, and other particulars, see page 196.

Continue to sow a variety of the best kinds of lettuce once every two weeks, that there may be a regular succession. Dig a spot of rich ground for them in an open situation, sow the seed even, not too thick, and rake them in lightly. Scatter a few seeds among general crops, and they will grow large and fine.

SMALL SALADING.

Sow small salading generally about once every week or fortnight; the sorts are lettuce, cresses, mustard, rape, radish, &c.

Dig a bed of light mellow earth for these seeds, and rake the surface fine. Draw some flat, shallow drills, sow the seeds therein, each kind separate, and cover them lightly with earth.

Water them moderately if the weather should be dry, which will greatly promote their growth.

For more particulars respecting small salading, see pages 132 and 199.

RADISHES.

Thin the general crops of radishes where they have arisen too thick, leaving the plants about two or three inches asunder, and clear them from weeds.

Radish seed, both of the short-topped, salmon-colored, and white and scarlet turnip sorts, should be sown at three different times this month, by which means a constant supply of young radishes may be obtained, allowing about twelve days between each time of sowing; choosing at this season an open situation for the seed; sow it evenly on the surface, cover, or rake it well in, and the plants will come up in a few days, and be of proper size for drawing in three or four weeks.

The crops of early radishes in general should be often watered in dry weather; this will promote their swelling freely, and will prevent their growing hot and sticky.

Sow a thin sprinkling of radish-seed among other low-growing crops; such will generally be found very good.

Turnip-rooted radishes, of both the white and red kinds, should now be sown, and treated as directed on page 198. Thin such of them as were sown last month to two or three inches apart. You may, likewise, sow some of the white Spanish radishes; but the general time for sowing that, and the black winter kind, is June, July, and August.

SOWING SPINAGE.

Continue now to sow seed of the round-leaved spinage every ten or twelve days, agreeably to the directions given on page 198, which see. Hoe the spinage sowed in the former months, and thin the plants to three, four, or five inches distance.

CARROTS AND PARSNEPS.

Carrots may now be sown for a full crop ; but in order to have tolerable sized roots, in some reasonable time in summer, let the seed be sown the beginning of the month.

Where, however, a supply of young carrots is required, it is proper to perform three different sowings this month ; the first in the beginning, the second about the middle, and the third towards the latter end.

Parsneps may also be sown in the beginning or middle of this month ; but if later, the crop will not succeed well, at least not to have large swelling roots in full perfection.

For the method of sowing both carrots and parsneps, see page 199.

Note.—There are several varieties of the garden carrot ; differing in the color of their roots ; such as the orange, white, yellow, and dark red. These variations may be continued by taking care not to mix them together in the same garden. There is another variety called the horn-carrot, differing in the *form* of its root, the lower part terminating in a round, abrupt manner, and not tapering off gradually like the others ; this is the earliest sort, is of an orange color, and very delicious ; and should always be sown for a first crop. The long orange carrot is the best for a principal crop. They all delight and thrive in a deep, rich, sandy loam.

CELERY.

The young celery plants, arising from the seed sown in February or March for an early crop, will be fit to prick out now, some in the beginning, and others towards the middle or latter end of the month, into a nursery-bed of rich light earth, or in a hot-bed, to forward them still more.

Prepare a spot of ground, form it into three or four feet wide beds, and rake the surface smooth ; then thin out a quantity of the best plants from the seed-bed, and plant them into the above, at about three inches distance ; or you may prick some of the earliest into a moderate hot-bed to forward them ; give a gentle watering, and repeat it occasionally till the plants have taken fresh root.

They should remain in these beds a month or five weeks, to get strength before they are planted out finally into the trenches.

As these early sown plants, after they become fit for use, will not continue long before they run up for seed, there should not be more of them raised or planted out than are necessary for an early supply.

Sow some celery seed in the first or second week of this month, to raise plants for a *general crop*, and to succeed those which were sown in March.

Dig for this purpose a bed of rich light earth, and make the surface even ; sow the seed thereon tolerably thick, and rake it in lightly ; in dry weather give frequent moderate watering, both before and after the plants come up, which being very essential should not be omitted.

The best kinds to sow are the white solid and red-stalked celery, both of which are very fine and blanch delightfully.

Those who have not the convenience of a hot-bed, to raise early plants, and wish to have celery as soon as possible, will find the following method of some importance. Make choice of a piece of very rich, light loam, that lies well to the sun; give it a good coat of manure, and dig it carefully in one spade deep at least; then at the distance of four feet form trenches, *north and south*, about ten inches deep, eight wide at bottom, and the edges sloping outward regularly towards the centre of the ridges formed by the earth thrown up, the better to admit the sun to the seeds and plants; in the bottom of these trenches lay three inches of *very old* horse-dung; cast over this the same depth of earth, and with your spade dig and incorporate both well together; cover the whole with mould previously made fine with the rake, and draw a shallow drill with your finger in the centre of each trench, not more than a quarter of an inch deep, in which sow your seed very thin, and draw the earth lightly over it, just to cover the seed and no more. This should be done as early in this, or the preceding month, as the ground can be got to work freely.

When the plants are up they must be kept free from weeds, and when grown a couple of inches, thinned to the distance of five from one another, always leaving the strongest and most promising.

When about eight inches high draw to their roots, on each side, three inches deep of mould, and let them grow on till of sufficient size to earth them up for blanching; then they are to be earthed in the general way. Plants thus treated will arrive at perfection three weeks earlier than those managed in the common method.

ASPARAGUS.

The forking, dressing, sowing, and planting of asparagus, if not done last month, should be performed the first week in this, particularly the forking and dressing; for the shoots will be advancing rapidly, and if not done in time they will be greatly injured, either by omitting it altogether, or performing it at an untimely season. New plantations ought to be made in the early part of the month; the seed may be sown at any time therein, but the earlier the better. For the methods of doing the whole, see pages 201, 202, and 203.

SOWING BEET SEED.

Beet of every kind may now be sown with good success. For the kinds and methods of sowing them, see page 203.

SOWING ONION AND LEEK SEED.

Onion seed, if sown in the first week of this month, agreeably to the directions given on page 204, will arrive at a tolerable size for

22

use the same season; but if sown for the purpose of raising seed onions, or small bulbs for planting next year, the middle of the month will be the proper time, or even towards the latter end. Seeds for the latter purpose should be sown pretty thick, and in poor gravelly ground; otherwise they will grow too large, or run to tops and not bulb well.

You may now sow a principal crop of leeks, either in drills, or as directed for onions on page 204; if in drills, they may be landed, as you do celery, when arrived at full size; or if in beds, they should be transplanted in June or July, as then directed.

PLANTING SEED ONIONS.

All your seed onions ought to be planted, if not done in the preceding months, as early in this as possible; for they never succeed so well as by early planting. (See page 205.)

GARLIC, ROCOMBOLE, SHALLOTS, AND CHIVES.

These useful culinary and medicinal plants, if not attended to in the former months, should now be planted as early as possible, and as directed on page 206.

TURNIPS.

You may sow any time this month, a full summer crop of the early Dutch, early stone, or early green turnip; they will succeed very well, and being of a quick growth, will arrive at good perfection before they are overtaken by the violent summer heats.

Sow the seeds in open quarters or beds, after the ground has been well dug and sufficiently manured, tolerably thin, and as evenly as possible; if the ground is dry, tread down the seed regularly, and rake it in with a light and even hand.

Hoe and thin the turnips which were sown last month, leaving the plants six, seven, or eight inches distant from each other, according to the richness of the soil.

SALSAFY.

Salsafy, or *Tragopogon porrifolium,* is a plant by some highly valued for its white eatable root, which grows a foot or more long, and in shape like a carrot or parsnip. Some have carried their fondness for it so far as to call it a vegetable oyster. Its method of cultivation, &c., you will find on page 207: the seed may be sown with good success any time this month.

SCORZONERA, OR VIPER'S-GRASS.

There are nineteen species of scorzonera described; but the *Scorzonera hispanica* is that principally cultivated in gardens, for its roots; which, if sown in this month in drills, and covered about half an inch deep, will produce fine eatable roots for autumn and winter use; they are boiled and eaten like carrots, &c., and are greatly esteemed by many. When the plants are up, they must be thinned to five or six inches apart, and be kept perfectly free from weeds. They may also be sown broadcast, in three or four feet wide beds, and, when up, thin them to six or seven inches distance every way.

SKIRRET.

The *Sium sisarum*, or skirret, is greatly esteemed as a garden vegetable; its root is composed of several fleshy tubers, as large as a man's finger, and joining together at top. They are eaten boiled, and stewed with butter, pepper and salt; or rolled in flour and fried; or else cold with oil and vinegar, being first boiled. They have much of the taste and flavor of a parsnep, but a great deal more palatable.

This plant is cultivated two ways; first by seed, and second by slips from the roots : the former method I think the more eligible, because the roots which are raised from seeds generally grow larger than those raised by slips, and are less subject to be sticky.

The seeds should be sown the latter end of March, or in the beginning of this month, either broadcast or in drills; the ground should be light and moist, for in dry land the roots are generally small, unless the season proves wet.

The seeds may be sown broadcast or in drills, and covered half an inch deep ; they will rise in five or six weeks, when they must be carefully weeded, and thinned to the distance of six inches asunder. In autumn, when the leaves begin to decay, the roots will be fit for use, and continue so till they begin to shoot in the spring. They may be taken up on the approach of winter, and preserved like carrots.

To propagate this plant by offsets, dig up the old roots in spring, before they begin to shoot, and slip off the side shoots, preserving an eye or bud to each ; plant them in rows one foot asunder, and six inches distant in the rows ; and in autumn they will be fit for use as before. Or you may separate the roots that you have preserved all winter, and plant them in the same manner.

SOWING COMMON AND LARGE-ROOTED OR HAMBURG PARSLEY.

Sow a full crop of the common and curled parsley ; and also of the large-rooted parsley, as directed last month, on page 207.

SEA KALE.

If you have yet omitted sowing the *Crambe maritima*, or sea kale, it may be sown the beginning of this month. For its general culture, see page 208, &c.

CORIANDER AND CHERVIL.

Coriander and chervil may yet be sown, as directed on page 208, which see. The latter particularly, is by many esteemed in salads and soups.

DRESSING, PLANTING, AND SOWING ARTICHOKES.

In the early part of this month, if omitted in the last, you may give a spring dressing to your artichokes, and it will be a very proper time to make new plantations of that delicious vegetable, or to sow the seed of it. For full instructions as to the performance of all the above, see pages 211, 212, &c.

CARDOONS AND ALEXANDERS.

Cardoons and Alexanders may yet be sown, as directed on page 214. For their further culture, see *June* and *July*.

PROPAGATING VARIOUS POT AND MEDICINAL HERBS.

For the various kinds of pot and medicinal herbs, and the different methods of propagating them, either of which will answer extremely well in this month, but more particularly that of sowing the seeds, see page 215, &c.

DILL AND AZORIAN FENNEL.

For an account of, and the method of propagating Dill and Finochio or Azorian fennel, see page 216.

HORSERADISH.

Horseradish may now be planted with good success, but the earlier in the month that it is done, the better. For the method of propagating it, see page 217.

RHUBARB.

For the general culture of rhubarb, see page 219. The seed, if neglected to be sown in the former months, will still succeed, by sowing it in the early part of this, but the plants from late sowings particularly, will require to be shaded, when up, from too powerful sunshine, till they have attained strength.

In the first week of this month, it may be successfully propagated by offsets from the root.

JERUSALEM ARTICHOKE.

Jerusalem artichokes may still be cultivated, as directed last month, on page 222.

POTATOES.

If omitted in the last month, plant potatoes in the beginning of this, as directed on page 217.

NASTURTIUM.

The *Tropæolum majus*, or large nasturtium, is very deserving of cultivation, as well on account of the beauty of its large and numerous orange-colored flowers, as their excellence in salads, and their use in garnishing dishes. The green berries or seeds of this plant, which it produces abundantly, make one of the nicest pickles that can possibly be conceived; in the estimation of many, they are superior to capers.

There are, of the nasturtium, a major and minor kind; the former being of a large running growth, and the most productive, is the proper sort for the above purposes.

A drill may be drawn for them as practised for peas, and the seeds dropped therein, at the distance of two or three inches from one another, and covered with earth near an inch deep. When the plants are grown about six inches, they should have sticks placed to them to run upon. Or they may be sown near hedges, fences, or palings of any kind, on which they can climb and have support, for they will always be more productive in this way than when suffered to trail on the ground.

LIQUORICE.

The *early* part of this month is a very good season, in the middle States, for planting liquorice. For its general culture, see page 218, &c.

SOWING OKRA.

The *Hibiscus esculenta*, or okra. The green capsules of this plant are an admirable ingredient in soups, and its ripe seeds, if burned and ground like coffee, can scarcely be distinguished therefrom. Numbers cultivate it for that purpose, and even say that it is much superior to foreign coffee, particularly as it does not affect the nervous system like the latter.

Between the middle or latter end of this month, is a proper time to sow the seed in the middle States; and in the eastern States, the early part of May; or generally, it may be sown, with certainty of success, at the time that Indian corn is planted. Draw drills about an inch deep and four feet asunder, into which drop the seeds at the distance of eight inches from one another, or rather drop two or three in each place, lest the one should not grow, and cover them near an inch deep. As they advance in growth, earth them up two or three times as you do peas, and they will produce abundantly. Some plant or sow them much thinner in the rows; but by the above method you will have more in quantity and as good in quality.

CAPSICUMS OR RED PEPPERS.

Sow capsicums towards the end of this month on a warm border, to produce plants for planting out towards the latter end of May, or beginning of June; the large heart-shaped capsicum is in the greatest estimation for pickling, but the small upright kinds are the strongest for pepper: if they are desired at an early season, sow them on a slight hot-bed the beginning of this month, and with due care they will be fit to transplant, where they are to remain, towards the middle of May. In the eastern States, the tenth of May will be soon enough to sow them in the open ground, but in the southern States they may be sown any time this month.

TOMATOES, OR LOVE APPLES.

The *Solanum lycopersicum*, tomato, or love apple, is much cultivated for its fruit, in soups and sauces, to which it imparts an agreeable acid flavor; and is also stewed and dressed in various ways and very much admired.

The seeds, may, towards the latter end of this month, be sown on a warm border, pretty thick, and about the end of May will be fit to plant out; or they may be sown where intended to remain for fruiting. They will require such support as directed for nasturtiums, on page 341, and must be planted in rows five feet asunder, and a foot or fourteen inches distant, plant from plant, as they run greatly. Some lay various kinds of old branches in their way for them to run upon; however, the better they are supported, the more numerous will their fruit be.

This fruit may be had much earlier by sowing the seeds in the first week of this month, if not done in March, on a slight hot-bed, and forwarding them in that way; they bear transplanting well, and may be set out finally about the middle of May.

EGG-PLANT.

The *Solanum melongena*, or egg-plant. There are two varieties of this plant, the white fruited and the purple, cultivated for culinary purposes; the latter kind is preferable, and when sliced and nicely fried, approaches, both in taste and flavor, nearer to that of a very nice fried oyster than perhaps any other plant.

This delicious vegetable may be propagated by sowing the seed on a slight hot-bed the beginning of this month, or in March; and towards the middle or latter part of May, they should be planted in a rich warm piece of ground, at the distance of two feet and a half asunder every way for the purple, or two feet for the white kind; and if kept clean, and a little earth drawn up to their stems, when about a foot high, they will produce plenty of fruit. Or, the seed may be sown about the end of this month on a warm border, and planted out finally in the beginning of June; but these will be rather late, and not produce fruit so abundantly in the middle or eastern

States, as by the former method. If any were sown last month, let them be pricked out into a fresh hot-bed the middle of this, at the distance of four or five inches, to gather strength, and prepare them for planting out about the fifteenth or twentieth of May.

SOWING CUCUMBERS, SQUASHES, MUSK AND WATER-MELONS.

In the middle States where the ground is light, dry, and warm, you may in the last week of this month sow cucumbers, squashes, water-melons, and early musk-melons in the open ground, agreeably to the directions given next month. If the weather proves favorable, and they are not attacked by frost after being up, they will succeed very well; but if you have hand or bell glasses for their protection, there is no doubt of their success.

It is generally observed, that cucumbers, squashes, and melons of every kind, may be sown in the open ground as early as Indian corn; but they are certainly somewhat more tender, and cannot be sown in the middle States with great certainty of success before the eighth of May.

KIDNEY-BEANS.

Towards the latter end of this month you may plant a first crop of kidney-beans in the open ground. Select a warm dry, and favorably situated spot, and having dug and manured it properly, draw drills an inch deep, and two feet or thirty inches asunder; drop the beans therein two inches apart, and draw the earth equally over them; do not cover them more than an inch deep, for at this early time they are liable to rot if cold or wet ensue. The kinds proper to be sown now, are the early cream-colored, speckled, yellow, and white dwarfs.

ENDIVE.

Those who are fond of endive as a salad, may now sow some of the seed, as directed in *June*, and blanch it when of sufficient size in the manner prescribed in *August*. But in the early summer months, lettuce has almost generally superseded the use of it.

SORREL.

Sow now a sufficient supply of the broad-leaved garden sorrel, and also of the round-leaved or French sorrel; these, or either of them, may be sown on narrow beds or borders and covered lightly or raked in; when the plants are up keep them free from weeds, and in June you may transplant them either in rows along the borders, or into three or four feet wide beds, at the distance of nine inches, plant from plant, every way.

GARDEN ORACHE.

The *Atriplex hortensis*, or garden orache, is cultivated for culinary purposes, being used as spinage, and is by some persons preferred to it. The French particularly are very partial to this plant. There are three or four varieties of it, differing only in color; one is of a deep green, another of a dark purple, and a third with green leaves and purple borders. The green-leaved variety, however, is that cultivated as an esculent herb, and is sown at the same time and treated in every respect like spinage.

CARAWAY.

The *Carum carui*, or common caraway, is a biennial plant: it produces its seed, which is highly aromatic and grateful to the stomach, the second year after sowing, and then generally dies. It may now be sown on a bed, either broadcast and raked in, or in drills, and covered half an inch deep; when up, thin the plants to six inches distance, and in the June twelve months following, it will produce its seed. Some of the plants that have not seeded abundantly will continue to bear the second season. Young plants rise in abundance where the seeds fall when ripe, and these will shoot and produce seed the following summer.

DESTROY WEEDS.

Weeds will now begin to appear plentifully from seed in every part of the garden. The utmost diligence should be used to destroy them while they are young, before they get the start of the crops, especially towards the middle and latter end of the month, when, if a forward season, they will be advancing in a rapid growth.

Pay particular regard, at this time, to your small crops, as onions, carrots, parsneps, and the like; weeds grow much quicker than they do; and if they are not weeded in time, either by small hoeing or hand-weeding, such will occasion much labor and trouble to clear them, and sometimes totally destroy the crops.

Take the opportunity of dry weather, and hoe the ground between the rows of beans, peas, cabbages, cauliflowers, and other crops that stand wide, to destroy the weeds.

A large piece of ground may soon be gone over with a hoe when the weeds are small; but when they are permitted to grow large, it requires double labor to destroy them.

IMPORTANCE OF WATER IN GARDENING.

The importance of water in gardening is too well understood to require anything to be said to enforce it. The proper mode of introducing it will depend upon the resources at hand and the means of the owner. The hydraulic ram is now much employed, and is found to be economical in its working; the reduced price of lead pipe

Fig. 31.

has resulted in a general introduction of this valuable invention long confined to the wealthy only.

    The accompanying figure, No. 31, represents an ornamental tower containing a reservoir, and serving also as a prospect tower. It is

Fig. 32.

filled by two water rams; the pipes are laid below the frost.

The water tower is eighteen feet square, and forty-five high, placed upon a terrace for beauty, and to gain elevation. Within is a reservoir seven feet square and thirty-four feet high, constructed in the strongest manner. From the bottom the water is conducted in 2-inch iron pipes, three and a half feet below the sod, and lateral pipes of lead, varying in size to supply hydrants for root culture, irrigation, the cattle-yard, stable, garden, the house, and fountains.

A useful and simple trough is represented by cut No. 32, which it will be well to adopt in watering ground that has a slight fall.

This simple trough may be six inches wide, with sluiceways every few feet, formed by pieces of the sides cut out and turning on pivots in the centre, which, when open, shut off the water from further progress down the trough by falling back against the side, and allows it to escape through an opening wherever it may be wanted.

For strawberry beds, and, indeed, all plants that require much water, this simple contrivance, which may be varied in many ways, will be found truly useful.

THE FRUIT GARDEN.

PLANTING FRUIT-TREES.

Such fruit-trees as are not yet burst into leaf may be transplanted in the early part of the month, but any that are either in leaf or flower will suffer considerably by such unseasonable removal. However, when late planting is from some cause unavoidable, and having a previous knowledge thereof, it would, in that case, be highly proper to take up the trees some time before, to check their shooting, and lay them by the roots in a trench of earth till they can be planted.

Where such planting is intended in the middle States, let it be done in the first week in the month, but in the eastern States it may be continued to the second, particularly with apples, pears, and plums, and even many other kinds, should the season prove late.

After planting, give each tree a plentiful watering, which will cause the earth to settle close about its roots, and prepare them for pushing fresh fibres; repeat it once every week or ten days till the new roots are established. For the method of planting, see the *Fruit Garden* and *Orchard* in *March*.

New planted trees, in general, but particularly such as are planted late in the spring, should be frequently watered in dry weather, once a week or ten days will be sufficient. In doing this, give a copious watering to reach the roots effectually, and let their heads be sometimes watered as well as their roots.

To preserve the earth moist about the roots of new planted trees, let some mulch or half rotted litter be spread on the surface of the ground; this will keep out the effects of the sun and wind, and the earth will retain a due moisture, with the assistance of a moderate watering now and then.

DESTROY INSECTS ON FRUIT-TREES.

Insects often do much damage to fruit-trees if not prevented. This is the time they begin to breed on the buds, leaves, and new advancing shoots of young trees, and also frequently on those of older growth. Proper means should be used to destroy them in time, before they spread over the general branches.

Where you perceive any of the leaves of these trees to have a crumpled, deformed, clammy appearance, &c., it is a sign of insects, notwithstanding it is sometimes produced by the extreme changes from warm, to wet and cold. Let the worst of these leaves be taken off as soon as they appear; and if the ends of any of the young shoots are also attacked, prune away such infected parts; and if furnished with a garden watering engine, it would be greatly serviceable therewith to dash the branches with water in dry weather, which, and the above precautions, if proceeded to in time will do a great deal in preventing the mischief from spreading considerably.

Or where wall-trees are much infested, first pull off all the curled or crumpled leaves, then get some tobacco-dust, or fine snuff, and scatter some of it over all the branches, but most on those places where the insects are troublesome. This should be strewed over the trees in the morning when the twigs and leaves are wet, and let it remain. It will greatly diminish the vermin, and not injure the leaves or fruit.

But fruit-trees are also sometimes attacked by insects of the caterpillar tribe, contained numerously in a minute embryo state in small webs deposited on the branches, &c.; animated by the heat of the weather they soon overrun and devour the young leaves, whereby neither the trees nor fruit prosper in growth, and which should be attended to, especially in young trees, by picking off the webs, &c., before the insects animate considerably; and, if accommodated with

a watering engine, as above suggested, you might play the water
strongly upon the trees, so as in the whole to diminish the increase
and spreading depredations of the vermin as much as possible.

PRUNING.

Pruning of all kinds of fruit-trees should be finished in the first
week of this month, if neglected so long, especially the forward blos-
soming kinds.   (See page 223.)

PROTECTING THE BLOSSOMS, ETC., OF WALL TREES FROM FROST.

Your early kinds of fruit-trees, particularly those planted against
walls, may in forward seasons require protection for their blossoms
and young setting fruit from night frosts; the doing of which will
be found of importance.   (For the method, see page 219.)
Where the sheltering of these trees is practised, it should be continued occasionally all this month; for although there are generally
some fine warm days and nights, yet the weather is so very uncertain at this season that we often have such severe hard frosts as to
prove the destruction of the blossoms and young fruit on such of the
above trees as are very forward and fully exposed.
They may be protected with mats every cold night, and taken
down in the morning; if cuttings of evergreens are used as devised
last month, let them remain constantly till the fruit is past danger.

GENERAL SPRING TREATMENT OF FRUIT-TREES.

For the general spring management of fruit-trees, see the *Fruit
Garden* and *Orchard*, last month.

GRAFTING.

For the various methods of grafting, &c., see the *Nursery* for last
month, and also for this.

RASPBERRIES.

New plantations of raspberries may be made in the first week of
this month, but it would have been much better if that business had
been performed in the last, except in the eastern States, where it
may now be done with good success, as directed on page 231, which
see.

STRAWBERRY BEDS.

Strawberry beds should now be kept perfectly free from weeds.
The runners produced from the plants should be constantly cleared
away as they advance.   But where new plantations are wanted, let
some of the strongest remain till June, to form young plants, then
to be transplanted, as directed in that month.
Water the beds of fruiting plants frequently in dry weather, when

they begin to advance for bloom; for if they are not supplied with that article in a dry time, the fruit will be smaller and of less abundant production; observing to give the water between the plants, and not over them. New plantations may be made in the first week of this month. For the method, see pages 232, 233.

EARLY FRUITS IN FORCING.

Let the same care be taken of the early fruits of all kinds now in forcing, as directed last month and *February*; but be very particular to give air in proportion to the increasing heat of the weather.

THE ORCHARD.

The orchard has been so fully treated of in the last month, beginning at page 234, as well as in *January* and *February* that there is little to be said respecting it in this; except to advise the completion of all that was directed to be done in the former, as early in this as possible. Late planting of deciduous trees, whether fruit or forest, seldom succeeds well, especially in warm climates; and to insure the best possible success everything should be attended to in due season, but more particularly planting; for "time waits for nobody." Apples and pears, however, may be planted with tolerable success in the middle States, but more particularly in a backward season, any time before the middle of April; though it is necessity alone that could warrant their removal at so late a period.

Let it be observed, as a general rule, always to plant or transplant your fruit-trees before a leaf expands, or a blossom appears; it is true that some plant later, but never with equal success.

The grafting of various kinds of fruit-trees, may be performed in the early part of this month, as directed in the *Nursery* for *March*, page 259, &c.

THE VINEYARD.

Vine cuttings, preserved since the time of pruning, as directed on page 256, may yet be planted in the method pointed out on page 258; and all the other work, directed to be done in the vineyard in March, should now be finished as early as possible. Rooted plants may also be planted out into rows at proper distances, but the earlier in the month the better.

If neglected last month, you must *early* in this, before the buds begin to shoot, either plough, dig, or deeply hoe the ground between the vines. This is indispensable; the surface must always be kept loose, clean, and free from weeds, or the consequence will be the having of few fruit, and these of a bad and insipid quality. Keeping the earth loose and pulverized by frequent working, will cause it to attract the dews, imbibe the rains freely, when such occur, and consequently to be constantly stored with a sufficient supply of nourishment for the plants and fruit; and moreover, the reflection of the sun from the clean surface, will dry and dissipate the damps that would otherwise cause the fruit to become mildewed, and render its quality crude and insipid.

In looking over the vines about the end of the month, observe to displace such young shoots or prominent buds as appear useless, or promise to be injurious to those intended for bearing fruit. Many small weakly shoots generally arise from the old stocks or branches, that seldom produce fruit, and are supernumerary; such should be rubbed off close, except in places where a supply of new wood or shoots for next year's bearing are wanted; in which case a suitable number should be carefully preserved. This operation ought, at this time, to be performed with the finger and thumb, nipping or rubbing them off close to where produced.

Where two shoots arise from one bud, take the worst away, the remaining one will grow stronger, and its fruit be numerous and large in proportion.

The vines should now have stakes placed to them, such as are directed to be made on page 60, and any old or decayed poles replaced with new, if not done in the former months, in order to tie and train the young advancing shoots thereto.

Any very long shoots of the last year, left upon strong and established stocks, for fruiting more abundantly, as directed before, may, about the first of this month, when the sap has arisen; and the shoots become pliant, be bent round the stake, in the form of a hoop, and made fast thereto with a willow twig, &c.; by this method it will break out into fruit more abundantly, and produce a less luxuriancy of wood than if left in the ordinary way; but it must be bent gently, so as not to crack the bark, lest it should bleed and be weakened thereby, or become totally abortive.

THE NURSERY.

As it is my plan to avoid repetitions as much as possible, in order to make room for more important matter, and having gone pretty extensively into the nursery business in March, I must refer you to that month for general instructions respecting the culture of trees and shrubs. You will there find the various methods and proper periods for grafting; the modes of raising, planting, and training all sorts of live hedges; the different ways of cultivating various kinds of shrubby plants, forest and fruit-trees, by layers, suckers, cuttings, seeds, &c., a repetition of which, in this place, would only swell the book to no purpose.

Let it, however, be observed, that the sowing of all kinds of tree and shrub seeds (except those that have had a year's previous preparation), and also grafting, may successfully be practised in the middle States in the early part of this month, and in the eastern States till near the latter end thereof; and that the earlier in the month such can be done, provided the ground is in good condition, and the weather favorable, the better. Propagation by layers, suckers, and cuttings, may also be practised in the early part of this month, both in the middle and eastern States, and indeed in the latter, it is the most eligible season for the performance of that work.

TRANSPLANTING.

All hardy evergreen trees and shrubs, seedling and others, may be taken up and transplanted in the first week of this month (earlier in the southern States, and not much later in the eastern), with great certainty of success.

Pines and firs of all kinds may now be removed. Likewise cedars, junipers, kalmias, and rhododendrons; pyracanthas, hollies, evergreen oaks and yews; and also alaternuses, phillyreas, arborvitæs and evergreen privet, with many others.

The seedlings are to be planted as directed in *March*, the others as on page 314, and immediately after, they should have a good watering to settle the earth about their roots. Likewise, any deciduous shrubs and trees of the late shooting kinds may yet be transplanted, if done early in the month.

CARE OF NEW PLANTED TREES AND SHRUBS.

Water the new plantations of evergreens and flowering shrubs, &c., but in particular those which were lately planted out from the seed-beds. Three times a week will be sufficient for these; and for those deciduous kinds that have been transplanted in autumn or early in spring, once a week will do; always observing, during this month, to give the water very early in the morning.

NEW GRAFTED TREES.

Examine the new grafted trees, the clay is sometimes apt to fall off or crack, so as to admit air and wet to the grafts.

When that is the case, the old clay must be taken entirely off, and immediately apply some more that is fresh and well wrought: let this be closed in every part, so that neither air nor wet can enter.

Where there are any shoots produced from the stocks below the grafts rub them off close; for these, if permitted to grow, would starve the young shoots: be careful also to eradicate all root suckers.

BUDDED TREES.

Budded trees should also be looked over about this time, for those that were worked last summer will now be making their first shoots, and therefore demand some attention.

The first shoots from the inoculated buds are, in some seasons, apt to be attacked by insects or blights; and these, if not prevented, will injure them greatly, and sometimes entirely spoil them; but by timely attention, it may be, in a great measure, prevented: where the ends of the young shoots appear crumpled, and the leaves curled, let them be carefully taken off, for they are full of small insects. By this practice the vermin may be prevented from spreading farther.

Likewise observe, that all shoots which put out from the stock, except the proper inserted bud, must be rubbed off constantly as they are produced, that its whole efforts may go to the support of the bud-shoots only.

THE MANAGEMENT OF SEED-BEDS.

Water occasionally the seed-beds of all kinds of trees and shrubs in dry weather: this must be practised both before and after the plants begin to appear.

Observe at all times to water these beds with moderation; a little and often must be the rule. Likewise be very careful not to apply the water over hastily at any time, for that would be apt to wash the earth away from the seed, and also from the young plants now beginning to come up: be particularly careful as to the more tender and delicate sorts: generally let the refreshments of water be repeated moderately once every two days in warm dry weather, which will be of great service to all kinds of seedling plants.

Shade will also prove *very beneficial* in the middle of hot sunny days, to many of the choice kinds of seedling-trees and shrubs, about the time of their first appearing, and for some time after.

These young plants may be shaded from the sun occasionally, by fixing hoops across the beds, then let mats, canvas or the like, be drawn over the hoops as often as occasion requires.

Where there are boxes, pots, or tubs of seedling plants, let them be placed in a shady situation, about the middle, or towards the latter end of this month, where they may have the morning and afternoon sun only, carefully protecting them from its mid-day influence.

All beds of seedling trees and shrubs whatever, must be kept perfectly clean from weeds. This should be carefully attended to, for the weeds are of much quicker growth than the young seedling plants, and would soon get the start of them if permitted to stand. Therefore, let such as soon as they appear in the beds be pricked out before they get to any great head, performing it by a very careful hand-weeding.

HOEING AND WEEDING.

Hoe and destroy weeds between the rows of young trees; they will now arise abundantly from seeds, but by applying the hoe to them while young, they may be very expeditiously destroyed. Choose dry weather, let the hoe be sharp, take advantage of the weeds while they are small, and cut them up clean within the ground.

There is nothing like destroying weeds in due time, for when they

are suffered to grow large, they are extremely hurtful to all young
trees and shrubs, and in particular to those plants which are not far
advanced in their growth; besides, if suffered to ripen and shed their
seeds these lay the foundation of a world of trouble afterwards, which
might be avoided by timely exertions and care.

GRAFTING HOLLIES, ETC.

Graft hollies with cuttings of the variegated kinds. The first fortnight in this month is the proper time to perform that work, in the
middle States.

The common green holly is the proper stock to graft the variegated
kinds upon, and the stocks for this purpose must not be less than three
or four years' growth from the seed; but those of five or six answer
perfectly well.

Get some cuttings or grafts of the best variegated kinds; they
must be shoots of the last summer's growth. Let them be grafted
with exactness, according to the general method of whip-grafting.
(See page 263.)

Likewise graft any other curious varieties of trees, on stocks of
their own kinds.

But in most fruit-trees and other deciduous kinds, where any grafting remains to be done, no time should be omitted in forwarding it
early in the month.

INARCHING.

Inarching may be performed now on evergreens, and on any kinds
of trees or shrubs that you desire to propagate that way.

This method of grafting is principally intended for those kinds
which are not easily raised by common grafting or budding, or by
seeds, layers, or cuttings, or any of the other general methods.

The evergreen kinds may be inarched towards the end of this
month, but deciduous sorts generally succeed best when done about
the middle of it. For the method, see page 267.

THE PLEASURE, OR FLOWER GARDEN.

HANGING VASES.

Those who study the ornamental will not omit the use of hanging vases, which may be placed in rooms, windows, and piazzas, to the great beautifying of the scene. In general, the plants for growth should be selected from those whose branches hang down gracefully, and are sufficiently vigorous to cover the vase. Ivy, carefully cultivated, forms an admirable plant for the house, as it bears a fire heat better than most. The following are also eminently suitable : Petunia, Nurembergia gracilis, Torenia ariatica, mesembryanthum, Pentas carnea, heliotropium Peruvianum, verbenas, maurandia Barclayana, lycopodium, tropæolum, hoya, &c. &c.

Fig. 33.

CHOICE HYACINTHS.

The earlier sorts of hyacinths will begin to open and show color in the beginning of this month ; it will be proper to screen the finer sorts from the too powerful effects of the sun, which, if not prevented, would bleach and tarnish their colors, particularly the reds and deep blues, but if they are properly defended from it, their colors will be preserved, and they will, in some measure, be kept back so as to be in full bloom with the later sorts, especially if the roots of the early kinds have been planted about an inch deeper than the rest : it is a very desirable object in a grand display of this delightful flower to have a uniform bloom.

It will be necessary to support the stems as they advance in height; for this purpose small sticks or wires, painted green, should be forced into the ground immediately behind the bulbs, either in an erect position or leaning a little backwards, to which the stems are to be rather loosely tied with small pieces of green worsted as soon as they begin to bend, or are in danger of being borne down by the weight of their bells ;* this operation must be repeated as they advance in height, for it is impossible to do it at one time, so as to answer the purpose. When the greater part of the bed appears in color, a covering or awning should be erected over it, and the walk to be in

* The Florist's usual name for the corolla of the hyacinth.

front: for the support of the awning a strong frame of wood should be erected, ten feet high in the centre, and seven feet at each side, and covered with strong sheeting, which will keep out the rain and admit a tolerable degree of light; it should come down close to the bed on the north side, in order to preserve it from cold winds, which are prejudicial to the bloom.

The covering ought to be so constructed by means of lines and pulleys, as to be easily and expeditiously rolled up or let down, as occasion requires, to afford the plants *the full benefit of light and air at all favorable opportunities;* that is to say, when the air is mild, and light clouds intervene, so as to blunt the sun's rays.

A bed of hyacinths never requires to be watered at any period; the rains that happen after planting are generally more than sufficient both for the roots and bloom; and after the bloom is over, they are rather prejudicial than otherwise, except when very moderate.

Although covering in the manner described presents and exhibits the bloom to the greatest advantage, yet it evidently has a tendency to weaken and injure the bulbs, and ought not, therefore, to be continued more than two or three weeks at most; but as soon as the general bloom declines, the bed should be immediately exposed to the open air, and the hoops replaced as before, that mats may be laid on occasionally for protecting the beds from heavy torrents of rain, which would prevent the bulbs from ripening well, and render them very subject to decay after having been taken up.

The common hyacinths in open beds and borders, will require no other care at this time than to support their flower stems, as directed above, without which they will generally fall down, and much of their beauty be lost.

A DESCRIPTION OF THE PROPERTIES OF A FINE DOUBLE HYACINTH

The stem should be strong, tall, and erect, supporting numerous large bells, each suspended by a short and strong peduncle, or footstalk, in a horizontal position, so that the whole may have a compact pyramidal form, with the crown or uppermost bell, perfectly erect.

The bells should be large and very double; that is, well filled with broad bold petals, appearing to the eye rather convex than flat or hollow: they should occupy about one-half the length of the stem.

The colors should be clear and bright, whether plain red, white, or blue, or variously intermixed or diversified in the eye; the latter, it must be confessed, gives additional lustre and elegance to this beautiful flower.

Strong bright colors are, in general, preferred to such as are pale; there are, however, many rose-colored, pure white, and light blue hyacinths, in high estimation.

Observations.—Some sorts consist of petals of different colors, such as light reds, with deep red eyes; whites, with rosy, blue, purple, or yellow eyes; light blues, with deep blue or purple eyes; and yellow, with purple in the eye, &c. Others again have their petals striped or marked down the centre with a paler or deeper color, which has a pleasing effect.

It sometimes happens, and with some sorts more frequently than others, that two stems are produced from the same root, one is generally considerably taller than the other; when this is the case, the weaker may be cut off near the ground soon after it makes its appearance, or suffered to bloom, and its bells be intermixed with the lower ones of the taller stem, so dexterously as to appear like one regular pyramid of bells.

TULIPS.

Towards the end of this month, some of your choice tulips will begin to show color; they should, when the greater part of the blossoms begin to open, be shaded from the sun, in the same manner as directed for your elegant hyacinths; for, when its heat is considerable, it will cause the colors to run and intermix in such a manner as to destroy the elegance and beauty of the flowers; some sorts are more particularly liable to this than others, and will be spoiled in five minutes.

The awning should be always kept rolled up, or totally off, except when the sun is powerful; for if kept too long, or too closely covered, the colors of the flowers would become faint and weak, and the grandeur of effect would be lost or considerably lessened.

Strong winds are extremely injurious to tulips when in flower, by dashing them against one another, and thereby bruising their petals, from the effects of which they must be guarded by letting down the awning at such times quite to the ground on the windy side; a line of bass mats sewed together, and their upper edge nailed to the frame on that side, may answer the purpose, if the cloth is not of sufficient length.

Tulips never require to be artificially watered in the hottest and driest seasons, at any period from planting to taking up the roots; nevertheless, moderate rains will be very beneficial to them in spring, and cause them to produce a strong bloom; after flowering, too much wet is very prejudicial to the roots. Immediately after the flowers are on the decline, the bed must be fully exposed to the open air.

Lines of small twine, painted green, should pass from one end of the bed to the other, corresponding with the rows of flowers, fastened at the ends and middle to nice painted sticks placed therein for that purpose; to these the stems of the flowers are to be loosely tied with short pieces of green worsted, which will preserve a pleasing regularity of appearance, without stiffness and formality. The covering may be continued at the necessary intervals for three weeks with safety, but continuing it too long will injure them.

When vacancies occur in the beds by the decay of some roots which might look awkward, you may immerse the lower end of the stems of flowers from other quarters, in phials filled with water, and sunk into the bed, so as not to appear above ground; these will continue in bloom, when shaded, for several days, and may be replaced with others, which will fill those vacancies and make a tolerable appearance.

Common tulips will require no other care in the borders, &c., than keeping them free from weeds.

RANUNCULUSES.

April showers, and frequent rains in May, are essentially necessary to the growth and vigor of ranunculuses: if these fail, soft water must be administered in sufficient quantities between the rows, by means of a common watering pot, with a long tube or spout held low, so as not to wash the earth into holes: for it is better to avoid watering the plants themselves, as it might chill them too much, and stagnate their juices, and has a tendency to rot the crowns. The consequences of omitting to water, when necessary, are these, viz: The plants will make little progress; the blossom buds of the strongest will be small, and the weaker plants will not bloom at all; the grass or foliage will put on a sickly yellowish appearance, from which it will not recover during the season; and lastly, the roots when taken up will be small and lean.

But such kinds of watering, however necessary, are by no means so salutary to these, or any other flowers or plants, as fine warm, natural showers; as they can neither be so equally dispensed, nor are the plants naturally disposed to receive them when the atmosphere is dry; because their pores and fibres are contracted, and they are, as it were, in the expectancy of dry weather.

Since it is evident that artificial waterings are, in all respects, so much inferior to natural, it is, therefore, better to wait a day or two, in hopes of a change of weather, than to be too hasty in affording these succors, although the plants may appear to suffer for the moment by the omission; for if such a change should fortunately take place, they will receive infinitely more benefit from it than when both themselves and the soil are already saturated or replenished with water, not so congenial to vegetation as that ordained by nature for the purpose. (For their further treatment, see the *Flower Garden* in *May*.)

ANEMONES.

The beds of anemones, for the present, will require exactly the same treatment as the ranunculuses therefore it is not necessary to say more in this place respecting them.

AURICULAS.

The auriculas, towards the middle of this month, will be advancing in their flower stems. If any plant is possessed of more than one or two principal stems, it is advisable to pinch off the pips or flower buds of the smallest and weakest, in order to render the blossoms of the remaining larger and more vigorous than they would be if this was omitted to be done in due time.

When the pips become turgid, and begin to expand, they must be preserved from rain; nor should the early plants be suffered to remain in a situation exposed to cold winds; on the contrary, they ought to be selected from the rest, and removed to a shady corner, where they should have hand-glasses suspended over them, or placed on brickbats or the like to admit air, and yet preserve the expanding bloom from rain.

The farina or mealy dust which overspreads and ornaments the surface of those flowers, contributes exceedingly to their lustre and beauty; this must therefore be preserved upon them; the least shower of rain would easily wash it off; it is also liable to be blown away by the winds; and the sun, if permitted to shine freely on the flowers, would occasion them soon to fade.

Therefore, where it is required to have the more curious or choice varieties to blow in the best perfection, the pots containing the plants should, according as the flowers begin to open, be immediately removed and placed on the shelves of the auricula stage or where the flowers may be protected occasionally from such weather as would deface the bloom. The stand or stage should have from three to five ranges of shelves, in proportion to the number of pots, about six inches wide, rising theatre-like, one above another, from the front; having the back generally placed against a shady wall, pale, or other building; it must be constantly covered at top, water-tight, sloping to the back part; but the front and ends should only be covered occasionally by having some canvas or mats fastened thereto by way of curtain, so contrived that it may be readily let down and drawn up at pleasure; which, when the air is very sharp, or in high winds, or driving rains, must be let down to shelter the flowers; but when the weather is mild and calm, let the front and ends be constantly open. Or this may also be used occasionally to shade the flowers from the sun, where it has access in the heat of the day; observing, however, generally, not to let the screen remain longer than is necessary for the defence of the bloom.

Regular waterings should be given during the time the plants are on the stage; examine them once every day to see where water is wanted, and let such pots as stand in need of that article be immediately supplied with it. In doing this suffer no water to fall on the flowers, for that would wash off the afore-mentioned farinaceous bloom, and greatly deface their beauty.

The waterings should be moderate and frequent; for these plants being rather of a succulent nature cannot bear too much without material injury.

Keep the surface of the pots perfectly neat, free from weeds and every sort of litter; suffer no decayed leaves to remain on the plants, but let such, as soon as they appear, be taken off.

By thus placing your auricula pots on a covered stage, it not only preserves the flowers much longer in beauty, but you also more readily view them, and they show themselves to much greater advantage than when placed on the ground.

The shelves and back of the stage should be painted black, or of some dark color, by way of contrast to the white eyes, &c., of the flowers; and if a large looking-glass be placed at each end of the stage, the effect produced will be very pleasing, by apparently lengthening the stage each way as far as the eye can reach.

A row of fine polyanthuses in pots may likewise be introduced on

the auricula stage ; it will add to the variety and form a pleasing contrast.

The tallest flowering auriculas should stand on the most distant
shelf, and the shortest in front; those stems which are weak and
bend, ought to be supported with small wires fixed in the earth behind them, so as not to be easily discerned. If the root of the stage
is covered with glass, it will be an additional advantage to the plants.

COMPOST FOR AURICULAS.

The compost proper for auriculas, should consist of the following
ingredients in the annexed proportions, viz :—

One-half rotten cow-dung, two years old.
One-sixth fresh sound earth of an open texture.
One-eighth earth of rotten leaves.
One-twelfth coarse sea or river sand.
One-twelfth moory earth.
One twenty-fourth ashes of burned vegetables.

These ingredients should be well incorporated, and placed in an
open situation, perfectly exposed to the action of the sun and air; it
should be laid in a regular heap or mass from fifteen to eighteen
inches thick, and turned frequently : in this state it should remain a
year or six months, turning it once every two months, and keeping
it always free from weeds : before it is used it should be passed
through a coarse screen, to free it from stones, &c., and to incorporate it more effectually.

NEW POTTING AURICULAS, AND INCREASING THEM BY SLIPS.

The most advisable time to transplant, or to slip auriculas, or as
it is usually termed, to pot them, is immediately or very soon after
their bloom is over ; and this should be repeated annually, for it preserves the health and constitution of the plants, by affording them a
fresh supply of nourishment, and affords an opportunity of curtailing
the fibres if grown too long, or if any are decayed and mouldy ; or
of cutting off the lower part of the main root, if in a rotting or decayed state, which is frequently the case. By this treatment, the
plants are brought into a state of action and fresh vegetation, which
will cause a continued circulation of the juices during the summer.

The pots should be hard baked, and for blooming plants, ought to
be seven inches in diameter at top, four and a half at bottom, and
about seven deep; but smaller plants and offsets should have shallower pots, and of a proportionate size, and very large plants must
have pots in proportion. These before being used, if new, should be
immersed in water for five or six hours or more.

In potting or transplanting auriculas, the plant ought to be carefully turned out of the former pot, and the earth shaken from its
fibres, which should be trimmed if found long and numerous, and
also any part of the old main root that appears in a sickly or decayed state must be cut clean out, whether on the lower part or side ;
and if near the leaves, a cement should be immediately applied, con-

sisting of beeswax and pitch, in equal quantities, melted together and laid on when soft, but not hot, to make it adhere more firmly. Place a hollow oyster shell, or the like, over the hole in the bottom of each pot, with the convex side upwards, and then more than half fill it with the compost; let it be higher in the middle than at the sides : the plant is next to be placed thereon, with its fibres regularly distributed all around, and the pot filled up, adding a little coarse sand close around the stem of the plant, on the surface; the bottom of the pot should then be gently struck two or three times against the ground, in order to close the earth about the roots, this will cause it to sink about half an inch below the top of the pot, which will prevent the loss of water when administered.

N. B. The true depth to plant an auricula, is within about half an inch of the bottom of its lowest or outside leaves.

Any offsets that have formed one or more fibres, of an inch or two in length, may be *slipped* off the old plant, and replanted around the sides of large pots, or singly in small ones, filled with the same compost ; and if hand-glasses are placed over them, such will cause their fibres to grow more rapidly ; but they ought not to be long continued on, lest the plants should be drawn and weakened thereby.

After potting, give each plant a little water, and place the pots in a shaded situation, where they may have the morning sun till ten o'clock, and the afternoon from four or five, but by no means under the drip of trees; there they are to remain till October, taking care to keep them regularly watered, and free from weeds. The pots may or may not be plunged in the earth, but in the latter case they will require more attendance. Those who wish to grow auriculas and polyanthuses without all the trouble of potting, may do so by planting eight inches apart, in the fall, in a common garden-frame, and after blooming, plant them out in an open but shaded situation.

CARE OF SEEDLING AURICULAS.

Seedling auriculas which were sown last autumn or this spring, now demand attention ; these plants when newly come up, or while quite young, must be carefully protected from the full sun in the heat of the day, and frequently refreshed with water.

The boxes or tubs in which they are growing should be removed to a shady border, toward the latter end of this month or beginning of next ; the place should be open to the morning sun till about nine o'clock, but shaded the rest of the day, and the plants watered frequently in dry weather. As soon as any of them appear with six leaves, such should be carefully taken out from the rest and planted in pots or boxes filled with compost, about two inches asunder; and if grown by the beginning of August so large as to touch each other, they may then be transplanted into separate small pots, to remain all winter.

POLYANTHUSES.

Polyanthuses blow at the same time, and the fine kinds require nearly the same treatment as auriculas, both with respect to soil and situation; they are, like the latter, very impatient of heat and drought, and agree with a much greater portion of moisture; they are fond of shade and will not succeed well when exposed to our summer heats, in a warm situation; at least so as to blow, even in tolerable perfection, the ensuing season.

The fine kinds may be grown in the same sized pots and in the same compost, as auriculas, with the addition of more loam; and the common or more indifferent sorts may be planted in *cool shady* beds or borders, being tolerably hardy, and having more to fear from the summer heats than the winter frosts.

Their propagation is by slips and seed, at the same time and in the same manner as directed for auriculas.

A DESCRIPTION OF THE PROPERTIES OF A FINE POLYANTHUS.

Its properties are, in most respects, similar to those of a fine auricula; that is, the stem, peduncles, or footstalks, and formation of the bunch or truss; therefore, a description of its pips or corollas only remains to be given in this place.

The tube of the corolla, above the calyx, should be short, well filled with the anthers or summits of the stamens, and terminate fluted rather above the eye.

The eye should be round, of a bright clear yellow, and distinct from the ground color; the proportion as in the auricula throughout the flower.

The ground color is most admired when shaded with a light and dark rich crimson, resembling velvet, with one mark or stripe in the centre of each division of the rim, bold and distinct from the edging down to the eye, where it should terminate in a fine point.

The pips should be large, quite flat, and as round as may be consistent with their beautiful figure, which is circular, excepting those small indentures between each division of the rim which divide it into several heart-like segments.

The edging should resemble a bright gold lace, bold, clear, and distinct, and so nearly of the same color of the eye and stripes as scarcely to be distinguished; in short, the polyanthus should possess a graceful elegance of form, a richness of coloring and symmetry of parts not to be found united in any other flower.

Fine double primroses are cultivated by offsets, in the same way and at the same time as polyanthuses, and require similar care and management in pots; they are somewhat more tender, and consequently must be treated accordingly.

CARNATIONS.

If you have omitted the potting or transplanting of carnations last month where necessary, let it be done in this, as early as possible, agreeably to the rules laid down on page 309.

Keep the pots perfectly free from weeds, and the plants from decayed leaves, and let the earth on the surface be stirred if it binds hard, for this will encourage the plants to shoot, and will also give an air of neatness.   Water the pots in warm weather, for they will require a little every second day, or oftener, if the season proves dry, which should not be omitted, otherwise the plants will shoot weakly, and produce but slender flower-stalks.

When the flower-stalks have advanced, let them be supported as directed in *May*.

Carnations may yet be finally planted into the borders or beds where intended to flower, but that should be done in the beginning of the month, removing them with balls, and watering them as soon as planted.

MANAGEMENT OF POTS OF PERENNIAL PLANTS IN GENERAL.

Give fresh earth to such pots of perennial plants as were not dressed and new earthed in March.   For the method of doing which, see page 311.

The plants will receive great benefit from this dressing ; and where it was not done in that month, it should not be put off longer than the beginning of this.

If you have plants of any kind in small pots, that require to be shifted into larger, it may be performed early in the month ; in doing of which, turn each plant out of the former pot with the ball of earth entire ; trim the outside roots and pare away some of the old earth ; having fresh mould or compost, replant it into a larger pot, filling the deficiency with new earth, and give some water immediately.

Be very particular in dry weather to supply all your plants with a sufficiency of water ; this is a material article, and should not be omitted.   Water should be always given as often as the earth begins to appear dry in the pots, as there is no other general rule by which it can be administered.

PINKS.

Pinks may yet be transplanted, slipped, and managed as directed in *March*, pages 312, 313, but it will be necessary to do this as early in the month as possible.

TENDER ANNUALS.

Such tender annuals as you have in an advanced state, are to be managed as directed on page 312 ; always observing to give them more and more air, in proportion to the increasing heat of the weather, and shade to the young and weakly plants from the mid-day sun, when too powerful.   As they advance in growth, it will be necessary to raise the frames, in order to give them full liberty to shoot, closing the vacancy below if thought necessary.

But where there is the convenience either of drawing-frame or glass case, for the purpose of drawing the tall growing tri-colors and other curious annual plants, it may be effected to greater advantage.

The drawing-frame is either composed of two, three, or more different frames, all of the same length and breadth, and each about nine or ten inches deep, except the upper glass frame, which should be ten inches deep in front, and eighteen at the back ; being all of equal dimensions in width and length, made in a very exact manner, to fit one on the top of another, appearing as but one frame when thus joined, and are to be made use of in the following manner :—

Begin first with the deepest frame ; then, when the plants have reached the glasses, let the said frame be taken up, and in its place set one of the others, and immediately fix the deepest frame upon that, as above ; and then, when they have filled that space, let another frame be added, observing, as above, to let the deepest or sloping frame be always placed uppermost in order to receive the glasses.

The *glass-cases* for this purpose are generally made about six, seven, or eight feet wide, and as long as may be convenient; the height should be five or six feet in front, and seven or eight in the back.

The front ought to be of glass sashes, perfectly upright, and facing the south; the back may be either of wood or brick, and both ends of the same materials, but if of glass, the better ; and the top must also be of glass sashes, sloping from the back to the front.

Within this, a hot-bed is to be made, for which a pit must be formed nearly the whole length, raised by brick-work or planking above the floor, having the whole about two feet and a half deep, and from four to five or six feet wide : this is to be filled with hot dung or tanner's bark, carrying it up a few inches higher than the top of the pit, to allow for settling; and if a dung-bed, lay earth or tan-bark at top five or six inches thick.

The pots are to be placed upon this, plunging them to their rims in earth, as before mentioned ; but if the bed be made of tan, plunge them therein, having no occasion for earth upon such beds.

In this frame or glass case, let the plants have fresh air daily, and give sufficient supplies of water, and towards the latter end of May they will be advanced to a large size, and may be removed in their pots into any principal compartment in the pleasure-ground, &c., or placed among the green-house plants.

When tender or curious annuals have been omitted to be sown in the former months, a slight hot-bed may be made for them in the beginning of this, to forward them as much as possible. The seeds are to be sown as directed on page 139.

SOWING ANNUAL FLOWER SEEDS.

All the varieties of annual flower-seeds that are capable of bearing the open air, and of arriving at perfection in our climates, may now be sown with good success. In the early part of the month, you may sow the following kinds with many others too tedious to mention in this place, viz: alkekengi, China aster in sorts, Moldavian-baum, belvidere or summer cypress, candy-tuft in sorts, Lobel's-catchfly, cyanus in sorts, flos-adonis, bladder-ketmia, heart's-ease, convolvulus tri-color, larkspurs in sorts, lavatera in sorts, and lupins of every kind; dwarf lychnis, curled, oriental, and Peruvian mallows, nigellas, roma nettle, sweet, Tangier, and winged peas, annual and ten-week stocks, strawberry spinage, persicaria, sunflower, and Venus's looking-glass; snails, horns, hedge-hogs, caterpillars and horseshoes; Venus's navelwort, purple and yellow hawkweed; Cassia chamæchrista, polygala sanguinea and silene in sorts, &c. &c. About the middle of the month you may sow sweet alyson, love lies bleeding, prince's feathers, mignonette, tree and spike amaranthus; cock's-combs, cape marigold, bastard saffron, and honey-wort; sweet sultan, China hollyhock, and China pinks; marvel of Peru, nolana, palma christi, annual snapdragon, zennia and xeranthemum, &c., and in the last ten days of the month, you may sow either of the preceding, and also the following kinds, viz : white, purple, and striped globe amaranthus, tri-color amaranthus, double balsams and martynia annua; browallia, scarlet ipomœa, capsicums in sorts, serpent cucumber and squirting cucumber, white and purple egg-plant; cleome, purple, white, and dwarf dolichos, with many other kinds.* The whole of the preceding sorts may be sown in small patches in the borders, interspersing the kinds, so as to form a well assorted variety and a long succession of bloom. If to be sown in patches, observe the directions given for sowing *hardy annual flower seeds*, on page 166, &c., which will now be perfectly applicable to these. Such as you wish to sow in small beds for transplanting, let them be sown as directed for *perennial and biennial flower seeds*, on page 365, observing always to give each kind a depth of covering in proportion to the size of the seed.

Let the beds or patches be frequently watered in dry weather, both before and after the plants appear; and when they have been up a few weeks, let all the large growing kinds be thinned where they have risen too thick, observing to transplant into other places where wanted some of the best you pull up of the kinds that succeed in that way. Thin the others as directed in May, &c.

Any of the smaller growing kinds, such as mignonette, ten-week stock, browallia, sensitive plant, ice plant, &c., may be sown in pots, and if duly watered and kept clean will arrive at good perfection; but the last two will require the protection of glasses for some time.

SOWING CARNATION AND PINK SEEDS.

Carnation and pink seeds may be sown any time this month. As it is from seed that all new varieties are obtained, you should sow some every year; and if you have but one good variety from each sowing, there can be no reason to complain, as this may afterwards be abundantly propagated by layers or slips. The fine double kinds seldom ripen seed, but semi-doubles do very plentifully. From the seeds of the latter, especially when growing near the finest varieties, you may expect some good and perhaps valuable flowers. For this purpose prepare a small bed of good rich ground, sow the seeds on

* This list contains most of the old and beautiful annual flowers, many of which are now seldom seen. The newer discoveries have in a great measure displaced them, without in all cases, being any improvement.

the surface tolerably thick, each sort separate, and sift over them about a quarter of an inch of fine light earth. If the weather should prove dry, water the beds occasionally; the plants will soon rise, after which it will be necessary to keep them free from weeds and refresh them now and then with a little water. For their further management, see the work of the following months.

SOWING PERENNIAL AND BIENNIAL FLOWER-SEEDS.

You may now with good success sow the seeds of most kinds of perennial and biennial fibrous-rooted flowers that prosper in the open ground, such as those mentioned last month on page 313, together with monk's-hood, nettle-leaved campanala, lobelias, phloxes, double soapwort, sneezewort, goat's-rue, and red garden valerian; crimson monarda, Chinese ixia, verbascums, night-smelling rocket, and aletris or star-root; asclepiases of various sorts; calceolarias, Maryland cassia, clinopodiums and coreopsises; dracocephalums, galega virginica, gerardias, cucubalis, hedysarums and huecheras; hibiscuses, liatrises, œnotheras and podalyrias; penstemons, rudbeckias, saxifragas and silphiums; solidagoes, spigelias, spiræas, chelone, trilliums and veronicas, with many other kinds.

These seeds may either be sown on borders or on three or four feet wide beds of rich earth, and covered evenly with fine light earth, the largest not more than from half to three-quarters of an inch deep, and the smallest from an eighth to a quarter of an inch.

But in sowing these or any other kinds you may draw shallow drills, proportioning the depth to the size of the seeds, and sow them therein, drawing the earth lightly over them, observing that it is much better to cover too light than too deep, for if covered shallow they will vegetate when moist weather ensues, but if overly deep never. Or you may practise the following method: first, rake the surface of the bed smooth, and with the back of a rake or a common trowel draw or push off the fine top mould, either into the alleys or the divisions intended to be left between each kind, and to a depth in proportion to the size of the seed intended to be sown in each space, then sow it on the surface, and cast the drawn-off earth evenly over it, after which pick or rake away the lumps with a fine rake, and pat the surface lightly and smooth with the back of the trowel.

Should dry weather ensue, it will be necessary to sprinkle the beds frequently with water, both before and after the plants appear, and to be very particular in keeping them free from weeds. Some of the more delicate kinds when up may not be able to bear the mid-day sun whilst young, and will consequently appear in a declining state. These must be shaded and protected from its influence by occasional coverings of mats until they have established their roots and obtained sufficient strength to withstand its force.

PLANTING AND PROPAGATING PERENNIAL FLOWERING PLANTS.

In the early part of this month you may continue to remove and transplant most sorts of fibrous and tuberous-rooted perennial flowering plants, and to slip and increase many of them by offsets. The following, together with those mentioned on page 314, may yet be removed with good success, that is, such of them as have not previously begun to shoot flower-stems, viz., dracocephalums of various kinds, but particularly the *virginicum* and *dentatum,* which are very beautiful; penstemons, podalyrias, gentianas in sorts, hibiscuses in great varieties, cypripedums and phloxes, monardas, coreopsises, sisyrinchiums and gerardias, aletrises, aconites, ranunculus, aconitifolius, dictamnuses, and dodecatheon, meadia, galega virginica, hedysarums, hemerocallises, napæa, pæonia, saponaria, silphiums and rhexias, with many others. A great number of the above kinds may now be taken up out of the woods and fields and transplanted into the flower-borders and pleasure-grounds, which will keep up a regular succession of bloom during the whole summer and autumn.

Let the plants be taken up carefully with balls of earth about their roots, and planted where necessary; then water them, and repeat it in dry weather, till they begin to grow freely : they will flower generally the same year, and those that are truly perennial will continue to reward your labors annually with a new display of their beauty as long as you deserve that compliment, by rendering them a fostering care.

Here again would I call attention to the necessity of introducing into our gardens and pleasure grounds, a variety of our beautiful field flowers, and not to suffer those departments to appear desolated in the autumnal months, whilst nature displays a profusion of its glory in the fields, woods, meadows, and swamps; but in doing this, let it be observed to give each kind a soil and situation as nearly similar to that in which it grew in its wild state as the nature and extent of your ground will admit. (See pages 91 and 92.)

Note. On pages 74, 87, you will find general designs, both ancient and modern, for laying out pleasure grounds, flower gardens, and all kinds of ornamental planting, to which I refer you.

DOUBLE DAISIES.

Double daisies may now be propagated abundantly by dividing and slipping the roots; but these should be planted in shady borders, or rather in shallow frames, where they can be protected from the too powerful influence of the summer sun, which would absolutely destroy them if left to its mercy. These frames will also be convenient for the laying of boards and mats over them, for the winter protection of the plants, without which most of them would perish. They may be either planted in small pots sunk in the earth, or in rows in the beds, ten inches asunder, and plant from plant six inches distant in the row. Water them immediately and give them shade for a few days.

PLANTING DECIDUOUS FLOWERING AND ORNAMENTAL SHRUBS.

Such deciduous kinds of trees and shrubs as are yet to be removed, should be transplanted in the first week or ten days of the month in the middle States, and not delayed longer in the eastern States than the fifteenth. (For the various kinds and methods of planting them, see page 314.)

PROPAGATING FLOWERING SHRUBS AND EVERGREENS.

For the methods of propagating all kinds of hardy flowering shrubs and evergreens, see the *Nursery* in *March;* and also the work of the *Nursery* in this month, *June* and *July*, &c.

PLANTING EVERGREENS.

Every kind of hardy evergreen trees and shrubs may be removed in the beginning of this month, with the best possible success; but the earlier the better. (See page 351.)

Neither the English broad-leaved laurel, Portugal laurel, sweet bay, laurustinus, arbutus or strawberry-tree, nor the evergreen cypress can withstand the severity of the winter frosts in the middle or eastern States, with very few exceptions, in the former; and, therefore, must in these places be treated as green-house plants. In most parts of the southern States they succeed extremely well; but all kinds of trees and shrubs will there require to be planted much earlier in the season.

In transplanting large evergreens, if the plants can be conveniently taken up, and brought with balls of earth about their roots, it should be done, placing them in the holes with the balls entire; or previously pour some water into each hole, and with your spade let it and the earth be worked up together, then plant the roots in the pap, and fill the earth in about them, tread it down gently around the stem, and form it in a little hollow at top, in order to retain about the roots any water that may afterwards be given when necessary.

Such as are not treated in this way must have a plentiful watering immediately after being planted, to settle and close the earth about the roots; and if some mulch is laid on the surface around each plant it will be very serviceable in preventing the sun and wind from drying the earth too fast.

Stakes should be immediately placed to such as require them, firmly fixed in the ground, and the plants tied thereto.

PLANTING ROSES.

Roses of every sort may still be planted with great success. (But for some remarks worthy of attention, see the article on page 316.) A well cultivated pot-rose should present the healthy appearance here figured.

Fig. 34.

PLANTING EDGINGS.

There is no plant that makes so neat and permanent an edging as box; it may be planted, for that purpose, in the first week of this month, but if slips or cuttings are to be used, they will require very frequent waterings till they throw out and establish fibres or young roots. Rooted plants, however, or slips with the roots attached to them, will succeed well in the early part of the month, if watered occasionally. (For the method of planting and forming box edgings, see page 316.)

Thyme, hyssop, winter savory and lavender are sometimes planted for edgings; but these grow rather out of compass or get stubby and naked by close clipping.

Pinks may likewise be occasionally planted for edgings, and will grow in tolerably close order for a year or two, and produce abundance of flowers.

Thrift, if neatly planted, makes handsome edgings to borders or flower-beds, both in its evergreen property and as a pretty flowering plant in summer. This may be planted either in a close edging as directed for a box, or with a dibble, setting the plants near enough to touch one another, so as at once to form a tolerable close row, or, however, not above two or three inches apart, giving occasional waterings for a week or two if necessary.

London-pride, that is, the *Saxifraga umbrosa*, will make a very neat edging, and is to be planted as directed for thrift.

Double daisies are made use of in many parts of Europe for edgings, and form very neat ones; but they are not able to bear the heat of our summers, which seldom fail to destroy them when fully exposed thereto; nor can they survive, without some slight protection, the severe winters of the middle and eastern States.

Any of our *Sisyrinchiums*, but particularly the *mucronatum*, will make beautiful edgings; they keep blowing a long time, look very gay, and may now be propagated by parting their roots and planting them as directed for thrift. They are indigenous, and bear our summers and winters well.

Strawberries may be occasionally used to make edgings for large walks, and answer the double purpose of pleasure and profit.

Where box-edgings want trimming, it should now be done, although this is not the general season for clipping them; but notwithstanding, when they appear in need of it, let them be handsomely dressed with a pair of garden shears, which will add much to their neatness.

The sisyrinchium will bear trimming extremely well, and continue to produce flower-stems and flowers notwithstanding.

Where any of the above edgings have, for want of care, grown into rude disorder, they should be taken up, slipped, or divided, and replanted in a close regular manner.

TUBEROSES.

To have this fragrant flower in tolerable early perfection you may, about the first of this month, or any time in March, plant a few roots in pots of light rich mould, one in each, first stripping off the offsets, for if these are left on they will draw away a considerable part of the nourishment, whereby the bloom will be greatly weakened. The *upper part* of the roots, when planted in *pots*, should only be covered

24

about a quarter of an inch deep. Immediately plunge the pots to their rims in a hot-bed, and give but very little water, if any, until the plants are up and growing freely; but afterwards they will require a good supply. As the weather gets warm, give them plenty of air, and also sufficient head-room, till the middle of May; then place them where designed to flower, first tying the advancing stems to small green painted sticks to prevent their being dashed about by the winds.

The time for planting these roots in the open ground is, in the southern States, between the first and twentieth of this month; the more northerly, the later; in the middle States, the last week in April or first ten days of May; and in the eastern States, between the fifteenth and twentieth of May.

Prepare for them beds of rich sandy loam, which, being well trenched or dug, divest the roots of all the larger offsets, or of the whole, if the flowers are the exclusive objects, and plant them in rows one foot asunder and eight inches distant from one another therein, making small drills for their reception, and covering their crowns or upper parts about an inch or an inch and a half deep with fine loose earth. They will require no further care but to keep them free from weeds, and to support their flower-stems till November, when the roots are to be taken up and managed as then directed, except to cut off the stems after the bloom is over. The offsets are to be planted in like manner, but somewhat closer, to produce blowing roots for the ensuing season, as the old ones seldom flower well the second year, though they will increase abundantly.

SCARLET AMARYLLIS.

Its management and season of planting are in every particular the same as directed for the tuberose; it flowers generally in about a month after its being planted, and its bulbs do not ripen sufficiently for taking up before November. It is increased by offsets from the roots, which are to be treated as those of the tuberose. In order to have a succession of the flowers, you may in the middle States plant some of their roots in the open ground, once a week, from the twentieth of April to the middle of June. And if the roots are strong and are preserved in saw-dust or the like, they will keep good and blow well, even when planted at that late period. However, the roots will not be so strong the ensuing season, nor the increase so numerous, as if they had been planted in due time.

These can be made to flower during any of the winter months, by planting some of the strongest bulbs, which were taken up in November and kept dry till the time of planting, in pots of light good earth, and plunging them into the bark-pit in the hot-house, or into a good hot-bed: in a month or five weeks after, or sooner, if the heat be regular and brisk, they will produce their very admirable flowers.

GERANIUMS, MYRTLES, BALM OF GILEAD, ETC.

For the methods of cultivating the above, and other green-house plants, see the article *green-house,* in this month, and in *March.*

TRANSPLANTERS.

Dibbers and trowels are well-known instruments for the removal of plants of various kinds. In using the pointed or semicircular trowel, the young plants may be taken up with a considerable ball of earth attached to the roots, while they suffer no injury by the process. A more perfect mode of transplanting by the use of the trowel, is that by taking two of these, one in each hand, thrusting them down on opposite sides of the plant, at the same time drawing the handles slightly outwards; the faces of the trowels are thus made to collapse so much as to press the soil about the roots, and enable the operator to take the plant, with ball entire, from the seed-bed to its destination, and to place it in its new abode without the least check to its growth. We have figured several transplanters, which have been employed for such plants as the brassicæ, &c. Fig. 35 is called Saul's transplanter. It may be thus described: the blades

| Fig. 35. | Fig. 36. | Fig. 37. | Fig. 38. |

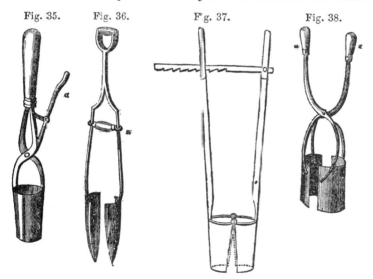

are opened by pressing the lever *a* toward the handle, when they open outwards, and in this state are thrust into the ground, having the plant within them; a counter-pressure causes them to collapse and embrace the ball firmly, and, in this state, the instrument being drawn upwards, brings with it the plant and ball entire; it is then taken to its new place, when the handle is again pressed inwards, and the blades open and are withdrawn, leaving the ball to be filled around with earth.

Fig. 36 shows a modification of the above instrument, wherein the blades are opened by moving the slider *a* upwards, and when thrust down around the plant, the blades collapse by pressing the slider downwards. The operation, afterwards, is the same as in Fig. 35.

Upon the same principle, but with much more mechanical ingenuity, is McGlashan's transplanter, Fig. 37, constructed, which is admirably adapted to such operations. These three collapse upon the ball firmly—and not only that, by their construction they embrace it tighter at the bottom than at top, rendering it next to impossible that the ball should be extracted, and, also, that it cannot slip out afterwards until relieved by the removal of the pressure upon it. All these transplanters are merely modifications of Fig. 38, long used in France for similar purposes. Its principle will be readily seen by the figure. The handles, *a a*, are pulled outwards when the blades are thrust into the ground. They are pressed inwards when the operation of lifting upwards is desired.

GRAVEL WALKS.

New gravel walks may be made any time this month; in the making of which, be very particular in the choice of good and suitable gravel; as to color, you must be governed by fancy and convenience, but as to quality, it should be coarse and lively, containing a due proportion of light sandy loam to make it bind close and firm at all seasons; but not so redundant in loam or clay as to stick to the feet in wet weather, nor so sandy, as to become open and loose in dry weather. As to the dimensions and distribution of gravel walks, see page 77, &c. Agreeably to the designs there laid down, or to any other fancy of your own, stake out the width of the walk, and proceed to level the boundary on each side, corresponding to the adjacent ground, and form the cavity of the walk for the reception of the gravel, observing that the whole space, to make a permanent and good walk, should be dug ten or twelve inches deep, to allow for a proper depth of gravel, both to prevent weeds rising from the ground below, and worms from casting up the earth therefrom; and also to allow a proper depth for turning the gravel occasionally, when the surface becomes foul : the earth dug out from the cavity of the walk, may be used to raise and level any hollow parts on each side, or contiguously situated, which, with the edgings, if of box, should always be completed before you begin to lay the gravel.

The walks being thus laid out, you may first lay any stony rubbish, such as brick-bats, small stones, &c., for several inches deep in the bottom, which will greatly obstruct worm casts, drain off any extra moisture, and thereby prevent the surface from becoming mossy or foul : the proper gravel is then to be laid on six or eight inches thick; and as you proceed in laying, observe to rake off the coarse parts into the bottom and to raise the middle of the walk higher than the sides in a gradual rounding form, just as much and no more as is sufficient to carry off the wet to each side. The proportion to be observed is, a walk of four feet wide should be one inch and a half higher in the middle than at the sides, and for every foot after that such increases in width, add to this a quarter of an inch for the centre elevation. Rounding the walk too much would make it very uneasy to walk on, and of an unpleasing appearance. Never lay more in one day than you can finish off and roll effectually.

Gravel walks should now, if not done in March, be broken up and turned; for such turnings will not only destroy weeds and moss, but will render them much more agreeable to walk on; besides, the fresh and lively surface will be sightly and pleasing.

Before you begin to turn the gravel, the edges of the walks, if of grass, should be first neatly dressed with an *edging iron*, such as described on page 90; or, if planted with box, they ought to be handsomely trimmed with garden shears; any borders near the walks should be neatly dug, and the surface raked smooth; for when the edges and borders are put in proper order they add much to the general neatness. Proceed then to dig the walk five or six inches deep, or whatever depth the fine gravel will admit of, turning the surface clean to the bottom, and the fresh gravel below to the top, rounding and dressing the walk neatly after you, and rolling the whole effectually when done.

In turning or laying down gravel walks, always choose dry weather, and let the work be done in the most complete order, as these contribute very materially to the beauty of the whole garden.

Roll the walks once a week regularly after being either turned or new laid; such will render them firm and neat, and also greatly prevent the growth of weeds. It is a general rule among neat gardeners, who are allowed sufficient help, to roll and sweep the gravel walks every Saturday. During the summer it is of much advantage to give a good rolling after rain, which will preserve a compact smooth surface.

GRASS-WALKS AND LAWNS.

Grass-walks and lawns may yet be laid in the middle and eastern States, if done in the beginning of this month; but if delayed till the weather becomes dry, it will scorch the turf and render the surface disagreeable. For the method of laying and making them, see page 317.

The grass-walks and lawns should be well rolled in the early part of the month; and afterwards, as the grass advances in growth, it should be mowed as often as the scythe can lay hold of it, for this is a season in which most people delight to walk out; consequently the walks ought to be kept in good order. Besides, were this neglected in spring, the grass would become coarse and rank, and be some time before it could be restored to its proper texture.

Always mow this short grass when yet either by dew or rain, otherwise it will be impossible to cut it close or even. (For the general care of grass-walks and laws, see page 89.)

The edges of all your lawns and grass-walks should now be neatly cut with an *edging iron,* if omitted in last month; but this should be particularly done to those edgings next to gravel walks always before the gravel is turned or newly laid on, and afterwards occasionally.

STICKING AND TRIMMING FLOWER PLANTS.

Examine all the beds and borders, and place convenient sticks to such advancing plants as require support; tying them neatly thereto, which should be repeated occasionally as they progress in growth. Let them be made or cut in proportion to the usual height of each respective kind, for it is awkward to see a tall stick set for the support of a plant of humble growth.

WEEDS.

Weeds of every kind, both from roots and seeds, will now make rapid progress; particular care must be taken to keep the beds and borders free from them, as on this, in a great measure, depends much of your success and the beauty of your improvements.

THE GREEN-HOUSE.

GIVING AIR TO THE PLANTS.

Many of the green-house plants will now begin to shoot freely, therefore it will be necessary to give as much air as possible, consistent with their safety. Open the windows every morning when the weather is mild and calm, and let them continue so till the cold of the afternoon begins to increase, provided that the air continues moderately warm all the time. Too much confinement at this season, especially towards the end of the month, when the heat of the weather increases, would do infinite injury to the plants in general, but especially to the early shooting kinds; for if drawn up weakly in the house, they would not be in so good a condition to bear a removal into the open air in the early part of next month, as if their vegetation had been retarded by the admission of a due and salutary circulation of air in the house at all favorable opportunities.

WATERING.

The plants will now require frequent waterings, giving only a little at a time; but especially the oranges, lemons, myrtles, oleanders, African heaths, jasmins, coronillas, justicias, arbutus, laurustinus, and most of the woody kinds; and also the herbaceous green-house exotics will require to be occasionally refreshed with moderate waterings.

Let all of the plants, in general, be often looked over, to see where

water is wanted, and let such as need it be supplied therewith according to their respective necessities, for it is now an indispensable article
But moderation and discretion ought to be observed in the dispensing
of it, especially while the plants are in the house, and particularly
to the succulent tribe.   The latter, such as aloes, agaves, euphorbias,
cactuses, crassulas, stapelias, mesembryanthemums, &c., being naturally replete with moisture, do not require much water; to those and
other plants of the same nature, it should be given only when the
earth in the pots appears very dry, as too much would rot them.

SHIFTING PLANTS INTO LARGER POTS AND TUBS.

Such of your plants as require to be shifted into larger pots or
tubs may now be brought out in a mild warm day, and taken out of
the pots or tubs in which they have stood, with the balls of earth
entire about their roots; then cut away such roots on the outside as
are rotted or appear dry or decayed, and also some of the earth around
the ball.*

Having good sound fresh earth in readiness, put some into each
new pot or tub, previously placing a hollow oyster shell or such like,
with the concave side under, over each hole in the bottoms; over this
put an inch or two, according to the size of the plant, of small lumps
of charcoal or broken crocks; then set each plant, with its ball of
earth prepared and dressed as above, into the middle of the pot or
tub, and fill it with fresh compost, so as that the new earth may cover
the crowns of the roots an inch deeper than before.

According as the plants are thus potted, let them be immediately
watered and returned to their places in the green-house, administering the water occasionally afterwards, as their respective necessities
may require.

FRESH EARTHING THE PLANTS.

Such of the plants as do not require shifting into larger pots, &c.,
should be refreshed with new earth, as directed on page 323; after
which, give them a moderate watering and replace them in the green-
house as before.

TRIMMING AND CLEANING THE PLANTS.

Where any decayed, straggling, or ill-placed branches appear, either
cut them off close, or prune them, so as to give the plants a neat and
becoming form.

Pick off all decayed leaves as they appear, and suffer no weeds
of any kind to grow in the pots; keep them free from moss, &c., by
stirring the surface earth frequently; wash and clean the floor of

---

* When the roots are healthy, it is best not to remove any of them, even
though they be matted, and always let the ball of earth be moist before
being removed into a larger pot, else, it remains dry, as the water, given
afterwards, runs down amongst the new soil without penetrating to the
centre.

the green-house, and let everything in and about it appear neat and lively.

When any large-leaved kinds have contracted foulness, wash them, one by one, with a sponge dipped in soft water; the small-leaved sorts may be taken out of the house, in a warm day, and water poured over them out of a watering pot, which will not only wash off the dust but greatly refresh them; then replace them as before.

HEADING DOWN SHRUBBY PLANTS.

Myrtles, oranges, lemons, geraniums, and several other woody plants that have got into a bad state of health, may now be headed down; observing that any of the budded kinds should not be cut off below where they were worked, except in cases of absolute necessity, that is, when the wood is either dead so far, or in such a state that no hopes remain of its producing new shoots—under such circumstances you may head them down to the fresh wood.

By this means they will put out plenty of strong shoots, near, or from the stems, and form full regular heads in two or three months.

Shifting, or fresh earthing the plants, as above directed, will be necessary upon this occasion, and in the case of unhealthy roots, they should be cut away to the sound parts, and the plants placed in smaller pots than those they previously occupied.

INARCHING.

Towards the latter part of this month you may inarch oranges, lemons, citrons, limes, shaddocks, pomegranates, and almost every other kind of shrubby plants, agreeably to the directions given on page 267.

By way of curiosity, or as required, you may inarch a branch of an orange or lemon-tree, that has young fruit on it, on one end of the common seedling stocks: it will be well united by the end of August, when it may be separated from the mother plant, in a full bearing state.

SOWING SEEDS OF GREEN-HOUSE PLANTS, ETC.

As *early* in this month as possible, sow the seeds of geraniums, myrtles, oleanders, coronillas, lemons, oranges, balm of Gilead, aloes, cannas, buddleias, and cactuses; callicarpa, caparis, celcias, mimosas, mesembryanthemums, centaureas and chrysocomas; cinerarias, cistuses, coluteas, cyclamens, dolichoses, ericas and euphorbias; ferrarias, gardenias, genistas, heliotropiums, indigoferas and lyciums; melias, melianthuses, oleas, passifloras, solanums, proteas, salvias, silenes, spartiums, teucriums, yuccas and xeranthemums, with many others. For the method of sowing them see page 323. Many kinds will not vegetate for two, three, four or six months, and some not sooner than twelve; therefore attend the pots carefully, and your patience and trouble will be ultimately rewarded.

PROPAGATING GREEN-HOUSE PLANTS BY CUTTINGS, SUCKERS AND
LAYERS, ETC.

There are few shrubby plants but may be propagated by layers;
these should be laid in the pots or tubs, agreeably to the methods
directed on page 300.

Suckers may now be taken off where they appear, and be planted
in separate pots, or several small ones in the same pot.

The far greater number of all the green-house plants may now be
plentifully propagated by cuttings or slips; such as laurustinus,
myrtles, geraniums, balm of Gilead, and all the fuchsias, jasmines,
garden ias, hydrangeas, English and Portugal laurels; oleanders, pas-
sion-flowers, justicias, lagerstroemia, heliotropiums, coronillas and
melianthuses; acuba, and camellia japonica, buddleias, solanums, teucriums, proteas, and salvias, with almost every other kind, if planted
in hot-beds, and carefully shaded and watered. Such as do not root
freely should have bell-glasses placed over them in the hot-bed till
rooted this is the most effectual way to insure the growth of many
hard-wooded kinds.

The roots of herbaceous kinds may now be separated and planted
in different pots for increase; the succulent kinds may also be propagated by slips, cuttings, and suckers, such as cactuses, stapelias,
mesembryanthemums, &c. The succulent sorts should not be planted
for a few days after having been taken off, that the wounds may
heal; during which time, they may lie on a shelf in the green-
house, and when fit, plant them in pots of good sandy earth.

The young orange and lemon stocks, raised last year for budding,
should now, if not done before, be planted into separate and suitable
sized pots; and if then plunged in a hot-bed till they have taken
fresh root, it will greatly promote their growth. Some of the strongest will probably be of sufficient size to bud in August, and all of
them at that time twelve months.

CAPE BULBS.

Many of the cape bulbs, mentioned on page 175, will be now in
flower; they should all be kept in the front parts of the green-house,
and have plenty of air, without which they will spindle up and never
show either strong or brilliant flowers; such as are in blow, however, are, when the sun shines too powerfully on them, to be, for the
moment, removed out of its rays, or it will facilitate their decline.

THE HOT-HOUSE.

PINE APPLES.

In this month it will be easy to distinguish which of the pines
are likely to produce the best fruit: this is not always common to

the largest plants. A few of the most promising being marked, a small iron rod, made with a sharp angular point, may be thrust down the centre of each sucker arising therefrom, which being turned two or three times around, will drill out the heart and prevent its growth. Thus the plants being sufficiently supplied with water, and having nothing to support but the fruit, will sometimes grow amazingly large. But this method is not to be practised on too many plants, as it would be attended with the entire loss of all the suckers.

WATERING THE PINES.

In the West Indies, where pines grow to the greatest perfection, rains are very unfrequent during the period that this fruit is coming to maturity; but the dews are remarkably heavy, therefore it is principally supplied with moisture from the latter, in imitation of which you should raise artificial dews in the hot-house by watering the walks and flues frequently in dry weather. This will be found extremely beneficial, not only to the pine-apple but to all other plants which are natives of similar climates, and by this management they will require much less water than they otherwise would. However, regular waterings, taking care to give but little at a time, just to keep the earth moderately moist, will be necessary.

TOP AND BOTTOM HEAT.

Continue to support the requisite heat in the hot-house by aid of moderate evening fires and a *constant good heat* in the bark-bed; the fruiting plants in particular will require this. If the bark was not turned and fresh tan added thereto in March it should be done in the first week of this month, as there directed; but if then attended to there is no necessity for it now, as the pit will yet continue to be in excellent order.

ADMITTING AIR.

Air should now be admitted in proportion to the increasing heat of the season. A great deal depends on this article, for without due attention to its utility and great influence on the plants they may, if deprived of a sufficiency, be soon rendered of little value.

Every warm sunny day, when the wind is not cold, let some of the glasses or lights be opened a little way, and more in proportion to the heat of the day; but this should not be done before nine or ten o'clock in the morning, and they ought to be continued open longer than while the air in the house keeps up to a proper degree of warmth.

Towards the end of the month you will find that a sufficiency of air cannot be admitted by the upright glasses, therefore it will be very necessary to have your roof-lights constructed so as to slide up and down by means of pulleys. Seventy or seventy-two degrees of Fahrenheit will be a good medium for sun-heat, but always when it rises above that give abundance of air; and in the early part of the month this is done with more safety by sliding open a sufficient number of the roof-lights.

SUCCESSION PINES.

The succession pines, especially those intended for fruiting next season, should be shifted as early in this month as possible if not done in March. For the method of doing it and the manner of treating them after, see page 325.

The crowns and suckers of last season should now also be shifted into larger pots and managed in like manner.

TREATMENT OF THE OTHER VARIOUS STOVE PLANTS.

The general treatment directed for the pines may be given in common to most other stove plants. With respect to shifting or adding fresh earth to the pots, that should now be done in the same manner as directed for the green-house plants; after which, if there be room in the bark-bed, let the pots be immediately plunged to their rims therein, and by the assistance of the kindly heat the plants will root freely in the new earth, which will give them strength, promote their health, revive their color, and prepare them the better for a removal into the open air towards the end of next month.

The woody kinds will now require frequent and gentle waterings, the herbaceous occasionally; but the succulent sorts should get only a little now and then, as the earth in the pots seems to stand in need of it.

When any of the stove plants have contracted much dust or other foulness, such must be cleaned off immediately; all decayed leaves should constantly be picked away, and the utmost cleanness preserved in all the house.

Where insects appear on the pines or on any of the other plants, immediate attention ought to be paid to the destruction of them, for, in a short time, if neglected, they would overrun the house and ruin many of the plants. For the methods of extirpating them, see article *Hot-house* for *February*, page 178, &c.

The paying of due attention to all the plants, giving them suitable care and culture, preserving them in good health, and keeping the house constantly clean and the plants free from decayed leaves and filth, is the surest method of not being much troubled with insects.

PROPAGATING VARIOUS STOVE EXOTICS.

You may now propagate by cuttings, layers, suckers, or seeds, the various plants of this department. Plant the cuttings in pots, plunge them in the bark-bed, and the kinds that grow by that method, which are very numerous, will strike root freely; and, indeed, there are very few sorts but may be cultivated in this way, if covered close for some time with bell-glasses to preserve a moist atmosphere around them till they establish themselves in the earth and are able to draw therefrom a sufficient supply of juices to replace those which might be exhaled by the open dry air.

You may, in like manner, strike cuttings of many sorts of green-house plants, and of any curious and valuable shrubs of the open ground departments.

Sow seeds of all hot-house plants that you are able to procure and wish to cultivate; let them be sown in pots, and if room can be had plunge these in the bark-bed, give them occasional watering, and you may expect many kinds to come up shortly, and several others not for months. The laying of panes of glass over these pots will facilitate the growth of the seeds by opposing the ascending moisture, and retaining it about the surface of the earth; but bell-glasses would more effectually answer this end.

CARE OF SEVERAL FRUITING, FLOWERING, AND ESCULENT PLANTS IN THE STOVE.

Pay due attention to the regular watering of the strawberries, kidney beans, cucumbers, and flowers now forcing in the stove, and early in the month introduce others to succeed them.

Continue to keep the grape-vines now fruiting free from all unnecessary shoots, and such as are produced from the axillas of the leaves, &c., and train the others close and regular.

A COLD PIT.

It must be recollected that to *flower* plants is a very different thing from merely preserving them. A structure that would answer perfectly for the latter, might be wholly unsuited for the former. A "cold pit" is simply a miniature green-house, without any facilities for producing artificial warmth. If the amateur gardener wishes to

Fig. 39.

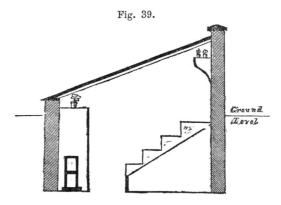

flower plants in winter, a small furnace and flue will be requisite. Indeed, under any circumstances, the means for producing heat are desirable to keep the atmosphere free from damp. As this is a kind of house which, we think, ought to be more generally used, we have prepared the accompanying plan. The arrangements are so apparent that no detailed description is deemed necessary. The dimensions of this pit are as follows : inside width, 8 feet, height of back wall the same, and the front five feet. As all the other parts are in proportion, they can easily be ascertained; of course, the length may vary to any extent. If under twenty feet, the flue should return on itself, as shown in the figure. It should be constructed either of brick or stone ; a dry situation should be chosen, and the bottom covered with six inches of gravel, sand, or coal ashes. It may be entered by a door at one end, or by merely lifting up one of the sashes. The best covering is water-proof cloth, hung on rollers, and elevated six inches from the glass by a portable framework of laths, so as to include a stratum of air between the glass and the covering. It is essential that the cover, when in use, should fit closely round the pit; as a protection from frost this system will be found more efficient and economical than any method of wooden shutters. Fire heat will seldom be found necessary, and all kinds of green-house plants may be kept in the highest state of health, and flower better than in a close, steaming green-house. The mere exclusion of frost only is required, and the day temperature may be allowed as high as 70° or 75° during sunny weather. Water must be carefully administered ; the dryer everything can be kept, compatible with healthy growth, the better will it be for the plants. A southeast aspect is best.

MAY.

WORK TO BE DONE IN THE KITCHEN GARDEN.

EARLY MELONS AND CUCUMBERS.

The early melons will now show fruit abundantly ; they must have plenty of air, and protection from the mid-day sun ; for a few hours sunshine at this season, if the glasses were close shut, would destroy the whole crop. The lights should be taken off, and the plants fully exposed to the open air, about the twentieth or towards the end of the month ; therefore the plants ought to be previously and gradually inured thereto. Should the beds happen to be greatly declined in heat about the first of this month, a fresh lining of hot dung ought to be applied, for at this period of their fruiting a brisk bottom heat is necessary to the free swelling of the fruit. The advantage of this will soon appear very evident. A slight covering ought to be kept over the glasses every night, till about the tenth of the month, after which they will need it no longer ; these should be taken off early every morning, for light and plenty of air will now be absolutely necessary.

According as the melons set, place a piece of board or shingle under each fruit; this will preserve them from the damp of the earth.

About the middle of the month the frames may be raised by means of any kind of support at the corners, and the plants be suffered to run out under them, and by the end thereof you may take them totally away.

A regular supply of water will be very necessary; and although melons do not require as much of it as cucumbers, yet a sufficiency must be given.

The early cucumbers will now be in full fruiting, and will require plenty of air and water; they may be fully exposed to the open air, in the middle States, about the twentieth of the month, and in the eastern States about the end thereof.

MAKING HOT-BED RIDGES FOR CUCUMBERS AND MELONS.

The cucumbers and melons which were sown last month, or late in March, may in the first week of this be planted in hot-bed ridges, as directed on page 329, or the seeds may be sown thereon in the following manner.

The ridges being made and earthed as directed in *April*, page 329, mark out the holes for the seed, four feet asunder, and in form of a shallow basin, about an inch deep, and nine or ten inches wide. In the middle of each, sow eight or nine seeds, and then put on bell or hand-glasses. After the plants have been up ten or twelve days, they must be thinned, leaving only three of the strongest in each hole, drawing a little earth about their stems, and giving a light watering to settle it close to the roots.

When the plants have two rough leaves, they must be stopped or topped, as directed on page 127, which see. This operation is very necessary to throw them into a fruiting state, before they run too much into vine.

As the plants advance in growth, they must have gentle and frequent waterings, and plenty of air admitted, by the raising of the glasses on props, under which suffer them to run out as they increase in growth. The glasses may be totally taken off about the end of the month.

SOWING MELONS AND CUCUMBERS, IN THE OPEN GROUND.

About the tenth of this month will be a good time, in the middle States, to sow a general crop of melons in the open ground; from a week to a month earlier, to the southward, according to the respective situations; and between the fifteenth and twentieth in the eastern States. It is remarked that musk and water-melons, cucumbers, pumpkins, squashes, gourds, and all the varieties of these families,* may be sown at the periods in which people *generally* plant Indian

---

* The different genera of this family ought to be kept as far asunder as the extent of the garden will permit, as they are very subject to fertilize with each other, and of course become mixed.

corn ; but in order to have them as early as possible in the open ground, a few patches may be sown ten days or more before the dates above mentioned, which, with good care, may succeed very well, especially if the season proves favorable.

For the varieties of the musk or cantaleupe melons, prepare a piece of rich sandy ground, well exposed to the sun; manure it and give it a good digging, then mark it out into squares of six feet every way; at the angle of every square, dig a hole twelve inches deep and eighteen over, into which put seven or eight inches deep of old hot-bed dung, or very rotten manure; throw thereon about four inches of earth, and mix the dung and earth well with the spade; after which, draw the remainder of the earth over the mixture so as to form a round hill, about a foot broad at top. Some people use hot stable dung, under an idea that its heat would promote the vegetation of the seed; this is a mistaken notion, as in a few hours it loses all it had for want of a sufficient quantity being together to promote fermentation, and becomes a dryish wisp, unfit, at least for the present, to afford either heat or nourishment to the plants.

When your hills are all prepared as above, plant in each, towards the centre, eight or nine grains of good melon seed, distant two inches from one another, and cover them about half an inch deep.

When the plants are up and in a state of forwardness, producing their rough leaves, they must be thinned to two or three in each hill; the extra number in some, may serve to fill up deficiencies in others: draw earth from time to time around the hills, and as high about the roots of the plants as the seed leaves; when fit, stop them as directed on page 127, after which keep the ground, by frequent hoeings, perfectly free from weeds.

SQUASHES.

Squashes of every kind may be cultivated as directed for cucumbers and melons, should be sown at the same time, and at similar distances, with this difference, that two plants of these will be plenty for each hill, and that they are easier pleased in soil and preparation than the others.

WATER-MELONS.

In order to have water-melons in good perfection, you must fix upon a piece of very light, rich, sandy soil; prepare, sow, and manage it in every respect, as directed for cucumbers and melons, only let the hills be nine or ten feet distant every way.

PUMPKINS AND GOURDS.

Pumpkins will require to be ten feet distant hill from hill, two or three plants will be sufficient in each; they are not so tenacious of a particular soil as either melons or cucumbers, but will grow freely in any dry and tolerably rich ground; they are to be sown at the same time as directed for sowing melons and cucumbers in the open ground, and should be kept constantly clean and free from weeds.

The various kinds of gourds, which are more cultivated for ornament than use, may be sown where they can be trained to trellises, fences, walls, or to cover arbors.

When you intend to cultivate either melons, cucumbers, squashes, pumpkins, or the like kinds, on a large or extensive scale, you can prepare the ground with a plough, which will save much labor; and also, afterwards, as the weeds advance, plough and harrow between the plants till they begin to run, after which, the hoe must be used.

SWEET POTATOES.

The sweet potato requires a very light, sandy, and tolerably rich soil to bring it to good perfection. The time to plant it in the middle States is the first ten days in May, or more generally it is planted about the eighth or tenth of the month. It is remarked that the earlier and more forward crops are always most productive and best for eating; and several people, to accomplish this end, first sprout them in hot-beds, and then plant them out in the following manner.

The ground being first well pulverized by ploughing and harrowing, &c., is afterwards laid out by the plough in squares of four or five feet each, and at the intersections of the scores or furrows, hills are made, in the manner directed for melons and cucumbers, on page 382; into each of these, one or two good sets are planted, and covered about an inch deep, or a little better; as they advance in growth the hills are enlarged by drawing the earth up around them with a hoe; or, by first cross ploughing the ground, harrow it with a very narrow harrow, and then finishing and rounding the hills with a broad hoe. They ought to be kept constantly free from weeds, and the frequent enlargement of the hills will encourage the growth and increase the number of roots.

When they are cultivated upon a small scale in gardens, all this work may be performed with a spade and hoe.

INDIAN CORN.

The *Zea mays*, or Indian corn, is frequently required from the gardener for early use. For this purpose, procure some seed of the *earliest* kind, and select a piece of dry, sandy, and tolerably rich ground, in a warm exposure. After preparing it as if for peas, &c., form shallow drills about two inches deep, at the distance of six feet from each other; drop the seed therein two feet and a half asunder, and two grains in each place; strew a little wood-ashes in the drills, then cover the seed as you would peas. As the plants advance in growth, earth them up two or three times. For an early crop you may plant the seed, in the middle States, about the first of this month, or ten days earlier should the season prove very favorable.

This method is exclusively intended for the garden culture of the small early kinds.

EARLY CAULIFLOWERS.

The early cauliflower plants, as they advance in growth, should have the earth drawn up about their stems, and in dry weather be occasionally watered, which will cause the heads to grow to a much greater size than they otherwise would.

Towards the latter end of the month the plants will begin to show their flowers, when they should frequently be looked over ; and as these appear in an advanced growth, not before, let some of the largest leaves be broke down over them to defend them from sun and wet, whereby they will be preserved in their natural color, firmness, and beauty; for, if left fully exposed to the weather, it would change their peculiar whiteness to a yellowish hue, and occasion them to open sooner than if treated in this manner.

PLANTING CAULIFLOWERS.

The plants from the late spring sowings should now, according as they arrive at a sufficient size, be planted out as directed on page 329. Very few of these will produce flowers till October, but then you may expect some fine heads.

SOWING CAULIFLOWER SEED.

You may now sow cauliflower seed for a late crop. Should the plants from this sowing not produce heads before November, they are then to be taken up and managed as directed in that month, by which means they will continue to produce fine flowers all winter, when such will be very acceptable.

CABBAGES.

Draw earth about the stems of your early cabbages, and all others that are advanced in growth; this will strengthen them considerably, and cause them to produce fine large heads.

The earliest will, towards the middle or latter part of this month, begin to form their heads, when they may be greatly forwarded in their whitening by tying their leaves together. For this purpose, get some strong bass or small osier twigs, go over the plants row by row, and tie such as begin to turn their leaves inward for heading, first gathering all the leaves up regularly. Do not, however, bind them too close, for that would occasion their rotting.

This method may be practised with a few early plants, but by no means with the principal crop, as those treated in that way never produce such large and firm heads as they would if left to nature. However, market-gardeners may derive some advantage from it, as the early produce will always command the highest price.

Continue to plant out your spring cabbage-plants for autumn and winter use agreeably to the directions given on page 331. Plant also at this time a full crop of red-pickling cabbage and savoys. All

25

these will require an open situation; they never thrive or head well near trees, walls, or shade of any kind, and the richer your ground the larger-sized heads will you have.   You may plant some between rows of forward kidney-beans and other low-growing crops, which will occupy the ground when those are off.

Let all be planted out, if possible, in moist or cloudy weather, and immediately after give each a little water, unless the ground is already sufficiently saturated.

Sow now some early York, sugar-loaf, and other close quick-hearting kinds for summer and autumn use; likewise savoys, large drumhead, flat Dutch, and any other of the large late-heading sorts for autumn and winter cabbages, and also some of the red-pickling cabbage.   Sow these seeds as directed on page 331, and transplant young advancing seedlings into beds as there directed, watering them immediately, giving them shade for a few days if necessary.

SOWING BORECOLE.

You may now sow a principal crop of green and red-curled borecole for autumn, winter, and spring use, for an account of which see pages 200 and 331.

By sowing the seed early you will have tall strong stems and large bushy heads, sometimes growing to the height of four feet; but the largest are always obtained from the spring sowings.   However, it is usual to continue sowing successive crops of them to the end of July.

The seed should be sown in beds of open ground tolerably thin and covered lightly or raked in regularly.   In dry weather it will be of use to water the beds occasionally, both before and after the plants are up.   When about three inches high, it will be proper to thin the seed-bed, and prick out a quantity therefrom at four inches' distance, that the whole may obtain proper strength for final transplanting.

Towards the end of the month those sown in April should be planted out into beds of rich sandy soil in the manner directed for cabbages, at three feet distance every way, and afterwards be kept free from weeds and the earth drawn to their stems as they advance in growth.   Those intended for winter use should never be planted in a rich fat loam, as there they would become too succulent, and consequently could not bear the frost as well as if growing on a gravelly soil.   Such as are designed for autumn use may be planted in any convenient open bed that is tolerably rich.

BRUSSELS SPROUTS AND JERUSALEM KALE.

The Brussels sprouts and Jerusalem kale are both cultivated in the same manner, at the same time, and for similar purposes, as the borecole.   They may be now sown and treated like the latter, with this difference, that two feet, or rather two and a half, will be a sufficient distance for the final transplanting of the Jerusalem kale, as it never grows as tall as either of the other kinds.

TURNIP CABBAGE AND TURNIP ROOTED CABBAGE.

For an account of both these varieties, see page 332.   The seeds
of the turnip cabbage may now be sown, and the plants afterwards
treated as directed for cabbages; only observing not to earth them up
above the swelling bulb on the stem.   The turnip rooted kind should
be sown on a bed of strong rich ground, as you would turnips, and
treated like them in every respect; observing to thin the plants with
the hoe, when advancing in growth, to the distance of about sixteen
inches apart.   Their roots will be much larger and better when treated
in this way than if transplanted.

The early sown plants of the former kind may now be planted out,
and afterwards treated as above observed.

BROCCOLI.

The early sown broccoli plants should now be planted out into beds
of good rich earth, in an open situation; the purple kind at two feet
and a half distance every way, and the white at the distance of three
feet.

Broccoli seeds of both these kinds, as well as of any other variety
which you would wish to cultivate, should be sown early in this month
for a second principal crop, for winter and spring use.   Sow them in
a bed or border of rich earth, in an open exposure, each kind separate, and rake them in regularly.

In the middle and eastern States, where the frost is too powerful
for the standing out of these plants during winter, on its approach
they must be taken up and planted in earth up to their leaves, either
in cellars or under sheds, where they can be protected from wet and
very rigorous frosts, and they will continue to produce their fine heads
during all the winter months, which are equal to any cauliflowers.
On the opening of spring, plant out the stalks of the purple kind,
and they will produce abundance of the most delicious sprouts; the
white do not answer for that purpose

These plants, even if hung up in a cellar, would shoot forth their
flowers or heads pretty much about their usual time.   (For a more
particular account of them, see page 333.)

MANAGEMENT OF BEANS IN BLOSSOM.

The early Mazagan, long-podded, Windsor, and all the varieties of
that species of bean, should be topped when arrived at full bloom
and the lower pods begin to set; this will greatly promote the swelling of the pods, as well as their early maturity; for, having no advancing tops to nourish, their whole efforts must go to the support
of the fruit.

This should be performed on the beans in general, which are now
in full blossom, observing to let the stems be first advanced to such
a due height as to have a *sufficient quantity* of pods; the early Mazagan bean may be topped when about two feet high, and the larger

sorts when from about two feet and a half or a yard, to three and a half high, according to the growth of the different varieties, and may be done with a finger and thumb.

But with respect to the small early beans, if you would have them come in as soon as possible, you should top them when the blossoms at the bottom of the stalks begin to open.

Be very particular to earth up the stems of your beans two or three times in the course of their growth, as this is absolutely necessary to their good success and plentiful production.

SOWING PEAS.

To have a regular supply of peas, let some be sown at least twice in this month; but where a constant succession is wanted, three or four sowings will be necessary.

The best sorts to sow now are the champion of England, Woodford's marrow, Flack's victory, and blue imperial—these being the finest and largest sorts—Prussian blue, &c.; those that are sown any time this month will yield tolerably good crops.

The earlier in the month, however, that those or any other kinds of peas are sown the more abundantly will they produce.

You may now sow some of the tall sugar peas, as directed on page 334, to which and its preceding page, I refer you for more general instructions on this subject.

Sow, early in the month, the dwarf sugar and dwarf Spanish peas, and also Bishop's dwarf, as directed on page 334. These are all very delicious, great bearers, and do not require sticks, particularly the two former; and when sown at this season, are generally more productive than the taller growing kinds.

Hoe and earth up the peas which were sown in April; this will greatly strengthen them and promote a plentiful bearing; and also pay due attention to the sticking or placing pea-rods to the young rising crops, as soon as they have attained the height of five or six inches. There is a great advantage in allowing sticks of a suitable height to the various kinds, for the produce is, generally, not only much superior, but by far more abundant, often to more than double the quantity produced by those that are permitted to trail on the ground. The sticks should not only be sufficiently tall, but also branchy, that the plants may readily take hold; and they should be prepared fan fashion, so as the side branches may extend only along the rows.

They should be placed, when in single rows, on the sunny side of the drills, as the plants will naturally incline that way, and more readily lay hold of the sticks; or there may be double rows of sticks placed to them, as directed on page 194.

TRANSPLANTING LETTUCE.

Take advantage of moist weather to transplant such of those sown in the two former months as are now fit for it. The ground should be fully exposed, not encumbered with trees, or near any kind of shade whatever, for these plants never form good heads in such situations, but start to seed immediately.

Dig the ground neatly and rake the surface smooth, then dibble in the plants, in rows ten or twelve inches asunder, and near the same distance from one another in the rows; water them immediately, and repeat it occasionally till they have taken good root.

Such as are intended to remain for heading, where sown, should now be thinned to about ten or twelve inches distance, every way, and those growing among other general crops ought not to be left nearer to each other than three feet.

SOWING LETTUCE SEEDS.

Lettuce seeds of various good kinds should be sown two or three times this month, that there may be a constant and regular supply of this very wholesome vegetable. The white Silicia, grand admiral, and India, are very proper kinds to sow now; the cos varieties do not head like the other kinds, but if tied up as you do endive they will blanch beautifully, and are extremely crisp and delicious; they, however, soon run up for seed. The white and brown Dutch, and large cabbage kinds are excellent sorts, and will succeed well if sown in the early part of this month.

An open situation must be chosen in which to sow the seeds; the ground should be light and rich, and each sort sown separately and very thin; for if drawn up close in the seed-bed, they will never head well.

The beds wherein these are sown, should be frequently refreshed with water in dry weather, to promote the vegetation of the seeds and encourage the growth of the young plants.

TYING UP EARLY LETTUCES.

The various kinds of cos or Roman lettuce which are now beginning to gather and whiten in the heart, should be tied up with strings of bass, which will forward their whitening, and render them crisp and tender for eating; but this must be done only by degrees, or as they are wanted, for it greatly promotes their shooting to seed.

SOWING SMALL SALADING.

Sow a variety of small salading every week or ten days, for these, at this season, shoot on to seed very rapidly, such as cresses or pepper-grass, lettuce, rape, radish, mustard, &c. Sow the seeds in shallow drills on shady borders, cover them lightly, and give them occasional waterings, without which they will be destroyed by insects.

KIDNEY BEANS.

A principal crop of kidney beans should be planted in the first week of this month, and successional crops about the middle, and also towards the end thereof.

Any of the dwarf kinds may now be planted; such as the black, brown, or red speckled, yellow, cream-colored, negro, Canterbury, white, Dutch, Mohawk, refugee, and Battersea dwarfs. The cream-colored, brown, speckled, yellow, Mohawk, and white, are the earliest sorts, and should be particularly chosen for the first crop.

Select for these a piece of light rich ground, for in such they will always be most productive. Let drills be made for them with a hoe, about two feet and a half asunder, and an inch and a half deep; drop the beans therein at the distance of two or three inches from one another, draw the earth evenly over them, and rake the surface lightly to give the bed a neat appearance.

These, upon a more extensive scale, may be cultivated to great advantage, and to the saving of much labor by the plough, in which culture the rows will require to be three or four feet asunder for the convenience of ploughing and harrowing between them, for the destruction of weeds, and also for the landing of them with that instrument.

The various kinds of running or climbing kidney beans may also now be sown in drills made four or five feet asunder, and the seeds planted double the distance from one another of the dwarf sorts. The large white Dutch, common white, and cream-colored runners are excellent sorts for this purpose, they are very productive, boil well, and eat very tender.

When the plants come up and begin to push their runners, then let some tall sticks or poles be placed to each row for them to climb upon. The runners will soon catch hold and twine themselves naturally around the stick or poles, to the height of eight or ten feet or more; or if some are planted in a row close against a wall or any high fence or building, you may suspend strong pack-thread from above, six inches distant, fastened tight at both ends, the lower of which may be tied to the main stem of the beans, and the runners will readily ascend around the strings.

The scarlet runner, though in Europe considered one of the best bearers, and very good for the table, is here neither productive nor esteemed, and is cultivated exclusively for the beauty of its flowers, and for covering arbors, &c.

CAROLINA AND LIMA BEANS.

What is commonly called the Carolina bean, is only a small and early variety of the Lima bean: it may be planted in the first week of this month, or in the last of April, if a favorable season, and the ground sandy and dry; they may be cultivated in the same manner as above directed for the running kidney-beans; or, in hills, as they are called, at the distance of four feet every way, planting five or six good beans in each hill, a few inches apart, and covering them about an inch and a half deep. When the plants are up a few inches, or before, if more convenient, place two or three tall poles to each hill for them to climb on, and as they advance in growth, draw the earth around the hills up to their stems.

The Lima beans should not be sown in the middle States before the first week of this month, when vegetation is very brisk; for they are very subject to rot if planted in cold weather, especially if the ground be replete with much moisture.

They delight in a light, sandy, and tolerably rich soil, and should be planted in hills, as directed for the Carolina beans, but at the distance of four feet or upwards, hill from hill, four or five beans in each, and the poles for their support ought to be strong and near ten feet high. They are very productive, will continue bearing till overtaken by the frost, and are extremely delicious. To these may be added the red and white cranberry beans, which may be treated in the same way as white Dutch.

RADISHES.

Hoe, weed, and thin the advancing crops of radishes, as directed on page 335; and continue to sow a fresh supply every two weeks, as at this time they soon shoot to seed after growing to any tolerable size.

The salmon-colored, white Naples, olive shaped, and white turnip-rooted, are the best kinds to sow now; you may likewise sow some of the white Spanish radish, they bear the warm weather rather better than the other kinds, but are not so crisp and tender. The purple and short-top kinds will yet do very well.

At this season these seeds must be sown in an open exposure, on beds of rich loose loamy earth, for if on a clay or gravelly soil they would become sticky and good for nothing; in order to have them crisp and nice they should be frequently watered in dry weather.

PLANTING RADISHES FOR SEED.

Transplant radishes for seed when the roots are just in their prime; if showery weather, it will be a particular advantage.

Choose for this purpose some of the best kinds, long, perfectly straight rooted, and with short tops; having also regard to the color of the root, that is, if of the purple, or short topped kind, those that are of a clear pale red are preferable, as they generally eat more crisp and mild than such as are of a darker color.

When intended to save seed of the salmon radish, always prefer the best and brightest colored roots, to preserve the kind in its purity, and particularly those that have the shortest tops.

The principal reason why radishes for seed are directed to be transplanted is, that, having drawn up a quantity for that purpose, you can the more readily judge of the goodness of the roots, taking only what are of the right sort, otherwise the transplanting of them would be unnecessary, and those not so treated would produce a much greater quantity of seed.

Plant the roots by dibble in rows four feet asunder, in an open situation, one foot from each other in the row, and give them a good watering immediately after.

Select, also, some of the best formed white and red turnip-rooted radishes of moderate growth, hoe the others out and let these remain for seed; or, if necessity requires, you may transplant them; in that case, plant the bulbs or roots entirely in the earth, leaving the tops free, and then water them.

SPINAGE.

When spinage is required in continuation, some of the round leaved sort may be sown in a cool moist loamy soil, every eight or ten days; for during the summer months it starts to seed immediately.

Weed and thin the spinage sown last month, especially what had been sowed in the broadcast way; and of your early crops, both of the round-leaved and pricklyseeded kinds, leave a sufficiency of the best plants for seed.

NEW ZELAND SPINAGE (TETRAGONIA EXPANSA).

This is a delightful vegetable for greens: it has a large luxuriant leaf, which it produces in great quantities in the dryest summers. Two or three dozen plants are sufficient for a family: the seeds require to be planted the beginning of this month, and covered about one inch deep. On the approach of frost if the plants are taken up and planted in a box and placed where they will be secure from it, and have light and air occasionally, they will continue to yield plenty of leaves.

SOWING CARROTS.

Carrots may yet be sown, especially in the eastern States, with a good prospect of success, if done in the first week of this month, and even in the middle States, if the season is any way backward. (For the proper soil and method of sowing them, &c., see pages 199 and 336.)

CLEANING AND THINNING CARROTS AND PARSNEPS.

Carrots and parsneps will now be advancing fast in their growth and should be properly encouraged. Clear them from weeds, and thin the plants out to due distances.

This work may be done either by hand or hoe, but for extensive crops particularly small hoeing is the preferable method, as being the most expeditious, and by loosening the surface of the ground with the hoe it will greatly promote the free growth of the plants.

Whatever method is pursued, it will be necessary to free the plants from weeds, and to thin them to proper distances, that they may have full liberty to grow and enlarge their roots. The general crops of carrots should be thinned to about six or seven inches, plant from plant, and the parsneps from eight to ten, in order that each kind should attain its utmost perfection.

Such crops of carrots, however, as are intended to be drawn gradually for the table, while young, need not be thinned at first to more than four or five inches distance, as the frequent pulling up of some for table use will in a little time afford the others sufficient room to grow large; but the main crops should be thinned at once to the proper distances.

PRICKING OUT AND PLANTING CELERY.

Some of the early celery plants from the seed-beds should now be pricked out to obtain strength previous to a final planting in trenches; by this method those left in the beds will have room to grow strong and stout. They should be planted at the distance of three inches from one another, in beds of rich loose earth, watered immediately, and afterwards occasionally, till growing freely. When they have acquired sufficient strength in these beds they are to be planted in trenches for full growth, as directed in *June*.

Let those remaining in the seed-beds be watered to settle the earth about their roots, which had been loosened in the act of pulling out the others.

When of sufficient size and strength, plant out into trenches some of your earliest sown plants, as directed in the *Kitchen Garden* for *June*.

For the best method of obtaining celery in early perfection, without the assistance of a hot-bed, see page 336.

SOWING CELERY SEED.

Sow more celery seed for a principal later crop; let this be done as directed on page 336. In hot sunny weather the shading of the bed with mats, raised a foot or more above the ground, from ten to four o'clock, would greatly facilitate the growth of the seed. Occasional waterings also will be very serviceable, and in a dry season indispensable.

ASPARAGUS.

Asparagus is in the best state for cutting when the shoots are from two to four inches above ground, and the top buds or heads remaining close and compact; soon after they become open and of less estimation. For the proper method of cutting them, see page 201.

Keep the asparagus beds perfectly free from weeds, and let it be remembered to terminate the general cutting as soon as you perceive the coming-up roots begin to appear small or weaker than usual; for, if the cutting be continued too late in the season, it will greatly exhaust the roots, and the next and succeeding years' produce will be diminished in proportion.

BEETS.

Weed or hoe your early crops of beets, and thin them, if in beds, to one foot asunder, or, if in drills, to eight or nine inches, plant from plant. Continue to sow more, especially of the turnip-rooted and long red beet, for a succession crop, which will succeed very well if sown in the early part of the month. A full and abundant supply of this very excellent vegetable ought to be cultivated in every garden. (For the methods of sowing, see page 203.)

ONIONS.

The onions which were sown at an early season, with an expectation of their growing to a sufficient size for table use the first year from seed, should now be perfectly cleared from weeds, and the plants thinned to about three inches from one another, being careful to leave the largest and best. They should be thinned at an early period, and kept totally free of weeds from the moment of their appearance·above ground to the period of their perfection.

This work may either be performed by hand or with a small hoe. The latter is the quickest method, and the stirring the ground therewith will be of great service to the growth of the plants. Have for this purpose a small one-hand hoe about two inches broad, or, in want of this, an old table-knife, bent a little at the end, about an inch, by heating in a fire, will answer very well for small or moderate crops, and use a six inch wide scuffle hoe between the rows.

The plantations arising from seed onions should now be kept very clean, and also the late sown crops intended to produce small bulbs for next year's planting.

TURNIPS.

Hoe and thin your advancing crops of turnips, and sow some more of the early Dutch or early stone kinds for a succession. This sowing should be performed in the first week of the month, in order that the roots should have time to grow to a good size before their being overtaken by the great summer heat and drought, which are very inimical to them. In the doing of this, take advantage of moist or cloudy weather or immediately after rain, and sow the seed on a bed of good mellow ground, thin and even; tread it down and rake it in regularly. It is only in very damp and cool seasons, however, that these late sowings will be of use.

HAMBURG PARSLEY, SCORZONERA, AND SALSAFY.

The young crops of Hamburg or large-rooted parsley, scorzonera, and salsafy, must now be carefully cleaned from weeds, and the plants should be thinned or hoed out to proper distances, that their roots may have room to swell, thinning them to about six inches asunder.

Early in this month you may sow principal crops of salsify and scorzonera, for autumn and winter use; for those that are sown now will not be so subject to run to seed as those which were sown in the former months, and their roots will be in excellent order for the table during the entire autumn and winter.* For a more particular account of these plants, see pages 207 and 338.

* Late sown salsafy does not always vegetate, although the roots of such are more tender for winter use. The seedsman sometimes gets blamed for this without reason. Sow early for surety.

CAPSICUMS OR RED PEPPERS.

Early in this month you may sow in a warm exposure, on a bed of rich earth, seeds of the various kinds of capsicums which you desire to cultivate; the large heart-shaped kind is that which is more generally used for pickling; it is also the best flavored. The small Cayenne is good for vinegar. The plants from this sowing may be planted out in rows about the first of June.

The early plants raised in hot-beds should, in the middle States, be planted out finally, as soon after the twentieth of this month as moist or cloudy weather may occur the rows must be two feet or a little better asunder, and the plants one foot distant from one another; when planted give each some water, and afterwards keep the ground free from weeds.

You may, likewise, at this time, sow the seeds in drills at the above distance, covering them about a quarter of an inch deep; and when grown an inch or two, thin them to proper distances; but as they bear transplanting extremely well, it will be attended with less trouble to raise them in the seed-bed, and afterwards plant them out.

TOMATOES.

Sow the seeds of tomatoes in the first week of the month, on a warm sandy soil, either to remain for fruiting or for transplanting, as directed on page 342.

Plant out from the hot-beds about the middle of the month, or a little later, if the season is not favorable, those plants which are forwarded therein, and at the distances mentioned on page 342. Or they may be planted close to palings or fences of any kind to which they may be trained; but a support of some kind will be necessary in order to have them in the best perfection, and in abundant bearing.

EGG-PLANT.

If omitted to sow the seed of the egg-plant last month, as there directed, some should be sown in the first week of this, on a rich warm border, to raise plants for planting out when about three or four inches high, as directed on page 342.

About the middle of this month or soon after, according to the season, you should plant out for fruiting the early plants of this kind which were forwarded in hot-beds. A rich sandy soil is the most suitable for them : the purple kind will require to be two feet and a half asunder; and for the white, two feet will be sufficient. As they advance in growth, draw some earth to their stems in like manner as to cabbage plants; keep the ground about them clean, and you may expect fine fruit.

ENDIVE.

Some endive may now be sown for an early crop; but at this season, it is very subject to run up to seed; however, when such is required, let it be sown on an open spot of rich ground, tolerably thick, taking care to cover it evenly, or to rake it in well.

The white and green curled endive are the proper sorts to sow now; when the plants are about three inches high, they should be transplanted into beds, at the distance of ten or twelve inches from one another, and immediately watered, taking care to transplant them in cloudy or wet weather, if such should occur in due season.

Towards the end of the month you may sow some more, to keep up a regular succession, and although it is very difficult to raise it in good perfection at this season, some families must have it at all events.

OKRA.

The first week of this month is a very proper time to sow a full crop of okra; and another sowing may be made about the middle thereof, for a succession crop; the seeds will now vegetate freely and the plants advance apace. For the method of sowing them, &c., see page 341.

NASTURTIUMS.

The seed of the nasturtium may be sown in the first week of this month, as directed on page 341; but the early crops of this kind are generally most successful.

SORREL.

Either the common garden broad-leaved, or the French round-leaved sorrel, may be sown in the first week of this month, as directed on page 343. Or, the old standing roots of either kind may be separated and planted for increase, in beds or borders, at the distance of ten or twelve inches asunder; this would have been better if done last month, but they will succeed any time in this if well watered immediately after planting, and repeated at intervals for a few days. When the plants shoot up to seed, cut them down close, and a new crop of leaves will be produced; this may be repeated from time to time during the summer and autumn.

SOWING POT-HERBS, ETC.

Common and curled parsley may now be sown where it had been omitted in the former months, as may also the seeds of chervil, sweet basil, coriander, pot-marigold, borage, and burnet; thyme, summer and winter savory, sweet and pot marjoram, together with many other sorts of pot, aromatic, or medicinal herbs; observing the same method as directed on page 215, which see. All those, with every other kind necessary, should be sown as early in the month as possible.

PROPAGATING AROMATIC, POT, AND MEDICINAL PLANTS, BY CUTTINGS AND SLIPS, ETC.

You may yet, if attended to in the early part of this month, propagate the various kinds of pot, medicinal, and aromatic plants mentioned on page 215, and in like manner as there directed; but they will now require to be frequently watered, and if shaded for some time after planting, the better.

SUPPORTING PLANTS FOR SEED.

Now support the stems or stalks of such plants as were planted for seed. The onions and leeks in particular will require this care, for the stalks of these will be run up to a good height, and if they are not secured in due time, the winds and heavy rains will break them down.

The best method of supporting these plants is to drive some firm stakes into the ground along the rows, placing them about two or three yards asunder; then let some thin long poles, or strong lines, be fastened from stake to stake, close along each side of the seed-stalks.

Let the advancing stems of the different kinds of cabbages and other tall growing plants, that are now shooting to seed, and are subject to be borne down by wind or wet, be likewise supported by placing stakes to them and tying them thereto securely, or by any other more convenient method.

CARDOONS.

The cardoons which were sown in March or April ought now to be thinned where they have risen too thick, that the plants may have room to grow and get strength by next month, when they should be planted where they are to remain for landing up to blanch.

Thin them to about four or five inches distance, or some may be pricked six inches asunder on a nursery-bed, to remain till next month, when the whole should be transplanted finally.

Give water immediately to those that you prick out, and if sunny weather, shade will be necessary for a few days.

DESTROYING WEEDS.

It is in vain to expect good crops, and folly to go to the expense of seed or labor, unless you keep them free from weeds, and particularly while they are young; therefore, more than common care should now be taken to destroy weeds throughout the whole garden, but more especially among the young rising crops. It is now the most important work in the garden; the hoe should be applied between all the rows of peas, beans, cabbages, and every other kind growing in drills, and the weeds which are close to the plants be pulled up by the hand.

The onions, carrots, leeks, parsneps, and all other close and low growing crops, should be always kept free from weeds, from the moment they appear above ground till grown to their full size. A small hoe may be applied where it will answer, but where not, hand-weeding must be practised.

WATERING.

Watering in dry weather is very necessary, but especially to the newly transplanted crops, whether young seedlings, or plants of larger growth finally transplanted, such as cabbages, cauliflowers, lettuces, celery, &c. A plentiful watering should be given to each plant immediately after planting out, and repeated occasionally till all have taken root and begin to grow. Most of the young seedling plants will require it now and then, till they have established their roots, and extended them to a sufficient depth to be out of the power of drought.

Water should generally be given late in the afternoon, or very early in the morning, but the former is preferable, that the plants may have as much benefit from it as possible before any part is exhaled by the heat of the ensuing day.

THE FRUIT GARDEN.

WALL TREES.

In the early part of this month look over your wall trees, and where you perceive a superabundance of young and unnecessary shoots appearing, either rub, nip, or cut them clean off close to whence they were produced, being particular to leave a plentiful supply of such as are good and well placed; and when of due growth, train them in at full length, close and regular. The long fore-right shoots, that is, such as project directly towards the front, ought generally to be displaced, except where some are wanted for laying in, to fill up vacant places; and likewise, any extraordinary vigorous growths arising in the middle of the tree, unless where necessary to be preserved for similar purposes.

Where any considerable opening appears, and that but one or two shoots offer in such place, you should, after these have grown about a foot long, shorten them to three or four eyes, and they will soon after shoot out again, probably one from each bud, to furnish the vacancy.

Be very particular as to apples, pears, plums, and cherries, not to shorten or rub off such advancing buds as nature has intended for fruiting-spurs, which are very distinguishable by their short thick growth.

ESPALIERS.

All unnecessary, ill-placed, and fore-right shoots on espalier trees of every kind, should now be rubbed off or cut away; they are only robbers, and should consequently be discarded; but in doing this discretion ought to be observed, and an abundant supply left to furnish the trees and to discharge such parts of the ascending juices as are not convertible into wood or fruit.

Apples, pears, plums, and cherries, continue bearing many years on the same spurs or branches, and do not require such a general annual supply of young wood as peaches, nectarines, &c., which always, with very few exceptions, produce their fruit from the preceding year's shoots: yet a sufficiency should be left to train in between the main branches, and a leading or terminal one to each branch, unless the tree has already extended as far as you desire; for it is essentially requisite to leave a sufficient number of the best placed shoots to choose from in the general winter pruning. The shoots now preserved should be trained in regularly to the espalier at full length, for the reasons assigned in the winter pruning; see the *Fruit Garden* in *January*.

Where there is any great vacancy it is proper, towards the latter end of this month, to shorten some of the adjoining young shoots of the year to three or four buds, to cause them to produce a supply of lateral branches to fill the vacant places.

Young wall and espalier trees that are advancing in a training state should also be attended to now, in their early shooting, to displace the improper and ill-placed growths, and retain all the well-placed shoots, both for an additional supply of branches in the general formation of the trees and to form future bearers for production of fruit.

THINNING OF FRUIT.

Apricot, peach, and nectarine trees, in favorable seasons, sometimes set superabundant crops of fruit often in thick clusters, and in greater quantities than they can supply with a sufficiency of nourishment, and which, if suffered to remain, would not only be poor and miserable but would so exhaust the trees as to render it impossible for them to produce good and sufficient shoots capable of bearing any tolerable quantity of fruit the ensuing season, or perhaps ever after

Therefore let them now be thinned, leaving only a good, moderate, regular crop on each tree; and the sooner it is done the better, both for the trees and remaining fruit, always leaving the best placed and most promising.

The young fruit that are thinned off are excellent for tarts, &c., particularly the apricots; but the others are also very good for that purpose.

Some people will consider this a very disagreeable task, both on account of casting away so many fruit, which they might think would do very well, and also on account of the time spent in performing the work; but this is a mistake, as the loss in number will be more than repaid by the size, flavor, and excellence of the remaining fruit; and, besides, the trees will be preserved in health and vigor for the production of future crops.

This thinning should not be confined only to wall and espalier trees, but ought to be extended generally, and for the same reasons, to all your standard peach, nectarine, and apricots, but more particularly to such as are young.

When trees are suffered to bear a superabundant crop, the extraordinary efforts made to support their too numerous offspring often so exhaust them as to bring on diseases, of which several do not recover, at least for two or three years.

PROTECTING CHERRIES FROM BIRDS.

As soon as your cherries begin to ripen, hang up nets before the wall-trees, and cast some over the espaliers, supporting them with sticks or branches at a sufficient distance to prevent the birds from reaching the fruit. Likewise, the casting of large nets over standard cherry-trees will prevent the depredations of birds.

CLEANING THE FRUIT-TREE BORDERS.

The borders where wall and espalier-trees grow should be kept remarkably clear from weeds, for these not only appear disagreeable and exhaust the nourishment, but afford harbor for snails, slugs, and other crawling insects, to the detriment of the fruit.

Therefore, when weeds appear in these parts, and where there is room to admit of hoeing between any crops that are growing on the borders, let a sharp hoe be applied to them on a dry day, by which you may stop their progress; and, as soon as hoed, rake off all the weeds and rubbish, leaving a clean smooth surface.

INSECTS.

At this season insects will probably appear on some of your fruit-trees; when that is the case, there should be immediate means used for their destruction before they increase and become numerous. See page 347.

Watering with common water proves very beneficial to trees infested with insects, especially if thrown against them with some force, by means of a small water engine. This will not only displace caterpillars and many other insects, but greatly refresh the trees, especially in dry weather, and if often repeated where insects appear, it will considerably diminish their number, and prevent their spreading.

The most eligible engines are such as have the pump and discharging pipe fixed in the vessel for containing the water, of which some are of a moderate size for carrying about by the hand, but larger ones are fitted upon a low, light, three wheeled carriage, for the more convenient removal from place to place.

This engine may be conveniently used for watering different parts of the garden in dry weather.

WATERING NEW PLANTED TREES.

The new planted fruit-trees will now be greatly benefited by occasional watering, which should always be given in the morning, and frequently over the branches, as well as about their roots; this will be of great service in washing off any dust and filth which their leaves may have contracted, and in opening their pores for the reception of the atmospheric moisture.

STRAWBERRIES.

Watering at this season will be extremely salutary to strawberries, by causing their fruit to set and swell freely; let it not be given over the plants, but between them, lest it should wash off the fecundating pollen from the flowers, and thereby prevent their setting fruit.

In those beds where the plants are kept apart from one another, and the fruit required in the greatest perfection, the young advancing runners should be trimmed off, to encourage the bloom and enlarge the fruit; but when a supply of those are wanted for forming new plantations, a sufficiency must be left for that purpose.

The edgings of strawberries, round beds or borders, &c., should be kept within due bounds, by occasionally cutting away their advancing runners.

NEWLY GRAFTED AND BUDDED TREES.

For the treatment of such trees as were grafted in the preceding months, or budded last summer or autumn, see the *Nursery* for this month.

THE IMPOSTOR'S GRAFT.

Mention is made by Pliny, of a tree in the garden of Lucullus, at Tivoli, which is described in his *Natural History*. On the trunk of one tree he saw branches which produced pears, others figs, apples, plums, olives, almonds, grapes, &c.; but he adds, that this wonderful tree did not live long. Even at the present day, the gardeners of Italy, especially of Genoa, Florence, and Rome, sell plants of jasmines, roses, honeysuckles, &c., all growing together from a stock of orange, or myrtle, or pomegranate, on which they say they are grafted. But this is a deception, the fact being that the stock has its centre bored out, so as to be made into a hollow cylinder, through which the stems of jasmines and other flexible plants are easily made to pass, their roots intermingling with those of the stock. After

26

Fig. 40.

growing for a time, the horizontal distension of the stems forces them together, and they assume all the appearance of being united. M. Thouin, who calls this "The Impostor's Graft" (*Greffe des Charlatans*), tells us that he himself tried the operation with perfect success upon both a linden and an ash-tree a foot in diameter. He contrived to give both of them heads of plums, hazels, wild and cultivated services, walnuts, peaches, and vines, the branches of which were thoroughly interlaced. Of one of these he gives a figure, which is here reproduced, and which perfectly illustrates the system.

THE ORCHARD.

You should now pay attention to the due formation of the heads of young or new planted trees; much may be done towards that by the timely displacing of irregular and unnecessary shoots, and by the shortening of luxuriant ones.

The new planted trees will require to be frequently watered, giving it occasionally to the branches as well as the roots, and always about the hour of sun-setting, or a short time before or after.

Such of your peaches, nectarines, and apricots, but more especially the young trees that are over-burdened with fruit, must be deprived of any superabundance by a judicious thinning, and only as many left on as they have sufficient strength to support without injury to themselves.

Take particular care to destroy caterpillars, &c., while yet in small

clusters, before they overrun the trees, and where worms or canker
appear in either stems or branches, let such parts be treated as directed on page 149.

THE VINEYARD.

The vines will now begin to shoot vigorously, and produce besides
bearing and other useful shoots, numbers that are totally unnecessary,
which ought to be carefully cleared away, for if left on, they would
rob the fruit, and also crowd and impoverish those shoots intended
for next year's bearing. But in doing this, you must be very particular not to break off, in going between the vines, such fruiting or
other shoots as are necessary, for at this time they are very easily
injured; nor to annoy in the least the blossom buds, which will early
in the month be very prominent. Where suckers from the roots, or
shoots from the under parts of the stems appear, let them be immediately stripped off. The principal part of this work, if attended to
in due time, may be done with the finger and thumb, but where that
will not answer, you may now use the knife with great safety, for
although these plants bleed copiously in spring when destitute of
leaves, yet afterwards the exhalation by the foliage becomes so great,
that the absorbent roots do not supply a fluid so fast as it could be
expended in the growth of the plant or dissipated into the air; hence
the cause of the drooping of various kinds of plants in hot weather.

All the shoots that have fruit on, and others that are strong, well
placed, and suitable for next year's bearing, should, when grown to
a sufficient length, be carefully and neatly tied up to the stakes, previously observing, as before directed, to clear away all unnecessary
young growths arising in places not wanted, and to leave a sufficiency
of the best for a proper choice in the general winter pruning.

It will not be proper at this time to cultivate the ground between
the vines, as many accidents might happen thereby to the blossoms
and young shoots; but towards the end of the month, or when all
the vines have had their first tying up (for this must be repeated as
they advance in growth), you should give the ground a general cleaning either by hoe or plough, &c., as most convenient.

THE NURSERY.

DESTROY WEEDS.

There is nothing more important at this season, than the destruction of weeds in all parts of the nursery, for if you let any of them
perfect seeds, your ground will thereby be stocked for years; therefore the hoe must be applied wherever you can use it, and always be

careful to rake and carry away all you hoe or pull up, for if left lying
on the surface or in the alleys, many of them would there ripen seed
which would afterwards considerably increase your labor. Weeds
should never be suffered to grow between the rows of trees, &c., for
those rob them of a great portion of the necessary nourishment; nor
should you, for the same reason, ever plant any kitchen vegetables
between them, as is practised by some unskilful and covetous persons.

The seed-beds of all young trees and shrubs should now, in particular, be kept remarkably free from weeds, and this must always
be done by a very careful hand-weeding.

WATERING THE SEED-BEDS.

If the weather should now prove dry, all the seed-beds, but particularly the evergreens, such as pines and firs, &c., ought to be
frequently watered, taking care not to administer it too hastily lest
it should wash the earth from about the young roots and expose them
too much to the sun, which would greatly retard their growth.

SHADING AND SIFTING EARTH OVER SEEDLINGS.

All the slow growing and tender seedlings, especially the evergreens, should, after having newly come up, be occasionally shaded
from the too powerful influence of the mid-day sun, which would destroy a great number of them, particularly while their small stems
are in a tender succulent state.

There is nothing that will be more beneficial to the young seedlings at this period of their growth, than to sift some fine, light
earth over them, just as much and no more as will cover their stems
up to the seed leaves; this will keep their roots cool and moist, and
protect their stems from the power of the sun. The pines and firs
in particular, are very subject to be cut off, when young, at the very
surface of the ground, by the burning heat thereof, melting away
the yet soft and tender stems, while the leaves do not appear in the
least injured.

WATERING NEW PLANTATIONS.

Watering will be extremely necessary for all the new plantations
of the more curious and valuable sorts of evergreens and flowering
shrubs, and indeed for as much of the general young plantations as
it can be extended to with any tolerable degree of convenience. It
should be occasionally given to the leaves and branches as well as
the roots, for it will not only wash off any dirt or filth which they
may have contracted, but open the pores of the plants, which, in dry
weather, are many times almost closed, whereby the trees suffer
greatly; nor is the water poured about the roots only capable of relieving them when in that condition; this is one reason why rain is
much more effectual than artificial watering: these waterings should
always be given in an evening after the heat of the day is over, that
the water may have time to soak down to the roots, and the moisture

be dried from the leaves by the morning sun; for if watered in the forenoon, and there should be a powerful sun soon after, the leaves are frequently scalded thereby, the spherical drops of water which remain on their surface, causing the rays to converge to a focus, and act upon them as a lens or burning-glass.

But in watering, let it be observed not to give too much, as that, in some cases, would be injurious. To avoid these bad effects, when water is necessary, let a good soaking be given, and a mulching of rotted dung or litter be applied on the surface around the roots, this will prevent the demand for frequent repetition.

Such plants as you have in pots, should be treated as directed hereafter for those of the green-house department.

PROPAGATING EVERGREENS, ETC., BY LAYERS.

About the latter end of this month begin to propagate such evergreens and other shrubs by layers of the young shoots of the present year as do not succeed well by layers of the old wood.

When the young shoots are from eight to ten or twelve inches long, bring them down to the earth, and if strong, you may slit them as directed on page 300, or if weak, give them a gentle twist and lay them into the earth from two to six inches deep, according to their size, leaving about two or three inches of the tops out of ground; fasten them securely with hooked pegs and draw the earth over the parts laid. When done give them a moderate watering, and repeat it occasionally, so as to keep the earth in a moist state, to encourage their rooting.

Trees and shrubs in general root very freely by this method, which may be practised on the various kinds as they advance in growth, both evergreen and deciduous, from the middle of this month to the end of July. Many kinds will be well rooted by October, and may then be taken off and removed. Such as are not rooted by that time must be suffered to remain another year.

NEWLY GRAFTED AND BUDDED TREES.

Examine all kinds of trees and shrubs which were grafted in the preceding months, and such as are well united, manifested by the free shooting of the grafts, the clay and bandages may be taken off, not, however, in most kinds, until the scions have grown five or six inches long; the latter part of the month will, generally, be the proper time for this examination.

Those that are not as well united as might be wished, should have the bandage slackened and fresh clay applied to them as in the first instance, or the clay may be applied without the bandage, which will preserve the wounds from the weather, and greatly promote the growth of the bark over the headed parts of the stocks; this may be left on till it falls off.

Suffer no shoots to remain that arise from the stocks below the grafts; all should be looked over once a week, and when such appear, let them be immediately rubbed off, that the whole nourishment may go to the support of the scions.

The trees which were budded last summer must also be carefully and frequently looked over, and all improper shoots rubbed off.

As the shoots from the inoculations advance in growth, they should be tied gently to the spurs, left for that purpose at the time of heading the stocks, that they may not be broken off by winds or other accidents.

SEEDLINGS IN POTS OR TUBS.

The pots and tubs of the more rare and delicate seedling plants should now be kept constantly in the shade where they may have only the morning sun till nine or ten o'clock, and that of the afternoon, after four; they must be frequently watered and kept free from weeds. A little earth sifted over them, as directed for other seedlings, will be of great service.

THE PLEASURE, OR FLOWER GARDEN.

DAHLIAS, OR GEORGIANS.*

Of this beautiful plant there is an endless variety; they are originally a native of Mexico, where they grow in great quantities. They were introduced into England in 1806, and were cultivated for some time before any of the double varieties were obtained, which is done by raising from seed. They generally produce seed, which is sown and treated as other annuals, generally flowering the first season; but you cannot judge of the quality of a fine flower until the second year; sometimes those which produce single or semi-double flowers the first season will give five double ones the second.

They are also propagated by dividing the roots, and by cuttings from the young shoots, which is the method employed to increase the double varieties. The proper time to plant the roots is the beginning of this month, and the plants about the twentieth; they will grow and thrive in any common garden soil, but are much finer when cultivated in fresh loam well enriched by rotted stable manure and guano. When you plant them it is necessary to place a good strong stake to each, and, as they advance in growth, tie them up to it, to prevent their being broken off by the wind. The dahlias vary in height from two to eight feet, so that when they are planted it is necessary to proportion the stake to the height of the plant, for it looks very awkward to see a low growing plant with a tall stake. Through the sum-

* The enthusiasm of florists has now brought this flower to perfection in symmetry, and it forms an indispensable requisite to our flower gardens in the fall months. There are all shades of color, excepting pure blue, from a snowy whiteness, down to maroon black.

mer, should the weather prove dry, it will increase their flowers materially to water your plants every evening.

In October, when the leaves and stalks are killed with the frost,
it is necessary to cut down the stalks to within six inches of the
ground, and let them remain so for a few days that the roots may
be well refined, otherwise they are not so likely to keep during the
winter or vegetate in spring. As you take them up label each plant
separately with the name, color, and height, as it will assist you to
diversify the different varieties in planting. The better way to label
them is to write the name on a small wooden tally, and tie it on the
root with good twine, or fine wire is preferable. Keep them in winter
secure from frost by putting them in dry sand or saw-dust, and placing
them in a cellar.

HYACINTHS.

Continue to defend the beds of the more curious hyacinths, yet in
full blow, as directed last month, or they may be defended either by
boards or by mats laid occasionally on hoops placed archwise over the
beds for their support. These should be laid on every day, when the
sun shines powerfully, about nine or ten o'clock in the morning, and
taken off at four or five in the afternoon.

When hyacinths are past flower, let them always be fully exposed
to the weather, except in very heavy torrents of rain, from which
they should be carefully protected.

It is the practice in Holland to take up the bulbs about a month
after the bloom is completely over, in the following manner: as soon
as the plants begin to put on a yellowish decayed appearance, they
take up the roots and cut off the stem and foliage within an inch or
half an inch of the bulb, but leave the fibres, &c., attached to it;
they then place the bulbs again on the same bed, with their points
towards the north, and cover them about an inch deep with dry earth
or sand in form of a ridge, or in little cones over each bulb: in this
state they remain about three weeks longer, and dry or ripen gradually; during which period the bed is preserved from heavy rains
or too much sun, but at all other times exposed to the full air: at the
expiration of this period, the bulbs are taken up, and their fibres,
which are become dry and withered, cut or gently rubbed off; they
are then placed in a dry room for two or three weeks, and are afterwards cleaned from any soil that adheres to them, their loose skins
taken off, with such offsets as may be easily separated.

When this dressing is finished; the bulbs are wrapped up in separate pieces of paper, or buried in sand, made *effectually dry* for that
purpose, where they remain till the return of the season for planting.

Another, and less troublesome mode of treatment after bloom,
though perhaps more hazardous, is to suffer the roots to remain in
the beds till the stems and foliage appear nearly dried up and consumed; this will seldom happen to be the case in less than two
months after bloom; the bulbs are then to be taken up, cleaned from
the fibres, soils, &c., and spread to dry and harden on the floor of an
airy room, for about three weeks, then to be preserved in sand or

paper as before directed. Or they may be deposited in dry barley chaff, saw-dust, or kept on open shelves out of the sun and wet; but too much exposure to the air often destroys many roots, and materially injures the whole.

Others again take up the roots at the first mentioned period, cutting off the flower stems but not the foliage, and prepare a bed of light earth, either where the hyacinths had grown, or in any other convenient place; forming it into a high sloping ridge, east and west; on the north side of which, they place the roots in rows, so as that the bulbs do not touch, and in a horizontal manner, covering the roots and fibres with the earth, and suffering the leaves to hang down the ridges; here they remain till the bulbs are sufficiently ripened, and then are taken up and treated as before.

TULIPS.

Continue to protect the fine late tulips, yet in flower, as directed last month on page 356, and treat them in every respect as there advised.

As soon as the petals or flowers fall, the seed-vessel of each should be immediately broken off, or if suffered to remain and ripen seed, it would procrastinate the maturity of the roots, and considerably weaken them.

Towards the end of the month, or rather when the grass or foliage becomes of a yellowish-brown, not before, which will happen sooner or later, according to season, climate, soil and situation, and a few inches of the top or stem appear dry, purplish, and withered, you are to take up the roots of such as you particularly esteem; for this is the critical period for that work, because if done earlier, they would be weak and spongy, and deferred later, their juices would become gross; which would appear manifest at the succeeding bloom, by too great a redundance of colorific matter in the petals, and the flowers would be what is generally termed foul.

When the roots are taken up, they are to be laid in a dry shady place and gradually dried; observing to keep each variety of the superb kinds separate, that in planting, you may know how to diversify the bed, according to fancy, either as to intermixture of colors, or the usual height and growth of the plants. About five or six weeks after the bulbs are taken up and properly dried, it is proper to take off their loose skins, fibres, and offsets; the last brown skin which is so intimately connected with the root, ought to be left on; after which they should be preserved in *dry* sand, barley chaff, saw-dust, or rolled up in separate papers, till the time of planting, for the action of the air during our warm summers and autumns would greatly weaken and injure them, by drying up part of their juices.

The smallest and weakest offsets, particularly such as are not provided with a brown skin, ought to be replanted as soon as they are taken up, about an inch and a half deep, in a fresh sandy loam, and in a dry situation; or instead of replanting these offsets so early, they may be preserved from the drying influence of the air by burying them in dry sand till October, when they are to be planted as already mentioned.

Common tulips, planted in the borders of the pleasure-ground, &c., need not be taken up oftener than once in two or three years, to separate the offsets, and replant the bulbs in fresh earth.

RANUNCULUSES.

The weather in this month is generally very clear and hot; the ranunculuses ought to be shaded at such times from the mid-day sun, by means of lofty hoops and mats, or by some better contrivance, that will admit light and air freely: a frame and cover, similar to that directed for hyacinths on page 354, would answer best, if expense and trouble were not to be considered: it will, however, be absolutely necessary to shade them, in some manner, during the period of bloom, otherwise they will continue but a short time, especially the dark rich colored sorts; for, in proportion as their colors approach to black, is the injury they will receive from the rays of the sun, if it is permitted to shine upon them in full force; some of the very darkest cannot stand it a day without being entirely deprived of their beauty. The light colored sorts will bear the sun's rays much better, reflecting them in proportion as they approach to white; green is the only color that reflects and absorbs the rays of light in equal proportion, and consequently, is more predominant in the vegetable kingdom than any other.

During the continuance of the bloom, the earth around the roots must be occasionally watered as directed on page 357, but when that is over, they will require it but seldom, and not at all should gentle showers of rain occur now and then, but shading in the middle of hot days will be very beneficial to the plants; it tends to prolong their vegetation, and the size and substance of the roots are thereby increased. For their further treatment, see the *Flower Garden* in *June.*

A DESCRIPTION OF THE PROPERTIES OF A FINE DOUBLE RANUN-CULUS.

The stem should be strong, straight, and from eight to twelve inches high, supporting a large well-formed flower, at least two inches in diameter, consisting of numerous petals, the largest at the outside, and gradually diminishing in size as they approach the centre, which should be well filled up.

The blossom should be of a hemispherical form, and its component petals imbricated in such a manner as neither to be too close and compact nor too widely separated, but have rather more of a perpendicular than of a horizontal direction, to display its colors with better effect.

The petals should be broad, and have perfectly entire well rounded edges; their colors should be dark, clear, rich, or brilliant, either consisting of one color throughout, or be otherwise variously diversified on an ash, white, sulphur, or fire color ground, or regularly striped, spotted, or mottled, in an elegant manner.

There are more numerous varieties of beautiful double ranunculuses than of any other flower, and we may add, that, neither them nor yet anemones will give satisfaction unless well attended to according to these directions.

ANEMONES.

Gentle and moderate waterings will be necessary for anemones, during their period of flowering, as well as for ranunculuses; the blossoms and petals of the former are of a more soft and flexible texture than those of the latter, and are consequently more liable to receive injury from high winds and heavy rains; their colors soon fade when exposed to a strong sun; it is, therefore, equally necessary to shade and shelter them whilst in bloom, in order to prolong the extreme beauty of their flowers.

Anemones continue longer after bloom in a state of vegetation than ranunculuses, probably because of their greater degree of succulency; and even at the proper time to take them up, it will sometimes happen, that part of their foliage will not be entirely divested of greenness and moisture; when it thus happens, which it does more frequently in rainy or wet seasons, much skill is necessary to ascertain the critical period to take up the roots; for if they are suffered to remain too long, especially if the season be moist, they will shoot afresh, and be thereby materially weakened and injured; it is indeed better to take them up too early, than suffer them to vegetate in this manner, but the roots will not be so firm and solid as if done at the exact time. The safest and most effectual method to preserve them from these disagreeable consequences, is to keep off all heavy rains after the bloom is quite over, by means of mats and hoops, but on no account suffer the ground to become too dry; the roots will then regularly and gradually mature, and the foliage in due time will become brown and dry, which will point out the true time to take up the roots, and this will usually happen to be about a month after bloom.

For their subsequent treatment, see the *Flower Garden* for next month.

EARLY FLOWERING BULBS.

Any curious bulbs that are now in flower, may be much prolonged in bloom and beauty by occasional shade from the sun.

Spring crocuses, snow-drops, fritillaries, crown-imperials, dens canises, and all other early flowering bulbs that have done flowering, should, where intended, be taken up as soon as their leaves decay.

This ought to be constantly practised with such as have stood unremoved two or three years, in order to separate the offsets, and to select the best roots for new planting, for without this care the bulbs would become numerous, and so small as to render the flowers very insignificant. The offsets, when separated, may be immediately

planted in beds or prepared borders, to increase the stock and enlarge
their size; or they may be kept up as well as the largest of the roots
till found convenient to plant them.

All these kinds, when taken up, should be placed in the shade to
dry, and when sufficiently so, preserved in dry sand or saw-dust, &c.,
till the time of planting, which, for these, should not be delayed later
than October, nor even till then if not taken good care of, as they do
not keep well out of ground, especially if exposed long to the air.

AUTUMN FLOWERING BULBS.

The autumnal crocuses, amaryllises, and colchicums, should be
taken up as soon as their leaves decay, the offsets separated, and all
replanted again before the end of July: they are by no means to be
kept longer out of the ground, as that would prevent their flowering
in due perfection in autumn, which is their proper season.

CARE OF SEEDLING BULBS.

The boxes of seedling tulips, hyacinths, narcissuses, and other
bulbous kinds, arising from the seeds sown last autumn, should be
now placed in the shade, carefully preserved from the mid-day sun,
and the plants refreshed now and then with a little water: a small
portion of loose earth sifted over them would be of great benefit.

AURICULAS AND POLYANTHUSES.

The first week of this month, or immediately after your fine auriculas and polyanthuses have done flowering, is a very proper time to
repot and slip them, as directed in the *Flower Garden* for last month;
after which they must be treated during the summer and autumn, as
there advised.   (See page 360.)

CARNATIONS.

The fine carnations in pots should now have due care and good attendance; they should be watered according to their necessities, and
as their flower stems advance, small neat sticks, for their support,
should be placed, one in each pot, to which they are to be tied; these
ought to be at least three feet long, tapering a little from the bottom
to top, and painted green; they should be substantial and straight,
and their lower ends are to be forced into the earth in the centre of
each pot, sufficiently deep and firm not to be shaken loose by the
wind.   As the stems continue advancing in height, the tying is to
be repeated at about every five or six inches.

The pots may now be removed to the stage, and remain there till
the time of bloom.

If any small, green winged insects appear on the stems or foliage
of the plants, they must be effectually extirpated, either by washing
the infested parts with a strong infusion of tobacco-water, or dusting

some Scotch or fine snuff over them early in the morning, whilst yet wet with the dew of the night.

The common carnations in the borders will require to be kept free from weeds, and as their stems advance they should be tied up neatly to sticks placed for that purpose. (For the further treatment of carnations see the *Flower Garden* next month.)

PINKS.

Your choice pinks in pots will require due attention at this time; they must be kept free from weeds—frequently watered, and not too much exposed to the mid-day sun in hot water. (For further particulars see next month.)

TUBEROSE AND SCARLET AMARYLLIS.

The first week of this month is, in the middle States, the best period for planting the roots of the tuberose and scarlet amaryllis; for the method, see pages 369 and 370.

SOWING ANNUAL FLOWER SEEDS.

Most kinds of annual flower seeds may yet be sown, if done in the early part of this month; but the first week thereof will be a very proper time to sow the seeds of the most tender kinds, such as the various sorts of flowering dolichos, tri-colors, mesembryanthemums, ipomœa quamoclit, browallia, sensitive plant, and vinca rosea, &c.; the last two, however, though often considered as annuals from their flowering the same season in which they were sown, are not truly so, as they will continue for several years if preserved in a hot-house: to do them justice they should be sown in pots, and forwarded under frames and glasses, or else the sensitive plant will not display its sensibility so well, nor will the vinca rosea flower in due time: the dolichoses should be sown to cover arbors, &c., as may also the ipomœa quamoclit, convolvulus purpureus, scarlet kidney beans, &c.; or they may be sowed in small patches, and neat poles placed for them to climb on.

(For the various kinds, &c., see pages 363 and 364.)

TRANSPLANTING ANNUALS.

You may now transplant various kinds of annuals from the early sowing into beds, borders, or pots, as you think proper, observing to give them shade and water till well rooted, or to transplant them in moist or cloudy weather.

Towards the middle of the month, the various beds, intended for the purpose, may be filled with verbenas, heliotropes, salvias, cupheas, petuneas, Nurembergias, tea-scented China, and Bourbon roses, remontant carnations, and all such continual blooming plants, that have been wintered in the green-house or cold frame.

SOWING PERENNIAL FLOWER-SEEDS, ETC.

The seeds of most kinds of perennial and biennial flower-seeds, may yet be sown as directed on page 365; but they will require occasional watering till up and well established in the earth.

PROPAGATING DOUBLE SCARLET LYCHNIS.

This beautiful flowering plant may now be propagated by cuttings of the stocks, as well as at an earlier period by slips from the root. Towards the latter end of the month, let some of the young flower-stalks be cut into lengths of six or seven inches, and planted in a *shady* border of rich light earth, leaving one or two joints of each cutting above ground; close the earth well about them, water them gently, and if bell or hand-glasses are placed over them, their rooting will be greatly facilitated thereby.

THE HESPERIS MATRONALIS, OR GARDEN-ROCKET.

The double white, and double purple varieties of the garden-rocket, are extremely beautiful and fragrant; I have not yet had the pleasure of seeing one of them in this country, nor have I been able to learn that such is to be found on this side the Atlantic: however, it is to be hoped we shall soon obtain that charming, showy, and delightful flower.* It is perfectly hardy, and may be cultivated at this season, as above directed, for the double scarlet lychnis, or by slips or offsets from the root, taken off and planted either in spring or autumn; it does not prosper well except when annually slipped or propagated by offsets; for the old roots are very subject to decay, especially the double varieties; the single sorts are much more permanent and easy of culture. The ladies of Europe are extremely fond of it, whence it obtained the name of dame's-violet, or queen's gillyflower.

DOUBLE WALL-FLOWERS AND STOCK-GILLYFLOWERS.

The fine double wall-flowers, and double stock-gillyflowers, may now be propagated by young slips of the present year : choose those of short and robust growths, from four to five, or six inches long, and let them be carefully slipped or cut with a knife from the mother plants. Take the lower leaves off, so that there may be two, three, or four inches of a clean stem to each, and plant them in a shady border or in pots, inserting them into the earth up to their leaves ; then give some water, and be particular to shade them from the midday sun till they have taken root. Water them occasionally during summer, and in September, such as are planted in borders may be taken up with balls of earth and potted, in order to lie placed in frames, &c., for protection from the winter frosts.

The double varieties are accidentally produced from seed, and it is

---

* The double white is now in many collections in this country, and the double purple has been often imported, but for some unknown cause it generally dies out after a short time.

very rare to meet with such among seedling plants of the wall-flower, perhaps not one out of five hundred would prove double, but the gillyflowers produce numbers of double flowers from seed, especially if it is saved from semi-double varieties; the full double never producing any. The beginning of this month is a very proper time to sow the seed of either of these or of their varieties.

GUERNSEY LILLY.

The *Amaryllis sarniensis*, or Guernsey lily. The leaves of this most beautiful flower will generally be decayed towards the end of this month, when the roots may be taken up, and the offsets separated; they may be re-planted in pots immediately, or if dried first in the shade, be preserved in dry sand, &c., and planted any time before the end of July, but are not to be kept up longer, as they flower in September or October. When the winter frost approaches, the pots are to be removed into a garden-frame, where they may have occasional protection during the winter months, or they may be placed in the front windows of the green-house. Their roots do not increase numerously when removed oftener than every third year, and in the summer months they ought to be kept in the shade and gently watered now and then; but as their roots are in a dormant state during that time, too much water would totally destroy them.

TRANSPLANTING PERENNIAL AND BIENNIAL SEEDLINGS.

Many of the early sown perennial and biennial flower plants, will in the course of this month be fit to transplant into nursery beds, where they should be set at a distance of six inches from one another, there to remain to get strength till September or October, when they should be removed with balls of earth, and finally planted where intended to flower.

SUPPORTING FLOWER-PLANTS.

Sticks must now be placed to such flowering plants as want support; in doing this, have regard to the natural size and height of each kind, and let the sticks be in proportion; fix them down firm on that side in which they can be least seen; for although the intent is to keep the plants upright and of neat appearance, yet the means should be concealed as much as possible, and similar care ought also to be observed in tying up the plants.

Likewise, climbing and trailing plants of every kind should have timely support of sticks or stakes proportioned to their respective growths, and their stems or shoots conducted thereto in a proper manner.

WEEDS.

More than ordinary care should now be taken, to keep all your beds and borders free from weeds, but more especially those in which small seedlings are growing.

GRASS AND GRAVEL WALKS.

The grass-walks and lawns should now be duly mowed and rolled, otherwise the grass will soon grow rank and unsightly; and where plantain or any other kind of weeds are mixed therewith, they ought to be picked or grubbed out, or else many of their seeds will ripen, and thereby increase their species, which will overpower the grass and render the verdure less agreeable.

The gravel-walks should also be kept in complete order, preserving them always free from weeds, and having them occasionally swept to clear away all loose litter, and likewise well rolled, generally once a week, but particularly after heavy showers of rain, which well consolidate them, and render the surface smooth and even.

THE GREEN-HOUSE.

AIR AND WATER.

During the first ten days of this month, and in the middle States, the last week of April, the doors and windows ought to be kept open, night and day, in order to harden and prepare the plants for a removal into the open air; an extraordinary change of weather, however, may sometimes render it prudent to close them at night, but that should not be done at this season except in cases of necessity.

Water must now be given to every plant according to its nature and in proportion to its necessity, as observed last month; the oranges, lemons, myrtles, and other woody kinds, will require it frequently; it is impossible to say how often : the state of the earth in which they grow will readily denote it; it should always be kept moist but not wet. The succulent tribe must yet get it but sparingly.

SHIFTING.

Such plants as were not removed into larger pots or tubs in the preceding months, and that still require it, may now be shifted as directed on page 375; but this must be done in the first week of the month, keeping them afterwards in the shade till they begin to grow freely.

Loosen the earth in the top of the pots and tubs, and refresh with new compost such as had been neglected in April.

PRUNING AND HEADING.

You may still prune, trim, and head such of your plants as are in need of that treatment; but let it be done early in the month, and as directed on pages 321, 322, and 376, which see.

PROPAGATING GREEN-HOUSE PLANTS.

Continue to propagate most kinds of plants, by cuttings, suckers, seeds, and layers, as directed on pages 324 and 377. The China, tea-scented, and Bourbon roses may now be increased abundantly by cuttings, they will strike root freely, and flower handsomely in autumn.

SEEDLING ORANGES AND LEMONS.

The seedling oranges and lemons raised from the late sowings of last year should, early in this month, if not done before, be transplanted into separate pots; they ought to be watered immediately, and shaded from the sun till newly rooted. If plunged into a hotbed or bark-bed for two or three weeks, and carefully shaded from the mid-day sun, it will greatly facilitate their rooting, and promote their growth.

The early sown seedlings may, towards the latter end of the month, be planted separately into small pots, and treated in like manner.

You may yet sow the seeds of oranges and lemons in pots or boxes, for stocks; they will rise freely without any artificial heat, and make tolerable progress during the season.

INARCHING.

Inarching may now be performed on oranges, lemons, and any other plants that you desire to propagate in that way, for the method see page 267.

BRINGING OUT THE GREEN-HOUSE PLANTS.

About the tenth of this month, two or three days earlier or later, according to the season and situation, you may, in the middle States, begin to bring out the more hardy kinds of green-house plants, such as the viburnum tinus, prunus lauro-cerasus, prunus lusitanica, nerium oleander, hydrangea hortensis, myrtles, pomegranates, oranges, lemons, magnolia grandiflora, lagerstrœmia indica, daphne indicum, and all the other hardy kinds: the more tender, and tenderest sorts, are to be brought out successively, so that the entire may be abroad by the twentieth of the month.

In the eastern States this work must be delayed for a week or two longer, according to the respective climates, and not attempted while there is any danger remaining from night frosts; but when this is over, the sooner the plants are taken out the better, especially the more hardy kinds: by no means ought they to be continued a day longer in the house than their preservation from frost and cold severe weather requires, as at this season the young shoots of many kinds will be growing freely, and if deprived of the benefit of the open air, they would become weak and sickly.

Generally, when the plants are first brought out of the green-house, it would be advisable to place them in a warm situation where the wind can have but little power; about ten or twelve days after they will be somewhat hardened to the open air, and may then be removed to the places where they are to remain during the season.

Every plant, as soon as brought out, should be cleared from all decayed leaves, dust and foulness of every kind, and the heads of the whole ought to be watered all over by means of a watering pot or a hand engine, which will greatly refresh and cause them to assume a lively appearance.

If not done before, take out the earth from the tops of the pots or tubs, and fill them up with fresh compost; this will greatly encourage their flowering and promote a free growth; and if their stems, &c., had not been pruned and dressed in the former months, it should now be done.

It would be very advisable, immediately on bringing out, to place the pots of small growing plants on a stage, and the larger kinds on boards or planks, supported on bricks or pieces of timber, in order to prevent the earth-worms from entering at their bottoms, which, if once admitted, never fail to destroy the texture of the soil, and render it like a honey-comb, consequently, it cannot long retain moisture, and becomes more pervious than necessary to wind and weather, to the great injury of the plants, and trouble of the gardener; for the pots or tubs so perforated will require to be watered double as often as those that are free from earth-worms.

When pots are plunged in the earth there ought to be a piece of shingle, board or slate placed immediately under the bottom of each to prevent the roots from working out through the holes into the surrounding earth; for although their rooting in this way will cause them to grow more vigorously, it, to many, when taken up, proves very injurious; therefore, to avoid this evil as much as possible the pots should be turned around, at least once a week during the season, to break off the extending fibres that may have pushed through those apertures at bottom.

The hard-wooded kinds are generally not so much injured by this as those of a more spongy texture, but it is ultimately of more injury than service to every plant, and, therefore, ought to be avoided as much as possible.

THE HOT-HOUSE.

Fire-heat should now be totally discontinued, except in the more northern parts of the eastern States, where a moderate fire at night, during the first week of the month, may, in some seasons, be necessary; but still continue for the pine-apples a constant moderate heat in the bark-bed agreeably to the intimations given last month.

27

PINE APPLES.

The pine apple plants will now require frequent and moderate refreshments of water, which, during the summer season, should be given late in the afternoon; let this not be given in too great quantities at any one time, for such would not only damp the heat of the bark but also loosen the plants in the pots.

As the weather increases in heat give air in proportion, both by the front and roof-lights; but especially when the thermometer rises above seventy degrees of Fahrenheit; for that is necessary in order to have large and good fruit. When the weather gets very hot the front lights must be kept open night and day, but the roof-lights should be closed every night, particularly in cloudy weather, to preserve the tan-pit from sudden rains, and ought to be opened again early in the morning, especially in warm weather.

GENERAL CARE OF ALL EXOTICS IN THE HOT-HOUSE.

Continue also to give plenty of air to the plants in all the hot-house departments; supply them duly with proper waterings; and if any want shifting into larger pots, let it be done now as soon as possible, keeping the whole clear from decayed leaves, &c. If casual irregularities occur in the shoots or branches, prune or regulate them as may be required, and cut away any decayed parts; observing the same general directions as in the two preceding months.

PROPAGATING THE PLANTS.

You may still continue to propagate such plants as you desire by cuttings, layers, suckers, and seeds in the manner directed in *March* and *April*.

Any time in this month you may plant cuttings or slips of cactuses, euphorbiums, aloes, agaves, sedums, mesembryanthemums, stapelias, and other succulent plants, laying them in a dry, shady place a week or ten days, according as they are more or less succulent, before they are planted, that the wounded parts may heal over, otherwise they are subject to imbibe too much moisture and rot. When they are planted they should be placed in the shade or plunged in the tan-pit till newly rooted, giving them a little water as necessity may require. The hardy sorts may be planted in a bed of light sandy earth, where, if they are screened with mats for some time, they will freely take root.

BRINGING OUT THE HOT-HOUSE PLANTS.

About the twenty-fifth of this month you may, in the middle States, begin to bring out the hardier sorts of hot-house plants; if they had been removed into the green-house eight or ten days previously, it would be of service, as there they would gradually be prepared, hardened, and become in a good condition for a removal into the open air.   The more tender kinds should not be brought out till the first week in June, but if previously removed into the green-house for a week or ten days it would be the better way; always ob-serving, wherever they are, to give them abundance of air to harden and prepare them for the transition.

In the eastern States the above work is to be deferred, in every instance, from one to two weeks later, according to climate and the local situation of the place; and to the southward of the middle States it may be done somewhat earlier.

Should you have no pine-apples in your hot-house, and there are plants permanently growing in any beds or borders therein, the roof-lights should be totally taken off when the other plants are out, that these may receive the full benefit of the open air during the summer months, &c.

As to the manner of placing and treating the pots when and after being brought out, I would advise the same as recommended for the green-house plants, which see.

You must be very careful when you plunge any of your pots, to make it a particular point to turn them around in their seats once a week, in order that such roots as run into the ground through the holes in the bottom may be broken off; for though these would, for the moment, encourage the growth of the plants, when you come to take them up for housing, the sudden deprivation of their usual sup-ply of nourishment would give them such a check as seriously to injure them : and, besides, they would be but ill rooted in the pots, and badly prepared to extract the necessary nourishment during winter.

TREES GROWN IN POTS.

The injury done to the roots of trees grown in pots, is a subject that the gardener should well consider.   By cutting round the roots before

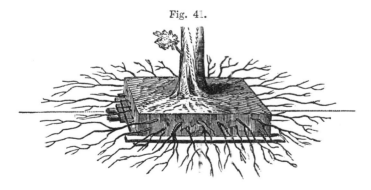

Fig. 41.

the removal of a tree (Fig. 41), we may have those rootlets preserved from injury which are too often destroyed : the main roots now radiate from the common centre as in Fig. 42. In the next figure, 43, is represented a tree circumscribed by the limits of pot culture. In

Fig. 42.

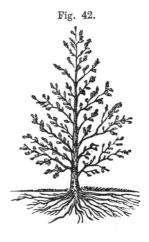

Fig. 43.

the former, the roots are extending in all directions, near the surface, in search of food; in the latter they have a direct tendency downwards, where they neither can derive food, nor from their position have the same effect as the former, in maintaining the perpendicular position of the tree.

Fig. 44.

The next figure, 44, shows the state of a fruit or forest tree, subjected in early life to pot culture; where the roots have been most confined and contorted, the supply of sap thrown into the tree immediately above them has been limited and irregular, as seen by the smaller and irregular portions of the annular rings in the transverse section of the trunk; whereas again, where the root *a* has had the means of penetrating deeper into the soil, and consequently been able to collect a greater amount of sap food, the annular rings above are larger, and more uniform in size. Sickliness, deformity, and premature death are the result. Great care should be employed in planting such a specimen, to disentangle and spread the roots carefully.

Where the corkscrew, or spiral direction has been once taken by the roots, they are very apt to retain it during their lives; and if when they have become large trees they are exposed to a gale of wind, they readily blow out of the ground. To prevent this occurrence, it is a good plan to place trees intended for transplantation in old baskets. Through their wicker sides the roots readily penetrate, and when this has happened, the half decayed baskets are lifted and " potted" in other baskets of a larger size.

Fig. 45 is a sketch of a root of Laricio, after having been planted ten years, illustrating the effects of corkscrewing better than any description.

Fig. 45.

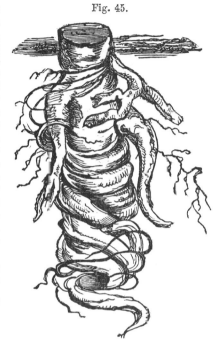

JUNE

WORK TO BE DONE IN THE KITCHEN GARDEN.

EARLY MELONS AND CUCUMBERS.

About the first of this month all your melons and cucumbers that have been hitherto under the protection of glasses or paper-frames, may be fully exposed to the open air, having been previously and gradually inured thereto. A piece of shingle or board should be laid under each fruit of the early melons to preserve them from the damp of the earth, which would injure their flavor. Occasional refreshments of water will be necessary, but particularly to the cucumbers.

Your principal or general crops of melons and cucumbers, in the open ground, should now be kept totally free from weeds, the ground between the plants must be frequently hoed, and the earth drawn gently to the stems of the latest sown : the vines should be laid off in a neat and regular manner, and when any of them are too luxuri-ant, check them by nipping off the extremities of the runners.

In the last week of this month sow general crops of cucumbers and melons for pickling, which is to be done in the same manner as directed on page 382. The long oval musk-melon, and the long prickly cucumber, are in general estimation for this purpose; but the cluster cucumber, on account of its numerous bearing and small fruit, is by many preferred.

WATER-MELONS.

If not done before, thin your water-melons, leaving but three of the best plants in each hill, and draw the earth with a hoe up around the hills till the stems of the plants are covered up to the seed leaves; the ground between them must be kept perfectly free from weeds, either by hoeing, or (if cultivated on a large scale), by ploughing and harrowing in the early part of the season.

SQUASHES AND PUMPKINS.

Squashes and pumpkins may be treated in the same way as di-rected for water-melons; they are more hardy, and do not require so very particular attention; however, the ground must be kept loose and free from weeds, for it will be in vain otherwise to expect pro-fitable crops.

SWEET POTATOES.

Your sweet potatoes must have earth drawn around the hills, to enlarge them and encourage the growth of the roots; lay off the vines regularly, and keep the ground very clean.

CAULIFLOWERS.

The early cauliflowers will now be producing their heads abund-antly; care must be taken to break down the leaves to preserve the flowers from sun and rain, as directed on page 385.

Those plants which are still advancing in growth, or part coming into flower, should, in very dry weather, be frequently well watered, which will greatly enlarge the size of the flowers. For this purpose, draw the earth around each plant, basin-formed, to retain the water till soaked down about the roots. This practice is absolutely neces-sary in dry seasons.

The cauliflower plants from late sowing, should now be planted out finally, as directed on page 329; taking care either to do it in moist or cloudy weather, or to give shade and water after planting: a large cabbage leaf laid over each plant will protect it considerably.

CABBAGES AND SAVOY.

Take opportunity of moist or cloudy weather, and plant out a full crop of cabbages and savoys, from the late spring sowings; also, of the red pickling cabbage, allowing each kind a sufficient distance according to the nature of its growth, as directed in the former months.

But in gardens, where there is no ground vacant, from other crops, or where there is a necessity of making the most of every piece of kitchen ground, you may plant the savoy and cabbage plants between rows of forward beans, and early cauliflowers, or such crops as stand distant, and are soon to come off the ground; observing to give each plant a little water immediately after planting, unless the ground is sufficiently saturated with moisture.

You may now sow seeds of any of the early heading kinds of cabbage, such as the early York, Sugarloaf, or Battersea, to come in both for small hearts and hard cabbages in autumn.

BORECOLE, BRUSSELS SPROUTS, JERUSALEM KALE, AND TURNIP CABBAGE.

The early plants of either of the above kinds may now be planted out, as directed in *May ;* the late sown crops should be thinned, and those pulled out planted in nursery-beds, four inches asunder, giving them a good watering when planted, and afterwards occasionally, till well established : here they are to remain till of sufficient strength for planting out finally.

BROCCOLI.

Plant out finally such broccoli plants as are of sufficient size, choose for this purpose a bed of rich mellow earth, and let them be planted at the distances mentioned on page 387.

Thin the late sown crops, and plant those pulled out into nursery rows, to obtain strength, giving them a good watering immediately after planting.

Early in the month sow some more seed for a succession crop, to produce their heads in February, &c.   For particulars see page 387.

CELERY.

The celery plants that have arrived to a sufficient size, should now be finally planted out into trenches.

Choose for this purpose a piece of rich ground, in an open exposure; mark out the trenches by line, ten or twelve inches wide, and allow the space of three feet between trench and trench, which will be sufficient for the early plantations.

Dig each trench a moderate spade deep, laying the dug out earth equally on each side, between the trenches; lay three inches deep of very rotten dung in the bottom of each trench, then pare the sides and dig the dung and parings with an inch or two of the loose mould at bottom, incorporating all well together, and put in the plants.

Previous to planting, trim the tops of the plants, by cutting off the long straggling leaves, and also the ends of their roots, leaving the former about six inches long, and the latter two.   When, however, the plants have been duly thinned and kept free from weeds they will be short and stubby, and will lift with small balls of earth to each. In this case they may be planted with a trowel and need no trimming.

Let them be planted with a dibble, in single rows, along the middle of each trench, allowing the distance of four or five inches between plant and plant; as soon as planted, give them a plentiful watering, and let them be shaded until they strike root, and begin to grow.

Small sticks may be placed across the trenches, and on those boards or pine planks laid lengthwise; or, pine or cedar boughs may be laid over the plants, which are to be taken off as soon as they begin to grow.

The plants when grown to the height of eight or ten inches should have their first landing; this must be done in a dry day; the earth should be broken small and laid in gently to both sides of the plants, always taking care to leave the hearts and tops free; repeating it every ten or twelve days till they are blanched of a sufficient length for use.

PEAS.

Though peas sown at this time do not always succeed in bearing abundantly, yet a few, to keep up a regular succession, may be sown at two or three different times in the month, and if the season should prove somewhat moist, there will be a chance of obtaining a handsome crop. The best kinds for this season are early Frame, early Warwick, or blue Prussian. The marrow and other such are more subject to mildew, while the above sorts are comparatively free.

If the weather and ground be very dry, it will be of some use to soak them a few hours in soft river or pond water previous to sowing, otherwise water the drills and then sow them.

Let those crops, if convenient, be sown in moist ground, but not in a shady place; in such a situation, the plants would draw up and be good for nothing; observe to allow plenty of room between the rows, for at this season much depends on their having air and liberty to grow.

ASPARAGUS.

The asparagus now running up to seed, should be cleared from weeds, and also your new plantations; likewise, the seedlings intended for next year's planting; for if suffered to be overrun with weeds, it would ruin them.

TRANSPLANTING LEEKS.

Select a piece of good ground for this purpose, manure and dig it well, then draw from the seed beds a sufficiency of the stoutest plants, trim the long fibres of the roots, and cut off the tops of the leaves; this done, plant them in rows a foot asunder, and six inches plant from plant in the rows, inserting their shanks into the earth up to their leaves; by this means they will grow very large, and the part inserted in the earth become white and tender.

LETTUCES.

Transplant and sow lettuces as directed last month, on page 388. Let this be done in moist weather, particularly the transplanting; for if in a great drought, the plants will not succeed well: the place must be open and fully exposed, otherwise they will start to seed before they arrive at any tolerable perfection. If you are under the necessity of planting them in dry weather, let it be done late in the afternoon, and immediately give them a plentiful watering.

SMALL SALADING.

Continue to sow cresses and other small salading once a week on a *shady border*. They should be often refreshed with water, in dry weather, and this ought to be repeated both before and after the plants appear.

KIDNEY BEANS.

Sow successive crops of kidney beans in the beginning, middle, and towards the latter end of this month, as directed on page 390; either of the dwarf or running kinds may now be planted with good success.

Should the ground happen to be very dry at the time of planting, the drills ought to be well watered previous to the beans being dropped therein; this should not be omitted in dry weather, as it will greatly promote the sprouting of the seeds, and the crops will rise sooner and be more regular.

Land up the rows of kidney beans planted last month, which will greatly strengthen and bring forward the plants, and place sticks or poles to the running kinds, which are now beginning to advance in growth.

CAROLINA AND LIMA BEANS.

Hoe and clean the ground between your crops of Carolina and Lima beans; see that all are properly supported with sticks or poles, and draw up some earth around the stems of the plants. A few of the early Carolina kind may be planted about the first of this month, for a late crop; for the method of planting, &c., see page 390.

RADISHES.

Although radishes do not generally succeed well at this season, yet a few of the salmon-colored may be sown at different times in the month: should the season prove moist, they may do tolerably well. Some of the short top and white turnip-rooted kinds may also now be sown, and toward the middle or end of the month you may sow a good crop of the white and black winter or Spanish radish, to draw early in autumn.

CARROTS, PARSNEPS, AND ONIONS.

The crops of carrots, parsneps, and onions, must now be kept clean and free from weeds; and if you observe that your onions incline more to tops and roots, you may with a long stick gently lay over their tops on one side, so as to bend them, and in a few days after, lay them back to the opposite side, which will check the ascent of the juices and cause the bulbs to swell.

BEETS.

The crops of beet should be kept very clean and the plants thinned to proper distances, that they may have room to swell and grow large.

The seeds of these plants are generally sown in drills, or rows, a foot or more asunder; and where that method was practised, you can now more readily clear out the weeds and thin the plants; observing to thin them to ten inches distance in the rows; also, where the seed was sown broadcast, so as the plants stand promiscuously, they must likewise be cut out to ten or twelve inches distance, plant from plant, and the roots will grow to a large size accordingly.

You may now sow succession crops of red, green, and white beet; and also of the *Mangel wurtzel*, or root of scarcity; they will all succeed well from this sowing, but the green and white kinds are generally cultivated for their leaves (see page 203), while the last is only useful for cattle.

TURNIPS.

The advancing crops of turnips should be hoed and thinned to proper distances, and this ought always to be done at an early period of their growth. As they do not grow large at this season, six or seven inches apart will be sufficient.

SCORZONERA, SKIRRETS, SALSAFY, AND HAMBURG PARSLEY.

Thin and clear from weeds the crops of scorzonera, salsafy, skirret, and large rooted parsley, which perform either by hand or small-hoeing, thinning out the plants to six inches distance, and cutting up all the weeds.

ENDIVE.

Transplant endive that is now of a sufficient size; for the method, see page 396.

Sow another crop of curled endive, to keep up a regular succession when wanted; and also some of the broad Batavian kind; this grows very large, whitens well if tied up, and is very palatable. Sow more towards the end of the month.

OKRA, TOMATOES, AND EGG-PLANTS.

Earth up your advancing crops of okra; where too thick, thin them to the distances mentioned on page 341, and keep the ground free from weeds.

In the early part of this month, plant out a general crop of tomatoes and egg-plant, as directed on pages 342, 395 and 396.

CARDOONS.

Plant out cardoons in a bed of good earth, at the distance of four feet from one another, every way: they may either be planted on the level, or in holes made basin-form, at the above distances, previously laying some rotten manure in each hole, and mixing the earth therewith; one good plant is sufficient in a place, as they rise to the height of three or four feet and require a considerable quantity of earth to blanch them. Observe, before planting, to dress the tops and roots as directed for celery; and as they advance in growth, they are to be earthed up for blanching, keeping the leaves close together.

These plants are a species of *Cynara*, or artichoke; the stalks of the leaves are used, when well blanched, in salads, soups, and for stewing, &c.

RED PEPPERS, OR CAPSICUMS.

In the early part of this month, you should plant out from the seed-beds full and general crops of the various kinds of capsicums, as directed on page 395.

PLANT POT AND OTHER HERBS, &C.

Plant out from the seed-beds the young plants of thyme, hyssop, marjoram, winter savory, &c. &c.; let this be done, if possible, in moist or cloudy weather. Prepare for that purpose some beds, three and a half feet wide, rake the surface smooth, and put in the plants in straight rows, setting them six or eight inches distant every way, and water them immediately. Many of these kinds may be planted occasionally as edgings, along the sides of any particular beds or borders.

All the large growing kinds of medicinal herbs, such as angelica, lovage, &c., ought to be planted a foot or eighteen inches asunder, in proportion to their usual growth. You may yet make slips or cuttings of lavender, rosemary, thyme, hyssop, &c., and plant them in shady borders.

THE FRUIT GARDEN.

GATHERING HERBS.

All kinds of herbs, such as mint, balm, lavender, clary, sage, rosemary, &c., that are gathered for drying, or for distillation and other purposes, should be cut off when just beginning to come into flower, and laid in the shade to dry gradually, which will render them much better for any purpose than if they were dried in the sun.

THE FRUIT GARDEN.

WALL AND ESPALIER FRUIT-TREES.

Where the apricot, peach, nectarine, and other wall or espalier trees were neglected last month, or not carefully attended to, you may in the early part of this thin the fruit as then directed; rub off all fore-right or ill-placed shoots, and train others regularly at proper distances : be not too officious with the knife at this season, nor pull off any of the leaves from the branches, unless they are distempered; for the pulling off the leaves will expose the fruit too much to the sun, and thereby greatly check their growth; besides it would greatly injure the buds which are formed at the footstalks of those leaves. For further particulars respecting fruit-trees, see the *Fruit Garden* for *May*, which are generally applicable in this month.

STRAWBERRIES.

The strawberry plants in general will, early in the month, be coming into full bearing, and if watered occasionally between the rows as directed on page 401, it will swell the fruit to a much larger size, and greatly encourage the bloom and setting of an abundant crop.

Should the weather prove moist or cloudy, this will be a very proper season, to make new plantations of the various kinds of straw-berries, observing the method directed on page 232. But it would be more advisable at this time to plant some of the best runner-plants of this year's production into nursery beds in shady borders, six inches asunder, there to remain and get strength till September or October, and then to plant them with balls of earth where they are to stand for fruiting. Frequent waterings will now be very neces-sary for the young plantations.

Be particular in selecting the best kinds, and of the stoutest and most vigorous growth; dress or trim their roots, and cut off all the strings or runners previous to planting.

Though it is not common to propagate strawberries at this season, yet if done, and duly watered till they are well rooted, the plants will be stronger, and bear much more abundantly next season, than if deferred till September or October; but if the weather should not happen to be peculiarly favorable, I would advise them to be planted for the present in nursery beds, in a shady border, as before observed, taking good care to water them frequently till well rooted.

You may, however, any time this month, plant out some of the young runner-plants of the Alpine or prolific strawberry, and if shaded and watered till they have taken fresh root, they will soon bear fruit on the present plants, and in August and September, on the runners produced in the intermediate time. The seeds of these latter kinds, if sown in March, are particularly productive; these will commence bearing in the September following, and continue on until destroyed by frost, or if placed in the green-house, all the winter.

THE ORCHARD.

At this time there is very little to be done in the orchard, but a repetition of what was recommended on page 402, to which I refer you.

It would be very proper, when you observe many of your young fruit punctured by insects, and consequently in a declining state, gently to shake the trees, and pick and carry away to the pigs such as fall to the ground, for the reasons assigned on page 151, &c., which see.

PRUNING.

Dr. Lindley, in his new edition of the *Theory of Horticulture*, has given some directions regarding pruning and trimming, which it is well to remember, and it is therefore here inserted. His views on this subject have become authority with many. They will not be unprofitable studies at all times.

THE PEAR-TREE.

This tree bears its fruit on wood more than one year old, but chiefly on spurs, and very rarely on two-year branches. The object of the pruner is to secure spurs by stopping branches and arresting luxuriance, at the same time maintaining the plant in perfect health.

There is no difficulty in obtaining the requisite number of branches, at proper distances, by observing the following directions: Plant a maiden tree in autumn; allow it to establish itself for one year, and then head it back to a good eye, a few buds from its base. Let one shoot grow as strong and upright as possible during the summer, and head it back to within thirteen inches of the ground in autumn, cutting very close to a bud, in order that the shoot springing from it may form little or no bending; train it upright, whilst three or four shoots, from buds immediately below it, should be more or less inclined to horizontal direction, according to their strength; the strongest should be most depressed. These three or four constitute the commencement of the first or lower tier. For the next tier, head back the upright leader to within eighteen inches of its base, if the soil is rich; if not, to fifteen inches; and from the shoots produced in the following season from buds, just under the cut, train a shoot for a leader, and three or four somewhat horizontally, as before, for a second tier. Precisely in this manner tier after tier must be started, till the tree attain its assigned height. All this can be effected in accordance with the natural disposition of the tree to form an upright stem, and with the tendency of the sap to develop the uppermost buds of a shortened shoot. But it is not to be done without serious difficulties.

The shoots started for horizontal branches will rarely take that direction; on the contrary, they will generally diverge at an angle of 45°. This may, and should be overcome by tying down. The disparity of vigor in the upper, as compared with the lower branches, is a more serious affair. If allowed, the former will soon overgrow the latter, and the pyramid will ultimately become inverted. It is, therefore, evident that, in order to have well-conditioned pyramid pear-trees, means must be adopted to maintain vigor in the lower tiers of branches, and repress over-luxuriance in the upper.

With the view of invigorating the lower, permit the shoots to grow without restraint till September, and then bend them towards a horizontal position. They will thus be much stronger than if they had been made to follow a horizontal direction from the beginning. Shorten them a little at the winter pruning, in order to obtain a stronger leading shoot than would otherwise be produced. Cut to a side bud; one on the upper side would produce a stronger shoot, but the latter could not be brought down without occasioning an unsightly bend. Besides a leader, some other shoots will probably be produced; let them grow, for their foliage will assist in forming channels or layers of wood containing channels, for the transmission of sap along these branches in the following season. The growing shoot should have its point elevated till September, as before. No reduction of foliage connected with the lower branches should be made by summer pruning. Their leading shoots must not be overshaded.

In order to prevent excessive luxuriance in the upper branches, recourse must be had to summer pruning as the most efficient means. The shoots should be trained horizontally from their origin, their points depressed instead of elevated. In short, they must be subjected to a treatment generally the reverse of that recommended for the lower branches.

Against *walls*, the horizontal mode of training answers well for the pear. When the young tree is planted, head down the shoot to a foot, or four courses of bricks, above the level of the ground. Train a shoot upright, and one right, another left, at an angle of 45°; if these prove unequal in point of vigor, depress the strong and elevate the weak. Lower them both about the middle of September to the horizontal line represented by the joint between the fourth and fifth course of bricks. Their origin on the stem was somewhat below this line, and therefore they must ascend a little to reach it. This, as regards the lower branches, is an advantage, for the sap flows more freely into limbs thus diverging, than it does when constrained to proceed from the stem directly at right angles. The lower branches being apt to become the weakest, may be afforded this advantage, whilst towards the top of the wall the branches may be made to proceed horizontally immediately from the stem.

The tree having now a central upright shoot, and two horizontal side shoots, shorten the latter at the winter pruning according to their strength; if weak, nearly to their bases; the upright one to the fourth course of bricks above that to which the first shoot was cut. Train the shoot from the uppermost bud in a perpendicular direction, and one on each side as before. Proceed thus to obtain an upright and two horizontal branches every year till the tree reach the top of the wall. When the horizontal branches are sufficiently strong, they may be trained along the courses of bricks without shortening.

If properly managed in summer, fruit-spurs will begin to form along these branches. The accompanying cut (Fig. 46) represents a spur in which *a* is progressing to form a blossom-bud, whilst *b b* are already blossom-buds, known by their plumpness; and from this period of the season such buds exhibit signs of active vegetation, but in *a* the surrounding scales remain undisturbed till late in spring. The scar at *c* is where a portion of spur that has borne fruit has been cut back, and at the winter pruning, after *b b* have produced fruit,

Fig. 46.

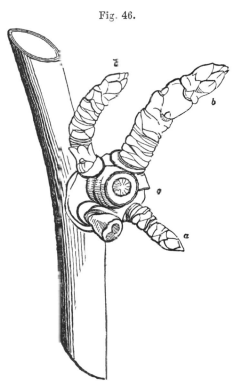

Spur of the pear-tree.

they must likewise be cut back to others likely to form at their bases, as they did at the base of *c*.

The pruning of the pear-tree trained against an *espalier* differs in nothing from that which it requires when trained against a wall, except that the spurs of espalier trees need not be so much shortened.

Fig. 47.

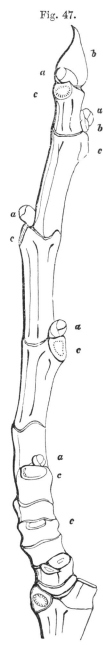

Shoot of a fig-tree.

THE FIG-TREE.—The accompanying figure represents a shoot of the last summer's growth; on
which *a, a, a, a, a,* are fruit-buds; *b, b,* wood-
buds; *c, c, c, c, c, c,* scars where the leaf-stalks had
detached themselves at the fall of the leaf. It
thus appears that the fruit-buds of the fig-tree
are formed on the young shoots, in the axils of
the leaves. Sometimes it happens that leaves
are not accompanied with fruit-buds; but they
are frequently formed in the axil of every leaf,
from the base of the shoot to its apex. In a
congenial climate, fruit-buds thus progressively
formed, result in a succession of ripe fruit. But
in our climate, although young figs are produced
in great abundance, they rarely acquire maturity
in the same season in which they originate, unless assisted by artificial heat. Shoots may be
seen plentifully furnished with green figs, some
of the latter attaining a considerable size before
autumn, but seldom ripening even at that period;
and then the temperature begins to decline below
that which is necessary for carrying on the active
vegetation of the plant; the leaves drop; the
fruits still hold on; but they wither even if protected from frost. Such being the case, those
fruit buds which may be expected to yield mature fruit in the open air, are not to be looked
for on the lower part of the shoots where the
fruit-buds have become developed. It is towards
the extremity of the shoots, where fruit-buds are
yet in embryo, compact and sessile, like those
represented by *a, a, a, a, a,* that we have to look
for a crop. Such buds retain their vitality till
the following spring, if they are not killed by
frost, or cut off by a badly directed pruning-
knife. The mode of bearing will thus be readily
understood, and the necessity of protecting the
extremities of the shoots of figs from frost.

"Whenever," says Mr. Knight, "a branch of
this tree appears to be extending with too much
luxuriance, its point, at the tenth or twelfth leaf,
is pressed between the finger and thumb, without letting the nails come in contact with the
bark, till the soft succulent substance is felt to
yield to the pressure. Such branch, in consequence, ceases subsequently to elongate; and
the sap is repulsed, to be expended where it is
more wanted. A fruit ripens at the base of each
leaf, and during the period in which the fruit is
ripening, one or more of the lateral buds shoots,
and is subsequently subjected to the same treat-

ment, with the same result. When I have suffered such shoots to extend freely to their natural length, I have found that a small part of them only became productive, either in the same or the ensuing season, though I have seen that their buds obviously contained blossoms. I made several experiments to obtain fruit in the following spring from other parts of such branches, which were not successful: but I ultimately found that bending these branches, as far as could be done without danger of breaking them, rendered them extremely fruitful; and, in the present spring, thirteen figs ripened perfectly upon a branch of this kind within the space of ten inches. In training, the ends of all the shoots have been made, as far as practicable, to point downwards."—*Hort. Trans.*, iv. 201.

Fig. 48.

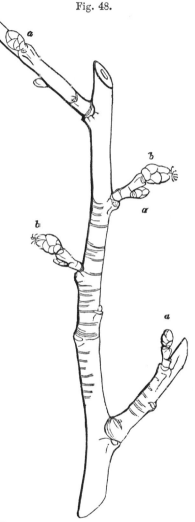

THE FILBERT-TREE.— The filbert-tree is one of those which does not contain all the parts necessary for the production of fruit in the same bud. Some buds develop only the male parts, and others only the female; the former are comprised in those pendent yellow catkins, easily recognized in the end of winter and early spring. The female portions are less conspicuous; all that appears of them are some slender, deep crimson stigmas, protruding beyond the apex of the buds, as represented at *b, b.* On these,

Branch of the Filbert. *a, a, a,* wood buds; *b, b,* blossom buds.

fertilizing particles from the catkins either fall naturally, or are otherwise brought in contact with them whilst being blown about by the winds; and fruitfulness is the result. If, on the contrary, there are

28

no catkins, or if they are prematurely cut away in pruning, there can be no fruit. Pruning should not be commenced till after the appearance of the crimson stigmas at the apex of such buds as *b, b,* and after the full expansion of the catkins. When the latter have fulfilled their purpose, they fall off. After fertilization, the buds *b, b,* lengthen into a twig much the same as other buds; but towards midsummer the formation of the cluster can be seen. The cluster is always terminal.

The county of Kent has been long celebrated for the production of large crops of filberts. The method pursued by the Maidstone cultivators is minutely detailed by the Rev. William Williamson in the fourth volume of the first series of the *Transactions of the Horticultural Society.*

" Plant the bushes unpruned, and after being suffered to grow without restraint for three or four years, cut them down within a few inches of the ground. From the remaining part, if the trees are well rooted in the soil, five or six strong shoots will be produced. In the second year after cutting down, these shoots are shortened; generally one-third is taken off. If very weak, I would advise that the trees be quite cut down a second time, as in the previous spring; but it would be much better not to cut them down till the trees give evident tokens of their being able to produce shoots of sufficient strength. When they are thus shortened, that they may appear regular, let a small hoop be placed within the branches, to which the shoots are to be fastened at equal distances. By this practice two considerable advantages will be gained—the trees will grow more regular, and the middle will be kept hollow, so as to admit the influence of the sun and air. In the third year a shoot will spring from each bud; these must be suffered to grow till the following autumn, or fourth year, when they are to be cut off nearly close to the original stem, and the leading shoot of the last year shortened two-thirds. In the fifth year several small shoots will arise from the bases of the side branches which were cut off the preceding year; these are produced from small buds, and would not have been emitted had not the branch on which they are situated been shortened, the whole nourishment being carried to the upper part of the branch. It is from these shoots that fruit is to be expected. These productive shoots will in a few years become very numerous, and many of them must be taken off, particularly the strongest, in order to encourage the production of the smaller ones; for those of the former year become so exhausted that they generally decay; but whether decayed or not they are always cut out by the pruner, and a fresh supply must therefore be provided to produce the fruit in the succeeding year. The leading shoot is every year to be shortened two-thirds, or more should the tree be weak, and the whole height of the branches must not exceed six feet. The method of pruning above detailed might, in a few words, be called a method of spurring, by which bearing shoots are produced, which otherwise would have had no existence. Old trees are easily induced to bear in this manner, by selecting a sufficient number of the main branches, and then cutting the side shoots off nearly close, excepting any should be so situated as not to interfere with the others, and there should be no main branch directed to that particular part. It will, however, be two or three years before the full effect will be produced."

The management of the laterals must be varied according to the nature of the soil, and the greater or less humidity of the climate. If the soil is rich and moist, strong shoots, too strong for any but wood buds being formed on them, will be produced. Instead of the fruitful laterals produced on the Kentish soil, rod-like walking canes will be produced when the plants are grown in many other parts of the kingdom. They must be cut back, otherwise they would form strong cross branches; but then we must consider that each of these rods, with their ample foliage, has contributed to the formation of roots during the summer; that these roots will be adequate to supply nourishment in the following season to all the shoots made in the present season; but when the shoots are necessarily reduced, say more than one-half, either by shortening or cutting out entirely, then the remaining portion has more than double the quantity of roots necessary for its nourishment; and it will, in consequence, be stimulated to grow with excessive luxuriance.

THE PEACH.—The mode of bearing is as follows: A, Fig. 49, represents the branch of a peach-tree. The figures 1, 2, 3, 4, 5, denote the respective ages of the portions of branch opposite. The asterisks at the sides of the shoots, indicate the place to which these may be shortened at the winter pruning. B, is a portion of a bearing shoot furnished with both wood and blossom buds; a, a, a, a, are blossom bubs; b, b, b, b, wood buds.

Peach and nectarine-trees bear their fruit exclusively on wood of the preceding summer's growth. For example, if one pull a peach in the summer of 1857, it must be from wood formed in the summer of 1856, and which had no existence, as a shoot, in 1855, although then its origin might have been traced to a vital point within a bud. Such an almost invisible point was the shoot B, in 1855. In summer, 1856, this point, developed from a bud, grew a shoot, furnished with leaves disposed singly, in twos or in threes, along the growing shoot. In the axil of each of these leaves, the rudiments of a bud were formed. The leaves, having accomplished their office, dropped in autumn, whilst the energy of the young buds continued to increase. Their winter appearance is represented in B. The blossom buds are distinguished by their plumpness; they have an ovate form, which gradually becomes globose; they have a hoary appearance, owing to the scales opening and exposing their downy integuments. The wood buds are slender and conical. Their scaly covering is less deranged by expansion of their interior parts in early spring, and consequently they exhibit less of that hoary pubescence by which the others are distinguished. In the case of triple buds the middle one is generally a wood bud.

The peach differs materially from the pear and apple-trees. In these a shoot may be shortened to any bud, and the one immediately below the cut will almost invariably produce a shoot; but the peach shoot must be cut to where there is a wood bud; for if cut to a blossom bud only, no shoot can result. Sometimes all the buds on a

Fig. 49.

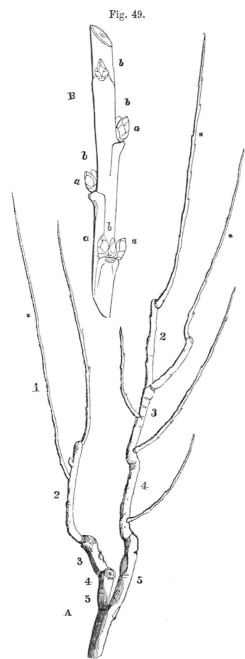

Shoot of Peach-tree.

shoot are blossom buds, except the terminal one and one or two at the base. Such shoot must either be left its entire length, or cut back to the wood bud at its base. The shoots of the peach naturally terminate with a wood bud. If this be cut off, the blossoms on the part left will expand and the fruit may set, but all will prematurely drop; thus, if all the buds marked *b* were blossom buds, they would expand; but the eight blossoms would either drop without setting, or the fruit would drop at the time of stoning; at all events, a leafless, budless shoot would result, incapable of further vegetation. It dies downwards to the first wood bud. The blossom buds, *a* of B, will produce four peaches, but one is enough to leave to come to perfection. From the wood bud, *b*, shoots will proceed; these, in the course of the summer, will form buds for future bearing; and a twelvemonth hence they will appear similar to those on B, which having once borne fruit can do so no more, and therefore its place must be supplied by the most appropriate shoot it produces at or near its base, or by a shoot from an adjoining branch.

These facts are the foundation of all the long intricate plans for pruning and training this tree The following are, I think, the best *concise* directions which have yet been given on this subject:—

"Commencing with the winter pruning, the first rule to be laid down as a basis for all the rest, is to shorten every shoot in proportion to its strength, and to prune where the wood is firm and well ripened: this will cause all the pithy and unripened wood to be removed, thence insuring a supply of that which is better ripened for the ensuing year. But in order to give every facility to the ripening of this wood, it must be trained thin, not in profusion according to the general custom, but such shoots only as may be required for the following year.

"Trees which have arrived at a bearing state should have their strongest bearing shoots shortened to twelve or fourteen inches, those next in strength to eight or ten, and the weaker ones to four or six inches, pruning each to what is termed a treble eye, or that where there is a blossom-bud on each side of a wood-bud; where branches are not in a bearing state, these treble eyes will not be found; they must, therefore, be pruned to a wood-bud alone, which is always known by its sharp point.

"In May, the season for disbudding the tree, all fore-right shoots, as well as those from the back, must be carefully removed with a sharp small-bladed knife, taking care to cut close to the branch, but not into the bark; a few, however, of these fore-right shoots had better be cut within a quarter of an inch only, which will leave two or three leaves to each, to shade the young fruit, and such slight wounds in the branch as have been occasioned by cutting the shoots off close.

"As soon as the young shoots have grown long enough, the leading one from each branch should be nailed neatly to the wall, selecting one or two of the side shoots produced lower down the branch, and training them parallel also. This applies to those of the stronger branches, at and near the extremity of the tree. Those in the middle and near the bottom will allow of but one shoot probably in addition to the leaders; this will depend upon the space left in the winter pruning; if sufficient, it is always better to have a young shoot on each side as well as the leader, than to have only one, for it is by this arrangement that a succession of young wood can be kept up throughout every part of the tree.

"Should young shoots, indicating extraordinary vigor, anywhere make their appearance, they should immediately be cut out, unless where a vacant part of the wall can be filled up, because an excessive vigor in one part of the tree cannot be supported without detriment to the other. Peach-trees, when in a state of health and vigor, generally throw out laterals from their stronger shoots; when this is the case, they should not be cut off close, but shortened to the last eye nearest the branch; and if there is room, one or two of those

Fig. 50.

Shoot of Gooseberry-bush.

a, a, a, a, wood-buds.
b, b, b, b, fruit-buds.
c, c, c, young shoots cut back.

first produced may be nailed to the wall; or the middle shoot may be cut out, leaving the two lowest laterals, and allowing them to take its place; thus frequently obtaining two fruit-bearing branches, when the former one would in all probability have been wholly unproductive of fruit the following year."

THE GOOSEBERRY-BUSH.—Left to its natural growth, the Gooseberry becomes an almost impenetrable thicket, not at all adapted for producing such fine fruit as is produced by plants properly cultivated and pruned.

In the accompanying cut it will be seen that the wood-buds, *a, a, a, a,* are on the last summer's shoot, whilst the fruit-buds, *b, b, b, b,* are on two-years old wood, and produce the largest and finest fruit, but they may be seen on wood much older. The buds marked *a,* are called wood-buds, because from them young shoots are produced, but usually not from all of them; for it appears, that of the buds on the two-years old wood, which, a twelvemonth back, were similar to those now marked *a,* three had produced shoots, *c, c, c,* and the others formed the fruit-buds, *b, b, b, b.*

After the plants have formed shoots, these must be shortened according to their strength; if moderately strong, to about six inches. In shortening, care must be taken to cut to a bud pointing the most towards the direction which the branch should follow, in order to complete the form in which the plants are intended to be kept. The general mode is to keep the bush hollow in the middle, and six, eight or ten branches at equal distances, or as nearly so as possible. If two branches are likely to approach too near each other, one or both must be cut to buds pointing in the opposite direction; thus, in the accompanying figure, supposing the branch were intended to be prolonged more towards the left, then the young shoot is properly cut, as represented, for

the uppermost bud *a* to proceed in that direction.   On the contrary,
if the uppermost bud *a* had been on the inside of a shoot, of which
it would have been desirable that the direction should be outwards,
towards the right, then it would have
been entirely wrong to cut at that bud.

Observing thus to cut at the proper
buds, each leading branch may be made
to diverge outwards, or to either side,
to an extent sufficient for ordinary cultivation.   The pruning of one of the
leading branches may now be detailed
from its commencement.   In autumn,
or early part of winter, the shoot ought
to be shortened to some extent, bearing in mind that generally the three
buds immediately below the section
will break into shoots; therefore, it
will be advisable to cut where another
leader is required to originate   This
is the first winter pruning.   The second will consist in shortening the
leading shoot about one-third; and
also the other shoot intended for an
adjoining leader.   If there should be
another young shoot growing strongly
where not wanted, it may be cut off
close; and others, weaker, may be cut
like that marked *c* on the right of the
engraving.   The next season the leader
should be shortened, and laterals cut
to one eye, if weak; but otherwise
three or four eyes may be left on these,
some of which will probably break into
shoots, and others will form fruit-spurs.
The other branches will require a similar treatment.   Young shoots should
be trained up to supply the place of
any branch exhibiting symptoms of
decay.

In the midland and northern counties, an open cup-form of bush is generally aimed at in pruning; on the contrary, in some cases in the South,
although the branches are pruned and
thinned, yet some are left in the centre for the purpose of shade, otherwise
the fruit would be scorched.

The CURRANT-BUSH.—Under every
mode of training, the red Currant, and
also the white, require to be regularly
pruned every year.   In rearing the

Fig. 51.

Shoot of Currant.

a, a, a, a, wood-buds. *b, b,* fruit-
buds. *c, c, c,* clusters termed fruit-
spurs; they consist chiefly of fruit-
buds, but amongst them there are
generally some wood-buds which
produce small shoots.

young plants, the first thing to be aimed at is a clear stem, about five inches in length, free from suckers. In preparing the cutting, care should be taken to remove all the buds on the portion intended to be inserted in the ground, otherwise many of them would form suckers, injurious to the plants, and troublesome to displace effectually. In some cases, cuttings can be obtained long enough to afford at once the proper length of stem; but when such cannot be had, when the cutting is altogether too short, or proves so after the necessary removal of the imperfectly formed wood at top, then three buds above the surface of the ground will be sufficient. These will generally produce three shoots, all of which may be allowed to grow during the first summer after the cutting has been planted, in order to assist in forming roots. Supposing the plant is intended for the open ground, and that it is to be trained in the usual way, open in the centre; then in autumn, after the leaves have fallen, two out of the three shoots which the plant has made should be cut off, and the third, selected as the most eligible for a stem, should be shortened, so that the third bud below the cut may be five inches above the ground. Three shoots will generally be produced in the following summer. In autumn the plants will require to be planted out where they are to remain, and at the same time the shoots should be cut back to about four inches, taking care to cut above buds pointing outwards. We have now a stem five inches high, and three branches diverging from it, each of them shortened to about four inches. Two shoots should be encouraged from each of these three, so that in autumn the plant will have six shoots, corresponding with the ultimate number of branches necessary. All other shoots must be spurred to within an inch of their bases. The six shoots selected for leaders should be cut back so as to leave them from four to six inches long; and, like those of the former season, they should be cut to buds pointing outwards. At every future winter pruning the terminal shoots of the six branches should be shortened to between four and six inches long, according to their strength. When the branches nearly attain the intended height, the terminals may be shortened to two or three buds. With regard to the lateral shoots, they must all be cut to within an inch of the old wood at every winter pruning.

No fruit is more improved than the Currant by good pruning. When left to itself, both bunches and berries are small and worthless; it is only when carefully thinned, skilfully pruned, and annually divested of old spurs, that the fruit acquires its proper excellence.

THE VINEYARD.

During the early part of this month, the vines will be in full bloom, which, in the middle States, generally happens about the first week thereof, a little earlier or later, according to the season; and although the vines may now require some attendance, it is dangerous to administer it until the bloom is over, lest the blossoms should be broken off thereby or otherwise injured; but when that period arrives, let the young shoots as they advance be neatly and regularly tied up to the stakes, not too close, that they may enjoy the full benefit of the sun and air; at the same time displace all weakly and unnecessary growths, any young side shoots growing out of the main ones should be nipt off at their first appearance, and the tops of the bearing spurs some three leaves above the fruit.

Towards the end of the month, or when the bloom is over and the fruit is set, if the weeds have made much progress, they should be extirpated by the most convenient means.

The young vines of one, two, or three years' growth, should now be carefully tied to the poles placed for their support, and never suffered to trail about on the surface of the earth; the ground must be kept perfectly free from weeds, as these would rob the plants of a great portion of their nourishment, and exhaust the ground to no purpose.

THE NURSERY.

WEED, SHADE, AND WATER.

You must observe in this month, as directed in the former, to keep the ground between your rows of trees entirely free from weeds, for these are very injurious to the plants, and nothing can have a worse appearance than a nursery overgrown with weeds; therefore, this caution cannot be too often repeated. Observe, also, to keep the seed-beds, in which the seeds of trees and shrubs were sown, perfectly clean, for these plants being young, are soon greatly injured, if not totally destroyed, when overrun with weeds.

The beds of small, young, tender seedlings should now be shaded from the mid-day sun, particularly the pines, firs, and other evergreens in general; and also the more delicate and rare deciduous trees, shrubs, and herbaceous plants. They, however, must not be kept close, nor shaded too long a time, for that would draw them up weak and tender; therefore, give but a slight shading from about ten to four or five o'clock, and that only when the sun is powerful and no clouds interrupt its rays.

The more choice sorts of new planted trees, that is, such as were planted late in the spring, should have occasional waterings; and observe to renew the mulch about their roots where it is decayed; for at this season the moisture of the earth will soon be exhaled and the young fibres dried up when this is neglected; besides, it will save much trouble in watering.

The seedling-beds of all kinds of trees and shrubs, but more especially the evergreens, will require frequent waterings in dry weather; let it always be given late in the afternoon, frequently and moderately, as observed on page 403.

TRANSPLANTING SEEDLING PINES AND FIRS.

It has been advised by some writers on gardening, of considerable celebrity, to plant out in this month pines, firs, &c., from the
seed-beds; and asserted " that they would be much stronger and
better prepared to live through the winter by this treatment than if
suffered to remain in the seed-beds, as their roots would be fixed in
the ground and their stems shorter." The reverse of this I have
experienced in upwards of twenty years' practice, and therefore have
here noticed it, lest my readers should be led astray by such respect-
able authorities. The true method of treating these and such plants
is, frequently during the summer months, as they advance in growth,
to sift some loose earth over them in the seed-beds till it comes up
to the seed leaves, by which the stems are protected, and, as it were,
shortened, without disturbing their roots or checking their growth;
and, besides, it tends to keep the moisture confined to the earth by
preventing its too sudden evaporation, and the loose sifted mould
attracts the dews and imbibes the rains, when such fall, by which
means the plants are kept cool, moist, and in a constant growing
state.

PROPAGATING EVERGREENS AND OTHER TREES AND SHRUBS BY LAYERS.

Most kinds of evergreens and deciduous trees and shrubs may now
be propagated by laying the present year's shoots; being soft and
tender, they will emit roots much more freely than the older wood;
and several sorts that would not root for two years if laid in spring
or autumn, by this method will be well rooted the autumn twelve
months after laying, and many kinds before the ensuing winter.
Virgin's bower, passion flowers, trumpet flowers, common jasmine,
and most of the climbing plants root immediately when laid in this
way. For the various methods of performing this operation, see
page 300.

After these are laid you should observe to water them occasionally
in dry weather, which will greatly promote their rooting. But these
waterings should not be too often repeated, nor too abundantly given
at a time, for that would rot the tender fibres as they proceed from
the layers; therefore the best method is to lay mulch on the surface
of the ground, after the layers are put down, to prevent the sun from
drying it too fast, then a little water will be sufficient, and the layers
will more certainly take root.

TRIM UP EVERGREENS.

Evergreens should now be trimmed up according to the uses for
which they are designed; for if you suffer them to grow rude in
summer, they cannot be so easily reduced afterwards; besides, the
ruder they grow the more naked they will be near the stems.

NEWLY GRAFTED AND BUDDED TREES.

Take off the clay and loosen the bandages of your grafted trees, and where any have made remarkably vigorous shoots and seem to need support to protect them from the power of violent winds, but more especially in exposed situations, let stakes be placed thereto, and the shoots bound to them with strings of bass or such like.

The vigorous shoots from the buds inserted last season may, under like circumstances, require similar support, which ought to be given when deemed necessary.

Be very particular to rub off such young shoots proceeding from the stocks as are independent of the grafts or the inserted bud-shoots; for those, if suffered to remain, would rob the grafts and budded shoots of a great portion of nourishment, and therefore ought to be displaced as often as they appear.

BUDDING.

Budding might now be practised on most kinds of trees and shrubs, but when done at this time, the inserted buds, generally, grow in the present year, and the shoots arising therefrom are much weaker, and worse prepared to withstand the winter frost than those produced in spring, from the buds inserted the preceding autumn; and, in fact, such seldom make but indifferent trees. Therefore, it will be much better not to attempt this work, except upon a *few* roses or other shrubs, until the latter end of July and the autumnal months, as hereafter directed. The method of performing the operation you will find in the *Nursery* for *July*.

THE PLEASURE, OR FLOWER GARDEN.

HYACINTHS AND TULIPS.

Most of your hyacinths and tulips will, in the course of this month, be fit for taking up, and then are to be treated as directed on pages 407 and 408.

TAKING UP EARLY FLOWERING BULBS IN GENERAL.

All the different kinds of spring flowering bulbs, such as fritillarias, crown imperials, crocuses, snow-drops, &c., whose leaves are now decayed, may be taken up and treated as directed more particularly in the *Flower Garden* for last month

GUERNSEY AND BELLADONNA AMARYLLISES.

The roots of the Guernsey and belladonna amaryllis may now, if their leaves are quite decayed, be taken up, their offsets separated, and all the roots treated as directed for the former in page 414, with this difference, that during the winter months the belladonna will require rather more care and protection than the Guernsey amaryllis; but both may be considered as *hardy* green-house plants. The roots ought to be replanted before the end of July, as both kinds flower late in autumn.   The soil in which to plant them should be a good fresh loam, mixed with about a fourth part of fine sand, and the roots are not to be covered, when planted in pots, more than half an inch above their crowns.

These plants commonly flower in October, and in some seasons not till November; but on taking in the green-house plants those should be removed with them, and placed in the windows, where they will display their beautiful flowers in great perfection.

In such of the southern States as the winter frosts are not very severe, both these kinds may be planted in the open ground, and two or three inches of tan laid over the beds on the approach of frost, to protect the bulbs therefrom, or the beds may be covered at such times with mats laid on hoops, placed archwise over them, for that purpose.

HARDY AUTUMNAL FLOWERING BULBS.

The beginning or middle of this month is still a proper time to take up your yellow amaryllises, colchicums, autumnal crocuses, and such other autumnal flowering bulbs as have their leaves decayed or in a declining state.

These may be planted again immediately after separating their offsets, or kept up dry till July or early in August, and then planted where they are to flower in October, &c.   The roots when taken up are to be carefully dried in the shade, as directed for tulips, &c.; and it will be well to plant them either in or before the last week of July or the first in August.   By planting them at this time they will blow stronger than if kept too long out of the ground.   All these sorts, in their flowering state, are generally unattended with leaves, which spring up after the flowers fade.

It is not absolutely necessary to take up these bulbs every year, once in two or three years will do; but then it must be done, in order to separate the offsets for increase, and to plant the strong roots in fresh earth, which will cause them to shoot and flower much more luxuriantly.

CYCLAMENS.

These are all too tender to bear the winter frosts of the middle and eastern States, and consequently must be treated as green-house plants, where they should be kept in the front windows, to have the benefit of as much light and air as possible.   The leaves being generally decayed about this time, the roots may be taken up and replanted immediately into a composition of one-half good loamy earth, one-fourth sand, and one-fourth light moory earth, or earth of rotten leaves, all being well incorporated together.   They do not require to be taken up oftener than every second or third year, and then only to give them fresh earth, as they never increase by offsets, and are only propagated by seed, or by cutting the roots through across the crowns, which latter method is, generally, very unsuccessful.

They continue a long time in bloom, and display flowers of a curious structure and delicately beautiful. The pots containing these roots must be kept, during the summer months, where they will not be much exposed to the sun, and in that time should have but little water, as their roots are, generally, then in an inactive state, and would soon rot by too much moisture.

All the sorts may be propagated by seed, which should be sown soon after being ripe, or early in spring, and covered near half an inch deep; they must always be protected from frost and also from the summer sun; the September following, you are to lay over the roots, not covering the leaves, half an inch or better of good loose sandy earth, and during the following winter and ensuing summer protect them as before. Any time in the summer of the second or third year that the leaves are decayed, take up the roots, and replant them in pots of fresh earth, covering them one inch deep; here they remain till they flower, which will generally be in the second and third years after sowing.

PINKS.

Your superb pinks, during the time of bloom, should be defended from the sun by an awning of some kind, and the soil ought to be kept regularly moist by soft water, administered between the plants, carefully avoiding to wet the blossoms.

The most approved method of propagating pinks, is by piping them as directed for carnations; they seldom fail to strike sufficient root in two or three weeks; when well rooted, they may be transplanted into an open part of the garden, on a bed of common garden mould, fresh dug up, where it will in a few weeks be easily discernible which are the most proper to place on the best bed for bloom. The time to pipe pinks is immediately previous to, or during the bloom, or, indeed, as soon as the new shoots are grown of a sufficient length for that purpose. The surest and readiest way, however, is to lay down the shoots two inches under the soil immediately after flowering.

New sorts of pinks are produced from seed, but this should be gathered from such as have superior properties.

A DESCRIPTION OF THE PROPERTIES OF A FINE DOUBLE PINK.

The stem should be strong and erect, and not less than twelve inches high. The calyx rather smaller and shorter, but nearly similar in form and proportion to that of a carnation, as well as the formation of the flower, which should not be less than two inches and a half in diameter.

The petals should be numerous, large, broad, and substantial, and have very finely fringed or serrated edges, free from large coarse deep notches or indentures; in short, they approach nearest to perfection when the fringe on the edge is so fine as to be scarcely discernible; but it would be a very desirable object to obtain them perfectly rose-leaved, that is, without any fringe at all.

The broadest part of the limina, or broad end of the petals, should be perfectly white and distinct from the eye, unless it be ornamented by a continuation of the color of the eye round it,* bold, clean, and distinct, leaving a considerable portion of white in the centre, perfectly free from any tinge or spot.

The eye should consist of a bright, or dark rich crimson, or purple, resembling velvet; but the nearer it approaches to black, the more it is esteemed; its proportion should be about equal to that of the white, that it may neither appear too large nor too small.

CARNATIONS.

The calyx of many sorts of carnations contains a great number of petals, which, as they increase in bulk, will distend and burst it, if not timely prevented: this will generally happen a few days previous to the proper time of the blossoms opening, and will, if neglected, by letting out the petals on one side, and thereby producing a loose irregular appearance, totally destroy that compact, graceful circular form, which a perfect flower ought to possess, and which is one of its greatest ornaments; but this disagreeable effect may be easily avoided by fastening a small narrow slip of bladder round the middle of the pod, where it is most swelled, and appears to have the greatest inclination to burst. The slip of bladder should be rather longer than is required to go once around, so that one end of it may lay over the other a little, which by the application of some strong gum water, will adhere firmly together, and answer the purpose completely. Small slips of wet bass may be substituted for those of bladder, and being tied with a single knot around the same part of the calyx, will answer the purpose.

Others place upon the calyx thin pieces of card, cut circular, of a proper size to suit the blossom, with a hole in the centre adapted to the size of the pod, and cut quite through from thence to the periphery, in order to admit the stem, after which to draw them up around the calyx; these are to be placed close to the guard leaves or outside petals, to support them horizontally, and will, when extended just as far as the extreme points of the petals, give the flower a neat and pleasing appearance; but these are apt to warp when long exposed to the weather, especially after being wet, and must, in such cases, be either taken off entirely or replaced with new ones, as they will no longer answer the intended purpose.

Either of the above methods may, and should be resorted to, in order to have the fine large bursting kinds of carnations and pinks to blow to the greatest advantage.

When the major part of your elegant carnations are in bloom, an

---

* When the corolla consists of petals of this description, it is denominated a Laced Pink.

awning should be placed over the whole, so as to be drawn up or let down by means of pulleys. The same frame that was used for tulips or hyacinths would answer this purpose extremely well.

In order that the flowers should appear to the greatest advantage, it is necessary that the pots should stand upon a stage erected theatre-like; and it would be an additional advantage to have the flowers suspended from the sticks placed in the pots for their support by small pieces of fine elastic wire of unequal lengths, to support them in a natural, easy, and graceful manner, neither too near together nor remote from each other; one end of the wire should be introduced into the stick by means of a small awl, and there fixed sufficiently tight, to prevent its being drawn out by the weight of the flower; the other end of the wire should be formed into a small ring about a quarter of an inch in diameter, to inclose the stem below the calyx; this ring should be a little open on one side to admit the stem freely without bruising it, which would materially injure the bloom.

The pots must be kept regularly and constantly watered during the bloom, and no favorable opportunity should be neglected to allow them the full advantage of exposure to light and air; but no rain should be admitted to the blossoms at any period of their bloom.

It is not advisable to let every pod blow, because it would render each blossom smaller than if only two or three were left on each plant; it is, therefore, proper, in this case, to cut off or draw out the small lateral pods close to the main stem as soon as they appear, in order that the remainder may have time to reap due benefit by it; but those sorts that have remarkably large short pods, abounding with petals (commonly called bursters) should be suffered to bloom them all, or the greater part, although, in general, three or four pods are as many as ought to be suffered to blow on one plant.

Modern florists divide the carnations into four classes:—

1. *Flakes;* of two colors only, and their stripes large, going quite through the leaves.

2. *Bizards;* with flowers striped or variegated with three or four different colors in regular spots and stripes.

3. *Piquettes* or *Piquettees;* having a white ground, and spotted or pounced with scarlet, red, purple, or other colors.

4. *Painted Ladies;* these have the petals of a red or purple color on the upper side, and white underneath.*

A DESCRIPTION OF THE PROPERTIES OF A FINE VARIEGATED DOUBLE CARNATION.

The stem should be strong, tall, and straight, not less than thirty, nor more than forty-five inches high. The flower should be at least three inches in diameter, and the petals well formed, neither so many as to appear crowded, nor so few as to appear thin. The lower or

---

* These classes are more particularly applicable to the *once flowering* kinds. The *remontants*, which bloom all the year round if protected in winter in the green-house, are far more preferable, and now may be had of all hues and kinds of stripes.

outer circle of petals, commonly called the guard leaves, should be particularly substantial; they should rise perpendicularly about half an inch above the calyx, and then turn off gracefully in a horizontal direction, supporting the interior petals, which should decrease gradually in size as they approach the centre, which should be well filled with them.   All the petals should be regularly disposed and lie over each other in such a manner as that their respective and united beauties may meet the eye altogether; they should be nearly flat, or, at most, have but a small degree of inflection at the broad end; their edges should be perfectly entire (or what is called rose-leaved), without notch, fringe, or indenture.   The calyx should be at least an inch in length, sufficiently strong at the top to keep the base of the petals in a close and circular body.   The colors should be distinct, and the stripes regular, narrowing gradually to the claws of the petal, and there ending in a fine point.   Almost one-half of each petal should be of a clear white, and free from spots.

Bizards, or such as contain two or more colors upon a white ground, are esteemed rather preferable to *Flakes*, which have but one, especially when their colors are remarkably rich and very regularly distributed.

Scarlet, purple, and pink, are the three colors most predominant in the carnation; the first two are seldom to be met with in the same flower, but the purple and pink very frequently.

PROPAGATING CARNATIONS BY LAYING AND PIPING.

When carnations, &c., are propagated in the open air, by their shoots or layers connected with the mother plant, the operation is called laying; but when they are propagated by cuttings taken from the original plant, and by the assistance of artificial means caused to strike root in a confined air, it is called piping them.

The operation of laying, or piping, is to commence as soon as the plants are in full bloom; nevertheless, those who are particularly desirous to preserve their bloom in the greatest perfection, may defer it till the flowers are on the decline; but others, anxious to have their plants strong and well rooted early in autumn, with a view that the layers may be better prepared to endure the severities of the ensuing winter, begin to lay at the commencement of the bloom; at which time, the plants being full of juices and vigor, the layers are the better nourished and supported, and soon strike root; but it must be allowed that the bloom is considerably impaired by the wounds inflicted in the operation, particularly so when performed in an early stage of it; the old plants seldom survive unless very strong and sound, or some of the upper young shoots be left, such as are too short to be laid with convenience; these will encourage and continue the circulation of the juices if suffered to remain.

Previous to entering on the operation of laying, you must be provided with a sufficient number of wooden or other pegs, each to be about five or six inches long, and formed somewhat like the figure 7, that is, with a short hooked end.   The operator should, likewise, be provided with a table, on which to place the pots, when the plants are so grown, for the greater convenience in the examination, dressing, and laying of the shoots, also with a sharp pen-knife, and some fresh compost earth.

The layer may be supposed to have four or five joints, more or less; the lower leaves next the root are all to be cut or stripped off close to within two or three joints of the extremity of the layer, and its extreme points are to be shortened by cutting the tops off with the knife, so as to leave them only an inch and a half or two inches in length from the joint whence they proceed.

All the layers in the pots, and also those in the open ground, are to be thus treated or prepared before any further procedure be made; the surface of the earth is then to be cleared of what has fallen on it, and should be stirred up about an inch deep : the pot is then to be filled up nearly level with some light rich compost, not of too fine a grain.

The incision immediately follows : the knife should have a small, thin, and very sharp blade ; it is to be introduced on that side the layer next the ground, in a sloping direction upwards, to commence a quarter of an inch below the second or third clean joint from the extremity, and continue through the middle of that joint, and half or three-quarters of an inch above it, the small portion left under and connected with the joint is to be cut off horizontally, quite close to the bottom of the joint, but not into it, as it is from the outer circle of the bottom of the joint that the fibres proceed, consequently, that part should not be injured.

After the incision is made, which should be through the middle of the joint, &c., and the lower part dressed as before directed, the layer is to be gently forced down to the earth with great care to avoid breaking it off, or even cracking it at the joint, which would prevent a due communication of the juices of the old plant, so necessary for the support of the layer, till it has formed sufficient root to support itself; it would likewise render it more likely to decay on the application of water.

The layer is to be held down to the surface of the earth by one of the pegs before described, which is to be forced into the soil close behind the joint where the incision was made, observing at the same time to keep the slit a little open; and it is to be observed that the joint from whence the fibres are expected to proceed should be covered about an inch deep with good compost earth, and not deeper ; for the influence of the air is necessary to the free rooting of the layer. The remainder of the stalk of the layer should lay, as much as possible, upon or above the surface, but must by no means be covered too deep.

Carnations and pinks, growing in the open ground, in beds or borders, &c., may be propagated by laying them in like manner as above, or either may be propagated by pipings, as follows :—

PIPING CARNATIONS AND PINKS.

For this purpose it is necessary to form a bed of fine light mould, or old compost earth, which should be moderately moistened and

29

rendered rather compact than otherwise; then take a hand or bell-glass, and with it mark its dimensions on the surface of the soil, in order to know where to stick in the pipings, so as to lose no room, or endanger their being disturbed when the glass is placed over them.

The cuttings intended to be piped are to have two complete joints, that is to say, they are to be *cut off* horizontally close under the second joint; the extremities or points of the leaves are likewise to be shortened as for laying, which will leave the whole length of the piping about two inches; as soon as thus prepared they may be thrown into a basin of soft water for a few minutes to plump. They are then to be taken out of the basin singly, and forced into the earth in their wet state not more than an inch deep, and about two inches asunder every way.

When a sufficient number for the glass are thus placed regularly, they are to be very gently watered, in order that the earth may adhere more closely to them, and thereby keep out the air; after this watering they are to remain open, *but not exposed to the sun*, till their leaves become perfectly dry, after which the glass is to be placed over them carefully, in the same mark that was made by it on the surface of the soil before the insertion of the pipings.

The bottom edges of the glass, or glasses, are to be forced a little into the earth to keep out the influence of the external air, and to preserve a moist atmosphere about the pipings, till their young radicles are established and begin to act; for if fully exposed to the air before that period, it would carry off from the leaves, &c., a greater portion of juices than the young plants could, for the present, extract from the earth, and consequently they must perish thereby. This is the particular reason why cuttings of every kind succeed better when thus treated than when left exposed to the influence of the weather.

The pipings should have a little of the morning sun, but must be shaded from it when the heat increases; this will easily be effected by placing mats upon a slight frame of hoops or laths, erected over the bed, about two feet above it.

The glasses should be occasionally taken off, for half an hour at a time, early in the morning, or late in the afternoon, to admit fresh air; if this material point is neglected, the consequence will be a green mossy appearance on the surface of the earth, and a universal mouldiness amongst the plants which will destroy them.

When the fibres are formed, which the additional verdure and growth of the plants will demonstrate, the glasses should be placed over them very lightly, in order that more air be admitted; and when they become tolerably well rooted, the glasses being no longer necessary, should be entirely taken away; continue to water them frequently, but moderately, as they progress in growth, and for their further treatment see the *flower garden* for next month.

Some sorts of carnations succeed much better by piping than laying, and make healthier plants: This is particularly the case with the remontants, but it requires attention and experience to distinguish such sorts in the other classes from the rest, which must depend wholly on the discernment of the cultivator.

PLANTING CARNATION AND PINK SEEDLINGS.

The carnation and pink seedlings sown early in spring, may now be planted into nursery beds, in rows, eight or nine inches asunder, and plant from plant five or six inches, there to remain till September or October, when they are to be planted at greater distances to remain for flowering.

Persons who are fond of carnations and pinks, ought to sow some seed of each sort every year, for it is by this means that all the fine new varieties of these charming flowers are obtained.

When new sorts are procured in this way, they are to be increased by layers or pipings, and will generally keep to their original colors; but when propagated by seed, very few will be found to possess the same colors and properties as the mother plant.

DOUBLE SWEET-WILLIAM.

The fine kinds of double sweet-william may now be propagated, either by slips or by laying the young shoots, as directed for carnations; in either way, they will root freely, but if the slips are planted, they will require shade as well as occasional waterings for ten or twelve days after.

TRANSPLANTING ANNUALS.

You may now transplant into the borders and other places where wanted, all the different kinds of annual flowers that succeed in that way, and that stand too close where they had been sown; such as French and African marigolds, China asters, cocks-combs, chrysanthemums, China pinks, China, hollyhocks, balsams, amaranthuses of various sorts, gomphrena globosa, and many other kinds, observing to do this in moist or cloudy weather, if possible, and to give them shade and frequent refreshments of water till newly rooted; let them be taken up and transplanted with as much earth as possible about their roots, whether into flower-pots or elsewhere.

THINNING AND SUPPORTING FLOWERING PLANTS, ETC.

Wherever you have sown annual flower seeds in patches, &c., and they have grown too thick, you must thin them to proper distances, according to their respective habits of growth, so as to allow them full liberty to attain the utmost perfection.

Place sticks for the support of the various kinds that require it, whether annual, perennial, biennial, or climbing plants, as directed on page 411, observing the method there recommended.

Cut off, close to the ground, the decaying flower-stems of such perennial plants as are past flowering, and clear the roots from dead leaves; but where intended to save seed from any of the kinds, leave for that purpose some of the principal stems.

Trim, dress, and tie up any disorderly growing plants, pick off all withered leaves, and cut out decayed parts.

PROPAGATING FIBROUS-ROOTED PLANTS BY CUTTINGS.

You may still continue to propagate the double scarlet-lychnis, double-rocket, lychnideas or phloxes, with many other like kinds, by cuttings of the flower-stalks, as directed for the scarlet-lychnis, in May.

TRANSPLANTING SEEDLING PERENNIALS AND BIENNIALS.

Transplant from the seed-beds the early sown perennial and biennial seedling flower plants, that are grown to a sufficient size ; such as sweet-williams, sweet scabious, Canterbury-bells, rose-campion and monk's-hood, soapwort, valerian, Chinese ixia, asclepiases, asters and rhexias; coreopsis, hibiscuses, dracocephalums, &c., &c., &c.

Prepare for these three or four feet wide beds of good earth, and plant them by line at six inches distance every way, water them immediately, and if the weather be very dry, give occasional shade and waterings till they have taken root and begin to grow. The plants are to remain in these beds until autumn or spring, and are then to be planted out finally into the beds or borders where they are intended to flower the ensuing year.

STOCK-GILLYFLOWERS AND WALL-FLOWERS.

The stock-gillyflowers and wall-flowers are not sufficiently hardy to bear the winter frosts of the middle or eastern states; therefore, it will be necessary to plant the seedlings of these kinds in some convenient place where a garden frame may be placed over them in winter, on which to lay boards or any slight covering for their protection, as directed in November. Or you may plant them now in the open borders to grow till September, then to be taken up and potted, and in November they are to be removed into their winter quarters: or, they may immediately be planted into small pots, which are to be plunged into some shady border, where you can give them water during the season according to their necessities.

TRIM BOX EDGINGS.

Take advantage of the first moist weather that happens after the middle of this month, in which to clip and dress your box edgings ; for if done in dry or parching weather they are apt to turn foxy, and consequently, lose much of their beauty.

The edgings should be cut very neat, even at top and both sides, and ought not to be suffered to grow higher than two or three inches, nor broader than two. When the edgings of box are kept near that size, they look extremely neat, but if permitted to grow to the height of four, five, or six inches, and perhaps near as much in breadth, they then assume a clumsy and heavy appearance, and deprive the beds and borders of that apparent roundness so necessary to set them off to advantage.

DRESSING THE FLOWER-BORDERS AND SHRUBBERIES, ETC.

The flower-borders, beds, shrubbery-clumps, and all other ornamental compartments, must now be kept remarkably clean and neat, and no weeds suffered to appear, or at least to grow to any considerable size in any of these places. The weeds must be exterminated immediately on their appearance either by hoe or hand, occasionally, and this should be performed on a dry day; if with the hoe, cutting them up within the ground and raking them off immediately.

Examine the evergreens and flowering shrubs, and where any have made disorderly shoots, let such be cut clean out or shortened, as you may deem expedient, in order to preserve the heads in due form and of an elegant appearance.

WATERING.

Occasional waterings must be given to all your late planted shrubs and flowers, and particularly to the annual, perennial, and biennial flower plants newly planted out into nursery beds.

Your entire stock of plants in pots and boxes, seedlings and others, must be watered as often as the earth about them becomes dry and unfriendly to vegetation; and your carnation and other layers must be duly attended to in this respect to preserve the earth about them moderately moist, and only so.

For some useful observations in respect to watering, see page 404.

GRASS AND GRAVEL-WALKS.

The grass and gravel-walks, &c., must be treated constantly during the summer and autumn, as directed on page 415.

THE GREEN-HOUSE.

GENERAL CARE OF THE GREEN-HOUSE PLANTS.

The plants being now out and fully exposed to the air, will require a constant supply of water; it is impossible to say how often it ought to be administered, or how much should be given at a time, as the state of weather, the different constitutions and habits of the plants, and also the size of the pots or tubs as well as of the plants themselves, make a material difference in that respect. The only true guide is the state of the earth in the pots or tubs, which should always be kept moist and in a proper condition to promote and encourage vegetation. In very hot weather, the plants that are in small pots will require some water both morning and evening, at other times once a day will be sufficient; but as the plants have no other nourishment but what they extract from the earth within the pots or tubs, it ought to be a general rule to keep it constantly moist, but not too wet.

The best water for this purpose is such as is taken from rivers or ponds where it is fully exposed to the sun and air, so that if you have no other than spring or well water, it should always be exposed in cisterns, &c., to the sun and air at least twenty-four hours before it is used.

You may, about once a fortnight, use a weak solution of guano in the proportion of one pound to twenty gallons, or the diluted drainings from a dunghill; but care must be taken that these materials are weak enough; for these strongly impregnated waters, instead of affording nourishment, cause the leaves to change to a pale sickly color, and ultimately bring on a general debility; they operate like hot liquors on human bodies, which, at first taking, seem to add new vigor, yet, after some time, leave the body weaker than before.

If mowings of short grass, or some moss, be spread on the surface earth of the large tubs or pots of oranges, lemons, &c., it will preserve the moisture and defend the upper roots from the sun and drying air.

Such of the pots with plants, as are plunged in the earth, must be turned fully around in their seats once a week to break off such fibres as extend through the holes at bottom into the surrounding earth; for the reasons of doing this see pages 416 and 417.

Some people thin what they consider the superabundant blossoms of oranges and lemons; this I do not approve of, as it is probable that such as would set the best fruit might be plucked off as well as any other; therefore it will be the better way to suffer the whole bloom to remain, and if too abundant a crop of fruit should happen to set, to thin them soon after to a sufficient number. However, where some are wanted for making orange-flower water, the smallest may be picked off where they appear in clusters, leaving the largest and most promising. Any declining myrtles, or other hard-wooded plants, may be greatly restored to strength and vigor by turning them out of their pots, earth and all, and placing the balls in baskets made of peeled or dried willows, and plunging these in the open borders till September; when they are to be taken up, the extending roots trimmed off, the baskets cut away, and the plants with the entire balls replanted in suitable-sized pots or tubs, after which they are to be placed in the shade till housed.

PROPAGATING THE PLANTS.

Myrtles may be propagated abundantly towards the middle or latter end of the month by slips or cuttings of the present year's wood, as may also hydrangeas, fuchsias, China and Otaheite roses; coronillas, bupthalmum fruticosum, geraniums, jasmines, heliotropiums, and almost every other kind of shrubby or under shrubby plants; observing when dressed and the under leaves taken off to plant them three, four, or five inches deep, according to their respective lengths, in wide garden pans or pots filled with light rich earth, or into beds of similar earth, where they can have occasional shade and waterings till rooted. However, the covering of them with bell-glasses will greatly facilitate their rooting and promote their growth, which is by far the most eligible method, but particularly for woody plants, and such others as are not of the succulent tribe.*

This is also a very proper time to propagate succulent plants of most kinds, which are to be treated as directed on page 416, under the article *Propagating the Plants.*

TRANSPLANTING SEEDLING EXOTICS.

You should now transplant, separately, into small pots, any advanced young seedling exotics, which were raised this year from seed; giving them shade and occasional waterings till newly rooted.

BUDDING.

Any time this month you may bud oranges, lemons, citrons, and shaddocks; the buds are not to be taken from the shoots made this season, as they are not yet sufficiently ripe, but from those produced last autumn, which will now take freely, and produce handsome shoots in the present year.

In about three weeks or a month the buds will be taken, when you are to untie the bandages, and soon after head down the stocks of such as are plump, fresh, and well united, to within four inches of the buds, cutting off all side branches and suffering no other buds to grow but the inserted ones: as the shoots advance tie them to the spurs left for that purpose to prevent their being broken off by winds, or displaced by any other accidents.

Budding, however, should not at this time be generally practised, for the buds now inserted will start in a few weeks, and the shoots produced thereby will not be as ripe, nor, consequently, in as good condition to stand the winter as those produced in the early part of the season from the buds inserted in August. For the method of budding see the *Nursery* in *July.*

CAPE AND OTHER GREEN-HOUSE BULBS.

The green-house bulbs and tuberous-rooted plants, natives of the Cape of Good Hope, &c., whose leaves are now decayed, such as gladicluses, ixias, watsonias, antholizas, ornithogalums, moreas, oxalis, &c., may be taken up and immediately transplanted, or they may be kept up till September, and if carefully wrapped in dry moss, it will tend greatly to their preservation; but there are some kinds which will require to be planted into pots of fresh earth immediately,

---

* The cuttings of geraniums (pelargonium) at this season, root the best and soonest when placed in the ground in a situation which is only shaded from the hottest of the mid-day sun. If put under glass and kept close they are subject to rot.

such as cyclamens, &c., and all the autumnal flowering bulbs, such as the Guernsey and belladonna amaryllises, must not be kept longer out of the ground than the end of next month, as that would greatly weaken their bloom.

THE HOT-HOUSE.

The more tender kinds of exotics, which could not with safety be brought out into the open air the latter end of last month, should now be placed where intended to remain during summer.

Their subsequent treatment whilst out, being exactly similar to that directed for the green-house plants, in this and the preceding month, induces me, in order to avoid repetitions, to refer you to those articles. But let it be observed, that although most of the shrubby kinds will require abundance of water at this season, yet that article must be administered with rather a sparing hand to the succulent tribe.

PINE-APPLES.

The pine-apple plants must now have abundance of air night and day, by keeping all the upright front lights slid open, and also the roof-lights, except during heavy rains, when the roof-lights must be kept close to preserve the bark-pit from too much wet. The plants will likewise require frequent refreshments of water, but this should not be given too copiously at one time.

Some of the most forward pine-apples will, about the end of the month, be advancing towards maturity; be careful at that time to give such plants but little water, for too much would spoil the flavor of the fruit.

The succession pines must likewise have abundance of air and a sufficiency of water, to keep them in a regular and constant state of vegetation.

PROPAGATING HOT-HOUSE PLANTS.

Continue to propagate the various kinds of plants belonging to this department, by cuttings, layers, offsets, suckers, and seeds, as directed in the preceding months.

All the succulent tribe may now be easily propagated by suckers, slips, cuttings, &c., laying them when taken off in a shady place for a week or ten days, more or less, according to the degree of succulency, before they are planted.

ORCHIDEOUS HOUSES.

These beautiful structures are now rendered highly ornamental, and are so general among the wealthy that a gardener is expected to understand their structure and conduct.

The *London Horticultural Society Journal* has published the annexed drawing and account of the orchideous house of J. Dillwyn Llewelyn, Esq., at Swansea, in Wales, whose description is as follows :—

" I inclose with this the section of the stove, which I promised to send. This will show the shape of the building ; the water for the supply of the cascade is conducted to the top of the house by means of a pipe communicating with a pond at a higher level. This pipe is warmed by passing with a single coil through the boiler, and terminates at the top of the rock-work, where it pours a constant supply of water over three projecting irregular steps of rough stone, each of which catches the falling stream, dividing it into many smaller rills, and increasing the quantity of misty spray. At the bottom the whole of the water is received into the pool which occupies the centre of the floor of the stove, where it widens out into an aquarium ornamented with a little island overgrown like the rock-work with Orchideæ, Ferns, and Lycopods.

" The disposition of the stones in the rock-work would depend much on the geological strata you have to work with : in my case they lay flat and evenly bedded, and thus the portions of the rock-work are placed in more regular courses than would be necessary in many other formations. In limestone or granite countries, designs much more ornamental than mine might, I think, be easily contrived.

" The account of the splendid vegetation which borders the cataracts of tropical rivers, as described by Schomburgk, gave me the first idea of trying this experiment. I read in the ' Sertum Orchidaceum' his graphic description of the falls of the Berbice and Essequibo, on the occasion of his first discovery of *Huntleya violacea.* I was delighted with the beautiful picture which his words convey, and thought that it might be better represented than is usual in stoves.

" With this view I began to work, and added the rock-work which I describe to a house already in use for the cultivation of Orchideous plants. I found no difficulty in rearranging it for its new design, and after a trial now of about two years can say that it has entirely answered the ends I had in view.

" The moist stones were speedily covered with a thick carpet of seedling Ferns, and the creeping stems of tropical Lycopods, among the fronds of which many species of Orchideæ delighted to root themselves.

" *Huntleya violacea* was one of the first epiphytes that I planted, and it flowered and throve in its new situation, as I hoped and expected. The East Indian genera, however, of *Vanda, Saccolabium,*

Aerides, and other caulescent sorts, similar in habit and growth, were
the most vigorous of all, and many of these in a very short time only

Fig. 52.

Interior of orchideous house, Wales.

required the use of the pruning-knife to prevent their overgrowing smaller and more delicate species.

" Plants that are grown in this manner have a wild luxuriance about them that is unknown to the specimens cultivated in the ordinary manner, and to myself they are exceedingly attractive, more resembling what one fancies them in their native forests—true air-plants, depending for their subsistence on the humid atmosphere alone.

" Different species thus intermingle together in a beautiful confusion, *Dendrobium*, and *Camarotis*, and *Renanthera*, side by side, with wreaths of flowers and leaves interlacing one another, and sending their long roots to drink from the mist of the fall, or even from the water of the pool below.

" Many species are cultivated upon the rocks themselves, others upon blocks of wood, or baskets suspended from the roof, and thus sufficient room is secured for a great number of plants. At the same time the general effect is beautiful, and the constant humidity kept up by the stream of falling water suits the constitution of many species in a degree that might be expected from a consideration of their native habits ; and I would strongly recommend the adoption of this or some similar plan to all who have the means of diverting a stream of water from a level higher than the top of their stove.

" This, I think, in most situations might be easily contrived. Our house lies on high ground, and the water is brought from a considerable distance, but yet I found very little difficulty or expense in its construction."

JULY.

WORK TO BE DONE IN THE KITCHEN GARDEN.

Clean and prepare the ground where your early crops of cauliflowers and cabbages grow, and also any other vacant spots, in order to receive such seeds and plants as are proper to supply the table with good vegetable productions in autumn and winter.

MELONS AND CUCUMBERS, ETC.

Your crops of melons and cucumbers should now be kept very clean and free from weeds, the spaces between the hills must be carefully hoed in dry weather without injuring the vines ; also, hoe and weed the crops of water-melons, squashes, pumpkins, &c., for unless they are kept perfectly clean, good fruit and numerous productions cannot be expected.

SOWING MELONS FOR MANGOES.

The first week of this month is a very proper time in the middle States to sow a principal crop of melons for mangoes; they are to be sown and managed as directed on pages 382 and 421. The long, smooth musk-melon is generally sown for that purpose.

SOWING CUCUMBERS FOR PICKLING, ETC.

Sow in the first week or ten days of this month, a general crop of cucumbers for pickling, and treat them in every respect as directed for like crops in May and June.

The long green Turkey cucumber is preferred by many for this purpose, but it is not very prolific; the long and short prickly, and particularly the green cluster cucumber being great bearers, will be more profitable, and are equally good for use. Some of the early frame or short prickly kinds may be sown in the middle or any time in the month for a late crop.

PLANTING CABBAGES, SAVOYS, BORECOLE, ETC.

Take advantage of moist or cloudy weather, and plant out your late crops of cabbages, savoys, borecole, broccoli, turnip-cabbage, Brussels sprouts, Jerusalem kale, and any other of the cabbage tribe that you wish to cultivate; let them be planted as directed in the former months, and immediately watered, which must be frequently repeated till they are newly rooted and in a free growing state. The laying of a fresh cabbage leaf over each plant when set, will afford protection from the sun for a few days, which will be of considerable service. Some seed of the green curled borecole may now be sown for a late crop.

TRANSPLANTING AND SOWING ENDIVE.

Plant out, to supply the table early in autumn, a sufficient quantity of the best and stoutest endive; it requires a good, strong, and (at this season) moist ground; if well dunged, it will be an additional advantage. Put in the plants a foot asunder every way, and water them immediately, which repeat every evening till the plants have taken root.

Sow endive seed in an open, cool, and moist situation, two or three times this month, for the greater certainty of procuring a regular supply; let it be of the curled kind, and sown tolerably thin, for when the plants grow too close in the seed-beds, they are more subject to start soon to seed than if they had been raised at moderate distances. Give occasional waterings to the seed-beds, both before and after the plants appear, which will greatly encourage their free growth.

KIDNEY-BEANS.

You may plant kidney-beans of the dwarf kinds any time this month; the refugee is the best for this time; or, in order to have a regular succession, some may be planted in the beginning, middle, and end thereof. The running kinds will also succeed well if planted in the early part of the month. It will, however, be necessary at this time to water the drills, or lay the beans to soak in river or pond water about five or six hours previous to planting, or if both be done, it will be still better.

CAULIFLOWERS.

The late sown cauliflowers intended for winter use may now be planted out finally, if not done before.

In planting this crop, it would be of essential advantage to take opportunity of showery or moist weather, if such should happen in proper time; plant them in rows two feet and a half asunder, and the same distance in the row; let them be directly watered, and afterwards at times, till they have taken good root.

SMALL SALADING.

Continue to sow crops of small salading every eight or ten days, as directed in the former months; but these must now be sown on shady borders, or else be shaded with mats, occasionally, from the mid-day sun, and frequently watered both before and after the plants appear above ground.

CARROTS.

Towards the end of this month you may sow some carrot seed to raise young roots for the table in autumn and winter. Choose an open situation and light ground, and let the seed be sown immediately while the earth is fresh after being dug. When the plants are up an inch or two, thin them to five or six inches every way.

CELERY.

This is a proper time to plant out into trenches a full crop of celery, for autumn and winter use; let this be performed, in every respect, as directed on page 423, which see. Seymour's White is extremely valuable, blanches very white, and is by most people, who have had the opportunity of cultivating it, preferred to any other.

The following method of planting out celery may also be practised, which for the ease of preserving the plants in winter will be found extremely convenient; besides, a greater quantity can be raised on the same complement of land. Lay out the ground into four feet wide beds, with alleys between of three feet; dig the beds a spade deep, throwing the earth upon these alleys; when done, lay four or five inches of good, *well-rotted* hot-bed or other dung all over the bottom of the beds, dig and incorporate it with the loose earth remaining, and cover the whole with an inch or an inch and a half of the earth from the alleys; plant four rows in each bed at equal distances, and eight inches apart in the rows; after which, give them a plentiful watering, and stick down small branches of cedar, or of any kind of evergreen shrubs between the rows, to shade them from the sun till well rooted, when the branches are to be taken away. The plants must be kept free from weeds till grown of a sufficient size for earth-ing, which is done with the assistance of boards, by laying them along the rows to support the leaves while you are putting in the earth from the alleys, and removing them as you progress in the business. For the method of preserving the plants in winter see the *Kitchen Garden* in *November*.

Land or earth up your early crops of celery, first breaking the earth fine with the spade, and then laying it up neatly to both sides, al-ways preserving the tops and hearts of the plants free, that they may continue in growth without any interruption; repeat this earthing at intervals of eight or ten days, till the plants are sufficiently blanched and of proper size for use.

RUTA BAGA, OR SWEDISH TURNIP.

This variety of turnip is the most important of all, and deserves to be ranked in the first class of vegetable productions. Its quantity of produce, richness of flavor, and extreme hardiness, render it of great importance and give it a pre-eminence over every other kind. The best time for sowing is from the twentieth of June to the twentieth of July, according to the season. The ground should be well prepared and manure scattered pretty thickly over it; which done, it should be laid off in ridges about three feet apart, two fur-rows together, with the plough, and the seed sown on the top. By this method you give a double portion of the manure for each row of turnips, and a better opportunity of attending to their after culture. When they are of sufficient growth thin them to the distance of twelve inches apart in the row; they will continue growing and in-creasing in size till late in autumn, when, if not used before, they may be taken up and preserved through the winter, in like manner as other turnips (or permitted to remain in the ground), than which they are more hardy, will keep better, and be as fresh in May as at Christmas.

The flesh of the root is yellow, sweet, and firm, being nearly twice as heavy as a common turnip of the same size; when dressed for the table it is by most people preferred to the garden turnip, and as well as the tops is peculiarly grateful to most sorts of cattle. Skirving's improved is one of the best.

LETTUCES.

Thin and transplant such lettuces as were sown last month, water them immediately after, and repeat it as often as necessary till the plants are well rooted.

Sow more lettuce seed in the beginning, middle, and particularly in the last week of the month, in order to have a regular and constant supply for the table. The white Silesia is the best to sow at this time, as it is not injured by the extreme heat.

SPINAGE.

In the last week of this month a good crop of spinage may be sown for autumn use; it will not then be so subject to run to seed as in the former months. The round seeded kind is always preferable for summer and autumn service.

RADISHES.

Radishes of every kind may be sown in the last week of this month with a good prospect of success; but particularly the white and black Spanish, or winter sorts, of which you ought to sow a full crop for autumn use.

Sow, likewise, some of the short-top, salmon, and turnip-rooted radishes; should the season prove any way moist, they will succeed tolerably well. Let all these kinds be now sown on moist loamy ground.

SOW CABBAGE SEED.

Sow some of the early York, Battersea, and sugar-loaf kinds of cabbage for a supply of young greens during the autumn; the hearts of these are very delicious when grown to a tolerable size, and are, by many, very much admired; when used in that state they are called coleworts, having totally superseded the true colewort, which was formerly cultivated for boiled salads. Some savoy seed may also be sown at this time for a late winter crop.

ARTICHOKES.

If you desire to have large artichokes you must, in the first week of this month, if not done in June, in order to encourage the main head, cut of all the suckers or small heads which are produced from the sides of the stems, and these may now be dressed for the table.

The maturity of a full grown artichoke is apparent by the opening of the scales; and it should always be cut off before the flower appears in the centre.

As soon as the head or heads are collected from any stem let it be immediately cut down close to the ground. This practice is too often disregarded, but such neglect is utterly wrong; for the stems, if permitted to remain, would greatly impoverish the roots, and injure them much more than is generally imagined.

Where cardoons are in request, and they were not planted out last month, it should be done in the first week of this, as directed on page 427.

COLLECTING SEEDS.

Collect all kinds of seeds that come to good maturity, cutting off or pulling up the stems with the seed thereon as they ripen; and spread them in some airy place where they can receive no wet, in order that the seeds may dry and harden gradually; observing to turn them now and then, and not to lay such a quantity together as might bring on a fermentation and hazard the loss of the whole. When they are sufficiently dry, beat out and clean the seeds, and put them by in boxes or bags till wanted.

LEEKS.

You may still continue to transplant leeks, as directed on page 424; by this method they will grow to a great size, and be much better for use than if suffered to remain in the seed-beds.

HERBS.

Gather herbs for drying and distilling as they come into flower, and dry them in the shade.

Sage, hyssop, thyme, lavender, winter savory, and many other kinds may still be propagated by slips of the present year's growth, giving them shade and occasional waterings till rooted. Plant them two-thirds of their length into the earth.

Gather chamomile, marigold, and such other flowers as may be wanted, and that are now in bloom; spread the flowers in the shade till sufficiently dry, and then put them up in paper bags, &c.

SOWING PEAS.

In the last week of the month, sow a crop of the early frame: Charleston, or golden hotspur peas. Water the drills, and let the peas be soaked in soft water five or six hours previous to sowing. Should the season prove moist, you will have a tolerable crop from these early in September.

EGG-PLANT, RED PEPPERS, AND TOMATOES.

In the first week of this month, if not done before, plant out sufficient crops of egg-plants, red peppers, and tomatoes, as directed last month; if the weather be unfavorable, give them shade and water till well taken with the ground, but on no account delay the final planting of the egg-plants longer; the red peppers may be transplanted any time in the month, but the earlier the better.

ORDINARY WORK.

Diligently destroy weeds before they seed in every part of the ground, and immediately carry them away out of the garden.

Give water to such plants and crops as require it, but let this be done always in an evening, that it may have time to soak down to the roots before the sun appears to exhale it.

Earth up your advancing crops of cabbages, and all other plants of that tribe; likewise okra, peas, kidney beans, &c.; this will greatly refresh them, and protect their roots and fibres from the powerful heat of the sun.

Pull up the stalks of beans, cauliflowers, cabbages, and the haulm of peas and other plants which have done bearing, that the ground may be clear, for if these are suffered to remain, they will harbor vermin to the injury of the adjoining crops.

THE FRUIT GARDEN.

WALL AND ESPALIER TREES.

In the beginning of this month, you must look carefully over your wall and espalier tress, rubbing off all fore-right shoots, and training in all such regular growths as are designed to remain close to the wall or espalier, at regular distances, and in their due position. Never pull off any leaves, nor thin the branches, in order to expose the fruit to the sun, as the sudden exposure would be extremely injurious to them; by it their skins would be hardened and contracted, and their growth greatly retarded. Though I am not fond of using the knife too freely at this season, which is a very common and pernicious practice, yet it will be proper to cut out irregular and disorderly shoots, but this must be done judiciously, and an abundant supply of young wood left for the winter pruning, particularly on the peaches, nectarines, figs, apricots, and morella-cherries, which generally bear their fruit on the preceding year's wood; the apricot bears on fruiting-spurs likewise.

Pick off all punctured and decaying fruit, and give them to the hogs; also such as have fallen in that state from the trees; for the worms that are in these fruit, which have been the cause of their decline, will soon arrive at their fly or winged state, and attack the remaining fruit.

Look carefully over the fruit-trees which have been grafted last spring, or budded in the former season, and suffer no shoots from the stocks to remain, for these will rob the grafts of their nourishment.

BUDDING OR INOCULATING.

Budding may be performed on some kinds of fruit-trees about the middle of this month, but as that subject is fully treated of in the nursery department, I refer you thereto for information.

30

DESTROY WASPS, ETC.

Hang up glass phials filled with honey or sugar water in different parts among the wall, espalier, and standard fruit-trees, in order to destroy wasps, ants, &c., which would otherwise infest and devour the choice fruit; by the sweetness of the water, they are tempted into the phials, and frequently drowned; but these should be hung before the fruit begins to ripen, for then the insects would be much sooner tempted to the water than after having tasted the fruit: where a sufficient number of glasses are placed in time, properly attended to, and the water occasionally renewed, very little damage is done by these insects.

CLEAN THE BORDERS, ETC.

Hoe and clean the ground about your espalier and wall trees, for if weeds are permitted to grow at this season, they will rob the trees of a great portion of their nourishment; cut off all suckers which arise from the roots of the trees as they are produced, for these are robbers, and would injure them much if suffered to remain.

THE ORCHARD.

Little remains to be done during this month in the orchard, but to feast on its delicious productions: however, it will be very proper to pick and carry away all decayed and fallen fruit, for the reasons assigned in the fruit garden for this month. Should any of the trees show canker or much gum, you may now cut out the decayed part clean to the fresh wood, and give it a dressing of the *medicated tar* prescribed on page 58, giving this medication a due consistence as there directed, to prevent its melting away by the heat of the weather; or you may apply Mr. Forsyth's composition, for which see page 235.

Where it can be done without injury, it would be of use to turn pigs into the orchard at this season to eat up the fallen, decayed fruit, and, consequently, to destroy the numerous brood of insects contained therein.

THE VINEYARD.

In the middle States the grapes are generally set or formed about the first week of this month; when all the loose hanging shoots are to be neatly tied up to the stakes, and the useless weak growths, as well as the suckers arising from the roots and lower parts of the stems, cleared or cut away; but by no means divest any of the branches of their leaves, as some unskilful persons too often practise; for these are absolutely necessary to the growth and protection of the fruit: the small side shoots growing on the main branches from the axillas of the leaves, should, if time permits, be nipped off as they are produced, which will tend considerably to strengthen the principal shoots.

When the vines are suffered for some time to hang loose, and trail about upon the ground, all their leaves grow upward; which, on the shoots being afterwards bound in an upright position to the stakes, are turned upside down; and until these leaves resume their natural position, which they are commonly eight or ten days in effecting, the fruit is at a stand, and consequently loses the advantage of that length of time in the principal season of its growth.

The ground should be kept constantly free from weeds, either by means of the plough and harrow or by the hoe; for where there are other plants suffered to grow, they not only rob the roots of the vines of their nourishment, but also by perspiring, cause a damp in the air, and prevent the sun and wind from exhaling and carrying away the vapors arising from the earth, whereby the fruit would be filled with crude nourishment, and rendered of much less value for making good wine, as well as unpalatable.

Continue to nip out the renewed extremities of the fruit-bearing shoots, to check the too great luxuriancy of their growth, and to afford the bunches of grapes a greater portion of nourishment; but this ought not to be done too close to the fruit, as it would check the free ascent of the juices into those branches, by depriving them of the means of discharging such a portion thereof as is not convertible into wood or fruit: and moreover, though the fruit might by this means be swelled to a greater size, it would be more replete with watery particles, and less with that refined saccharine juice so pleasing to the palate, and so necessary for the making of good wine.

Such shoots as are intended to be cut down in the pruning season, *for next year's fruiting*, are by no means to be topped, but should be suffered to grow at full length, taking care to keep them constantly divested of any side branches, which ought always to be rubbed off as they appear. Were those to be topped at this season, it would force out at an untimely period, many of the flower-buds which nature had designed for the ensuing year, and, consequently, at that time render the vines barren and unproductive.

THE NURSERY.

BUDDING OR INOCULATING.

The budding or inoculating of cherries and plums, and all such other trees and shrubs as are subject to become bark-bound in autumn, is generally commenced in the middle States about the fifteenth of this month, earlier or later, according to the season or the quantity to be budded ; these and others of the like nature should now be attended to, as they seldom work freely after the twenty-fifth of July. But this you may always easily know by trying the buds, and when they readily part from the wood, and also the bark of the stock rises or separates freely, then the work may be done.

But let it be particularly remarked, that every kind of tree or shrub that makes new autumn shoots, or that continues in a free growth, or flow of sap, should be budded either in August or before the twentieth of September, according as each kind is early or late in ripening its wood, that is, to bud each sort before it becomes bark-bound; and likewise observe that all those kinds which are likely to become bark-bound early in autumn ought to be budded in this month, while the juice flows freely in the stocks and buds.

If trees or shrubs are inoculated in the early part of this month, whose nature it is to take a second growth in autumn, the buds will then start, and the shoots produced therefrom not having a sufficient length of season to ripen the wood, will either be destroyed the ensuing winter, or so much injured as never to make good trees; therefore, budding ought to be performed on the respective kinds at such periods as there will be no hazard of their growing before the ensuing spring, when they will have the advantage of the whole season for perfecting their wood, and of acquiring a sufficient strength and texture before winter.

Apricots, if worked on plum stocks, or on those of its own kind, should be budded in this month, but if on peach or almond, August will be a preferable period.

Pears may, likewise, be inoculated late in this month, but as to peaches, nectarines, almonds, and apples, if done now, the inserted buds would shoot in the course of the present season, and consequently be of little value.

The stocks of cherries, plums and pears that were budded last summer, or grafted in spring, and that have miscarried, may now be inoculated with the same kinds of fruit, for those will succeed either by grafting or budding.

Budding generally succeeds best when performed in cloudy weather, or in the morning or evening; for the great power of the mid-day sun is apt to dry and shrivel the cuttings and buds, and prevent the free union that might be expected immediately to take place in a favorable season ; at all events let the operation be performed on the north side of the stocks, which will give the buds every possible advantage of the sun.

In performing this work it will be necessary to observe that where trees are intended for walls, espaliers, or to be trained as dwarf standards, the buds must be inserted low in the stocks, that is, at the height of five or six inches from the ground; but if intended for tall standards, the stocks may be worked at the height of three, four, five, or even six feet; or, the low inserted buds may be trained up on single stems to a proper height for standards, or half standards, and then be headed for the production of lateral branches.

Where there are wall or espalier trees that do not produce fruit of approved kinds, such may be budded with any favorite sorts; this may be performed either upon strong shoots of the present year, or on clean young branches of two years' growth or more; several buds may be inserted in each tree, in different parts, by which means they will be furnished with a sufficiency of new wood of the desired kinds; and in two or three years they will bear abundantly.

Should it be found necessary to immerse the cuttings from which you take your buds in water, place therein only about an inch of their lower ends; the upper parts will be more congenially refreshed by that means than if the cuttings were entirely covered; and, moreover, the buds which are soaked for any considerable time in water will be so saturated with moisture as to prevent their imbibing the more congenial sap of the stocks, so that they often miscarry. For the proper stocks to work the various kinds upon see page 259, &c.

When the stocks are from about half an inch, or a little less, to an inch or more in diameter in the places where the buds are to be inserted, they are then of a proper size for working.

In order to perform the operation you must be provided with a neat sharp budding-knife, having a fat thin haft to open the bark of the stock for the admission of the bud, and, likewise, with a quantity of new bass-strings, which are certainly the best of all bandages, or if such cannot be obtained, some soft woollen yarn to tie round it when inserted.

Observe that the head of the stock is not to be cut off as in grafting; that the bud is to be inserted into the side, and the head suffered to remain until the spring following, when it is to be cut off above the bud, as directed on page 239.

METHODS OF BUDDING OR INOCULATING.

1. Having your cuttings, knife, and bandages ready, fix upon a smooth part on the side of the stock at whatever height you intend to bud it; with your knife make a horizontal cut across the bark of the stock quite through to the firm wood; then from the middle of this cut make a slit downwards, perpendiculary, about an inch and a half long, going also quite through to the wood, so that the two cuts together may be in the form of the letter T; then with the point of your knife raise the bark a little at the angles formed by the two cuts, in order to make room for the flat part of the haft to enter and raise the bark.

This done, proceed with all expedition to take off a bud, having immediately previous to the commencement cut off all the leaves, leaving about an inch of the footstalk to each bud, and holding the cutting in one hand, with the thickest end outward; then enter the knife about half an inch, or rather more, below a bud, cutting nearly half way into the wood of the shoot, continuing it with one clean slanting cut about as much more above the bud, so deep as to take off part of the wood along with it, the whole from an inch and a quarter to an inch and a half long; directly take out the woody part remaining in the bud, which is easily done by placing the point of the knife between the bark and wood, at either end, but the upper is the more preferable, and with the assistance of the thumb, pull off the wood from the bark, which ought, if in good condition, to part freely; then quickly examine the inside, to see if the root of the bud be left, and if there appears a small hole, the rudiment of the young tree is gone with the wood, the bud is rendered useless, and another must be prepared; but if there be no hole, the bud is good; then place the footstalk or back part of the bud between your lips, and with the flat haft of the knife, separate the bark from the stock on each side of the perpendicular cut, clear to the wood for the admission of the bud, which, directly slip down close between the wood and bark, till the whole is inserted to within the eighth of an inch; let this part be cut through into the first transverse incision made in the stalk, and the bud will fall neatly into its place; then draw the bud up gently so as to join the upper or cut end of it to the bark of the stalk, where it will most generally first unite.

Let the parts be then bound with a ligature of bass, previously immersed in water to render it pliable and tough, or, in want of this, with woollen yarn; beginning below the bottom of the perpendicular slit, and proceeding upwards close around every part, except over the eye or bud, which is to be carefully preserved, and continue it a little above the horizontal cut, not binding it too tight, but just sufficient to keep the parts close, exclude the air, sun, and wet, and thereby to promote the junction of the stalk and bud; finish by making the ligature fast.

2. Although it is universally recommended by every author who has written on the art of gardening to take the woody part out of the bud before its insertion into the stalk, as above directed, I find such practice by no means necessary; for if the bud be taken off with a less portion of wood than in the former method, and immediately inserted as above directed, it will succeed full as well, if not better; and as to expedition, there is no comparison; certainly double the number can be inserted in the same period of time by this method as by the former. It will be found particularly convenient for the budding of lemons and oranges, and may also be practised at periods in which the first method would be totally unsuccessful, that is, when the buds are not sufficiently ripe to exist without the young wood, or too much so for the bark to separate freely. This method may be practised, when desired, at a much earlier period than the former, and also as late in the season as the bark of the stalk will *rise freely* for the admission of the bud.

In three weeks or a month after inoculation, you will see which of them have taken, by their fresh and plump appearance, and at that time you should loosen the bandages, for if kept on too long they would pinch the stalks, and greatly injure, if not destroy, the buds. Those that appear shrivelled, black, or decayed, are good for nothing.

In this dormant state the buds should remain till the March following, when the stalks are to be headed down, as directed in the *nursery* for that month.

Note. The cuttings should not be taken off the trees in the middle of the day, if the weather be hot and dry, for at such times they will perspire so fast as soon to leave the buds destitute of moisture;

but if you are obliged to fetch them from some distance, as it often
happens, you should be provided with a tin case about twelve inches
long, and a cover to the top, which must have five or six holes; in
this case you should put as much water as will fill it about two inches
high, and place your cuttings therein in an upright position, so that
the parts which were cut from the tree may be set in the water, and
then fasten down the cover to keep out the air; the holes in the cover
will be sufficient to let the perspiration of these branches pass off,
which, if pent in, would be very hurtful to them; you must also be
careful to carry it upright, that the water may not reach to the buds,
which would so saturate them as to deprive them of any attractive
force to imbibe the sap of the stalk.

INOCULATE AND LAY CURIOUS TREES AND SHRUBS.

Agreeably to the preceding directions and observations, inoculate
roses, jasmines, and such other kinds as you desire to propagate in
that way. The moss rose may, in particular, be increased by this
means, as it is not very free in producing suckers; this may be
budded on stalks of any kinds of common roses that have been either
raised from seed or suckers.

The proper stalk to bud any of the more curious kinds of jasmines
on, is that of the common white jasmine.

Continue also to propagate the various kinds of trees and shrubs
by layers and cuttings, as directed last month.

ORDINARY ATTENDANCE.

Weeding, shading, and watering, must now be particularly attended
to as directed last month; without which, much injury will be sustained, especially by the seedlings, layers, and late transplanted trees
and shrubs.

You should continue to train your evergreens for the purposes they
are designed; and when any of your forest-trees shoot too vigorously
near the roots, those branches may be pruned off, to encourage their
heads.

THE PLEASURE, OR FLOWER GARDEN.

BULBOUS AND TUBEROUS ROOTS.

Take up the bulbs of such late flowers as were not sufficiently ripe
nor their leaves decayed last month, as ornithogalums, bulbous irises,
martagon, and other lilies; transplant the roots of fritillaries, crown
imperials, dens canis, and such other bulbous and tuberous-rooted
flowers as do not endure to be kept long out of ground; and this
being the season in which their roots are not in action, is the most
proper time for transplanting them, before they put forth new fibres;
after which it would be very improper to remove them.

ANNUAL FLOWERS.

You may still transplant any of the late sown balsams, cock's-combs, amaranthuses, China-asters, &c., into the border or flower-beds where wanted, taking them up with balls, or with as much earth as possible about their roots, and giving them a good watering when planted, which is to be occasionally repeated till they are well rooted; if some shade could be afforded them for a few days, it would the better insure their success.

CARNATIONS.

The choice carnations now in flower should be taken care of and assisted in their blowing, as directed last month; you may likewise assist those of inferior qualities and that have a tendency to burst, by splitting the pod or calyx a little way at top, on the opposite side to where it shows an inclination to burst in two or three different places, so as to promote the spreading of the flower regularly each way. This should be done just as the flower begins to break the pod with a pair of small, narrow pointed scissors, or with a sharp pointed knife, taking care not to cut the calyx too deep, but rather to open it a little at each place, and to leave as much of the bottom of the cup entire as will be sufficient to keep the petals or flower-leaves regularly together.

Some florists take great pains in the opening of the flowers to assist nature in spreading and displaying the petals, so as to enlarge the circumference and dispose the flower-leaves in such a manner as to show the stripes and variegations to the best possible advantage, and for this purpose make use of a small pair of wire nippers, the points of which are flattened and bound around with silk or thread to prevent injury. With these they extract such of the petals as do not please, and display the others so as to suit their fancy.

Continue to propagate your choice carnations and pinks by layers and pipings, as directed on page 448, for the performance of which, the early part of this month is a very practicable time. Give the necessary shade and water to the plants now in flower, and see that those layers which were laid last month are kept sufficiently moist to promote their free rooting.

When the layers are properly rooted, which will be the case with most sorts in a month after laying—provided due care be taken to keep them regularly moist, and to shade them from the heat of the meridian sun—they are then to be taken off from the old plant with about half an inch of the stalk which connects them to it, and be immediately planted in small pots, one, two, three, or four in each. The pots should be filled with the compost recommended on page 309, previously adding thereto a little more loam and coarse sand, and when the plants are neatly planted therein, the pots should be buried to their rims in a convenient airy place, and arches of hoops placed over the bed on which to lay mats to shade the plants from the sun till well rooted and growing freely; and these mats are to be afterwards laid on occasionally as necessity may require, to protect the plants from too powerful sunshine or heavy torrents of rain, which are both injurious to them.*

Here they are to remain till November, when they must be removed into their winter repository, as then directed; during this time they must have a sufficiency of water as often as it may appear necessary, to keep them in a constant growing state and good health.

The layers of the common kinds of carnations should, when taken off, be planted in beds of rich earth in rows about six inches asunder, where they are to be watered and shaded until well taken with the ground, and growing. They may remain in these beds till September, October, or March, and are then to be taken up with balls of earth and planted where intended to flower.

PINKS.

The most valuable kinds of pinks should be treated in every respect as directed for carnations.

SENSITIVE PLANTS.

The sensitive plants which have been raised in hot-beds, may about the first of this month, if not done in June, be brought out into the open air and placed in a very warm situation, for they delight in much heat; but some ought to be kept constantly under glasses, for, when fully exposed to the weather, they lose much of their sensibility.

The species I particularly allude to, is the *Mimosa pudica*, or humble and sensitive plant.

Those plants which are placed in the greatest warmth in winter, continue vigorous, and retain their faculty of contracting on being touched; but those that are in a moderate warmth have little or no motion.

TRANSPLANTING BIENNIAL AND PERENNIAL FLOWERING PLANTS.

If not done in June, you should now transplant from the seed-beds the various kinds of perennial and biennial seedling flowering plants, as directed on page 452.

AURICULAS AND POLYANTHUSES.

Exame your auriculas and polyanthuses; when dead leaves at any time appear upon the plants, let them be immediately picked off, and suffer no weeds to grow in the pots.

Preserve those plants carefully from the mid-day sun, which at this season would destroy them, particularly the auriculas, and keep the earth in the pots always moderately moist.

---

* Pot culture of carnations is only applicable to the enthusiast. They bloom equally well in the open ground, where they are grown with ordinary care.

When any of them have furnished strong offsets, such may be taken off in the last week of this month, and planted in small pots; for about that time these plants begin to grow afresh, and advantage ought to be taken of that critical period. The offsets will require shade and water till newly rooted : the latter must be sparingly administered till the plants take and are in a growing state, before which too much water would cause the roots to rot; but, notwithstanding, the earth must still be kept a little moist.

The auricula and polyanthus seedlings that were sown last autumn or early in spring, if having grown well and of sufficient size, should in the last week of this, or first in August, be transplanted into boxes or pots, as directed on page 360, and placed in the shade to grow on till the middle of October, when they may be rather more exposed to the sun, and early in November remove the pots or boxes into a warm situation, to remain till taken into their winter quarters.

GRASS AND GRAVEL WALKS.

The same care and attention must now be paid to the grass and gravel walks, and lawns, as directed in the preceding months.

BOX EDGING.

Such box edgings as were not clipped in June, should now be dressed, observing the same directions in every particular as given on page 452.

CLIP HEDGES.

Hedges in general, of every kind, should be clipped in the early part of this month; for that purpose, advantage ought to be taken of moist or cloudy weather to do the work in, as hedges always look better after being clipped in wet weather than in dry.

Another dressing of the same kind towards the latter end of September will keep them in a neat condition the year round.

ORDINARY ATTENDANCE.

The principal flower-borders, beds, &c., must now have more than ordinary attention paid to the keeping of them clean, as well as the shrubbery-clumps and other similar compartments. Where any of the flowering-shrubs or evergreens have grown rude or disorderly, let such be trimmed or pruned into neat form; that is, if any have produced strong and rambling shoots, cut out, shorten, or reduce them to a pleasing regularity.

Stake and tie up the stems of such flowering plants as stand in need of support, to prevent their being borne down by winds or heavy rains, &c.

Cut down the stems of such fibrous-rooted plants as are past bloom, except a few of the best, where the seeds are wanted. Those have always an unpleasing appearance, and ought to be removed as soon as possible; by which means the plants, though past flowering, will appear more lively and decent, and the advancing bloom of others will show to greater advantage.

LAYING OUT A GARDEN.

It is one of the difficult things for a novice to arrange a small garden so as to produce the greatest effect in a moderate space. In the following cuts, the house is supposed to be pleasantly situated in a village, having its entrance towards the public road, and looking from the garden side on a level country. In the front of the house a garden extends itself flanked by a shrubbery on both sides, and bounded by a piece of water. On the right is the green-house, &c., inconsiderately placed so close to the garden as to make it impossible to conceal it without too much encroaching on the ground. Further to the right stands the coach-house, and stables, &c., and beyond these a large kitchen-garden.

Fig. 53.

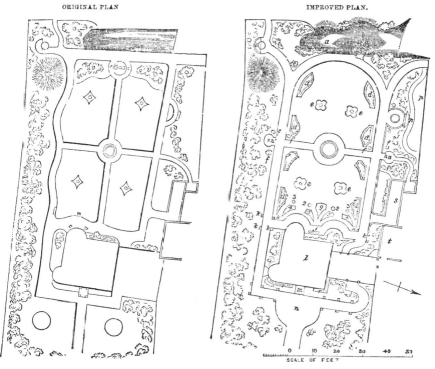

ORIGINAL PLAN

IMPROVED PLAN.

SCALE OF FEET

a. Pond.	*f.* Irish Yews.	*k.* Vases on pedestals.
b. Mass of Water Lily.	*g.* Parterre on turf.	*l.* House.
c. Large Chinese Arbor-vitæ.	1. Blue with white margin.	*m.* Porch.
d. Clump on turf for herbaceous plants and small flowering shrubs, and bordered by clipped evergreen hedges of Cotoneaster, &c.	2. Scarlet.	*n.* Coach ring.
	3. Light pink.	*o. p.* Alcoves.
	4. Brownish orange.	*q.* Background for reserve, &c.
	5. Deep violet or purple.	*r.* Border for creepers against house.
e. Beds on turf, with Jupiter in centre, flowering plants round.	*h.* Statues on pedestals.	*s.* Green-house.
	i. Fountain.	*t.* Laundry.
	j. Seat on centre line.	

The great faults in this case are the shutting out of the prospect, and the complete exposure of all the walks, as though they were the most important features of the garden. The first of these is to be rectified by cleaning away the clumps near the piece of water, the second by destroying the centre walk, and the third by fringing the broad turf-plat so obtained with clumps for flowering shrubs.

In the new arrangement a centre will be obtained upon a line from the fountain, at right angles with the building; and to give a balance to the basis of operations, a large projecting mass of close-clipped evergreen was introduced, to correspond with the shape of the draw-ing-room bow, which also served to aid in concealing the offices and yard on the right side of the house, and the yard itself was contract-ed, that it might be effectually planted out on both sides from the garden. The walks in the "improved plan" are judiciously altered. The house itself, and the laundry, are to be covered with clematis, honeysuckles, and wistaria.

The apparent breadth of the garden, indeed its general extent, being so much increased, the four beds *e, e, e, e,* are introduced, and it is admissible to fill these with flowering plants. A juniper will have a satisfactory effect in the centre of each. The plans almost explain themselves.

THE GREEN-HOUSE.

Orange, lemon, citron, and shaddock-trees, on which there are now set a superabundance of young fruit, should have them thinned to a reasonable number on each, in proportion to its strength; after which they may be divested of all flowers subsequently produced, especially when wanted for domestic purposes, such as to make orange-flower water, &c.

It would be of considerable utility to those trees to have the earth in the top of the tubs or pots now taken out, for two or three inches deep, and replaced with fresh compost; this would greatly encourage their autumn growth.

PROPAGATING THE PLANTS.

Still continue to propagate the various kinds of green-house plants which you wish to increase, by cuttings, layers, suckers, &c., as di-rected in the preceding months; most kinds will yet succeed by cut-tings of the present year's wood if carefully planted, duly shaded, and moderately watered; such as xeranthemums, salivias, geraniums, pelargoniums, and erodiums, hermannias, phlomises, ericas, cinera-rias, camellia japonica and acuba japonica, cotyledon orbiculata, ono-nis natrix, polygala bracteolata, lavendulas, anthyllises, proteas, &c. &c. These kinds, with many others, will now take freely, in suit-able earth, without the assistance of a hot-bed. Let the cuttings be taken from healthy plants; they should be from four to eight inches in length, and of a stout and robust growth. The leaves should be stripped off more than half way up, and the cuttings planted about two-thirds of their length into pots, garden-pans, or beds of earth, adopting for each kind its favorite soil; then give shade and water, as directed on former occasions.

The ericas, anthyllises, and other kinds that do not root freely in this way, should have bell-glasses placed over them, which will greatly facilitate their rooting.

Continue to propagate the various kinds of succulent plants belonging to this department, as directed on page 418.

PROPAGATING BY MERE LEAVES.

Several plants may be propagated from mere leaves. The wax plant, hoya, is a common instance. Gesnera, clianthus punicens, gloxinia speciosa, are also well known, but it is probable that most leaves, when separated from their parent, are incapable of doing so for reasons which we are not yet able to explain. The scales of a bulb will, with some certainty, produce new plants under favorable circumstances, viz : a strong bottom heat, moderate moisture, and a rich, stimulating soil.

Leaves intended for cuttings, should be taken from about the middle of a branch. Gloxinia, bryophillum, lilies, &c., may be experi-

Fig. 54.

mented upon by the amateur. If we wish to get on very quickly, the midrib on the lower face of the leaf may be broken in several places, without injuring the limb, and so lightly that the broken places can scarcely be distinguished; the lower face of the leaf is then placed on the earth of a pot. Soon at each fracture a little callus develops itself which gives rise to roots as seen above at *c*.

Some leaves, when employed as cuttings, send out roots and buds at each incision, as in hemionitis palmata, bryophillum, &c.; *d* shows how this effect is produced. Time is required to accomplish this, and especial attention must be paid to burying the end of the petiole, or the base of the leaf; *e* represents theophrasta latifolia, with its leaf cut in two, which struck and developed buds; the dotted part, shown in the upper half of the leaf, *e*, was removed, in order to put the leaf into a little pot, but this did not prevent the success of the cutting. The above is abridged from Dr. Lindley's new edition of his "*Theory of Horticulture.*" *a* indicates at what place we may cut the leaf without hurting the plant; the leaf being placed in the earth forms a callus at its base, *b*, whence the roots, and, consequently, more shoots, spring up.

TRANSPLANTING SEEDLINGS AND CUTTINGS.

Such seedlings of green-house plants as were raised from the spring sowings, and that are now three inches high, or more, should be transplanted into small pots separately, or several into large pots, and immediately watered; they must be kept duly shaded till well taken with the earth, and in a growing state; and even then it will be proper to place them where they can avoid the mid-day sun for the remainder of the season.

Many of the cuttings planted in spring will be well rooted by this time, and may now be taken up with as much earth as possible about their roots, planted separately in suitable sized pots, and shaded for eight or ten days from the mid-day sun; always observing to keep the earth in the pots moderately moist. The geraniums in particular may be taken up when too thick, and transplanted at any time after the cuttings have grown four or five inches.

SHIFTING INTO LARGER POTS.

You may now shift such of your plants as require larger pots or tubs; this is the best of the summer months for that purpose, as the greater number will have made their summer progress, and are now rather at a stand previous to the commencement of their new autumnal vegetation. This is particularly applicable to the camellia.

The operation of shifting is to be performed in every respect as directed on page 375.

Such plants as are now shifted must be immediately watered and removed into the shade, where they can have free air and protection from the sun in the heat of the day; there to remain for two, three, or four weeks, according to the time the respective kinds may take to re-establish themselves, and get into a fresh state of growth, when they may be replaced among the general collection.

LOOSENING AND GIVING FRESH EARTH.

It will be very proper at this time to examine the pots and tubs in general, and where the earth is inclinable to bind let the surface be carefully loosened to a little depth, breaking the earth small with the hands, and at the same time add thereto, if not done in any of the preceding months, some fresh compost; then level the surface neatly.

This dressing will do the plants more good than many people might imagine; but in particular to such as are in small pots.

GATHERING AND SOWING SEEDS.

Collect all the different sorts of seeds as they ripen, spread them upon paper in a dry shady place, and when sufficiently hardened, let them be carefully preserved in their pods or husks, or in paper bags, till the proper season for sowing them.

The seeds of geraniums, and of any other quick growing kinds of green-house plants, may now be sown, and if properly attended to will attain to a neat size before winter.

THE HOT-HOUSE.

PINE-APPLES.

The pine-apples being now arriving at maturity, it may not be unacceptable to give some account of the different varieties.

Of the *bromelia* there have been many distinct species described, viz: the B. ananas, B. pinguin, B. karatas, B. lingulata, B. humilis, B. acanga, B. bracteata, B. nudicaulis, B. paniculigera, &c.; but as the first species is the only one cultivated on account of its fruit, I shall confine myself exclusively to it, at least for the present.

From the *Bromelia ananas*, or pine-apple, as it is called, on account of the resemblance of the shape of its fruit to the cones of some species of pine-tree, particularly to that of the *Pinus pinea*, or stone-pine, there arise six principal varieties which have been cultivated for their fruit, &c. 1. The variety *ovata*, or queen-pine. 2. The *pyramidalis*, or sugar-loaf pine. 3. The *lucida*, or king pine. 4. The *glabra*, or smooth pine. 5. The *serotina*, or late pine; and 6. The *viridis*, or green pine.

The queen pine is the most commonly cultivated, but seems daily to decrease in esteem. Its flesh is of a fine yellow color, but in the hot summer months it is very apt not to cut firm, is liable to crack in the middle, and often contains an insipid watery juice; but when it ripens late in the season it is not so subject to any of these defects.

The sugar-loaf pine is easily distinguished from all the others by its leaves having purple stripes on their inside the whole length. The fruit is paler when ripe than the former, inclining to a straw color. This was brought from Brazil to Jamaica, where it is esteemed far beyond any other kind. But of this there are three varieties. 1. The brown leaved. 2. The green leaved, with purple stripes, and spines on the edges. 3. The green leaved, with purple stripes and smooth edges. The fruit of these is of exquisite flavor, filled with a lively delicious juice, and the flesh of a yellow color.

The king pine has grass-green smooth leaves, and produces a pretty large fruit; but as its flesh is hard, stringy, and sometimes not well flavored, it is not much cultivated.

The smooth pine is preserved by some persons for sake of variety, but the fruit is of little value.

The late pine is not of much importance for cultivating on account of its ripening at an untimely season, and therefore its description is considered unnecessary.

The green pine is considered tolerably good. The fruit, if suffered to ripen well, is of an olive color; to have it green, it must be cut before it is ripe, and suffered to lie by till fit for use. Plants of this kind may be procured from Barbadoes and Montserrat; but the fruit of the sugar-loaf is much to be preferred to it, and indeed to any other kind yet introduced.

There is, likewise, the Surinam, or silver-striped pine, which exceeds in beauty the whole tribe of variegated plants. The leaves are variously striped with a dark green and delicate white; and the whole is tinged with a lively red, which produces a contrast that gives the plant a gay and most beautiful appearance. Nor is there less beauty in its fruit, the protuberances of which swell large, and when ripe, are variously marbled with red, green, yellow, and white; which, together with the variegated crown on the top of the fruit, add a singularity and elegance to the whole beyond the power of description. The fruit is tolerably good, and therefore the plant is doubly worthy of cultivation.

Many other varieties of this fruit have arisen from seed, such as the black or brown Antigua; the Ripley queen pine, which is a very good fruit; the Grenada pine, with marbled leaves and very large fruit; the bog-warp pine, with broad green leaves; the smooth, long, narrow-leaved pine; the Surinam pine with gold-striped leaves, and the Enville pine; and there are also varieties with red-fleshed fruit.

COMPOST PROPER FOR PINE PLANTS.

You should, in the first place, twelve months previous to the time of its being wanted for use, pare off the sward or turf of a pasture not more than two inches deep, where the soil is a strong, rich loam, and carry it to some convenient place to be piled together for rotting; observing to turn it over once a month at least, spreading it so as to expose a considerable surface to the summer sun, as well as to the frosts in winter; but in wet weather it will be proper to gather it up into a high ridge to prevent its rich juices being dissolved and carried away by water. If a quantity of sheep dung could be collected fresh and mixed therewith, in the first instance, it would greatly improve it.

1. Having the above prepared and made fine with the spade, but not screened; to three barrowfuls of it, add one of vegetable mould of decayed oak leaves, and half a barrowful of coarse sand, observ-

ing, however, that if the soil, from which the turf had been taken, inclined any way to sand, that should be now omitted. This makes a proper compost for *crowns, suckers* and *young plants*.

2. To make a compost for *fruiting plants* use three barrows of the above reduced sward, two of the vegetable mould, one of coarse sand, and one-fourth of a barrow of soot.

The above compost should be made some months before wanted, and very frequently turned during that time, that the different mixtures may get well and uniformly incorporated. As to the quantity of sand to be added, you must be governed by the nature of the soil from whence the turf was taken; for too great a portion of sand would be injurious, and subject many of the young plants to go into fruit before the proper period.

Where oak leaves are not used in hot-houses, or for hot-beds, &c., the vegetable mould may be made by laying a quantity of them together, as soon as they fall from the trees, in a heap sufficiently large to ferment. They should be covered at first for some time, to prevent the upper leaves from being blown away; the heap must afterwards be frequently turned, and kept clean from weeds; the leaves will be two years before they are sufficiently reduced to be fit for use.

Keep the different heaps of compost at all times free from weeds, turn them frequently, and round them up in rainy seasons; but they should be spread out in continued frosts, and in fine weather.

RAISING THE PINE BY CROWNS.

The crown is perfected at the time when the pine-apple is quite yellow; therefore the crowns of such fruit may be planted in two or three days after being taken off; but if the fruit be cut green, as is practised by some persons with the queen pine, or if only the top of the fruit be green when cut, as is the case frequently with the sugar loaf kinds, even when the principal part is thoroughly ripened, then it will be necessary to let the crowns of such fruit lie five, six, or seven days, after they are taken off, in a shady part of the hot-house, in order that the wounds should dry, and particularly to give them that degree of maturity to which nature was not allowed to conduct them.

The crowns may then be planted in small pots and plunged into the tan-pit, where they will soon strike root, and get into a growing state. But before the crowns are planted their lower or bottom leaves should be cut off close with a knife or a pair of scissors, which will cause them to decay much sooner, and make room for the roots to be produced with greater ease.

The crowns will require but very little water till they have taken root, and are in a growing state; when it may be administered more freely, but always with a sparing hand.

RAISING THE PINE BY SUCKERS.

As the fruit of the pine-apple is the principal object and sole

31

reward of the great expense attendant on its management, few persons choose to permit the suckers to remain on the plants till they grow very large, as they would injure the fruit and prevent its swelling; they are, therefore, generally stopped in growth, or taken off as soon as it can be done with safety; but when a stock of plants is the object, the additional advantage which might be gained in the fruit is given up, or at least of as many as will produce the number of suckers required, in order to encourage their growth, and are permitted to remain on the old stocks or plants even for some time after the fruit is cut.* In this situation the suckers will grow very large, provided the stools are plentifully supplied with water.

The suckers should not be taken from the plants till they are grown to the length of about twelve inches, when their bottoms will be hard, woody, and full of round knobs, which are the rudiments of the roots.

In taking off each sucker, remove it two or three times backward and forward, in a side-way direction, and it will come out with its bottom entire, which should be cut smooth, and deprived of any raggedness.

Place these in a shady part of the hot-house for two or three days, and then plant them in small sized pots, just so deep as to keep them fast in the earth; after which they are to be treated as directed for the crowns. The proper size of the pots to plant full grown crowns and suckers in, is six inches diameter in top, and five and a half deep.

CARE OF THE FRUITING PINES.

The fruiting pines must now have abundance of air, which adds much to the flavor of the fruit; but though the heat of the day, at this season, is very intense, yet, when northwesterly winds prevail, the night sometimes happens, though not frequently, to be rather cold for the fruiting plants; in which case it may be prudent to close the lights at night, taking care to slide them open early in the morning; this, however, must be governed by circumstances and by the heat of the bark pit, which, if any way brisk, will render it the more necessary to give plenty of air at all times.

As the pine-apples come to maturity, care should be taken to cut them off when in due perfection and before they become too ripe; generally cutting them in a morning, each with several inches of the stalk, and with the crown of leaves at top, till served to the table.

When the fruit is eaten, it will be proper to preserve the crowns and any young suckers growing round at the base,† particularly if wanted for increase.

---

* Much of the expense here spoken off may be obviated by planting out in beds in the hot-house, and having a part of the hot-water pipes sunk in a chamber underneath for bottom heat. All potting, bark beds, and repeated shiftings are thus avoided.

† The brown Antigua, the king, and the sugar-loaf kinds, commonly

SHIFTING THE SUCCESSION PINES.

The pine plants which are to fruit in the ensuing season, should be shifted either in the last week of this month or the first in August, into full sized pots, of about eleven or twelve inches diameter at top, and ten deep; by doing this so early in the year they will have time to make good roots before spring, for otherwise they seldom produce very large fruit.

Having the pots and new compost ready, take the plants out of the bark-bed, and shift them in the following method :—

First, place a shell in the bottom of the new pot, and put in two inches deep of fresh compost: then turn the plant out of the old pot with the ball entire, and place it immediately into the new, fill up around the ball with more of the compost, and let the top thereof be covered with it an inch deep.

In this manner let the whole be shifted and immediately watered, then plunge them again into the bark-bed.

Previous to plunging the pots, the bark-bed must first be stirred up to the bottom to revive the declining heat, observing at the same time to add about one-third or at least one-fourth of new tan thereto, if the old is much wasted, become earthy, or not likely to produce a sufficient degree of bottom heat to promote the fresh rooting and growth of the plants.

CARE OF THE VARIOUS HOT-HOUSE PLANTS.

The general care and propagation of the various exotics of the hot-house department, are the same now as directed in *May* and *June*, and therefore unnecessary to be repeated; but it would be very proper at this time to refresh the earth in the top of the pots or tubs, as directed on page 478, and also to shift such of the plants as require it. The hibiscus rosa sinensis, vinca rosea, plumeria rubra, allamanda cathartica, asclepias curassavica, lantanas, begonias, &c. may now be easily propagated by cuttings, and where an increase of the various kinds is wanted, that business ought not to be delayed to a later period, that the cuttings may have time to become well rooted before winter; nor should you despair of being able to propagate any kind of tree or shrub by cuttings; for with due care there are few but may be increased that way, especially with the assistance of bell-glasses and a suitable bottom heat.

produce suckers at the top of the stem, immediately under the fruit; but these are generally small, and of much less value than those produced about the surface of the earth.

AUGUST.

WORK TO BE DONE IN THE KITCHEN GARDEN.

SAVOYS, COLEWORTS, AND BORECOLE.

In the first week of this month finish planting your savoys; they will not, at this season, require a greater distance than two feet every way. This plantation will be tolerably well cabbaged in November, and may, with a little care, be preserved in fine condition all winter.

The early York, Battersea, and sugar-loaf plants, arising from seed sown last month, should now be planted out for autumn coleworts; they will yet form nice heads; and some more of the same kinds should be sown in the first week of this month, from which you will have delicious hearts late in October, &c. In the southern States, where the plants can stand out all winter, this will be a very useful practice. Plant also your last crop of borecole.

SPINAGE.

Now prepare some ground and sow a good crop of spinage; that sown in the first week of the month will be fit for use in September, and what you sow in the second will be in fine condition in October.

In the last week of the month, you should sow a principal crop of the prickly seeded spinage for early spring use; this ought to be sown on dry gravelly ground, for on such it will stand the winter much better than on any other. A second sowing will, however, be necessary for the same purpose in the first week of September, as it will always be proper to have a double chance. With either or both of these sowings, you may throw in a thin scattering of brown Dutch or cabbage lettuce, and if the winter is any way mild, you will have good early plants in spring, which you are then to take up and transplant into beds for heading.

SOWING RADISHES.

In the early part of this month you should sow a sufficient supply of short-top and salmon radishes; also, some of the white Naples and turnip-rooted kinds; these will be fit for the table in September. About the middle of the month, you ought to sow a second crop to come into use in October.

A full crop of the black and white Spanish or winter radishes may be sown at either, or both of the above periods, for fall and winter use.

ASPARAGUS.

The plantations of asparagus should now be kept perfectly clear from weeds, but particularly those which were planted last spring, and likewise the seedling beds, but this must be done by a very careful hand weeding.

TURNIPS.

The first week in this month is a very principal time for sowing your general crop of turnips for autumn and winter use, whether in the field or garden; you may continue in the middle States to sow as opportunity offers, or as the season proves favorable, till the middle of the month; after which, it will be too late to expect any tolerable produce. In the eastern States, the last sowing ought to be performed in the first week of this month, and the earlier in that, the better. If any be sown after the above periods, it ought to be of the early six weeks kind; this will arrive at maturity at an earlier period than any other sort. In the southern States, turnips may be sown somewhat later. Sow very thinly in drills, one foot apart and one inch deep. The purple-top strap leaf, and yellow stone, are two good kinds.

CELERY.

Plant now a full crop of late celery; let this be done as early in the month as possible, and as directed on pages 423 and 461.

Continue to earth up your advancing crops of celery once every ten or fourteen days, observing to do this on a dry day, and previously to break the earth fine with the spade; take care to gather up all the leaves neatly, and not to bury the hearts of the plants.

ARTICHOKES.

The late spring plantations of artichokes should be now looked over and treated as directed for the older plants on page 463.

SMALL SALADING.

Where a constant supply of small salading is wanted, such as lettuce, cresses, radish, rape, and mustard, they should now be sown every eight or ten days on a shady border, and frequently watered, both before and after coming up.

SOWING PEAS.

You may any time between the first and fifteenth of this month, or at each period, sow a crop of the early frame, Charlton, or Warwick peas; these, should the season prove favorable, will afford you tolerable crops in October. If the weather be dry, soak the peas and water the drills, as directed on page 464.

PLANTING KIDNEY-BEANS.

At any time before the middle of the month you may plant a crop of the early cream-colored, early yellow, or early China dwarf kidney-beans; they will yet succeed very well; but should the ground and weather be dry at the time, the drills ought to be watered, and the beans soaked in soft water four or five hours before planting.

SOWING AND TRANSPLANTING LETTUCES.

Early in the month sow a good supply of lettuces for fall use; the kinds proper to sow now are the brown Dutch and Silesia lettuces; both these kinds succeed well at this season. Sow them as directed in the former months. A succession crop should also be sown about the middle of the month.

In the last week of the month sow some of the brown Dutch and hardy green cabbage lettuce, to transplant into frames and on warm borders in October, for winter and spring use; for the method of protecting them from frost, see *November.*

Transplant from the seed-beds such of your advancing young crops of lettuces as are grown to a sufficient size; let this be done as directed in the preceding months, and, if possible, in moist or cloudy weather; giving them a plentiful watering when planted, and repeat it frequently if necessary. Be particular always to sow and plant your lettuces in an open situation, and not to suffer them to be drawn up, or to remain too long in the seed-beds, otherwise they will never form good heads.

ENDIVE.

Tie up your endive, which is full grown, or cover them with boards or tiles to blanch: this must be performed when the leaves are very dry, otherwise the plants will rot. Select the large and full-hearted plants, and with bass or other strings, or with small osier twigs, tie them a little above the middle, not too tight, previously gathering up the leaves regularly in the hand,

Transplant, agreeably to the directions given on page 460, such young endive as is now of a proper size, and water it immediately, which repeat, occasionally, till the plants begin to grow freely. These plants must be set in an open situation, and by no means near any kind of shade whatever.

In the early part of the month sow a full crop of endive for late autumn and winter use; the green curled sort is by much the most preferable for this sowing, as being more hardy and keeping better than any other kind. It would be proper to sow some more of the same sort about the middle of the month; for these, provided they have time to grow to a proper size, will keep better than those which were sown earlier.

CARDOONS AND FINOCHIO.

The cardoons, which were planted in June, will now be arrived at some considerable height, so that you may begin to tie up some for blanching; bind the stalks round, rather loosely, as practised with endive, and draw the earth up to the stems, as you would to celery; repeat this earthing from time to time, as they advance in growth, till whitened to a sufficient height.

Earth up finochio, which is full grown, in order to blanch and render it fit for use.

MELONS AND CUCUMBERS.

Your crops of melons and cucumbers, whether in an advancing or fruiting state, should be kept very clean, which will much improve the flavor and encourage the growth of the fruit. If the weather proves very dry, a gentle watering, now and then, given in the evening, will be of considerable service to the late crops, but more particularly to the cucumbers.

CARE OF THE GENERAL CROPS.

All your crops should be kept clear from weeds, using the hoe where it can be done with safety, and where not, they must be carefully hand-weeded. Earth up your advancing crops of cabbages, peas, beans, and all others that require that treatment. Water all new plantations, and such young advancing seedlings as may be improved thereby. Pull up the haulm and stalks of peas, beans, and cabbages, &c., which have done bearing, and carry them out of the garden, as well as all weeds, hoed or picked up.

HERBS.

Cut such herbs as are now in flower to distil, or to dry for winter use, always observing to do it when they are dry, and spread them in a dry, shady place; for if they are dried in the sun, they will shrink up, turn black, and be of little value.

You may now, if omitted in spring, or in the preceding months, plant slips of sage, rue, lavender, mastich, thyme, hyssop, and winter savory, &c., but these will not be near so strong, nor so capable of resisting the severity of the winter as those planted at an earlier period.

Cut down the decayed flower-stems of any kinds that appear unsightly; and at the same time it will be proper to shorten all the straggling young branches in order to keep the plants in due compass, which will cause them to produce fresh shoots, and make the plants appear neat during the remainder of the season. This should be done, if possible, in moist or cloudy weather.

CORN-SALAD.

The *Valeriana locusta*, variety *olitoria*, grows commonly in the cornfields in many parts of Europe; hence, it is called corn-salad; and from its being sufficiently hardy to stand the winter, and of early growth in spring, has acquired the appellation of lamb's lettuce, from its affording them an early pasturage.

This is an annual plant, and is cultivated as an esculent herb in salads for winter and early spring use. It should be sown in the middle States in the last week of this month, or first in September, on a dry soil and open situation, and raked in; the plants will come up soon after, and should be thinned to two or three inches asunder; they are used during the winter and early spring months in composition with lettuce and other salad herbs, and as a substitute for these where deficient.

WINTER CRESSES.

The *Erysimum barbarea*, or winter cress, is used for the same purpose, sown at the same time, and treated in like manner as directed above for corn-salad. This plant is, by the market-gardeners about Philadelphia, called scurvy-grass, to which it is by no means allied; the latter being the *Cochlearia officinalis* of Linn., a good antiscorbutic, which has rather a disagreeable smell, and a warm, bitter taste, by no means palatable as a salad. The winter cresses, if sown in the last week of this month, or first in September, on a dry soil and warm exposure, will afford an early salad in spring, very pleasing to some palates, and perfectly resembling in taste and flavor, and somewhat in appearance, the *Sisymbrium nasturtium*, or water-cress.

LIMA AND CAROLINA BEANS.

Hoe and clean between the hills or rows of Lima and Carolina beans, and cut off any runners that are found to trail on the surface of the ground, which only tend to rob the bearing vines.

SOUTHERN STATES.

In the southern States, particularly the Carolinas and Georgia, this month being the commencement of their rainy season, it is common to sow cauliflowers, cabbage, carrot, parsnep, onion, leek, and endive; and in short, the general variety of seeds that are sown in the middle States in the months of March and April. These kinds arrive there at a tolerable degree of perfection before their winter sets in, which is so very mild as scarcely to injure any of their esculent crops; and such of them as do not come to maturity before winter attain it early in spring.

DUNG-HILLS AND WEED-HEAPS.

The dung-hills should, during the summer months, be kept free from weeds, for if the seeds of such are permitted to ripen and fall, the dung when carried into the garden will poison the whole ground. The manure produced by the heaps of weeds taken out of the garden, should not be introduced therein again, until it is three or four years old, lest the seeds which happened to ripen should stock the ground afresh

---

THE FRUIT GARDEN.

The care of your wall and espalier fruit-trees, &c., being the same in this month as directed in the former, page 465, I refer you there-to to avoid repetition.

Should any of the shoots be displaced by winds or other accidents, let them be immediately made fast again in a secure and neat manner.

FIG-TREES.

The wall and espalier fig-trees will now be ripening their fruit; they should be kept neatly trained, but the knife must not be used except to the fore-right and other irregular productions, as it is from the young shoots of this season's growth that you are to expect fruit next year; and these bearing principally towards their extremities, ought not to be shortened.   Lay in the shoots regularly, not across one another, and let them be well secured, for the wind and rain have great power over them on account of their broad leaves.

BUDDING.

For the budding necessary to be done in this month, see the *nursery* department.

THE ORCHARD.

Such of your standard peach and other trees as are overburthened with fruit, and likely to break down, should be supported with sub-stantial stakes, to which the pending branches ought to be bound by strong hay-bands, taking care to place part thereof between each stake and the branch lest the bark should be injured : these supports are to be taken away as soon as the fruit are off.   See the article *Orchard*, on page 466; what is there directed is very applicable at this time.

THE VINEYARD.

Keep your vines in neat, regular order, trained up and tied to the poles, and suffer none to trail upon the ground; by this means the influence of the sun and free air will be admitted to the fruit, which are essentially necessary to its timely maturity.

You should now be very particular in keeping the ground between the vines free from weeds; for at this time a clean surface answers, in a great degree, to reflect the sun's heat upon the vines and fruit, which will cause them to ripen soon, and acquire an improved richness of taste and flavor; and besides, neither the vines nor fruit will be so subject to contract mildew, as if the vapors and damps were confined round them by weeds, or by their own branches laying trailing about. Some of the early sorts of grapes will begin to ripen about the end of this month, but the general vintage may be expected some time in September, early or late, according to the season.

Continue to divest the main shoots of all young side productions, but be careful not to pull off or injure the leaves. Such fruit bearing branches as were topped, ought to be likewise divested of young shoots as they are produced, at least of the greater number.

THE NURSERY.

BUDDING.

This is the proper season for budding or inoculating peaches, nectarines, almonds, apples, and pears; also apricots on peach or almond stalks; but when the apricot is to be worked on the plum, it ought to be done in July.

Cherries, plums, or any other fruit-trees may also be budded in this month, if the bark parts freely from the stalk. Pears ought to be inoculated in the early part of the month, or while the sap flows freely; but the peach, nectarine, almond, and apple will succeed any time between the first of August and twentieth of September, provided that the stalks are young and vigorous.

You may now inoculate all such curious trees and shrubs as you wish to propagate in that way; there are very few but will succeed at this time if worked on good and suitable stalks; but when you find the bark not to part or rise freely, it will be almost in vain to attempt the work. Many kinds now take a second growth, and when that is perceivable it will be a very proper time to inoculate them. For general instructions on this subject see page 467.

NEW BUDDED TREES.

You should now look carefully over the stalks which were budded in July, and in three weeks, or at most a month after their being worked, loosen the bandages, lest the buds should be pinched thereby; and where there are any shoots produced below the buds, they should be rubbed off. You ought, also, to examine the trees which were budded in the former year, or grafted in the spring, and cut off all the shoots that are produced beneath the inoculations or grafts; for if these are permitted to grow they will starve the proper shoots.

PRESERVING THE STONES OF FRUITS.

Preserve peach, plum, cherry, and apricot stones, &c., to sow for raising stocks to bud and graft on. These may either be sown immediately, or preserved till October or any of the following months, in common garden earth or moist sand; but it will be necessary to embrace the first opportunity in spring, if not before, to sow them before the stones open and the radicles begin to shoot, otherwise a great number of these would be injured in the act of sowing. You may mix the stones with either earth or sand, which put into garden pots or boxes, and plunge these to their edges, and no deeper, in some dry border, till the time of sowing. Every day that they are kept out of the ground is an injury to them, and if preserved in a dry state till spring, very few will vegetate for a year after, and the far greater number not at all.

WEED AND WATER SEEDLINGS, ETC.

The seedling trees and shrubs of all kinds must now be kept perfectly clean from weeds; for these, if permitted to grow among the young plants, would totally ruin them.

In dry weather you must be careful to give frequent waterings to the seedling plants, whether in beds, boxes, or pots, according to their respective necessities.

Keep the ground between the rows of trees well hoed, and train up the various sorts of forest-trees and shrubs for the several purposes for which they are designed; but do not trim the stems of standard trees too close, for it is necessary to leave some small shoots to detain the sap for the purpose of strengthening those parts.

PREPARING GROUND FOR AUTUMN PLANTING.

Towards the end of this month you should begin to clear and trench the vacant quarters in which you intend to plant fruit-stocks, or trees or shrubs of any kind, in October or November, &c., that the rain may soak and mellow the ground before the season of planting; and if the land be of a stiff nature, the laying of it up in high sloping ridges, by exposing more surface to the sun, rain, and dews, will greatly improve it, and it can be the more expeditiously levelled down and rendered in a fit condition for planting, when necessary.

THE PLEASURE, OR FLOWER GARDEN.

CARNATIONS AND PINKS.

Transplant the layers and pipings of carnations and pinks that are sufficiently rooted, and treat them in every respect as directed on page 472, which see. You may yet lay pinks and carnations, if omitted in June and July, taking care to keep the earth moderately moist about them till well rooted; but it would be much better to have done this in the beginning of July, as in that case the layers would be strong and well established before winter. For the method, see page 449.

AURICULAS AND POLYANTHUSES.

The first week in this month is a very proper time to shift into fresh compost such of your choice auriculas as were not new potted in April or May; for which compost, and the method of shifting, see page 359, &c. You may at the same time take off any strong slips that have fibres attached to them, and plant them as there directed; this fresh earth will strengthen the plants greatly, and improve their flowers the following spring. All your auriculas will require, at this season, is to be kept where they can be free from the mid-day sun, and enjoy that of the morning till nine or ten o'clock, and that of the afternoon after four or five.

The choice polyanthuses, under similar circumstances, should be treated in every respect as recommended for the auriculas.

Transplant auricula and polyanthus seedlings, as directed on pages 359 and 360, observing to give them proper shade and occasional waterings, and also to close the earth well about their roots, otherwise the worms will draw them out of the ground.

REMOVING AND PLANTING BULBOUS ROOTS.

In the first week of this month, if not done in July, you should plant all the autumn flowering bulbs which you have yet out of ground; such as crocuses, colchicums, autumnal narcissuses, amaryllises, &c., and likewise any spring flowering bulbs that do not agree with being kept too long in a dry state; as fritillaries, crown imperials, snow-drops, spring crocuses, martagons, red and white lilies, bulbous irises, &c. Any of the latter kinds may now be taken up and immediately transplanted; but this should be done early in the month, before they begin to push out new fibres; after which they would be considerably weakened by a removal. You may also at this time take up, separate, and transplant the roots of pæonias, flag irises, and any other hardy kinds of fleshy or tuberous-rooted flowers, whose leaves are now decayed. When the roots are taken up the small offsets should be separated and planted in beds, to increase the kinds, and the large roots replanted in any beds or borders where wanted for flowering. Each respective kind is to be covered from two to four inches deep, generally in proportion to the size and strength of the roots.

TRANSPLANTING SEEDLING PERENNIALS AND BIENNIALS.

Transplant into nursery-beds the seedlings of the various kinds of perennial and biennial flowers that are now of a proper size, as directed on page 452; or such may now be planted finally where they are to flower next season. As the wall-flower and stock-gilly flower plants will, in the middle and eastern States, require some protection in winter, such should now be transplanted into pots, or into beds where frames may be placed over them, on the approach of severe frosts.

SOWING SEEDS OF BULBOUS-ROOTED FLOWERS.

The seeds of tulips, hyacinths, narcissuses, irises, crown imperials, fritillaries and lilies, or of and other kinds of bulbs, whose seeds are ripe, may now be sown, in order to obtain new varieties. These, if sown as soon after being ripe as they are sufficiently dry and hardened, will vegetate the ensuing spring; but if kept out of the ground till that period, very few of them will come up for a full year after. (For the method of sowing the seeds, &c., see the *Flower Garden* for next month.)

PROPAGATING FIBROUS-ROOTED PERENNIAL PLANTS.

Most of the early flowering fibrous-rooted plants, whose flower-stems have been cut down in June or July will, some time in this month, have thrown up new suckers from the roots; then such may be carefully taken off and planted in nursery beds; or the whole roots may, towards the end of the month, be taken up and divided into many separate parts, taking care to do it in such a manner as that every plant or part, so separated, may be furnished with roots. Trim or cut off from each slip, or part, any long or bruised roots; pick off all decayed or declining leaves, and plant the sets or divisions in a shady border, or where they can be conveniently covered with mats or other covering till newly rooted.

They should be watered immediately, and that repeated from time to time, till they are well taken with the ground, and in a free growing state.

Pinks, sweet-william, rose-campion, scarlet lychnis, gentianella, polyanthuses, primroses, double daisies, double chamomile, double perennial catchfly, double ragged-robin, perennial cyanus, monardas, penstemons, phloxes, violas, campanulas, dracocephalums, spiræa trifoliata, and various other kinds, may now be propagated in this way.

COLLECTING FLOWERING PLANTS FROM THE WOODS, FIELDS, AND SWAMPS.

Many beautiful ornamental plants may now be collected from the woods, fields, and swamps, which would grace and embellish the flower garden and pleasure grounds, if introduced thereinto: and that at a season when the general run of cultivated flowers are out of bloom: such as lobelias of various kinds, aletris farinosa, asclepiases in sorts, asters, cassia marilandica, chelones, cucubalus stellatus, cypripediums, dodecatheon meadia, dracocephalums, eupatoriums, euphorbias, and galega virginiana; gentianas, hardy herbaceous geraniums, gerardias, glycines, gnaphaliums, hedysarums, helianthuses and heucheras; hibiscuses, hypoxises, irises, liatrises, lysimachias, melanthiums, monardas, napæas, and ophryses; orchises, oxalises, podalyrias, penstemons, phloxes, polygala senega, rhexias, rudbeckias, sarrasenias and saxifragas; sylphiums, sisyrinchiums, solidagoes, spigelia marilandica, trilliums, veratrums, and veronicas; limadorum tuberosum, lilium superbum and canadense, erythronium americanum, together with an immense number of other delightful plants.

All the above, and any other kinds you meet with, that are worthy of notice, may be taken up, whether in or out of flower, with balls of earth, brought home, and planted immediately; on taking them up, cut off the flower-stems, if any, and when planted give water and shade for a few days to the fibrous-rooted kinds; next year they will flower luxuriantly, after which, each sort may be propagated in its proper season. Observe in planting, to give each respective kind a soil and situation as nearly similar as possible to that in which you found it in its wild state.

FLOWERING PLANTS IN POTS.

Such annual and other flowering plants as are in pots must now be carefully supplied with water, some kinds requiring it twice a day in very dry weather, others once a day, and a few sorts not so often. As to the consumption of water, there is an astonishing difference in the constitutions of plants, some absorbing and discharging it so quickly as to excite surprise, and others but very slowly; therefore you must supply each respective kind according to its habit and necessity.

ORDINARY ATTENDANCE.

Give water as often as necessary to all the young plantations of herbaceous flower-roots; cut down the stems of such as are past bloom; loosen the earth in the tops of all your pots containing flowering-plants; clip hedges, if omitted in the last month; clip box edgings, and trim the various other kinds used for that purpose into a neat and becoming form; but let this be done early in the month, and if possible in moist and cloudy weather. Mow grass-walks and lawns once a week or fortnight, according to the growth of the grass. Sweep, dress, and roll the gravel-walks once a week; hoe and clean the flower-borders, beds, alleys, and shrubbery compartments; and let the weeds be raked up and carried away immediately out of the garden, &c. Trim and tie up any loose growing or straggling plants; dress disorderly growing shrubs, and inoculate such kinds as you wish to propagate in that way.

Gather flower-seeds as they ripen and preserve them till the season of sowing; most kinds will keep better and longer in their pods or husks than when rubbed out.

THE GREEN-HOUSE.

SHIFTING AND GIVING FRESH EARTH TO THE PLANTS.

In the first week of this month, if not done before, you may shift into larger pots, &c. young oranges, lemons, citrons, and shaddocks, and also such other plants as are too much confined, and that have perfected their spring or summer shoots previous to their beginning to push their autumn growths; such is the critical period in which plants ought to have a summer shifting, and should be particularly noticed in any climate or country where such practice is necessary. Let this operation be performed as directed on page 375; after which treat the plants as recommended on page 478.

Loosen the earth in the tops of such pots or tubs as it appears hard or stiff in, and add some fresh compost thereto, if not done last month; this and the picking off of any decayed leaves, together with the trimming of disorderly branches, will give a fresh and pleasing appearance to the collection, add to the beauty, and promote the vigorous growth of the plants.

PROPAGATING THE PLANTS.

You may still continue to propagate various kinds of plants by cuttings, layers, and suckers, as directed in the former months.

BUDDING ORANGES AND LEMONS, ETC.

Any time this month you may successfully bud oranges, lemons, citrons, limes, and shaddocks; beginning in the first week thereof and continuing to the end; observing to work each tree as you perceive it to put forth its fresh autumn shoots; some trees, even of the same species, will produce those earlier or later in the month, and so soon as you perceive a few of them grown to two or three inches in length, seize upon that time to perform the operation, as then the sap being in a fresh state of circulation, the bark of the stock will separate freely for the reception of the bud, and the necessary nourishment will be copiously supplied.

Observe at this time to take the buds from shoots produced in the early part of the present season. The proper stocks are those raised from the kernels of either of the species. For the methods of budding, and general observations on that subject, see page 467, &c.

It will be very proper on budding those, or any other kinds of plants in pots, to place them in the shade for three or four weeks, after the operation is performed; or at least to turn the budded side of each plant to the north, in order to avoid the drying influence of the sun.

Cut off oranges, lemons, jasmins, and other exotics, which were inarched in April or May, provided that you find them sufficiently united. For the method of doing this, see the article *grafting by approach, or inarching,* on page 267.

WATERING.

Carefully attend to the watering of all the plants, giving it to each as often as necessary, and in proportion to its consumption, observing always to administer it sparingly to the succulent kinds.

The pouring of water, occasionally, through the rose of a watering-pot, over the branches of the shrubby kinds would greatly refresh them, and wash off the dust collected on the leaves, which would give them a clean and pleasing appearance; but this should be done late in the evening, when the sun has lost its power for the day.

Such pots as are plunged, must be turned full around in their seats at least once a week, to prevent the roots penetrating into the surrounding earth, through the holes in the bottoms of the pots.

THE HOT-HOUSE.

PINE-APPLES.

The care of the fruiting pines being the same in this month as in the last, is unnecessary to be repeated; as likewise the propagation of the plants by crowns and suckers, as well as the shifting of those succession pines which are expected to produce fruit next season.

Let this shifting, where neglected last month, be done, if possible, in the first or second week of this, that the plants may have time to establish strong roots, and to be advanced in free and vigorous growth before winter. (For the method of shifting, see page 483.)

Besides the watering of the pine plants in the common way, it will be of great service to them in very warm weather, to water the walks and flues of the hot-house occasionally; this should always be done late in the evening, and the glasses ought to be immediately closed. The great heat of the house will exhale the moisture, and raise a kind of artificial dew, which will soon stand in drops on the glasses; the leaves of the pine being succulent, they will imbibe the watery particles and be greatly benefited thereby.

RAISING THE PINE FROM SEED.

New varieties of the pine may be obtained from seeds, and when such is found in the fruit, which is very uncommon, even in the West Indies, they should be carefully preserved in dry sand till March when they will vegetate and succeed better than if sown at an earlier period.   The pots for this purpose should be then filled to within an inch of their rims, with light rich earth, and plunged into a warm part of the tan-bed for a day or two before sowing the seeds, which should be placed therein, about an inch apart, and covered not more than a quarter of an inch deep.   Cover the pots immediately with pieces of glass that will fit the tops very close; this, by preventing the mould from drying and giving an additional heat to it near the surface, will soon cause the seeds to vegetate.   After the plants appear sprinkle them over with water occasionally; as they advance in size give them increased portions of air and water, and by the time they have five or six leaves, they will be able to withstand the general air of the hot-house.

By the end of August these seedlings will be grown to a proper size for transplanting; when they should be put into small pots, filled with the same mould recommended for crowns and suckers on page 481; and from that time their treatment requires no difference from that of those.

SHIFTING THE VARIOUS EXOTICS, ETC.

The beginning of this month is a very proper season for the shifting of aloes, sedums, cactuses, mesembryanthemums, and all other succulent exotics ; they will now take fresh root sooner than at any other time of the year; you should at the same time take off any off-sets that may be produced, and plant them into small pots filled with fresh sandy earth, placing them where they may have only the morning sun for ten or twelve days, and observe to refresh them, now and then, with a little water.

The several kinds of tender exotics that require it, should now be shifted, in order to establish strong and fresh roots before winter ; observing to place them in the shade immediately after, till they shall have recovered the check occasioned by the removal.   This work should be performed early in the month; for if they are shifted too late in the season, they do not recover before the cold comes on, which checks their growth, prevents their free rooting, and consequently renders them not so well prepared to maintain themselves in winter, as if done at an early period; and many kinds that have stood too long in the same pots without shifting, will have their roots so matted, as to grow mouldy in winter and decay; which has often been destructive to many choice plants.

The other plants, which do not require shifting at this season, should have some of the earth taken out of the tops of the pots, if not done last month, and replaced with fresh compost; this will greatly encourage their autumn growth, and should not be neglected.

32

The regular watering of the plants must now be duly attended to, for one day's neglect, at this season, might destroy many of your most valuable plants. Keep all the collection free from decayed leaves, and such pots as are plunged in the earth must be turned quite round in their seats once a week, for the reasons mentioned in the preceding months.

Keep all the pots and tubs free from weeds, and continue to propagate the various kinds by suckers, layers, or cuttings.

LABELLING THE PLANTS.

In large collections all the plants should be labelled, having the *generic* and *specific* name of the plant on each label. These may be made of small slips of pine or cedar, each from six to ten inches long, near an inch broad at top, tapering to a point at the lower end, and about a quarter of an inch thick. When the sticks are ready, the parts to be written on should be rubbed lightly with white oil paint; then with a black lead pencil, *while yet wet*, write the generic and specific name of the plant thereon, which will soon dry and become completely permanent; the label is then to be stuck into the pot near the rim, and so deep as to leave the writing easy to be seen. These labels will continue good for three years, or longer.

SEPTEMBER.

WORK TO BE DONE IN THE KITCHEN GARDEN.

SOME persons who write on gardening, content themselves by simply saying that such a thing should be sown in such *a month;* this gives a latitude in the present, of thirty days, so that an inexperienced person may be led to think that he is within due bounds, if he sows on the 30th of September what ought to have been sown in the first week, perhaps about the first day thereof, whilst experienced gardeners well know that a difference of three or four days, particularly in this month, makes a greater odds, in crops, than most people could imagine would be consequent on the difference of as many weeks.

I am not an advocate for sowing seeds on a particular day of the week or month, nor in the full or wane of the moon, nor when the wind blows from the east, west, or any particular point of the compass; these ridiculous and superstitious notions have been long since deservedly banished out of the well-informed world; but in this month, above all others in the year, there is an absolute necessity of sowing certain crops within a *few* days of particular periods, in order to insure the best possible success, so that the plants may not become too strong before winter, and consequently be subject to start to seed early in spring, previously to their attaining due perfection, nor be too weakly to endure the severities of the ensuing winter.

SPINAGE.

Hoe and clean your advancing crops of spinage, and let the plants be thinned out to proper distances in order to afford sufficient room for the production of large succulent leaves.

In the first week of this month prepare some good dry ground for a full crop of spinage for winter and spring use. In the eastern States, particularly, this work should not be delayed later, nor, indeed, in the middle States, if it can be well avoided; but in a favorable season, and a warm soil and exposure, it may succeed very well in the middle States if sown so late as the fifteenth or even the twentieth of the month; the more to the southward, the later it may be sown.

The best sort to endure cold is the prickly seeded kind, which is what most people sow at this season, it being much hardier than the round seeded sort; of this there are two or three varieties, differing only in the size of their leaves; but the largest and most profitable sort is what gardeners call the burdock spinage. A thin sprinkling of the brown Dutch and hardy green cabbage lettuces may be sown among the spinage, and if the winter is any way favorable you may have some good plants from these to transplant early in spring for heading. A few of the early short-top salmon and white turnip rooted radishes may also be sown among the spinage for use in October and November. Sow the seed thinly in drills about twelve inches distant from one another, or broadcast, and tread it in, then rake the ground effectually so as to cover the seed well; or if it be cultivated on a large scale it may be harrowed in with a light harrow, wrong end foremost.

When the plants are up, and have got leaves an inch broad or a little better, they must be thinned, either by hand or hoe to three or four inches asunder, and the weeds effectually cleared away from among them; by this treatment the plants will get stalky, gather strength, and be the better able to stand the winter frosts.

LETTUCES.

The various kinds of lettuces sown last month should be planted out as early in this as they have attained to a proper size for that purpose; let them be set in beds of good, well prepared ground, about ten inches asunder, and watered immediately, which should be frequently repeated if the weather proves dry.

In the last week of the month prepare a dry, warm, well sheltered south border, on which to plant the lettuces sown in the latter part of August, for standing over winter for spring use. Take up the best plants from the seed-bed, pick off the decayed leaves, trim the ends of their roots, and plant them in rows six inches asunder every way;

if the plants survive the winter, every other one may be taken up in spring and planted in new beds, which will give the others abundance of room to grow to the best perfection. They are to be protected during winter as directed in *November*. Sow more lettuce seed in the first week of this month, to plant out in the beginning of October, for the same purpose. The kinds proper to be sown now are the brown Dutch and Hammersmith hardy green. Also, about the middle of the month, sow another crop of the same kinds, to be planted in frames in October, for their winter preservation.

To have lettuces in good perfection in November, December, and January, you should, about the latter end of this month, prepare one or more beds of rich earth, in a warm part of the garden, where the ground is dry, and lies well to the sun. Make the bed or beds the length and width of one or more cucumber frames; plant therein some good plants, and give them water occasionally till well rooted and growing freely.

Towards the middle of next month, when the nights begin to grow cold, place the frames and glasses on the beds; keep on the glasses every night; but let them be kept totally off in the day time till the November frosts commence; after which you must be governed by circumstances, always admitting as much air every day as the safety and free growth of the plants will warrant.

SOWING RADISH SEED.

In the first week of this month you should sow a good supply of the early short-top, white and red turnip-rooted and salmon radishes; also, a sufficient quantity of the black and white winter, or Spanish kinds; the latter, on the approach of frosts, must be taken up and preserved for winter use, as you do carrots or turnips.

ENDIVE.

As early in the month as possible, transplant a full crop of green curled endive for late autumn and winter use; let this be done as directed on page 460. Tie up the leaves of full grown endive for blanching, as advised on page 486.

CELERY AND CARDOONS.

Earth up celery as it advances in growth, but be careful to avoid covering the hearts of the plants; this work should always be done in a dry day; lay up the stalks neatly without injuring them, for if bruised they will become mouldy and be subject to rot.

If your crops of celery be scanty, and you have got strong plants, you may, about the first of this month, plant them out in trenches. Should the season prove very favorable, this crop may succeed tolerably well.

The cardoons will now be considerably advanced in growth, and consequently should be earthed up regularly for blanching; as these plants spread considerably, they must be tied up neatly with bass strings, or willow twigs, &c., but not too close, so that the hearts may freely advance in growth; then gather the earth up all around each plant, first breaking it fine, and as you lay it up, pat it with the back of the spade to make it keep its place and cast off the rain : as the plants progress in growth continue earthing them still higher till well whitened and fit for use; on the approach of frost they may be protected as directed in November for celery, if not made use of before that time.

WINTER CRESSES, CORN-SALAD, AND CHERVIL.

Sow corn-salad and winter cresses the beginning of this month, if not done in August, for winter and early spring use; let these be sown as directed on page 488. Likewise, sow a supply of chervil for soups and salads; this may be sown in drills nine or ten inches asunder and covered about a quarter of an inch deep, or broadcast and raked in.

SMALL SALADING.

Continue to sow once every ten days the different kinds of small salading as directed in the preceding months. The seeds may now be sown in an open situation where the earth is light and rich, but what you sow towards the end of the month should have a warm exposure.

HOE TURNIPS.

As your crop of turnips advances in growth, hoe and thin the plants to proper distances; let this be done in a dry day, cutting the weeds up clean with a sharp and middle sized hoe.

SOWING CABBAGE SEED.

The proper period for sowing cabbage seed in the middle States, to produce *early* summer cabbages, is between the sixth and tenth of this month, if intended to be transplanted into frames in October for winter protection, which is the most preferable method; but if they are designed for remaining in the seed-beds till spring, the period is between the fifteenth and twentieth. However, it will be very proper to make two or three sowings within that time, as it is impossible to say whether the fall may be favorable or otherwise, and therefore the better way is to be prepared in either case by successive crops.

The consequence of having plants too forward or early is, that they are very subject to run to seed in the spring soon after being planted out; and if the seeds are sown too late, the plants do not acquire sufficient strength before winter to withstand its rigor without extraordinary care. But in either case there is a remedy; that is, if the plants are likely to become too luxuriant and strong, transplant them once or twice in October, and if too backward and weakly, make a slight hot-bed towards the latter end of that month, and prick them out of the seed-bed thereon; this will forward them considerably.

At all events, I would advise, particularly in the middle States, the first sowing to be made about the tenth or before it, the second four days after, and the third on the eighteenth day of this month, or at any rate within two or three days of these periods; for the difference occasioned at this time by one or two days will in a few weeks be very perceivable and striking. In the eastern States, the first of the month will be a suitable period for sowing a principal crop.

The kinds proper to be sown now are the early Enfield, early York, and early Battersea.

Sow these seeds in beds of good garden mould, and either cover or rake them in so that they may be lodged about a quarter of an inch deep; if the weather should prove dry, water the beds occasionally in the evening till the plants are up, and in about five weeks they will be fit for transplanting into their winter quarters, as directed in *October*.

SOWING CAULIFLOWER SEED.

The critical period, in the middle States, for sowing cauliflower seed, is between the twentieth and twenty-eighth of this month; if sown earlier the plants would be very subject to button (as the gardeners term it) or flower in April or early in May, which flowers seldom exceed the size of a common button, and thereby the hopes and expectations of the cultivator are lost.

I would recommend to sow the seed at three different periods, say the twentieth, twenty-fourth and twenty-eighth of this month; for each sowing let a small spot of rich ground be neatly dug, mark out the bed three and a half feet wide, and immediately sow the seed and rake it in carefully; or you may first rake the bed smooth, and with the back of the rake push the loose mould evenly off the surface for near half an inch deep into the alleys, one half to each side, then sow the seed, and with a spade or shovel cast this shoved off loose earth over it about a quarter of an inch deep, or a little more, and finish by picking off the lumps or small stones with your hand, or drawing them off neatly and lightly with the rake; or you may sow the seed on the smooth raked surface, and sift over it about a quarter of an inch of light earth.

Should the weather prove dry, water the bed both before and after the plants are up, and in a month after sowing they must be transplanted into beds of good·rich earth, covered with garden frames, at the distance of three inches from one another, there to remain during winter, and to be taken care of as directed in the following months.

In the southern States, the most forward of these may be finally planted out in November, as directed on page 329, and covered with bell or hand-glasses during winter; but in the middle or eastern States this practice will not succeed on account of the severity of the weather at that season.

If the plants should happen to be late and of a weakly growth, when you are planting them into frames in the latter end of October, let a trench be dug about ten inches deep in a dry, warm, and well sheltered situation, the breadth of a frame and the length of one, two, or more, according to the quantity of plants; then fill it in with new horse-dung to the height of eighteen inches from the bottom, and set on the frame; earth the bed over five or six inches deep with rich earth, and set the plants in rows three inches apart every way, immediately give them a moderate watering and place on the glasses; observing to leave them open about four or five inches at top that the steam may pass away.

It will also be proper to lay a mat over the glasses in sunny weather till the plants have taken fresh root; after which the lights must be totally taken off by day till the weather becomes too severe, and every advantage must subsequently be taken to give the plants as much air as possible, consistent with their preservation.

The plants, with the assistance of this slight bottom heat, will soon take root and be greatly forwarded thereby, so as to acquire a due degree of strength before the setting in of very severe weather.

Note.—Late sown cabbage plants would be greatly benefited by treating them as directed above for cauliflowers.

LATE CAULIFLOWERS AND BROCCOLI.

If the weather should prove dry, give occasional waterings to the crops of late cauliflowers and broccoli which you expect to flower in October, &c., otherwise the heads will be small, especially if the ground is naturally dry.

SOWING WELSH ONION SEED.

Sow some Welsh onion seed for early spring salad, &c. This kind never bulbs and is very hardy; for a though the tops will sometimes die down in winter, yet the roots will continue sound, and push up new leaves on the eve of the first spring vegetation.

It will be necessary to sow this seed in the first week of the month on beds of light rich ground, in a warm exposure, and afterwards to keep the rising plants perfectly free from weeds.

MUSHROOMS.

This is a proper time to prepare for making beds, in which to cultivate the *Agaricus campestris*, Champignon, or common mushroom. Of two hundred and thirteen species of agaricus, enumerated by Dr. Withering, this is the only one selected for cultivating in gardens. The *gills* of this are loose, of a pinky red, changing to liver color, in contact but not united with the stem; very thick set, some forked next the stem, some next the edge of the cap, some at both ends; and generally in that case excluding the intermediate smaller gills. *Cap*, white, changing to brown when old, and becoming scurfy, fleshy, and regularly convex, but with age flat, and liquefying in decay;

flesh white; diameter commonly from one inch to three or sometimes four or more. *Stem* solid, one to three inches high, and about half an inch in diameter.

I consider the description of this species the more necessary, as many of the others are poisonous. This is the most savory of the genus, and is eaten fresh, either stewed or boiled; and preserved either as a pickle or in powder. The sauce commonly called *catchup* is made from its juice with salt and spices. Dr. Withering asserts that those gathered from fresh undunged pastures are more delicate than those which are raised in artificial beds. Mr. Miller is of a different opinion, probably because the cultivated ones are more sightly, and may be collected more easily in a proper state for eating.

It will be necessary in the early part of this month to provide a quantity of fresh horse-dung, and to throw it up in a heap, out of the reach of rain, to ferment; when it has lain two or three weeks, turn it again, that all the parts may be equally dried and fermented, and the violent heat passed away. In this state it should remain till about the first week of October, when the bed is to be made as directed in that month, or the preparation may commence in August, and the beds be made any time this month at pleasure.

The reason for the previous preparation of the dung is to prevent a too violent fermentation when the bed is made, which would totally destroy the spawn; and, moreover, by this management it will preserve a slow temperate warmth much longer than if put together when quite fresh.

You must likewise provide a sufficiency of good mushroom spawn; this is frequently to be found in rich pasture fields, old mushroom beds, old cucumber beds, dung-hills or dungy composts; but that of the true kind from the pastures or old mushroom beds is to be preferred; it may also be found where horses are employed under sheds in turning mills, riding-houses, livery-stable yards, &c.

The spawn is a white fibrous substance, running and spreading itself in the rich pasture grounds and in lumps of dryish rotten dung, and if of the true sort, has the exact smell of the cultivated kind.[*]

Take up the earth or dung in which you find it in lumps, observing to preserve these entire, and lay them in a dry shady place till wanted; you may cover them with straw or garden mats, for much wet would totally destroy the spawn. But if the pieces are wet or very damp when collected, they must be spread to dry gradually; the spawn is seldom, if ever, destroyed by drought, especially when mixed with earth or dung. For the method of making and spawning the bed, &c., see the *Kitchen Garden* for *October*.

---

[*] This spawn may be made artificially. Mix together equal portions of horse and cow droppings, and turfy sods; work all into a stiff mortar by the addition of a little water. Form into the shape and size of common bricks, dry in an open shed, then make a hole in each, on the side, one inch cubic; place in this a small piece of good spawn, and plaster up with a little cow-dung; build the whole in a heap, and cover with a layer of fresh litter from the stable; in three or four weeks it will be fit for use, and will keep several years.

GATHER SEEDS.

Gather all kinds of seeds as they r pen, which may be necessary in the ensuing season, and spread them to dry on mats or cloths ; when sufficiently hardened, beat them out clean, and put them up carefully till wanted for sowing.

PERENNIAL HERBS.

Towards the latter end of this month you may safely transplant all kinds of hardy perennial pot, aromatic and medicinal herbs, which will take fresh root, and be well established before winter ; but this should be done, if possible, in moist weather.

SOUTHERN STATES.

In the southern States, particularly where the winters are mild, you may sow at this time, carrots and onions for early spring use, as well as all the other articles recommended to be sown in this month; and also plant out late crops of borecole, broccoli, celery, cabbages for winter, coleworts, endive, &c. &c

THE FRUIT GARDEN.

FRUIT-TREES.

Examine your wall and espalier trees, and where you find any long loose branches, train them in and make them firm in their proper places.

The early kinds of fruit-trees against the walls of your forcing-houses should, towards the end of this month, be pruned and trained close to the wall or trellis, that the r buds may be preparing before the season for applying artificial heat.

GATHERING RIPE FRUIT.

Gather apples and pears as they r pen, and treat them as directed under the head *Orchard*, for next month.

PREPARE FOR PLANTING.

Begin towards the end of this month to prepare the borders, &c., in which you intend to plant fruit-trees, in October or November ; it is of consequence to add a good supply of thoroughly rotten dung, and to trench the ground to the depth of eighteen inches or two feet, provided that the natural good soil admits thereof.

STRAWBERRIES.

Of the *Fragaria vesca*, or esculent strawberry, there are five *principal* varieties cultivated in gardens for their very delicious fruit. 1. *F. virginiana*, or scarlet strawberry. 2. *F. vesca pratensis*, of *Aiton*, or hautboy strawberry. 3. *F. Chiloensis*, or Chili strawberry. 4. *F. Alpina*, Alpine or monthly strawberry, and, 5, *F. Ananas*, or pine-apple strawberry. There are besides these, the varieties *sylvestris*, or common wood strawberry, and *caroliniana*, or Carolina strawberry, with many others arising from these, differing principally in the color of their fruit.

The first, or scarlet strawberry, has dark green leaves, and is of a more even surface than the others; the flowering stems are shorter, and the fruit is frequently concealed among the leaves. It is the earliest in ripening its fruit, for which reason it merits esteem, had it nothing else to recommend it; but the fruit is so good as to be generally preferred to most others.

The second, or hautboy strawberry, has larger and thicker leaves than the scarlet, oval-lanceolate, and rough; the fruit is of a pale red, much larger than the scarlet, and of a musky flavor, of which there are several varieties, differing in shape and color, but that called the globe hautboy is the best and most approved fruit.

The third, or Chili strawberry, has oval hairy leaves, of a much thicker substance than any sort yet known, and stands upon very strong hairy footstalks; the runners from the plants are very large, hairy, and extend to a great length, putting out plants at several distances. The peduncles are very strong; the leaves of the calyx are long and hairy. The flowers are large and are often deformed, and when cultivated in strong loamy land, the plants produce plenty of large, firm, well-flavored fruit; in a light soil this kind is not generally very productive.

The fourth, or Alpine strawberry, has small oval leaves, small flowers, and middle-sized, oblong, pointed fruit; the plants and fruit are considerably larger than the wood strawberry, and are particularly valuable for their continuing to bear fruit successively from June till the autumn frosts put a stop to them, but with the help of hot-beds, &c., they may be kept in a bearing state the whole year round. The reason of its long continuance in fruit is, that the runners which it throws out during the summer, shoot up into flowers and fruit the same year. Of this there are four varieties, the scarlet fruited, red fruited, white fruited, and scarlet blossomed. This is said to be a native of the Alps, in Europe.

The fifth, or pine-apple strawberry, has leaves which much resemble those of the scarlet strawberry, but are larger, of a thicker substance, and the indentures of their edges are blunter; the runners are much larger and hairy; the peduncles are stronger, the flowers much larger, and the fruit approaches in size, shape, and color, to the Chili strawberry. As this produces a great quantity of fruit, when the plants are kept clear from runners (and the fruit is very large) it is well worthy of cultivation. The fruit of this variety has somewhat of the smell and taste of the pine-apple, from whence it takes its name.*

In the cultivation of strawberries, much depends upon the choice of plants; for if they are promiscuously taken from the beds without care, a great number of them will become barren; these are by the gardeners termed blind, which is when there are plenty of flowers but no fruit produced; if these flowers are well examined they will be found to want the female organs of generation, most of them abounding with stamina, but there are few, if any, styles; so that it frequently happens among these barren plants that some of them have a part of an imperfect fruit formed which will sometimes ripen. The hautboy strawberry is more subject to this than any of the other kinds. The plants of either sort should never be taken from old neglected beds where the stools had been suffered to spread or run into a confused multitude of vines, nor from any plants which are not *very fruitful*, and those offsets which stand nearest to the old plants should always be preferred.

Strawberries in general, love a strong loamy ground, in which they will thrive and bear fruit more abundantly than in a light soil. The ground should be somewhat moist, for if it is very dry, all the watering which is given to the plants in warm dry seasons, will not be sufficient to procure abundant crops; nor should the ground be made *overly rich* with *dung*, for that would cause the plants to run into suckers, grow too luxuriant, and render them less fruitful.

Any time this month that the weather proves moist, you should take advantage of it for making your general plantations of strawberries, but if dry and hot, it will be better to defer that work to the last week thereof, or first in October, not later if possible, as the plants will be greatly benefited by having time to form good roots before winter. But should the weather then prove unfavorable you should proceed to planting, after which, plentiful and frequent waterings must be given till the plants are well rooted.

The sets proper for planting at this time, are those produced in the present year from the young runners, selecting them as before noticed, or such as were taken off in June and transplanted into nursery beds. When taken up, the roots should be trimmed, the decayed leaves picked off, and also any small vines or runners issuing from the plants.

The ground should be well dug and, if necessary, previously manured with a sufficiency of old well rotted dung, then laid out into four feet wide beds with alleys between, of eighteen or twenty inches, for the convenience, of going in occasionally to weed and water the plants and to gather the fruit. Each bed is to contain four rows of plants, the large kinds eighteen inches distant in the rows, and the small sorts fifteen. Close the earth well about the roots of each plant,

* This division applies to the more primitive state of the strawberry; we have now got them so mixed up by cross-breeding, that we recognize them as Pistillate and Staminate, or Hermaphrodite varieties. The Pine or aromatic, and the Hautboys, are somewhat distinct classes, notwithstanding there are many kinds of them, and also that they have partaken of the general mixing up.

and when finished, water the whole plentifully should the weather happen to be dry at the time.

The old strawberry beds will require to be kept clear from large overgrown weeds, and in October are to have their autumn dressing as there directed.

N. B. If you intend to force strawberries in the winter or early spring months, this is the time to pot them for that purpose. The alpine and scarlet kinds are the best for forcing; they should be strong plants of two years old, and in a proper state for full bearing. Provide as many pots of about seven inches diameter at top, and made in proportion, as you think may be sufficient, and at the same time get some good loamy earth, made fine with a spade, place a few inches thereof into the bottom of each pot, previously laying a shell over each hole as directed on former occasions, then take up each plant with a ball of earth to its roots, pare the ball neatly round with the knife, clear the plant from decayed leaves and runners, place it in the pot and fill up the spaces around the sides and over the surface of the ball with fine earth. Water the whole when potted, and remove them to the shade for eight or ten days till newly rooted; then you may plunge them to their rims in any open part of the garden, there to remain, watering them occasionally till the approach of winter, when the pots are to be placed under the protection of frames and glasses till taken into the forcing departments.

This practice is absolutely necessary, in the middle and eastern States, as during winter the earth is so hard frozen as to render it impracticable to take up the plants out of the open ground, when wanted, without injury; moreover, when they are potted at this season, their roots will be well established before the time of forcing commences, and consequently the plants will be much more productive of fruit.

THE ORCHARD.

COLLECTING RIPE FRUIT.

Apples and pears that attain now to full maturity, rarely keep as well as those which ripen in the ensuing month; but when it is desirable to preserve them as long as possible, they must be treated as directed in *October*.

When planting of fruit-trees is intended in the months of October or November, opportunity ought to be taken of any leisure time that may now occur for the preparation of the ground, as directed in March, under the head Orchard.

THE VINEYARD.

PROTECTING THE FRUIT.

Your early varieties of grapes will now be ripening very fast, and will sometimes be subject to the annoyance of birds, which are more apt to attack the fruit a little before sun rising and about the time of its setting, than in any other part of the day; it will be, therefore, prudent to have boys with rattles to frighten them away, particularly about those hours.

You should also destroy poke, wild cherries, and any other uncultivated productions growing near the vineyard, the fruit of which might invite a resort of birds. Should you observe an extraordinary resort of wasps in any quarter, and that they are destructive to the fruit, hang up phials of honeyed or sugared water in such places, in which numbers of them will be caught and destroyed.

The ground between your vines must now be kept perfectly free from weeds, and all the branches tied up neatly, in order to afford the fruit the full advantage of air and sun for its due perfection.

THE METHOD OF MAKING WHITE WINES.

In the middle States, the general vintage will happen some time in this month, earlier or later, according to the season; it will, therefore, be necessary to be provided with a sufficient number of clean, sweet casks, new, if for white wines, to prevent their coloring the liquor; but red wines may be put into any cask, without injury, provided they are sweet and clean. You must also be provided with a vat for mashing the fruit in, and with a suitable contrivance for pressing out the juice.

Let it be observed that white wines are made from black as well as from white grapes; that the former generally makes the strongest and best wines, and that it is from the skin of the *black* grapes, *when fermented with the juice and pulp*, that the red tinge is obtained.

When you perceive the grapes to be fit for gathering, which you may judge of by the eye and taste, for when perfectly fit for eating they are then in the best condition for making wine; make choice of cloudy weather, if such should occur, and early in the morning, or very late in the afternoon, being provided with a sufficient number of careful people, each furnished with a basket to hold the fruit, and a crooked pointed knife or a pair of strong scissors to cut off the bunches, let them begin their work, collecting only such bunches as are open, ripe, and perfectly sound, passing over all that are green, not matured, dry, rotten, or bursted. The stalk of every bunch should be cut off close to the fruit, and the bunches laid gently into the basket without bruising or pressing them together.

The grapes which are not sufficiently ripe must be gathered at another time, and treated in like manner.

As the grapes are collected, they must be immediately carried to the press or vat, for the sooner they are pressed after gathering the finer and whiter the wine will be, and not only that, but it will be more mellow, have a more exquisite flavor, and be greater in quantity.

As your vat is filling, the grapes are to be trampled and mashed effectually by men, having their legs and feet previously washed very clean; then let your machine for pressing fall down thereon, which will force out the liquor plentifully, having a cask conveniently placed to receive it.

When the liquor ceases to run from the press, raise it and cut up the cake to pieces with steel shovels, and press it again, together with all the loose grapes that happen to be scattered, and you will have another plentiful running of good liquor.

This is called wine of the first cutting, which will be of a fine color and flavor, little inferior to the other, having a stronger body, and will keep longer than that of the first pressing.

The cutting and pressing is to be repeated as often as you find the liquor to run, and that from the second and third cutting will be still good, of a sufficient body to keep for a length of time, and with age will acquire mellowness and an improved flavor.

The liquor which first runs from the grapes without any other violence than the weight of the press, is called *le vin de gout*, and is fine, thin, and lively; of a pleasant flavor and relish, appears sparkling in the glass, but has not body enough to keep a long time without being mixed; but when incorporated with that obtained from the first, second, and third cuttings, it makes then what is called the best *champaign*.

The different pressings being mixed as you think proper, should be immediately put into clean casks or hogsheads, placed in a warm room or dry cellar, and filled to within two inches of the bungholes, which should be covered with pieces of cloth, laid loosely on to prevent dirt from falling into the liquor.

It is to be observed that the finest wines ferment the soonest, the rest in proportion to their goodness. The first cask that ferments, take some of the froth which works therefrom, and put a little of it into those casks which are backward in fermenting, which will greatly help their working.

The fermentation may continue for eight, ten, or twelve days, or some time longer, according to the season or quality of the *must*, but at whatever time you perceive it to cease, which you will see by the froth not rising as before, fill your casks within about an inch or two of the top and bung them up tight, at the same time making small vent-holes to carry off what may be thrown up by the fermentations not being quite ceased.

Continue to fill up your casks every three or four days, as before, until the fermentation completely ceases, lest the foulness which should work through the vent-holes sink down for want of passage, and foul the wines. When all appearance of fermentation is over, fill the casks and stop the vent-holes; however, open the latter occasionally whilst there is any chance of the liquor continuing to work. Observation and discretion will best guide on these occasions.

About the middle of December, or so soon as the wines have settled and become clear, draw them off into new well-bound casks, previously well impregnated with salt and water, to extract the injurious bitterness of the wood; after which, rinse the casks with fair water, and an infusion of peach leaves or flowers, fill them quite full and bung them as tight as possible. Repeat this racking off in February, and likewise in the latter end of March; after which it may remain so till bottled, disposed of, or used.

You must be particularly careful in racking off the wine to draw it as clear as possible from the lees, which will render it brisk, lively, and sparkling in the glass; while the contrary produces a muddy dreg, or sediment, which makes the wine thick, dull, and sometimes ropy; and besides, when drawn off foul, principles capable of maintaining fermentation would be introduced into the hogshead, which would be productive of the decomposition of the saccharine part, and consequently, deprive the wine of its sweetness.

The lees after the wine is racked off, may be distilled for brandy, and also the cakes of pulp and skins, after being pressed and then properly fermented.

THE METHOD OF MAKING RED WINES.

Red wines must always be made from black grapes, for besides the main pulp or core, which is white in these as well as the others, there sticks to the inside of the skin a considerable body of rich pulp of a deep red, more so in some kinds than others; this gives the color to the wine when extracted by a due process of fermentation. The color of red wine is said to be heightened by gathering the grapes in the heat of the day, but this is productive of a considerable deficiency in the quantity, though the quality may be improved thereby.

Taking these considerations into view, your grapes are to be collected with the same care as before directed in the making of white wines. Having a sufficient quantity gathered, put them into the vat, by degrees treading and mashing them effectually as you fill it, till quite full, and the liquor floating above them; then work the pulp and the liquor effectually together, leaving all the parts as loose as possible, and so let it remain to ferment.

You ought to be provided with a cover for the top of the vat, perforated with holes, and made so as to easily slip down into it and sink a little under the superficies of the liquor, to keep the skins and pulpy parts from coming into contact with the air during the process of fermentation; for when this is exposed, and it tends to swim on the top, it very shortly becomes *acid*, and communicating this to the liquor, greatly injures it. As the skins give the color to the wine, nothing is better than the keeping of them down, without pressing, during this process, for to believe that these and other dregs floating on the top impede the evaporation of the spirit, is a thing improbable, since it requires a good cork to stop it.

The moment of drawing off the wine is of great importance, but

generally, however, without rule. It would be impossible to pre-
scribe a certain number of days for an operation liable to so many
vicissitudes, as much through the qualities of the grapes as other
circumstances. But as the great object of fermentation is the con-
version of the *must* or expressed juice into wine, no drawing should
take place until that is effected. This moment, which might appear uncertain, may be ascertained with tolerable precision by means
of a tin tube open at one end and perforated all over with holes of a
small size, that the grains or stones of the fruit may not pass through
when dipped into the vat; inside of this a small wooden cylinder
must be placed, upheld at its bottom by a cork plate that can work
up and down freely in the tube: this instrument is to be plunged
into the vat and kept there, the liquor getting in through the holes
of the tube, will raise the cork to the surface, to which cork the
wooden pin or cylinder is affixed. This latter must be marked in
different heights, which will be seen to rise as the vinous fermentation increases.

With this instrument, the precise moment in which the wine is to
be drawn off, may be established with great exactness; this is generally done when the cylinder has attained to the highest and become
stationary, the fermenting mass always swelling in bulk till the vinous fermentation is completely accomplished, becoming then stationary previous to the commencement of an acetous fermentation, and
sinking with that, which if suffered without drawing off the liquor,
would ruin all. Berthollet and other authors recommend not to
draw off the wine till you are able to perceive the cylinder begin to
lower a little.

When the liquor is drawn off into clean sweet casks, place them in
the cellar, fill them up within an inch or two of the top, and lay a
piece of leather with a small weight on it over each bung-hole that
may yield to a second fermentation, which generaly takes place.
When the wine has settled or ceased to ferment, bung the casks as
close as possible, and the subsequent treatment is exactly the same
as directed for white wines.

In the making of red wines it is customary to mix with the fruit a
small portion of what is called the claret grape, to heighten the color,
as the entire juice of this variety is of a deep red.

It is also customary, and even necessary, with wine of a weak body,
made from newly established vineyards, or from worn-out old ones,
to add two or three gallons of very nice brandy, and five or six of old
strong wine of the same color, and as near the intended flavor as
possible, to every hogshead of sixty or sixty-three gallons of the new
wine; this is usually done after the fermentation is over.

In Spain and other parts of Europe, if the season proves wet, or
if they think the *must* or expressed juice too replete with watery particles, they boil the whole or part thereof, to evaporate the superabundance; but this is done immediately after the juice is expressed
before the least fermentation takes place.

The evaporation ought not to be by an intense ebullition, and
although the fire may be ardent, the ebullition may be prevented by

pouring some cold *must* into the kettle every time you perceive it ready to boil.

The acid contained in the *must* being capable of dissolving copper and converting it into verdigris, you must, therefore, be careful not to boil it in any kettle but such as is perfectly well tinned; and some people, after cleaning the inside effectually, rub it all over with a woollen rag dipped in sweet oil ; if these precautions are neglected the dissolution of the copper will give a disagreeable brass taste to the wine, and perhaps render it pernicious to the health of those who drink it.

The kettle should be large, wide in the mouth and flat in the bottom, which will produce a saving in the consumption of fuel and expedite the process.

The whole of the *must* may be boiled, or if only a part thereof be so reduced, this should be mixed with the remainder, and if intended for white wine, put into casks to undergo the process of vinous fermentation as before noticed. But if designed for red wine it must be poured into the vat, when of a temperate degree of heat, on the pulp and skins, there to undergo with them the necessary degree of fermentation to extract the color and to form the wine ; after which it is to be treated as before directed, observing to take similar pains in pressing the juice out of the pulp when sufficiently fermented, as recommended under the article *White Wines*, but this will not be so difficult.

GENERAL REMARKS.

Ideal, as well as intrinsic qualities, cause one kind of wine to be preferred to another, so that one nation or country admires what another does not like, or perhaps despises; and even this ideal fancy is not uncommon among individuals of the same country, town, or place ; consequently, it will be well to know how to vary the properties of wine according to fancy.

If a taste of wine slightly acid, similar to that of the Rhenish, is desired, some tartareous acid may be added to the *must*.

If the wine is required sweet, the *must* should be drained in such a manner that it may retain as little as possible of the lees, and let it afterwards ferment of itself. Some sugared matter might be joined with it.

If the wine should be wanted delicate and of a light color, the *must* should not be suffered to have a long action on the lees, from which it takes principles that augment the fermentation, and dissolve in consequence the mucilaginous parts, together with the coloring matter.

Should a strong wine of good body be preferred, the *must* ought to be suffered to remain the longer on the dregs, in case the grapes do not afford it of sufficient strength. Or the boiling of the *must*, in the manner before observed, will accomplish this.

If besides it be desired to have a heady or intoxicating wine, add some tartar and sugared matter to the *must*, which will produce a greater portion of spirit.

33

If the wine be required to have a great deal of body, add, after the ceasing of the fermentation, fresh sugared matter, such as strong *must* deprived of its tartar.

It has been suggested to me, that exposing the casks of weak wine to the winter frost till the watery particles contained in the liquor are converted into ice, and then drawing off the pure wine, would be the best method of giving it a sufficient body. If this answers the end, and it is very probable it may, as pure wine requires a much greater degree of cold to freeze it than water, the middle and eastern States of the Union possess an advantage in that respect over most of the wine countries of Europe, as the cold of their winters is not sufficiently intense to answer that end.

Should the wine be required with much, little, or no color, let it be remembered that this quality resides exclusively in the skin of the fruit, so that you may conduct the process according to your desire.

Different flavors and fragrancies are communicated by the different kinds of grapes, and also from other ingredients : the odor of Muscatel, for example, is given with the flowers of elder and other herbs ; some use peach flowers, and consider them to communicate an agreeable flavor to wine.

The absolute and essential qualities in wine are to have no defect, nor be liable easily to contract any, to be able to keep long, and bear transportation.

An essential article in the preservation of wine is to keep the air totally excluded out of the vessels, for which purpose Davanzati advises to "take off the rind of a piece of dried bacon, and leave a little fat adhering to it in the centre ; after that make use of it in the manner of a bung, and cram it in with might, that the cask may be well stopped up ; extend out the rind afterwards over the cask after having done it over with ashes ; then cover it over again with very dry ashes ; and that they may not fall off, nail a piece of stuff over the same. The cask being then sufficiently shut up, the air will not penetrate into it, and the wine cannot change its nature."

I mention this to show the necessity of the casks being kept airtight and bunged effectually, not doubting but many other methods may be used equally effectual, perhaps much more so than that recommended by Davanzati.

A wine cellar should be dry, and so deep under ground that the temperature of its heat may be nearly the same winter and summer : it should be at a distance from streets, highways, workshops, sewers, and necessaries ; if arched over the better.

Of all other methods wine is best preserved in bottles, well corked and sealed ; but this should not be done till it is clear and fine, and all fermentation subsided.

Tartar and the lees of wine are the principles of its destruction, and none but sweet wines can bear the existence of them ; by often drawing it off in order to purge it of these, there is too great a superfices exposed to the action of the air, which greatly injures the wine.

To obviate this evil, the people of Champagne and other wine

countries make use of the following expedient, viz : To a leather
pipe from four to six feet in length and two inches in diameter are
adapted, at each end, wooden pipes nine or ten inches in length,
which decrease in diameter towards the ends, and are fastened to the
leather pipes by means of a piece of twine. The bung of the cask
intended to be filled is taken out and one of the pipes put into it.
A good cock is fixed in the cask to be emptied, two or three inches
from the bottom, and in this is inserted the extremity of the other
pipe. A pair of bellows of two feet long, including the handles, and
ten inches in diameter, with a wooden pipe, to the extremity of which
is fixed a small leather valve to prevent the air from rushing out when
the bellows are opened, is introduced through a hole made in the bung
and fitted *exactly* thereto. When the bellows are worked, the pressure exercised on the wine obliges it to issue from the cask and to
ascend and pass through the leather pipe into the other cask. When
the pipe is once filled, the wine will pass through without the application of any further force till each cask is half full; but then by
working the bellows the artificial pressure of the air on the surface
of the wine will oblige the remainder to pass off, without any agita-
tion or shaking. When a hissing is heard at the cock, it is a sign
that all the wine has passed. This operation may be performed in
another manner, without the assistance of a cock, by making one of
the wooden pipes so long as to reach within five or six inches of the
bottom, and introducing it through the bung, together with the pipe
of the bellows, which when worked, will force up the liquor as before.

CLARIFICATION OF WINES.

When wines have been racked off three or four times, in the preceding manner, they may be fined or clarified as follows : For white
wines, mix a quart of new milk and about an ounce of salt with two
or three quarts of wine and pour it into the cask; then with a strong
lath or flat stick, stir the wine in the cask *very well*, observing not
to put the stick to the bottom, lest you disturb the lees or sediment.
This will be sufficient for sixty-three gallons.

Some for this purpose use a solution of isinglass, about the quantity
of an ounce to every fifty gallons of wine; but Chaptal observes,
" the use of this substance is dreaded in warm climates, and its place
is supplied by whites of eggs : ten or twelve are sufficient for half a
muid, or seventy two gallons English. They should be well beaten
up, and mixed with a pint of new milk."

For a hogshead of red wine, beat up effectually the whites of ten
or twelve *fresh* eggs, and incorporate this well with three or four
quarts of wine, which pour into the cask, stirring it as above directed. In five or six days after, the wines will be fit to draw off
for bottling, &c.

METHODS OF CURING RAISINS.

R. Twiss, Esq., says, in his *Travels through Portugal and Spain*,
page 334, " Raisins are of two sorts; those which are called sun-

raisins are made thus : when the grapes are almost ripe, the stalk is half cut through, so that the sap may not penetrate farther, but yet the bunch of grapes may remain suspended by the stalk ; the sun, by darting on them, candies them, and when they are dry they are packed up in boxes.

"The second sort is made after this manner : when the vines are produced, the tendrils or claspers are preserved till the time of vintage, a great fire is made, when the tendrils are burned, and in the ley made of their ashes the newly gathered grapes are dipped, after which they are exposed to the sun to dry, which renders them fit for use."

Mr. Swinburn, in his *Travels through Spain*, informs us that "the raisins dried on the coast of *Valencia* are dipped in a ley of *wine* and ashes."

PRESERVING GRAPES FRESH FOR WINTER USE.

Grapes may be kept fresh a long time by the following method : before the autumn frosts have killed the leaves, let the bunch, with the shoot, be carefully cut off the vine ; then let the lower end of the shoot be put into a bottle filled with water ; which hang up with the shoot and branch in a warm room, or in a green-house.

The bottle should be filled with fresh, clear water every ten or twelve days, and at the same time a thin paring should be cut off the bottom of the shoot, whereby the pores will be made to imbibe the water with greater facility.

By this method, grapes may be kept fresh and good till the middle of February.

Or, let the grapes hang on the vines as long as they will continue on with safety ; the late ripening kinds will be best for this purpose, provided they are of good flavor and have attained full maturity. When the frosts begin to set in sharp then gather them. Where there are several bunches on one branch, cut it off, leaving about six inches in length, or more, of the wood, according to the distance between the bunches, and a little on the outside of the fruit at each end ; seal both ends of the branch with some common sealing wax, or with such as wine merchants use for sealing their bottles with ; then hang them across a line in a dry room, which is to be kept perfectly free from frost, taking care to clip out with a pair of scissors any of the berries that begin to decay or become mouldy, which if left would taint the others. In this way grapes may be kept fresh a long time ; if they are cut before the bunches are very ripe, they will keep longer, but their flavor will not be so fine.

Having plenty of fresh grapes in winter makes a great addition to the table, and if properly kept they will be of a much superior flavor to the imported grapes.

Grapes may also be kept in jars ; every bunch, when well aired and perfectly dry, should be wrapped up loosely in soft, white paper, laid in layers, and each layer covered with bran, which should be perfectly well dried before it is used ; first lay a little of the dry bran in the bottom of the jar, then a layer of the wrapped up grapes, and so on, a layer of bran and a layer of grapes alternately, till you have filled the jar; then shake it gently and fill it to the top with bran; cover the top with paper, and over this a piece of bladder doubled, which tie firmly around to exclude the air; then put on the top or cover of the jar, observing that it fits as close as possible. These jars should be kept in a room where they will not be exposed to damps, frosts, or too much heat.

In order to preserve a few of your finest bunches for this purpose, from the depredations of birds and insects, let some small bags made of thin gauze or crape be drawn over them, or rather let the bunches be put into the bags; the sun and air will have free access through the crape, and when wet it will dry very soon.

VINERIES.

Much attention is now paid to vineries for forcing grapes, and, as an example of the combination of the ornamental vinery and green-houses combined, Figs. 55 and 56 are given.

It exhibits a perspective view and ground-plan of one erected on Staten Island, New York, from designs by William Charlton. It was required to have an early and a late grapery, a large general conservatory, and a suitable apartment for camellias, and other beautiful, polished-leaved green-house plants which are subject to be scorched by the rays of the mid-day sun. The most available spot was on a level spot, so situated that the longitudinal extension of the structure should be east-southeast, and west-northwest. It was also desirable that no parts should appear as "sheds" or other nuisance; consequently, the ordinary conveniences are provided for by a cellar, forty feet long by nine feet wide, being sunk under the northwest part of the building, and which contains the two boilers and sufficient room for the winter's fuel. There are two cisterns, each fourteen feet wide by fourteen feet deep, under ground, and beneath the stage of the central house. Each house is furnished with a tank for tepid water, having a hose-coupling attached, with faucets so arranged, that one force-pump placed under the stage answers all the purposes of drawing water from the cisterns into the tanks, or from any one of the tanks to shower over the whole or any part of the interior, at pleasure. The centre house is twenty-one feet wide by forty-six feet long, and seventeen feet from the ground-level to the ridge. The two wings are fifty feet long by twenty feet wide, and fourteen feet to the ridges, which are on a level with the eaves where they join. This is a good example to imitate.

Figs. 55, 56.

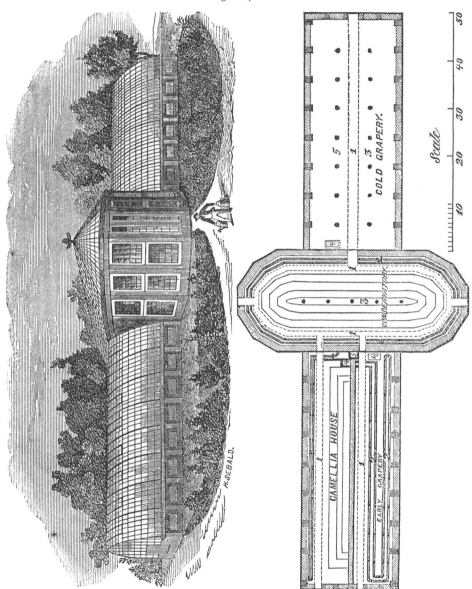

Fig. 57.

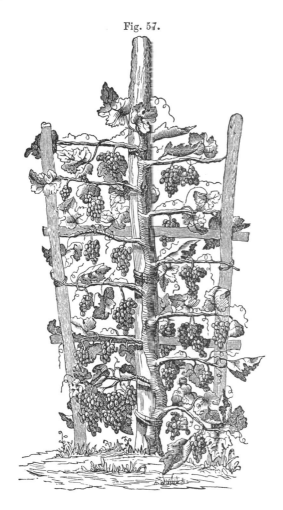

PRUNING THE VINE.

In addition to the rules heretofore enforced regarding pruning the vine, we give a representation of the results of a judicious system to induce and evenly distribute its fruitfulness. The vine here represented occupied a space four feet high and three feet wide, and produced and perfectly ripened sixty-seven bunches of fruit.

THE NURSERY.

BUDDING OR INOCULATING.

Continue to inoculate peaches, nectarines, almonds, and apples; the three former will succeed very well if done any time before the middle of the month, and even later in some seasons, especially in the middle and eastern States; the budding of apples should be finished as early in the month as possible; but these or any other kinds may be inoculated as late as you find the bark to separate freely from the stock.

Untie the bandages of such plants as have been budded three or four weeks; this must not be neglected, for the swelling growth of the stocks would cause the bandages to sink into the bark, which would injure both stocks and buds.

PREPARE GROUND FOR PLANTING.

If omitted in August, it will be very proper to embrace every leisure moment at this time, to dig and prepare all vacant quarters and borders in which you intend to plant fruit-tree stocks, or trees or shrubs of any kind in October or November; this will forward your business, and not only that, but the ground will be mellowed and moistened by the rain, which will be of much advantage in exciting the plants to produce new fibres before winter.

TRANSPLANTING.

When absolute necessity requires it, and only in that case, you may in the last week of this month remove and transplant evergreens and such deciduous trees and shrubs as are much declined in leaf; but should the season prove dry, these must be carefully and frequently watered for a month or five weeks after, not giving too much at a time, nor too frequently, lest an over quantity should rot the young fibres as they are produced.

PROPAGATING TREES AND SHRUBS BY CUTTINGS AND LAYERS.

In the last week of this month you may begin to propagate gooseberries, currants, honeysuckles, and several other hardy trees and shrubs by cuttings; but it will be necessary at this time to plant them in a shady border; however, I would not advise this to be done before October, except in cases of necessity; for wood imperfectly ripened, when cut off and planted in this month, seldom can bear the power of the sun in our climates, unless it is for some time after covered and protected therefrom.

The general propagation by layers may, with great propriety, be commenced towards the latter end of this month. (For the method see page 300.)

FRUIT STONES.

Peach, plum, and cherry stones, &c., may now be sown as already directed, or they may be preserved as recommended, till October, November, or February; but in the southern States they should be sown in or before January if possible.

TRIMMING PINES AND FIRS, ETC.

Where firs, pines, and other resinous trees are grown so rude as to require some of their branches to be cut off, this is the best time in the year for so doing; now they are not subject to weep as in the spring, and there will be time for their wounds to harden and partly heal before winter. Walnut-trees and maples should also be trimmed at this season where necessary, for the same reason.

GENERAL CARE OF YOUNG NURSERY PLANTS.

Thoroughly clean from weeds all the seed-beds and young plantations of trees, shrubs, &c.; this must be done occasionally by hand and hoe, taking opportunity of dry days when you work with the hoe; and weeding will be easier performed when the ground is moist.

Continue to give water in dry weather to all the plants in pots or boxes, and also to new plantations of flowers, &c.

Towards the latter end of the month begin to pot off singly such young *tender* plants as were raised from seed this year, and that stand too close together where growing. These should be immediately placed in the shade for about three weeks till newly rooted, after which place them in a warm exposure till the approach of frost, when they must be removed into the green-house or placed under the protection of frames and glasses, &c.

THE PLEASURE, OR FLOWER GARDEN.

CARNATIONS AND PINKS.

Your late carnation and pink layers must now be taken off as soon as they are well rooted, and be treated as directed in July and August; the earlier in the month that you can do this the better will the plants be rooted before winter.

Towards the end of the month you may transplant from the nursery-beds the seedling pinks and carnations, into such beds and borders as you intend them to flower in; observing to take each plant up with a ball of earth, and to give it some water when newly planted.

AURICULAS.

The auricula plants still require due attention, but particularly those shifted last month; they must yet be kept in the shade and moderately watered, as often as the earth appears rather dry, to promote a free growth and a good supply of new roots before winter.

If the shifting had been neglected last month it may yet be done, but the beginning of August is a more eligible period.

Particular care must now be taken to keep the auricula seedlings, as well as the old plants, free from decayed leaves and weeds of every kind, to keep the earth about them in a *moderate* state of moisture, that the plants may grow freely and obtain strength before winter.

SOWING SEEDS OF BULBOUS-ROOTED FLOWERS.

This will be a very proper time to sow the seeds of tulips, hyacinths, and of every other kind of bulbous rooted flowers that have perfected seed in the preceding part of the season. These seeds should be sown separately in boxes filled with good sound garden mould, mixed with a small portion of sand or with hyacinth or tulip compost; sow the seeds pretty thick and cover them about half an inch deep. The depth of earth in each box should be at least six inches, the bottoms of the boxes should be perforated with holes, each about an inch in diameter, and covered with shells, in order that any extra moisture may drain off thereby. The boxes are then to be placed in a warm exposure, and will require no water, or any other attention than the keeping of them perfectly free from weeds, and slightly protecting them from frost till the spring following, when the plants will appear. Early in May place the boxes in the shade, but not under the dropping or shade of trees; and in very dry weather give the plants a small portion of water; but this should be administered sparingly, lest it should rot the young bulbs. In June, when the leaves are decayed, sift half an inch of fresh earth over that in the boxes, and on the approach of winter place them again in a warm exposure where you can give them some slight protection from severe frost. Continue the same treatment, winter and summer, till the month of June or July, in the third year; the roots may then be taken up, dried, and treated in the same manner as directed for large bulbs or offsets on pages 407 and 408; a few of the strongest roots will flower the fourth year, about one-half may be expected to flower the fifth, but the sixth year every healthy root will exhibit its bloom; and the hopes and expectations of the cultivator will be realized or disappointed. He may, however, think himself fortunate if one-half of the plants that first appeared are in existence at this period, and if he can at last find one tulip or hyacinth in five hundred deserving a name or a place in a good collection, he may rest perfectly content.

The *tulips* raised from seed will each consist of one plain color on a white, dark, or yellow bottom; the period of their breaking into different stripes is very uncertain, so much so that it is not uncommon to wait ten or twenty years without the desired success, although it sometimes happens, fortunately, to take place the first, second, or third year after their blooming; where the collection of *breeders* is numerous (a name given to those self-colored tulips), there may be reasonable expectations of procuring one or two valuable flowers annually : a poor dry soil is most likely to produce these effects; and a single instance has occurred where forty breeders out of fifty became broken or variegated in one season in a situation of this description.

New sorts of breeders are procured from seed, but such only as have tall strong stems, with large well formed cups, and clear in the bottom, are worth cultivating.

Note.—The various kinds of *tender* bulbous-rooted flowering plants may be propagated as above directed, but the boxes in which the seedlings grow must be placed in a green-house or hot-house in winter, according to the respective necessities of the various kinds.

TRANSPLANT PERENNIAL AND BIENNIAL FLOWER ROOTS.

The latter end of this month is a very proper period for transplanting the various kinds of seedlings, perennial and biennial flowers, out of the flower-nursery into the beds, borders, and pleasure-grounds, where they are designed to bloom. You may likewise slip and plant out double catchfly, pinks, London pride, phlox, dracocephalums, sweet-william, thrift, scarlet-lychnis, Virginian spiderwort, double rose-campion, double rocket, Virginian lungwort, creeping Greek valerian, and every other kind or hardy fibrous-rooted perennials that are past bloom.

Cut down the stalks of such flowers as are decayed, and where they are not to be transplanted, dig the ground about them and add some rotten dung or fresh earth to the borders, which will greatly strengthen their roots.

This will also be a very good time to collect from the fields, swamps, and woods, some of the favorites of the Most High, which he has decorated with such a profusion of lustre and beauty, that "Solomon in all his glory" was not equal to. These are to be taken up and treated as directed on page 493.

The various kinds of tuberous-rooted flowering plants may now be propagated by slipping or parting their roots, such as pæonias, spiræa filipendula, flag-irises, helleborus hyemalis or winter aconite, &c. This last should have its roots planted in small clusters; for, small solitary flowers scattered about the borders are scarcely seen at a distance ; but when these, snowdrops, crocuses, and dwarf Persian irises are alternately planted in bunches, they will have a very good effect, as they flower at the same time and are much of a size. You may also divide and transplant the roots of the helleborus niger, or Christmas rose, helleborus viridis, or green hellebore, helleborus ranunculinus, and helleborus fœtidus, stinking hellebore, or bear's-foot. The helleborus lividus, purple, or great three-flowered black hellebore, is a very desirable plant; it is usual to keep this in the green-house, where it will flower in February and continue a long time in bloom. It may now be propagated in like manner as the other species.

PLANTING VARIOUS KINDS OF BULBOUS ROOTS.

Spring crocuses, snowdrops, fritillaries, crown-imperials, dens-canises, dwarf Persian, English, and Spanish bulbous irises, scarlet martagons, white, superb, Canada, and red lilies, and all other kinds of bulbs that do not agree with being kept long out of ground should now be planted if possible: for although these roots may be kept up much longer if preserved from the air, in dry sand, sawdust, dry chaff or the like, yet they would not flower near so well next season as if planted in due time.

Common tulips, hyacinths, narcissus, &c., may now be planted in the borders of the pleasure grounds, in small clumps of four or five in a place, covering the roots about four inches deep if the soil be dry and light; if stiff and heavy, three inches will be sufficient; but the latter kind of soil should not be chosen for this purpose if possible: where the borders are naturally inclined to clay, proper earth should be brought on barrows, and holes made in the spots where you intend planting about a foot in diameter, and at least the same in depth, which fill with the good soil and plant the roots therein, covering as above.

Van Thol and other early tulips may now be planted in a warm soil and exposure for an early spring bloom.

FLOWER BORDERS AND SHRUBBERIES.

Towards the latter end of this month begin to dig the vacant beds and borders where the plants are mostly declined in their flowering, to prepare them for the reception of any plants or roots, to kill weeds, and to give a neat and becoming appearance to the whole; if they require it add some fresh earth or very rotten dung to them, and in the planting of flowers in borders along the principal walks observe to dispose them in such a manner as that there may be a regular succession of flowers throughout the season in the different parts, planting the low growing kinds in front and the taller more remote from the walks.

Continue to keep the general flower borders, clumps, and other similar districts very clean, and in neat order, and go around all the beds, borders, and shrubbery compartments once a week to cut down decayed flower stems, for such detract much from the beauty of the plants in flower as well as from that of the general appearance.

Regulate disorderly growths, tie up straggling branches, and pick off all decayed leaves; likewise prune or cut away any branches or twigs that appear in a mouldy or declining state on any of the flowering plants or shrubs.

BOX EDGINGS.

Clip box edgings where it was omitted in the two former months, but let this be done as soon now as possible, that the box may have time to grow a little and put on a fresh appearance before winter ; it will be best to do this in wet or cloudy weather, if such should happen in due time.

In the last week of this month, should the season prove moist, you may begin to plant box edgings where wanted, as directed on page 316, but if the weather sets in dry and hot immediately after, it will be necessary to shade them with boards, &c., for a month ; about that period they will be newly rooted, and appear neat all winter. However, should the weather not prove favorable in this month, it would be more advisable to defer that work till the early part of October.

If you have low bunches of dwarf box, that the offsets are generally rooted, you need be under no apprehension of their striking fresh root and growing freely at this time if kept regularly watered ; but where you form edgings of box *cuttings*, these will require to be carefully shaded from the sun, at least for a month after, if planted at this season.

CLIP HEDGES.

Such hedges as have not been trimmed in the preceding month should be clipped in the early part of this, before the shoots get hard.

In clipping hedges, always take particular care to have the shears in perfect good order, that you may be able to make neat and expeditious work. Let the sides of the full grown hedges be always clipped in nearly to the former year's cut, and as even and straight as possible ; for it looks awkward and not workmanlike to see the sides of hedges, especially garden hedges waved and uneven : and always observe to clip a hedge in such a way as to *slope in a narrow manner upwards*, that the top may be a little narrower than the bottom, and at the same time as even and level as possible.

In clipping young hedges under training be cautious not to cut them too close above, but clip the top off regularly to retard the luxuriant shoots, and cause them to branch out and thicken the hedge, and also to give the moderate growths an equal advantage of air and room to advance as equally as possible; cut the sides with similar care but closer, and always sloping inwards or narrowing towards the top; for by thus exposing the sides and bottom of the hedge to the influence of the air, rain and dews, all parts are equally encouraged in growth, and the whole becomes close and well furnished ; but when the top overhangs the bottom, the lower branches, for want of those advantages, decay, and the hedge becomes thin below, and consequently much more unfit to answer the end than if judiciously trained.

GRASS AND GRAVEL WALKS, AND LAWNS.

Continue to treat your grass and gravel-walks, and lawns as directed on page 415, and let the rough edges of all grass lawns, &c., adjoining gravel-walks and principal borders, be cut close and neat with a very sharp edging iron, &c., which will give an additional neatness and becoming appearance to the whole.

PREPARING FOR PLANTING.

Prepare now, at all leisure hours, the different beds, borders, and composts for your plantations of choice tulips, hyacinths, anemones, ranunculuses, and other flower roots which are to be planted next month; also for the various flowering shrubs, &c., that the hurry of business may not press upon you too much at once, and that you may be the better able to do everything in its proper season.

TRANSPLANTING EVERGREENS.

In the last week of this month, *should necessity require*, you may transplant such evergreens as seem to have ceased growing, provided you can remove them with balls of earth, or that they are to be planted in shaded places; but in either case it will be necessary to water them occasionally in dry weather for three or four weeks after planting; however, if the season proves hot and dry, it will be better to defer that work till October.

THE VALLISNERIA AMERICANA.

Some account of the *Vallisneria Americana* may not prove unacceptable to the curious, the more especially as it tends to cast some light on the "*loves*" and sexes of plants; and it is also the best subject to place under a microscope to exhibit the circulation of the sap.

This extraordinary vegetable production grows in the river Delaware, not far from Philadelphia, and may, with care, be introduced by means of seeds or roots, into rivers, ponds, and canals, &c. Another species, the *Spiralis*, is found in the East Indies, in Norway, and various parts of Italy. The American species flowers generally in the latter part of August or in September.

The *Vallisneria* belongs to the class *Diœcia*, and order *Diandria*, bearing male and female flowers on separate plants. The female plant produces long, tubular, purple flowers, which stand singly on the top of a stalk, curiously twisted in the form of a screw, which is common to both *species;* when the flowers are about to expand, this screw or spiral stalk relaxes more or less according to the depth of the water, and suffers the flowers to rise up to the surface, where they float in expectation of a visit from their husbands.

The flowers of the male plant are very numerous, small, and of a white color; they are contained within a spathe or sheath, which stands on a short footstalk that never rises to the top of the water;

the flowers being arrived at maturity they burst open the spathe in which they are contained, detach themselves from the receptacle to which they are fixed, and rise up to the surface of the water, where they float about as if in search of their mates, and suddenly, with a kind of elasticity, open themselves and discharge their pollen, which being conveyed to the female flowers growing near them, or scattered thereon, impregnates the seeds contained within the germen.

The pollen being discharged on the stigma, the embryo seeds are impregnated, but how this impregnation is effected it is difficult to say; indeed, while the affair of impregnation in animals is involved in so much obscurity, we can scarcely expect to discover more of it in vegetables.

It has been the opinion of some of the early writers on the sexes of plants, that the pollen in substance passed through the style, and so impregnated the seeds in the ovary; but this is a very irrational supposition, for it is not probable that the pollen, which is nothing more than a case for the true sperm, should pass through a part which has every appearance of being impervious to it.

Whether the sperm itself be conveyed through the style is perhaps what never will with certainty be determined.

The hint of there being different sexes in plants, seems first to have been taken from the *Diœcia* class, or such as produce (male) flowers with stamina on one plant, and (female) flowers with pistilla on another.

"If the dust of the branch of a male palm-tree," says Aristotle, "be suspended over the female, the fruit of the latter will quickly ripen; and if the male dust be carried along by the wind, and dispersed upon the female, the same effect will follow as if a branch of the male had been suspended over it."

"Naturalists," says Pliny, "admit of distinction of sex not only in trees but in herbs and all plants; yet this is nowhere more observable than in palms, the females of which never propagate but when they are fecundated by the dust of the male."

Note.—Those who wish to become scientifically acquainted with the *Linnæan*, or sexual system of plants, will be greatly edified by consulting that very valuable work, the *Elements of Botany*, published in 1803 by the late Benjamin Smith Barton, M. D., Professor of Materia Medica, Natural History, and Botany in the University of Pennsylvania. The botanist will also consult Longman and Green's *Structural Botany*, Gray's *Text-Book*, and Lindley's *School Botany*.

THE GREEN-HOUSE.

In the *eastern States*, between the fifteenth and latter end of this month, according to local situations, the nights will be getting cold, and consequently the more tender kinds of green-house plants must be taken in before they change their color by too much cold, leaving the hardy sorts out as long as there is no danger of their being attacked by frost.

Some people are desirous to keep out their plants as long as possible; this is very right, but it ought not to be extended to too hazardous a period, for one night's frost would cause the leaves to lose their fine green color, which perhaps might not be restored during the whole winter, and if any way severe, serious injury might be sustained.

If the windows and doors are kept open day and night, as long as there is safety in so doing, the plants will be nearly as well off as if in the open air, and no danger is encountered: the mere difference of five or six days in the taking in of the plants will insure safety; but on the other hand, it is not right to be too precipitate in housing them before the common appearance of the weather indicates the necessity.

For further particulars respecting the housing of the plants, see next month, which is the period for doing that business in the middle States.

In the *middle* and other States where frosts do not frequently appear before the middle of October, the plants are to be taken care of as directed in the preceding months; observing to decrease the usual supply of water in proportion to the moistness and coldness of the weather, for the administering of it too copiously when there is not a necessity, would be very injurious. And let it be particularly observed, that as soon as the cold nights set in, which may be about the middle of this month or sooner, the water must be given to the plants in the morning, for if given late in the afternoon as in the preceding months, the chill occasioned by it and the coldness of the nights, would change the color of the foliage from a fine green to a yellowish cast, whereby much of their beauty would be lost, as well as the plants themselves in some degree injured.

If any are in want of larger pots or tubs, they may be shifted in the beginning of this month, but on no account defer it later, that the plants may have time to strike some fresh roots before winter. And if, in consequence of a bad state of health, any had been planted in baskets in the borders as recommended on page 454, they must, early in this month, be taken up and re-potted; observing to take them up carefully, to trim off the wide extended roots, cut the baskets away, and plant them with the entire balls in the pots or tubs destined for their reception; after which give them water and place them in some shady warm situation, till the time for housing them.

Any young green-house plants raised this or last year from seeds, slips, cuttings, or suckers, and that are growing too close together in pots, &c., should, if well rooted, be transplanted in the early part of this month into pots, singly, and be immediately watered and placed in the shade for a week or two; or of such as are very small, two, three, or more may be planted in a pot, and treated in like manner. But those that have been raised from slips or cuttings and that are not well rooted, and consequently not much advanced in top-growth, should be suffered to remain in their present pots till spring or autumn next.

Any green-house plants propagated in the open ground, or in beds, during the course of the summer, should be taken up in the first week of this month, with balls of earth, potted and treated as above.

About the middle of this month you should plant your ixias, walchendorfias, oxalises, gladioluses, Watsonias, oyanellas, babianas, tritonias, Massonias, melasphærulas, antholizas, moreas, Laperousias, lachenalias, melanthiums, geissorhizas, with all the other different kinds of the more tender bulbs, either obtained from the Cape of Good Hope or elsewhere; especially such of them as show the least disposition to produce fibres from the roots; for if kept out of the ground much longer, after this appearance, they would be greatly injured thereby.

The proper compost for the generality of the above kinds, is one-half rich fresh loam, one-half bog earth, or earth of rotten leaves, and a small portion of drift or river sand.

They are to be planted in pots of quart size, from one to five roots in each, a greater number if very small, and covered about an inch deep; the pots are then to be placed in the green-house windows, and to get but very little water till the foliage appear above ground, and even after, it is to be but sparingly administered, for too much moisture would infallibly rot the bulbs.

Towards the end of the month take into the green-house all your succulent and other tender plants, such as stapelias, cactuses, aloes, cycas revoluta, agaves, &c., and place them in front near the windows, where they can have the benefit of the sun and air. Collect your geraniums, at the same time, and all other plants that tend to succulency, and arrange them in front of the green-house, there to remain till it is found necessary to take them in. (*See next month.*)

THE HOT-HOUSE.

REPAIRING THE LIGHTS AND CLEANING THE HOUSE.

If the roof-lights had in the course of the summer been taken off any of the hot-house departments, they should be replaced early in the month, and all the glass-work of the entire house or houses put in the best possible repair. Examine the wood-work and see that all is tight and in good condition. If new painting of the timbers, sashes, or any other part is necessary, and it has not been done in the preceding months, it should be no longer neglected.

Indeed it would be of considerable advantage at this time, previous to the taking in of the plants, to give a complete and thorough cleaning, painting, and white-washing to the entire house; and if infested with insects, to fumigate it effectually; and also to wash the entire of the inside with a very strong solution of corrosive sublimate, and, if thought necessary, to clean away every morsel of old bark out of the pits, carry it off to a considerable distance, and replace it with fresh tan. Any plants remaining in this department may be removed

34

into the green-house while this work is going on, and these should be effectually washed and cleaned, if infested with these insects, before their being replaced.

This cleansing, fumigating, &c., will destroy most, if not all, of the lurking insects which have taken shelter in the various parts of the house, and which, by and by, if not destroyed, would sally forth and make a formidable and, perhaps, destructive attack upon your plants; every timely precaution ought to be taken to keep the house clean and sweet, and the plants free from vermin.

TAKING IN THE PLANTS.

The more tender kinds of hot-house exotics which are arranged out of doors should, *in the middle States*, be taken into the green-house about the tenth of this month, and the others successively, according to their respective degrees of tenderness, so that the whole collection may be in by the eighteenth or twentieth thereof, or a few days earlier should the weather happen to be cold. Here they are to remain, closing the windows at night and giving them all the air possible on warm and mild days, till towards the end of the month, or sooner if you have the hot-house ready for their reception.

When you have everything in readiness dress the plants by picking off all decayed leaves, and especially those which are annoyed with insects, cut away all awkward and ill-placed branches, give each pot a fresh top dressing of suitable compost, and place the smallest in front and the tallest behind, on the shelves of the stage. The succulent sorts may be set on shelves arranged over the flues, &c.

Now the plants being in order and placed in their winter quarters, it will be of much importance to give them plenty of air every favorable day by sliding open the upright glasses, and also the roof-lights if necessary, in order to prevent their being drawn up too tender before winter, for the fresh bottom heat will give new action to the plants, and render abundance of air the more necessary; observe, however, to close the lights every evening when the house is tolerably warm, and to open them as early in the morning as you find the thermometer up to 60 degrees of Fahrenheit.

It is scarcely necessary to mention that every plant must have a due supply of water, from time to time, according to its nature and necessity.

PINE-APPLE.

Succession pine plants which are expected to produce fruit next year may, in the first week of this month, if omitted in July and August, be shifted as directed; but on no account should this be delayed longer. Where it has been done in the preceding months, and at that time no fresh tan added, it will now be necessary to examine the heat of the bark-bed in the succession house, wherein the plants in general are plunged, and if you find it very weak fork up the tan to the bottom, and plunge in the pots again immediately to their rims.

This will revive the heat of the bed, and continue in a due temperature till next month, when the plants must be removed into the fruiting-house, and plunged in a bed made wholly of new tan.

The younger succession pines intended to succeed those, if not lately done, should not be shifted into larger pots, the tan forked up, and the pots replunged immediately after having received a little water.

CROWNS AND SUCKERS.

The crowns and suckers of this year's production will require a brisk bottom heat to enable the plants to make good roots before winter; therefore examine the bed, and if it is declined in heat fork it up and replunge the pots immediately; but if these were placed on a dung hot-bed it may be necessary to renew the heat by a lining of fresh hot dung applied to the sides, or to the sides and ends; or if the bed is much sunk to work it up afresh, adding some new dung thereto, laying on the top, as before, several inches of light earth or tan in which to plunge the pots. After this it will be necessary to give a considerable portion of air to the plants, and to raise the glasses behind when you find the steam rising in the bed. When the nights begin to grow cold cover the glasses carefully with mats, and be very cautious not to keep your lights close in sunny days.

All your succession pines should have plenty of air at this season, which, with a moderate and steady bottom heat, will keep them in a growing and prosperous state, but by no means are they to be forced too much nor too much confined, as by such treatment some of the most forward might start into fruit at an untimely season, and all would be rendered more unfit to bear the vicissitudes of the winter season than if they were properly inured to the air and gradually hardened; but still there may be an excess in this as well as the other, both of which are equally to be avoided.

PROCURING FRESH TAN.

About the latter end of this month you should procure a quantity of fresh tan, if you employ this article, from the tan-yards, for the purpose of making new beds in the next month for those plants which you expect to produce fruit in the ensuing year, and also for the succession pines. When the tan is brought home it will be proper to throw it up in a heap to drain and ferment for ten or twelve days before it is put into the pits. But if it is very wet, as is commonly the case when thrown up out of the tan-vats, it should be spread thinly for two or three days, that the sun and air may draw off or exhale the superabundant moisture; for if used too wet, it would be a long time before it would acquire a sufficient degree of heat.

PREPARE COMPOSTS.

The composts proper for pines are described on page 480, and if you have not hitherto prepared such as may be wanted next season, that business should be delayed no longer.

For most of the shrubby tribe and herbaceous plants of the hot-house, prepare equal parts of good light garden earth and mellow surface loam from a rich pasture ground, with the turf; add to these a fourth of very rotten or old hot-bed dung, and let the whole be duly incorporated and exposed to the weather several months before it is used, turning the heap over every five or six weeks.

A PLANT CABINET.

A " plant cabinet," while it scarcely aspires to the dignity of a conservatory, possesses the attractions of one, and gives the family of the possessor as much pleasure as a more expensive arrangement.

A bay-window, in one of the most frequented rooms (Fig. 58), suggested itself as a suitable place for bringing the plants as they bloomed, from a small green-house too distant from the dwelling to be visited in bad weather.

Simple glass sashes to fit the opening were procured; they open like a double door; shelves on one side support the plants, and small wooden brackets screwed on to the walls here and there, assist to furnish this little jewel of beauty. In the centre is an ornamental post, of red cedar varnished, up which climbs two different colored Maurandia Barclayanas, and the top is ornamented with a golden fern. In front are seen two China seats; on these are placed ornamental long-stemmed climbing plants, and hanging vases assist materially in the effect. During winter the cabinet is gay with the finest camellias and other flowers. Chrysanthemums, at the proper season, give it their peculiar attractions. In short, there are few plants that are not exhibited in succession; even orchideous, and other tender varieties, are introduced with success. In extremely cold weather the door is left a little ajar to admit the warmth of the room, especially at night, and the thermometer has not yet fallen below 45°.

The whole cost of fitting up this beautiful case, exclusive of the flowering plants, did not exceed twenty-five dollars. It gives completeness and beauty, and an expression to the house that could be produced in no other mode so cheaply. But it has a higher object; it embues all connected with the mansion with a love of flowers, and gratifies many senses. A pair of Canary birds are sometimes let out of their cages to enjoy the liberty of the cabinet.

Cowper, in his happiest manner, has alluded thus to the love of Nature's works :—

> " The love of Nature's works
> Is an ingredient in the compound, man,
> Infused at the creation of the kind.
> And, though th' Almighty Maker has throughout
> Discriminated each from each, by strokes
> And touches of his hand, with so much art
> Diversified, that two were never found
> Twins at all points—yet this obtains in all,
> That all discern a beauty in his works,
> And all can taste them."

Fig. 53.

W.T.RICHARDS DEL   R. TELFER SC

A Plant Cabinet.

By introducing such a cabinet into a sitting-room, the beauties of
nature are made accessible in the severest season. There would be
no necessity of having a green-house to resort to, to fill such a case;
without leaving their comfortably warmed rooms, ladies can attend
to their pets, which by employing water in dishes for the sake of the
evaporation, will possess as healthy an atmosphere as the gardener's
case. As much light as possible should be given. The cactus tribe
would thrive here remarkably well.

OCTOBER.

WORK TO BE DONE IN THE KITCHEN GARDEN.

WINTER SPINAGE.

Weed and thin your advancing crops of spinage; in doing this observe to leave the best plants, and at the distance of three, four, or
five inches asunder, according to the progress in growth of the successive crops, leaving the greatest space between the most forward in
growth; or the plants may only be moderately thinned now in order
to admit of drawing some out by degrees for use.

Some of the spinage sown in August will now be fit for the table,
and if the plants were left too thick let them be thinned out regularly by pulling some up by the roots as they are wanted for use;
but if the plants were properly thinned before, gather only the outside large leaves, and the others will advance for culinary purposes
in regular succession.

Let it be particularly observed that spinage will rot off wherever
the weeds spread over it, and that consequently it is necessary to
keep it very clean.

LETTUCES.

In the first week of this month transplant from the seed-beds into
others, of light rich earth, in a warm exposure, and of such dimensions as to be covered with your frames on the approach of frost, the
lettuce plants arising from the late August or early September sowings. Plant them in rows five or six inches distant every way, so
that every second plant may be taken up either for use or future
planting, leaving the others sufficient room to grow and to head in
the greatest perfection.

Likewise plant some stout plants immediately in frames for use in
the latter end of November, December, &c., covering them only at
night till severe frosts set in.

Lettuces designed to remain where sown till spring, should be duly thinned as they advance in growth, and always kept free from weeds.

The various successive crops of lettuces should be transplanted where they are to remain during winter, whether on warm borders, in slight hot-beds, or under frames and glasses, as early in this month as they shall have attained to two or three inches in growth ; and indeed a judicious gardener will always have a regular succession of these plants to guard against every kind of disappointment, and the better to insure a constant supply.

In the middle States, if the winter is tolerably mild, but particularly in the southern States, lettuces will stand in warm south borders of light sandy ground with a very slight protection, and afford an early supply in spring; in these beds or borders they may be planted at the distance of three or four inches every way, and the supernumerary plants may be taken up in March and planted either in hot-beds for forcing, or into other beds in warm exposures for heading in due season.

The lettuces which you plant in warm borders in the open ground may, on the approach of winter, be protected by placing hoops over the beds, on which to lay mats or other covering in severe weather, or by placing a frame of boards around them, on which to lay others slightly covered with litter when necessity requires; or by sticking in small branches of pine or cedar between the rows, which will yield them considerable protection, especially if some long, dry straw be laid over these in frosty or cutting weather. Or you may stick down forked sticks about a foot high, lay long poles from one fork to another, and on these boughs of pine or cedar pretty thick, and likewise around the edges of the beds; those branches being supported ten or twelve inches above the plants will admit a free circulation of air and prevent mouldiness. This protection is not to be given until the severe frosts commence, nor is it then to be taken entirely off, especially in sunshine, until after the general thaw takes place in spring; on very dry, mild days, when the sun does not shine, or when it is not powerful, you may take off the covering for a few hours to air the plants; but you must as carefully guard against strong sunshine, especially towards the latter end of February, as against the most severe frosts; for after tender plants are severely pinched by frost, a too powerful sun literally dissolves and destroys them ; whereas, if they were protected from such till gradually recovered and the commencement of free vegetation, there would not be the least danger of their success. This is not common to lettuces only, but to cabbage and cauliflower plants, stock-gilly flowers, wall flowers, and every other kind that can be in the least affected by frost.

In the beginning of this month sow some of the brown Dutch hardy cabbage, and Hammersmith hardy green lettuces in a frame or frames, to be kept where sown, during winter, under the protection of glasses, &c., in order to afford a supply of young plants for forcing or planting out in the early spring months.

CABBAGE PLANTS.

The young cabbage plants arising from the seeds sown last month, and intended for the production of early summer cabbages should, as soon in this month as they shall have attained a sufficient size, be planted into the beds in which they are to remain during winter.

Let a bed or beds be prepared for them in a warm, well sheltered part of the garden, where the sun has the greater power; for although direct sunshine, when the plants are in a frozen state, is almost certain destruction to them, yet its influence will prevent that intense frost so prevalent in colder aspects; and when the plants at such times are screened from the direct rays of the sun, its reflected heat comforts without injuring them.

The beds should be made the width of your garden-frames, and the plants set therein up to their leaves in rows about three or four inches distant every way. When thus transplanted they will survive the winter much better than in the seed-beds, for their long stems being buried into the earth, are protected thereby from alternate freezing and thawing, and the effects of the various changes of weather, than which there is nothing more injurious to tender plants. The stems of these and cauliflower plants are injured before the foliage, and it is of importance to keep those tender parts in an equal temperature, by which they will be preserved much longer even if in a frozen state than if they were exposed to alternate frost and heat.

Select good plants from the seed-beds, and, when planted, give them a gentle watering to settle the earth about their roots, observing not to apply it too hastily lest you wash the earth into their hearts.

Put on the frames immediately, and also the lights, but the glasses are now to be continued on only four or five days till the plants have taken fresh root; observing during that period to shade the plants with mats or other protection from the mid-day sun; but when they have taken sufficient root the lights are to be taken totally off, and the plants left fully exposed till the setting in of smart frosts, except in very cold nights or during the prevalence of cold heavy rains; for it is of considerable moment to have the plants tolerably hardy on the commencement of severe weather.

But if they happen to be in a backward state you should keep on the glasses every night to encourage their growth.

When you have not the convenience of glass, you may defend the plants sufficiently in winter by means of boards and mats.

Or, in the middle and southern States, you may plant some in a warm border to be defended in like manner, as before directed for lettuces; and if the winter proves tolerably mild, they may happen to stand it pretty well. But if at any time, particularly towards the end of February or early in March, you expose the plants to a warm sun, while they or the earth in which they stand are in a frozen state, it will inevitably destroy them.

You should in mild warm weather, when the sun is not powerful, give them an occasional airing, and the oftener this can be done, so that they are covered up again in due time, the better.

Similar precautions are to be used with plants in frames that are frozen, but such as are not, will be improved by exposing them occasionally to as much air and sun as prudence may warrant till planted out finally in March, &c.

By pursuing this method you will have much earlier and larger cabbages than can be expected from plants sown in the early spring months.

CAULIFLOWERS.

The cauliflower plants are to be treated in every respect as directed for cabbage plants, with this difference, that as they are somewhat more tender they will require the protection and advantage of glasses and a good substantial covering to defend them from severe frosts, though in mild winters they, with due care, will survive under the protection of garden frames covered with boards and mats.

As the cauliflower plants advance in growth, it will be proper to strew between them some dry tan, sawdust, or chaff, so as to cover the stems completely up to the leaves; this will afford great protection to those parts which are always found to be the most vulnerable to frost, &c.

If you find, in consequence of an unfavorable season or of your not sowing the cauliflower seed in due time, the plants to be rather backward, you should prick them from the seed-bed on a slight hot-bed to promote their growth; but in this case you must be particularly attentive to give them plenty of air, that the plants may be stout and hardy on the approach of severe weather.

You should carefully protect the cauliflower plants from excessive heavy rains, especially when the nights get pretty cold, for such are very injurious to them and frequently cause their stems to turn black, which always proves destructive.

In the southern States, where the winters are mild, and where it is difficult to have good cauliflowers, except they can be obtained at an early season before the great summer heat sets in, which is very inimical to those plants, the only sure way of obtaining them in the best perfection is, to be provided with a sufficient number of bell or hand-glasses, under which to plant them out finally about the latter end of this month.

The ground for this early crop should be very rich, tolerably light, in a warm situation, and where water is not apt to stand in winter. The ground is to be previously well manured with old hot-bed or other well rotted dung, and then dug one good spade deep at least, breaking it effectually and incorporating the dung well therewith.

Then lay it out into beds three feet wide, and allow alleys a foot wide between them, for the convenience of going in to take off, put on, or raise the glasses, &c., stretch your line along the middle of the bed from one end to the other, and at every three feet and a half mark the places for the glasses, and for each, put in three, four, or more plants according to the size of the glasses, and within about six inches of one another; close the earth well about their roots and stems, and give them a moderate watering. When the whole are planted set on your glasses, observing to place one over every patch of plants as above.

The glasses are to be kept close down for about eight days till the plants have taken fresh root and begin to grow, when they are to be raised on one side and supported with pieces of wood, stone, or brickbats, &c., about two or three inches thick, or they may be supported with notched wooden pegs or forked sticks, placing them on the south side, one prop under each glass. In this manner they are to remain night and day until the frosts set in; but if the plants are much advanced in growth before that period, which will seldom be the case, except in the more southern States, it will be proper to set the glasses off in the middle of mild, dry days, but keep them always over the plants at night and in wet or frosty weather; in keeping the glasses over the plants to defend them from excessive or incessant rains, if open mild weather, they must be raised two or three inches on the warmest side, in the manner before observed, to admit a sufficiency of air.

When the frost sets in, close down the glasses, and keep them so during its continuance; observing on a favorable change to give the plants a little air occasionally, and to pick off any mouldy or decayed leaves. As early in spring as it can be done with safety, plant out the extra plants into other beds similarly prepared, or rather as directed in April, leaving only one or two of the best under each glass; at the same time draw the earth up around the stems of those left, and raise the glasses on props as the plants advance in growth till they become too much confined; then take off the glasses totally, observing to earth them up occasionally, and finally to treat them as directed in May.

In places where the winters are somewhat severe, mats or straw should be placed over and around each glass during the prevalence of hard frost.

This method may be practised successively in warm soils and exposures in the middle States; but it will require more than ordinary care to preserve them in good perfection.

The late spring sown cauliflowers will now begin to show their heads; therefore they must be diligently looked over two or three times a week, to break down some of the inner leaves upon the flowers, which will protect them from sun, frost, and wet, either of which would change their color and cause them to be unsightly.

BROCCOLI, CABBAGES, ETC.

Early in this month give a general hoeing and earthing up to all the late planted advancing crops of broccoli, cabbages, savoys and borecole, in order to forward and strengthen their growth as much as possible before winter; likewise to the late cauliflowers and every other of the cabbage tribe.

MUSHROOMS.

Having the dung for the mushroom bed duly prepared, and the spawn in readinesss, as advised in September, you should in the first week, or rather about the first day of this month, begin to make the bed.

With respect to the situation in which to make the bed, it should be in an elevated part of the hot-bed yard, or in some dry and well sheltered place. The bed ought to be made entirely on the surface of the ground, rather than forming a shallow trench in which to make the bottom part, as practised by some; for by the former method it can be spawned quite to the bottom, and the lower part will not be chilled by standing water in cold or wet weather, and particularly as the part sunk in the ground may be considered as totally useless.

The width of the bed at bottom should be from three to four feet, and any length you please, in proportion to the quantity of mushrooms required, or the quantity of spawn with which you are provided.

Being furnished with a three tined fork, begin to make the bed by shaking some of the longest of the prepared dung evenly all along the bottom four or five inches thick; then take the dung in general as it comes and work it into the bed, gradually narrowing it upwards, shaking and mixing the dung as you proceed and beating it down with the fork layer by layer: proceed in this manner, still drawing in the sides of the bed till it terminates in a narrow ridge at top, so that the bed may be formed like the roof of a house : be careful that each end shall be sloped in like manner as the sides, and that *all* parts are made *full* and *firm* by beating with a fork as you proceed, to preserve uniformity and to prevent its settling down too much in an unequal manner : it should be full three or three and a half feet perpendicular height when settled.

When the bed is finished, it should be covered with long straw, laid on neatly to keep out wet, and also to prevent its drying ; in this state it is to remain about ten or twelve days, by which time it will be in a fit condition to be spawned ; but to ascertain the state of the bed with the greater certainty, put in a few long sharp-pointed sticks into several parts thereof, pull out and feel these occasionally, carefully attending to the progress of its fermentation, and when you find the heat on the decline, and temperate, that is the time to put in the spawn ; for a violent heat, as well as too much wet, would inevitably destroy it.

The bed being in a proper temperature, the covering of straw should be taken off and the sides made smooth and even; then lay all over the bed about an inch thick of light rich earth, not wet. In this the spawn is to be planted in rows six inches asunder along the sides and ends, making the first or lowest row six inches from the surface of the ground, and proceeding upwards row by row to the top, observing to place the pieces of spawn about six inches asunder, and so far in as to touch the surface of the dung. This done, lay on the top of the ridge part of the loose or scattered spawn, and shake some all over the bed; then cover the whole about an inch and a half deep with light rich earth, smooth the surface neatly, and lay on a light covering of straw as before, just so thick as to keep out wet and prevent the bed from drying.

As you find the bed decrease in heat and the weather grow cold, increase the covering to a foot, eighteen inches, two feet, or, in severe frost, to such a thickness as may be effectually sufficient to prevent its reaching the bed.

Two or three beds may be made parallel to each other in this way, with wide alleys between them, and if the whole were to be covered with a shed, especially in the middle and eastern States, it would be found of considerable advantage in effectually preserving them from too much wet, which is as essentially necessary as their preservation from frost.

If your bed is in a due temperature, the mushrooms will begin to appear in about four or five weeks after its being made, and with proper care will continue in bearing several months: when you find it ceasing to produce, in consequence of cold, lay a covering of hot stable dung seven or eight inches, or in hard frosts, near a foot thick all over the bed, observing to leave under this, between it and the bed, about three inches thick of dry straw, covering the hot dung over with the remainder of the straw or litter; this will revive the heat, give new action to the spawn, and should be repeated as often during winter as it may be found necessary, always observing to preserve the bed from wet, cold, and frost.

Sometimes it happens that the beds do not produce any mushrooms till they have lain five or six months, so that they should not be destroyed though they do not at first answer the expectation; for such frequently produce great quantities afterwards, and continue bearing a long time.

A good bed may continue productive for three, four, five, or even twelve months; but by that time it is generally worn out; the dung then makes excellent manure, and the interior part sometimes furnishes very good spawn.

The great skill of managing these beds is that of keeping them in a proper degree of warmth and moisture, never suffering them to receive much wet: during the summer season they may be uncovered occasionally to receive gentle showers of rain, when thought necessary, and in very dry seasons the beds should be now and then opened, gently watered, and covered up soon after; but the summer covering need be no thicker than what is necessary to preserve the bed from the drying influence of the weather.

This method of propagating mushrooms by the *spawn*, or the white fibrous radicles, is the most common; but they may also be increased by seed. When the latter method is used, the gills are cut out and put into the beds: or else they are infused in water and the beds sprinkled with the infusion.

When the bed is in full bearing, it should be examined two or three times a week, to gather the produce, turning off the straw carefully, and collecting the mushrooms white, and of a moderate size : taking care to detach them from the bottom by a gentle twist, pulling the stems out clean, for if broke or cut off, the remaining parts would become putrid and full of maggots, and consequently infectious to the successional plants.

Where mushrooms are greatly admired, and expense not considered an object, they may be had with more certainty, in greater abundance, and in a regular succession, by making the beds as before directed, under a range of wood framing, made in the manner of a hothouse, or the top sloped both ways like the roof of a house ; in such a place, they could be effectually defended from excessive wet, cold, frost, and snow, and would consequently be very productive. Likewise, if in this place there are shelves fixed three feet apart, each having a front board, a bed of dung may be made in each, raised at top in a rounding manner, on which the spawn is placed, earthed over near two inches thick, and then covered well with straw. Or you may, by mixing a quantity of strong horse dung, moist stable litter, and rich loamy earth together, have the spawn generated; by filling a pit with this mixture, the dung predominating so as to produce a slow and lasting fermentation, and covering the whole over with about an inch deep of light earth and a good coat of straw, the spawn will be produced; and from this, abundant crops of mushrooms, in regular succession for several months.

You may likewise make beds in the common hot-bed way, place thereon frames and glasses, and when the violent heat is abated, spawn the top all over, cover it with an inch and a half or two inches of earth, then thickly with straw, and lay on the glasses to protect the beds from rain.

Mushroom beds may be made in any month, when the weather is mild and dry, but those made in the beginning of this, are generally most productive, and besides, they retain more heat on the approach of winter than if made in September   However when a second bed is to be made it would be well to make one in each month.   The most suitable temperature is between 55° and 60°, and the nearer the mushroom house is kept to this, the better they will succeed.

ENDIVE.

Continue every week to tie up some full grown endive for blanching, as directed on page 486, tying no more at a time than in proportion to the demand or consumption; for if it is not used soon after being sufficiently blanched, it becomes tender, and is subject to rot, especially if the season proves wet.   Some people blanch endive by laying boards or tiles flat on the plants; they will whiten tolerably well by this method, but their growth during the period of whitening is greatly checked thereby which is certainly of some importance.

Others draw earth around the endive plants after their being tied up in the usual manner; this may do very well in dry weather, but if rain ensues, many of the leaves will rot, and the whole be greatly injured.

If you have stout endive plants, and neglected in September to set out a sufficient number, that work may be done in the first week of this month, but it ought not to be deferred longer; these late plants will keep better, if the season should prove favorable that they may attain a tolerable size, than those of a more forward growth.

Or, to preserve late endive for winter use, as well from the effects of too much wet as frost, you may in the first week of this month prepare a sloping bank of light earth in a warm situation, the sloping side fronting the south, and the bed raised two feet higher behind than in front; on this plant, tolerably close, some stout, middle sized plants, and on the approach of severe weather place a frame and glasses over the bed, and in hard frost fill the inside immediately over the plants with *dry* straw; thus they will be protected from wet and frost, and will whiten effectually under the covering of straw, which should be turned occasionally to prevent that part next the plants and earth from becoming mouldy.

For further particulars repecting the preservation of endive, see next month.

RAISING YOUNG MINT AND TARRAGON FOR USE IN WINTER.

Where young mint and tarragon are in request at all seasons, you may, towards the end of this month, make a slight hot-bed, and set the plants therein, as directed on page 27; this done, put on the glasses, and observe to raise them behind every day to admit air, and prevent the young rising shoots from being scorched by the effects of a too powerful sun beaming on the lights whilst close shut. The young productions will be fit for use in about three weeks or a month, and afford a supply for a considerable time.

WINTER DRESSING OF ARPARAGUS BEDS.

Towards the end of this month if the stalks of your asparagus turn yellow, which is a sign of their having finished their growth for the season, cut them down close to the earth and carry them off the ground; clear the beds carefully from weeds, eradicating them effectually and drawing them into the alleys.

Asparagus beds in general will be greatly benefited by an annual dressing of good manure, and nothing is better or more suitable for them than the dung of old hot-beds; but if that is not to be had, well rotted stable manure will answer; let it be laid equally over the beds, one, two, or three inches deep, according to necessity, after which stretch a line, and with a spade mark out the alleys from about eighteen inches to two feet wide, agreeably to their original dimensions.*

Then dig the alleys one spade deep, and spread a considerable part of the earth evenly over the beds; and as you advance let the weeds which

---

* Asparagus, being a marine plant, is greatly benefited by an annual dressing of salt, and there is no kitchen vegetable that is more improved than this by the addition of guano, applied previous to commencing growth.

were raked off into the alleys be dug into the bottom of the trenches and covered a proper depth with earth; observe to make the edges of the beds straight, full, and neat, and to finish your work in a becoming manner, giving a moderate rounding to the beds, especially if the ground be inclined to wet.

In the southern States there may be planted in each alley a row of early cabbage plants; but in the middle and eastern States it would be well to fill them up with straw or old litter, well trampled down, which would in some measure prevent the frost from entering that way to the asparagus roots.

The seedling asparagus which was sown last spring should also now have a slight dressing, that is, to clear the bed from weeds, and then to spread an inch or two in depth of dry, rotten dung over it to defend the crowns of the plants from frost.

The asparagus which is intended for forcing, will likewise require to have the stalks cut down and the weeds drawn off into the alleys, which must be dug to bury them, and as you proceed spread a little of the earth over the beds, after which they are to be treated as noticed next month.

I would not advise to attempt the forcing of asparagus sooner than November, as before that period the roots will not be completely matured; however, you may, about the middle or towards the latter end of this month, begin to prepare hot-beds for the reception of the roots early in November. (See the method on page 128.)

CELERY AND CARDOONS.

In dry weather continue to earth up celery and cardoons, to blanch them, as directed on page 500. (For the method of preserving them in winter, see next month.)

AROMATIC AND MEDICINAL HERBS, ETC.

Cut down all the decayed flower stems and shoots of the various kinds of aromatic, pot, and medicinal herbs close to the heads of the plants, or to the surface of the ground, according to the nature or growth of the different sorts; at the same time clear the beds very well from weeds and litter, and carry the whole off the ground.

Lavender, thyme, hyssop, winter savory, southernwood, sage, rue, and the like undershrubby kinds will require only their tops or heads to be neatly dressed; but pot marjoram, baum, burnet, tarragon, tansy, pennyroyal, sorrel, chamomile, fennel, marsh mallows, horehound, mint of every kind, angelica, lovage, and every kind of *herbaceous* perennial herbs should be cut down pretty close to the ground.

After this it will be proper in beds where the plants stand distant from one another, to lightly dig and loosen the ground between them; or, in old beds it would be a great advantage to spread some very rotten dung equally over the surface, and with a small spade or trowel to dig it in, lightly between the plants; if they are in beds with alleys between them, dig the alleys and spread a little of the loose earth over the beds, leaving the edges full and straight.

But the beds of close growing running plants, such as mint, pennyroyal, and the like creeping herbs will not well admit of digging; therefore, after the stalks are cut down and the beds cleared from weeds, dig the alleys and strew some of the loose earth evenly over the beds; and if the ground be rather poor, a *light* top dressing of very rotten dung will be of considerable service.

This dressing will give proper culture and protection to the roots of the plants, a neat appearance to the whole, and in spring the shoots will rise with renewed vigor.

Early in the month you may plant, where wanted, well rooted young plants of thyme, hyssop, winter savory, lavender, or the like, into four feet wide beds, or in any warm borders, in rows a foot asunder. You may also divide and plant roots of mint, chamomile, horehound, and likewise any of the preceding or other herbaceous perennial herbs that you are desirous of propagating. (For further particulars, see former pages.)

SMALL SALADING.

Where a constant succession of small salad herbs is required, continue to sow the seeds accordingly every ten or fourteen days, particularly cresses, radish, rape, mustard and lettuce, to cut while young. But in the middle and eastern States, these should be sown at this season, particularly towards the latter end of the month, in very warm borders under the protection of frames and glasses, for the greater certainty of having a constant supply. The glasses should be kept totally off every warm day, and only put on at night or when the weather is very cold or excessively wet.

In the middle States, when the season is favorable, small salading will grow free enough anytime this month in warm borders, but it will be proper to have frames and glasses to place over them if necessity should require it.

DILL, ALEXANDERS, SKIRRETS, RHUBARB, AND SEA-KALE.

The seeds of dill, alexanders, skirrets, rhubarb, and sea-kale should now be sown, for if kept out of the ground till spring, many of them would not vegetate for a year after; but when sown in this or the next month, if the seeds are fresh and perfect, good crops may be expected to rise therefrom in March or April. (For the methods of sowing and treating them, see the *Kitchen Garden* for *March*.)

SHALLOTS, CHIVES, GARLIC, AND ROCAMBOLE.

This is a very proper season to plant roots of shallots, chives, garlic, and rocambole; for the method of planting them, see page 206.

PLANTING LARGE ONIONS FOR PRODUCING SEED.

For this purpose make choice of a piece of good, rich, light ground, which dig a full spade deep, breaking it fine as you proceed; when ready, select a number proportionate to the quantity of seed you intend to save, of the firmest, largest, and best shaped onions, and of the most desirable kinds, observing that each variety is to be planted separately and remote from any other.

The middle of October, or any time between that and the end of the month is the most eligible time for planting, as the bulbs will have time to establish roots or fibres which will greatly support them during winter, and render them less liable to injury from frost than if planted at a later period.

Having your ground dug and the roots in readiness, lay it out into four feet wide beds with a fourteen inch alley between each; then strain a line about six inches within the side of a bed, and with a spade throw out an opening or drill about five inches deep the length of the bed, in which lay the onions, seated handsomely on their bottoms, about nine inches distant one from the other; then with a rake draw the earth into the opening so as to cover the bulbs from three to four inches above their crowns; remove the line a foot farther back, plant another row as before, and so continue till the first bed is planted containing four rows; after which proceed with the others in the same way to the end; then with a spade or shovel cast over the beds a slight dressing from the alleys, and finish by raking them neatly, drawing off the stones and any large lumps of earth from the surface.

In March the leaves will appear above ground, after which they are to be kept perfectly free from weeds; many of the roots will produce three or four stalks each, which towards the latter part of May will have grown to their full height, when you must be provided with a sufficient number of stakes, about four feet long, to drive into the ground in the rows of onions, at the distance of from six to eight feet stake from stake in each and every row, to which are to be fastened double lines of packthread, rope-yarn, or small cord, to run on each side of the stems of the onions a little below their heads, to support and prevent them from breaking down by wind and rain, and if those are tied together at intervals between stake and stake, they will the more effectually support the plants. This is the more necessary, as when the seeds are formed, the heads become very heavy, and often break down even by their own weight, where they are not well secured, in which case there will be a considerable loss both in the quantity and quality of the seed.

When the seed is ripe, which is very perceivable by the capsules opening, and the seed turning black, the heads are to be cut off and spread thinly upon coarse cloths, in the sun, till quite dry, observing to keep them under shelter at night and in wet weather; then beat or rub out the seed, fan it clean, expose it to the sun for a day or two after, and put it up in bags till wanted for sowing.

Some people plant the onions which they intend to produce seed

35

in spring, but when planted at that season they are never so productive of seed as those planted in October, and are much more subject to blight; however when it is so determined, it should be done as soon after the middle of February as it is possible to get the ground in a fit condition to receive them, and should not be covered more than from two to three inches over their crowns; observing to select for that purpose such roots as have good properties and no growths from their tops.

A slight covering of straw or light litter laid over the October planted beds, on the approach of hard frost, and raked clean off as soon as the leaves *begin* to appear in spring, would be of use, though it is not absolutely necessary to the preservation of the roots.

HORSERADISH AND SCURVY-GRASS.

You may now plant roots of the *Cochlearia armoracia*, or horse-radish, in dry, rich ground, agreeably to the directions given on page 217, but in moist soil; March will be a preferable time.

This is a proper season to sow some seed of the *Cochlearia officinalis* or common officinal scurvy-grass; from this sowing the plants will rise freely in spring, and generally succeed better than if sown at that season. I do not mean what is commonly used for an early spring salad, and generally called scurvy-grass, for the sowing of which I have given directions on page 488, under the name of *Winter Cresses.*

ORDINARY WORK.

Give a general hoeing and weeding to all your crops, and carry the weeds immediately out of the garden, lest they shed their seeds and lay the foundation of much trouble; likewise clean all vacant quarters from weeds, and from the decayed stalks of peas, beans, cabbages, &c.

Such spaces of ground as are now vacant should be dunged and dug, or trenched, that it may have the true advantage of fallow in the winter season.

If the ground is of a stiff or heavy nature, throw it up into high sloping ridges, for the reasons assigned on page 17.

TAKING UP THE ROOTS OF CARROTS, BEETS, ETC.

About the latter end of the month you may begin to take up the roots of full grown carrots, beets, parsneps, turnips, Jerusalem artichokes, &c., which are to be preserved as directed in November.

SOUTHERN STATES.

In Georgia, South Carolina, and the parts of North Carolina south of the 35th degree of latitude, you may now sow the seeds of carrot, parsnep, beet, onion, parsley, cresses, spinage, and several other kinds of hardy garden vegetables; plant out from the seed-beds cabbage and cauliflower plants; sow peas, and plant early Mazagan and Windsor beans, with every other variety of the *Vicia Fuba*.

In North Carolina, generally, Tennessee, and the southern parts of Virginia and Kentucky, you may sow peas, plant the above species of bean, sow carrot, parsnep, onion, parsley, and other hardy seeds; plant out cabbages, and also cauliflower plants; but the cauliflowers, if the winter is any way severe, will require the protection of hand glasses, oiled-paper caps, frames, or the like, as directed on page 537.

THE FRUIT GARDEN.

GATHERING WINTER PEARS AND APPLES.

Gather your winter pears and apples as they ripen; but for particulars see the article *Orchard* for this month.

PRUNING.

Towards the latter end of the month, you may begin to prune such trees as have completely shed their leaves, but by no means lay your knife to a tree, for a general pruning, till this is the case.

In the middle States I would not recommend the pruning of peach, nectarine, almond, and apricot-trees before the latter end of February, nor in the eastern States before the first week in March; but they should not be much longer neglected. In the southern States they may be pruned at any time between the periods in which they shed their leaves and the latter end of January.

Apples, pears, plums and cherries being perfectly hardy, may be pruned, in any part of the United States, immediately after they drop their leaves, or in November, December, or January, &c. But were it not on account of performing work *when it can most conveniently be done*, I would prefer *early* spring pruning of all kinds of trees to any other, on account of the recent *wounds* healing and covering over with bark more immediately when vegetation soon follows, than those anteriorly inflicted.

For the method of pruning the various kinds of wall and espalier fruit-trees, &c., see page 32, &c.

PLANTING FRUIT-TREES.

Towards the latter end of this month you may safely transplant most sorts of fruit-trees, but particularly such kinds as shall have by that time shed their leaves. This may be done to advantage during the entire of next month if the season continues open, provided the ground in which you plant be dry and does not lodge water in the winter months; and likewise that sufficient pains be taken to make each tree fast in its place by nailing or binding it up in such a manner as not to be rocked about by the winds; otherwise spring planting, if done early in March, will be more successful, particularly for the peach, nectarine, and almond.

Note.—In the more southern States of the Union the planting of the more hardy kinds of fruit and other trees should be completed before the end of January, on account of the early vegetation in those regions.

If the borders wherein trees are to be planted, either for the wall or espalier be new, they should be trenched at least two feet deep if the good soil admits thereof; but if not, they should be made of that depth by adding thereto a sufficiency of good mellow fertile soil, such as fresh surface loam, &c.; this should be worked to the depth of two feet, at least, with the soil of the border, and it would be of great advantage to add some good rotten dung previous to the trenching. But if a sufficient quantity of fresh soil cannot be conveniently obtained for the whole, you may sink one, two, or three wheelbarrows full, together with some rotten dung, in the place where each tree is to be planted.

However, where the ground is already of a good quality, as that of a common kitchen garden, &c., the above assistance will not be necessary, as trees will prosper sufficiently well in any soil that is productive of good garden vegetables.

As to aspect, your latest ripening fruits, particularly late peaches, should have a warm exposure, and also some of the earliest ripening of the various kinds of fruit, on account of having them in perfection at an early period. For the method of planting, and proper distances, &c., see page 229.

PLANTING GOOSEBERRIES.

Towards the latter end of this month, or early in November, is the best time in the year to plant trees of this delicious and very valuable fruit.

You may plant them around the borders of the best quarters of your kitchen garden about two feet and a half or three feet from the walks, and from six to eight feet distant from one another. Or they may be planted in continued plantations, the rows from eight to ten feet asunder, and the plants six or seven feet apart in the rows. In the latter case the ground between the rows may be occupied with winter spinage, corn salad, lettuces, and winter cresses; and in spring and summer with rows of salading of various kinds, dwarf peas and beans, or any other low growing crops; but it must be particularly observed, *always* to keep the ground under and immediately contiguous to each bush, free from weeds or crops of any kind; for if damps and moisture are confined about the bushes in this way, the fruit will mildew and become useless. If mildew shows itself, dust some sulphur amongst the bushes.

It will be in vain to expect fine fruit unless you have *good kinds*, and give them the best ground possible, a plentiful supply of manure annually, frequent culture and regular pruning.

The best time to plant them out finally is, when they have had one or two years' growth from cuttings ; or indeed the cuttings may, with great propriety, be planted where they are to remain for fruiting. Old gooseberry bushes seldom bear large fruit after being transplanted, unless they are carefully removed with large balls of earth around their roots.

Previous to planting, each young tree should be pruned up to one clean stem of eight to ten or twelve inches before you form the head; for when they are suffered to branch away immediately from the bottom, they, by spreading out so near the ground, will impede the growth of any crops that grow near them, and in the occasional and very necessary business of manuring, digging, hoeing, weeding, &c., will be very troublesome to work between.

For further observations on the planting of gooseberries, see pages 146 and 306.

PRUNING AND PROPAGATING GOOSEBERRIES.

The latter part of this month, and the entire of the next, will be a very suitable season for the pruning of gooseberries. It is a practice too common in pruning these trees to let them branch out with long naked stems, suffering them to remain in that state for many years. When that is already the case they should be cut down, or considerably shortened, to promote a free growth of healthy young shoots, which will bear fruit abundantly the second year. But for general instructions on this head, see page 42.

You may now plant cuttings of the various kinds of gooseberries which you wish to propagate; for the necessary instructions, see page 306.—*Note.*—New varieties of gooseberries may be obtained by sowing seeds of the best kinds you are able to procure, either in this or any of the autumn months, in beds in the open ground, or in boxes of good earth. From these sowings the plants will rise freely in spring, and by the autumn or spring following may be planted in nursery rows to remain another season, after which they are to be finally planted out for fruiting; or they may remain where planted from the seed-bed till they show specimens of fruit ; then those that are good are to be taken due care of; the others, which, by the by, will be the far greater number, may be thrown away.

If the seed is kept out of the ground till spring scarcely any of it will vegetate till that time twelve months; therefore it is necessary either to sow it in autumn, or to preserve it in damp earth or sand till February or March. If sown in autumn cover it near half an inch deep with loose, rich earth ; but if in spring a quarter of an inch will be sufficient.

PLANTING RASPBERRIES.

There are many varieties of the *Rubus idæus*, or European raspberry, but the most preferable are the red Antwerp, the white Antwerp, Fastolf, Victoria, Knevitt's giant, and Dr. Brincklé's seedling raspberries.

The smooth cane double bearing raspberry is cultivated in some places, as it produces one crop of fruit in June, and another in October; but the fruit are few and small, which has occasioned its being neglected.

Of the *Rubus occidentalis*, or American raspberry, we have two varieties, the black fruited, and the red fruited; the latter is preferable in taste and flavor to the black variety.

Raspberries do not thrive well under the shade of trees, nor in such situations are their fruit well flavored; therefore they should be planted in a detached airy piece of ground, naturally good, or artificially made so. As to the choice of plants and method of planting them, I refer you to page 231.

Such as you plant between the middle and latter end of this month, will make new roots before winter, and produce some good fruit next season; but in the year following they will bear plentifully.

DRESSING AND PRUNING RASPBERRIES.

When your new plantations are finished, and all the stout, straggling suckers taken away for that purpose, dig the ground of the old standing plantations carefully, clearing out by the roots the remaining useless and scattered suckers, leaving an ample supply of the best shoots for pruning.

In the middle and eastern States, I would not recommend the pruning of raspberries before spring; for by deferring that work to the latter end of February or beginning of March, there will be a greater chance of the shoots not being injured by frost; and moreover, you can then make choice of such as received the least injury. But in the southern States they may be pruned now with safety; for the method see page 146.

It is necessary to observe that the shoots which had borne fruit last summer, must be cut down to the ground either now or in the spring, as they will never bear again, and that it is from the shoots of the present season, immediately rising from the roots, that you are to expect fruit in the ensuing year.

The Antwerp raspberries being somewhat more tender and subject to be injured by frost than the common kinds, it will be of considerable advantage to protect them therefrom in the manner directed next month.

PROPAGATING FRUIT-TREES BY LAYERS AND SUCKERS.

The young shoots of mulberries, figs, filberts, codlins, vines, &c., may now be laid in the earth, as directed on page 300, and they will be all well rooted by this time twelve months.

Suckers may be taken off and planted from codlins, berberries, filberts, &c., digging them up with good roots to each, and planting the largest at once where they are to remain, and the rest into nursery-rows.

DRESSING THE STRAWBERRY BEDS, AND MAKING NEW PLANTA-TIONS.

The old beds of strawberries should some time in this month have their winter dressing, in doing of which, they should be cleaned from weeds, and the vines or runners taken off close to the plants; then if there be room between the plants by having been kept to distinct heads or single bunches, which is certainly the most preferable method, loosen the earth to a moderate depth with a small spade or hoe, observing not to disturb the roots. And if the plants are in beds with alleys between, line out the alleys and let them be dug a moderate depth, breaking the earth very fine and spreading a sufficiency of it over the beds between and around the roots of the plants, being careful not to bury their tops. A slight top dressing of well rotted dung may sometimes be necessary. This dressing will prove very beneficial, and promote strength and a plentiful crop the ensuing season.

When it was omitted last month, new plantations of strawberries may now be made, but the earlier in the month the better, that the plants may have time to establish new roots before winter. (For full instructions on that head see page 506.)

PRESERVING STONES AND KERNELS OF FRUITS.

Preserve in damp earth or sand, the stones of the various kinds of fruit you intend to sow for stocks, &c., and let apple, pear, and quince kernels be preserved in dry sand till you wish to sow them. Observe not to place them in the way of mice, rats, or squirrels, which would immediately destroy them; and when sown, every precaution must be taken to preserve them from these animals.

THE ORCHARD.

Winter pears and apples should generally be gathered this month; some will be fit for pulling in the early part, others not before the middle or latter end thereof.

To know when the fruits have had their full growth, you should try several of them in different parts of the trees, by turning them gently one way or the other; if they quit the tree easily, it is a sign of maturity and time to gather them.

But none of the more delicate eating pears should be suffered to remain on the trees till overtaken by frost, for if they are once touched with it, it will occasion many of them to rot in a very short time. Indeed, it would be needless, even wrong, to suffer either apples or pears to remain on the trees after the least appearance of ice upon the water, as they would be subject to much injury, and receive no possible kind of benefit afterwards.

Observe in gathering the principal keeping fruits, both pears and apples, to do it when the trees and fruit are perfectly dry, otherwise they will not keep so well; and that the sorts designed for *long keeping* be all carefully hand pulled, one by one, and laid gently into a basket, so as not to bruise one another.

According as the fruits are gathered carry them into the fruitery or into some convenient dry, clean apartment, and lay them carefully in heaps, each sort separate, for about ten days or two weeks, in order that the watery juices may transpire, which will make them keep longer, and render them much better for eating than if put up finally as soon as pulled.

When they have lain in heaps that time wipe each fruit, one after another, with a clean dry cloth, and if you have a very warm dry cellar where frost is by no means likely to enter, nor the place subject to much dampness, lay them singly upon shelves coated with dry straw, and cover them with a layer of the same.

Or you may wrap some of the choice sorts, separately, in white paper, and pack them up in barrels, or in baskets, lined with the like material. Or, after being wiped dry, lay layer about of fruit and *perfectly dry* sand in barrels, and head them up as tight as possible. In default of sand you may use barley chaff, bran, or *dry* saw-dust.

Another method, and a very good one, is to be provided with a number of large earthen jars, and a quantity of moss, in a perfectly dry state; and when the fruits are wiped dry as before directed, your jars being also dry, lay therein layer about of fruit and moss till the jars are near full, then cover with a layer of moss.

Suffer them to remain in this state for eight or ten days, then examine a stratum or two at the top to see if the moss and fruits are perfectly dry; and if you find them in a good condition, stop the jars up with good cork plugs, and cover them with some melted rosin to keep out air. The pears and apples to be used this way should be of the latest and best keeping kinds, and such as are not generally fit for use till February, March, or April.

After the jars are sealed as above, place them in a warm, dry cellar or room, on a bed of *perfectly dry* sand, at least one foot thick; and about the middle of November, or sooner if there is any danger to be apprehended from frost, fill up between the jars with very dry sand until it is a foot thick around and over them. Thus you may preserve pears in the greatest perfection for eight or nine months, and apples twelve.

Be particularly careful to examine every fruit as you wipe it, lest it is bruised, which would cause it soon to rot and communicate the infection, so that in a little time much injury might be sustained in consequence of a trifling neglect in the first instance: but, above all things place your fruit, whatever way they are put up, completely out of the reach of frost.

The common kinds, for more immediate use, after being sweated and wiped as before directed, may be packed in hampers or barrels, layer about of fruit and straw, and placed where they will neither be exposed to damps nor frost.

PLANTING AND PRUNING FRUIT-TREES.

What I have said under the article *Fruit Garden* for this month, is perfectly applicable, inasmuch as it has relation to the planting and pruning of orchards at this season.   But for general instructions on these heads, I refer you to the article *Orchard*, in January, page 57, February, page 150, and March, page 234, &c.   After a careful perusal of what is there said, you will be perfectly able to judge (taking into consideration the nature of your soil and local situation of the place), whether it is more prudent for you to plant and prune in the autumn, or to defer that business till the opening of spring.

If any of your fruit-trees are cracked and rough in the bark when the fruit is pulled, scrape off the loose parts, and, with a large painting brush apply a mixture of cow-dung and urine made to the consistence of a thick paint, covering the stem and any other parts so affected carefully over therewith.   This will soften the old rough bark, which will peal off with it during the following winter and spring, leaving after it the smooth fresh bark only.   Your trees being freed from that incumbrance and harbor for worms, insects, &c., will thrive much more luxuriantly than before.

THE VINEYARD.

Having given ample instructions last month for the making of wines, curing of raisins, and preserving the fruit fresh for a length of time, &c , it is unnecessary to touch upon those subjects in this place; therefore, I have only to refer you to the article *Vineyard*, on page 509, &c., for information respecting anything yet remaining to be done of what was there recommended.

In the southern States vineyards may now be planted, and vines propagated by cuttings, &c., and indeed where the winters are mild and but little or no frost, this is the most suitable season for so doing, particularly towards the latter end of the month.   But in the middle States the month of March, and in the eastern States the early part of April will be the most preferable periods in which to perform this business.

The subject of planting and propagating the vine being treated of at full length in March, beginning at page 244, I refer you thereto for the necessary information.

In the middle States, rooted vines may now be transplanted if necessity requires it, but in no other case would I recommend it; and these should be protected by laying litter around their roots, or some other suitable defence from the severity of the frosts.   Layers, however, may now be made with good prospects of success; and if you find it more convenient to procure cuttings at this season than in spring, you may plant them; but observe that it will be necessary to cover them lightly with straw, fern, leaves of trees, or some other light covering during winter or many of them will miscarry. Though these plants are extremely hardy when once established, they are rather tender in their infancy, and every advantage of season ought to be afforded them, especially in those parts of the Union where the winters are severe.

As to the practice of pruning grape-vines in autumn, it is not advisable, except where the winters are very mild. In the southern States this may be done with great propriety as soon in this or the ensuing month as the foliage shall have been shed, but by no means before, as while the leaves remain on the vines will not have done growing, and consequently the wood will not be sufficiently ripe and hard.

For further observations, together with the methods of pruning, see page 155, &c. (See also the *Vineyard* for next month.)

PLANTING WILLOWS FOR TYING THE GRAPE-VINES, ETC.

In the latter end of this, or the early part of next month, you should make plantations of willows for the purpose of tying up the vines with the small flexible twigs thereof.

Osiers or willows are also very useful in a garden for tying the branches of espalier-trees to trellises, binding up lettuces, cabbages, endive, &c., for blanching, tying bundles of trees or shrubs, making garden baskets, &c., so that a small plantation or hedge-row of willows would be very useful in every garden department.

The kinds most suitable for this purpose are the *Salix viminalis*, or true osier; *S. fissa*, or basket osier; and *S. vitillina*, or golden willow.

Willows of those kinds particularly, delight in low moist situations (though they grow to good perfection in a strong loam), consequently, soil that is generally useless or of but little value, may be profitably occupied by them. Make choice of such ground and plough it deep if possible for the reception of the cuttings; if too wet for the plough, form it with a spade and shovel into four feet wide ridges with deep trenches between, casting up the earth out of the trenches to form the ridges high and rounding; in each ridge plant two rows of cuttings, each row a foot from the edge, and the sets two feet and a half distant from one another in the row.

The cuttings or sets should be about two feet long, made from strong shoots of two or three years' growth, and about two-thirds of each set planted or drove into the earth, leaving the rest out to form the stool; each of these will throw out several shoots, and if kept free from weeds for the ensuing season, they will provide for themselves afterwards.

The year old shoots being what are generally used for the various purposes noticed, the whole produce must be cut down annually, either in autumn or spring, to promote such growths. However, a sufficiency may now be suffered to grow for two or three years when sets are wanted for an additional plantation.

If the ground can be ploughed, it will be attended with less trouble, and the rows may be planted three feet asunder: the distance of

the sets from one another in each row, should be about two feet and
a half.

I would advise to plant the cuttings with a dibble, in preference
to *forcing* them in, as by the latter method the bark would be injured.

This work may be done with equal propriety, and sometimes with
more success in the early part of spring. Cuttings may also be
planted at either season in the face of moist ditches, where they will
succeed extremely well.

THE NURSERY.

TRENCHING AND DRESSING THE GROUND.

In the beginning of this month continue to trench and prepare
the several quarters in which you intend to plant stocks, to graft and
bud the several sorts of fruit upon and also for the various other
planting and sowing that may be necessary.

Carry dung into such parts of the nursery as it is wanted, and
spread it upon the surface of the ground around the stems of young
trees ; this will contribute to the preservation of their roots from frost,
the rains will wash in the salts to the roots of the trees, and in spring
you may dig in the dung between the respective rows.

PROPAGATING TREES AND SHRUBS BY LAYERS.

Any time this month you may lay the various kinds of trees and
shrubs that you wish to propagate in that way ; for the methods of
doing which, together with several useful observations, see page 300,
&c.

Towards the latter end of the month take off such layers of the
preceding year as are well rooted, trim their stems, and plant them in
nursery-rows, or elsewhere as may be necessary.

This is the best season to lay elms, limes, maples, and most kinds
of hardy forest-trees and flowering shrubs ; for the moisture of the
ground during winter will prepare them for pushing out roots early
in the spring.

PROPAGATING TREES AND SHRUBS BY CUTTINGS.

This is a proper time to plant cuttings of all *hardy* trees and
shrubs, that will grow by that method, especially in the southern
States ; but it will be necessary to plant them where water does not
lodge in winter. Poplars, willows, plane-trees, honeysuckles, &c.,
will grow freely in this way ; but for more particulars, see page 304.

Cuttings of all sorts planted a year ago, or last spring, that are
well rooted and have shot freely at top, may, towards the latter end

of this month, be transplanted, if necessary, into open nursery-rows, to advance in growth and to have occasional training for the purposes intended.

SOWING HAW AND HOLLY BERRIES, ETC.

In the southern States you may any time in this or the three ensuing months, if the ground is open, sow haw, holly, yew, and mezereon berries, ash, hornbeam, and any other kind of seeds that require a year's previous preparation; but in the middle States, I would recommend to defer the sowing of these till the latter end of February, or very *early* in March, and in the eastern States, as soon in the latter month as possible. Indeed it would not be wrong to defer the sowing of them, even in the southern States, till January or February, according to the respective climates, always endeavoring to sow them before they begin to vegetate.

Observe that each kind has undergone a full year's preparation, previous to sowing, as directed in the *Nursery* for *February* and *March*, where you will find ample instructions for the cultivation of these and many other kinds of trees and shrubs, and which I would particularly recommend to your perusal at this time.

SOWING OAK ACORNS, CHESTNUTS, WALNUTS, HICKORY-NUTS, ETC.

The best season in the year for sowing the acorns of every kind of oak, is immediately after they fall from the trees; for when kept up much longer, especially in a dry state, they lose their vegetative power.

The only evils they have to encounter by sowing them at this season are, the depredations of mice, rats, and squirrels, &c.; if these animals can be caught, poisoned, or kept off by any means that may be devised, the seeds should be sown immediately; but if not, it will be better to preserve them till the early spring months, in sand or earth, or in moss, and although they will soon sprout, their progress in vegetation before the opening of spring will not be such as to do them any material injury, provided they are placed immediately in the coldest place possible till winter, and further, that you do not break the small radicles when planting them in spring.

The acorns, if sown or planted at this time, should be laid within one inch of one another in drills about two feet apart, and covered about an inch deep; here they may remain till they shall have had two years' growth, when they must be taken up and planted into nursery-rows at proper distances, there to acquire a sufficient growth and strength for a final transplanting, which will generally be the case in about two or three years.

Chestnuts of every kind, walnuts, and hickory-nuts may be planted now, or immediately after being ripe; they have the same enemies to encounter as the acorns; but all these kinds will keep well till spring in dry sand, or even in bags or boxes, and if planted *early* in that season will vegetate freely.

But if you find it more convenient to plant the nuts in autumn, let that be done, if possible, when they are perfectly ripe, and in their outward covers or husks, the extreme bitterness of which will be a good preservative against the attacks of vermin of every kind.

When you desire to cultivate the *Juglans regia*, or European walnut, for its fruit, and likewise any of the other species, make choice of the best varieties of nuts, such as are large, thin shelled, and have the finest flavored kernels; for although the best sorts will vary or degenerate, when raised from seeds, yet, by planting the most valuable varieties, there will be the better chance of having good kinds continued.

For the method of planting, and the subsequent treatment of chestnuts, walnuts, &c., see page 282.

Note.—When oaks, chestnuts, or walnuts, &c., are planted exclusively on account of their timber, it will be the better way, when it can conveniently be done, to sow or plant the acorns and nuts where they are intended to remain for full and mature growth; for trees of either of these kinds seldom attain to as great magnitude after having been transplanted, as if suffered to remain undisturbed where the seeds were sown.

TRANSPLANTING STOCKS, TO BUD AND GRAFT UPON.

About the latter end of this month you may plant out into nursery-rows all the hardy kinds of seeding stocks, to bud and graft the different varieties of fruits upon.

Let these be planted out in rows three feet asunder, and one foot or more distant from one another in the rows.

Plant also for the purpose of stocks, suckers from the roots of plums, codlins, pears, quinces, &c., but seedlings are much more preferable if you are sufficiently supplied therewith.

Transplant likewise from nursery beds and layer-stools all the well rooted cuttings and layers that were planted or laid a year ago, or in the last spring, for the purpose of raising stocks for fruit-trees; particularly quinces and codlins, to bud and graft dwarf pears and apples upon, in order to form dwarf trees for walls and espaliers, planting them in nursery-rows as above.

PLANTING HARDY DECIDUOUS TREES AND SHRUBS.

All manner of hardy deciduous trees and shrubs may be planted now into nursery-rows, or finally where they are to remain, immediately after they have shed their leaves, or as soon as the general foliage is turned yellow and on the decline; but observe that planting at this season should always be done in ground that lies dry in winter. When that is the case, the trees, shrubs, &c., will establish new roots before they are overtaken by the heats of the ensuing summer, and will require but very little trouble in watering.

PRUNING.

In the latter part of this month you may begin to prune and re-

duce into proper form most kinds of hardy forest and fruit-trees,
flowering shrubs, &c., clearing their stems from lateral shoots, eradicating suckers, and dressing their heads in a neat and becoming
manner.

PLANTING HARDY EVERGREENS.

Between the middle and latter end of this month you may plant
pines, firs, cedars, junipers, and every other kind of hardy evergreen trees and shrubs. However, I would not advise to plant
small seedlings of any kind at this season, especially in the middle
and eastern States, as many of them would be thrown out of the
ground by the winter frosts, and most of them so loosened in the
earth as to be subject to great injury from the parching winds in
spring; consequently, March will be a more eligible season for this
purpose.

SOWING STONES OF FRUIT-TREES.

If you are not apprehensive of the ravages of mice, rats, squirrels,
&c., you may now sow the stones of plums, peaches, nectarines,
apricots, &c., or you may, if you think it more prudent, preserve
them in sand, &c., as directed on former occasions, till February or
March.

These stones may now be sown pretty thick in drills, two feet
asunder, and covered from one to two inches deep, according to the
size of the respective kinds and lightness of the soil; and at this time
twelve months such of them as shall have attained to a good growth
may be transplanted into nursery-rows.

SOWING BEECH-MAST, MAPLES, ETC.

Beech-mast, maple, and several other kinds may now be sown as
directed in March, or they may be preserved in dry sand till that
season.

Note.—Many sorts of seeds may now be sown, but as I treated on
the subject of the *Nursery* at considerable length in March, and there
noticed what kinds might be sown with safety in autumn, I refer you
thereto for particular information.

SOWING APPLE, CRAB, AND PEAR PUMICE.

The pumice of apples, crabs, and pears, after having been pressed
for cider or perry, may be sown, kernels and all, in four feet wide
beds, laid on very thick and covered about an inch deep with good
light earth. In spring the plants will rise freely and produce you
a good supply, either for stocks, or for making live hedges. (See
page 274.)

PRESERVATION OF FRUITS.

A fruit room much commended is now in use among many fruit
raisers, which it may be as well to describe. There is a cavity be-

tween the boarding and walls, which is important, and so is the
wooden lining, because air and wood are known to be slow conductors
of heat.   The ceiling is double, and the floor is wood above a ceiling,
which to a considerable extent insures a uniformity of temperature.

Fig. 59.

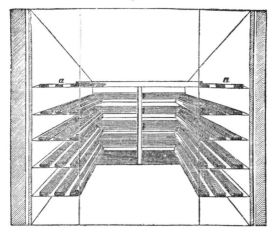

There is a small stove in the room, but it is only used when the
temperature is below the freezing point, or to remove damp; the
fruit is therefore kept cool.   A swing window is occasionally a little
opened, but should be at all times covered with a roller blind, so that
the fruit is kept in the dark.   The shelves a, a, have a layer of clean
straw laid across them; on this the fruit is laid singly. (Fig. 59.)

THE PLEASURE, OR FLOWER GARDEN.

AURICULAS, POLYANTHUSES, AND PRIMROSES.

The auriculas in pots must now be kept very clean, all decayed
leaves picked off occasionally, and moderate waterings administered
as often as necessary, that the plants may attain due strength before
winter.

The choice of polyanthuses and double primroses are to be treated
in every respect as the auriculas; the common kinds may now be
planted in beds and borders of good ground, where they will flower
early in spring in tolerable perfection, especially if they have a
slight covering of straw or light dry litter laid over them during
severe frosts.

The seedling plants of each of the above kinds must be kept free
from weeds and filth of every sort, and receive regular but gentle

waterings to promote their growth and strength as much as possible before winter.

For the methods of preserving the choice kinds of auriculas, polyanthuses, and primroses during winter, see the *Flower Garden* in *November*.

CARNATIONS.

The carnation layers that were taken off in August or September, and all other choice carnations in pots should now be kept clean and duly watered, and towards the latter end of the month be placed in a warm situation, there to remain until disposed of as directed in November.

The seedlings and common kinds may be transplanted into beds and borders where wanted.

PINKS.

Your choice double pinks in pots, will require the same treatment as the carnations; but as pinks are extremely hardy, they may be cultivated in great perfection in the open ground.

A good fresh loamy soil trenched about two feet deep, well pulverized, and manured with a stratum of cow-dung two years old, mixed with an equal portion of sound good earth; this stratum to be about six inches thick, and placed about four inches below the surface, is all the preparation or compost that appears necessary for this flower.

The bed should be raised three or four inches above the surrounding paths, and its sides may be supported with an edging of boards to come up even with, or one inch higher than its surface; this last for the sake of neatness, more than any particular utility it will be of to the plants.

The plants intended for the principal bloom should be planted in it in the first week of this month or in September, as they do not blow quite so strong if removed late in the season: they should be planted at the distance of nine inches from each other, and the bed should be laid rather convex or rounding, to throw off excess of rain, but it will require no other covering than a very slight one in case of severe frosts.

The bed should be kept free from weeds, and its surface stirred up a little if it inclines to bind.

Carnations will prosper very well if treated in the above manner.

The more indifferent kinds of pinks may be planted in the common borders, &c.

PLANTING SUPERB TULIP ROOTS.

The most proper season for planting tulip roots in general is from the middle to the latter end of this month, and indeed I should prefer the middle to any other period, for about that time you will perceive a circle around the lower end of each bulb, disposed to swell, preparatory to the emission of fibres, and also a disposition at the upper end of some to show foliage.

By keeping the roots out of ground after this predisposition to vegetation, they would be greatly weakened thereby.

The situation for the best bed of *superior tulips*, should be in an open airy part of the garden, protected at the same time from north and west winds by some distant shelter; when that is fixed upon, the ground should be marked out agreeably to its intended dimensions, and the soil taken out twenty inches deep; the bottom is then to be filled up with sound fresh earth ten inches thick, upon which is to be placed a stratum of two years old rotten cow-dung and earth of the above description, one-half of each, well mixed together and laid on twelve inches thick; upon this is to be placed another stratum of the same kind of earth as that of the bottom; this latter is only to be two inches thick at the sides, and three in the middle of the bed, which will give it a small degree of convexity.

The bed should be thus prepared a week or ten days previous to planting the roots, in order to give it time to settle, so as to be about two inches higher than the circumjacent paths; but if heavy rains intervene between this preparation of the bed and planting, it will be proper to keep them off in order to preserve the earth from becoming too compact by a redundancy of moisture, for the young fibres to pass freely through it.

On the day made choice of for planting, rake the surface of the bed smooth, and level any inequalities, still preserving its convexity, and mark the exact situation for every root upon it. The proper distance between each root is seven inches every way.

A bed consisting of seven rows makes the most grand appearance when it is of sufficient length, with a path around it about two and a half or three feet wide; but where the number of roots is small, five rows may suffice, and the path in that case may either extend quite around the bed, or only on one side, at pleasure.

If the bed consists of seven rows it should consequently be fifty inches wide, which will allow a space of four inches between the outside rows and the sides of the bed; but if the bed contains only five rows, it will only require to be three feet wide to give the roots similar distances.

Having sprinkled a little clean sand where the roots are to be set, place them with great exactness, and add some very sandy earth, so as to completely envelope each root in a little cone of it; then cover the whole very carefully with strong, sound, fresh loam, about four inches thick or a little better, if the roots are strong, so as to allow the covering to be from three and a half to four inches thick, after the earth shall have settled, still observing to preserve the original convexity of the bed.

The tallest growing kinds should be placed in the middle, and the lower towards the outsides. No tulip root, whatever may be its size or strength, should be planted more than four inches deep from the upper side of the root; nor should any *blooming* root be planted less than three inches deep, however small it may be. The soil made use of for covering the bulbs, should be frequently turned over and

36

thoroughly exposed to the sun and air some time before it is made use of, that it may be rendered perfectly sweet and free from the acrid quality that most soils are most subject to when taken considerably below the surface.

If the bed is only to contain five rows, with a path in the front and not behind, then it will be proper to plant the smallest and lowest growing kinds in the front next the path, and so gradually to increase in the size to the fifth or last row, which should contain the strongest and tallest of all. Board edgings may be placed around the beds as high or an inch higher than the surface; this will not only keep the earth from crumbling down from the outside rows, but give a degree of neatness to the whole.

When the operation of planting is concluded, in order to preserve the bed from heavy rains or severe frosts, it should be arched over with hoops at convenient distances, on which to lay mats or canvas on such emergencies; but it will not be necessary to defend it from moderate rains or slight frosts: for too frequent and long covering will deprive the roots of the due action and influence of the air, which ought to be avoided as much as possible : it were even better not to cover at all than over do it to the certain detriment of the plants.

Having procured roots of the *finest sorts*, and pursuing the preceding instructions, you may depend on having those incomparable flowers in the greatest perfection possible.

The common kinds of tulips, being of little value, may be planted in small patches of three, four, or five roots together, around the borders of the garden or pleasure-ground, and covered the same depth as the others.

PLANTING THE BEST HYACINTH ROOTS.

The roots of hyacinths may be planted with good expectation of success at any time from the beginning of this month to the middle of November; but I would prefer the middle of the present month, as being the best period in which these roots can be planted; for about that time they will show a natural inclination to vegetate, manifested by a swelling of the circle from whence the fibres proceed, which will be soon followed by an actual appearance of their points, together with that of the foliage at the other extremity of the root, in the form of a small cone of a greenish color.

The bed on which the finest sorts are to be planted should be situated in rather a dry and airy part of the garden; a southern aspect is to be preferred, sheltered on the north and northwest by walls, trees, or buildings, at a distance from it proportionate to their elevation; that is, the distance of the bed from either should be equal to the height of the wall, fence, or hedge, &c.

When the situation is determined on, the dimension of the bed should be marked out and the soil entirely taken away to the depth of at least two feet; the earth in the bottom should then be dug and well pulverized for about nine inches deep, and the space above filled with the following compost :—

One-third sea or river sand ; one-third fresh sound earth ; one-fourth rotten cow-dung at least two years old ; and one-twelfth of earth of decayed leaves.

The fresh sound earth of the compost should be of the best quality that the garden or adjacent country affords, and entirely free from noxious vermin of every description. These ingredients should be well mixed and incorporated a considerable time before wanted, and about ten days previous to planting, the bed should be filled up with the compost to about three inches above the level of the path on the south or front side, and seven inches on the north side, so as to form a regular slope or inclination towards the sun.

On planting the roots the surface of the bed should be covered with fresh sandy earth about one inch thick, raked perfectly smooth and even, and have the exact situation for every bulb marked on it, as follows :—

R	B	W	R	B	W	R	B	W	R	B
	W	R	B	W	R	B	W	R	B	W
R	B	W	R	B	W	R	B	W	R	B
	W	R	B	W	R	B	W	R	B	W
R	B	W	R	B	W	R	B	W	R	B
	W	R	B	W	R	B	W	R	B	W

This plan, on minute investigation, will appear superior to any other that can be devised for simplicity and an elegant and advantageous display of the colors; each bulb, those of the outside rows excepted, will be in the centre of a hexagon, and the whole at equal distances from each other. The width of the surface of the bed is to be four feet, the six rows along it eight inches asunder, and the outside rows each four inches from the sides of the bed; consequently the space between the centre of each bulb will be about nine inches and a quarter. The letters R, B, W, denote the color of the flower to be placed there, viz: Red, Blue or White. Under these three heads all hyacinths may be comprehended, except a few sorts of yellow, which may be classed with the whites.

On planting the hyacinths a little clean sand should be placed underneath, and likewise upon the roots, to prevent the earth ad-*hering too close to them; the whole are then to be covered with sound, fresh, sandy earth, from three to four inches deep, according to the size of the bulbs; when this is completed, the bed will be about six or seven inches above the level of the walk in front, or on the south side, and about ten or eleven inches on the north side; it should be supported all around with a strong frame of thick boards or with brickwork; this frame should be six inches or more higher all around than the surface, and of course sloping towards the front to support such covering as may be necessary for the preservation of the roots from heavy rains and severe frosts. For their further treatment see the ensuing months.

The extraordinary preparation and trouble above recommended, are only necessary to bring the finest kinds of hyacinths to the best possible perfection; but the nearer you can make it convenient to approach to said method, in the cultivation of all the other varieties, the greater perfection you may expect to have them in; this, how ever, must be governed by circumstances, and you need not despair of having very fine flowers in any *good*, rich kitchen garden soil that lies dry and inclines a little to sand; and even without any kind of protection during winter.

The common sorts of hyacinths, of every species and variety, may be planted in open beds, or in small clumps round the borders, three, four, or five roots in a place, and covered from three to four inches deep, according to the strength of the roots and lightness of the soil.

PLANTING RANUNCULUSES.

Ranunculus roots may either be planted before or after winter; if the soil and situation is remarkably cold and wet, it will be better to defer planting till the first opening of spring, but then the earliest opportunity of planting them should be embraced.

In favorable situations, and where due attention can be paid to the protection of the roots from severe frosts, the early part of this month is the most preferable period and should be embraced, as the roots will have more time to vegetate, and form themselves, and will, of consequence, bloom stronger and earlier than those planted in spring.

The ranunculuses are originally natives of a warm climate, where they blow in the winter, or more rainy season of the year; they are of course partial to coolness and moisture, *exempt from wet and frost*, which the more delicate sorts cannot bear, in any considerable degree, without injury.*

A fresh, strong, rich, loamy soil, is preferable to all others for ranunculuses.

The bed should be dug from eighteen inches to two feet deep, and not raised more than four inches above the level of the walks, to preserve a moderate degree of moisture; at about five inches below the surface should be placed a stratum of two years old rotten cow-dung, mixed with earth, six or eight inches thick; but the earth above this stratum, where the roots are to be planted, must be free from dung, which would prove of more injury than benefit, if too near them. The fibres will draw sufficient nourishment from it at the depth above mentioned; but if the dung were placed deeper it

* The best method of growing both ranunculuses and anemones is to plant in frames covered with glass, and treat them in the same way as Neapolitan violets, or else in pots in a cool green-house; by this treatment they will bloom strong, and perfect their growth before the hot weather commences.

would not receive so much advantage from the action of the air, which is an object of some importance.

The surface of the bed should be raked perfectly even and flat, and the roots planted in rows at the distance of about five or six inches from one another. It is better to plant in shallow trenches, made nearly two inches deep, than to make holes for the reception of the roots; there should be a little clean sand sprinkled in the trench, and the roots placed with their claws downwards, each distant from the other about three or four inches according to its size and strength; when the roots are thus laid in fill the trenches up level, with the same earth that was taken out so as to cover the roots exactly one inch and a half deep, which is the only true depth to produce a good bloom; it is pointed out by nature in a singular manner; for when these roots have been planted either too shallow or too deep, in either case, a second root is generally formed at a proper depth, by which the plant is weakened to such a degree that it seldom survives a repetition of it. It will be of considerable service to have the bed framed around with boards, or brickwork, a few inches higher than its surface, in front, and rising gradually to the back part, in order to make it the more convenient to protect the roots from severe frosts, as directed in the following months.

PLANTING ANEMONES.

Anemones require nearly the same treatment as ranunculuses, are hardier, and consequently may be planted in the autumn with more safety; the most eligible period is between the first and fifteenth of this month, for if the winter sets in early and proves severe, late planted roots will not have time to vegetate before frosty weather takes place; in which case, there will be great danger of their perishing, as they are then replete with moisture, and in a state of inactivity, which renders not only them but all other roots more susceptible of injury from frost, and more subject to mouldiness, than after vegetation has commenced. To avoid which, as much as possible, a suitable covering or protection must be put on and taken off the beds, as often and in such proportion, as the exigency or circumstances of the case may require.

The beds should consist of the same kind of soil, and be prepared in the same manner as for ranunculuses; the roots should be at nearly similar distances from each other, and be planted in the same manner, except that they require to be covered rather deeper; that is, they should be planted two inches deep. It requires some care and attention to distinguish which side of the root is to be placed uppermost, especially if the small thread-like fibres had been entirely cleaned off, when the roots were taken up.

The roots are in general rather flat, and their eyes, from whence the stems and flowers proceed, are easily distinguished on one side of the root, which of course should be planted uppermost. For their further treatment see the ensuing months.

PLANTING VARIOUS KINDS OF BULBOUS-ROOTED FLOWERS.

A good, sound, fresh soil, either of the black or loamy kind (with the addition of a little coarse sea or river sand placed round the roots on planting), and manured with rotten cow-dung, two years old at least, if the soil and situation be dry and warm, or rotten horse-dung, if it be cold and moist, is all the compost or preparation required for the greater part of those flowers; observing that the dung should never come in contact with the bulbs, or be placed at so great a depth from the surface of the soil as to lose the advantage of the due action of the air upon it, which would render it poisonous instead of nutritious: in short it should never be placed more than eight or ten inches deep upon any occasion, where it can possibly be avoided.

The polyanthus-narcissus consists of many varieties; each sort produces several flowers on one stalk; the roots may be planted any time this month, about three or four inches deep; they succeed best in rather a warm dry soil and situation: but if the soil happens to be the reverse, the bed should be raised seven or eight inches above the common level, and in either case it would be well to cover the bed with straw in case of severe frost, for the roots of these are more tender and subject to be injured by the severity of the winter, than either hyacinths or tulips. The bed should be formed rather rounding, to cast off the wet, for which a good fall or descent should be in some convenient direction. The roots may remain two or three years in the ground without being disturbed; but then it will be necessary to take them up to separate their offsets, which by being longer connected with the old roots, would cause them to blow small and weak.

Double-narcissus (daffodils) consist of several varieties; they are hardier than the former, the Italian excepted, and may be treated in a similar manner, but are in less danger from the effects of frost.

Jonquils, English, Spanish, and Persian bulbous iris: the three first consist of several varieties; they may be planted from two to three inches deep, according to the looseness of the soil and strength of the bulbs, and treated in the same manner as the polyanthus-narcissus: they are all hardy.

Crown imperials, lilies, pæonias, and the ornithogalum pyramidale, or star of Bethlehem, should be planted now, if not done before, and covered about four inches deep; these do not require to be taken up oftener than once in two or three years, and then only to separate their offsets.

Martagons (lilies with revolute petals) consist of many species and varieties, and may be treated as other lilies; they however make the best appearance in beds by themselves, and will grow stronger if the ground is well manured and the roots planted from five to six inches deep. The lilies called martagons are, the *Lilium chalcedonicum,* or scarlet martagon lily, *L. catesbæi,* or Catesby's lily, *L. pomponium,* or pomponian lily, *L. superbum,* or superb lily, *L. martagon,* or purple martagon lily, *L. canadense,* or Canada martagon lily, and *L. japonicum,* or Japan white lily, with their varieties; the latter obtained by sowing the seeds of the different species.

If not done in the preceding months, you should no longer defer the planting of spring crocuses, snowdrops, hardy gladioluses, Persian fritillarias, erythroniums, pancratium maratimum, orchises, limadorum tuberosum, snake's-head iris, musk, feathered, grape, and other hyacinths; the scilla maritima, or officinal squill, scilla peruviana, or starry hyacinth, together with all the other kinds of hardy bulbous or tuberous-rooted flowers which you intend planting before spring. These may be planted separately in beds, or along the borders of the flower garden and pleasure grounds and covered from two to three or four inches deep over the crowns of the roots, according to their respective size and strength, and the lightness or stiffness of the soil.

In planting any of the above or other sorts in borders, observe that the lowest growing kinds are to be planted next the walks, and the larger farther back, in proportion to their respective growths, that the whole may appear to advantage, and none be concealed from the view. Likewise observe to diversify the kinds and colors, so as to display, when in bloom, the greatest possible variety of shades and contrasts.

In assemblage with other flowers in the borders, these should be planted in small clumps of six, seven, or eight inches in diameter, three, four, five, or more roots in each, according to size and growth, and these at suitable distances from one another, say one, two, or three yards. Some of the common anemones and ranunculuses may also be planted with those roots in the borders, either in rows towards the edges, or in small clumps or patches as above.

As much elegance of taste and fancy is necessary, and may be displayed in setting off a border of intermixed flowers to advantage as perhaps in any other part of gardening.

SOWING SEEDS OF BULBOUS-ROOTED FLOWERS, ETC.

You may still continue to sow the seeds of bulbous and tuberous-rooted flowers, as directed on page 522.

TRANSPLANT PERENNIAL AND BIENNIAL FLOWER ROOTS.

The entire of this month is a very proper time to divide and transplant the various kinds of hardy perennial and biennial flower-roots, as noticed on page 523, which see.

Observe to plant the different sorts in a diversified order, the low growing kinds next the walks, and the largest more remote therefrom, so that the whole may rise in a regular gradation as they advance in growth.

Collect ornamental plants from the woods, fields, and swamps, as directed on page 494; this will be a very good time to procure the late flowering kinds, many of which are extremely beautiful.

NEAPOLITAN AND RUSSIAN VIOLETS.

These may be planted in frames having glazed sashes, at the beginning of the month. Dig in a third of rotted leaves or decayed vegetable refuse; put out single crowns six inches apart, give a good soaking of water, and after they have taken root, give air freely in all favorable weather; when winter sets in cover with thick straw mats at night. In this way they will bloom all winter, and repay for the extra labor.

DOUBLE DAISIES, ETC.

About the middle of this month, prepare a warm border in a south aspect, on which to plant the double daisies that you preserved in shaded situations during summer; the bed should be raised four or five inches above the common level, and if surrounded with a frame the better; take up the roots with balls of earth and plant them on this bed in rows, five or six inches plant from plant, every way; give them water immediately, and if shaded from the sun for a week or two, it would be of considerable service.

Primroses, polyanthuses, and common auriculas, may be treated in this way. (For their further management see the ensuing months.)

STOCK-GILLYFLOWERS AND WALL-FLOWERS.

Any double stocks and wall flowers that you have growing in beds or borders, should be potted in the beginning of this month, if not done in September, and placed in the shade for about three weeks, then removed to a warm aspect, there to remain till it is found necessary to house or place them in a frame.

PLANTING BULBOUS ROOTS IN POTS AND GLASSES FOR FLOWERING EARLY.

In the beginning of this month you should plant some of the earliest kinds of tulips, hyacinths, polyanthus-narcissus, &c., in pots of light, rich, sandy earth, one, two, or three roots in each, and of different colors, in order to force them into an early bloom in winter. If the pots are large the roots may be covered one inch above their crowns, but if small the bare covering of the crowns will be sufficient, in order to give the fibres the more room to extend themselves.

Ranunculuses, anemones, crocusses, snowdrops, dwarf Persian irises, and any other early blooming kinds, may be planted in pots for the same purpose, covering them generally about an inch deep over their crowns.

When the roots are planted the pots are to be sunk to their rims in a good stout garden frame, on a bed of very light sandy earth, elevated above the common level of the ground, where they are to be kept gently moist and no more; but they must be carefully protected from heavy torrents of rain, which would tend greatly to rot or weaken the bulbs. The glasses are to be kept off, except in rainy weather, till the approach of frost, after which the bed must be defended therefrom as directed in the following months.

In this month you should put the bulbs of tulips, hyacinths, jonquils, narcissuses, &c., in bulb-glasses filled with water, to flower in rooms early in spring; the glasses should be then placed where they may have as much free air as possible while the weather continues mild; if they are placed near the windows of a green-house, where they may have free air in favorable weather, and be protected from cold and frost, they will produce fine, strong flowers, and at a very acceptable season.

The water should be changed as often as it turns greenish, and the glasses well washed inside. Particular care must be taken not to suffer the water to be frozen in winter, which would not only injure the roots but burst the glasses.

POTTING ROSES, ETC., FOR FORCING.

Pot roses, honeysuckles, double-flowering almonds, peaches, cherries, and thorns, and any other desirable shrubs, whether evergreen or deciduous, either for the convenience of affording them protection in winter, decorating any compartments in spring or summer, or for placing some of them in the forcing departments in December or January, to force an early bloom. This must be done with care, not injuring the roots, and taking up as much earth with them as possible. When potted, place them in the shade for ten or twelve days after, or until you find it necessary to house or otherwise protect them.

PRUNE FLOWERING SHRUBS.

This is a very proper season to prune roses, lilacs, honeysuckles, and indeed all kinds of hardy trees and shrubs, whether deciduous or evergreen. Let this be performed with a sharp knife, and not with garden shears, as sometimes practised. But to avoid repetition I refer you for further instructions on this head, to page 172.

All suckers which arise from the roots should now be taken clean away, for when suffered to remain they starve the old plants and prevent their flowering; many kinds of shrubs, for instance the lilac, will send forth great numbers of suckers from their roots, which, if not annually taken off, will spread over the ground to the great injury of your plants. These suckers, if wanted, may be planted in nursery rows for a year or two, and will then answer for renewing the old or for forming new plantations.

FORMING NEW ORNAMENTAL PLANTATIONS, ETC.

This being a very proper season for laying out and planting pleasure-grounds, I refer you for general information on these subjects to page 74, &c., which though given in a month not favorable for such work, in the middle or eastern States, I considered it a period in which there would be leisure time for contemplating the designs and making preparations for the carrying of them into execution on the opening of spring.

All kinds of hardy deciduous trees and shrubs may be planted as soon in this month as they shall have shed their leaves; the evergreen kinds may be planted towards the latter end thereof, always, but particularly for the latter, making choice of moist or cloudy weather, if such should occur in due season.

In this place I think it proper to remark, that I always have had better success in the planting of evergreens in general, when done in the spring of the year immediately before their vegetation commenced, than at any other season.

The early part of next month will be an excellent time to plant all kinds of deciduous forest-trees and flowering shrubs, &c. that shall not have shed their foliage before that time.

For general directions respecting the best methods of planting trees and shrubs of every kind see page 315.

PROPAGATE TREES AND SHRUBS.

Various kinds of trees and shrubs growing in the pleasure-ground, borders, &c. may now be propagated by suckers, layers, and cuttings; but having described the methods of doing this in the nursery for March, a repetition is unnecessary in this place.

PLANTING BOX AND OTHER EDGINGS.

Box edgings may be planted any time this month with good success, if some care be taken to give them shade and water for about a month : for the method see page 316.*

Many other kinds may now be planted for edgings, but particularly those mentioned on page 369, which see.

PLANT HEDGES.

This is a fine season to plant all sorts of live hedges, whether for fences, shade, or ornament; especially ground hedges, or such as are to be established on the plain surface of the earth; but having treated on this subject at full length, in the *Nursery* for *March*, beginning at page 271, to which I refer you, it is unnecessary to repeat here what has been said before.

It may, however, be proper to observe, that evergreen hedges are, generally, more successful when planted in spring than at this season; notwithstanding, in cases of necessity, I would not hesitate to plant them now.

CLIPPING HEDGES AND EDGINGS.

If any hedges or box edgings want trimming, let them be clipped early in this month, observing the directions given on page 525.

Be very particular to finish the clipping of *evergreen hedges* as early in the month as possible, for if cut too late the cold will occasion the cut leaves, and others suddenly exposed thereto, to change

---

* If box edging is planted at this time in the northern States it will need covering during the first winter to prevent the lifting by frost.

to a rusty disagreeable color, which they will not recover before the ensuing spring.

ORDINARY WORK.

Mow grass-walks and lawns close and even, and roll them, in order that they should appear neat all winter; clean and roll your gravel-walks once a week; hoe, weed, cut, rake, and carry away clean off the ground, all weeds, decayed flower-stems, fallen leaves, &c.; prepare ground by trenching, laying it up in ridges, &c. for spring planting, which will be of considerable advantage both in meliorating the ground and expediting your business at that season.

THE GREEN-HOUSE.

Having in the preceding month, page 527, intimated the proper time for taking in the green-house plants, in the eastern States, I shall now notice the period for doing that business in the middle States. In the southern States, the plants may be left out a few days later than hereafter mentioned, say from four to ten, according to climate, season, and local situation.

About the first day of this month, if not done before, take into the green-house all the more hardy species of cactuses, aloes, mesembryanthemums, sedums, stapelias, agaves, cotyledons, cycas revoluta, and other succulent and tender plants; place them in front where they can have plenty of air in mild weather, and give them water but sparingly.

Let it be observed for the benefit and encouragement of those who have no hot-houses, that although all the above genera or families are commonly considered as hot-house plants, the far greater number of species thereunto belonging, may be preserved in excellent perfection in a good green-house, and also many other plants hitherto considered as too tender to be preserved therein: experience is the true criterion, and where there are duplicates of doubtful plants, an ingenious gardener will make an experiment with one of each. Several kinds of plants commonly kept in hot-houses, would thrive much better in a well constructed green-house, if kept comparatively drier at the roots during winter.

Between the sixth and tenth of this month, according to the season, situation, and shelter of the place, you should take in your orange, lemon, citron, lime and shaddock-trees, and also your geraniums, and every other sort of plant that slight frosts could injure or discolor the leaves thereof. Myrtles and the more hardy kinds will not be in much danger before the middle of the month, nor will the hardiest sorts, such as prunus lusitanica, or Portugal laurel, prunus lauro-cerasus, or Levant laurel, viburnum tinus, or laurustinus, arbutus unedo, or strawberry-tree, lagerstrœmia indica, daphne odora, fuchsia coccinea, cupressus sempervirens, hydrangea hortensis, &c.,

before the twentieth or twenty-fifth thereof: indeed in warm soils and situations, most of these would bear the winters of the middle States, in the open ground, if sheltered with mats or straw, &c.*

Before they are taken in, pick off all decayed leaves, prune any decayed, ill-formed, disorderly, or irregular shoots or branches, and stir the earth a little in the tops of the tubs or pots. Such as appear weakly, should have some of the old earth taken out and the vacancy filled up with fresh compost.

In placing the plants in the green-house, be particular to arrange them in regular order, the tallest behind, and the others according to their height, in regular gradation down to the lowest in front, being careful to dispose the different sorts in such varied order as that the foliage may effect a striking contrast and variety, by intermixing the broad and narrow leaved, the simple and compound leaved, the light and dark green, the silvery, &c., in order that the whole collection may exhibit a conspicuous and agreeable diversity.

When all are thus arranged give their heads a good watering, which will wash off any dust they have contracted, refresh them considerably, and add lustre and beauty to their foliage; then wash clean and wipe dry all the stage, benches, floor, &c., after which the whole will assume a neat, gay, lively, and becoming appearance.

The plants now should have as much free air as possible during the continuance of mild weather, for if kept too close the damps occasioned by a copious perspiration would cause many of their leaves to become mouldy and drop off, and, besides, they would be less hardy on the approach of winter; therefore, on every warm or mild day keep the windows open; and even on mild dry nights, during the remainder of this month, you may slide down the upper front lights so as to admit a little air at top. But observe to keep the windows close shut in cold weather, frosty nights, and during the continuance of cold rains or fogs.

It will still be necessary to water the plants frequently but moderately, especially the shrubby kinds; the succulent sorts will not require it so often.

Pick off, from time to time, all decayed leaves, and keep every part of the house constantly clean and free from filth of any kind.

The deciduous green-house plants, such as the *lagerstrœmia indica*, *punica granata*, or double-flowering pomegranate, *Croton sebiferum*, or tallow-tree, &c., may be placed on a platform erected at the back of the stage, as noticed on page 103, or they may be preserved very well during the winter in a dry warm cellar that has windows to admit light, air, &c., as necessity may require.

PRESERVING GREEN-HOUSE PLANTS IN GARDEN FRAMES.

There are but few green-house plants of a small size but may be

* It is much the best plan to keep camellias, during the summer months, inside a well ventilated green-house, as the roots are often rotted by the excessive rains of summer. A free use of the syringe will keep down insects.

preserved during winter, in great perfection, in garden frames of the following construction :—

The frame should be erected on a bed of earth, in a remarkably dry and warm exposure; it should be made of strong planks, four, five, or six feet high in the back (according to the size of the plants), eight or nine inches high in front, and four or five feet wide, with the ends sloping accordingly. The length should be in proportion to the number of plants you have to winter, but at every nine or ten feet there should be partitions or stays in the inside for the support of the back.

Around this frame you are to form another at the distance of two feet therefrom, made of any kind of rough boards, supported by pots, and of the same height. The vacancy between both frames is to be filled up to the top with tanner's bark, dry litter, leaves of trees, or any other substance that will keep the frost from penetrating to the plants.

Your frame being thus made, plunge the pots containing the plants to their rims in the inside, either in tan or light sandy earth, placing the lowest in front and the tallest behind, and cover the whole with well glazed and well fitted sashes. During the most severe winter the generality of green-house plants may be effectually preserved in this or the like frame by laying on, as occasion requires, a sufficient quantity of mats over the glasses, and over these a covering of boards.

The plants are to have light and air given to them at every favorable opportunity, and should be treated, generally, as directed for those in the green-house, only kept drier at the roots.

Many other similar contrivances may be made, and with the desired effect, as nothing more is necessary for the preservation of these plants than light, air, a less share of moisture, and an effectual protection from the frost.

THE HOT-HOUSE.

PINE-APPLES.

In the early part of this month the pine plants that are to produce fruit next season should be removed out of the nursery stove, &c., into the fruiting-house; but previous to this you should take out of the pit all the old bark, if you use such material, and fill it with new fresh tan, previously prepared, as directed last month, page 530; observe not to put it into the pit in too wet a state, for in that case it would be a long time before it would come to a kindly heat, and sometimes not at all, so as to answer the end.

Some people sift the old bark, and use the coarse part with new, about one-half of each; but if you can conveniently procure a sufficiency of new tan to fill the pit entirely, it will answer much better for this purpose.

When the bed begins to heat, and the warmth has reached the

surface, bring in your fruiting-plants, and plunge them in the bark-bed to their rims; or if you are apprehensive of the new bark heat-ing too violently at first, plunge the pots only half-way for about a fortnight; if, however, you plunge them wholly at first, you must examine the bed frequently, and if you find the heat at any time violent, then draw the pots up half-way or quite out of the tan, as you see convenient, to prevent its burning the roots of the plants, and plunge them again as soon as it can be done with safety.

The plants thus finally placed in the fruiting-house, are to get the usual and necessary attendance; air must be admitted every mild and warm day, and gentle waterings given when necessary.

Towards the latter end of the month the nights will be growing very cold, and sometimes it may be found necessary to kindle a small fire in the evening; but you should never resort to this while the heat of the house keeps up at night to fifty-two degrees of Fahrenheit, which will generally be the case during the whole of this month if you take care to shut the house in the afternoon when pretty warm; but should cold, cloudy weather continue for a few days, it may render a little fire necessary notwithstanding.

SUCCESSION PINES.

The succession house should now be replenished from the pits, &c., with the pines next in growth to the fruiting plants taken out of it; also the younger successions in the next advancing stage should be placed in the pits, frames, or other winter departments.

All these will now require to be renewed with a proper quantity of new tan, one-half at least, so as to support a regular heat for a considerable time; the whole of the old tan must be sifted, and what goes through the screen, may be used for covering beds wherein are planted bulbous roots, &c., to protect them from frost: as much new tan, previously made sufficiently dry, must be added to the coarse part as will fill up the pits again a little above the top, mixing both well together as you proceed in the filling. This done, plunge the pots as directed on other occasions.

GENERAL CARE,

The pines and all the other exotics must have regular care and attendance; let water be given once or twice a week to some, oftener to others, as you see necessary, being careful not to give too much at a time, for that would not only injure many plants, but destroy the heat of the bark-bed.

Admit fresh air into the house every calm or warm day, especially when the sun shines, by sliding open some of the glasses from nine or ten o'clock till two, three, or four, always observing to close the house in the afternoon while the air is warm, to supersede the neces-sity of fire as long as possible; and if you must have recourse to it towards the latter end of the month, use it but moderately at this season.

The advantages of keeping the house as cool as may be consistent with the safety of the plants, during this and the next month, are very obvious ; all the plants are gradually hardened and rendered thereby capable of bearing the vicissitudes of the winter season better than if they were drawn up tender and weakly by too much heat ; but the pines in particular, if forced at this season, would, many of them, start to fruit at an untimely period, which would get stunted and misshapen before the commencement of the free spring vegetation, and would consequently be totally lost, or not worth their room in the house.

When the leaves of any plants decay, they should be picked off, and the house kept constantly clear from fallen leaves, cobwebs, or any other filth, which not only renders the house neat, but is very necessary to preserve the plants in health.

WINTERING HOT-HOUSE PLANTS IN GARDEN FRAMES.

There are few tropical plants but may be preserved during winter, while in a small state, in garden frames well constructed and attended, so that an ingenious and careful gardener may not despair of preserving the most rare plants in winter, without the aid of a hot-house ; and even where there is one, and the stock of plants too numerous, such auxiliary convenience will be found of considerable utility.

A frame for this purpose should be made about nine or ten feet long, four to five wide, three and a half high in front, and five in the back part, with sashes well glazed and fitted as close and neat as possible, so as to slide up and down freely. This frame should be placed in a dry well sheltered situation, exposed fully to the south, and where it can have the benefit of the sun during the whole day. It should be filled with fresh well prepared tan, to the depth of three feet when settled, and the pots plunged therein to their rims, the smallest sized plants in front, the largest towards the back part.

The frame should be entirely surrounded with a large quantity of the fallen leaves of trees to its full height, having still more in reserve to add, as the others sink and contract in bulk, in consequence of fermentation and pressure, always keeping them full up to the *top* of the frame an *every side ;* the leaves will soon heat and cause the tan to ferment, and between both a fine glow of warmth will be kept up in the frame during the whole winter ; this, with the assistance of a suitable covering of mats, boards, &c., at night and in severe weather, will keep the most tender plants in health and good condition.

Linings of hot horse-dung may be substituted in place of leaves, but the latter is preferable on account of its slow, steady, and long continued heat.

OAK LEAVES USED AS A SUBSTITUTE FOR TAN.

As oak leaves abound in almost every part of the United States, it is of some importance to know that they may be used in forcing pits of every kind, in place of tanners' bark, and with advantage, their heat being constant, regular, and continuing for a long time.

often for an entire year; whereas bark generally turns cold soon after its violent heat is gone off, which obliges the gardener to fork it up frequently in order to revive the heat.

The sooner the leaves are raked up after they fall from the trees the better, as the quality and fermenting substance will naturally decrease during the time they are exposed to the weather.

When raked up they should be carried immediately into some open shed, and there thrown into a heap to settle and ferment. In this place tread them well, and water them a little if you find they are rather dry. The heap should be at least six or seven feet in thickness, and covered with old mats, as well to promote a general fermentation as to prevent the upper leaves from being blown away by the wind. They should be suffered to remain in this state for four or five weeks, by which time they will be properly prepared for the pits, and will not settle down much after. In putting them into the pits, if they appear dry, water them a little and tread them in layers, exceedingly well, till the pits are quite full: then cover the whole with tan to the thickness of two inches, and tread it well till the surface becomes smooth and even. On this place your pots of pines or other tender plants in the manner they are to stand, filling up the spaces between them with tan as you proceed, row by row.

After this, the leaves require no further trouble the whole season through, as they will retain a constant and regular heat for twelve months, without either stirring or turning.

Leaves mixed with stable dung make excellent hot-beds, which preserve their heat much longer than when made of dung only.

NOVEMBER.

WORK TO BE DONE IN THE KITCHEN GARDEN.

As this is a period in which much may be done towards the laying out and preparing of new kitchen gardens for the ensuing season, &c., I refer you for general instructions on that subject to page 115, &c.

SPINAGE, CORN-SALAD, AND WINTER-CRESSES.

You should now be very attentive to the keeping of your winter spinage free from weeds, and to the thinning of the plants where they stand too close; otherwise they will not be sufficiently strong and firm to endure the severity of the approaching frosts.

Corn-salad and winter-cresses should be treated as directed for spinage, and for the same reason; but the distance of two or three inches, plant from plant, will be sufficient for these. This should be done early in the month, for it is not prudent either to thin or weed succulent plants of any kind immediately on the eve of a severe frost, as the sudden exposure of the shaded and tender parts to it would prove very destructive.

WINTER DRESSING OF ASPARAGUS BEDS.

Where omitted last month, dress your asparagus beds as directed on page 542. Indeed there is no better season than the first or second week of this month for that business.

LETTUCES.

The lettuces which were planted in frames last month, should be still suffered to enjoy the free air every day while the weather continues mild and dry, by taking the glasses entirely off early in the morning; but let them be put on again in the evening, or whenever the weather becomes cold or wet; for if these plants are kept too close, they will draw up and become weakly, tender, and of little value.

When the weather is very wet or cold, keep the glasses on, and should the frost set in rather too severe towards the end of the month, you must give the necessary covering, so as to prevent the plants from getting frozen; but be careful to admit air to them at every favorable opportunity.

In the first week of this month, you should plant into the frames, if omitted in October, such lettuces as are designed to be wintered therein; this should on no account be delayed to a later period.

On the approach of severe frost protect your lettuces on warm borders, &c., as directed on page 544.

N. B. Lettuces make a most delicious boiled salad, which, in the estimation of most people who have tried it, is much superior to spinage. This observation escaped my recollection while writing the work of the summer months, where it might have been more appropriately inserted; as then, thousands of heads start to seed and are totally lost, which might be profitably used in this way. They are generally in an excellent condition for this purpose, at any time from the period of their having attained a sufficient size, till the hearts or centre stems have shot towards seeding six or eight inches high, so that when they are past use for a raw salad, they are yet good for a boiled one.

SMALL SALADING.

Small salading of every kind will now require to be sown *on a slight hot-bed*, under the protection of frames and glasses; otherwise disappointment will ensue, especially if the cold sets in early. In mild weather admit plenty of air, to give strength to the plants.

37

GARLIC, ROCAMBOLE, AND SHALLOTS.

You may now plant garlic, rocambole, and shallots; the earlier in the month that this is done the better. When planted at this season in dry, light, rich ground, the roots will be much larger than if deferred till spring. The bulbs of the common garlic, or *Allium sativum*, grow to a larger size than those of the rocambole, or *Allium scorodoprasum*, but some people conceive the latter to be of a better flavor.

The true shallot, or *Allium ascalonicum*, is considered to possess the most agreeable flavor of any of that genus, and is, consequently, highly deserving of cultivation.

For the method of planting each of the above sorts see page 206; but in planting the bulbs produced on the tops of the garlic and rocambole stalks, observe to cover them only about two inches deep, as they are not so large or strong as the cloves of the roots.

CABBAGE AND CAULIFLOWER PLANTS.

During the continuance of mild weather, give your cabbage and cauliflower plants every advantage of free air, to inure them by degrees to bear the cold, by taking the glasses off totally, in the warm part of the day; but be attentive to lay them on again at night, and in wet or cold weather. On coldish days, except there is a cutting, frosty wind, you may raise the glasses a little behind for the admission of air; however, if a severe frost should set in, in the course of the month, you must cover the beds carefully at night, and at other times when necessary, to protect the plants therefrom. But having given general instructions for the methods of treating cabbage plants on page 536, and cauliflower plants on page 537, I now refer you thereto for further information.

Observe that the cauliflower being much more tender than the cabbage plants, will require more care and covering to protect them from frost; and that either will be greatly injured by being deprived of light or air longer than their safety or preservation requires.

PRESERVING CABBAGES AND BORECOLE FOR WINTER AND SPRING USE.

Immediately previous to the setting in of hard frost, take up your cabbages and savoys, observing to do it on a dry day; turn their tops downward, and let them remain so for a few hours to drain off any water that may be lodged between the leaves; then make choice of a ridge of dry earth, in a well sheltered, warm exposure, and plant them down to their heads therein, close to one another, having previously taken off some of their loose hanging leaves. Immediately erect over them a low temporary shed, of any kind that will keep them perfectly free from wet, which is to be open at both ends to admit a current of air in mild, dry weather. These ends are to be closed with straw when the weather is very severe. In this situation your cabbages will keep in a high state of preservation till spring; for, being kept perfectly free from wet as well as from the action of the sun, the frost will have little or no effect upon them. In such a place the heads may be cut off as wanted, and, if frozen, soak them in spring, well, or pump water for a few hours previous to their being cooked, which will dissolve the frost and extract any disagreeable taste occasioned thereby.

Some plant their cabbages, after being taken up and drained as above, in airy or well ventilated cellars, in earth or sand up to their heads, where they will keep tolerably well; but in close, warm, or damp cellars they soon decay.

Others make a trench in *dry* sandy ground, and place the cabbages therein, after being well drained and dry, and most of their outside loose green leaves pulled off, roots upward, the heads contiguous to, but not touching each other; they then cover them with the dryest earth or sand that can be conveniently procured, and form a ridge of earth over them like the roof of a house: some apply dry straw immediately around the heads; but this is a bad practice, as the straw will soon become damp and mouldy, and will of course communicate the disorder to the cabbages.

Upon the whole, the first method is, in my opinion, the most preferable, as there is no way in which cabbages will keep better if preserved from wet; and, besides, they can be conveniently obtained whenever they are wanted for use.

The green and brown curled borecole being very hardy, will require but little protection; they may now be taken up and planted in a ridge tolerably close together, and during severe frost covered lightly with straw; this will preserve them sufficiently, and during winter the heads may be cut off as they are wanted for use; the stems, if taken up and planted in rows, as early in March as the weather will admit, will produce abundance of the most delicious sprouts.

In the southern States, and even in warm soils and exposures in the middle States, borecole will stand the winter in open beds without any covering whatever.

CAULIFLOWERS AND BROCCOLI.

Your late cauliflowers and broccoli will now be producing their heads; therefore it will be necessary to break down some of the largest leaves over the flowers to preserve them from the effects of sun, rain, and frost.

Such plants of either sort as are not likely to flower before the commencement of severe frost should be taken up and planted as recommended in the first instance for cabbages, where, if *well protected* from wet and frost, they will continue to produce fine flowers all winter.

Or, they may be planted in a dry, warm cellar, in the same manner as directed for cabbages, where they will also flower in winter:

indeed I have had tolerably good flowers from strong plants *hung up* in a damp, warm cellar.

PRESERVING TURNIPS, CARROTS, PARSNEPS, BEETS, SALSAFY, ETC.

Previous to the commencement of severe frost you should take up, with as little injury as possible, the roots of your turnips, carrots, parsneps, beets, salsafy, scorzonera, Hamburg or large rooted parsley, skirrets, Jerusalem artichokes, turnip-rooted celery, and a sufficiency of horseradish for the winter consumption; cut off their tops and expose the roots for a few hours till sufficiently dry. On the surface of a very dry spot of ground, in a well sheltered situation, lay a stratum of sand two inches thick, and on this a layer of roots of either sort, covering them with another layer of sand (the drier the better), and so continue layer about of sand and roots till all are laid in, giving the whole on every side a roof-like slope; then cover this heap or ridge all over with about two inches of sand, over which lay a good coat of drawn straw up and down, as if thatching a house, in order to carry off wet, and prevent its entering the roots; then dig a wide trench around the heap and cover the straw with the earth so dug up to a depth sufficient to preserve the roots effectually from frost. An opening may be made on the south side of this heap, and completely covered with bundles of straw, so as to have access to the roots at all times when wanted, either for sale or use.

Some people lay straw or hay between the layers of roots and immediately on the top of them; this I do not approve of, as the straw or hay will become damp and mouldy, and very often occasion the roots to rot, while the sand would preserve them sweet and sound.

All these roots may be preserved in like manner in a cellar; but in such a place they are subject to vegetate and become stringy earlier in spring. The only advantage of this method is, that in the cellar they may be had, when wanted, more conveniently during winter, than out of the field or garden heaps.

Note.—All the above roots will preserve better in sand than in common earth, but when the former cannot be had, the sandiest earth you can procure must be substituted.

CELERY, ENDIVE, AND CARDOONS.

Continue during the early part of this month to blanch your celery, endive and cardoons, as directed in the preceding months; but when the severe frosts approach, they must be preserved therefrom, either in the following or some other more convenient and effectual manner.

Every third row of the celery may be suffered to stand where growing, opening a trench on each side of every standing row, within six or eight inches thereof, for the reception of the plants of the other two rows, which are to be carefully taken up with as little injury as possible either to their tops or roots, and planted in those new trenches, in the same order as they formerly stood. The whole being thus planted, three rows together, they are to be earthed up near the extremities of their leaves, and as soon as the frost becomes pretty keen, in a very dry day cover the whole with straw, and over this a good coat of earth.

When this plan is intended, the celery should in the first instance be planted in rows, east and west, so that when the whole is covered for winter use as above, the south side, especially if protected a little with straw, &c., may be easily opened to take out the plants when wanted for use.

Or, if you have the convenience of a deep garden frame, you may almost fill it with fresh sand, and then take up and plant therein, so close as nearly to touch one another, a quantity of your best and largest celery, and so deep as to be covered within five or six inches of their tops ; place on your glasses immediately, and suffer neither rain nor water to reach the plants, except a very gentle shower, occasionally, in warm weather.

When severe frosts set in, lay dung, tan, leaves of trees, or other litter around the sides and ends of the frame, and cover the glasses with mats, &c., so as to keep out the frost.   By this means you can have celery during winter in the greatest perfection, and as convenient as you could desire.

Or, celery may now be taken up when dry, well aired, and planted in sand in a dry cellar, in the same manner as directed for planting it in the frame ; observing, in either case, to lay up the stalks and leaves neat and close, and to do as little injury to either as possible; it does not keep so well, however, as by the above method.

The beds of celery which were planted as directed on page 461, should, in the early part of this month, be earthed up to within six or eight inches of the tops of the plants, and on the approach of hard frost, additionally earthed to the very extremities of their leaves ; then lay a covering of dry sandy earth on the top of each bed, the whole length, so as to give it a rounding; on this, place a coat of dry straw, drawn and laid on advantageously to cast off the wet, and of a sufficient thickness to effectually resist the frost; after which cut a trench around the bed to carry off and prevent any lodgement of water.   Here you can have access to your celery, and it will continue in a high state of preservation during the whole winter and early spring months.

Endive may be preserved in a frame, or cellar, as directed for celery, or as recommended on page 541.

Cardoons may be preserved either in sand in a cellar, or by banking up a sufficiency of earth to them where they grow, and covering the tops, &c. with straw or long litter.

N. B. All the above work must be performed in dry weather, and when the plants are perfectly free from wet, otherwise they will be very subject to rot.

SOWING RHUBARB, SEA-KALE, AND OTHER SEEDS.

You should now sow the seeds of rhubarb, sea-kale, skirrets, alesanders, dill, and any other kinds of seed that do not vegetate freely if kept out of the ground till spring; sow them as directed in *March*, and be not under the least apprehension of the frost doing them any injury.

MUSHROOMS.

The mushroom beds must be carefully protected from wet and frost, as directed on page 539, &c.

WINTER-DRESSING OF ARTICHOKES.

The winter dressing of artichokes is an important operation, and on it depends much of their future success. This should not be given them as long as the weather continues mild, that they may have all the advantage possible of growth, and be gradually inured to the present increasing cold; but it should not be deferred till the setting in of hard frost, lest the entire work be prevented thereby.

In the first place, cut all the large leaves close to the ground, leaving but the small ones which rise from the hearts of the plants; after this, line and mark out a trench in the middle between each row, from fourteen to sixteen inches wide, presuming that the rows are five feet apart, as directed under the article *planting artichokes*, on page 212. Then lightly dig the surface of the beds from trench to trench, burying the weeds, and as you proceed, gather the earth round the crowns of the plants to the height of about six inches, placing it in gently between the young rising leaves without burying them entirely under it; this done, dig the trenches one spade deep, and cast the earth thereof equally between and on each side the plants, so as to level the ridges, giving them at the same time, a neat rounding form; finish by casting up with a shovel the loose earth out of the bottoms of the trenches evenly over the ridges, in order that the water occasioned by heavy rains, &c., may immediately run off: on which account the trenches ought to have a gentle declivity, as a lodgement of water about the roots in winter is the greatest evil and danger they have to encounter; even greater than the most severe frost of our climate.

The beds are to remain so until there is an appearance of hard frost, when they should be covered with light dry litter, straw, leaves of trees, fern, peas-haulm or the like, the better to preserve the crowns and roots from its rigor. In this manner the roots will remain in perfect safety all winter, and in March they are to have their spring dressing as directed on page 212.

When your artichoke plantation wants manure, lay on a coat of old rotten dung previous to the digging of the trenches, and cover it over with the earth as you throw it up; in the spring following dig it in.

FORCING ASPARAGUS.

This is a very proper time to begin to force asparagus in hot-beds; for the method see page 128, &c.

You should now, previous to the setting in of hard frost, cover the asparagus beds containing the plants which you intend to force during the ensuing months, with as much straw, or light litter of some kind, as will prevent the ground from becoming frozen, so that you can take up the roots with convenience and without injury when wanted. This method is preferable to taking them up and depositing them in a cellar, in sand or earth, which is practised by some gardeners.

ONIONS.

The young crops of Welsh onion or *Allium fistulosum*, should be kept free from weeds ; some may be thinned out for use in salads, &c., the remaining plants will stand the winter even if their foliage decay, and produce a plentiful supply early in spring.

Dried onions should be occasionally examined, and such as show a tendency to rot carefully picked out.

PATIENCE DOCK.

The *Rumex patientia*, or patience dock, being a plant that affords an early spring salad for boiling, and being perennial in root, is deserving of a place in the garden. The leaves are very large, long and succulent, and are produced in great abundance ; the plant may be propagated by sowing the seed any time this month while the ground continues open, and the plants will rise freely in spring; or you may sow the seeds in March or early in April, but those sown at this time will make stronger and earlier plants; the seeds may be sown pretty thick in drills eighteen inches asunder, and covered about half an inch deep; when the plants are about two inches high, thin them to the distance of eight inches from one another, and so let them remain, always keeping them free from weeds. It may also be propagated by offsets from the root taken off in the spring or late autumn months, and planted in rows at the above distances, and by heading it down frequently during summer, as it starts to seed, you will increase the crops of foliage.

DUNG AND TRENCH GROUND.

In the beginning of this month, dung and trench the ground that is intended for early crops, and lay it up in high narrow sloping ridges, particularly if it be any way stiff, or of a heavy nature, to receive the benefit of the winter frosts, &c., which will enrich, mellow, refresh, and sweeten it ; besides, by getting as much of this work performed now as can be conveniently done, it will greatly forward and assist your affairs in spring, when hurried by a pressure of other business.

Should the frost set in towards the latter end of the month so as to bind up the ground, and prevent the operation of trenching, you may cart or wheel manure into the different quarters where wanted, which will help to forward your business considerably.

SOUTHERN STATES.

Transplant finally cabbage and cauliflower plants, but where the winter frosts are rather severe, the latter will want occasional protection of some sort; plant early Mazagan, Windsor, and long-pod beans, and sow a succession crop of early peas; earth up your advancing crop of the cabbage tribe, celery, and cardoons, blanch endive, sow spinage, radish, lettuce, and likewise small salading of every kind on warm borders; the latter will require the protection of a frame and glasses in cold or frosty weather.

THE FRUIT GARDEN.

PLANTING ESPALIER AND WALL TREES, ETC.

In the early part of this month, plant apple, pear, quince, plum, cherry, peach, nectarine, almond and apricot-trees, either for espaliers against walls, or for half or whole standards; observing that the ground in which you plant at this season lies perfectly dry during winter. (For further particulars, see the *Fruit Garden* for last month, page 547, and also page 229.)

GOOSEBERRIES AND CURRANTS.

This is a very suitable and proper season for the planting and pruning of gooseberries and currants; but for particulars I refer you to pages 548 and 549.

Cuttings of either kind may now be planted as directed on page 306, but they must be stout and pretty long, so as to be planted about ten inches deep, or the frost during winter will be very apt to throw them out of the ground.

Gooseberry seed may now be sown as directed on page 549, with a view to obtain new varieties. Currants and raspberries may in like manner be raised from seed, and improved sorts obtained thereby.

RASPBERRIES.

As long as the weather continues open you may transplant and make new plantations of raspberries; but the earlier in the month that this can be done the better, especially if you have to transplant the Antwerp varieties. (For further information on the subject of planting and pruning raspberries, see page 550, &c.)

The red and white Antwerp kinds are excellent fruit, and less hardy than the other varieties; consequently, it will be necessary, in the eastern and middle States, to lay down the young shoots of the present season immediately previous to the commencement of hard frost, first cutting off close to the ground the shoots which had borne fruit the preceding summer. The supernumerary weakly shoots may also be cut off, and likewise the straggling tops of those you intend to lay down; or, they may now have a general and final pruning as directed on page 146.

This done, dig the earth between the rows, clearing out all useless suckers and weeds, previously adding some very rotten manure, if the ground seems to need it; then, being provided with some hooked wooden pegs and a number of long, small hoop-poles, or the like, lay down each row of shoots gently on one side, on which lay the hoop-poles, lengthwise the rows, pegging them down with the hooked sticks, so as to keep the shoots close to the earth; after which cover all over with light litter, straw, hay, barley chaff, fern, leaves of trees, or any other light covering that will protect the plants from the effects of the various changes of the weather, which, and not the frost only, are the causes of their destruction. Here they will remain in safe and good condition till the beginning of March, when the litter is to be taken off, the plants raised up, and the ground receive its spring dressing.

Some lay the shoots into, and cover them with the earth; but although this has a clean appearance, and sometimes will answer very well, the buds will be more liable to receive injury in this way than when covered with light litter as above.

FIG-TREES.

The more tender kinds of fig-trees which are planted against walls or board fences, should now be gone over, and all fruit found thereon, whether ripe or unripe, picked off; for these would rot in winter, and injure the young branches intended for next year's bearing.

At the same time nail up close to the wall or fence, all the principal shoots, the better to secure them from the frost and power of the wind; and if bass mats are likewise nailed up so as to cover the trees, an important protection will be afforded thereby to the young shoots. As to pruning, that should not be done either in the middle or eastern States till March. (See page 225.)

Fig-trees, growing in the espalier way, may also be protected from frost by laying bass-mats over them and making them fast, or by laying boughs of pine or cedar up to them. It would also be proper, in a severe season, to lay some long litter around the roots of the trees.

PRUNING OF FRUIT-TREES.

Having in the *Fruit Garden* for October expressed my opinion respecting the pruning of fruit-trees at this season, it is unnecessary to repeat it in this place. (See page 547.)

THE ORCHARD.

PLANTING, ETC.

This being an eligible period for the planting of orchards on dry ground, and indeed they never should be planted on a cold, wet, or swampy soil, I refer you to the article *Orchard* in *March*, where you will find ample instructions respecting the extent, aspect, situation and soil, the preparation of the ground, the choice of trees and method of planting, &c., all of which are equally applicable in this month as in that, and a reference thereto will, at present, supersede the necessity of a repetition.

Apples, pears, quinces, plums, cherries, peaches, nectarines, apricots, and almonds may now be planted; also, walnuts, chestnuts, filberts, persimmons, berberries, medlars, and every other kind of hardy fruit-trees, agreeably to the directions given in *March*.

PRUNING.

As you may now commence the pruning of apple and pear-trees, &c., I would strongly recommend to your perusal at this time, the entire of the article *Orchard* in *January*, beginning at page 56, and also the same article in *February*, page 149, &c.

Old fruit-trees having scaly, rough bark, should in this month, if not done in the former, be brushed over with a mixture of cow-dung and urine, as directed on page 553.

THE VINEYARD.

PRUNING OF VINES.

The pruning of grape-vines at this season, will answer extremely well in the southern States, and ought to be duly attended to; but the severity of the frosts in the middle and eastern States, renders it more prudent to defer this work to the latter end of February, or if the season proves late, the first week in March; but upon no account should you delay it longer: indeed, upon the whole, the late February pruning will be the safest. In the city and neighborhood of Philadelphia, vines that were pruned on the first and second days of March, 1805, wept copiously a few days after, but some cold weather ensuing, they stopped bleeding; this shows the necessity of pruning in February, especially in warm situations or exposures.

Those who prefer pruning their vines at this time, as well as those who from the temperateness of their climate ought to do it, will find the necessary instructions on page 155, &c.

WINTER DRESSING OF VINES.

You should now plough between the rows of vines in your vine-yard where practicable, having first tied up all the trailing runners to the stakes; observing to lay up the earth as much as possible to the stems of the vines : to effect this the better, the ground must be cross-ploughed. *The one and two year old plants* will particularly require this earthing; and after the ploughing is finished, the earth should be drawn up around them with a hoe, the better to preserve the lower parts of the stems with the buds from alternate freezing and thawing, which is much more injurious to them than a continued frost. In this state they are to remain till the proper time for pruning in spring, when the earth is to be drawn from around them, and the plants dressed as directed on page 156.

When the ground does not admit of this culture with the plough, it should be given with the spade and hoe, as it is of considerable importance, not only to protect the plants, but to destroy weeds, and ameliorate the soil, by throwing it up loosely to the influence of the frost and weather. A dressing of manure, where wanted, should be given previous to the ploughing, &c.

This is a very proper period to manure, trench, or plough the ground which you intend to plant with grape-vines next spring, as observed on page 253, leaving it as rough and high as possible.

In the southern States, vineyards may now be planted, vines pruned and propagated by layers and cuttings, and everything also done in that way, as directed in March for the middle and eastern States.

THE NURSERY.

TRANSPLANTING.

All the principal nursery transplanting should be finished as early in this month as possible, in order that the plants may have time to push out new fibres before the frosts set in; for when planted at a late period, they seldom put out fibres before spring, and have to live principally on their own substance during winter, which greatly weakens them. However, where that cannot be conveniently done, and that necessity requires it, you may continue to transplant all kinds of hardy trees and shrubs while the ground continues open.

PROTECTING SEEDLINGS AND TENDER PLANTS.

In the early part of the month you should sift some dry, fresh earth over the seedling pines, arising from the seed sown last spring, so as to nearly reach the foliage, in order to protect their yet tender stems from the inclemency of the approaching season; and immediately on the setting in of hard frost, spread some dry straw, fern, leaves of trees, or other light covering, thinly over the beds, to afford additional protection, and in some measure to prevent the frost from entering the ground as deep as it otherwise might; for, without the above care, many of the plants would be spewed up by the frost, and most of them be destroyed by the dry parching winds of the ensuing spring. Observe that the covering must be *light*, or that it be supported above the plants by some means, or a serious injury may accrue by its rotting the foliage, &c. The branches of common cedar are good for this purpose.

The top covering is not necessary except when the winter frosts are severe: but sifting earth between and among the plants, so as nearly to come up to the leaves, will be of use in every climate and country; and not only to pine and fir seedlings, but to every other sort that are subject from their diminutive first year's growth to be thrown out of the earth by frost, or injured by drought.

Any kind of seedlings that are rather tender should have hoop arches made over the beds, and on the approach of severe frosts, thick mats, &c. laid on these for the protection of the plants.

All hardy plants in pots should now be removed to where they can have sufficient protection in severe weather; for if left fully exposed to the frost, the plants will not only be injured, but the pots burst by the expansion of the earth and water.

Pots containing tolerably large and *hardy* exotic plants may be plunged to their rims in a warm border, and covered six or eight inches deep over their edges with tanners' bark, leaves of trees, long litter, &c., which will considerably preserve the roots of the plants. But the more curious kinds of hardy evergreens and other plants in pots should now be removed into the green-house, or into garden-frames with glasses and other covering, the more effectually to protect them.

DIGGING BETWEEN THE NURSERY ROWS.

You should now continue to dig the ground between all such trees and shrubs as are to remain another year in the nursery rows; this will destroy the weeds, improve the plants, and add neatness to the whole during winter and spring.

CARE OF NEW PLANTED TREES, ETC.

Stake and tie up all new planted trees that are in open exposures, in order to prevent their being rocked about by the winds, than which there is nothing more injurious to them.

Lay light litter of some kind, a good thickness, over the roots of the more tender and choice kinds of trees and shrubs, to protect them from frost; this will be of considerable service, and encourage them to shoot vigorously in spring.

PRUNING TREES AND SHRUBS.

You may now reduce to proper form any hardy forest or ornamental trees, flowering shrubs, &c., cutting out any disorderly or straggling branches, and trimming up the stems of such as require it. But the more tender sorts should not be pruned till spring.

PREPARATIONS FOR MAKING NEW PLANTATIONS.

Continue to dig and trench the ground, or to plough it extremely deep, where you intend making new plantations in spring, by which it will be greatly improved, and your business thus forwarded.

Where dung is wanted, it should be given previous to the digging, &c., and advantage ought to be taken of dry weather to carry it in and spread it on the ground. It will be much better to give it at this season than immediately before planting, as it will have more time to incorporate with the earth, and to be deprived of its rancid qualities.

THE PLEASURE, OR FLOWER GARDEN.

PROTECTING TULIP, HYACINTH, ANEMONE, AND RANUNCULUS ROOTS.

As it is not unfrequent in the eastern and middle States for hard frost to set in towards the latter end of this month, you should previous thereto, lay a good lining of fresh tanners' bark, horse-dung, leaves of trees, or dry straw, around the outsides of the beds containing your choice hyacinths, anemones and ranunculuses; this should be quite as high as the upper parts of the surrounding frames, and of a sufficient body to keep the frost effectually from penetrating in at the sides, &c. Tulips will only require to lay a light covering of any kind over and around the beds, such as straw, fern, leaves, &c., for although the frost will not kill the roots, yet by slightly protecting them therefrom the flowers will blow much stronger and more perfect than they otherwise would.

Hyacinths, though very hardy, will also be greatly improved in their flowers by protecting the bulbs in winter from severe frosts, which may be effected by laying boards and mats over the frames in which the finest sorts are planted; but these should be taken off every mild day, or when the sun is so powerful as to prevent an accumulation of frost in the beds. The less valuable and common sorts may be protected as directed for tulips; any kind of light covering will be of use, and indeed they often flower very well without it.

Two inches deep of one or two years old tanners' bark, if laid over your beds of tulips, hyacinths, polyanthus-narcissuses, &c., in the open ground, will afford the roots considerable protection; but be cautious not to use for this purpose new or fresh tan from the vats, as the astringent juice thereof would work down to the roots, and do them much more injury than the entire omission of covering, or of affording them any manner of protection.

Ranunculuses and anemones being much more tender than tulips or hyacinths, will require *in severe frost*, a good effectual covering of glasses, mats, and boards; or in default of glasses, mats and boards only, or any other suitable protection. This covering is to be supported by the frames surrounding the beds wherein the roots are planted, and it must be taken off *every mild day*, while there is no danger of the beds accumulating frost, in order to ventilate and sufficiently air the plants that are up, so that they may neither be drawn too much, the foliage turn yellow, nor the roots become mouldy. But particular care must be taken to place the covering on again, as soon as the day becomes cold and before the beds begin to freeze. The ranunculuses are somewhat more tender than the anemones, and will require a proportional protection.

PLANTING VARIOUS KINDS OF BULBOUS AND TUBEROUS FLOWER-ROOTS.

You may still continue to plant the various kinds of bulbous and tuberous flower roots, as directed on page 566, but the earlier in the month that you can get this accomplished the better.

TRANSPLANTING PERENNIAL AND BIENNIAL FLOWER-ROOTS.

Where omitted in the preceding months, you should as early in this as possible divide (where necessary) and transplant the various kinds of hardy perennial and biennial fibrous-rooted plants, agreeably to the directions given on pages 523 and 567.

AURICULAS, POLYANTHUSES, CARNATIONS, PRIMROSES, ETC.

The pots containing your choice auriculas, polyanthuses, carnations and double primroses should, immediately previous to the setting in of hard frost, be plunged to their rims close together in a garden frame, and there defended from heavy rains and severe frost by putting on the glasses and a suitable covering of mats, &c., occasionally, according to the necessity of the case. But observe, that as all these kinds are of a hardy nature, they must be fully exposed to the weather every day that is tolerably mild and dry, and even at night until the frost becomes rather rigorous. However, it will be proper to line the outside of the frame, as directed on page 589, for ranunculuses and anemones, the better to keep out the most severe frosts of the winter; for when properly protected, and not drawn or forced too much, they always flower better than when cut up by severe weather.

Where there is not the convenience of glasses, mats and boards may be laid over the frame; or, if no frame, the pots may be plunged close together in a raised bed of dry soil or tan in a warm situation, and low arches made of old cask hoops, or the like, erected over them, on which to lay thick mats in wet or frosty weather. But in February, and early in March, while the frost is in the ground, or the leaves in a frozen state, and especially if they had been covered with snow, you must be particular not to expose them to a *hot* sun, which would be almost certain death to them.

DOUBLE DAISIES.

The beds wherein were planted your double daisies, &c., as directed in October, page 568, should towards the latter end of this month, or when the frost is likely to become severe, be protected occasionally therefrom by a covering of mats, or when very severe, boards and mats, but let them have the benefit of the air as long and as often as the weather is mild; observing always to defend them from heavy rains and snow, either of which would have a tendency to rot and melt them away.

Daisies will survive the winter in a warm border, covered with a light coat of clean straw, which should be taken off and laid on occasionally in mild weather to air and harden the plants; but these will not blow as well nor as early in spring as those taken better care of.

The daisies which were potted in September or October with a view to force them in winter, should be particularly attended to during the whole of this month, in order to strengthen and encourage their growth. But if the potting of them were omitted, it should be done in the beginning of this month; selecting for that purpose the largest and best plants, and carefully removing them with good balls of earth round their roots.

PROTECTING SEEDLING BULBS.

You should now plunge the pots or boxes in which you sowed the seeds of bulbous-rooted flowering plants, and also those containing the one or two year old seedling bulbs, up to their rims or edges in a raised bank of light, dry earth, or you may set them on the bank and fill the spaces between them with tanner's bark, or leaves of trees well crammed in; then on the approach of severe frosts cover them all over with dry straw or peas-haulm, which is to be taken off occasionally in mild dry weather, and aired, in order to prevent its getting mouldy, and communicating the disorder to the seeds or roots.

STOCKGILLY-FLOWERS AND WALL-FLOWERS.

Your double stockgilly-flowers and wall-flowers in pots should now be either taken into the green-house or warm close rooms, or plunged to their rims in a dry, warm exposure, surrounded with a deep garden frame, where they may be protected during winter. These plants being tolerably hardy, will keep well by a very slight protection of boards and mats, or boards covered with straw or other litter when the frost is severe: they will seldom be injured before February, but a warm sun about the end of that month, if suffered to shine on them whilst the leaves or stems are in a frozen state, would totally destroy them.

It would be of additional advantage to lay three or four inches of old tanners' bark over the surface of the pots, the better to preserve the roots from the frost. The plants must be aired occasionally in mild weather, for if kept too closely covered they would become blanched, weak and tender, and lose their robust growth, so necessary to a good bloom of flowers.

PLANTING BULBOUS ROOTS IN POTS AND GLASSES.

You may continue to plant the various kinds of early flowering bulbs in pots, as directed on page 566, but the earlier in the month that this is done the sooner you may expect them to flower. The pots are then to be placed either in a warm room, where there is plenty of light, or in garden frames, and treated as directed last month. Some of them may be immediately placed in the hot-house, or in a forcing frame, to be forced into an early bloom for the decoration of rooms, windows, &c., and others placed in the green-house for a succession.

The early part of this month is still a very proper time to set the bulbs of early tulips, hyacinths, polyanthus-narcissuses, jonquils, dwarf Persian iris, &c., in bulb-glasses filled with water, which should never be suffered to come higher around the roots than about the eighth of an inch, replenishing the water occasionally as it evaporates, so that it may just touch the bottom of the bulbs. Some of the glasses may be immediately placed in the hot-house for an early bloom, the others to be treated as directed on page 568.

TAKING UP AND PRESERVING THE ROOTS OF TUBEROSES, AND SCARLET AMARYLLISES, ETC.

As soon in this month as you observe the frost to injure the foliage of your tuberoses and jacobæa lilies or scarlet amaryllises and other very tender bulbs, which generally lie dormant in winter, take up the roots and spread them in a warm room, where they will be perfectly secure from frost—if in a stove-room the better; in the course of eight or ten days, divest them of the decayed foliage and root fibres, and continue them spread as before till well dried, always taking care to preserve them from frost; when sufficiently dry pack them up in *small* boxes, in very dry sawdust, chaff, dry moss, or the like, and then place the boxes in some very warm room to remain during winter, where they can be effectually secure from frost, the least touch of which would totally destroy the roots.

DRESSING THE BEDS AND BORDERS, ETC.

The beds of young succession or other flower-bulbs which were not disturbed in the present year, should now be carefully weeded, raked over, and if any moss appears thereon, it ought to be picked off; after which lay an inch or two, as may be deemed necessary, of good light compost all over the beds—this will assist in defending the roots from frost, and add much to their health and vigor in the ensuing spring.

Clear the beds, borders, and other compartments from fallen leaves of trees, and the dead stalks of annual and other plants; pulling up the annuals by the roots, as they never flower again, and cutting down the decayed perennials to the ground. After this, hoe and clear the ground from all manner of weeds, and where there are no bulbs planted, slightly dig the ground without injuring any plants growing therein, and rake the surface smooth and even. This will prepare the borders, &c., for the reception of other plants, and give a neat and becoming appearance to the whole during winter.

Dig and neatly rake all the shrubbery compartments, especially those contiguous to the principal walks, excepting such as are laid down with grass, or wilderness plantations—this will destroy weeds, enliven the prospect, and encourage the growth of the shrubs.

PLANTING FOREST-TREES AND ORNAMENTAL TREES AND SHRUBS.

All kinds of hardy trees and shrubs, especially the deciduous sorts, may be planted *in dry soil* any time this month while the weather continues mild, but the earlier in it that this is done the better. For an account of the sorts, see page 314; for designs in ornamental planting, see page 74, &c., and for the method of planting, see page 314, &c.

TRANSPLANTING LARGE TREES, ETC.

It frequently happens that people are desirous of removing large favorite trees or shrubs from one place to another, and as this is the best time to prepare for that business, I refer you for the necessary information to page 241, &c.

PRUNE FLOWERING-SHRUBS, ETC.

You may now prune and reduce into due form any hardy flowering-shrubs and forest-trees, whether evergreen or deciduous; but the more tender sorts ought not to be pruned till spring. For the method of doing which, see page 172.

PLANTING AND PLASHING HEDGES.

Ground hedges of hawthorn, beech hornbean, honey-locust, or any other hardy kinds of deciduous plants, may be made any time in this month while the weather continues open. For ample instructions on this subject, see page 270, &c.

Old hedges which are overgrown and thin, may now be plashed or cut down, as directed on page 279.

ORDINARY WORK.

Rake and carry away out of the walks, borders, and lawns, the fallen leaves of trees and other rubbish; stake and tie up any large new planted trees, to prevent their being rocked about by the wind, and lay mulch, long litter, or leaves, around the roots of such as are rather tender, to protect them from frost.

Place small stakes and bass-mats, or evergreen branches, bound around such plants of the hydrangea hortensis, prunus lauro-cerasus, China and Otaheite roses, &c., as you have planted out in warm, well-sheltered borders. Many plants that are commonly kept in green-houses would abide during winter in the open ground if thus protected; but this should not be done till the keen frosts are just commencing.

Dress gravel-walks, and mow grass-walks and lawns, after which roll them with a heavy roller, which will render the surface firm, smooth, and neat during winter. Observe to do this work in dry open weather. Some people break up their gravel walks at this season, and throw them in ridges to lie so all winter, under an idea of destroying weeds, &c.; but as this renders walks unserviceable at a time when a foot can scarcely be set with pleasure on any other part of the ground, and that a turning in spring would answer the end proposed, this practice ought to be abandoned.

Lay roses and other shrubs for propagation, and in the early part of the month take off well rooted layers, and dig up suckers of desirable kinds, which plant immediately where wanted, or into nursery-rows, to obtain age and strength.

Turn your compost heaps of every kind and spread them so thin that the frosts may penetrate to the very bottoms of them; let the lumps be well broken, and all parts properly mixed.

Provide materials and make new composts, agreeably to the directions given in the preceding part of this work, in order to have them ready for use in the ensuing year; for the longer they are in a state of preparation, and the more effectually incorporated, the better will all sorts thrive which may be planted therein.

THE GREEN-HOUSE.

In the beginning of this month all the hardy exotic plants which have been permitted to remain abroad till this time, but which require protection in winter, should be removed into the green-house, or into the other places destined for their preservation. In the middle States, the viburnum tinus, hydrangea hortensis, prunus lauro-cerasus, magnolia grandiflora, China and Otaheite roses, lagerstrœmia indica, daphne odora, aucuba japonica, double flowering pomegranate, double stocks and wall-flowers, cyclamen, belladonna and Guernsey lilies, with several other shrubby and herbaceous kinds, will seldom suffer by being left out before the middle of this month; but leaving them much longer unprotected would be imprudent, unless your stock is so numerous that you wish to try experiments on their hardness.

In mild weather your green-house plants should have plenty of free air admitted to them every day, by opening the glasses, &c., always observing to close the house in due time in the afternoon, and in wet or frosty weather; even in very severe weather, you may happen to find an hour or two in the middle of the day in which to slide down the upper lights, to admit fresh air and suffer the foul to pass out; this may be often done when it would be quite imprudent to raise the lower sashes. But if a very rigorous frost should set in towards the latter end of the month, it may be necessary to make a fire in the evening, to prevent its penetrating into the house; however, this should not be resorted to while you can keep out the frost by means of good shutters, or by fastening mats in front of the windows at night; for too much heat at any time, but particularly in the early part of the season, is of serious injury to the green-house plants, which require nothing more than merely to be kept from frost.

Occasional, but gentle waterings, must now be given to all the plants; some will require to be watered three times a week, while others, particularly the succulent kinds, will not need it more than a little once a week; but as the state of the weather sometimes makes a very material difference in this, there is no saying how often, or how much at a time, ought to be administered; however, it will be safer to give a little and often, than too much at a time, which should now be administered in the forenoon of fine days, that the damp may pass off before the windows are shut, lest the steam occasioned thereby might create a mouldiness, and injure the plants.

Pick off all decayed leaves from the plants, and throw them out of the house; for if they are suffered to remain in it, they will rot and infect the air, which foul effluvia being imbibed by the plants, will infect them also, and bring on disease and vermin.

Examine the tubs and pots occasionally, and if the earth cakes or binds at top, loosen it to a moderate depth; and where decayed branches or shoots occur, prune them off as soon as observed, and cast them out of the house.

The myrtles and other plants which are in frames, or pits, must now be duly attended to, in like manner as those in the green-house. The frames or pits, to the full height of the glasses, must be lined around with horse-dung, leaves, straw, fern, or the like, to keep the frost from penetrating in at the sides and ends; the plants must have plenty of fresh air at all favorable opportunities, and be effectually protected at night and in frosty weather, by laying a sufficient covering of mats, straw, boards, &c., over the glasses, observing not to deprive them of the benefit of light but while absolute necessity requires it.

PRESERVING TENDER BULBS, ETC.

As some persons who have not the convenience of a hot-house, may be desirous of having some tender exotic bulbous and tuberous-rooted plants, such as crinums, pancratiums, arums, amomum, zinziber, or true ginger, &c., these and such like roots may, in the beginning of this month, be taken up and carefully dried as you do tuberoses, and then packed up in very dry sand, or in extremely dry moss, observing to keep them during winter completely out of the reach of frost or moisture. About the beginning or middle of April, you may plant them in pots, which should be plunged in a temperate hot-bed, and give the roots but very little water till they produce foliage, and are growing freely: towards the latter end of May the pots may be placed in the open air, to remain till the latter end of September, when they should be taken in, and placed in the green-house, or in the windows of some warm room till this time; then to be treated as above. Or, you may keep up the roots till the middle of May, and then plant them even in the open ground; after which they will grow considerably before autumn, but not flower quite as strong as if properly kept in a hot-house.

THE HOT-HOUSE.

It is to be presumed that your tan-pits have been renewed, and all your pots containing pine and other tender plants, duly arranged in the course of the last and preceding month, as then directed; but should it happen by any disappointment, that this could not have been effected, it ought on no account to be omitted in the first week of this month.

As the cold weather advances the fires in the stove should be increased proportionably, being careful not to overheat the air, lest thereby the plants shoot too freely, which would be a serious injury to them at this season, by rendering them more tender, and consequently less able to endure the vicissitudes of the ensuing winter; besides, the most forward of the pine plants might start to fruit, which would ruin all your expectations; nor should the air be kept too cold—that is, the spirits in the thermometer of Fahrenheit suffered to get lower in the night than 52 or 54 degrees, and in the day than 65° or 70°, lest the pines become stunted, and many of the curious exotics lose their leaves, and perhaps their extreme parts decay for want of that degree of heat so necessary and so congenial to their constitutions.

Give water occasionally to such plants as want it, in moderate proportions, and not too much at a time, for they cannot now discharge it so freely as in summer; observing that it stands at least twenty-four hours in the stove before you use it, to acquire the same degree of heat as the air of the house.

Fresh air must be admitted into the house every mild and warm day while the weather continues open, but especially when the thermometer is above 70°; you must be attentive, however, to close the house immediately on any sudden unfavorable change of weather, and always sufficiently early in the afternoon to retain a considerable warmth in the house during the night, which will, sometimes, in the early part of the month, supersede the necessity of fire, or at least of but very little.

The art of managing tender exotic plants consists principally in keeping the air of the stove or hot house in a proper and regular temperature of heat, in duly proportioning the quantity of water to the different natures and necessities of the various kinds of plants, in judiciously admitting a sufficiency of air at suitable opportunities, and in keeping the bark-pits, when they are used, in a proper state of fermentation; all which must be duly attended to, or the desired success cannot be expected.

Pick off constantly all the decayed leaves from the plants, and throw them out of the house; clean their leaves and stems from filth, which many kinds are subject to contract; wash off and destroy all insects which infest any of them, frequently stir the surface earth in the pots to keep it from contracting moss, &c., and keep all the house clean, sweet, and in neat order.

CARE OF YOUNG SUCCESSION PINES AND OTHER PLANTS.

The young pines or other plants in succession houses must have the same care as above; and those in bark beds, under garden frames, are to be diligently attended to; the outside lining must be kept to the full height of the frame all around, and in a regular and constant state of warmth; the glasses must be carefully and sufficiently covered every night, and by day in a very severe frost, but the plants should have as much light as possible, and air whenever it can be given with safety: decayed leaves must constantly be picked off and taken out of the frame, but watering will seldom be necessary at this season, as the steam arising from the bed will occasion a moist atmosphere about the plants. Observe that the more succulent kinds will not keep as well in such a place as in a dry stove, or on shelves in the hot-house.

The garden pits erected with brick and furnished with flues, in which you have tender exotic plants, must also have a lining of hot dung placed around them to their full height, in order to prevent the frost from penetrating in through the wall; moderate fires must be made in the flues every evening, and in severe weather, to keep up the internal heat when that of the pit is found not to be sufficiently strong: the glasses must be well covered with mats, &c., every night, and even by day when the weather is cloudy and the frost very severe.

VINE BORDERS HEATED ARTIFICIALLY.

It may be as well here to mention the following method, lately introduced, of the artificial mode employed for heating vine borders. It is described by A. L. Gower, Esq., in the Horticultural Society's *Journal.* "The bottom of the border," he says, "is gently sloped from the houses to the extreme edge, where is built a box drain extending the whole length of the border, as shown in the accompanying section, marked 1; this drain is one foot square, the top of it being level with the bottom of the border, as also shown.

"*Ground Plan of Houses, showing Cross-Walls beneath the Vine Borders. Section.*—When this was completed, dwarf walls, marked 3, were built across the border, three and a half feet apart, in the pigeon-hole manner; on the top of these walls are laid rough flags; these, in reality, form the bottom of the border, and upon these is placed about six inches of broken stones and bricks, marked 4; then covered with turf, with the grassy side down, to prevent the soil from mixing with the stones. There are flues or chimneys at each end of the border and centre communicating with the drains in the bottom, as shown in the section, marked 2. The top of these flues is nicely made of stone ten inches square, through which is cut a hole of six

Fig. 60.

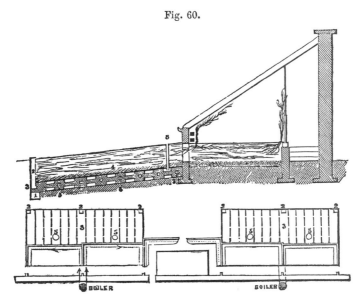

inches square, into which is inserted a plug of a wedge-like form, so as to fit tightly, but removable at pleasure; these flues are about an inch above ground. At the back of the border are placed cast-iron pipes (marked 5) perpendicularly, and also communicating with the drains underneath; these being higher than the flues in front, cause a motion in the air beneath the border. After a long continuance of rain, the plugs in the flues in front are taken out, thereby creating a great circulation of air, and thus, to a vast extent, accelerating the proper drying of the borders, which is deemed of much importance. In the winter season, the borders are covered with leaves and stable manure, to the depth of twelve inches. It is obvious that the whole aim of the constructor of this border was to do that which experience shows to be so very important. He not only got rid of superfluous water, but he introduced air in abundance, and, at the same time, the natural warmth which it carries with it. The result was, Black Hamburg Grapes, weighing from two pounds nine ounces to five pounds a bunch—beautiful fruit, of admirable quality, on vines just seven years old.

The experiments with *concreting vine border* were all made with the same end in view—the elevation of the temperature of the soil in which vine roots are formed; this is found to be of great importance.

DECEMBER.

WORK TO BE DONE IN THE KITCHEN GARDEN.

This is very frequently one of the most severe of our winter months, and every judicious gardener will be well provided against its rigor by having all his frames lined around as directed in *November*, and being well supplied with the necessary mats and other covering. If this provision he neglected, he may be taken, as it were, by surprise, and in one or two nights lose a great number of valuable plants.

Should the weather prove mild, and the ground continue open in the beginning of the month, which seldom happens in the middle or eastern States, you may complete any work recommended to be done in November, and then unavoidably omitted; such as dressing asparagus and artichoke beds, taking up and putting into a state of preservation, cabbages, turnips, parsneps, carrots, beets, celery, endive, cardoons, salsafy, scorzonera, &c. But the many chances that are against your being able to accomplish this work in December, ought to induce you to double your diligence in November, and complete everything in due season.

CAULIFLOWER AND CABBAGE PLANTS.

Every mild day observe to uncover your cauliflower plants which are under frames and glasses, that they may enjoy the free air, otherwise they will draw up and become weak: constantly pick off all decayed leaves, which, if suffered to remain on, would be very injurious to the plants, especially if it should happen, as it frequently does in this month, that the weather should be so severe as to render it imprudent to uncover the beds for several days successively; for when these decayed leaves rot, they emit a rancid vapor, which, mixing with the confined air of the beds, renders it very unwholesome for the plants.

When it is not safe to take off the lights entirely, in the middle of the day, let them be raised upon props two or three inches at the back of the frames, to let in fresh air to the plants.

The glasses must be covered every night with mats, straw, fern, or some other long dry litter, and even in the day-time when the frost is very rigorous; but no opportunity ought to be missed to admit light to the plants, and to give them air when it can be done with safety. The frame containing them must be carefully lined all around the outside, as directed in *November*, to prevent the frost from penetrating in at the sides and ends thereof.

Some will consider this rather troublesome, but it will be found much less so than to sow the seed in January or February, and nurse, and once or twice transplant the young seedlings during the remainder of the winter and spring; besides, the autumn sown plants when taken proper care of, will produce much larger and better heads than those sown in winter or spring, and be earlier and more certain.

The early York, sugar-loaf, and other tender kinds of cabbage plants, require exactly the same treatment as the cauliflower, but being more hardy less covering will be necessary, and more air may with safety be admitted. There is nothing more injurious to either, than to be kept too closely covered; therefore no opportunity, if but for half an hour at a time, ought to be omitted to admit light and air, when it can be done with any tolerable degree of safety.

The Savoy, flat Dutch, drum-head, and other late kinds, will keep when planted in warm borders with very little protection; arches made of old hoops, &c., should be erected over them on which to lay mats, straw, branches of evergreen trees, or shrubs, &c. (For further particulars, see page 536.)

CARE OF LETTUCE PLANTS.

The care of lettuce plants being the same now as in the ensuing month, I refer you for the necessary instructions to page 26, and also to page 534, &c.

SMALL SALADING.

Where small salading, such as cresses, rape, mustard, lettuce, radish, &c., is required at this season, these seeds must be sown in a hot-bed, protected with a good frame and glasses, and also sufficient covering of mats, &c., or in the green-house; but care must be taken not to cover the seeds deeper with earth than what is barely sufficient to hide them.

Keep the glasses constantly over them, and admit air to the plants every day when the weather is mild, by raising the lights a little behind, otherwise they will be apt to become mouldy and decay. It is almost unnecessary to say that the glasses must be kept well covered every night, and even in the day-time during extremely severe weather.

MUSHROOMS.

Particular care must now be taken to preserve the mushroom beds out of doors from frost or wet, either of which would destroy the spawn, and render the beds unproductive. They must consequently be covered with a sufficient depth of dry straw, and over this mats: after heavy rains or snow they should be examined, and if you find the covering next the earth of the beds wet, take it totally away and immediately replace it with dry straw. Where the necessary and proper care is taken, there will be a constant supply of mushrooms for the table even in the most rigorous seasons. Observe the general directions given on page 539, &c. This necessity for covering and continual renewal shows the advantage of having the beds inside. Where there is not a suitable house erected for the purpose, the winter beds may be made in the sheds where the heating apparatus is.

FORCING ASPARAGUS.

Hot-beds may now be made for forcing asparagus, to supply the table about the latter end of January; for at this season it will be full six weeks from the time of making the beds before the asparagus will be fit to cut, presuming the beds to be kept of a due temperature of heat. (For the method of making and managing them, see page 128, &c.)

ORDINARY WORK.

If the weather continues open, carry dung into the quarters of the kitchen garden, spread it, and trench the ground, laying it in high sloping ridges to be mellowed by the frost, &c.

When the ground is frozen that it cannot be dug, cart or carry in manure, and lay it down in convenient places, to have it at hand when the frost goes off; repair the fences of the garden where necessary; if you have any seeds remaining in their pods or capsules, beat or rub out and clean them, so as to be ready for sowing when wanted; prepare all tools which may be necessary in spring, that there may be no delay when the season is favorable for commencing your early cropping.

Provide from the woods, &c., pea sticks and bean poles of every size; dress and point them, that they may be in complete readiness when wanted; collect all your old sticks and poles which are yet fit for use, and lay them with the new ones under the protection of some shed, to prevent their rotting by wet, &c.

SOUTHERN STATES.

In such of the southern States as have but very slight frosts in winter, you may, in addition to other necessary work, sow on warm borders for early crops, small quantities of carrots, parsneps, onions, beets, radish, lettuce, spinage and parsley, &c.; earth up late celery and cardoons, tie up endive for blanching, and plant out in rows up to their heads such of the cabbage tribe as are intended for seed, covering their heads with straw if found necessary, to preserve them from frost or wet. Take care to set each kind apart by itself, and at a considerable distance from any other, for if contiguous, the farina of the one when in blossom would impregnate the seeds in the ovaries of the other, whereby the whole would become bastardized, and you would have neither kind in its original purity.

Plant early Mazagan, Lisbon, long-pod, and Windsor beans, and sow early-frame, Sangster's early, and Charleton peas; earth up the crops of peas and beans which were sowed in the preceding months, as they advance in growth, and if there is any danger to be apprehended from frost, cover them at night and in severe weather with long dry straw, which can be conveniently removed when a favorable change takes place, and laid on again when found necessary.

Plant out garlic, rocambole, and shallots, likewise large onions, for seed, and sow as directed in March, the seeds of rhubarb, sea-kale, skerrets, alesanders, dill, and such other kinds of seeds as do not vegetate freely when kept out of the ground till spring.

THE FRUIT GARDEN.

IMPROVING THE BORDERS, ETC.

You may now carry well-rotted old dung, rich earth, or compost, and spread it on the borders in which are planted wall or espalier trees—this will protect the roots during winter; in spring, when dug in, it will add new vigor to the trees, and the advantage will be very evident in the ensuing crops. Standard fruit-trees of every kind will be greatly improved by similar treatment, especially if the ground is become poor, or any way exhausted.

PROTECTING THE ROOTS OF NEW-PLANTED TREES.

In the early part of this month, if omitted in November, you should lay wispy dung, straw, or long litter of some kind over the roots of those trees which were planted last spring or in the preceding months, to prevent the frost from having too great an effect on their young and yet tender fibres; this in very rigorous seasons often does considerable injury to young trees, and sometimes lays the foundation of diseases which ultimately destroy them.

Figs in particular will require this attention, and besides, the tops and stems of the tender kinds should be covered with mats, or other suitable protection where the frosts are extremely severe.

PRUNING APPLES AND PEARS ON ESPALIERS, ETC.

Apples and pears being perfectly hardy, may now be pruned if the weather happens to be mild, agreeably to the directions given on page 35; but if this is not deemed necessary on account of dispatching business when it can conveniently be done, it will be rather better to defer pruning till the latter end of February, unless you do it before the severe frosts set in.

As to the pruning of stone fruit-trees, I would not recommend it to be done in the middle or eastern States at this season, for the reasons assigned on page 234, &c., but in the southern States it may be now performed with the greatest safety.

Gooseberries and currants being extremely hardy, may be pruned in any of the winter months; but where it is intended to propagate the best kinds from the cuttings, it will not be advisable to prune or dress them when the ground is so frozen as to prevent your being able to plant the good cuttings taken off in pruning.

OTHER NECESSARY WORK.

You must be careful to keep the frost out of the apartments where the choice winter fruits are put up, for should any of them get frozen they would certainly decay soon after, and rot the others about them. Examine the fruit which you have on shelves in dry warm cellars, once every ten days, and take away any that you find tainted; continue over them near a foot thick of clean dry straw, and secure the windows and doors from the admission of frost.

Take off all moss from your fruit-trees, and when it is gathered, carry it quite out of the garden to prevent its multiplying by seed, which is is very apt to do.

Nail or tie up the dangling shoots which are loose on walls or espaliers, to prevent their being dashed about by the winds, and consequently their bark injured.

Repair all your decayed espaliers, or prepare stakes and other materials for so doing as soon as the frost gets out of the ground.

Make or provide and paint such new frame-work trellises as you intend to erect next spring, and do every other work that may have a tendency to forward your business at that season.

PREPARE FOR FORCING FRUIT-TREES.

Towards the latter end of this, or the beginning of next month, put on the glasses or lights on your fire-heat forcing-frames, such as are described on page 51, and immediately prune and nail up the trees in regular order, if not done before.

By this method the trees will not be so sensible of the sudden transition from the depth of winter to spring, when you kindle fires, as they would if the lights were not now put on; and it will gradually bring your trees to a state of vegetation, for the works of nature are performed by degrees, and not in a hurry.　For general information respecting the construction of forcing-frames and houses, of every kind, and the methods of working them, see the *Fruit Garden* for *January*, &c.

SOUTHERN STATES.

In such of the southern States as have not severe frost in winter, you may now prune apples, pears, plums, cherries, peaches, nectarines, and apricots; quinces, raspberries, currants, gooseberries, and every other kind of fruit-tree, the orange family and the fig excepted. You may also plant all the above, and any other sorts with great propriety at this season, excepting the orange family only.　For the methods of pruning, see *January*, and of planting, see *March*.

THE ORCHARD.

Apples and pear-trees that are in good health, may now be pruned agreeably to the directions given on page 56, &c., to which I particularly refer you; but it will be better to defer the pruning of stone fruit-trees to February, and of all trees that are in a bad state of health to the beginning of March, in which month (page 234, &c.) you will find the best methods of treating them for the restoration of their health and vigor.

Rub and scrape off moss wherever it appears on your fruit-trees, it robs them of their nourishment, prevents their free perspiration, and is an enemy to them in every way.

You may now cart manure into the orchard, and spread it over the whole ground, if necessary, or over the roots of such trees as you think are in most need of it; this will not only be of very considerable service to the trees, but also to any crops of grass or grain, &c., that you expect off the place the ensuing seasons.

It will be of considerable advantage to new planted trees to lay long litter, &c. around their roots to protect them from frost, as directed in the *Fruit Garden* for this month.

The hedges which enclose your orchard and other compartments, and that are grown tall, straggling, and thin, may now be cut down and plashed, as directed on page 279; you need be under no apprehension of their suffering by frost, especially the white thorns.

SOUTHERN STATES.

When the ground continues open in winter, or so much so as not to interrupt the operation of ploughing, you may manure your orchards, and plough such of them as you intend to lay down with clover, or grass of any kind, or to raise crops of grain or potatoes in.

You may likewise continue to plant and prune all manner of hardy fruit-trees, but particularly those mentioned in the *Fruit Garden* for this month.   Here I would recommend to your attention, the perusal of the article *Orchard* in *January,* page 56, *February,* page 149, and *March,* page 234.

THE VINEYARD.

In the middle and eastern States, little remains to be done in the vineyard at this season; indeed it sometimes happens in the former that the ground is open in the beginning of the month, in which case you may plough between the young vines and earth them up, as directed in *November,* if then omitted.   It will be of considerable use to lay some litter around the roots and a little way up the stems of such tender kinds as were planted in the preceding spring and autumn, to protect them from very severe frost, till they are once fully established.   For further particulars of what may be done in this month, in and for the vineyard as well as in the ensuing, see page 60.

In the southern States you may row prune vines, as directed in *February ;* and south of the thirty-fifth degree of latitude, vineyards may be planted agreeably to the instructions given in *March.*

THE NURSERY.

NEW PLANTED TREES.

Continue the care of the more curious and tender sorts of new-planted trees and shrubs ; where there was no litter laid between the rows in November, let it be no longer neglected, and bring it up close to their stems the better to protect all the roots from frost, should the winter prove so severe as to destroy their tops, which may also be protected as directed on page 614.   The roots and lower parts of their stems being thus preserved they will generally shoot out freely in the ensuing spring from the near surface of the ground.

SEEDLING TREES.

Seedlings which make but slow progress in growth the first year, such as pines, &c., must now be taken due care of, as directed on page 587.

The beds of acorns, and of any other tree seeds that were sown in the preceding months, would be greatly benefited by laying peas-straw, fern, leaves, straw, or other long litter over them during the continuance of hard frost ; but this must be removed as soon as the frost is out of the ground in spring, otherwise it will invite a resort of mice, &c., to destroy the seeds.

PROTECTING TREES AND SHRUBS, ETC., IN POTS.

The tall growing plants in pots which are plunged in warm borbers, and the pots covered with tan as directed on page 588, may, if the kinds are rather tender, require an awning of mats or strong canvas over them to protect them from cutting winds, which are always very injurious to tender plants. The other tender plants, both shrubby and herbaceous, which you have in pots in frames, must be duly attended to, as directed on page 595.

SOUTHERN STATES.

Where the ground is open and in *good condition for working*, this is a very proper time to sow hawthorn, holly, yew, mezereon, red cedar, juniper and pyracantha berries, and all other seeds that require a year's previous preparation, such as Stewartia malacodendron, ash, euonymus, hornbean, celastrus scandens, nyssa, and many other sorts. (For the method of performing this work, see the *Nursery* for *February*.)

Continue to dig between the rows of young trees and shrubs, and forward the manuring and trenching of such pieces of ground as are to be planted with young trees in the ensuing months.

You may still continue to make layers and plant cuttings of any kinds of trees and shrubs that succeed by these means, and also dig up and transplant suckers. Prune roses and other hardy shrubs, also forest and young fruit-trees in training. Plant out into nursery rows the various kinds of hardy deciduous trees and shrubs, as directed in March ; but let it be remembered that these instructions are exclusively intended for such parts of the Union as have not frost during winter sufficient to prevent the ploughing of ground.

THE PLEASURE, OR FLOWER GARDEN.

TULIPS, HYACINTHS, ANEMONES, AND RANUNCULUSES.

Continue to protect your beds of choice tulips, hyacinths, anemones and ranunculuses as directed last month ; this will be indispensable at present, as December is generally one of the most severe and cutting months in the year. It would be unnecessary in this place to repeat all the instructions given in November for that purpose, and therefore I refer you to page 589, &c., for information.

Some of the Van Thol and other early tulips which were planted in pots in October, may, towards the end of this month, be placed in the hot-house, or in any other forcing department, to produce a winter bloom of flowers. Early hyacinths, spring crocuses, snow-drops, dwarf Persian iris, and polyanthus-narcissus may now be forced in like manner; but observe that you are to reserve a sufficiency of each sort for several successions, so as to have a constant supply of flowers until those in the open ground begin to blow.

When the plants are just beginning to flower some of them may be taken in to decorate parlors and other rooms.

CARE OF AURICULAS AND CARNATIONS.

Your choice auriculas and carnations must now be defended from heavy rains, frost, and snow; but large portions of air must be admit-ted to them at every favorable opportunity, otherwise the auriculas will start to flower at an untimely season, and the carnations will draw, become weakly, and be good for nothing. Neither of them are very tender, and consequently should not be kept too closely shut up.

POLYANTHUSES AND DOUBLE PRIMROSES.

The fine polyanthuses and double primroses require exactly the same treatment as the auriculas and carnations, which need not be repeated; the common polyanthuses and primroses will succeed very well in the open borders, but will be the better of a slight covering of straw during the continuance of severe frost.

SOWING ANEMONE AND RANUNCULUS SEEDS.

The *double* varieties of the *Anemone hortensis*, or broad-leaved garden anemone, and *Anemone coronaria*, or narrow-leaved, as well as of the *Ranunculus persica*, or Persian ranunculus, being generally extremely beautiful, are peculiarly deserving of attention; as all those delightful flowers, displaying such a diversity of shades and colors, are only seminal varieties, and as the number of them may be annually increased, and superior varieties obtained, no good florist will neglect to sow seeds of each sort every year.

The seeds of either kind should be procured from semi-double flowers, for the full double seldom bear any, and those produced by the single rarely give double flowers. Care should be taken to save the seeds from flowers possessed of good properties, that is, such as have tall strong stems, a considerable number of well formed petals of rich, good and brilliant colors.

The seed of the ranunculus should remain on the plant till it has lost its verdure and becomes brown and dry, it may then be cut off and spread upon paper in a dry room exposed to the air; when per-fectly dry it should be put into a paper bag and kept free from all dampness till the time of sowing, otherwise it would be in danger of contracting a mouldiness that would infalibly destroy it. The ane-mone seed must be gathered from time to time as it opens; for, being very downy and light, it will otherwise be blown away by the first breezes of wind, or fall to the ground and be lost.

It would be found very difficult to sow anemone seed in a regular manner: it is united with, and enveloped in a downy substance, that, upon being put together in quantity, adheres in such a manner as to render it necessary to rub it between the hands for a considerable time in dry sand previous to sowing; otherwise the young plants would rise in clusters, and not have space enough to form their roots.

When you are ready to sow your ranunculus seed, take it out of the bag, and if the weather be damp, spread it thin upon a sheet of paper, before a moderate fire, till it is just warm, *and no more;* then rub it out and clean it perfectly from any pieces of the stalk, dried petals of the flower or other extraneous matter, which, if sown with it, would create a mouldiness of very destructive consequence.

The last ten days of December, any time in January, or even the first week of February, the seeds may be sown, but when convenient, the early sowing is preferable. Each kind should be sown separately in shallow frames (of either one, two, or three lights, according to the quantity), provided with glasses, similar to those made use of for cucumbers and melons; the soil should be taken out at least two feet deep, and replaced with good and suitable soil such as is directed on page 564; out of which the earth-worms should be carefully picked, for these are extremely destructive to the young plant, which they draw from a considerable distance into their holes for nutriment.

When the pit is filled, so as to reach about six inches up the sides and ends of the frame, it should be suffered to remain a few days to settle; then the surface should be made perfectly smooth and even, and the seed sown upon it with the utmost regularity, in such quantity as nearly to cover it, for accidents will befall many of them; the glasses should be placed on immediately, and the frame kept closely covered with them for two or three days, till the seeds begin to swell, observing to cover the glasses effectually at night and in severe weather, to keep out the frost, and also line the outside of the frame all around to its full height with tan, leaves, or horse-dung, for a similar purpose: a little light earth should then be sifted over the seed through a fine sieve, but not sufficient to cover it; this should be repeated once or twice a week till the greater part of the seed disappears. It is proper to remark in this place that such seed as happens to be covered deeper than the thickness of a dollar will never vegetate, and must of course inevitably perish.

It is necessary to keep the seed moderately moist by gentle occasional waterings with soft water, that has been exposed to the sun or to fire heat till the cold chill is off; this should be given from the rose of a small watering pot, which rose should be of a hemispherical form, and perforated with very small holes that will discharge fine streams of water in a very distinct and regular manner; this should be made of copper, it being less liable to corrode than iron.

But although it is necessary to the vegetation of the seed that it be kept moderately moist, too great a degree of moisture is nevertheless injurious, especially to the commencement of the spring heat, and indeed at any period.

When the young plants begin to appear, which, if sown in De-

cember or early in January, will generally happen about the latter
end of February, earlier or later, according to the temperature of
the weather and the care taken of the frame, refresh them occasionally with gentle waterings, and give them air at every favorable opportunity; but be sure to keep the glasses close in very cold weather,
and well covered at night; observing, also, as the sun gets powerful,
to screen the plants from its mid-day influence, which sometimes
would in one hour destroy the whole.

As the spring advances, more and more air must be admitted, and
on fine days the plants totally exposed, except to a scorching sun,
so as to have them by the latter end of April, or as soon as the
smart night frosts are over, so hardened as to bear the open air night
and day; observing to keep them regularly watered, and to give them
the advantage of fine warm showers of rain, when such happen in
due time.

This kind of management is to be continued till the roots are
matured, always taking care to protect the plants by a screen of
hurdles or thin bass-mats laid over the frame from the too powerful
influence of the sun, but never keeping this covering over them
longer than necessary. Their maturity will be known by the foliage
becoming brown, dry, and nearly consumed, which generally happens in the middle States towards the latter end of June, or early in
July.

The speediest and safest method of taking up these small roots, is
to pare off the earth three inches deep, having previously picked off
the dried leaves and any other extraneous matter that may be found
on the bed. The earth and roots thus collected are to be thrown
into a fine wire sieve that will not permit the smallest roots to pass
through it, which is to be worked in a large vessel or tub of water
nearly filled: the earthy parts will dissolve and wash away and the
roots remain in the sieve, which may be easily picked from the
stones, &c. The upper rim of the sieve must at all times be held
above the surface of the water, otherwise some of the small roots
will float over and be lost. The roots are then to be dried and preserved, as directed for the large roots on pages 407 and 408, till the
latter end of September or early in October, when they are to be
planted and managed as on pages 564 and 565; observing that they
(being small) may be planted somewhat closer than the large roots,
and will not require to be covered quite so deep.

The ensuing season several of the largest roots will flower, especially the ranunculuses, and all of them the third year, at which
time you should carefully mark such as are worthy of being preserved; the others may be planted in small clumps in the warm borders of the garden and pleasure-grounds, there to take chance. The
valuable kinds must be subsequently increased by offsets.

Those who desire to raise these plants upon a small scale, may
sow the seeds in boxes, large pots, or garden pans, of good compost,
observing to have the bottoms of the boxes, previous to their being
filled, bored with several auger holes, which are to be covered with
shells or the like, to suffer any extra moisture to pass away freely.
But the former method is much more preferable.

39

SOWING AURICULA, POLYANTHUS, AND CYCLAMEN SEEDS.

The surest and best method to obtain fine auriculas from seed, is as follows : In the first place the seed should be saved from young, healthy, strong plants, of capital high-colored sorts, possessing the first-rate properties : these, on the approach of bloom, should be detached from the rest, to some distant part of the garden, for fear of the farina of indifferent sorts contaminating them, and there exposed to the full air, the sun (except when too violent), and *moderate* rains; from an excess of which, the plants are to be protected by mats laid on hoops, or by small hand-glasses. In dry weather these plants must be regularly watered, as often as they appear to require it : much depends on a due attention to this particular point.

The seed will commonly ripen in June; it is advisable frequently to visit the plants at that season, and carefully to gather such pods or heads of seed as appear perfectly dry, brown, and begin to open; if all the pods on the same stem are ripe together they may be cut off with part of the stem to which they are connected; but if some of the pods are not sufficiently ripe, such as are, should be carefully picked from the rest as they become so. The seed thus collected, should remain in the pericarpiums or seed-vessels, in a dry room, till the season of sowing.

In the last week of December, any time in January, or in the early part of February, the seed may be sown with every prospect of success, provided you have the necessary conveniences. The early sown seeds, *if well managed*, will vegetate better, and the plants raise more numerously than the late : besides, it will be of serious importance to give the plants the advantage of a long spring vegetation, that they may be as strong as possible before the summer heat sets in, which to seedling auriculas and polyanthuses is very destructive, and even to the full grown plants; but if there is not a suitable convenience, and an opportunity of paying the necessary attention, it will be better to defer the sowing till February.

A hot-bed must be prepared, as for early seedling cucumbers, and a good frame and glass-light set thereon, with five or six inches of fine earth laid all over the bed, to keep down the steam. Provide a box or boxes about five or six inches deep, with several holes on the bottom; fill it with compost, and gently shake and strike it against the ground, till the earth settles a little; make the surface perfectly smooth and even, and sow the seed with the utmost regularity; then sift through a fine wired sieve a little compost or vegetable mould upon it, sufficient only to just cover the seed, and place the box in the frame on the surface of the bed; the glass must be set on immediately and the bed so managed as to preserve a moderate and equal degree of warmth both day and night, but must be occasionally opened, or the light raised up at the higher end, to admit fresh air, and to suffer the exhalations from the bed to pass away, which is a very essential point.

The earth must always be kept moderately moist, both before and after the plants appear, but never wet; the best method of watering it is by means of a hard clothes-brush dipped into soft water which has had its chill taken off by standing for some time in the sun or in the frame; the hair side being quickly turned upwards, and the hand rubbed briskly over it, will cause the water to fly off in particles almost as fine as dew; a sufficient watering may in this manner be given in a few minutes. If it is found impossible to preserve a due heat in the first bed till the seed has all vegetated, it will be proper to prepare a second into which to remove the box; but if there are cucumber frames, &c., at work, the box may be removed into any of them that supports a good temperate heat.

At the expiration of four or five weeks, if well managed, the young plants will have all made their appearance; it then becomes necessary to give them, very gradually, more air, in order to harden and render them fit, in due time, for an entire exposure to it. In the month of March the plants, if forward, should be fully exposed to the open air for a few hours in the middle of mild days, when the sun is not too powerful, but particularly to light warm rains. As to their subsequent treatment, see the *Flower Garden* for *April* and the months following.

If you are apprehensive of the young seedlings being attacked by snails, &c., which they are very subject to, place a hair band round the box when you sow the seed, as directed on page 167.

Polyanthus seed and seedlings are to be treated exactly in the same manner as those of Auricula.

Cyclamen seeds of every kind may be sown in boxes during any of the autumn or winter months, even to the middle of February; but when kept out of ground much later, most of them will not vegetate till the spring following: they may be treated generally as directed on page 444, observing always to protect them from frost. The *Cyclamen indicum* being a hot-house plant, its seed must be treated accordingly: this species differs from the others in not having the divisions of the corolla or flower reflexed or turned back, but hanging down, and in the whole corolla being much larger than either of the Persian or European kinds. The former kinds will require no bottom heat, but should be carefully protected by a good frame and glasses, well covered at night and in severe weather, so as to prevent the earth in the inside from becoming frozen, but more particularly after the plants appear; the latter kind must be sown in a box, which is to be placed in a good hot-bed, as directed for anemone seed, and constantly treated as a hot-house plant; or, it may be plunged in the bark-bed of any forcing department and there taken proper care of.

DOUBLE DAISIES.

Continue to protect and treat your double daisies as directed on page 591. You may now place a few of the best plants which you have in pots, in some of the forcing apartments, to promote an early bloom.

PLANTING BULBOUS ROOTS.

In the early part of this month, should the weather continue open, or that it is practicable to work the ground, you may plant hyacinths, jonquils, tulips, double narcissus, star of Bethlehem, crocuses, snowdrops, or any other hardy kinds of bulbs that yet remain out of ground; but it is wrong, if it can be avoided, to defer the planting of them to this time. However, it will be better at all events, to plant the above kinds now, should it be practicable, than to keep them up till spring: but it will be very proper, and indeed I may say necessary; to cover the newly-planted beds immediately with straw or other light covering; for such roots as have not produced fibres before the setting in of frost, are much more vulnerable to it than those that have.

Polyanthus-narcissus, anemones, or ranunculuses, should not be planted in the middle or eastern States at this season, unless they are effectually protected afterwards from rain, snow, and frost; I would rather advise to preserve them carefully in dry sand till the early part of March, or even the middle of that month.

PROTECT SEEDLING BULBS, ETC.

The various kinds of seedling bulbs should now be carefully protected as directed on page 591, otherwise many of them will be injured. The boxes in which were sowed, in the preceding months, the seeds of bulbous-rooted flowers, should be treated in like manner.

PROTECTING STOCKS, WALLFLOWERS, ETC.

Your double stock-gillyflowers, wallflowers, and other plants of similar constitutions, which are in frames, must have protection from rain, snow, and severe frost; and it will be necessary, during winter, to give them the full benefit of the air for a few hours in the middle of mild days, but by no means to expose them or any other tender plants to a hot sun whilst in a frozen state.

NEW-PLANTED SHRUBS AND TREES.

The more tender or choice kinds of shrubs and trees which were planted last spring, or in the preceding month, should now have their roots well protected from frost by laying some wispy dung, or long litter all around the plants. Some kinds may even require to have their tops matted around, or each to be completely enveloped in a coat of long straw, reaching from the ground to the top of the plant, and terminating there in a point, the whole assuming the form of a sugarloaf. The straw is to be supported by placing slender sticks in the earth around the shrub, the tops of which are to be tied together over it; a few willow twigs should be worked in between these sticks to prevent the straw from falling in, or lying close to the plants, which, when laid on, is to be bound around by hay bands, willows, or the like.

Hydrangea hortensis, China and Otaheite roses, prunus lauro-cerasus, and small plants of magnolia grandiflora, lagerstroemia indica, double pomegranate, and many other valuable shrubs may be preserved in good condition by this means, and ultimately inured to the winter frosts without much injury; observe that the covering is not to be disturbed before the middle of March in the middle States, or the beginning of April in the eastern States; and even then it is to be taken off by piecemeal and not all at once, for too sudden an exposure might do them considerable injury should a hard frost or cutting winds ensue.

OTHER USEFUL WORK.

Should the weather prove open in the early part of the month, you may continue to prune hardy shrubs and trees; spread your compost heaps if not done last month, and prepare more if necessary; rake off the fallen leaves of trees and dig among your clumps and shrubbery plantations.

In hard frosty weather, when little else can be done in the garden than the covering and uncovering of tender plants, &c., prepare label sticks to mark or number the various flowers and seeds when they are planted or sown, and prepare all the tools and every other necessary convenience for your spring operations.

THE GREEN-HOUSE.

It generally happens that the weather is extremely rigorous in this month; therefore, more than ordinary attention must be paid to the green-house plants. In cold or frosty weather keep the windows and doors closely shut, and close your window-shutters carefully every night, and also in *extremely rigorous* frosts, except while the sun shines on the windows.

When green-houses are so constructed as to have no window-shutters, which is certainly wrong, large thick mats should be hung and nailed, or made fast by small hooks, in front of the lights, every cold night, and also in the daytime when the weather is very severe, and no sun. It may sometimes be necessary, even when there are shutters, to hang and nail up mats in front of the windows, to check the piercing wind. If there are short roof-lights, they must be covered with mats, or strong canvas during the continuance of severe weather; these may be so contrived as to roll up, and fall down, by means of lines and pulleys, at pleasure.

During the continuance of severe frost, *accompanied by piercing cutting winds*, the windows must never be opened—that is, you must neither slide the lights up nor down, but always keep them and the door or doors closed; and any plants that are too near the glass must be removed into the interior of the house, especially at night and in cloudy dark weather.

If you find the frost likely to reach your plants, notwithstanding all this care, you must heat the flues by gentle fires at night, and also in the daytime when the frost is very piercing and the weather dark; and, indeed, without such a convenience it is almost useless to attempt the erection or trouble of a green-house, either in the middle or eastern States, on account of their extremely rigorous winters. But you must be particular never to heat the air in the night-time above 40 or 45 degrees of Fahrenheit's thermometer; for all the heat that the plants require at this season is only just as much as will preserve them effectually from frost.

However, be very particular every day, when the weather is mild and the sun shining on the windows, to slide down the sashes, even for but half an hour in the middle of the day, to admit fresh air and ventilate the house; for if the plants are kept too close they will become tender and weak, and besides it will cause the leaves of some kinds to turn of a yellowish sickly color, and afterwards to get mouldy and drop off.

N. B. The plants must never be deprived of light by keeping the shutters closed a moment longer than it is found absolutely necessary for their preservation; and though I am not an advocate for much fire-heat in a green-house, yet I would prefer it to keeping the plants too long in darkness, which has an extremely bad effect upon them.

For particulars respecting watering and other information, I would recommend to your perusal at this term the entire of the article green-house in January, and also in February, pages 98 and 174. The general care during each of these months is nearly the same.

The plants which you are wintering in garden-frames must now be carefully attended, agreeably to the directions given in page 594.

THE HOT-HOUSE.

The frost generally sets in very severe in this month, and the winds are keen and cutting; therefore it will be necessary to keep up your fire-heat in proportion to the severity of the weather, which must be regulated by a thermometer, never letting the air of the house in the night or cloudy days be colder than 52 degrees of Fahrenheit, nor warmer at this season *by fire heat* than 62° or thereabouts—with sunshine it may rise to 70° or 75°—for it is very injudicious to force the plants now into a fresh state of vegetation. All that they want at present is to be kept comfortably warm and rather in an inactive state; consequently, as the heat of the day in sunny weather increases, you must slacken your fires or put them totally out, as the case may be, always renewing them in the afternoon or whenever you find the due warmth on the decline.

It will be generally necessary to attend the fires till eleven or twelve o'clock at night, when, if wanted, a sufficiency of fuel must be added to support a proper degree of heat till morning; and in extremely severe weather it may sometimes be necessary to sit up all night to guard against untoward consequences. At all events, you must be up very early in the morning to renew the fires.

If the hot-house is furnished with shutters or covering of any kind, as noticed in January, they will now be of considerable use, both for the preservation of the plants and the saving of fuel. It will, however, be very proper to hang thick mats every severe night in front of the upright sashes, which will prevent the wind from rushing in immediately on the plants through any deficiencies that may be in the work.

If the bark bed was properly made or renewed in October, or in the beginning of November, it will yet be in a proper state of warmth, which is now essentially necessary; if, however, towards the end of the month it is found to be much declined in heat, it should be forked up to revive it, as directed in *January*, but more particularly so if it contains pines for fruiting next season, which must be now kept rather in a slow state of vegetation than dormant.

Succession pines, or other plants in pits or in the succession-house, require the same care as above, observing not to force them by too much heat, lest the pines start to a fruiting state at an untimely period. They are never fit to produce handsome-sized fruit until they are two years old, at which age they in October should be placed in the fruiting-house for the ensuing year's bearing.

The pines and other plants in the hot-house, &c., will still require to be watered occasionally, the former not oftener than once a week, the shrubby kinds in small pots perhaps twice a week; but the succulent sorts should at this season have but very little, and that only when you are able to perceive that they are in absolute want of it; and then let it be given round the edges of the pots, and not to the plants themselves, for if it should stagnate about the stems it would infallibly rot them. The varieties of cactus melocactus, or Turk's cap, with many others of the most succulent kinds, should at this season have no water given them, except in cases of great necessity.

When there happens to come a fine sunny calm day, it will be proper to admit some fresh air into the house by sliding some of the glasses, in the warmest part of the day, a little way open, even if but for half an hour; but be sure to close them again in due time, and especially if the weather changes to cold or cloudy. This is best effected at this season by sliding open a few of the roof-lights, if it can be done with convenience.

Pick off such decayed leaves as you perceive on the various plants, keep them free from insects and filth of every kind, and the whole house as sweet and clean as possible.

Sprinkle your flues and walks occasionally with water to raise a comforting steam of moisture in the house; especially when you are obliged to burn fires constantly night and day. This will preserve the plants from the bad effects produced by the parching influence of a constant fire-heat, and also tend to prevent an increase of insects.

You may, towards the latter end of this month, introduce into the hot-house pots of strawberries and flowering plants of various kinds; sow cucumber seed and plant kidney beans, as directed in *January*, in order to force them into early perfection. Pots or tubs of bearing grape-vines may also be now introduced for early bearing if there are none trained in from the outside. Such vines as are planted in front of the house, and trained in under the lights, should have the parts of their stems which are exposed to the weather well wrapped around with hay or straw neatly tied on; also their roots covered sufficiently with long litter; for, their juices being put into full circulation by the forcing heat, renders the exposed parts much more vulnerable to frost than if the entire plants stood inactive in the open air.

Having now gone through the work of the several months, and endeavored to adapt the whole to the seasons and local situations of the different parts of the Union, to explain and simplify the various operations, and to render the work of as much general utility as possible, it is offered to the public as the result of many years' experience, solely devoted to horticultural and botanical pursuits, without presuming to say that it is either infallible or incapable of improvement.

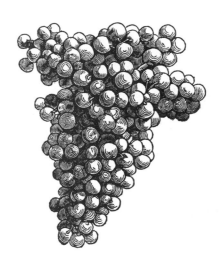

A CATALOGUE

OF

KITCHEN GARDEN ESCULENT PLANTS AND HERBS.

COMMON NAMES.	BOTANICAL NAMES.
ARTICHOKE, Garden	*Cynara Scolymus*
1. Green Globe. 2. White Globe. 3. French.	
Artichoke, Jerusalem	*Helianthus tuberosus*
Asparagus, the Garden	*Asparagus officinalis*
1. Dutch. 2. Gravesend. 3. Battersea. 4. Large Jersey.	
Bean, the common Garden	*Vicia Faba*
1. Early Mazagan. 2. Early Lisbon. 3. Long Podded. 4. Common Field or Horse. 5. Dwarf Cluster. 6. White Blossom. 7. Red Blossom. 8. Large Windsor. 9. Large Toker. 10. Broad Spanish. 11. Mumford. 12. Green Nonpareil. 13. Turkey Long Pod. 14. Green Genoa, &c.	
Bean, the Dwarf Kidney	*Phaseolus vulgaris*, v. *Pumilæ*
1. Early Yellow Dwarf. 2. Early Cream-colored do. 3. Early Speckled do. 4. Early White do. 5. Early Brown-speckled do. 6. Negro Dwarf. 7. Large White do. 8. Purple-speckled do. 9. Black-eyed do. 10. Red-speckled do. 11. Mohawk. 12. Early China, &c.	
Running Kinds.	v. *volubilis*
1. Corn Beans. 2. Large White Runners. 3. Cream-colored Runners. 4. Round White Runners, &c.	
Bean, Scarlet Runners	*Phaseolus multiflorus*
Lima Beans	*Phaseolus lunatus*
Carolina do.	v.
Beet, The Common	*Beta vulgaris*
1. Red Beet	v. *rubra vulgaris*
2. Long Red do.	v. *rubra major*
3. Turnip-rooted Beet	v. *rubra, radice rapæ*
4. Yellow-rooted do.	v. *lutea major*
5. Green or White do.	v. *pallide virens major*
6. Mangel-Wurtzel, or Root of Scarcity.	*Cicla*
Borage, Common	*Borago officinalis*
Borecole, Purple-curled	*Brassica oleracea laciniata*
Green-curled	*oleracea selenicea*
Siberian or Scotch	*oleracea sabellica*
Brussels Sprouts	
Finely Fringed	

Broccoli, Italian   *Brassica oleracea italica*
    1. Early Purple. 2. Early Green.
    3. Large Late Purple. 4. Large
    White. 5. Walcheren. 6. Early
    White Cape. 7. Dwarf Russian, &c.

Cabbage, Heading   *Brassica oleracea capitata*
    1. Early York. 2. Early Heart-
    shaped. 3. Early Battersea. 4.
    Early Antwerp. 5. Early Dwarf.
    6. Early Sugar-loaf. 7. Large Late
    Sugar-loaf. 8. Large Scotch. 9.
    Large English. 10. Large Drum-
    Head. 11. Flat Dutch. 12. Large
    Late Battersea. 13. Red Pickling.
    14. Enfield Market. 15. Early
    Vanack, &c.

Cabbage, Turnip   *Brassica oleracea Napobrassica*
    Turnip-rooted   *Napus sativa*
    Jerusalem Kale

Cabbage, Savoy   *Brassica oleracea sabauda*
    1. Green. 2. Yellow. 3. Milan.

Calabash, or Bottle-gourd   *Cucurbita lagenaria*

Cardoon, Spanish   *Cynara Cardunculus*

Carrot, Long Orange   *Daucus Carota*
    Early Horn do.
    Altringham
    Long Surrey, &c.

Cauliflower, Early   *Brassica oleracea botrytis*
    Late do.

Celery, Italian upright   *Apium graveolens*
    1. Solid-stalked. 2. North's Large.
    3. Red-stalked Solid. 4. Seymour's
    White Solid, &c.

Celeriac, Turnip-rooted Celery   *Apium graveolens rapaceum*

Chervil   *Scandix Cerefolium*

Chives or Cives   *Allium Schœnoprasum*

Coriander   *Coriandrum sativum*

Corn, Indian. Twelve-round sweet. *Zea Mays*
    Stowell's Evergreen, &c.

Corn-salad   *Valeriana Locusta olitoria*

Cress, or Pepper-grass   *Lepidium sativum*
    1. Narrow-leaved. 2. Broad-leav-
    ed. 3. Curled-leaved.

Cress, Winter, or Salad Scurvy-grass   *Erisymum Barbarea*

Cress, Water   *Sisymbrium Nasturtium*

Cucumber, Common   *Cucumis sativus*
    1. Early Frame. 2. Early Prickly.
    3. Early Cluster. 4. Long Prickly.
    5. Long Green Turkey. 6. Long
    White Turkey. 7. Long Roman.
    8. White Spined. 9. Walker's Im-
    proved, &c.

Cucumber, Round Prickly   *Cucumis Anguria*

Egg-Plant   *Solanum Melongena*
    1. Purple-fruited.
    2. White-fruited.

Endive, Green-curled   *Cichorium Endivia*
    White-curled
    Broad-leaved
    Batavian

Finochio   *Anethum azoricum*

Garlic, Cultivated   *Allium sativum*

Gourd-Squash. Early Bush. Bergen *Cucurbita Melopepo*
    Root. Boston Marrow, &c.

Ground Nut   *Arachis hypogea*

Leek, Common   *Allium Porrum*
    Narrow leaved

Leek, Broad-leaved

Lettuce, or Salad *Lactuca sativa*
    1. White Cos. 2. Green Cos. 3. Egyptian Cos. 4. Black Cos. 5. Aleppo. 6. India. 7. Brown Dutch. 8. Common Cabbage. 9. Imperial. 10. Grand Admiral. 11. Hammersmith Hardy-green. 12. Tennisball. 13. Silesia. 14. Large Royal. 15. Madeira. 16. Saxony Cabbage, &c.

Melon, Musk *Cucumis Melo*
    1. Early Romana. 2. Early Cantaleupe. 3. Early Small Zatte. 4. Early Succado. 5. Black Portugal. 6. Golden Rock. 7. Large Mogul. 8. Minorca. 9. Large African. 10. Rock Cantaleupe. 11. Nettled Green-flesh. 12. Japan Rock. 13. Nutmeg. 14. Mexican. 15. Beechwood, &c.

Melon, Water *Cucurbita Citrullus*
    1. Long Red-flesh. 2. Long Yellow-flesh. 3. Large Round Red-flesh. 4. Green-flesh do. 5. Sweet Mountain, &c.

Mushroom *Agaricus campestris*
Mustard, White *Sinapis alba*
           Black *nigra*
Nasturtium, Large *Tropæolum majus*
Okra *Hibiscus esculentus*
Onion, Common *Allium Cepa*
    1. Strasburg. 2. White Spanish. 3. Silver-skinned. 4. Madeira. 5. Long-keeping. 6. Blood-red. 7. Welsh. *fistulosum*
    8. Tree. *canadense*
Orach, or English Lamb's-quarter *Atriplex hortensis*
           Large Green-leaved
           Red-leaved
Parsley, Common *Apium petroselinum*
           Curled *crispum*
           Hamburg, or Large-rooted *latifolium*
Parsnep, Long Garden *Pastineca sativa*
Patience Dock *Rumex Patientia*
Pea, Garden *Pisum sativum*
    1. Early Frame. 2. Sangster's Early. 3. Early Charleton do. 4. Spanish Dwarf. 5. Dwarf Sugar. 6. Bishop's Dwarf. 7. Tall Sugar. 8. Woodford's Marrow. 9. Blue Prussian. 10. Green Imperial Marrow. 11. Dwarf Marrowfat. 12. Champion of England. 13. Fairbeard's Surprise. 14. Early Warwick. 15. Knight's Dwarf Marrow. 16. Common Field. 17. Pearl, or Nonesuch. 18. Flack's Victory. 19. Albany. 20. Hare's Dwarf Mammoth. 21. Large Marrowfat. 22. Ward's Incomparable

Pepper, Red or Guinea *Capsicum annuum*
    1. Long-podded   v. *longioribus siliquis*
    2. Heart-shaped   v. *cordiforme*
    3. Bell   v. *tetragonum*
    4. Cherry, &c.   v. *cerasiforme*
Potato, Common *Solanum tuberosum*

Potato, Sweet	*Convolvulus Batatas*
Pumpkin, or Pompion	*Cucurbita Pepo*
Many varieties.	
Radish, Garden	*Raphanus sativus*

    1. Early Frame. 2. Early Purple Short-top. 3. Salmon Short-top. 4. Common Salmon. 5. White Short-top. 6. White Turnip-rooted. 7. Red Turnip-rooted. 8. White Winter Radish. 9. Black Winter do. 10. White Naples. 11. Olive shaped. 12. Wood's Early Frame, &c.

Radish, Horse	*Cochlearia Armoracia*
Ruta Baga, or Swedish Turnip	*Brassica Rapa*
Rampion, Esculent	*Campanula Rapunculus*
Rape, or Cole-seed	*Brassica Napus*
Rocambole	*Allium Scorodoprasum*
Salsafy	*Tragopogon porrifolium*
Scorzonera	*Scorzonera hispanica*
Sea-Kale, or Cabbage	*Crambe maritima*
Shallot	*Allium Ascalonicum*
Skirret	*Sium sisarum*
Sorrel, Broad-leaved	*Rumex Acetosa*
Round-leaved	*scutatus*
Spinage. 1. Prickly seeded	*Spinacia oleracea*
2. Burdock. 3. Round-leaved	
Squash, Warted	*Cucurbita verrucosa*
Many varieties.	
Tomatoes, or Love-apple, Cherry, Red Burlington, Common Red, Yellow, &c.	*Solanum Lycopersicum*
Turnip, Cultivated	*Brassica Rapa*

    1. Early Dutch. 2. Early Stone. 3. Early Six Weeks. 4. Snowball. 5. Large Red-topped. 6. White Round. 7. Tankard. 8. Large English Field. 9. Swedish, or Ruta Baga. 10. Long French.

AROMATIC, POT, AND SWEET HERBS.

Anise	*Pimpinella Anisum*
Basil, Sweet	*Ocymum Basilicum medium*
Bush	*minimum*
Caraway	*Carum Carui*
Clary	*Salvia sclarea*
Coriander	*Coriandrum sativum*
Chamomile	*Anthemis nobilis*
Dill	*Anethum graveolens*
Fennel, Common	*Anethum Fœniculum*
Sweet	v. *dulce*
Hyssop	*Hyssopus officinalis*
Lavender	*Lavendula Spica*
Lovage	*Ligusticum Levisticum*
Marigold, pot	*Calendula officinalis*
Marjoram, Sweet	*Origanum Majorana*
Pot	*Onites*
Winter Sweet	*heracleoticum*
Mint, Spear	*Mentha viridis*
Pepper	*piperita*
Pennyroyal	*Pulegium*
Mint, Horse	*Monarda punctata*

Rosemary	*Rosmarinus officinalis*
Sage, Common	*Salvia officinalis*
Savory, Summer	*Satureia hortensis*
Winter	*montana*
Smallage	*Apium graveolens*
Tarragon	*Artemisia Dracunculus*
Thyme, Common	*Thymus vulgaris*
Lemon	*serpyllum*

PLANTS CULTIVATED FOR MEDICINAL PURPOSES, &c.

Ague-weed, Thoroughwort	*Eupatorium perfoliatum*
Angelica, Garden	*Angelica Archangelica*
Betony, Wood	*Betonica officinalis*
Bugloss	*Anchusa officinalis*
Carduus benedictus	*Centaurea benedicta*
Celandine	*Chelidonium majus*
Comfrey, Common	*Symphytum officinale*
Cucumber, Bitter	*Cucumis Colocynthis*
Elecampane	*Inula Helenium*
Flax, Common	*Linum usitatissimum*
Fenugreek	*Trigonella Fœnum Græcum*
Feverfew	*Matricaria Parthenium*
Foxglove	*Digitalis purpurea*
Gromwell	*Lithospermum officinale*
Hemlock	*Conium maculatum*
Horehound	*Marrubium vulgare*
Hound's-tongue	*Cynoglossum officinale*
Liquorice	*Glycyrrhiza glabra*
Madder, Dyers'	*Rubia tinctorum*
Mallow, Marsh	*Althæa officinalis*
Mugwort, Common	*Artemisia vulgaris*
Nep, or Catmint	*Nepeta Cataria*
Nettle, Stinging	*Urtica urens*
Palma Christi, or Castor-oil Nut	*Ricinus communis*
Pimpernel	*Anagallis arvensis*
Pink-root, Carolina	*Spigelia marilandica*
Poppy, Opium	*Papaver somniferum*
Rue, Garden	*Ruta graveolens*
Rhubarb, True Turkey	*Rheum palmatum*
Common	*Rhaponticum*
Scurvy-grass	*Cochlearia officinalis*
Snakeroot, Virginia	*Aristolochia serpentaria*
Southernwood	*Artemisia Abrotanum*
Tansy	*Tanacetum vulgare*
Tobacco, Cultivated	*Nicotiana Tabacum*
Common English	*rusticum*
Weld, Woad, or Dyers'-weed	*Reseda Luteola*
Winter Cherry	*Physalis Alkekengi*
Wormseed, Goosefoot	*Chenopodium anthelminticum*
Wormwood	*Artemisia Absinthium*
Yarrow	*Achillea Millefolium*
Sweet or Milfoil	*Ageratum*

GRASSES AND OTHER PLANTS USED IN FARMING.

The following are selected as the most important and valuable plants used in rural economy; the grasses and other plants cultivated for their foliage, are particularly such as have been found to merit attention; a knowledge of their true names is the first step towards obtaining them, and when obtained it is of serious importance to cultivate each sort in the soil and situation best adapted to its nature, which is carefully pointed out in the following list.

The judicious cultivation of grasses, though the least expensive and most profitable part of husbandry (for on it every other part may be said to depend), has hitherto been too much neglected by the generality of our farmers, and in this they have been blind to their best interests.

In order to be successful, a farmer should endeavor to procure and cultivate such grasses and other vegetable productions as are peculiarly adapted to the various soils of which his plantation is composed; so that every spot, from the dryest hill to the wettest swamp, may be employed in yielding him profitable productions.

Those marked thus * are indigenous, or native plants of the United States; and such as are marked thus †, of the West Indies and warmer parts of America.

GRASSES.

*Brome, Purging	*Bromus purgans (wet soil)*
Barnet, Field	*Poterium Sanguisorba (dry good soil)*
*Blue	*Poa compressa (dry fields)*
Canary, Reedy	*Phalaris arundinacia (wet soil)*
Clover, Red	*Trifolium pratense (moderately dry)*
White	*repens (rich dry soil)*
Yellow	*ochroleucum (dry ground)*
*Cock's-foot, Swamp	*Dactylis Cynosuroides (swamps)*
*Canadian, Reedy	*Cinna arundinacea (moist soil)*
Dog's-tail	*Cynosurus cristatus (dry ground)*
Fox-tail, Meadow	*Alopecurus pratensis (moist soil)*
Fiorin	*Agrostis stolonifera (wet or moist soil)*
*Fescue, Flote	*Festuca fluitans (swamps)*
*Tall	*elatior (moderately moist)*
*Meadow	*pratensis (moderately dry)*
*Green	*Poa viridis (rich and tolerably moist)*
†Guinea(a)	*Panicum maximum (strong warm soil)*
*Herd	*Agrostis stricta (wet or moist soil)*
Lucern	*Medicago sativa (a rich, dry, sandy loam)*
Meadow, Rough-stalked	*Poa trivialis (moist soil)*
Soft	*Holcus lanatus (moist soil)*
Water	*Poa aquatica (swamp)*
*Creeping	*Poa stolonifera (wet)*
*Smooth-stalked	*Poa pratensis (dry soil)*
*Five-nerved	*Poa nervata (wet)*
Medic, Yellow	*Medicago falcata (dry soil)*
Hop	*lupulina*

(a) This grass is by much too tender to bear the winter frosts of the middle or eastern States, but succeeds well in Georgia, and in the warmest parts of South Carolina.

Oat, Tall Meadow	*Avena elatior* (moderately dry)
Yellow	*flavescens* (good dry ground)
*Orchard	*Dactylis glomerata* (orchards and moderately dry meadow)
†Peruvian (b)	*Paspalum stoloniferum*
Ray, English	*Lolium perenne* (rich and tolerable moist)
Saintfoin	*Hedysarum Onobrychis* (dry deep soil, but answers well on poor ground)
Sweet-scented Vernal	*Anthoxanthum odoratum* (moderately dry)
Timothy	*Phleum pratense* (moist and upland)
Trefoil	*Medicago lupulina*

GRAINS, ETC.

Barley, Spring	*Hordeum vulgare*
Winter	*hexastichon*
Two-rowed	*distichon*
Naked	v. *nudum*
Buckwheat	*Polygonum Fagopyrum*
Corn, Indian	*Zea Mays*
Guinea	*Holcus Sorghum*
Broom	*saccharatus*
Millet, Large	*Panicum miliaceum*
German	*Germanicum*
Italian	*Italicum*
Oat, Cultivated	*Avena Sativa*
Varieties, 1. White. 2. Black. 3. Brown. 4. Potato. 5. Poland. 6. Friesland. 7. Siberian. 8. Tartarian.	
Oat, Naked	*Avena nuda*
Oriental	*orientalis*
Peas, Field	*Pisum sativum*
Rye, Spring	*Secale cereale* v. *vernum*
Winter	v. *hybernum*
Upland	v. *montanum*
Rice, Common	*Oryza sativa* (c)
Tares, Common	*Vicia sativa*
*Tobacco, Virginian	*Nicotiana Tabacum*
Teasel, Fuller's	*Dipsachus fullonum*
Wheat, Spring	*Triticum æstivum*
Winter	*hybernum*
Egyptian	*compositum*
Weld, Dyer's	*Reseda luteola*
Woad, do.	*Isatis tinctoria*
Liquorice, Common	*Glycyrrhiza glabra*

ROOTS, ETC.

Potatoes, Common	*Solanum tuberosum*
†Sweet	*Convolvulus Batatas*
Scarcity Root	*Mangel wurtzel*

(b) This is nearly as tender as the preceding, and therefore not answerable for the middle or eastern States. The Avena elatior or tall oat-grass, is, by mistake, called Peruvian and Andes grass in the County of Delaware, near Philadelphia, and in part of the State of Delaware, where it is cultivated; it is called meadow oats about Lancaster, Pennsylvania.

(c) There is a variety of this that grows well on dry lands, which is now cultivated near the Muskingum and in other parts of the United States, and is likely to become of considerable importance.

Rhubarb, True   *Rheum Palmatum*
Turnip, Common   *Brassica Rapa*
    Swedish, or Ruta Baga, *a va-*
      riety

ARTICLES FOR MANUFACTURING.

*Cotton   *Gossypium herbaceum*
Flax   *Linum usitatissimum*
Hemp   *Cannabis sativa*

INDEX.